Contributor:
Betty Kehl Richardson, RN, PhD, BC, LMFT, LPC

Instructor's Manual and Resource Guide for

Medical-Surgical Nursing Care

Third Edition

Karen M. Burke, RN, MS
Elaine L. Mohn-Brown, RN, EdD
Linda Eby, RN, MN

Pearson

New York   Boston   San Francisco   London   Toronto
Sydney   Tokyo   Singapore   Madrid   Mexico City   Munich
Paris   Cape Town   Hong Kong   Montreal

Notice: Care has been taken to confirm the accuracy of the information presented in this book. The authors, editors, and the publisher, however, cannot accept any responsibility for errors or omissions or for consequences from application of the information in this book and make no warranty, express or implied, with respect to its contents.

The authors and the publisher have exerted every effort to ensure that drug selections and dosages set forth in this text are in accord with current recommendations and practice at time of publication. However, in view of ongoing research, changes in government regulations, and the constant flow of information relating to drug therapy and drug reactions, the reader is urged to check the package inserts of all drugs for any change in indications of dosage and for added warnings and precautions. This is particularly important when the recommended agent is a new and/or infrequently employed drug.

The authors and publisher disclaim all responsibility for any liability, loss, injury, or damage incurred as a consequence, directly or indirectly, of the use and application of any of the contents of this volume.

10 9 8 7 6 5 4 3 2 1
ISBN-10:   0-13-608010-3
ISBN-13: 978-0-13-608010-7

Contents

Preface

Nurses today must be able to grow and evolve to meet the demands of a dramatically changing health care system. *Medical-Surgical Nursing Care* addresses the many concepts of contemporary professional nursing that students will need to learn and embrace to be effective members of the collaborative health care team. This Instructor's Manual and Resource Guide is designed to support your teaching in this stepped-up environment and to reduce your preparation for class. It will help you provide an optimal learning experience for your students and their many learning needs.

Each chapter in the Instructor's Manual and Resource Guide is thoroughly integrated with the corresponding chapter in *Medical-Surgical Nursing Care*. Chapters are organized by learning outcomes, and the teaching unit flows from these outcomes. You will find the following features to support the outcomes.

- ***Concepts for Lecture.*** This outline of the key concepts presented in each chapter may be used in its entirety or in conjunction with the classroom activities for a mixture of teaching styles that will meet the needs of students with various learning styles.
- ***PowerPoint Slides.*** The corresponding slide numbers for each learning outcome are found in the margin notes. The PowerPoint slides contain lecture outlines, integrated images, videos and animations, Connection Checkpoint questions, and classroom response system questions.
- ***Suggestions for Classroom and Clinical Activities.*** Ideas from educators to address learning styles and make the learning more process more interesting.
- ***Guide to Resources.*** In the margin you will also find a listing of additional resources that pertain to each learning outcome. These include figures, tables, and boxes from the textbook, additional references and websites, animations and videos available from the image library and more!
- ***General Chapter Considerations.*** At the end of each chapter is a list of additional resources for you and your students. These include the student workbook, MyNursingKit, Pearson eText, MyNursingLab, and other separate resources. Have your students take advantage of all these resources to help them succeed in the classroom!

This Instructor's Manual and Resource Guide also contains a Strategies for Success module that includes discussion on learning theories, planning for instruction, how to use effective pedagogies, assessing learning, and more. There is also a guide on *Teaching Students Who Speak English as a Nonnative Language*. This tool is intended to guide you in reaching across cultural barriers to train nurses.

The following additional resources are also available to accompany this textbook. For more information or sample copies, please contact your Pearson sales representative or visit www.mypearsonstore.com:

- ***MyNursingKit (www.mynursingkit.com).*** This student and instructor resource gives you everything you need in one place! Students can use this site as an online study guide and source for additional resources. Instructors can find chapter specific PowerPoint lecture notes, test item questions, and instructor manual materials.
- ***Student Workbook and Resource Guide.*** This workbook incorporates strategies for students to focus their study and increase comprehension of concepts of nursing care. It contains a variety of activities such as multiple-choice, fill-in-the-blank, case studies, and more.
- ***Instructor Resource Kit.*** This cross-platform CD-ROM provides lecture note PowerPoint slides, image library PowerPoint Slides, classroom response questions in PowerPoint, Test item questions in TestGen, word, and PAR test, and a video and animation library. This supplement is available to faculty upon adoption of the textbook.
- ***Online Course Management Systems.*** Instructor and student resources are available within our Course Compass platform. For more information on Course Compass and other course management systems such as Blackboard or WebCT, please contact your Pearson sales representative or visit www.mypearsonstore.com.
- ***MyNursingLab.*** A valuable tool for formative assessment and customized student remediation. This online tool gives students the opportunity to test themselves on key concepts and skills in pharmacology. By using MyNursingLab, students can track their own progress through the course and use customized, media-rich, study plan activities to help achieve success in the classroom, in clinical, and ultimately on the NCLEX-RN. MyNursingLab allows instructors to monitor class progress a students move through the curriculum.

TEACHING NURSING TO STUDENTS WHO SPEAK ENGLISH AS A NON-NATIVE LANGUAGE

We are fortunate to have so many multinational and multilingual nursing students in the United States in the 21st century. As our classrooms become more diverse, there are additional challenges to communication, but we in the nursing education community are ready. Our goal is to educate competent and caring nurses to serve the health needs of our diverse communities.

We know that ENNL students experience higher attrition rates than their native English-speaking counterparts. This is a complex problem. However, there are teaching strategies that have helped many students be successful.

The first step toward developing success strategies is understanding language proficiency. Language proficiency has four interdependent components. Each component is pertinent to nursing education. **Reading** is the first aspect of language. Any nursing student will tell you that there are volumes to read in nursing education. Even native speakers of English find the reading load heavy. People tend to read more slowly in their non-native language. They also tend to recall less. Non-native speakers often spend inordinate amounts of time on reading assignments. These students also tend to take longer to process exam questions.

Listening is the second component of language. Learning from lectures can be challenging. Some students are more proficient at reading English than at listening to it. It is not uncommon for ENNL students to understand medical terminology, but to become confused by social references, slang, or idiomatic expressions used in class. The spoken language of the teacher may be different in accent or even vocabulary from that experienced by immigrant students in their language education. ENNL students may not even hear certain sounds that are not present in their native languages. *Amoxicillin* and *Ampicillin*, for example, may sound the same. Asian languages do not have gender-specific personal pronouns (he, she, him, her, etc.). Asian students may become confused when the teacher is describing a case study involving people of different genders.

Speaking is the third component of language proficiency. People who speak with an accent are often self-conscious about it. They may hesitate to voice their questions or to engage in discussion. Vicious cycles of self-defeating behavior can occur in which a student hesitates to speak, resulting in decreased speaking skills, which results in more hesitation to speak. Students may develop sufficient anxiety about speaking that their academic outcomes are affected. Students tend to form study groups with others who have common first languages. Opportunities to practice English are therefore reduced, and communication errors are perpetuated. When the teacher divides students into small groups for projects, ENNL students often do not participate as much as others. If these students are anxious about speaking, they may withdraw from classroom participation. ENNL students may feel rejected by other students in a small group situation when their input is not sought or understood.

The fourth aspect of language is **writing**. Spelling and syntax errors are common when writing a non-native language. Teachers often respond to student writing assignments with feedback that is too vague to provide a basis for correction or improvement by ENNL students. When it comes to writing lecture notes, these students are at risk of missing important details because they may not pick up the teacher's cues about what is important. They might miss information when they spend extra time translating a word or concept to understand it, or they might just take more time to write what is being said.

Another major issue faced by ENNL nursing students is the culture of the learning environment. International students were often educated in settings where students took a passive role in the classroom. They may have learned that faculty are to be respected, not questioned. Memorization of facts may have been emphasized. It may be a shock to them when the nursing faculty expect assertive students who ask questions and think critically. These expectations cannot be achieved unless students understand them.

Finally, the European American culture, which forms the context for nursing practice, creates challenges. Because they are immersed in Euro-American culture and the culture of nursing, faculty may not see the potential sources of misunderstanding. For example, if a teacher writes a test question about what foods are allowed on a soft diet, a student who understands therapeutic diets may miss the question if he or she does not recognize the names of the food choices. Nursing issues with especially high culture connection are: food, behavior, law, ethics, parenting, games, or choosing the right thing to say. These topics are well represented in psychiatric nursing, which makes it a difficult subject for ENNL students.

MINIMIZING CULTURE BIAS ON NURSING EXAMS

Our goal is not really to eliminate culture from nursing or from nursing education. Nursing exists in a culture-dependent context. Our goal is to practice transcultural nursing and to teach nursing without undue culture bias.

Sometimes our nursing exam questions will relate to culture-based expectations for nursing action. The way to make these questions fair is to teach transcultural nursing and to clarify the cultural expectations of a nursing student in the Euro-American-dominated health care system. Students must learn the cultural aspects of the profession before they can practice appropriately within it. Like other cultures, the professional culture of nursing has its own language (medical terminology and nursing diagnoses, of course). We have our own accepted way of dress, our own implements, skills, taboos, celebrations, and behavior. The values accepted by our culture are delineated in the ANA Code of Ethics, and are passed down to our young during nursing education.

It is usually clear to nursing educators that students are not initially aware of all the aspects of the professional culture, and that these must be taught. The social context of nursing seems more obvious to educators, and is often overlooked in nursing education. Some aspects of the social context of nursing were mentioned previously (food, games, social activities, relationships, behavior, what to say in certain situations). Students must also learn these social behaviors and attitudes if they are to function fully in nursing. If they do not already know about American hospital foods, what to say when someone dies, how to communicate with an authority figure, or what game to play with a 5-year-old child, they must learn these things in nursing school.

Try for yourself the following test. It was written without teaching you the cultural expectations first.

CULTURE BIASED TEST

1. Following radiation therapy, an African American client has been told to avoid using her usual hair-care product due to its petroleum content. Which product should the nurse recommend that she use instead?
   a. Royal Crown hair treatment
   b. Dax Wave and Curl
   c. Long Aid Curl Activator Gel
   d. Wave Pomade

2. A Jewish client is hospitalized for pregnancy-induced hypertension during Yom Kippur. How should the nurse help this client meet her religious needs based on the tradition of this holy day?
   a. Order meals without meat/milk combinations.
   b. Ask a family member to bring a serving of *Marror* for the client.
   c. Encourage her to fast from sunrise to sunset.
   d. Remind her that she is exempt from fasting.

3. Based on the Puerto Rican concept of *compadrazco,* who is considered part of the immediate family and responsible for care of children?
   a. Parents, grandparents, aunts, uncles, cousins, and godparents
   b. Mother and father, older siblings
   c. Mother, father, any blood relative
   d. Parents and chosen friends (*compadres*) who are given the honor of childcare responsibility

4. A 60-year-old Vietnamese immigrant client on a general diet is awake at 11 PM on a summer night. What is the best choice of food for the nurse to offer to this client?
   a. warm milk
   b. hot tea
   c. ice cream
   d. iced tea

5. Which of the following positions is contraindicated for a client recovering from a total hip replacement?
   a. side-lying using an abductor pillow
   b. standing
   c. walking to the restroom using a walker
   d. sitting in a low recliner

When you took this test, did it seem unfair? It was intended to test nursing behaviors that were based on culture-specific situations. Your immigrant and ENNL students are likely to face questions like these on every exam.

Item 1 is about hair-care products for black hair. Option C is the only one that does not contain petroleum products. Students could know this, if they were given the information before the exam. Otherwise the item is culture-biased.

Item 2 is about the Jewish holiday Yom Kippur. To celebrate this holiday, it is customary to fast from sunrise to sunset, but people who are sick, such as the client in the question, are exempted from fasting. This question is only unfair if students did not have access to the information.

Item 3 expects you to know about *compadrazco,* in which parents, grandparents, aunts, uncles, cousins, and godparents are all considered immediate family. This can be an important point if you are responsible for visiting policies in a pediatrics unit.

Item 4 tests knowledge about the preferred drink for an immigrant Vietnamese client. Many people in Asia feel comforted by hot drinks and find cold drinks to be unsettling.

Item 5 does not seem so biased. If you understand total hip precautions, it is a pretty simple question, unless you have never heard of a "low recliner." An ENNL student who missed this question said, "I saw the chairs in clinical called 'geri chairs' and I know that the client cannot bend more than 90 degrees, but 'low recliner' was confusing to me. I imagined someone lying down (reclining) and I think this would not dislocate the prosthesis."

The best way to avoid culture bias on exams is to know what you are testing. It is acceptable to test about hip precautions, but not really fair to test about the names of furniture. The same is true of foods. Test about therapeutic diets, but not about the recipes (an African immigrant student advised us to say "egg-based food" instead of custard).

Behavior in social and professional situations is especially culture-bound. Behavior-based questions are common on nursing exams. Make behavior expectations explicit. Especially when a student is expected to act in a way that would be inappropriate in his or her social culture, these are very difficult questions. For example, we expect nurses to act assertively with physicians and clients. It is inappropriate for many Asian students to question their elders. When a client is their elder, these students will choose the option that preserves respect for the client over one that provides teaching. We must make our expectations very clear.

Finally, talk with your ENNL and immigrant students after your exams. They can provide a wealth of information about what confused them or what was ambiguous. Discuss your findings with your colleagues and improve your exams. Ultimately your exams will be clearer and more valid.

SUCCESS STRATEGIES

The following strategies were developed originally to help ENNL students. An interesting revelation is that they also help native English speakers who have learning styles that are not conducive to learning by lecture, or who read slowly, or have learning disabilities or other academic challenges.

STRATEGIES FOR PROMOTING ENNL
STUDENT SUCCESS

1. You cannot decrease the reading assignments because some students read slowly, but you can help students prioritize the most important areas.
2. Allow adequate time for testing. The NCLEX®-PN is not a 1-minute-per-question test anymore. Usually 1.5 hours is adequate for a 50-item multiple-choice exam.
3. Allow students to tape lectures if they want to. You might have lectures audiotaped and put in the library for student access.
4. Speak clearly. Mumbling and rapid, anxious speech are difficult to understand. If you have a problem with clarity, provide handouts containing the critical points. Provide the handouts anyway. You want to teach and test nursing knowledge, not note-taking skills.
5. Avoid slang and idiomatic expressions. This is harder than heck to do, but you can do it with practice. When you do use slang, explain it. This is especially important on exams. When in doubt about whether a word is confusing, think about what the dictionary definition would be; if there are two meanings, use another word.
6. Allow the use of translation dictionaries on exams. You can say that students must tell you what they are looking up, so they cannot find medical terminology that is part of the test.
7. Be aware of cultural issues when you are writing exams. Of course you will test on culture-specific issues, but be sure you are testing what you want to test (e.g., the student's knowledge of diets, not of recipes).
8. Feel free to use medical terminology, after all this is nursing school. However, when you use an important new term, write it on the board so students can spell it correctly in their notes.
9. In clinical, make the implied explicit. It seems obvious that safety is the priority, but if a student thinks the priority is respecting her elders, when a client with a new hip replacement demands to get out of bed there could be a disaster.
10. Hire a student who takes clear and accurate lecture notes to post his or her notes for use by ENNL and other students. The students will still attend class and take their own notes, but will have this resource to fill in the details that they miss.
11. SOA (spell out abbreviations).
12. Many international students learned to speak English in the British style. If something would be confusing to a British person, they will find it confusing.
13. Provide opportunities for students to discuss what they are learning with other students and faculty. A faculty member might hold a weekly discussion group where students bring questions. It can be interesting to find a student having no trouble tracing the path of a red cell from the heart to the portal vein, but having difficulty understanding what cream of wheat is ("I thought it was a stalk of grain in a bowl with cream poured on it").
14. Make it clear that questions are encouraged. When a student is not asking questions, and you think he or she may not understand, ask the student after class if he or she has questions. Make it easier for students to approach you by being approachable. Learn their names, and learn to pronounce them correctly. Hearing you try to pronounce their name might be humorous for them, and it will validate how difficult it is to speak other languages.
15. Take another look at basing grades on class participation. You may be putting inordinate demands on the ENNL students. Of course nurses must learn to work with others, but the nurse who talks most is not necessarily the best.
16. Be a role model for communication skills. You might even say in class when you talk about communication that if you respect a person who is trying to communicate with you, you will persist until you understand the message. Say, "Please repeat that," or "I think you said to put a chicken on my head, is that correct?" or "You want me to do what with the textbook?" It may be considered socially rude to ask people to repeat themselves repeatedly. Make it clear that this is not a social situation. In the professional role, we are responsible for effective communication. We cannot get away with smiling and nodding our heads.
17. In clinical, if a student has an accent that is difficult for the staff to understand, discuss clarification techniques (see 16 above) with the student and staff members. Make it explicit that it is acceptable for the student to ask questions and for the staff to ask for clarification.

18. If your college has a writing center where students can receive feedback on grammar and style before submitting papers, have students use it. If you are not so fortunate, view papers as a rough draft instead of a final product. Give specific feedback about what to correct and allow students to resubmit.

19. Make any services available to ENNL students available to all students (such as group discussions and notes). These services may meet the learning needs of many students while preventing the attitude that "they are different and they get something I don't."

20. Faculty attitudes are the most important determinant of a successful program to promote the success of ENNL nursing students. Talk with other faculty about the controversial issues. Create an organized program with a consistent approach among the faculty. The rewards will be well worth the work.

STRATEGIES FOR SUCCESS

Sandra DeYoung, Ed.D., R.N.

IMPROVING OUR TEACHING

Every faculty member wants to be a good teacher, and every teacher wants her or his students to learn. In particular, we want to achieve the student learning outcomes that our educational institutions say that we must achieve. How can we best meet both goals? We cannot just teach as we were taught. We have to learn a variety of teaching methods and investigate best practices in pedagogy. We also have to learn how to measure student learning outcomes in practical and efficient ways. The next few pages will introduce you to principles of good teaching and ways to evaluate learning. Keep in mind that this is only an introduction. For a more extensive study of these principles and pedagogies, you might consult the resources listed at the end of this introduction.

LEARNING THEORY

In order to improve our teaching, we must have some familiarity with learning theory. Nurses who come into educational roles without psychology of learning courses in their background should read at least an introductory level book on learning theories. You should, for example, know something about stages and types of learning, how information is stored in memory and how it is retrieved, and how knowledge is transferred from one situation to another.

BEHAVIORIST THEORIES

Behaviorist theories are not in as much favor today as they were 25 years ago, but they still help to explain simple learning. Conditioning and reinforcement are concepts with which most educators are familiar. Conditioning explains how we learn some simple movements and behaviors that result in desired outcomes, such as a nurse responding when an alarm sounds on a ventilator. Reinforcement refers to the fact that behavior that is rewarded or reinforced tends to recur. Therefore, reinforcement is a powerful tool in the hands of an educator.

COGNITIVE LEARNING THEORIES

Cognitive learning theories are much more sophisticated and deal with how we process information by perceiving, remembering, and storing information. All of these processes are a part of learning. One of the most useful concepts in cognitive theory is that of mental schemata.

Schemata (plural) are units of knowledge that are stored in memory. For example, nurses must develop a schema related to aseptic technique. Once a schema is stored in memory, related information can be built on it. For instance, changing a dressing is easier to learn if the learner already has a schema for asepsis.

Metacognition is another concept identified in cognitive theories. This concept refers to thinking about one's thinking. To help learners who are having difficulty mastering certain material, you might ask them to think about how they learn best and to help them evaluate whether they really understand the material.

Transfer of learning occurs when a learner takes information from the situation in which it is learned and applies it to a new situation. Transfer is most likely to occur if the information was learned well in the first place, if it can be retrieved from memory, and if the new situation is similar to the original learning situation. Educators can teach for transfer by pointing out to students how a concept is applied in several situations so that learners know that the concept is not an isolated one, and the students begin to look for similar patterns in new situations.

ADULT LEARNING THEORIES

Adult learning theories help to explain how learning takes place differently for adults than for children. Adults usually need to know the practical applications for the information they are given. They also want to see how it fits with their life experiences. When teaching young adults and adults, nurse educators need to keep in mind adult motivation for learning.

LEARNING STYLE THEORIES

Learning style theories abound. Research has shown that some learners are visually oriented; some are more auditory or tactile learners; some are individualistic and learn best alone whereas others learn best by collaboration; some deal well with abstract concepts while others learn better with concrete information. Measurement instruments that can determine preferred learning styles are readily available. Although not many educators actually measure their students' learning styles, they should at least keep learning styles in mind when they plan their instruction.

PLANNING FOR INSTRUCTION

With some background knowledge of how students learn, the nurse educator can begin to plan the learning experiences. Planning includes developing objectives, selecting content, choosing pedagogies, selecting assignments, and planning for assessment of learning. All nurse educators come to the teaching process already knowing how to write objectives. Objectives can be written in the cognitive, psychomotor, and affective domains of learning. In the cognitive domain, they can be written at the knowledge, comprehension, application, analysis, and synthesis levels of complexity. The critical aspect of objectives is that you need to keep referring to them as you plan your lesson or course. They will help you focus on the "need to know" versus the "nice to know" material. They will help you decide on which assignments will be most suitable, and they will guide your development of evaluation tools.

SELECTING ASSIGNMENTS

Selecting and developing out-of-class assignments calls for creativity. You may use instructor manuals, such as this one, for ideas for assignments or you may also develop your own. To encourage learning through writing, you can assign short analysis papers, position papers, or clinical journals, all of which promote critical thinking. Nursing care plans of various lengths and complexity may be assigned. You may create reading guides with questions to help students read their textbooks analytically. You might also ask students to interview people or observe people to achieve various objectives.

USING EFFECTIVE PEDAGOGIES

Selecting teaching methods or pedagogies takes considerable time. You must consider what you are trying to achieve. To teach facts, you may choose to lecture or assign a computer tutorial. To change attitudes or motivate learners, you may use discussion, role-playing, or gaming. Developing critical thinking may be done effectively using critical thinking exercises, concept maps, group projects, or problem-based learning. There are what I will call *traditional* pedagogies, *activity-based* pedagogies, and *technology-based* pedagogies.

TRADITIONAL PEDAGOGIES

Traditional pedagogies include lecture, discussion, and questioning. Lecturing is an efficient way to convey a great deal of information to large groups of people. However, the lecture creates passive learning. Learners just sit and listen (or not) and do not interact with the information or the lecturer. Research has shown that students learn more from active learning techniques—that is, from being able to talk about, manipulate, reduce, or synthesize information. So, if you are going to lecture, it would be wise to intersperse lecture with discussion and questioning.

Discussion gives students an opportunity to analyze and think critically about information that they have read or were given in a lecture. By discussing key concepts and issues, they can learn the applicability of the concepts and see how they can transfer to varied situations. Discussions can be formal or informal, but they generally work best if they are planned. For a formal discussion, students must be held accountable for preparing for it. The teacher becomes a facilitator by giving an opening statement or question, guiding the discussion to keep it

focused, giving everyone a chance to participate, and summarizing at the end.

Questioning is a skill that develops over time. The first principle to learn is that you have to give students time to answer. Most teachers wait only one second before either repeating the question or answering it themselves. You should wait at least three to five seconds before doing anything, to allow students time to think and prepare a thoughtful answer. Research has revealed that most instructor-posed questions are at a very low level (lower-order), eliciting recall of facts. But questioning can be used to develop critical thinking if it is planned. Higher-order questions are those that require students to interpret information, to apply it to different situations, to think about relationships between concepts, or to assess a situation. If you ask higher-order questions during your classes or clinical experiences, students will rise to the occasion and will be challenged to provide thoughtful answers.

ACTIVITY-BASED PEDAGOGIES

Activity-based teaching strategies include cooperative learning, simulations, games, problem-based learning, and self-learning modules, among others. Cooperative learning is an old pedagogy that has received more research support than any other method. This approach involves learners working together and being responsible for the learning of group members as well as their own learning. Cooperative learning groups can be informal, such as out-of-class study groups, or can be formally structured in-class groups. The groups may serve to solve problems, develop projects, or discuss previously taught content.

Simulations are exercises that can help students to learn in an environment that is low risk or risk free. Students can learn decision making, for example, in a setting where no one is hurt if the decision is the wrong one. Simulations in skills laboratories are frequently used to teach psychomotor skills. Simulations can be written (case studies), acted out (role-playing), computer-based (clinical decision-making scenarios), or complex, technology-based (active simulation mannequins).

Games can help motivate people to learn. Factual content that can be rather boring to learn, such as medical terminology, can be turned into word games such as crossword puzzles or word searches. More complex games can teach problem solving or can apply previously learned information; board games or simulation games can be used for these purposes.

Problem-based learning (PBL) provides students with real-life problems that they must research and analyze and then develop possible solutions for. PBL is a group activity. The instructor presents the students with a brief problem statement. The student groups make lists of what they know and don't know about the problem. They decide what information they must collect in order to further understand the problem. As they collect the information and analyze it, they further refine the problem and begin to investigate possible solutions. The educator serves as a facilitator and resource during the learning process and helps keep the group focused.

Self-learning modules are a means of self-paced learning. They can be used to teach segments of a course or an entire course or curriculum. Modules should be built around a single concept. For example, you might design a module for a skills lab based on aseptic technique; or you could develop a module for a classroom course around the concept of airway impairment. Each module contains components such as an introduction, instructions on how to use the module, objectives, a pretest, learning activities, and a posttest. Learning activities within a module should address various learning styles. You should try to include activities that appeal to visual learners and tactile learners, conceptual learners and abstract learners, and individual and collaborative learners, for example. Those activities could be readings, audiovisuals, computer programs, group discussion, or skills practice. The educator develops and tests the module and then acts as facilitator and evaluator as learners work through the module.

TECHNOLOGY-BASED PEDAGOGIES

Technology-based pedagogies include computer simulations and tutorials, internet use, and distance-learning applications. Computer simulations were discussed briefly in the previous section. They include decision-making software in which a clinical situation is enacted and students are asked to work through the nursing process to solve problems and achieve positive outcomes. They also include simulation games such as SimCity, which can be a useful tool in teaching community health principles.

Computer tutorials are useful for individual remedial work such as medication calculations or practice in answering multiple-choice test questions.

The internet is a rich resource for classroom use and for out-of-class assignments. The World Wide Web contains hundreds of websites that can be accessed for health-related information. Students need to be taught how to evaluate the worth of these websites. The criteria they should apply to this evaluation include identifying the intended audience, the currency of the information, the author's credentials or the affiliated organization, and content accuracy. Students may not know how to identify online journal sources compared to other websites. It is worth spending time, therefore, teaching students how to use the Web before giving them assignments that include Web use. If your classroom is internet-access enabled, you can visually demonstrate how to identify and use appropriate websites. For example, if you want students to find relevant information for diabetic teaching, you can show them the differing value of information from official diabetes associations versus pharmaceutical sites versus chat rooms or public forums.

You may be using this instructor manual in a distance-learning course. Distance learning takes the forms of interactive television classes, Webcasting, or online courses. In any form of distance learning, students are learning via the technology, but they are also learning about technology and becoming familiar with several computer applications. Those applications may include synchronous and asynchronous applications, streaming video, and multimedia functions.

ASSESSING LEARNING

You can assess or evaluate learning in a number of ways. Your first decision is whether you are just trying to get informal, ungraded feedback on how well students are learning in your class, or whether you are evaluating the students for the purpose of assigning a grade. Following are a number of techniques that can be used for one or both purposes.

CLASSROOM ASSESSMENT TECHNIQUES

Classroom assessment techniques (CATs) are short, quick, ungraded, in-class assessments used to gauge students' learning during or at the end of class. Getting frequent feedback on students' understanding helps educators to know if they are on the right track and if students are benefiting from the planned instruction. If you wait until you give a formal quiz or examination, you may have waited too long to help some students who are struggling with the material. The most popular CAT is probably the *minute paper*. This technique involves asking students to write down, in one or two minutes, usually at the end of class, the most important thing they learned that day or points that remain unclear. A related technique is the *muddiest point*, in which you ask the class to write down what the "muddiest" part of the class was for them. In nursing, *application cards* can be especially useful. After teaching about a particular concept or body of knowledge, and before you talk about the applications of the information, ask the students to fill out an index card with one possible clinical application of the information. This technique fosters application and critical thinking. Always leave class time during the following session to give feedback on the CAT results.

TESTS AND EXAMINATIONS

Tests and examinations are also used to assess or evaluate learning. Tests should be planned carefully to measure whether learning objectives have been met. You should form a test plan in which you decide the number of test items to include for each objective as well as the complexity of the items. Just as objectives can be written at the knowledge through synthesis levels of knowing, test items can be written at each level, too. Some types of items lend themselves to the lower levels of knowing, such as true-false and matching items, while multiple-choice and essay questions can be used to test higher levels.

TRUE-FALSE QUESTIONS

True-false questions are used simply to assess whether the student can determine the correctness of a fact or principle. This type of question should be used sparingly, because the student has a 50% chance of guessing the correct answer. Well-written true-false questions are clear and unambiguous. The entire statement should be totally true or totally false. An example of a question that is ambiguous is:

(T F) A routine urinalysis specimen must be collected with clean technique and contain at least 100 mL.

The answer to this question is false because the specimen does not require 100 mL of volume. However, the clean technique part of the question is true. Because part of the statement is true and part is false, the question is misleading. A better question is:

(T F) A routine urinalysis specimen must be collected with clean technique.

True-false questions can be made more difficult by requiring the student to explain why the statement is true or false.

MATCHING QUESTIONS

Matching questions also test a low level of learning—that of knowledge. They are most useful for determining if students have learned definitions or equivalents of some type. They should be formatted in two columns, with the premise words or statements on the left and the definitions or responses on the right. You should have more responses than premises so that matching cannot be done simply by process of elimination. Instructions should be given that indicate whether responses can be used more than once or even not used at all. An example of a matching question is:

Match the definition on the right with the suffix on the left. Definitions can be used only once or not at all.

____1.	____-itis	a. presence of
____2.	____-stalsis	b. abnormal flow
____3.	____-rrhage	c. inflammation
____4.	____-iasis	d. discharge or flow
____5.	____-ectomy	e. contraction
		f. surgical removal of

MULTIPLE-CHOICE QUESTIONS

Multiple-choice questions can be written at the higher levels of knowing, from application through evaluation. At these higher levels they can test critical thinking. A multiple-choice question has two parts. The first part, the question, is also called the *stem*. The possible answers are called *options*. Among the options, the correct one is called the *answer*, while the incorrect options are termed *distracters*. You can word stems as questions or as incomplete statements that are completed by the options. For example, an item written as a question is:

WHAT IS A QUICK WAY TO ASSESS THE APPROXIMATE LITERACY LEVEL OF A PATIENT?

a. Pay attention to her vocabulary as she speaks.

b. Give her an instruction sheet to read.

c. Administer a literacy test.

d. Ask her whether she graduated from high school.

The same knowledge can be tested by a stem written as an incomplete statement:

A QUICK WAY TO ASSESS THE APPROXIMATE LITERACY LEVEL OF A PATIENT IS TO

a. pay attention to her vocabulary as she speaks.

b. give her an instruction sheet to read.

c. administer a literacy test.

d. ask her whether she graduated from high school.

Notice the differing formats used here. When the stem is a question, each option is capitalized. When the stem is an incomplete statement, it does not end with a period, so the options do not begin with a capital letter. This style may vary. In this manual's test bank, all options begin with a capital letter, regardless of whether the stem is a complete or incomplete sentence. Stems should be kept as brief as possible to minimize reading time. Avoid negatively stated stems. For example, a poor stem would be, "Which of the following is not a good way to assess a patient's literacy level?" It is too easy for readers to miss the word "not" and therefore answer incorrectly. If you feel compelled to write negative stems occasionally, be sure to capitalize or underline the word "not," or use the word "except," as in the following example: "All of the following are good ways to assess a patient's literacy level, EXCEPT." In this case, the reader is less likely to miss the negative word because of the sentence structure and also because the word "except" is capitalized.

Options usually vary from three to five in number. The more options you have, the more difficult the item. However, it is often difficult to write good distracters. Be sure that your options are grammatically consistent with the stem. Next is a test item in which all of the options do not fit grammatically with the stem:

THE LECTURE METHOD OF TEACHING IS BEST SUITED TO

a. when the audience already knows a lot about the topic.

b. large audiences.

c. times when you are in a hurry to cover your material and don't want to be interrupted.

d. young children.

Not only are the options grammatically inconsistent, they are also of varied lengths. Attempt to keep the options about the same length. The following restatement of the item corrects the problems with grammar and with length:

THE LECTURE METHOD OF TEACHING
IS BEST SUITED TO

a. an audience that already knows the topic.

b. an audience that is very large.

c. times when you must cover your material quickly.

d. an audience of young children.

Distracters that make no sense should never be used. Instead, try to develop distracters that reflect incorrect ideas that some students might hold about a topic.

ESSAY QUESTIONS

Essay-type questions include short answer restricted-response questions) and full essays (extended-response questions). These types of items can be used to test higher-order thinking. Extended-response essays are especially suited to testing analysis, synthesis, and evaluation levels of thinking. An example of an essay question that might test these higher-order levels of thinking is: "Explain how exogenous cortisone products mimic a person's normal cortisol functions and why long-term cortisone administration leads to complications. Also explain how nursing assessment and intervention can help to reduce those complications."

The educator must plan how the essay is going to be graded before the test is given. An outline of required facts and concepts can be developed and points given to each. Then a decision must be made as to whether it is appropriate to give points for writing style, grammar, spelling, and so on.

TEST ITEM ANALYSIS

After a test is given, an analysis of objective items can be conducted. Two common analyses are *item difficulty* and *item discrimination*. Most instructors want to develop questions that are of moderate difficulty, with around half of the students selecting the correct answer. A mixture of fairly easy, moderate, and difficult questions can be used. The difficulty index can be easily calculated by dividing the number of students who answered the question correctly by the total number of students answering the question. The resulting fraction, converted to a percentage, gives an estimate of the difficulty, with lower percentages reflecting more difficult questions.

Item discrimination is an estimate of how well a particular item differentiates between students who generally know the material and those who don't. Another way of saying this is that a discriminating item is one that most of the students who got high scores on the rest of the examination got right and most of the students who got low scores got wrong. The discrimination index can be calculated by computer software or by hand using a formula that can be found in tests and measurement textbooks.

These few pages are but an introduction to teaching techniques. For more information, you might consult the following resources:

Book: DeYoung, S. (2003). *Teaching Strategies for Nurse Educators*. Upper Saddle River, NJ: Prentice Hall.

Websites:

www.crlt.umich.edu/tstrategies/teachings.html

www.gmu.edu/facstaff/part-time/strategy.html

www.ic.arizona.edu/ic/edtech/strategy.html

CHAPTER 1
NURSING IN THE 21ST CENTURY

LEARNING OUTCOME 1

Discuss current trends and issues in health care and nursing.

Concepts for Lecture

1. Health care today is a vast and complex system reflecting changes in society and changes in populations requiring nursing care.
2. Currently, there is an emphasis on health promotion as well as illness care.
3. There is recognition of the need to refocus on the quality and safety of health care.
4. The National Academy of Sciences (2004) identified core competencies for all healthcare providers.
5. Core competencies of healthcare providers include providing client-centered care, working in interdisciplinary teams, using evidence-based practice, applying quality improvement principles, and using information technology.

LEARNING OUTCOME 2

Explain client-centered care and describe its impact on the nurse's role and responsibilities.

Concepts for Lecture

1. The nurse attends to the uniqueness of the individual client, planning and adapting care to the needs of that person.
2. The nurse advocates for wellness, healthy lifestyles, and disease prevention with the client assuming the primary role.
3. The nurse listens to and respects the client's wishes and desired outcomes of care.
4. Care is planned with respect for the client's culture and values.
5. Attention is paid to relieving pain and suffering.
6. Nursing care and activities are coordinated to meet the needs of the individual (and as appropriate to the family), not the desires of the healthcare team.
7. When the client has a chronic disease or condition, the nurse advocates for lifestyle changes and disease management, with the client assuming the primary role.
8. For the dying client, the nurse provides client-centered care, advocating for comfort care and pain relief, and supports the family.

POWERPOINT SLIDES 22–23

Tables and/or Figures
- **Box 1-1** Healthy People 2020 Leading Health Indicators

SUGGESTIONS FOR CLASSROOM ACTIVITIES
- Ask students to bring newspaper clippings about proposed changes in health care, quality and safety of health care, health promotion, and evidence-based practice in health care. Display these articles on the classroom wall or on a bulletin board, or make a class scrapbook of these articles.

SUGGESTIONS FOR CLINICAL ACTIVITIES
- Discuss health promotion with students in preconference or prior to clinical. Ask students to include health promotion in their care plan. Call on students in postconference to talk about the health promotion they performed and their client's response to it.

POWERPOINT SLIDES 24–25

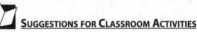

SUGGESTIONS FOR CLASSROOM ACTIVITIES
- Break students into small groups to discuss how culture would impact care in a variety of cultures. Give each group one of the cultures found in their community, with each group having a different culture. Each group should pick a spokesperson to share the discussion of that group with the class.
- Have each student select a country and then research the customs, foods, dress, language, and healthcare beliefs and customs of that country. Ask the students to write a paper on their research and present it in class.

SUGGESTIONS FOR CLINICAL ACTIVITIES
- Select clients from a variety of cultures to assign to students in clinical. Ask students to discuss in postconference what they learned about the culture of their client and how culture impacted client care.

LEARNING OUTCOME 3

Describe the role of the LPN/LVN as caregiver, manager of care, advocate, and teacher.

Concepts for Lecture

1. The roles of the medical-surgical nurse include caregiver, manager of care, client advocate, and teacher.
2. Roles of the medical-surgical nurse include promoting and maintaining health, preventing illness, and helping clients cope with disability or death in any setting.
3. The caregiver role is both independent and collaborative.
4. As a caregiver, the nurse practices both the art and science of nursing.
5. All nurses must learn to coordinate care and be leaders.
6. As an advocate, the nurse communicates with other healthcare team members, provides or reinforces client and family teaching, assists and supports client decision making, suggests referrals as appropriate, and identifies community and personal resources.
7. The framework for the role of teacher is the teaching-learning process.

LEARNING OUTCOME 4

Discuss the steps of the nursing process: assessment, diagnosis, planning, implementation, and evaluation.

Concepts for Lecture

1. The nursing process is a model of care that differentiates nursing practices from the practices of other healthcare providers.
2. The five interdependent and cyclic steps of the nursing process are assessment, diagnosis, planning, implementation, and evaluation.
3. Licensed practical/vocational nurses use all steps of the nursing process except making a nursing diagnosis.
4. Nursing process is a basis for improving clinical practice and evaluating the quality of care.

LEARNING OUTCOME 5

Explain how critical thinking and clinical reasoning are used to determine priorities of nursing care and to promote, maintain, or restore health.

Concepts for Lecture

1. Critical thinking is goal directed.
2. Critical thinking uses knowledge and skills to select the best action for the circumstances.
3. Critical thinking and clinical reasoning involve more than just knowledge.
4. Critical thinking and clinical reasoning involve both attitudes and skills, such as independent thinking, ability to use analytic processes to sort out relevant data, intuition, intellectual courage, empathy, fair mindedness, self-discipline, creativity, and confidence in self.
5. Critical thinking and the nursing process are essential in nursing practice.

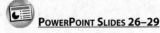 **POWERPOINT SLIDES 26–29**

Tables and/or Figures
- **Figure 1-1** Nurse as Caregiver
- **Figure 1-2** Nurse as Teacher

 **SUGGESTIONS FOR CLASSROOM ACTIVITIES**

- Post large sheets of paper in the classroom with each sheet listing at the top one of the roles of the nurse: caregiver, manager of care, advocate, and teacher. Ask each student to go around the room and put a post it note on each sheet describing an activity the nurse would carry out in that role. When completed, have a class discussion on the comments on the sheets of paper.

 **SUGGESTIONS FOR CLINICAL ACTIVITIES**

- Assign students to shadow a primary care nurse and make note of the nurse's activities that fall under the roles of caregiver, manager of care, advocate, and teacher.

 **POWERPOINT SLIDES 30–33**

Tables and/or Figures
- **Figure 1-3** Steps of the Nursing Process

SUGGESTIONS FOR CLASSROOM ACTIVITIES

- Post large sheets of paper in the classroom with each sheet listing at the top one of the benefits of the nursing process. Ask each student to go around the room and put a pertinent comment on each sheet. For example, the student could describe how the nursing process involves the client, how the nursing process increases client satisfaction, or how a written care plan ensures continuity of care.

SUGGESTIONS FOR CLINICAL ACTIVITIES

- Have students keep a log of their clinical activities for 1 to 3 days and then categorize each activity according to the steps in the nursing process. In postconference, have the students discuss the method and rationale used to categorize each activity. Have students discuss their thoughts and feelings about their competency in using the nursing process.

 **POWERPOINT SLIDES 34–38**

Tables and/or Figures
- **Figure 1-4** Sample Clinical Reasoning Care Map

LEARNING OUTCOME 6

Describe the nature of laws regulating nursing practice in the United States.

Concepts for Lecture

1. Nurses work with clients in vulnerable positions.
2. Nurses must have a good understanding of laws regulating nursing, the legal system within which nurses practice, and ethical principles that guide nursing practice.
3. Nursing is governed by nurse practice acts in every state in the United States.
4. Nurse practice acts are made up of both statutory law and administrative law.
5. The National Council of State Boards of Nursing (NCSBN) adopted a model practice act and standards for LPN/LVN nursing practice.
6. The American Nurses Association (ANA) Code for Nurses states principles of ethical concern. It guides the behavior of nurses and defines nursing for the general public.
7. The National Association for Practical Nurse Education and Service developed the code of ethics for licensed practical/vocational nurses.

LEARNING OUTCOME 7

Identify key features of the LPN/LVN scope of practice.

Concepts for Lecture

1. LPN/LVN nursing practice is under the direction of the registered nurse, advanced practice registered nurse, licensed physician, or other authorized healthcare provider.
2. LVN/LPN nursing practice is guided by established nursing standards.
3. LVN/LPN scope of practice includes collecting data, conducting focused nursing assessments, planning nursing care for stable individuals, participating in the development and modification of the comprehensive plan of care for all types of clients, and implementing appropriate aspects of care within the client-centered healthcare plan.
4. The LVN/LPN scope of practice includes participation in nursing care management through delegating to assistive personnel and assigning to other LVNs/LPNs nursing interventions within their scope of practice or assigned responsibilities.
5. Each LVN/LPN is accountable for the quality of nursing care given.
6. Each LVN/LPN must recognize the limits of his or her knowledge and experience and plan for management of situations beyond the nurse's expertise.

LEARNING OUTCOME 8

Describe how ethical standards and codes guide nurses in providing medical–surgical nursing care.

Concepts for Lecture

1. Nurses need a good understanding of laws regulating nursing, the legal system within which they practice, and ethical principles that guide nursing practice.

 SUGGESTIONS FOR CLASSROOM ACTIVITIES

- Discuss the role of the licensed practical nurse in each step of the nursing process.
- Have students list the attributes of a critical thinker and describe actions they need to take to have each of these attributes.

 SUGGESTIONS FOR CLINICAL ACTIVITIES

- Have students discuss how they appropriately used empathy with clients, as well as other critical thinking and clinical reasoning attitudes and skills.

 POWERPOINT SLIDES 39–40

 **SUGGESTIONS FOR CLASSROOM ACTIVITIES**

- Have students work in pairs or small groups. Provide each group with a copy of the state nurse practice act governing the practice of the LPN/LVN, or 3 to 4 weeks prior to this class, instruct students to go online to their state board of nursing and learn how to request a copy from the licensing board. Have students discuss the section on professional behavior and unprofessional behavior and the possible consequences for unprofessional behavior.

 SUGGESTIONS FOR CLINICAL ACTIVITIES

- Discuss health promotion with students in preconference or prior to clinical. Ask students to include health promotion in their care plan. Call on students in postconference to talk about the health promotion they did and their client's response to this.

 **POWERPOINT SLIDES 41–46**

SUGGESTIONS FOR CLASSROOM ACTIVITIES

- Ask students to identify activities that would be beyond the scope of practice of an LVN/LPN and to discuss the rationale for these activities being beyond the scope of practice.

 **SUGGESTIONS FOR CLINICAL ACTIVITIES**

- In postconference, role play in pairs the following situations, assigning students to play the role of student and the role of nurse and then having them switch roles.
  - Situation 1. A nurse on the unit asks the student if she would like to put down a nasogastric tube. The student has not been taught the procedure in class or lab. The nurse tells the student, "It will be easy and I'll be right there to help you."
  - Situation 2. The patient asks the student to give her a pain medication and not to mention it to the registered nurse assigned to her care because the registered nurse does not like her and withholds her pain medications.

2. Nursing is governed by nurse practice acts in every state in the United States. These acts contain both statutory law and administrative law.
3. Statutory law includes regulatory law, civil laws, and criminal laws.
4. Civil action or torts may be filed when the nurse's actions fall outside accepted standards and the client is harmed.
5. Torts are classified as intentional or unintentional.
6. Examples of intentional torts include assault, battery, invasion of privacy, deflammation, and false imprisonment.
7. Examples of unintentional torts include negligence and malpractice.
8. The Health Insurance Portability and Accountability Act (HIPAA) and the Standards for Privacy of Individually Identifiable Health Information contain laws to protect an individual's health information yet allow information to be shared for effective care.
9. Ethics is a set of principles of conduct concerned with moral duty, values, obligations, and the distinction between right and wrong.
10. Nursing codes of ethics, including ANA Code of Ethics for Nurses and the NAPNES Code of Ethics for LPN/LVNs, provide a framework for nurses to use in making moral and ethical decisions.
11. The nurse must maintain professional boundaries.
12. A legal or ethical dilemma involves a choice between two unpleasant alternatives. It is not the nurse's responsibility to solve ethical dilemmas.
13. Each nurse needs to have an understanding of guiding principles, legal responsibilities, and available resources to deal with legal and ethical dilemmas.

GENERAL CHAPTER CONSIDERATIONS

1. Have students study and learn key terms listed at the beginning of the chapter.
2. Have students complete end of chapter exercises either in their book or on the MyNursingKit Website.
3. Use the Classroom Response Question PowerPoints to assess students prior to lecture.

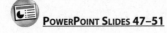
POWERPOINT SLIDES 47–51

SUGGESTIONS FOR CLASSROOM ACTIVITIES

- Divide the class into groups of five to six students. Using the nursing codes of ethics and the standards for nursing practice, assign each group to discuss the following situations: (1) A young man was involved in a motor vehicle accident and is now in a brain-damaged state, and the healthcare facility is asking the family to donate his organs. (2) How can the nurse working in a clinic for chemical and substance abuse assist the client in maintaining dignity and uniqueness? (3) How does the nurse who has had a personal experience involving a drunken driver objectively care for an alcoholic who has been involved in a motor vehicle accident in which the victim died? (4) When caring for a client with AIDS, what code of ethical behavior is mandated by the American Nurses Association?

SUGGESTIONS FOR CLINICAL ACTIVITIES

- During postconference, discuss legal and ethical dilemmas encountered in nursing care assignments in the clinical setting. If a student encounters no dilemmas, the student is to ask nurses on the unit to share a legal or ethical dilemma they have encountered.

MYNURSINGKIT
(www.mynursingkit.com)

- Websites
- NCLEX® Questions
- Case Studies
- Key Terms

STUDENT WORKBOOK AND RESOURCE GUIDE

- Chapter 1 activities
- *Separate purchase*

PRENTICE HALL NURSE'S DRUG GUIDE

- *Separate purchase*

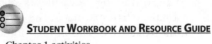
CLASSROOM RESPONSE QUESTION POWERPOINTS

TESTBANK

CHAPTER 2
HEALTH, ILLNESS, AND SETTINGS OF CARE

LEARNING OUTCOME 1

Define health, the health–illness continuum, and high-level wellness.

Concepts for Lecture

1. Health is "a state of complete physical, mental, and social well-being, and not merely the absence of disease or infirmity" (World Health Organization definition).
2. The health–illness continuum is a dynamic process, with high-level wellness at one extreme of the continuum and death at the opposite extreme.
3. High-level wellness is a way of functioning to reach one's maximum potential at a particular point in time.

LEARNING OUTCOME 2

Explain factors affecting health status, health promotion, and health maintenance.

Concepts for Lecture

1. Many different factors affect a person's health or level of wellness.
2. Major factors affecting health include genetic makeup; cognitive abilities and education; race, age, gender, and developmental level; lifestyle and environment; socioeconomic status; and geographic area.
3. The emphasis in nursing is shifting from a focus on acutely ill clients toward prevention and community-based care.
4. Two essential aspects of medical–surgical nursing today are teaching healthy behaviors and health maintenance and providing for continuity of care.
5. Certain practices are known to promote health and wellness.

LEARNING OUTCOME 3

Compare and contrast disease and illness.

Concepts for Lecture

1. Disease is a medical term describing disruptions in structure and function of the body or mind.
2. Manifestations are signs and symptoms exhibited by disruption that prompts a person to seek treatment.
3. Many diseases have a biologic cause. Environmental factors often play a major role in the development of disease, and lifestyle impacts on the development of disease.

 **POWERPOINT SLIDES 22–24**

Tables and/or Figures
- **Figure 2-1** The Health–Illness Continuum

 SUGGESTIONS FOR CLASSROOM ACTIVITIES

- Discuss the wellness–illness continuum. How does it differ from the definition of health by the World Health Organization? In what ways does it differ from Dunn's description of wellness? This discussion could take place in small groups in the classroom.

 **SUGGESTIONS FOR CLINICAL ACTIVITIES**

- Assign students to interview assigned clients to determine their concept of health and wellness.

  **POWERPOINT SLIDES 25–26**

 **SUGGESTIONS FOR CLASSROOM ACTIVITIES**

- Initiate a discussion on factors affecting health status, promotion, and maintenance by having the students compare their present health status and the ways in which they promote personal and family health.

 SUGGESTIONS FOR CLINICAL ACTIVITIES

- Have students help with teaching health promotion and maintenance at a health fair.

 **POWERPOINT SLIDES 27–29**

Tables and/or Figures
- **Table 2-1** Disease Classification Definitions

4. Diseases rarely result from just one cause. Common causes include genetic defects, developmental defects, biologic agents or toxins, physical agents, chemical agents, generalized response of tissues to injury or irritation, alterations in the production of antibodies, faulty metabolic processes, and continued unabated stress.
5. Illness is the response a person has to a disease. Illness integrates pathophysiologic alterations; psychologic effects of those alterations; effects on roles, relationships, and values; and cultural and spiritual beliefs.

LEARNING OUTCOME 4

Describe the sequence of acute illness behaviors.

Concepts for Lecture

1. Acute illness occurs rapidly, lasts a relatively short period of time, and is self-limiting, usually with a full recovery and return to normal pre-illness functioning.
2. Suchman describes five stages of acute illness behaviors.

LEARNING OUTCOME 5

Discuss chronic illness, including characteristics, needs of clients who are chronically ill, and the effects of chronic illness on the family.

Concepts for Lecture

1. The National Commission on Chronic Illness defines a chronic illness as any impairment or deviation from normal functioning that has one or more of the following five characteristics: it is permanent; it leaves permanent disability; it is caused by nonreversible pathologic alterations; it requires special teaching for rehabilitation; and/or it may require a long period of care.
2. A chronic illness or disease is one that typically has a slow onset and lasts for a prolonged time.
3. Chronic illness is characterized by impaired function in more than one body system.
4. The intensity of a chronic illness and its related symptoms ranges from mild to severe, and the illness is usually characterized by periods of remission and exacerbations.
5. The response of a person to chronic illness and the client's needs are unique and are influenced by many complex interrelated factors.
6. Adaptation to chronic illness is influenced by many variables such as anger, depression, denial, self-concept, locus of control, hardiness, and disability.
7. Nursing interventions for a client with a chronic illness focus on education to promote independent functioning, reduce healthcare costs, and improve well-being and quality of life.
8. Chronic illness in a family member is a major stressor that may cause changes in family structure and function, as well as changes in performing family developmental tasks.

SUGGESTIONS FOR CLASSROOM ACTIVITIES

- Divide the class into small groups of four. Have the students develop the following scenarios and role play the nurse–client interaction.
  - Scenario A: A 22-year-old male seen in the hematology clinic with sickle cell disease
  - Scenario B: A 45-year-old recently divorced female who had a hysterectomy
  - Scenario C: A 55-year-old postmenopausal female with a high cholesterol level
  - Scenario D: A 42-year-old client with esophageal cancer with metastasis to the liver who drinks alcohol ("in moderation") and smokes cigarettes ("just a few a day")
  - Scenario E: A 30-year-old type I diabetic who is not adhering to the diabetic diet or the insulin regimen
  - Scenario F: A 75-year-old client with chronic obstructive lung disorder

POWERPOINT SLIDES 30–31

SUGGESTIONS FOR CLINICAL ACTIVITIES

- Prior to clinical, assign students to interview clients and ask them what factors they think played a role in their disease or illness. Ask them about genetic factors, environmental factors, lifestyle factors, and stressors. Assess the client and see if you agree with the client's assessment of his or her own factors.

Tables and/or Figures

- **Figure 2-2** A Client With an Acute Illness Assumes the Dependent Role

SUGGESTIONS FOR CLASSROOM ACTIVITIES

- Define and discuss acute illness. Describe the steps of the sick role in acute illness.

SUGGESTIONS FOR CLINICAL ACTIVITIES

- Assign students to observe clients in a physician's office or other setting. Have them identify and journal about the behaviors that the clients exhibit in the various stages of acute illnesses.

POWERPOINT SLIDES 32–40

Tables and/or Figures

- **Figure 2-3** In Chronic Illness, the Client Learns How to Adapt to and Manage the Disorder

SUGGESTIONS FOR CLASSROOM ACTIVITIES

- Invite a home health nurse to speak to the class about caring for a client with chronic illness at home.

LEARNING OUTCOME 6

Compare and contrast the role of the LPN/LVN across different settings of care.

Concepts for Lecture

1. The setting for most health care has changed from the hospital to other settings depending on the acuity of the client's needs.
2. Hospitals are primarily acute care centers, with clients rarely remaining for long.
3. Health and illness care has changed from a fee-for-service inpatient method of delivery to a managed-care, community-based system.
4. To control costs, Congress created a system of healthcare payment based on diagnosis-related groups (DRGs).
5. In the acute care setting, clients often require a high level of professional and technologic care. LPNs/LVNs provide care in acute settings under the direction of the registered nurse.
6. The number of LPNs/LVNs working in rehabilitation and long-term care has increased in recent years, whereas it has decreased in acute care settings.

LEARNING OUTCOME 7

Describe the philosophy of and nursing care to facilitate rehabilitation.

Concepts for Lecture

1. Rehabilitation is the process of learning to live to one's maximum potential with a chronic impairment and the resulting functional disability.
2. Rehabilitation nursing is based on a philosophy that each person has a unique set of strengths and abilities that can enable him or her to live with dignity, self-worth, and independence.
3. The philosophy on which rehabilitation nursing is based applies to clients with both acute and chronic illnesses.
4. Nursing care to facilitate rehabilitation involves prioritization of the needs of multiple clients, the use and management of equipment, effective communication with physicians and other members of the healthcare team, and practicing cost-effective care.
5. In nursing care, to facilitate rehabilitation, managing and organizing care and client advocacy are major nursing roles.
6. In the rehabilitation setting, the nurse must maintain focus on the client and his or her needs, using technology only as a tool to provide care.
7. The nurse, working as part of a team of healthcare providers, assesses the level of function of the client, develops an individualized and holistic plan of care with ongoing evaluation of outcomes, includes the family in the plan of care, and implements discharge planning to ensure a smooth transition home.

 **SUGGESTIONS FOR CLINICAL ACTIVITIES**

- Assign students to care for clients in a rehabilitation facility. They should compare the care of a client with a chronic illness to a client with an acute illness in an acute healthcare facility.

 POWERPOINT SLIDES 41–42

Tables and/or Figures

- **Figure 2-5** A Client Receives Therapy in a Long-Term Care Facility
- **Figure 2-6** The Home-Like Setting of a Residential Care Facility
- **Box 2-2** Criteria for Medicare Reimbursement for Home Care

 SUGGESTIONS FOR CLASSROOM ACTIVITIES

- Invite several nurses, each from a different healthcare setting, to appear on a panel and speak about their roles in their respective settings. Advise the students of the settings where the panel members work. Ask students to each write questions they would like to ask panel members. Collect the questions and review them for relevance to the learning outcome, and give panel members the relevant questions prior to the panel presentation. Also, allow for some live question and answer time.

 **SUGGESTIONS FOR CLINICAL ACTIVITIES**

- Before clinical assignments in both long-term care settings and acute care settings, assign students to observe and interview LVNs/LPNs about their roles. Have the students write down what they observe and what they learn in the interviews. This information can be discussed in postconferences. Over a semester, the students will probably go to more than one setting, so as students move from one setting to another, they can compare and contrast the roles they have learned about.

 **POWERPOINT SLIDES 43–46**

Tables and/or Figures

- **Figure 2-4** The Rehabilitation Team Discusses the Client's Plan of Care

 SUGGESTIONS FOR CLASSROOM ACTIVITIES

- Assign students to go to the library and find an article in a journal about rehabilitation nursing or a person who is getting or has gotten rehabilitation. Ask students to summarize the article and share it with the class.
- Ask students to break into small groups and to imagine what it would be like not to be able to walk or feed themselves and to be in a rehabilitation hospital. What would their fears be, and what would they want from the nurse and from their families and friends?

LEARNING OUTCOME 8

Define community-based nursing care and describe settings in which it occurs.

Concepts for Lecture

1. Community-based nursing focuses on culturally competent individual and family healthcare needs.
2. Nurses practicing community-based care provide direct services to individuals to manage acute or chronic health problems and to promote self-care.
3. Community-based nursing occurs in many different settings, including community-based health centers and clinics, day care programs, churches, schools, and correctional facilities.

LEARNING OUTCOME 9

Describe nursing care guidelines and special considerations for home- and community-based care.

Concepts for Lecture

1. Clients receiving home healthcare services are under the care of a physician, and the LPN/LVN provides care based on physician orders.
2. Clients whose care is paid for by Medicare reimbursement must meet the criteria for Medicare reimbursement for home care.
3. The nurse's care is guided by the home health agency's bill of rights, which the LVN/LPN will share with the client.
4. Nurses employed in home health care are invited into homes as guests; they cannot assume entry as they do in clinical settings.
5. Nurses must establish trust and rapport quickly because the care given is usually for only 1 hour a few times a week.
6. The client in home health is both the person receiving care and the person's family, which is not limited to those related by birth, adoption, or marriage.
7. The success of home care heavily depends on the supports in place, so it is crucial to address the needs of the support network.
8. Safety and infection control in the home and in residential care are priority concerns for the home health nurse.

 SUGGESTIONS FOR CLINICAL ACTIVITIES

- Arrange a tour of a rehabilitation hospital or facility. Arrange to have someone demonstrate the various types of equipment and exercises used in rehabilitation. Have an LVN/LPN on staff talk about the philosophy of nursing at this facility; how he or she works with the other healthcare professionals on the team; the process of assessment and care planning; how he or she manages and organizes care and advocates for the client; how the team works with the family; and about discharge planning.

 **POWERPOINT SLIDES 47–49**

Tables and/or Figures

- **Figure 2-7** Community Care Settings Serve People Where They Work, Worship, or Play
- **Box 2-1** Community-Based Nursing Care Settings

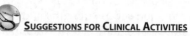 **SUGGESTIONS FOR CLASSROOM ACTIVITIES**

- Assign students to interview a nurse of their choice who works in a community care setting. Have the students write a paper on how this nurse came to work in this setting, the nurse's philosophy of nursing in this setting, what type of client the nurse serves, and how the nurse serves his or her client population. Have students present their papers in class or post them in an area where the rest of the class can read them.

 **SUGGESTIONS FOR CLINICAL ACTIVITIES**

- Arrange a tour of a jail or prison that employs LPNs/LVNs and have students observe what the nurse does when working in this particular community care setting. If this tour is not feasible, select a community care setting from the list in Box 2-1 and arrange a tour of that facility.

 **POWERPOINT SLIDES 50–59**

Tables and/or Figures

- **Box 2-2** Criteria for Medicare Reimbursement for Home Care
- **Box 2-3** A Home Health Agency's Bill of Rights
- **Table 2-3** Suggestions for Effective Home and Residential Care

SUGGESTIONS FOR CLASSROOM ACTIVITIES

- Assign students to compile a resource manual containing information about home-based and community health care. Students can collect information about the services of a variety of agencies providing these services. Information might include brochures, advertisements, interviews with marketing personnel, and information from the agency Website.

GENERAL CHAPTER CONSIDERATIONS

1. Have students study and learn key terms listed at the beginning of the chapter.
2. Have students complete end of chapter exercises either in their book or on the MyNursingKit Website.
3. Use the Classroom Response Question PowerPoints to assess students prior to lecture.

SUGGESTIONS FOR CLINICAL ACTIVITIES

- Arrange for students to have an observational experience with a home-based or community healthcare nurse.

MYNURSINGKIT (www.mynursingkit.com)

- Websites
- NCLEX® Questions
- Case Studies
- Key Terms

STUDENT WORKBOOK AND RESOURCE GUIDE

- Chapter 2 activities
- *Separate purchase*

PRENTICE HALL NURSE'S DRUG GUIDE

- *Separate purchase*

CLASSROOM RESPONSE QUESTION POWERPOINTS

TESTBANK

CHAPTER 3
CULTURAL AND DEVELOPMENT CONSIDERATIONS FOR ADULTS

LEARNING OUTCOME 1

Recognize and consider cultural differences in contributing to client assessment and care planning and implementation.

Concepts for Lecture

1. The United States is a multicultural society that is becoming ever more diverse.
2. Six cultural characteristics can help the nurse provide culturally appropriate care. These characteristics include communication, space, social orientation, time, environmental control, and biologic variation (Giger & Davidhizar, 2008).

LEARNING OUTCOME 2

Demonstrate respect for the client's cultural background.

Concepts for Lecture

1. In the United States, the biomedical model of health care, emphasizing effects of disease and treatment on the structure of the body, is prevalent. In some cultures, illness and disease are seen as the result of magic or forces of evil.
2. The nurse needs to respect cultural beliefs and accommodate folk practices whenever possible, e.g., encouraging prayer in addition to medicine in treating a disease or allowing the presence of a healer.
3. While respecting cultural beliefs, it is vital that the nurse recognize that some folk remedies are harmful. The nurse needs to ask clients what treatment was tried before seeking care.

LEARNING OUTCOME 3

Recognize cultural differences that may affect the client's response to illness and plan of treatment.

Concepts for Lecture

1. The social organization of a cultural group includes its religious practices and beliefs. The religions of the world have different religious practices and beliefs that bring care considerations.
2. Clear differences exist among cultures in regard to the concept and measurement of time. Some cultures measure by social time, and some measure by clock time. Some cultures are future oriented, and some are present oriented. People with a present orientation may be less willing to engage in preventative efforts and may arrive late to appointments.

 POWERPOINT SLIDES 21–22

Tables and/or Figures
- **Figure 3-1** The LPN/LVN Cares for Culturally Diverse Clients and Their Families
- **Figure 3-2** Giger and Davidhizer's Transcultural Assessment Model

 SUGGESTIONS FOR CLASSROOM ACTIVITIES

- Assign students to work with clients from other cultures. Ask students to observe and assess clients for the cultural characteristics of communication, space, and social orientation. Have students present in postconference about how they adapted their plan of care to provide culturally competent care based on what they found in regard to these three cultural characteristics.

 SUGGESTIONS FOR CLINICAL ACTIVITIES

- Assign students to work with clients from other cultures. Ask students to observe and assess clients for the cultural characteristics of time, environmental control, and biologic variation. Have students present in postconference about how they adapted their plan of care to provide culturally competent care based on what they found in regard to these three cultural characteristics.

 **POWERPOINT SLIDE 23**

 **SUGGESTIONS FOR CLASSROOM ACTIVITIES**

- Ask students to bring in information about folk remedies and healing practices of other cultures to share with the class. Students could find information from family and friends, on the Internet, or from interviewing people from other cultures.

POWERPOINT SLIDE 24

3. Biologic differences among people of various cultural groups affect food preference and food tolerance. Most Mexican Americans, African Americans, Native Americans, and Asians are lactose intolerant. If a client ingests milk products and has lactose intolerance, the undigested lactose in the intestine can cause cramping, flatulence, abdominal bloating, and diarrhea.

LEARNING OUTCOME 4

Compare and contrast the physical status, risks for alterations in health, and health behaviors of the young adult and middle adult.

Concepts for Lecture

1. From age 18–25, the healthy young adult is at the peak of physical development; then during the 30s, some normal physiologic changes begin to occur.

LEARNING OUTCOME 5

Provide teaching to reduce high-risk behaviors, such as information about the risks associated with smoking or drug use.

Concepts for Lecture

1. The nurse promotes health in adult clients by teaching the activities that maintain wellness.
2. The nurse provides information about known risk factors and recommended screening for early detection of disease, adapting teaching to cultural variations in risk.
3. The nurse provides specific information about decreasing risk factors, such as recommended immunizations.
4. The nurse promotes health by following healthy practices and serving as a role model.

LEARNING OUTCOME 6

Describe the functions and developmental stages and tasks of the family.

Concepts for Lecture

1. The nurse must consider both the needs of the client at a specific developmental stage and the needs of the client within a family with specific developmental tasks.
2. The family carries out tasks necessary for its survival and continuity such as providing shelter, food, clothing, and health care; sharing money, time, and space; determining roles and responsibilities; ensuring socialization of members by establishing socially acceptable ways to interact with others; rearing and releasing children appropriately; relating to the larger community; maintaining morale and motivation; rewarding achievement; dealing with personal and family crises; setting attainable goals; and developing family loyalties and values.

 **SUGGESTIONS FOR CLASSROOM ACTIVITIES**

- Assign students to clients from a variety of cultures. Have students talk with their assigned clients to find out if they know of any folk remedies and healing practices in their family of origin. Ask students to share about what they learned. Students can also describe any folk remedies and healing practices in their own family of origin and discuss if and how they impact their care.

 POWERPOINT SLIDES 25–33

Tables and/or Figures

- **Table 3-1** Major Religions of the United States
- **Table 3-2** Care Considerations for Selected Denominations

 SUGGESTIONS FOR CLASSROOM ACTIVITIES

- Ask students to share their own measurement of time (social or clock) and how this affects their daily life. Ask students to think about how people they interact with measure time and if the way they measure time is at all affected by culture.

 **POWERPOINT SLIDES 34–35**

SUGGESTIONS FOR CLINICAL ACTIVITIES

- Assign students to clients from different cultural backgrounds. Ask students to assess their client's food preferences and tolerances and help them communicate this to the dietary department and the staff. Have students ask their clients if these food preferences and tolerances are affected by culture or influenced by other factors.

Tables and/or Figures

- **Table 3-3** Physical Status and Changes in the Young Adult Years
- **Figure 3-3** Young Adults Are at the Peak of Physical Development and Health
- **Figure 3-4** In the Middle Adult, Physical Activity Contributes to Good Health

SUGGESTIONS FOR CLASSROOM ACTIVITIES

- Divide the class into four groups. Assign two groups to role play being 18–25 and two groups to be in their 30s. Ask the groups to do a role play about what it is like physiologically at their assigned ages.

 POWERPOINT SLIDES 36–37

LEARNING OUTCOME 7

Participate in health screening or health promotion activities for the young or middle adult.

Concepts for Lecture

1. There are recommended health maintenance examinations and recommended frequencies for these screenings that differ for a young adult and a middle adult.

GENERAL CHAPTER CONSIDERATIONS

1. Have students study and learn key terms listed at the beginning of the chapter.
2. Have students complete end of chapter exercises either in their book or on the MyNursingKit Website.
3. Use the Classroom Response Question PowerPoints to assess students prior to lecture.

 SUGGESTIONS FOR CLINICAL ACTIVITIES

- Assign students to care for a client who is 18–25 and another client who is in the 30-year-old range. Ask students to share in postconferences the differences in thinking, behavior, and physiology between the clients from these two different age groups.

Tables and/or Figures

- **Box 3-1** Client Teaching Health Promotion for the Adult

 **POWERPOINT SLIDES 38–44**

 SUGGESTIONS FOR CLASSROOM ACTIVITIES

- Ask students to think about how they can promote health by following healthy practices and serve as a healthy role model for clients. Have them write a page on how they will do this and turn it in for comments from the instructor.
- Ask students to make posters about unhealthy practices such as drug use and smoking and obtain permission to post these posters in public areas at the school.

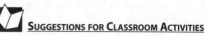 **SUGGESTIONS FOR CLINICAL ACTIVITIES**

- Have students share in postconference any data they collected while working with their assigned clients on unhealthy practices that can put the clients' health at risk.
- Ask students how they would deal with a situation in which the client smokes and has a respiratory problem but the students also smoke.

 **SUGGESTIONS FOR CLASSROOM ACTIVITIES**

- Have students identify how their families of origin reward (or rewarded) achievement and how that impacts their success as a nursing student.

SUGGESTIONS FOR CLINICAL ACTIVITIES

- Ask students to assess their assigned client(s) in clinical for how the client's family of origin and/or the client's current family carries out tasks necessary for survival and continuity.

Tables and/or Figures

- **Table 3-5** Recommended Health Screening for Healthy Adults (without Specific Risk Factors)

SUGGESTIONS FOR CLASSROOM ACTIVITIES

• Have students divide into small groups to discuss health maintenance examinations and recommended frequencies for young adults and middle adults. Prepare a list of questions and topics to cover, such as: Do young adults tend to get their recommended health examinations? Why or why not? The same questions can be asked about middle adults.

SUGGESTIONS FOR CLINICAL ACTIVITIES

• Find a healthcare fair that will be occurring in the community at an industrial site or community site, such as a senior center, and ask the charge person if your students can participate. Have students think of health teachings they can do and have them make posters or other items to help them teach (e.g., a large paper-mâché tooth to use in teaching how to brush teeth or a poster on healthy ways to prevent and manage hypertension). A typical activity for students to do is to take blood pressures and teach about hypertension.

• Clinical Reasoning Care Map

MYNURSINGKIT
(*www.mynursingkit.com*)

• Websites
• NCLEX® Questions
• Case Studies
• Key Terms

STUDENT WORKBOOK AND RESOURCE GUIDE

• Chapter 3 activities
• *Separate purchase*

PRENTICE HALL NURSE'S DRUG GUIDE

• *Separate purchase*

CLASSROOM RESPONSE QUESTION POWERPOINTS

TESTBANK

CHAPTER 4
THE OLDER ADULT IN HEALTH AND ILLNESS

LEARNING OUTCOME 1

Describe what is meant by the term *old*, including who is considered an *older* adult.

Concepts for Lecture

1. Aging may be defined in many ways, including by age in years as well as by personal definition. The older adult period begins at age 65. Older adulthood may be divided into three periods: *young-old* (ages 65 to 74), *middle-old* (ages 75 to 84), and *old-old* (ages 85 and older).
2. The rapid increase in older adults in the United States is the result of the baby boom and an increased growth of minority populations. Life expectancy has also increased over the years. By 2030, the largest increase in population groups will be in adults over age 75.

LEARNING OUTCOME 2

Discuss selected theories of aging, including those involving genetics, immunity, free radicals, and apoptosis.

Concepts for Lecture

1. The theories of why people age include genetics, immune factors, free radicals, and cell death (apoptosis). Scientists also study the factors that influence having a long and healthy life, which include genetic inheritance, physical environment, physical activity, and diet.
2. Genetic/biologic clock theories emphasize the role of genes in aging. A major idea is that there is a programmed code for aging stored in the DNA of body cells.
3. Immunity theories are based on the knowledge that components of the immune system are affected by aging, which means a person has fewer defenses against foreign organisms with aging.
4. Free radical theory suggests that unstable and reactive molecules known as free radicals interact with and damage cellular components. This theory maintains that antioxidants, which are one of the major protective mechanisms of the body, become less effective with aging.
5. The programmed aging theory proposes that cells stop dividing as they age, resulting in cell death or apoptosis. This apoptosis occurs throughout life and is regulated by opposing genes but becomes imbalanced or ineffective with increasing age.
6. The wear and tear theory holds that over time, aging cells lose their ability to repair damage, so tissues of vital organs are unable to regenerate.
7. Longevity and senescence (aging theories) focus on why people live as long as they do.

POWERPOINT SLIDES 22–24

Tables and/or Figures
- **Figure 4-1** Number of People Age 65 and Over, by Age Group, for Selected Years 1900–2000 and Projected 2010–2050

SUGGESTIONS FOR CLASSROOM ACTIVITIES
- Break into small groups and have students share about family members and acquaintances that fall into each of the older age groups (young-old, middle-old, and old-old). Ask students to decide whether they agree with the age ranges set for each of the groups and to explain their answer.

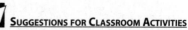

SUGGESTIONS FOR CLINICAL ACTIVITIES
- Assign students to care for clients in each of the older age groups (young-old, middle-old, and old-old). If they are caring for one client each clinical day, the assignments could be carried out over 3 clinical days.

POWERPOINT SLIDES 25–26

SUGGESTIONS FOR CLASSROOM ACTIVITIES
- Discuss healthy behaviors that lead to people living longer.

SUGGESTIONS FOR CLINICAL ACTIVITIES
- Interview two clients in a nursing home and compare their beliefs about living longer.

Tables and/or Figures
- **Table 4-2** Common Myths About Older Adults

LEARNING OUTCOME 3

Define ageism, incorporating common myths of older adults.

Concepts for Lecture

1. Ageism is a form of prejudice in which older adults are stereotyped by characteristics found in only a small number of their age group. Most older adults are satisfied with their lives, have adequate income, live in their own homes, are close to family and friends, and take part in community activities.
2. Myths and stereotypes may lead healthcare workers to have negative perceptions of older adults.

LEARNING OUTCOME 4

Compare and contrast the cognitive, psychosocial, moral, and spiritual development of the older adult with that of the young and middle adult.

Concepts for Lecture

1. Older adults continue to have developmental tasks. Cognition does not normally change with age. As people age, it is important for them to review their lives through reminiscence in order to achieve ego integrity.
2. Havighurst developed tasks for old age and later maturity. He believed the major tasks of old age centered on maintaining social contacts and relationships, with successful aging depending on one's ability to adapt to age-related roles.
3. Most older adults are at the moral development stage of conventional level and find strength in spirituality and transcendence.
4. Healthcare workers need to respect the moral and spiritual development of the older adult.

LEARNING OUTCOME 5

Explain age-related physical and psychosocial changes common to older adults.

Concepts for Lecture

1. Aging brings many physical changes, as well as the strong probability of psychosocial changes involving widowhood, retirement, and living arrangements.

LEARNING OUTCOME 6

Describe common threats to the health of the older adult, including chronic illness, accidental injuries, medication management, and dementia and confusion.

Concepts for Lecture

1. The most frequently occurring common health threats to the older adult include hypertension, arthritis, heart disease, cancer, diabetes, sinusitis, and Alzheimer's disease.

SUGGESTIONS FOR CLASSROOM ACTIVITIES

- Tape 2 large sheets of paper on the wall and title one as "Myths and Stereotypes About Older Adults" and the other one as "Facts and Positive Things About Growing Old." Ask the students to write down pertinent comments pertaining to each topic, on a sticky note provided or directly on the paper. Discuss the comments in class.
- Compare and contrast the ideas Americans have about older adults with the ideas of other countries such as Mexico and/or Japan. Assign students to research this topic prior to class.

POWERPOINT SLIDES 27–28

SUGGESTIONS FOR CLINICAL ACTIVITIES

- Instruct students to ask assigned older clients what they think are the myths and stereotypes about older adults.

POWERPOINT SLIDES 29–32

SUGGESTIONS FOR CLASSROOM ACTIVITIES

- Initiate a discussion on the developmental stages of the older adult client.
- Divide the class into three large groups. The groups should discuss the developmental stage for the young adult, middle adult, and older adult. Each group should describe the nursing role in promoting health and decreasing the risks for health alterations in each stage.

SUGGESTIONS FOR CLINICAL ACTIVITIES

- Assign students to care for older adults. Have them compare and contrast cognitive, psychosocial, moral, and spiritual development of the older adult with that of the young and middle adult.

POWERPOINT SLIDES 33–35

Tables and/or Figures

- **Table 4-3** Age-Related Physical Changes in the Older Adult
- **Figure 4-3** Multisystem Changes Associated With Aging

SUGGESTIONS FOR CLASSROOM ACTIVITIES

- Identify psychosocial changes related to the older adult. Discuss ways to assist the older adult with these changes.

SUGGESTIONS FOR CLINICAL ACTIVITIES

- Perform physical assessments on the older adult. Identify changes related to the aging process.

2. The three major causes of injury in the older adult are falls, fires, and motor vehicle crashes. Falls resulting in hip fractures are the most significant.

3. Adverse effects of prescription and over-the-counter drugs taken by older adults can have more serious consequences than in younger adults.

4. Nurses must have knowledge of how the effects of medications can differ for older adults.

5. Dementia refers to different kinds of organic disorders that progressively affect cognitive function and is not part of the normal aging process. Alzheimer's disease is the most devastating common cause of cognitive impairment.

6. Sometimes confusion and depression in an older adult are mistaken for true dementia. It is important to assess for other causes, including circulatory or metabolic problems, electrolyte imbalances, effects of medications, nutritional deficiencies, and changes and losses.

LEARNING OUTCOME 7

Incorporate actions to promote health and quality of life into nursing care of older adults.

Concepts for Lecture

1. Nursing care to promote health in older adults includes teaching healthy behaviors and encouraging healthy lifestyles, preventive medication (including screening examinations and immunizations), injury prevention, and self-management of illness.

GENERAL CHAPTER CONSIDERATIONS

1. Have students study and learn key terms listed at the beginning of the chapter.

2. Have students complete end of chapter exercises either in their book or on the MyNursingKit Website.

3. Use the Classroom Response Question PowerPoints to assess students prior to lecture.

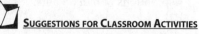

POWERPOINT SLIDES 36–41

Tables and/or Figures

- **Table 4-4** Nursing Care to Promote Health in the Older Adult
- **Box 4-2** Client Teaching Health Promotion for the Older Adult
- **Table 4-5** Recommended Health Screenings and Immunizations for Older Adults
- **Figure 4-4** Creative Outlets During Retirement
- **Figure 4-5** Regular Program of Exercise

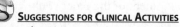

SUGGESTIONS FOR CLASSROOM ACTIVITIES

- Discuss ways to promote healthy behaviors in the older adult client, especially screening for diseases and the necessity of immunizations.

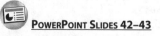

SUGGESTIONS FOR CLINICAL ACTIVITIES

- Have students develop charts or posters with large print to teach healthy behaviors to a group of older adults.
- Administer immunizations at a health clinic or long-term care facility.

POWERPOINT SLIDES 42–43

MYNURSINGKIT (www.mynursingkit.com)

- Websites
- NCLEX® Questions
- Case Studies
- Key Terms

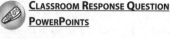

STUDENT WORKBOOK AND RESOURCE GUIDE

- Chapter 4 activities
- *Separate purchase*

PRENTICE HALL NURSE'S DRUG GUIDE

- *Separate purchase*

CLASSROOM RESPONSE QUESTION POWERPOINTS

TESTBANK

CHAPTER 5
GUIDELINES FOR CLIENT ASSESSMENT

LEARNING OUTCOME 1

Discuss the purposes of a client assessment.

Concepts for Lecture

1. Assessment is the collection of data that provide information about the client's individualized healthcare needs. Assessment is mandated by nursing standards, nurse practice acts, accrediting bodies, and institutional bodies.
2. Assessment data includes objective data and subjective data about and from the client; information about the client's family, community, culture, ethnicity, and religion; past and present client behaviors that support health or increase risk of illness; and data that suggest risk for or actual health problems (the RN will label these items as nursing diagnoses).
2. Nurses collect these data through the health assessment, which comprises a health history and a physical examination.

LEARNING OUTCOME 2

Describe the types of client assessment.

Concepts for Lecture

1. Types of assessment vary depending on the setting, the situation, and the needs of the client.
2. Types of assessment include comprehensive, partial, and focused assessments. An emergency assessment is a special type of focused assessment. It is a very rapid assessment to determine life-threatening situations.

LEARNING OUTCOME 3

Compare sources and accuracy of assessment data.

Concepts for Lecture

1. The primary source of data is the client. Secondary sources include the client's family or friends, client records, and other healthcare professionals.
2. Assessment data must be accurate and factual.

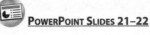 **POWERPOINT SLIDES 21–22**

Tables and/or Figures
- **Table 5-1** Information Included in a Health History
- **Table 5-3** Guidelines for a Physical Examination

 SUGGESTIONS FOR CLASSROOM ACTIVITIES

- Initiate a discussion on the importance of performing the assessment according to the standards of the Joint Commission on Accreditation of Healthcare Organizations (JCAHO).
- Discuss the difference between objective and subjective data. Have the students describe the sources for collection of data and give examples of subjective and objective data.

 SUGGESTIONS FOR CLINICAL ACTIVITIES

- Provide students with a two-column page. The first column is entitled "Subjective Data," and the second column is entitled "Objective Data." Ask students to use this sheet with an assigned client in clinical and to put what they hear from the client and what they observe in terms of subjective symptoms and objective signs into the correct column. A second page could be divided in half, with information collected about the client's family, community, culture, ethnicity, and religion put in the first half and the past and present client behaviors that support health or increase the risk of illness put in the second half. The student can circle data that suggest risk for or actual health problems.

 **POWERPOINT SLIDE 23**

Tables and/or Figures
- **Table 5-1** Information Included in a Health History

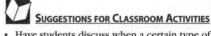 **SUGGESTIONS FOR CLASSROOM ACTIVITIES**

- Have students discuss when a certain type of assessment is appropriate to perform.

 SUGGESTIONS FOR CLINICAL ACTIVITIES

- Have students practice the steps in performing an emergency assessment.

POWERPOINT SLIDES 24–27

LEARNING OUTCOME 4

Describe components of the health history.

Concepts for Lecture

1. The health history, collected through an interview with the client, provides subjective and objective data.
2. Principles of therapeutic communication help the nurse collect accurate data.

LEARNING OUTCOME 5

Demonstrate the methods of physical examination.

Concepts for Lecture

1. The four methods of physical examination are inspection, palpation, percussion, and auscultation. The skills of physical examination take practice.

LEARNING OUTCOME 6

Prepare a client for a physical examination.

Concepts for Lecture

1. Preparation for a physical examination includes ensuring that room temperature is comfortable, area is quiet, lighting is adequate, all equipment is in working order, hands are clean, gloves are worn, Standard Precautions are followed, mask and eye goggles are worn (if appropriate), and privacy of client is maintained.
2. The purpose and the techniques of the physical examination should be explained to the client to decrease anxiety and feelings of embarassment.
3. The length of the examination should be adjusted to the physical condition and age of each client.

LEARNING OUTCOME 7

Describe the body systems and characteristics assessed in a physical examination.

Concepts for Lecture

1. A comprehensive physical examination is conducted in a head-to-toe sequence or system-by-system. If a focused or emergency assessment is being conducted, the nurse assesses only the specific client problem.

POWERPOINT SLIDES 28–30

SUGGESTIONS FOR CLASSROOM ACTIVITIES

- Have students discuss the methods of obtaining accurate and factual data.

SUGGESTIONS FOR CLINICAL ACTIVITIES

- Ask students to note instances of when they have used any of the general guidelines, in Chapter 5, for ensuring that data collected are accurate and factual and to discuss these instances in postconference.
- Have student review a client's record to obtain information needed to develop a plan of care.

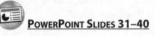
POWERPOINT SLIDES 31–40

Tables and/or Figures
- **Table 5-1** Information Included in a Health History

SUGGESTIONS FOR CLINICAL ACTIVITIES

- In the clinical setting, review a health assessment form with the students.
- Have students interview clients using therapeutic communication techniques.

SUGGESTIONS FOR CLASSROOM ACTIVITIES

- Initiate a discussion on the importance of cultural and social differences when obtaining a health history or performing a physical assessment.
- Partner students in groups of two or three. Have students role play methods of collecting data for a health history. Have students use methods of therapeutic communication such as closed-ended and open-ended questions to collect data.

POWERPOINT SLIDES 41–42

Tables and/or Figures
- **Table 5-2** Characteristics Assessed by Palpation
- **Figure 5-1** The Position of the Hand for Light Palpation

SUGGESTIONS FOR CLASSROOM ACTIVITIES

- Initiate a discussion on the methods of physical assessment. Have the students identify the methods of assessment to use in the following scenarios:
  - Scenario A: A 49-year-old male is admitted with a productive cough and shortness of breath.
  - Scenario B: A 30-year-old male is admitted with complaint of severe abdominal pain with nausea and vomiting.

POWERPOINT SLIDES 43–60

LEARNING OUTCOME 8

Document a health assessment.

Concepts for Lecture

1. Documenting assessments factually and accurately provides the base for evaluation of healthcare outcomes, provides evidence to support healthcare cost reimbursement, and is legal evidence of the health status of the client at that point in time.

GENERAL CHAPTER CONSIDERATIONS

1. Have students study and learn key terms listed at the beginning of the chapter.
2. Have students complete end of chapter exercises either in their book or on the MyNursingKit Website.
3. Use the Classroom Response Question PowerPoints to assess students prior to lecture.

- Scenario C: A 68-year-old female is diagnosed with a fractured femur and has a cast applied to the right lower extremity.
- Scenario D: A 78-year-old female admitted with an acute onset of congestive heart failure has a complaint of shortness of breath and edema of the lower extremities.

 **SUGGESTIONS FOR CLINICAL ACTIVITIES**

- Pair up students in the clinical laboratory and have them practice methods of physical assessment on each other.

Tables and/or Figures

- **Box 5-1** Focus on Older Adults: Age-Related Assessment Findings in the Older Adult

 POWERPOINT SLIDES 61–62

 **SUGGESTIONS FOR CLASSROOM ACTIVITIES**

- Pair students and have them practice explaining the purpose and the techniques of the physical examination to decrease anxiety and feelings of embarrassment. The students can take turns in the role of nurse and the role of client.

 SUGGESTIONS FOR CLINICAL ACTIVITIES

- Assign students to observational experiences in physicians' offices so they can observe the nurse in the office explaining the purpose and the techniques of the physical examination to decrease anxiety and feelings of embarrassment. Ask students to write about the experience and what they would do differently from the nurse they observed, if anything. If they would not change anything, ask the students to state why.

Tables and/or Figures

- **Table 5-3** Guidelines for a Physical Examination
- **Box 5-2** Assessment: Assessing the Pupils

 SUGGESTIONS FOR CLASSROOM ACTIVITIES

- Divide students into groups of three to four. Assign each group to perform an assessment on a body system and document its findings.

 SUGGESTIONS FOR CLINICAL ACTIVITIES

- Assign students to perform a beginning-of-shift physical assessment on the assigned client and document findings using the principles of factual and accurate documentation found in the chapter.

SUGGESTIONS FOR CLASSROOM ACTIVITIES

- Review examples of documentation to discuss how to document accurately and factually.
- Have students attend a documentation class at the healthcare facilities at which they will be doing clinical rotations.

SUGGESTIONS FOR CLINICAL ACTIVITIES

- Review examples of documentation to discuss how to document accurately and factually.
- Have students attend a documentation class at the healthcare facilities at which they will be doing clinical rotations.
- Have students practice documenting factually and accurately before documenting in a client's medical record.

- Clinical Reasoning Care Map

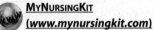

MYNURSINGKIT (*www.mynursingkit.com*)

- Websites
- NCLEX® Questions
- Case Studies
- Key Terms

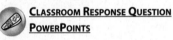

STUDENT WORKBOOK AND RESOURCE GUIDE

- Chapter 5 activities
- *Separate purchase*

PRENTICE HALL NURSE'S DRUG GUIDE

- *Separate purchase*

CLASSROOM RESPONSE QUESTION POWERPOINTS

TESTBANK

CHAPTER 6
ESSENTIAL NURSING PHARMACOLOGY

LEARNING OUTCOME 1

Describe the naming of drugs and the laws that govern the prescription, storage, and administration of drugs.

Concepts for Lecture

1. All drugs have four names: chemical, generic, trade, and official. The chemical name describes the chemical compounds and the molecular structure of the drug. Since the chemical names are long and seldom used, drugs are given a shorter name called a nonproprietary or generic name, which is approved by the United States Adopted Names (USAN) Council. The official name is usually the trade name (brand name), which identifies drugs sold by a specific manufacturer.
2. Laws regulate generic and nongeneric drugs with respect to the amount and purity of each drug as well as whether prescriptions can be filled with generic drugs or must be filled by the trade name.
3. Laws governing drugs include the Food, Drug and Cosmetic Act, which outlines regulations regarding labeling and packaging of drugs and requirements for toxicity tests on lab animals, and the Controlled Substances Act of 1970, which lists five schedules of drugs based on potential abuse and medical effectiveness.

LEARNING OUTCOME 2

Describe the processes of pharmacokinetics: absorption, distribution, metabolism, and excretion.

Concepts for Lecture

1. Pharmacokinetics is the study of how drugs are processed by the body.
2. The processes of absorption, distribution, metabolism, and excretion make up the pharmacokinetic action of a drug.
3. Older adults have physiologic changes that affect pharmacologic processes.

LEARNING OUTCOME 3

Explain factors that affect pharmacokinetics in older adults.

Concepts for Lecture

1. Older adults have physiologic changes that affect pharmacokinetic processes. These changes include changes in absorption, distribution, metabolism, and excretion.
2. The practice of polypharmacy (use of many prescribed and over-the-counter drugs at the same time), along with pharmacokinetic changes, often leads to drug toxicity in the older adult.

 POWERPOINT SLIDES 21–28

Tables and/or Figures
- **Table 6-1** Schedule for Controlled Substances

 SUGGESTIONS FOR CLASSROOM ACTIVITIES

- Ask a pharmacist to talk to the class about laws involved in dispensing drugs from the pharmacy and provide students a chance to ask questions.
- Develop a matching quiz to match generic names to trade names to help students identify drug names.
- Compare and contrast drugs in each of the controlled substance schedules.

 **SUGGESTIONS FOR CLINICAL ACTIVITIES**

- Have students familiarize themselves with the controlled substances kept on the unit or units where they are assigned. Discuss with students the facility and nursing school policies and procedures associated with signing out and giving a controlled substance to an assigned client.
- Have students look up assigned clients' drugs in the *Hospital Formulary* or the *Physician's Drug Reference* while in the clinical setting.

 REFERENCE
- www.fda.gov

 **POWERPOINT SLIDES 29–36**

Tables and/or Figures
- **Table 6-2** Drug Absorption Routes
- **Box 6-1** Focus on Older Adults: Pharmacokinetic Changes in Older Adults
- **Figure 6-1** The Four Processes of Drug Movement

 SUGGESTIONS FOR CLASSROOM ACTIVITIES

- Discuss disease processes and physiologic changes of aging that may affect the processes of pharmacokinetics.
- Discuss how to administer medications to bypass the blood–brain barrier.
- Compare and contrast injection sites for speed of absorption.

POWERPOINT SLIDE 37

LEARNING OUTCOME 4

Identify how pharmacodynamics affects drug action.

Concepts for Lecture

1. Pharmacodynamics is the study of how drugs produce their effects in the body to result in a pharmacologic response.
2. The effectiveness of a drug depends on its action and dose.
3. The response to any drug depends on the amount of drug given.
4. Drug interactions are the effects that occur when actions of one drug are affected by another drug, food, or herbal therapy.
5. Adverse drug reactions (ADR) range from expected side effects to toxic effects. The most common toxic effects include liver and kidney damage.

LEARNING OUTCOME 5

Apply the nursing process to administering medications.

Concepts for Lecture

1. The nursing process, when correctly applied to drug therapy, reduces the potential for errors and promotes sound decision making.
2. Assessment begins by collecting data on the client's medication history.
3. Diagnosing focuses on identifying the client's actual and potential health problems based on the assessment data. Examples of appropriate nursing diagnoses include: deficient knowledge, ineffective health maintenance, noncompliance, and risk for injury related to side effects.
4. During the planning step, the nurse reviews the drug's purpose, recommended dose, potential side effects, and therapeutic effects. The nurse plans when medications are scheduled according to the physician's orders and plans client teaching about taking medications at home.
5. Before giving medications, the nurse must have an order from an authorized healthcare provider and take all precautions to administer the right medication safely and correctly.
6. The success of the nursing interventions is measured by evaluating the client's outcomes and the success of the teaching.

LEARNING OUTCOME 6

Explain the six rights of medication administration and the nursing implications of each right.

Concepts for Lecture

1. Safe medication administration means implementing the "six rights" in order to prevent a medication error. The six rights are right medication, right client, right time, right route, right dose, and right documentation.
2. Preventing medication errors requires everyone to make a commitment to client safety.

 SUGGESTIONS FOR CLINICAL ACTIVITIES

- Have students explain factors affecting the speed of absorption of medications to assigned clients.

 POWERPOINT SLIDES 38–44

Tables and/or Figures

- **Box 6-1** Focus on Older Adults: Pharmacokinetic Changes in Older Adults

SUGGESTIONS FOR CLASSROOM ACTIVITIES

- Ask each student to ask one to four older adults how many medications they take, including both prescription and over-the-counter medications. Can they name their medications, and do they know what they are for? Ask students what health practices they would follow to reduce the number of medications they would have to take when they are older.

SUGGESTIONS FOR CLINICAL ACTIVITIES

- Assign students to compare the number of medications taken by older clients assigned to them and the number of medications taken by younger clients. Have students compare the number of medications taken among the older clients.

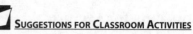 **POWERPOINT SLIDES 45–51**

Tables and/or Figures

- **Figure 6-2** First Pass Effect
- **Figure 6-3** Receptor Site Action
- **Figure 6-4** Potency and Efficacy

SUGGESTIONS FOR CLASSROOM ACTIVITIES

- Discuss effective nursing interventions to help manage the adverse effects of medications.
- Research foods or drugs that should be avoided with medication administration.
- Assign students to present a case study on a client, including the factors of drug effectiveness, variables in drug response, and possible adverse reactions of the drugs the client is taking.

SUGGESTIONS FOR CLINICAL ACTIVITIES

- In postconference, discuss drugs in which the therapeutic effects vary when administered to different clients with different disease processes.
- Have students look up medications on a drug incompatibility chart to determine which drugs are incompatible.
- Interview a client with a hypersensitivity to a medication and explore the signs and symptoms the client exhibited.

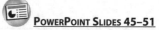 **POWERPOINT SLIDE 52**

LEARNING OUTCOME 7

Describe nursing strategies to reduce medication errors.

Concepts for Lecture

1. To reduce medication errors, the nurse must follow the six rights; question unfamiliar abbreviations, unusual drug name or dose, confusing drug name, or ambiguous drug orders; and when transcribing orders to the MAR, use only acceptable abbreviations and symbols.
2. The nurse needs to ask the following questions: Does the drug make sense for the client's diagnosis? Has the client achieved the desired therapeutic effect with a drug?
3. If pharmacy sends multiple tablets, ampoules, or vials for a single dose, the nurse must question the dose. If a dose seems unusually small or large, the nurse must ask the pharmacist or physician for clarification.
4. The nurse needs to take the MAR into the client's room and compare the drug to be given with the MAR for accuracy.

GENERAL CHAPTER CONSIDERATIONS

1. Have students study and learn key terms listed at the beginning of the chapter.
2. Have students complete end of chapter exercises either in their book or on the MyNursingKit Website.
3. Use the Classroom Response Question PowerPoints to assess students prior to lecture.

POWERPOINT SLIDES 53–54

Tables and/or Figures
- **Box 6-4** Medication History

SUGGESTIONS FOR CLASSROOM ACTIVITIES
- Have students develop patient teaching sheets on the most common drugs administered.
- Discuss which assessments are necessary prior to administration of medications.

SUGGESTIONS FOR CLINICAL ACTIVITIES
- Have students develop a plan for teaching an assigned client about a medication. Ask students to do a self-evaluation on the success of the teaching.
- Have students develop a care plan for a client receiving medication, including the outcome criteria for evaluating the effectiveness of the medications.
- Have students prepare drug cards to use in the clinical setting.

SUGGESTIONS FOR CLASSROOM ACTIVITIES
- Compare and contrast medication administration routes and techniques.
- Discuss the steps to take when a medication error occurs.

SUGGESTIONS FOR CLINICAL ACTIVITIES
- Administer medications in the clinical setting, using the six rights of medication administration.

SUGGESTIONS FOR CLASSROOM ACTIVITIES
- Have students find articles, in healthcare and nursing journals, that address avoiding medication errors or learning from errors nurses have made.

SUGGESTIONS FOR CLINICAL ACTIVITIES
- Have students write the six rights on an index card and read it before giving medication to assigned clients.
- In postconference, ask students to discuss ways to avoid medication errors.
- Ask a nurse on the clinical unit to share his or her observations with the students on how to avoid medication errors.

MyNursingKit
(www.mynursingkit.com)

- Websites
- NCLEX® Questions
- Case Studies
- Key Terms

Student Workbook and Resource Guide

- Chapter 6 activities
- *Separate purchase*

Prentice Hall Nurse's Drug Guide

- *Separate purchase*

Classroom Response Question PowerPoints

Testbank

CHAPTER 7
CARING FOR CLIENTS WITH ALTERED FLUID, ELECTROLYTE, OR ACID–BASE BALANCE

LEARNING OUTCOME 1

Identify the functions and regulatory mechanisms that maintain water and electrolyte balance in the body.

Concepts for Lecture

1. The volume and composition of body fluid are normally maintained by a balance of fluid and electrolyte intake; elimination of water, electrolytes, and acids by the kidneys; and hormonal influences. Change in any of these factors can lead to a fluid, electrolyte, or acid–base imbalance that affects health.
2. Fluid, electrolyte, and acid–base imbalances can affect all body systems, especially the cardiovascular and central nervous systems, and the transmission of nerve impulses.

LEARNING OUTCOME 2

Compare and contrast the causes and effects of fluid volume deficit and excess.

Concepts for Lecture

1. Fluid volume deficits may be due to excessive fluid losses, insufficient fluid intake, or both.
2. Fluid volume excess usually results from sodium and water retention.
3. Fluid and sodium imbalances commonly are related; both affect serum osmolality.
4. Potassium imbalances are due to excess or deficit in potassium intake, resulting in cardiac dysrhythmias.
5. Three hormones interact to regulate serum calcium levels: parathyroid hormone, calcitriol, and calcitonin.
6. Magnesium is critical to intracellular metabolism and extracellular functioning of neuromuscular transmission. The kidneys control extracellular magnesium.
7. Phosphorus is found in all body tissue, but most of it is combined with calcium in bones and teeth. It is the primary anion in intracellular fluid, with very small amounts in extracellular fluid. An inverse relationship exists between phosphorus and calcium levels.

LEARNING OUTCOME 3

Identify tests used to diagnose and monitor treatment of fluid and electrolyte imbalances.

Concepts for Lecture

1. Diagnostic studies, laboratory tests, and invasive monitoring help determine and monitor fluid volume imbalances.

 **POWERPOINT SLIDES 21–32**

Tables and/or Figures
- **Table 7-1** Average Fluid Intake and Output in Adults
- **Table 7-2** Normal Laboratory Values for Electrolytes, Osmolality, and Urine Specific Gravity
- **Figure 7-1** A Comparison of the Major Fluid Compartments of the Body
- **Figure 7-2** The Principal Electrolytes in Extracellular and Intracellular Fluids
- **Figure 7-9** The Renin-Angiotensin-Aldosterone System
- **Figure 7-10** The Effect of Antidiuretic Hormone (ADH) Release

 **SUGGESTIONS FOR CLASSROOM ACTIVITIES**
- Divide the class into small groups. Assign each group to present one hormone associated with regulating body fluids: renin-angiotensin-aldosterone system, antidiuretic hormone, or atrial natriuretic factor. Present the regulatory mechanisms and the disorders associated with each hormone.
- Have students keep a log of their fluid intake for 3 days and compare this to the recommended normal intake of fluids.

 **SUGGESTIONS FOR CLINICAL ACTIVITIES**
- Have the students review their assigned clients' lab tests to compare the clients' electrolytes with the normal range for these electrolytes and discuss their findings in postconference.

 **POWERPOINT SLIDES 33–38**

Tables and/or Figures
- **Table 7-3** Fluid Volume Deficit
- **Box 7-1** Focus on Older Adults: Fluid Volume Deficit in Older Adults
- **Box 7-8** Nursing Care Checklist: Fluid Restriction Guidelines

 SUGGESTIONS FOR CLASSROOM ACTIVITIES
- Discuss the key terms used in discussing the transportation of fluids across cell membranes and capillary walls.

 **POWERPOINT SLIDES 39–42**

LEARNING OUTCOME 4

Recognize normal and abnormal values of electrolytes in the blood.

Concepts for Lecture

1. The normal range of sodium is 135 to 145 mEq/L. Hyponatremia and hypernatremia lead to neurologic manifestations. Excessively low or high sodium levels are considered critical and require immediate attention.
2. The normal serum extracellular fluid (ECF) level of potassium (K) is 3.5 to 5.3 mEq/L, and the normal intracellular fluid (ICF) level is 140 to 150 mEq/L. Both hypokalemia and hyperkalemia affect cardiac conduction and function. Carefully monitor cardiac rhythm and status in clients with very low or very high potassium levels.
3. The normal level of calcium (Ca) is 4.5 to 5.5 mEq/L or 9 to 11 mg/dL. Calcium imbalances primarily affect neuromuscular transmission. Too little calcium causes increased neuromuscular irritability; too much calcium depresses neuromuscular transmission. Magnesium imbalances have a similar effect.
4. Magnesium imbalances affect neuromuscular transmission, the central nervous system, the cardiovascular system, and metabolism of potassium and calcium.
5. The normal serum phosphorus level in adults is 2.5 to 4.5 mg/dL (1.7 to 2.6 mEq/L). Within cells, phosphorus is important for energy (ATP) production, metabolism, and red blood cell function. A very small portion of phosphorus (1%) is in the extracellular fluid, but it is essential for normal neuromuscular activity.

LEARNING OUTCOME 5

Use arterial blood gas results to identify the type of acid–base imbalance present in a client.

Concepts for Lecture

1. Acid–base imbalances may be caused by either metabolic or respiratory problems.
2. Buffers, lungs, and kidneys work together to maintain acid–base balance in the body. Buffers respond to changes almost immediately; the lungs respond within minutes; the kidneys, however, require hours to days to restore normal acid–base balance.
3. The lungs compensate for metabolic acid–base imbalances by excreting or retaining carbon dioxide. Increasing or decreasing the rate and depth of respirations accomplishes this.
4. The kidneys compensate for respiratory acid–base imbalances by producing and retaining or excreting bicarbonate and by retaining or excreting hydrogen ions.
5. There are two major categories of acid–base imbalances: acidosis and alkalosis.

 **SUGGESTIONS FOR CLINICAL ACTIVITIES**

- Assign students to care for clients who are on restricted intake and clients who are on forced fluids and to determine why the clients are being instructed to drink less or more than normal.

 **POWERPOINT SLIDES 43–52**

Tables and/or Figures

- **Table 7-14** Normal Arterial Blood Gas Values

SUGGESTIONS FOR CLASSROOM ACTIVITIES

- Discuss the use of arterial blood gas findings to identify the types of acid–base imbalances present in a client.
- Review the procedures for performing the laboratory and diagnostic studies. What preparation needs to be done prior to conducting the studies? What needs to be done after completing the procedure? What teaching needs to be done with the client?

SUGGESTIONS FOR CLINICAL ACTIVITIES

- Assign students to hospital clients who are recovering in a post-intensive care unit. Review with students the laboratory and diagnostic studies and arterial blood gas results of clients. When clients were experiencing significant imbalances, what was the clinical picture? What treatments were ordered? What was the client's response?

Tables and/or Figures

- **Table 7-7** Sodium Imbalances
- **Table 7-8** Potassium Imbalances
- **Table 7-10** Calcium Imbalances
- **Table 7-12** Magnesium Imbalances
- **Table 7-13** Phosphorus Imbalances

SUGGESTIONS FOR CLASSROOM ACTIVITIES

- Divide the class into four groups. Assign each group to present the functions of each major electrolyte. Include the manifestations of each excess or deficit and the corrections for the excess or deficit. Have the groups formulate a nursing care plan for each imbalance.

 **POWERPOINT SLIDE 53**

SUGGESTIONS FOR CLINICAL ACTIVITIES

- Review with students which of their clients are receiving diuretic therapy. What are the classifications of diuretics? How do diuretics affect the electrolyte results? Do the clients follow any diet modifications or take supplements? What teaching should be given to the individual clients?

Learning Outcome 6

Provide appropriate nursing care and teaching for clients with fluid, electrolyte, or acid-base disorders.

Concepts for Lecture

1. Careful monitoring of respiratory and cardiovascular status, mental status, neuromuscular function, and laboratory values is an important nursing responsibility for all clients with fluid, electrolyte, or acid-base imbalances.

General Chapter Considerations

1. Have students study and learn key terms listed at the beginning of the chapter.
2. Have students complete end of chapter exercises either in their book or on the MyNursingKit Website.
3. Use the Classroom Response Question PowerPoints to assess students prior to lecture.

PowerPoint Slides 54–133

Tables and/or Figures
- **Box 7-8** Nursing Care Checklist: Fluid Restriction Guidelines
- **Box 7-13** Nursing Care Checklist: Interpreting Arterial Blood Gases

Suggestions for Classroom Activities

- Divide the class into four groups. Have the groups present the causes and manifestations of primary acid-base imbalances. Include the normal lab values, the abnormal lab values, and compensatory mechanisms for each imbalance.

Suggestions for Clinical Activities

- Arrange for students to observe arterial blood gases being drawn. Review the client's record for arterial blood gas results. Assist the students to determine the type of acid-base imbalance. Have the students identify causative factors in the client's case that led to the acid-base imbalance.

Tables and/or Figures
- **Table 7-3** Fluid Volume Deficit
- **Table 7-5** Fluid Volume Excess
- **Box 7-3** Nursing Care Checklist: Intravenous Infusion
- **Box 7-4** Procedure Checklist: Changing an Intravenous Bag, Tubing, and Site Dressing
- **Box 7-5** Procedure Checklist: Initiating an Intravenous Infusion
- **Box 7-7** Foods High in Sodium
- **Table 7-6** Giving Medication Safely: Fluid Volume Excess
- **Box 7-9** Client Teaching: Low-Sodium Diet
- **Table 7-9** Giving Medications Safely: Potassium Replacement
- **Box 7-10** Foods High in Potassium
- **Table 7-11** Giving Medications Safely: Calcium Preparations
- **Table 7-15** Primary Acid-Base Imbalances
Nursing Care Plan: Client With Excess Fluid Volume
Nursing Care Plan: Client With Hypokalemia

Suggestions for Classroom Activities

- Use the nursing process case studies in the textbook to show the appropriate nursing care and teaching for clients with fluid, electrolyte, or acid-base disorders.

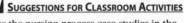

Suggestions for Clinical Activities

- Assign the students to care for clients with acid-base imbalances. Have them report the clinical manifestations that the client exhibited, compare them with the textbook, and report observations.

- Assign the students to clients receiving intravenous therapy. Have them calculate the rate of infusion and discuss the potential complications for a client with intravenous therapy.
- Assign the students to care for clients who are receiving enteral feedings. Calculate the total calories and intake and output. Are daily/weekly weight measures being performed? How does weight relate to the intake and output? Do clients exhibit behavior consistent with fluid deficit or overload?

- Clinical Reasoning Care Map

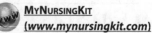

MyNursingKit
(www.mynursingkit.com)

- Websites
- NCLEX® Questions
- Case Studies
- Key Terms

Student Workbook and Resource Guide

- Chapter 7 activities
- *Separate purchase*

Prentice Hall Nurse's Drug Guide

- *Separate purchase*

Classroom Response Question
PowerPoints

Testbank

CHAPTER 8
CARING FOR CLIENTS IN PAIN

LEARNING OUTCOME 1

Describe the physiology of pain.

Concepts for Lecture

1. Pain impulses are initiated by direct tissue damage and by release of internal chemicals. The ability of the body to produce pain depends on *nociceptors*, which are nerve endings in the skin, viscera, blood vessels, muscle, and joints. Nociceptors are activated when noxious (unpleasant) stimuli are applied. This activation starts the pain process. Once noxious stimuli cause tissue damage, inflammation begins, and this inflammation causes the release of bradykinins and prostaglandins, which also activate nociceptors. Pain impulses are initiated by direct tissue damage and by the release of internal chemicals.
2. Long-lasting, intense stimulation produces greater pain than does brief, mild stimulation.
3. Pain is transmitted through the four steps of transduction, transmission, perception, and modulation.
4. The gate-control theory of pain states that pain impulses traveling from the skin to the spinal cord can be stopped at the spinal cord or allowed to be transmitted to the brain by opening or closing the gate by stimulation of nerve fibers.

LEARNING OUTCOME 2

Identify the characteristics of acute, chronic, cancer, neuropathic, and psychogenic pain.

Concepts for Lecture

1. Acute pain is usually temporary, has a sudden onset, and is localized. It normally lasts for less than 6 months and has an identified cause. Acute pain is caused by tissue injury from trauma, surgery, or inflammation.
2. Acute pain is classified into four major types: cutaneous pain, deep somatic pain, visceral pain, and referred pain.
3. Chronic pain is prolonged pain, usually lasting longer than 6 months. There may not be an identifiable cause, and often it is unresponsive to conventional medical treatment.
4. Cancer pain can result from the disease itself (tumor pressing on nerves or other structures), stretching of viscera, or metastasis to the bones.
5. Neuropathic pain is pain caused by damage to the central nervous system or peripheral nerves or following surgical or traumatic amputation of a limb.
6. Psychogenic pain results from emotional rather than physical causes.

 **POWERPOINT SLIDES 23–33**

Tables and/or Figures
- **Table 8-1** Pain Stimuli
- **Figure 8-1** Pain Conduction
- **Figure 8-2** Substance-P Transmits Pain Impulse, and During Modulation, Endorphins Are Released
- **Figure 8-3** Diagram of Gate-Control Theory

 **SUGGESTIONS FOR CLASSROOM ACTIVITIES**
- Initiate a discussion on the different methods of pain conduction.
- Assign students to groups of four. Have each group present a theory of pain and role play the therapeutic measures for the theory.
- Initiate a discussion on the types of pain pathways. Divide the class into groups of four, and assign each group to present a pathway.

 **POWERPOINT SLIDES 34–41**

Tables and/or Figures
- **Table 8-2** Comparison of Acute and Chronic Pain

 **SUGGESTIONS FOR CLASSROOM ACTIVITIES**
- Ask the students to relate their personal experiences with acute and chronic pain. Ask them to describe their pain threshold and pain tolerance levels. Were these levels different as a child? What cultural factors influence the coping skills for pain?

 **SUGGESTIONS FOR CLINICAL ACTIVITIES**
- Interview a client with pain. Determine the signs and symptoms the client is exhibiting. Classify the type of pain as to whether it is acute or chronic.

 **POWERPOINT SLIDES 42–44**

Tables and/or Figures
- **Box 8-1** Nursing Care Checklist: Client Receiving Intraspinal Analgesia

LEARNING OUTCOME 3

Identify factors that may affect a client's response to pain.

Concepts for Lecture

1. A person's response to pain is shaped by age, sociocultural factors, emotional state, past experiences with pain, meaning of pain, and person's knowledge base.
2. Pain management includes medications, such as nonopioids, opioids, and adjuvant analgesics, and nonpharmacologic therapies, including relaxation, distraction, massage, and TENS.
3. Nonopioids are used to manage mild to moderate pain; opioids are given for moderate to severe pain; and adjuvant analgesics are used in chronic pain.
4. Route of administration affects the onset and duration of pain relief.

LEARNING OUTCOME 4

Discuss the interdisciplinary care for the client in pain, including medications, surgery, transcutaneous electrical nerve stimulation, and complementary therapies.

Concepts for Lecture

1. Effective pain relief involves collaboration among a variety of healthcare professionals.
2. Medication is the most common approach to pain management; drugs include nonopioids, opioids, and adjuvant analgesics.
3. As a pain-relief measure, surgery is performed only after all other methods have failed. Clients need to understand thoroughly the implications of surgery for pain relief.
4. Types of surgery include cordotomy, neurectomy, sympathectomy, and rhizotomy.
5. A transcutaneous electrical nerve stimulation (TENS) unit is a low-voltage transmitter connected by wires to electrodes that are placed on the client. The client experiences a vibrating sensation that decreases pain.
6. Complementary therapies are often used with analgesics to treat pain. These methods are nonpharmacologic and include acupuncture, biofeedback, relaxation, distraction, hypnotism, and cutaneous stimulation.

LEARNING OUTCOME 5

Describe nonpharmacologic interventions clients may use in reducing or relieving pain.

Concepts for Lecture

1. Nonpharmacologic interventions are often used together with analgesics to treat pain. Their success is highly individualized.
2. Nonpharmacologic methods include acupuncture, biofeedback, relaxation, distraction, hypnotism, and cutaneous stimulation.

SUGGESTIONS FOR CLASSROOM ACTIVITIES

- Divide the students into groups of four. Assign each group a method of pain relief, such as pharmacology and surgery.
- Divide the students into groups of four and ask them to discuss the factors shaping a person's response to pain and to give a report to the group.
- Divide the students into groups of four. Assign each group a method of pain relief and ask the group to discuss when that method would be especially appropriate, what the nurse should assess before giving that method of pain relief, and what the nurse should chart.

SUGGESTIONS FOR CLINICAL ACTIVITIES

- Assign students to care for clients who are having pain. Have students observe the clients' responses to pain and report their observations in postconference, as well as what methods of pain relief were used for the clients.

POWERPOINT SLIDES 45–49

Tables and/or Figures

- **Table 8-3** Giving Medications Safely: Acetaminophen, NSAIDs, and Opioids
- **Table 8-4** Equianalgesic Dosage Chart
- **Table 8-5** Methods of Cutaneous Stimulation
- **Figure 8-5** Transdermal Patch

SUGGESTIONS FOR CLASSROOM ACTIVITIES

- Invite someone using a TENS unit to demonstrate it in class, or borrow a unit and have the students familiarize themselves with it.

SUGGESTIONS FOR CLINICAL ACTIVITIES

- Assign students to care for someone with pain and to discuss with that client the treatments the client has undergone for pain. Ask the students to share this information in postconference. Ask the students to share their thoughts and feelings about this client's pain and pain treatment and caring for this client.

POWERPOINT SLIDES 50–51

Tables and/or Figures

- **Table 8-5** Methods of Cutaneous Stimulation
- **Figure 8-8** TENS Unit

SUGGESTIONS FOR CLASSROOM ACTIVITIES

- Have students research alternative or complementary therapies of pain relief and present their findings to the class.

LEARNING OUTCOME 6

Describe pain rating scales and their use in assessing pain.

Concepts for Lecture

1. The first step in relieving the client's pain is to conduct an accurate, unbiased, and thorough assessment of the client's pain.
2. Pain rating scales include the McGill Pain Questionnaire, the visual analog scale, the numeric pain intensity scale, the simple descriptive pain intensity pain rating scale, and the Wong–Baker Faces Pain Rating Scale, which is used for clients who do not understand English or numbers.

LEARNING OUTCOME 7

Use the nursing process in care of clients experiencing pain.

Concepts for Lecture

1. All pain relief measures must incorporate an individualized and preventive approach.

LEARNING OUTCOME 8

Explain the nurse's role in administering medications to reduce or relieve pain.

Concepts for Lecture

1. The nurse assumes an important role in assessing the client's pain and working collaboratively with the physician to implement appropriate pain-reducing methods.
2. Clients receiving opioids must be monitored for side effects of sedation, respiratory depression, nausea, and constipation.

GENERAL CHAPTER CONSIDERATIONS

1. Have students study and learn key terms listed at the beginning of the chapter.
2. Have students complete end of chapter exercises either in their book or on the MyNursingKit Website.
3. Use the Classroom Response Question PowerPoints to assess students prior to lecture.

SUGGESTIONS FOR CLINICAL ACTIVITIES

- Assign students to attend a pain management clinic and have them observe the nonpharmacologic types of pain management used with the clients.

POWERPOINT SLIDE 52

Tables and/or Figures

- **Box 8-2** Assessment: Assessing for Pain
- **Figure 8-10** Examples of Commonly Used Pain Scales

SUGGESTIONS FOR CLASSROOM ACTIVITIES

- Discuss each step in assessing clients for pain.
- Explain how to use various forms of pain-rating scales.

POWERPOINT SLIDE 53

SUGGESTIONS FOR CLINICAL ACTIVITIES

- Have the students utilize pain rating scales in the clinical setting. Discuss which pain rating scale is appropriate to use based on age, developmental level, and culture.

Tables and/or Figures

- **Box 8-2** Assessment: Assessing for Pain
- **Box 8-3** Misconceptions About Pain Management
- **Figure 8-9** The McGill Pain Questionnaire
- **Figure 8-10** Examples of Commonly Used Pain Scales
- **Figure 8-11** Flow Sheet for Nursing Documentation of Pain Management

SUGGESTIONS FOR CLASSROOM ACTIVITIES

- Using the nursing process, discuss the nurse's role as caregiver in pain relief.

SUGGESTIONS FOR CLINICAL ACTIVITIES

- Have students develop a plan of care for pain management for assigned clients.

POWERPOINT SLIDES 54–59

Tables and/or Figures

- **Box 8-4** Focus on Older Adults: Pain Management Guidelines for the Older Adult
- **Table 8-3** Giving Medications Safely: Acetaminophen, NSAIDs, and Opioids

SUGGESTIONS FOR CLASSROOM ACTIVITIES

- Using Box 8-4, initiate a discussion on the guidelines and rationales for managing pain in the elderly.
- Discuss the responsibilities of the nurse in pain management.
- Discuss the Clinical Reasoning Care Map, and have the students answer the questions associated with the map.

SUGGESTIONS FOR CLINICAL ACTIVITIES

- In postconference, discuss pain management used with assigned clients in the clinical setting. Compare signs and symptoms of pain exhibited by the clients. Evaluate whether pain management was effective or not.

- Clinical Reasoning Care Map

MYNURSINGKIT
(www.mynursingkit.com)

- Websites
- NCLEX® Questions
- Case Studies
- Key Terms

STUDENT WORKBOOK AND RESOURCE GUIDE

- Chapter 8 activities
- *Separate purchase*

PRENTICE HALL NURSE'S DRUG GUIDE

- *Separate purchase*

CLASSROOM RESPONSE QUESTION POWERPOINTS

TESTBANK

Chapter 9
Caring for Clients With Inflammation and Infection

Learning Outcome 1

Differentiate between the local and systemic manifestations of acute inflammation.

Concepts for Lecture

1. Local manifestations of acute inflammation develop at and around the site of injury and include redness, warmth, edema, pain, and loss of function.
2. Local manifestations also include cellulitis, which is an infection that develops when inflammation spreads to the surrounding connective tissues.
3. Other local manifestations include abscesses, which is when pus develops and accumulates in pockets as the body's way of walling off infection, or the formation of a fistula.
4. Systemic responses to inflammation include enlargement of the lymph nodes (lymphadenopathy), fever, leukocytosis, tachycardia, increased respirations, loss of appetite, and fatigue.

Learning Outcome 2

Describe diagnostic tests used to identify inflammation and infection.

Concepts for Lecture

1. Diagnostic tests can identify the source and extent of inflammation and include WBC count with differential, erythrocyte sedimentation rate, and C-reactive protein. Cultures of the blood and other body fluids can help determine whether infection is the cause of the inflammation. Other tests used include sensitivity studies, antibiotic peak and trough levels, lumbar puncture, and ultrasound.
2. Fever and WBC count greater than 10,000/mm^3 may indicate a generalized infection.

Learning Outcome 3

Explain treatments and nursing care for inflammation.

Concepts for Lecture

1. Medications prescribed to relieve the effects of inflammation include antibiotics, acetaminophen, anti-inflammatory agents, and corticosteroids.
2. Inflammation and wound healing require adequate nutrition, blood supply, and oxygenation.
3. The client with inflammation needs a diet high in carbohydrates, protein, and vitamins.

 PowerPoint Slides 23–29

Tables and/or Figures

- **Figure 9-3** Lymph Nodes That May Be Assessed by Palpation
- **Box 9-1** Focus on Older Adults: Inflammatory Changes in the Older Adult
- **Box 9-2** Manifestations of Inflammation

 **Suggestions for Classroom Activities**

- Break students into small groups and have each group discuss manifestations of local and systemic infection that they would assess for when caring for a client with a diagnosis of acute inflammation. Ask students to identify personal experiences with local and systemic infections and to recall the manifestations they found in these personal experiences.

 Suggestions for Clinical Activities

- Assign students to care for any clients on the clinical area who have a diagnosis of cellulitis, abscess, or fistula. In postconference, discuss the manifestations of cellulitis, abscess, and fistula that were found in these clients.

 PowerPoint Slides 30–31

Tables and/or Figures

- **Table 9-1** White Blood Cell Count and Differential
- **Figure 9-5** Neutrophils by Stage of Maturity and Normal Distribution in the Blood Versus Shift to Left Caused by Severe Infection

Suggestions for Classroom Activities

- Discuss the use of laboratory tests to diagnose inflammation and infection.
- Invite a nurse practitioner working with inflammatory and infectious conditions to speak to the class about use of diagnostic tests to identify inflammation and infection and interpretation of these diagnostic tests.

 Suggestions for Clinical Activities

- Have students review diagnostic tests done on clients with inflammation and infection and discuss their findings in postconference. Ask the students to present the progress of the infection based on the laboratory tests. What were the presenting symptoms, and is there improvement in symptoms?
- Review proper techniques and instruction for obtaining cultures and other laboratory tests.

4. Topical treatments for inflammation include aloe to treat minor skin irritation, camphor to relieve pain from cold sores and warts, and comfrey to relieve inflammation of bruises and strains.

5. Care of minor wounds may be gentle cleansing with soap and water. More extensive wounds may involve irrigations and debridement of necrotic tissue.

6. Nursing care needs of the client are related to the manifestations of inflammation and altered tissue integrity.

7. Priority nursing diagnoses include Pain, Impaired Tissue Integrity, and Risk for Infection.

8. The nurse must identify potential complications that can prolong inflammation and tissue healing.

LEARNING OUTCOME 4

Review the mechanisms by which infection occurs and progresses.

Concepts for Lecture

1. Key elements of the chain of infection include a microorganism, a reservoir, a portal of exit from the reservoir, a mode of transmission from the reservoir to the host, an entry point, and a susceptible host.

2. Infectious disease usually follows a predictable course through five stages as it develops.

LEARNING OUTCOME 5

Identify common healthcare-associated (nosocomial) infections.

Concepts for Lecture

1. Healthcare-associated (or *nosocomial*) infections are infections acquired in a healthcare setting, such as a hospital or long-term facility.

2. Antibiotic-resistant microorganisms have developed that make common antibiotics ineffective for treating infections.

3. Community-acquired infections are usually referred to as communicable diseases because they can be transmitted to other people and are monitored by the World Health Organization (WHO).

LEARNING OUTCOME 6

Explain the types and spread of common multidrug-resistant organisms, emerging infectious diseases, and biologic threats.

Concepts for Lecture

1. Many microorganisms can develop resistance to one or more antimicrobial agents, so the pathogen lives and grows in the presence of the antimicrobial.

2. Resistance can occur as a result of a few hardy bacteria surviving every time an antibiotic is given, and when these bacteria reproduce, they pass along their antibiotic resistance. Overuse of antibiotics and insufficient medication doses are the most frequent cause of resistance.

3. Resistance can also occur because the pathogen develops a new form or mutation, allowing the organism to survive.

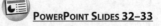 **POWERPOINT SLIDES 32–33**

 **SUGGESTIONS FOR CLASSROOM ACTIVITIES**

• Have students work in pairs to design a menu for a day or several days for a client with inflammation or infection; the diet should be high in carbohydrates, protein, and vitamins.

SUGGESTIONS FOR CLINICAL ACTIVITIES

• Assign students to care for clients who have wound care ordered, or have students assist a nurse assigned to wound care or to clients getting wound care.

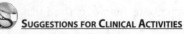 **POWERPOINT SLIDES 34–36**

Tables and/or Figures
• **Figure 9-4** The Chain of Infection
• **Box 9-5** Pathogenic Organisms
• **Table 9-3** Common Infectious Diseases and the Causative Organism

 SUGGESTIONS FOR CLASSROOM ACTIVITIES

• Describe the chain of infection.

SUGGESTIONS FOR CLINICAL ACTIVITIES

• Arrange for students to attend a wound care clinic or to spend time with an enterostomal therapist to see wounds in different stages of the infectious process. Discuss various treatments used to promote wound healing. Discuss the educational needs of the client.

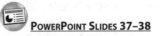 **POWERPOINT SLIDES 37–38**

Tables and/or Figures
• **Box 9-6** Risk Factors for Healthcare-Associated Infections

SUGGESTIONS FOR CLASSROOM ACTIVITIES

• Discuss the risk factors in the hospital for acquiring a healthcare-associated infection, such as exposure to infectious microorganisms, invasive procedures, indwelling tubes, nutritional status, and medications that lower immunities.

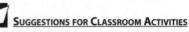 **SUGGESTIONS FOR CLINICAL ACTIVITIES**

• Arrange for students to work in an immunization clinic or a nursing home. Have them administer vaccines for influenza and pneumonia to the clients. Review contraindications for receiving immunizations.
• Assign students to perform an assessment on patients who are at risk for healthcare-associated infections, and review principles that will help prevent them.

4. The most common multidrug-resistant organisms include methicillin-resistant *Staphylococcus aureus* (MRSA), vancomycin-resistant *Enterococcus*, penicillin-resistant *Streptococcus pneumococcus*, and extended-spectrum beta-lactamase. *Clostridium difficile* is another healthcare-associated organism that is very difficult to treat.
5. Emerging infectious diseases are defined as diseases that have increased in the past 20 years or that threaten to increase in the near future.
6. Emerging infectious diseases include multidrug-resistant tuberculosis, HIV, West Nile virus, severe acute respiratory syndrome (SARS), avian influenza, and noroviruses. Infectious diarrhea results from organisms such as *E. coli*, *Salmonella*, *Shigella*, *Campylobacter*, and *Giardia*.
7. Infectious diarrhea is transmitted by contaminated food or water.
8. The most likely pathogens to be used for biologic threat infections are anthrax, smallpox, botulism, plague, and viral hemorrhagic fevers.
9. Anthrax is caused by *Bacillus anthracis*, which is a gram-positive spore producing organism that can be contracted by inhalation, ingestion, and skin contact.
10. Smallpox spreads by direct contact or by inhalation of respiratory droplets.

LEARNING OUTCOME 7

Explain age-related changes and other factors in older adults that increase their risk for infection, and apply nursing implications for these.

Concepts for Lecture

1. Older adults are at greater risk for developing pneumonia, influenza, and urinary tract and skin infections.

LEARNING OUTCOME 8

Identify the common antimicrobial medications, nursing implications, and client teaching guidelines.

Concepts for Lecture

1. Antibiotics, antiviral, antifungal, and antiparasitic medications are the common medications used to manage infections.
2. Antibiotic peak and trough levels monitor therapeutic blood levels of prescribed medication.

LEARNING OUTCOME 9

Apply the guidelines for Standard and Transmission-Based Precautions to clients with infectious diseases.

Concepts for Lecture

1. Most infectious organisms are spread by direct contact with healthcare workers.
2. There are a number of good hygiene practices that healthcare workers can follow to prevent and control infection.

POWERPOINT SLIDES 39–43

Tables and/or Figures
- **Table 9-4** Transmission-Based Precautions

SUGGESTIONS FOR CLASSROOM ACTIVITIES

- Have the students each locate a recent journal article on a multidrug-resistant organism, an emerging infectious disease, or a biologic threat infection and give a brief report in class.

SUGGESTIONS FOR CLINICAL ACTIVITIES

- Locate the policy and/or procedure for treatment of a client with MRSA on the clinical unit of the facility where students have their clinical experience. Discuss this policy and/or procedure in preconference, or if you don't have preconference, provide the students with a copy prior to clinical and discuss this information in postconference.

POWERPOINT SLIDES 44–45

Tables and/or Figures
- **Table 9-5** Special Population: Common Infectious Diseases in Older Adults, Age-Related Changes, and Nursing Implications

SUGGESTIONS FOR CLASSROOM ACTIVITIES

- Discuss the risk factors for developing infections in the older adult.

SUGGESTIONS FOR CLINICAL ACTIVITIES

- Assess nutrition in an older adult. Is the older adult getting the proper nutrition to prevent infections? What teaching needs to be done to promote good nutrition?

POWERPOINT SLIDES 46–50

Tables and/or Figures
- **Table 9-6** Giving Medications Safely: Antibiotic Therapy
- **Table 9-7** Giving Medications Safely: Antifungal and Antiviral Drugs

3. Effective hand washing for at least 15 seconds using friction and antimicrobial soap is the single most important measure in infection control.
4. Standard Precautions are guidelines to protect the healthcare worker as well as prevent transmission to other clients and are used with all clients, whether they have a known infectious disease or not.
5. Standard Precautions apply to blood; all body fluids, secretions, and excretions except sweat, regardless of whether they contain visible blood; and nonintact skin and mucous membranes.
6. Personal protective equipment (PPE) is the use of a barrier protection to prevent exposure of skin and mucous membranes to blood and body fluids.
7. The CDC has added a guideline called Respiratory Hygiene/Cough Etiquette.
8. There are three types of Transmission-Based Precautions: Airborne Precautions, Droplet Precautions, and Contact Precautions. These three types of Transmission-Based Precautions may be combined for diseases with multiple routes of transmission.

LEARNING OUTCOME 10

Use the nursing process to collect data, establish outcomes, provide individualized care, and evaluate responses for clients with inflammation and infection.

Concepts for Lecture

1. Nursing management of clients with an inflammation or infectious disease focuses on prevention, health promotion, and health maintenance. The nursing process is used to guide the nurse in client care.

GENERAL CHAPTER CONSIDERATIONS

1. Have students study and learn key terms listed at the beginning of the chapter.
2. Have students complete end of chapter exercises either in their book or on the MyNursingKit Website.
3. Use the Classroom Response Question PowerPoints to assess students prior to lecture.

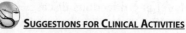

SUGGESTIONS FOR CLASSROOM ACTIVITIES

- Using the tables in the chapter, discuss the different categories of anti-infective medications, emphasizing the purposes, nursing implications, and client teaching needed for each medication.

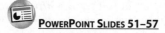

SUGGESTIONS FOR CLINICAL ACTIVITIES

- In the clinical setting, have students review the medical history of their clients for immunization status. Have them ask their clients if they know why immunizations are important.
- Assess laboratory studies for antibiotic peak and trough levels. Discuss what to do if the levels are too high or too low.

POWERPOINT SLIDES 51–57

Tables and/or Figures

- **Box 9-7** Standard Precaution Guidelines
- **Table 9-4** Transmission-Based Precautions

SUGGESTIONS FOR CLASSROOM ACTIVITIES

- Obtain policies and procedures for Standard Precautions and Transmission-Based Precautions from the clinical facilities in which your students have clinical experiences, and have students review these policies and procedures in class.

SUGGESTIONS FOR CLINICAL ACTIVITIES

- Assign students to work with a primary nurse who is caring for a client who has Transmission-Based Precautions. In postconference, the student will share about the client's need for these precautions as well as what precautions were taken.

POWERPOINT SLIDES 58–62

Tables and/or Figures

- **Box 9-3** Assessment: Clients With Inflammation
- **Box 9-8** Assessment: Clients With Infection

Nursing Care Plan: Client With MRSA Infection

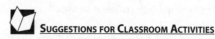

SUGGESTIONS FOR CLASSROOM ACTIVITIES

- Review the steps of the nursing process and how it can be used for the client with an inflammation or infection.

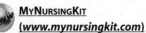

SUGGESTIONS FOR CLINICAL ACTIVITIES

• Assign students to clients with an inflammation or infectious process. Have them develop an appropriate nursing care plan for the clients.

• Clinical Reasoning Care Map

MYNURSINGKIT
(*www.mynursingkit.com*)

• Websites
• NCLEX® Questions
• Case Studies
• Key Terms

STUDENT WORKBOOK AND RESOURCE GUIDE

• Chapter 9 activities
• *Separate purchase*

PRENTICE HALL NURSE'S DRUG GUIDE

• *Separate purchase*

CLASSROOM RESPONSE QUESTION POWERPOINTS

TESTBANK

CHAPTER 10
CARING FOR CLIENTS HAVING SURGERY

LEARNING OUTCOME 1

Describe the classifications of surgical procedures.

Concepts for Lecture

1. Surgical procedures can be classified according to purpose, risk factor, and urgency.
2. Two types of surgeries are performed: inpatient or ambulatory. Inpatient surgery requires admission to a hospital before the procedure. Inpatient surgery may be a planned event or an unanticipated emergency situation.
3. Classification of surgical procedures according to purpose includes *diagnostic surgery* to determine or confirm a diagnosis (example: breast biopsy); *ablative surgery*, to remove a diseased organ or extremity (examples: appendectomy and amputation); *constructive surgery*, to build tissue/organs that are absent (example: repair of cleft palate); *reconstructive surgery*, to rebuild tissue/organ that has been damaged (example: skin graft after a burn); *palliative surgery*, to alleviate symptoms of a disease and not to cure the disease (example: bowel resection in client with terminal cancer); and *transplantation*, to replace organs/tissue to restore function (example: heart, lung, liver, and kidney transplant).
4. Classification of surgical procedures according to risk includes minor and major surgical procedures.
5. The minor surgical procedure has minimal physical assault with minimal risk, such as removal of skin lesions, dilation and curettage, and cataract extraction.
6. The major surgical procedure has extensive physical assault and/or serious risk, such as transplantation and total joint replacement.
7. Classification of surgical procedures according to urgency includes elective, urgent, and emergency.
8. The elective surgical procedure is suggested, although there are no foreseen ill effects if postponed (example: cosmetic surgery).
9. The urgent surgical procedure needs to be performed within 1 to 2 days (example: heart bypass surgery).
10. The emergency surgical procedure needs to be performed immediately (examples: obstetric emergencies, bowel obstruction, ruptured aneurysm, life-threatening trauma).

LEARNING OUTCOME 2

Discuss the meaning and implications of informed consent, including the nurse's responsibilities related to informed consent.

Concepts for Lecture

1. Informed consent is a legal document required for certain diagnostic procedures or therapeutic measures, including surgery.

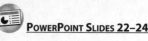 **POWERPOINT SLIDES 22–24**

Tables and/or Figures
- **Table 10-1** Classification of Surgical Procedures

 SUGGESTIONS FOR CLASSROOM ACTIVITIES
- Describe the classifications of surgical procedures.

SUGGESTIONS FOR CLINICAL ACTIVITIES
- Assign the students to the preoperative intake room, the operating room, and the postanesthesia care unit. Have the students write their observations of the events occurring in these units. Also ask the students to identify the healthcare professionals who work within these units and their duties.

 **POWERPOINT SLIDES 25–26**

Tables and/or Figures
- **Figure 10-1** Informed Consent to Operation, Administration of Anesthetics, and the Rendering of Other Medical Services

2. Informed consent protects the client, nurse, physician, and healthcare facility.
3. Specific information is required and contained within the informed consent.
4. While the surgeon is the one who should discuss the information in informed consent with the client and family in language they can understand, ideally the nurse should be present.
5. The nurse can discuss and clarify what the physician has presented.
6. If the client's questions or concerns were not answered or if the nurse questions the client's understanding, the nurse should contact the surgeon who is responsible for giving further information before the client signs informed consent.
7. After a thorough discussion of the informed consent, the nurse may witness the client's signature on the form, indicating the correct person signed the form and the client was alert and aware of what he or she signed.

LEARNING OUTCOME 3

Describe interdisciplinary perioperative care, including laboratory and diagnostic tests and related nursing responsibilities.

Concepts for Lecture

1. The Universal Protocol is a safety initiative established by the Joint Commission in 2003 to reduce the "wrong site, wrong procedure, and wrong person" surgery risk.
2. All members of the healthcare team, including the client whenever possible, are involved in carrying out the Universal Protocol, which starts with the decision to schedule surgery and continues into the intraoperative phase.
3. The Universal Protocol calls for three specific actions by the healthcare team: conducting a preprocedure verification process; marking the procedure site; and taking time out before starting the procedure to conduct a final verification of the correct client, site, positioning, and procedure and that all relevant documents, information, and equipment are available.
4. The LVN/LPN will monitor laboratory and diagnostic test values for the preoperative client and report abnormal values to the charge nurse or the physician.
5. The LPN/LVN plans and implements care with the registered nurse to meet the needs of the client. In many facilities, the LPN/LVN obtains focused assessment data and may perform presurgical procedures such as starting an IV, inserting a Foley catheter, and preparing the surgical area.
6. See Table 10-3, Laboratory Tests for Perioperative Assessment.

LEARNING OUTCOME 4

Describe nursing implications for medications prescribed for the surgical client.

Concepts for Lecture

1. The nurse is responsible for administering preoperative medications at the time ordered or when called for by the operative personnel so that desired effects can be obtained.

SUGGESTIONS FOR CLASSROOM ACTIVITIES

• Provide samples of informed consent forms from various health facilities where students will be doing clinicals during their current term or the next term.

SUGGESTIONS FOR CLINICAL ACTIVITIES

• Ask the nurses in the facility/facilities where students are doing clinicals to advise you of when the physicians and the nurse or nurses are giving information for informed consent and getting informed consents signed, so that a student can observe.

REFERENCE

• American Medical Associations. Informed consent. Available at http://www.ama-assn.org/ ama/pub/physician-resources/legal-topics/ patient-physician-relationship-topics/ informed-consent.shtml

POWERPOINT SLIDES 27–29

Tables and/or Figures

• **Table 10-3** Laboratory Tests for Perioperative Assessment

SUGGESTIONS FOR CLASSROOM ACTIVITIES

• Break students into small groups. Provide each group with laboratory and diagnostic test results for a fictitious client or an actual person. If an actual person, black out identifying data except for factors pertinent to the interpretation of results (age and gender). Ask students to discuss what abnormalities they would report to their instructor and the charge nurse.

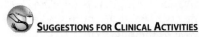

SUGGESTIONS FOR CLINICAL ACTIVITIES

• Arrange for students to have an observational experience in a surgical setting. Ask students to focus on the interdisciplinary team's application of the Universal Protocol and the nurses' roles (LPN/LVN and RN) in applying Universal Protocol as well as other responsibilities. Ask students to write about their observations and to report their observations in postconference.

REFERENCE

• Joint Commission: Updated Universal Protocol. Available at http://www.jointcommission.org/ PatientSafety/UniversalProtocol/

2. Anesthesia is the use of chemical substances to produce loss of sensation, reflex loss, or muscle relaxation during a surgical procedure, with or without loss of consciousness.

LEARNING OUTCOME 5

Discuss appropriate nursing care for the client in the preoperative, intraoperative, and postoperative phases of surgery.

Concepts for Lecture

1. Perioperative nursing includes care of the client through three phases: preoperative, intraoperative, and postoperative.
2. Care of the surgical client should focus on psychologic as well as physiologic risk factors.
3. Thorough nursing assessment is the key to identifying potential risk factors that may lead to perioperative complications.
4. All surgical team members have a vital role in the success of the surgery, but nurses are responsible for maintaining the safety of the client and the environment and for providing physiologic monitoring and psychologic support.
5. Nursing interventions are developed to prevent development of perioperative complications.
6. Nursing care of the postoperative client focuses on preventing and monitoring for complications.

LEARNING OUTCOME 6

Identify variations in perioperative care for the older adult.

Concepts for Lecture

1. Because of cardiovascular and tissue changes associated with aging, surgeries lasting longer than 2 hours place the older adult at increased risk for complications.
2. The older adult is more prone to hypotension, hypothermia, and hypoxemia resulting from anesthesia and the cool temperature in the operating room. The nurse can anticipate the possibility of these complications, assess for them, report them to the physician, and take measures to correct the problem(s).
3. Intraoperative positioning of arthritic joints can result in postoperative joint pain that is unrelated to the surgical procedure. The nurse needs to be aware of this, assess for it, and report postoperative joint pain to the physician.
4. The older client is at increased risk for skin breakdown and delayed wound healing because of decreased subcutaneous fat tissue and reduced peripheral circulation. Elderly clients undergoing lengthy surgeries have increased risk of this complication.
5. Some older adults have hearing or visual impairments. Sensory impairments, coupled with an unfamiliar environment, can make the operating room a frightening, disorienting place. By effectively communicating with the client, the nurse can provide support and reassurance postoperatively to minimize these problems.

POWERPOINT SLIDES 30–31

Tables and/or Figures
- **Table 10-4** Giving Medications Safely: Preoperative Medications

SUGGESTIONS FOR CLASSROOM ACTIVITIES

- Divide the class into small groups. Assign the students to research the types of anesthesia used for different surgical procedures.
- Invite a nurse anesthetist to talk to the class about the types of anesthesia used for different surgical procedures.

SUGGESTIONS FOR CLINICAL ACTIVITIES

- Have the students review the client's operative record and postanesthesia record for the types of medications used. Have them make drug cards for these medications.

POWERPOINT SLIDES 32–45

Tables and/or Figures
- **Table 10-2** Nursing Implications for Surgical Risk Factors
- **Table 10-5** Common Surgical Positions
- **Figure 10-5** Surgical Areas to Be Scrubbed
- **Box 10-5** Wound Drainage Devices

Nursing Care Plan: Preoperative Care for Client Having Inpatient Surgery

SUGGESTIONS FOR CLASSROOM ACTIVITIES

- Divide the class into small groups. Assign the groups to present the common risk factors and the nursing interventions for the client undergoing surgery.

SUGGESTIONS FOR CLINICAL ACTIVITIES

- Assign the students to the preoperative intake room, the operating room, and the postanesthesia care unit. Have the students write their observations of the events occurring in these units. Also ask the students to identify the healthcare professionals who work within these units and their duties.

POWERPOINT SLIDE 46

Tables and/or Figures
- **Box 10-4** Focus on Older Adults: The Older Adult Undergoing Surgery

LEARNING OUTCOME 7

Describe principles of pain management for postoperative pain control.

Concepts for Lecture

1. Control of postoperative pain is a major concern to the surgical client, surgeon, and nurse.
2. Established, severe pain is more difficult to treat than pain that is at its onset.
3. Pain stimulates the stress response and actually slows healing and recovery.
4. Initially, postoperative analgesics are administered at regular intervals or by a patient-controlled analgesia device to maintain a therapeutic blood level.
5. PRN administration of analgesics allows blood levels to fall below the therapeutic range, and delays in medication increase pain intensity and make its management more difficult.
6. In treating mild to moderate postoperative pain, NSAIDs are given often along with opioids, unless contraindicated, because NSAIDs allow for lower doses of opioids and fewer side effects.
7. Certain NSAIDs (e.g., ketorolac), when given in higher doses after surgery, may be administered safely for only 2–3 days before the dosage must be reduced.
8. NSAIDs can be given safely to older clients, but the nurse should observe closely for side effects, especially gastric, hepatic, and renal toxicity.

LEARNING OUTCOME 8

Compare and contrast outpatient and inpatient surgery.

Concepts for Lecture

1. Outpatient surgery (also called ambulatory or same-day surgery) is performed on a nonhospitalized client under general or conscious (local) anesthesia.
2. Ambulatory surgery has advantages and disadvantages.
3. Inpatient surgery is performed on a hospitalized client under regional, general, or conscious sedation anesthesia.
4. The major difference in postanesthesia care for the ambulatory versus the hospitalized client is in the extent of teaching and emotional support that must be provided.

GENERAL CHAPTER CONSIDERATIONS

1. Have students study and learn key terms listed at the beginning of the chapter.
2. Have students complete end of chapter exercises either in their book or on the MyNursingKit Website.
3. Use the Classroom Response Question PowerPoints to assess students prior to lecture.

SUGGESTIONS FOR CLASSROOM ACTIVITIES

- Break students into small groups with the following instructions: Select a leader to lead discussion, select a recorder, and decide who will report to the whole class later. Provide written instructions for the students to identify variations in preoperative, intraoperative, and postoperative care for the older adult; determine the impact the client's medical history might have on the surgery experience; and discuss risk factors for surgery complications present in the older adult.

SUGGESTIONS FOR CLINICAL ACTIVITIES

- Assign students to care for older adults who have recently had surgery. Assist the students to identify risks for variations in the perioperative experience, based on the client's medical history and type of surgery. What interventions can be performed to decrease the likelihood of complications?

POWERPOINT SLIDES 47–50

SUGGESTIONS FOR CLASSROOM ACTIVITIES

- Discuss medications used for postoperative pain, dosage, routes, side effects, and nursing implications for administering the medications.
- Have students make medication cards for the various medications used for postoperative pain. If they already have medication cards, have the students work together in small groups to develop posters about these medications that can be displayed in the classroom.

SUGGESTIONS FOR CLINICAL ACTIVITIES

- Assign the students to administer pain medications to postoperative clients. Have them make and/or use drugs cards on these medications.

POWERPOINT SLIDES 51–52

SUGGESTIONS FOR CLASSROOM ACTIVITIES

- Ask students to volunteer to role play a healthcare professional, a client who is undergoing inpatient surgery, and a client who is undergoing outpatient surgery. Compare and contrast the preparation needed for each type of surgery. Compare the psychologic impact of a client undergoing inpatient versus outpatient surgery.

SUGGESTIONS FOR CLINICAL ACTIVITIES

- Arrange for students to attend an outpatient surgery unit. Have the students assist with the preoperative checklist, preoperative teaching, and preparing the client for surgery. Have the students observe during the surgical procedure and in the postoperative unit. In postconference, have students compare this experience with a surgical rotation in the healthcare setting.
- Arrange for students to have a clinical experience in a surgeon's office. Have them follow several clients through the office visit, observing preoperative and postoperative visits. Ask the students to answer the following questions: What assessment data do the office personnel obtain? What teaching is completed, and what educational materials are made available for the clients?

- Clinical Reasoning Care Map

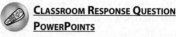

MYNURSINGKIT
(*www.mynursingkit.com*)

- Websites
- NCLEX® Questions
- Case Studies
- Key Terms

STUDENT WORKBOOK AND RESOURCE GUIDE

- Chapter 10 activities
- *Separate purchase*

PRENTICE HALL NURSE'S DRUG GUIDE

- *Separate purchase*

CLASSROOM RESPONSE QUESTION POWERPOINTS

TESTBANK

CHAPTER 11
CARING FOR CLIENTS WITH ALTERED IMMUNITY

LEARNING OUTCOME 1

Describe nursing interventions used to promote active and passive immunity in adult clients.

Concepts for Lecture

1. Nurses have an important role in preventing the spread of communicable diseases, including encouraging immunization.
2. Before immunizations are given, the nurse collects assessment data to determine whether immunization is appropriate.
3. Nursing care focuses on preventing injury from the vaccination and on providing client education.
4. Nurses must check the expiration date and the manufacturer's instructions for administration guidelines, dosage, routes, sites, precautions, and contraindications.
5. The nurse must not administer immunizations to a client with an upper respiratory infection or other infection.
6. The oral polio vaccines or MMR must not be given to immunosuppressed clients or to clients who are in close household contact with an immunosuppressed person.
7. The nurse must keep epinephrine 1:1,000 available when administering immunizations.
8. The nurse must provide instructions in several areas regarding immunizations.

 **POWERPOINT SLIDES 22–34**

Tables and/or Figures
- **Box 11-1** Assessment: Assessing Clients' Immune Status
- **Table 11-3** Recommended Immunizations for Adults

 SUGGESTIONS FOR CLASSROOM ACTIVITIES
- Have students work in pairs to make posters about the importance of vaccinations in preventing the spread of disease.

SUGGESTIONS FOR CLINICAL ACTIVITIES
- Arrange for students to do assessments prior to vaccinations at a public health clinic or other site. Supervise students giving flu vaccinations for the public.

LEARNING OUTCOME 2

Identify laboratory tests used to diagnose and monitor immune response.

Concepts for Lecture

1. Laboratory and diagnostic tests can measure the level of immunity in the body.
2. Several tests may be ordered to diagnose hypersensitivity reactions.
3. Serum assays are used to identify increased levels of antibodies to diagnose specific autoimmune disorders.
4. Basic laboratory and diagnostic tests are performed prior to any surgery, but additional studies are performed before organ or tissue transplant.
5. Diagnostic studies are performed to provide evidence of tissue rejection.
6. A radioallergosorbent test (RAST) measures the amount of IGE to specific allergens.
7. Skin tests are used to identify specific allergens to which a person may be sensitive.
8. The prick test may be done first to avoid a systemic reaction.

 POWERPOINT SLIDES 35–39

Tables and/or Figures
- **Table 11-2** Immunoglobulin Characteristics and Function
- **Figure 11-5** Skin Testing on the Forearm

 **SUGGESTIONS FOR CLINICAL ACTIVITIES**
- Assign students to clients who will have intradermal tests. Ask the client's primary nurse to demonstrate the intradermal injection and have students observe. Once they have observed the procedure, supervise them in giving another client an intradermal injection that is ordered.
- Arrange for students to have an observational experience at the office of a physician who does allergy testing so the students can observe the testing.

9. An intradermal test involves a small amount of allergen being injected on the forearm or intrascapular area.

10. The patch test involves a 1-inch patch impregnated with the allergen applied to the skin for 48 hours. Positive responses range from mild redness to severe redness, papules, or vesicles.

LEARNING OUTCOME 3

Describe nursing implications for medications given to clients with altered immunity.

Concepts for Lecture

1. Hypersensitivity reactions range from mild, such as hay fever, to severe (e.g., blood transfusion reactions, anaphylaxis, and organ transplant rejections).
2. Before administering immunizations, the nurse should collect assessment data to determine whether the immunization is appropriate.
3. Medications can provide symptomatic relief for reaction to an allergen.
4. Treatment of autoimmune disorders focuses on medications that relieve symptoms.
5. Specific medications are given before and after transplantation to prevent tissue rejection.

LEARNING OUTCOME 4

Teach clients with altered immune responses and their families the importance of care and follow-up.

Concepts for Lecture

1. Autoimmune disorders develop when the body fails to identify self from nonself (e.g., rheumatoid arthritis).
2. Because autoimmune disorders are chronic, the client and family need to understand care for the client and the long-term effects of the disorder.

LEARNING OUTCOME 5

Use the nursing process to collect data, establish outcomes, provide individualized care, and evaluate responses for the client experiencing altered immunity.

Concepts for Lecture

1. Nursing care is individualized for the client with an autoimmune disorder.
2. The client who has undergone an organ or tissue transplant has immediate and long-term nursing care needs. Pre- and posttransplant care focuses on reducing the risk of tissue rejection.

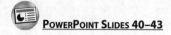 **POWERPOINT SLIDES 40–43**

Tables and/or Figures

- **Box 11-1** Assessment: Assessing Clients' Immune Status
- **Box 11-2** Natural Rubber Latex Products
- **Table 11-4** Types of Hypersensitivity Reactions
- **Table 11-5** Giving Medications Safely: Antihistamines
- **Table 11-6** Transplant Rejection Episodes
- **Table 11-7** Giving Medications Safely: Immunosuppressive Agents

 **SUGGESTIONS FOR CLASSROOM ACTIVITIES**

- Have a surgical nurse who works with people who have organ transplants talk to the students about organ rejection and the medications given to prevent rejection.
- Discuss the nursing implications for medications ordered for clients with altered immunity.

SUGGESTIONS FOR CLASSROOM ACTIVITIES

- Ask students to locate products in their clinical assignment area that can be used as alternatives to latex products for staff and clients with latex allergies.

 **POWERPOINT SLIDE 44**

Tables and/or Figures

- **Box 11-3** Autoimmune Disorders

 **SUGGESTIONS FOR CLASSROOM ACTIVITIES**

- Have students break into small groups and assign them one of several autoimmune disorders. Each group should have a different disorder. Ask each group to discuss three to four key things the client and family would need to know about care for a person with these disorders and to report back to the class.

 **SUGGESTIONS FOR CLINICAL ACTIVITIES**

- Assign students to care for clients with autoimmune disorders. Have them develop a discharge teaching plan for the assigned client.

 **POWERPOINT SLIDES 45–50**

Tables and/or Figures

- **Table 11-6** Transplant Rejection Episodes

LEARNING OUTCOME 6

Identify ways to prevent the transmission of HIV infection.

Concepts for Lecture

1. The human immunodeficiency virus (HIV) is the cause of acquired immunodeficiency syndrome (AIDS).
2. HIV attacks helper T4 lymphocytes, which decrease a person's ability to remain immunocompetent and increases the risk for developing opportunistic infections.
3. Education and counseling are the key elements for HIV prevention.

LEARNING OUTCOME 7

Use the nursing process to collect data, establish outcomes, provide individualized care, and evaluate responses for the client with AIDS.

Concepts for Lecture

1. Nursing care is individualized for the client with AIDS.
2. The client who has undergone an organ or tissue transplant has immediate and long-term nursing care needs. Pre- and posttransplant care focuses on reducing the risk of tissue rejection.

GENERAL CHAPTER CONSIDERATIONS

1. Have students study and learn key terms listed at the beginning of the chapter.
2. Have students complete end of chapter exercises either in their book or on the MyNursingKit Website.
3. Use the Classroom Response Question PowerPoint to assess students prior to lecture.

SUGGESTIONS FOR CLASSROOM ACTIVITIES

- Discuss the nursing process to collect data, establish outcomes, provide individualized care, and evaluate responses for clients experiencing altered immunity.
- Divide the students into groups of four. Have the groups design care plans for clients with altered immunity.

POWERPOINT SLIDES 51–52

SUGGESTIONS FOR CLINICAL ACTIVITIES

- Arrange for students to have a clinical experience in a hospital with a transplant program. Arrange for students to observe transplant surgeries and for students to participate in the care of clients during the first few days posttransplant. In postconference, have them discuss the nursing process in relation to the care of these clients.

POWERPOINT SLIDES 53–63

Tables and/or Figures
- **Box 11-6** Guidelines for Safer Sex

SUGGESTIONS FOR CLASSROOM ACTIVITIES

- Initiate a discussion on HIV infection; emphasize transmission, prevention of transmission, laboratory tests used for diagnosis and treatment, infections associated with HIV, and the treatment modalities.

SUGGESTIONS FOR CLINICAL ACTIVITIES

- Have students review the infection control policy of their facility.
- Have students observe how the staff institutes infection control on the unit and report their observations in postconference.
- Assign students the task of contacting the employee health department in the hospital. Review the follow-up protocol for healthcare workers who have experienced needle sticks. What is the policy about HIV testing on hospital clients and the employees involved in needle sticks? What blood tests are drawn? What medical protocols are prescribed? Review the nursing program policy on needle sticks.

REFERENCE

- Centers for Disease Control and Prevention: HIV/AIDS. Available at http://www.cdc.gov/hiv/

Tables and/or Figures

- **Box 11-5** Manifestations of HIV Infection
- **Box 11-7** Assessment: Assessing Clients With HIV Infection and AIDS
- **Table 11-9** Giving Medications Safely: Antiretroviral Agents
- **Table 11-10** Pharmacologic Treatment of Opportunistic Infections and Malignancies

Nursing Care Plan: Client With HIV Infection

SUGGESTIONS FOR CLASSROOM ACTIVITIES

- Ask the students to explore their feelings about taking care of a client with AIDS. Ask them to describe how they would dispel any negative feelings they may have toward the client.
- Discuss medications used for clients with HIV; include the use, dosage, route, side effects, and nursing implications of each medication.

SUGGESTIONS FOR CLINICAL ACTIVITIES

- Assign students to care for clients using Isolation Precautions. In postconference, ask the students to describe their feelings and thoughts while caring for the client.
- Assign students to administer medications to clients with AIDS. Have students make drug cards on each of the medications they administer.

REFERENCE

- Mayo Clinic: HIV/AIDS. Available at http://www.mayoclinic.com/health/hiv-aids/DS00005/DSECTION=symptoms

- Clinical Reasoning Care Map

MYNURSINGKIT (www.mynursingkit.com)

- Websites
- NCLEX® Questions
- Case Studies
- Key Terms

STUDENT WORKBOOK AND RESOURCE GUIDE

- Chapter 11 activities
- *Separate purchase*

PRENTICE HALL NURSE'S DRUG GUIDE

- *Separate purchase*

CLASSROOM RESPONSE QUESTION POWERPOINTS

TESTBANK

CHAPTER 12
CARING FOR CLIENTS WITH CANCER

LEARNING OUTCOME 1

Define cancer and describe its incidence and trends.

Concepts for Lecture

1. Cancer is a disease that results when normal cells mutate into abnormal, deviant cells and continue to reproduce within the body. Cancer can affect people of any age, gender, ethnicity, or geographic region.
2. Neoplasms are masses of abnormal cells that grow at a rate uncoordinated with the needs of the body, do not benefit the host, and may be harmful.
3. Cancer is a disease associated with aging; 77% of cancer diagnoses occur after age 55.
4. With advances in cancer prevention, early detection, and treatment, the 5-year survival rate for individuals with cancer continues to improve in the United States.
5. Minority ethnic groups bear a disproportionate burden of cancer.
6. African Americans have the highest death rate from cancer and the shortest survival of any ethnic group in the United States for most cancers.

LEARNING OUTCOME 2

Discuss the pathophysiology of cancer and factors associated with carcinogenesis.

Concepts for Lecture

1. Pathophysiology of cancer is a disruption in the genetic information coded in the DNA of genes that can produce abnormal cells, which may become cancerous.
2. Metastasis is the spread of malignant cells in the blood or lymph or shed into body cavities. An impairment or alteration of the immune system is a major factor in the establishment of metastatic lesions.
3. Causal factors may act together or in sequence to initiate or promote carcinogenesis. Factors are both external and internal.
4. Many cancer risk factors are controllable; prevention is key.

LEARNING OUTCOME 3

Describe the effects of cancer on the body.

Concepts for Lecture

1. Early detection and treatment are the factors that most influence the prognosis of people with cancer.
2. Clients with cancer need a great deal of emotional support because fear and anxiety are common responses to a diagnosis of cancer.

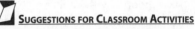

POWERPOINT SLIDE 22

Tables and/or Figures
- **Table 12-1** Top Ten Cancer Sites and Cancer Deaths in Men and Women in the United States
- **Box 12-1** Focus on Diversity: Cancer Incidence and Death

SUGGESTIONS FOR CLASSROOM ACTIVITIES
- Find newspaper articles about cancer and its incidence and circulate them in the classroom. Ask students to bring articles also. Make a notebook of articles for students to read. You can also ask students to present briefly on their articles.
- Obtain local health department and state health department statistics on the incidence of cancer by age, race, gender, and type. Share these statistics with students and discuss whether they match what is in the textbook or deviate in any way.

SUGGESTIONS FOR CLINICAL ACTIVITIES
- Assign students to clients with a diagnosis of cancer. Have the students ask clients to talk about what they think cancer is. Some people imagine cancer in a way that is unique. In postconference, have students discuss what they learned.

POWERPOINT SLIDES 23–31

Tables and/or Figures
- **Table 12-2** Comparison of Benign and Malignant Neoplasms
- **Figure 12-1** Benign and Malignant Tumors of the Breast
- **Figure 12-2** Metastasis Via the Bloodstream
- **Table 12-3** Selected Cancers and Sites of Metastasis

SUGGESTIONS FOR CLASSROOM ACTIVITIES
- Discuss the pathophysiology of cancer and the factors associated with carcinogenesis.

SUGGESTIONS FOR CLINICAL ACTIVITIES
- Assign a group of students to show poster presentations on risk factors and guidelines to prevent the different categories of cancer.

POWERPOINT SLIDES 32–37

3. Both physiologic and psychosocial sequelae of cancer and its treatment have been identified. The physiologic effects of cancer may vary, depending on the body system affected and the treatment undergone.
4. Routine cancer checkups should include counseling to improve health behaviors, physical examination, and instructions for self-examination.

LEARNING OUTCOME 4

Describe the laboratory and diagnostic tests used for cancer diagnosis.

Concepts for Lecture

1. A number of laboratory and diagnostic tests are used to diagnose cancer and monitor progress and treatment.
2. Early detection and treatment have the most influence on the prognosis of people with cancer.
3. Tumor identification provides some standardization in diagnosis and treatment protocols.

LEARNING OUTCOME 5

Discuss the use of surgery, radiation therapy, chemotherapy, and biotherapy in the treatment of cancer.

Concepts for Lecture

1. Cancer treatment is aimed at cure, control, or palliation of symptoms. Cancer may be treated through surgery, radiotherapy, chemotherapy, and/or biotherapy.

LEARNING OUTCOME 6

Use the nursing process as a framework for providing individualized care for the client with cancer.

Concepts for Lecture

1. The LPN/LVN is responsible for conducting focused assessments of the client, contributing to the identification of nursing care problems and care planning, delivering direct care, providing and reinforcing client and family teaching, and contributing to evaluation of the effectiveness of care.
2. Nurses have the responsibility of assisting and supporting clients during their treatment, recovery, and rehabilitation for cancer.
3. Evaluating the effectiveness of nursing care for the client with cancer requires ongoing assessment through the nursing process.
4. In caring for clients with cancer, nurses may encounter a number of emergency situations in which their role may be crucial to the client's survival.

- Assign students to care for clients who will undergo surgery or have had surgery to treat cancer in the surgical unit of a hospital. Assist students to correlate the specific type of cancer with this individual client in regard to risk factors, why the client sought medical attention, and associated signs and symptoms. What additional types of treatment are planned for the client after discharge from the hospital?

POWERPOINT SLIDES 38–41

Tables and/or Figures
- **Box 12-3** Possible Cancer Warning Signs
- **Box 12-4** American Cancer Society Guidelines for Cancer Screening

SUGGESTIONS FOR CLASSROOM ACTIVITIES
- Discuss the effects of cancer on the body, including physiologic and psychologic manifestations.
- Have students develop posters to demonstrate how to perform self-examinations for cancers.

SUGGESTIONS FOR CLINICAL ACTIVITIES
- Arrange with an organization having a health fair for the students to have a booth where they can educate attendees on how to perform self-examinations for cancer.
- Have students teach assigned clients how to perform self-examinations for cancers.

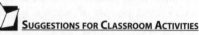
POWERPOINT SLIDE 42

Tables and/or Figures
- **Table 12-4** TNM Staging Classification System

SUGGESTIONS FOR CLASSROOM ACTIVITIES
- Discuss the laboratory and diagnostic tests used to diagnose cancer. Identify tissue markers that are specific to certain types of cancers. What are the treatment options for positive markers?
- Look at tumor identification systems and discuss what the grading and staging mean.
- If possible and time permits, invite an oncologist or an oncology nurse to talk to the class about grading and staging.

SUGGESTIONS FOR CLINICAL ACTIVITIES
- Assign students to care for clients on an oncology unit. Have the students look at the laboratory and diagnostic studies that were performed on assigned clients. Discuss the findings in postconference.

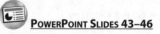
POWERPOINT SLIDES 43–46

Tables and/or Figures
- **Box 12-6** Caregiver Safety: Brachytherapy
- **Box 12-7** Nursing Care Checklist: Clients Receiving Radiation Therapy

LEARNING OUTCOME 7

Provide teaching for the client experiencing cancer.

Concepts for Lecture

1. Nurses should educate all clients about preventive strategies and lifestyle.

LEARNING OUTCOME 8

Discuss nursing care of the client experiencing an oncologic emergency or long-term effects of cancer and its treatment.

Concepts for Lecture

1. In caring for clients with cancer, nurses may encounter a number of emergency situations in which their role may be crucial to the client's survival.
2. Emergency situations require acute observation, accurate judgment, and rapid action once the problem has been identified. The first step is notifying the physician or emergency team.
3. Emergency situations include superior vena cava syndrome, pericardial effusion and cardiac tamponade, sepsis and septic shock, spinal cord compression, obstructive uropathy, hypercalcemia, hyperuricemia, and tumor lysis syndrome.
4. People with cancer are surviving longer, so they may experience long-term physiologic and psychosocial effects of cancer and its treatment.
5. Common physiologic long-term effects of cancer include chronic pain, fatigue, changes in mental processing, nonpitting edema of extremities, and increased risk of developing another malignancy.
6. Long-term psychosocial effects include fear of cancer recurrence or fear of dying, sexual dysfunction, difficulty with family relationships and parenting, depression, changes in self-esteem and body image, and possible discrimination.
7. Nursing measures to promote quality of life and identification of possible long-term effects of cancer begin with a focused assessment.
8. The nurse must acknowledge the validity of the client's concerns and symptoms.
9. The nurse needs to report any indications of cancer spread or recurrence and provide referrals to appropriate healthcare team members.
10. The nurse provides information to the client and family about available community services such as cancer survivor support groups and other resources.

- **Box 12-8** Focus on Older Adults: Chemotherapy
- **Box 12-9** Nursing Care Checklist: Immunotherapy
- **Box 12-10** Complementary Therapies: Clients With Cancer
- **Table 12-5** Giving Medications Safely: Selected Chemotherapeutic Drugs

 **POWERPOINT SLIDES 47–52**

 **SUGGESTIONS FOR CLASSROOM ACTIVITIES**

- Compare and contrast the use of surgery, radiation therapy, chemotherapy, biotherapy, and complementary therapies in the treatment of cancer.
- Assign groups of students to present a paper on different categories of chemotherapeutic drugs, emphasizing target malignancies, adverse or side effects, and nursing implications for each category.

POWERPOINT SLIDE 53

SUGGESTIONS FOR CLINICAL ACTIVITIES

- Assign students to observe an oncology nurse administering chemotherapy to a client. Have students report observations on the protocol for administering chemotherapeutic drugs. What safeguards are in place to protect the nurses who administer the medications? What side effects are associated with the specific chemotherapeutic drugs? What collaborative interventions are used to minimize these side effects? Review with the students the client's blood counts during the hospitalization, noting the effects of chemotherapy.
- Arrange for students to have clinical experience in an outpatient oncology clinic or in an oncologist physician's office. Assign students to observe the administration of intravenous fluids and chemotherapy to clients who have various types of venous access devices. How are the venous access devices maintained? Are any premedications given to minimize side effects for the clients? Have the students describe the care done to maintain the devices outside the office.

Tables and/or Figures

- **Box 12-9** Nursing Care Checklist: Immunotherapy

Nursing Care Plan: Client With Terminal Cancer

 **SUGGESTIONS FOR CLASSROOM ACTIVITIES**

- Discuss the baseline physical assessment needed for a client experiencing cancer who is admitted to a health service facility.
- Using the nursing process case study in the chapter, initiate a discussion on the nursing diagnoses used in the care of the client experiencing cancer.
- Assign groups of students to present nursing care plans on clients experiencing cancer pain and nutritional deficiencies.

GENERAL CHAPTER CONSIDERATIONS

1. Have students study and learn key terms listed at the beginning of the chapter.
2. Have students complete end of chapter exercises either in their book or on the MyNursingKit Website.
3. Use the Classroom Response Question PowerPoints to assess students prior to lecture.

 SUGGESTIONS FOR CLINICAL ACTIVITIES

- Invite an oncology nurse and/or a hospice nurse to talk about their careers in caring for clients experiencing cancer. Ask them to explain how they keep physically and psychologically fit when caring for these clients. Also ask them to describe how they use the nursing process in caring for clients with cancer.

Tables and/or Figures

- **Box 12-11** Client Teaching: When to Call for Help

SUGGESTIONS FOR CLASSROOM ACTIVITIES

- Discuss the client teaching needed for the client and family experiencing cancer.

SUGGESTIONS FOR CLINICAL ACTIVITIES

- Arrange for students to attend a meeting of a cancer support group. Who is attending the meetings: clients, family members, or both? What are the concerns brought by group participants? What advice is given by group members? How does the group leader facilitate meaningful discussions?
- Arrange for students to accompany a hospice nurse on client rounds or to visit an inpatient hospice unit. Discuss the needs of these clients and the support given to the client and families as death approaches.

SUGGESTIONS FOR CLASSROOM ACTIVITIES

- Divide the class into two to four teams to answer questions about the various cancer emergencies with a point given for each correct answer. Compose a number of questions about cardiac emergencies that can be answered by a word or a sentence.
- Have the teams take turns answering the questions and give a small reward to the team answering the most questions. Make the questions and answers available to the students for study later.

SUGGESTIONS FOR CLINICAL ACTIVITIES

- Assign students to care for clients who have long-term effects of cancer and cancer treatment. Have students assess for the physiologic and psychologic effects and share what they learned in postconference.

- Clinical Reasoning Care Map

 MYNURSINGKIT
(*www.mynursingkit.com*)
- Websites
- NCLEX® Questions
- Case Studies
- Key Terms

 STUDENT WORKBOOK AND RESOURCE GUIDE
- Chapter 12 activities
- *Separate purchase*

PRENTICE HALL NURSE'S DRUG GUIDE
- *Separate purchase*

 CLASSROOM RESPONSE QUESTION POWERPOINTS

 TESTBANK

CHAPTER 13
LOSS, GRIEF, AND END-OF-LIFE CARE

LEARNING OUTCOME 1

Define loss, grief, and death.

Concepts for Lecture

1. Loss occurs when a valued object, person, body part, or situation, formerly present, can no longer be seen, felt, heard, known, or experienced.
2. Loss may be temporary or permanent, complete or partial, subjective, physical, or symbolic.
3. Grief is the emotional response to loss, whereas grieving may be thought of as the internal process the person uses to work through the response to loss.
4. The stress of loss may initiate physical or emotional changes in a person or family. To deal with the resulting changes, people must resolve their feelings about the loss through a process called grief work.
5. Death is an irreversible cessation of body functions and an inevitable part of life and is the most critical loss of all.

LEARNING OUTCOME 2

Explain the stages of loss and the commonly experienced emotional responses for each stage.

Concepts for Lecture

1. When a valued object, person, body part, or situation is lost or changed, the experience of loss occurs. Grief is the emotional response to loss. Grieving responses are individualized to each person but commonly include the stages of denial, anger, bargaining, depression, and acceptance.

LEARNING OUTCOME 3

Discuss factors that influence responses to loss.

Concepts for Lecture

1. Death is an immensely difficult loss for both the person who is dying and for his or her loved ones. Family, friends, and spiritual practices often facilitate grief work.
2. Rituals of mourning are an important part of the work of mourning and grieving a loss. Culture dictates the rituals of mourning.

 **POWERPOINT SLIDES 22–24**

Tables and/or Figures
- **Table 13-1** Development of the Concept of Death
- **Figure 13-1** Nurses Who Work With Dying Clients Need Support From Their Colleagues

 SUGGESTIONS FOR CLASSROOM ACTIVITIES
- Have students write their own definitions of loss, grief, and death. Have them compare their own definitions with the text definitions.

SUGGESTIONS FOR CLINICAL ACTIVITIES
- Have students assess assigned clients for losses in their lifetime and current losses.

 **POWERPOINT SLIDES 25–26**

Tables and/or Figures
- **Table 13-1** Development of the Concept of Death

SUGGESTIONS FOR CLASSROOM ACTIVITIES
- Initiate discussion of the chapter by asking students if they have had to deal with the loss of someone close to them or how they have coped with any loss, such as a job or a social relationship. Ask whether they remember if and how they proceeded through Kübler-Ross's grieving stages.

 **SUGGESTIONS FOR CLINICAL ACTIVITIES**
- Assist the students to identify the losses that each of their assigned clients has experienced within the last several years. Losses may be death, health, functionalities, or loss of extremity. Assist the students to identify behaviors of grieving.

 **POWERPOINT SLIDES 27–34**

Tables and/or Figures
- **Table 13-2** Examples of Cultural Responses to Dying and Death

LEARNING OUTCOME 4

Discuss legal and ethical issues of dying, including advance directives, living wills, do-not-resuscitate orders, and euthanasia.

Concepts for Lecture

1. The dying person may control his or her own care through advance directives, living wills, and a durable power of attorney for health care. The client and family may request that the physician write a do-not-resuscitate (DNR) order.
2. Euthanasia signifies a killing that is prompted by some humanitarian motive. Natural death laws seek to preserve the notion of voluntary versus involuntary euthanasia.
3. Two models of care that focus on the dying client's quality of life are hospice and palliative care.

LEARNING OUTCOME 5

Explain the philosophy and services of hospice and palliative care.

Concepts for Lecture

1. Hospice is a model of care for clients and their families when clients are faced with a limited life expectancy.
2. Hospice is a model rather than a place of care and may be provided in free-standing clinics, hospitals, long-term care facilities, and the home by an interdisciplinary team.
3. Hospice care is care provided to meet emotional, spiritual, and comfort needs to ensure death with dignity based on wishes of the client and needs of the family.
4. Hospice care emphasizes quality rather than quantity of life.
5. Hospice regards dying as a normal part of life, and care is palliative rather than curative.

LEARNING OUTCOME 6

Assess physiologic changes in the dying client and signs of death.

Concepts for Lecture

1. As death nears, specific physiologic changes take place. These changes result in manifestations that indicate impending death. Death is pronounced when respiratory and circulatory functions stop or when all brain function ceases.

LEARNING OUTCOME 7

Use the nursing process to collect data and provide interventions for the client who is experiencing loss and is at the end of life.

Concepts for Lecture

1. Nursing care for clients who experience loss, grief, or death is implemented to meet the physical, emotional, and spiritual needs of the client and family.

 SUGGESTIONS FOR CLASSROOM ACTIVITIES

• Ask students to role play how they would interact with the family of the dying client using verbal and nonverbal communication.

 **SUGGESTIONS FOR CLINICAL ACTIVITIES**

• Arrange for students to have a clinical experience in an inpatient hospice or to accompany a hospice nurse making home visits. Assist the students to identify methods of therapeutic communication used by nurses to facilitate clients and families verbalizing concerns and spiritual beliefs.

 POWERPOINT SLIDES 35–37

Tables and/or Figures

• **Box 13-1** Types of Advance Directives

SUGGESTIONS FOR CLASSROOM ACTIVITIES

• Discuss the types of end-of-life considerations. Assign the students to write their advance directive and/or living will. Explain that this exercise is to help the student to explore his or her own fears, thoughts, and beliefs about dying.
• Discuss the ethical and legal considerations involved with euthanasia. Compare and contrast voluntary euthanasia and involuntary euthanasia.

 **POWERPOINT SLIDES 38–39**

 SUGGESTIONS FOR CLINICAL ACTIVITIES

• Have students review the advance directives and living wills used in their facility. Have students discuss their findings at a postconference.
• Arrange for students to attend a team meeting for a hospice client. Assist the students to identify the role of different members of the interdisciplinary team. What common client problems are identified? How do members of the interdisciplinary team support the clients and family members through the grief process?

 POWERPOINT SLIDES 40–41

Tables and/or Figures

• **Box 13-5** Nursing Care Checklist: Providing Physical Comfort for the Client Nearing Death

Nursing Care Plan: Client Experiencing Loss

SUGGESTIONS FOR CLASSROOM ACTIVITIES

• Invite a hospice nurse to talk to the class and answer students' questions about hospice care.

 **POWERPOINT SLIDES 42–44**

2. Nurses must also be aware of their own responses to these experiences to provide care more effectively.

GENERAL CHAPTER CONSIDERATIONS

1. Have students study and learn key terms listed at the beginning of the chapter.
2. Have students complete end of chapter exercises either in their book or on the MyNursingKit Website.
3. Use the Classroom Response Question PowerPoints to assess students prior to lecture.

SUGGESTIONS FOR CLINICAL ACTIVITIES

- Arrange to have students accompany hospice nurses on home visits for an observational experience.
- If there is a free-standing hospice house or an in-hospital hospice in your area, arrange for students to each be assigned to a primary nurse at one of these facilities sometime over the term.

Tables and/or Figures

- **Box 13-2** Manifestations of Impending Death
- **Box 13-3** Manifestations of Death
- **Box 13-4** Nursing Care Checklist: Postmortem Care

SUGGESTIONS FOR CLASSROOM ACTIVITIES

- Divide the students into groups of four and assign each group to write a nursing care plan for physiologic changes in the dying client such as anorexia, pain, incontinence, and fatigue.
- Role play the death of a client. What are the responsibilities of the nurse? How does the nurse interact with the family? How does the nurse deal with the death of a client?

SUGGESTIONS FOR CLINICAL ACTIVITIES

- If a death occurs during the clinical rotation, assign a student to assist with the postmortem care. In postconference, have the student discuss the procedure and the student's feelings about the experience.

Tables and/or Figures

- **Box 13-5** Nursing Care Checklist: Providing Physical Comfort for the Client Nearing Death
- **Box 13-6** Client Teaching: End-of-Life Checklist
- **Box 13-7** Client Teaching: Clients Experiencing a Loss
- **Figure 13-2** The Nurse Establishes a Trusting Nurse–Client Relationship Demonstrating Respect for the Person's Age, Culture, Race, and Values

Nursing Care Plan: Client Experiencing Loss

SUGGESTIONS FOR CLASSROOM ACTIVITIES

- Divide the class into four groups. Assign each group to explore the elements of each component of the nursing process as it relates to the grieving and dying process. Have each group present its findings to the class.
- Divide the class into groups of four. Have each group research the nursing interventions from the "Nursing Interventions Classification Project" and present their findings to the group. Ask the students to explore how the interventions might help in planning and implementing client care. What method can the students use to help when providing care for the dying client?

SUGGESTIONS FOR CLINICAL ACTIVITIES

- Arrange for students to have a clinical experience in caring for clients in a palliative care unit or a hospice unit. Assist the students to identify how the nurses assess for pain and evaluate pain relief. What comfort measures are commonly employed? How are nutritional, fluid, and elimination needs addressed?

- Clinical Reasoning Care Map

 MyNursingKit
(www.mynursingkit.com)

- Websites
- NCLEX® Questions
- Case Studies
- Key Terms

 **STUDENT WORKBOOK AND RESOURCE GUIDE**

- Chapter 13 activities
- *Separate purchase*

PRENTICE HALL NURSE'S DRUG GUIDE

- *Separate purchase*

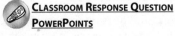 **CLASSROOM RESPONSE QUESTION POWERPOINTS**

 TESTBANK

CHAPTER 14
CARING FOR CLIENTS EXPERIENCING SHOCK, TRAUMA, OR DISASTERS

LEARNING OUTCOME 1

Describe common causes, pathophysiology, and manifestations for each type of shock: hypovolemic, anaphylactic, cardiogenic, septic, and neurogenic.

Concepts for Lecture

1. The five types of shock are hypovolemic, anaphylactic, cardiogenic, septic, and neurogenic.
2. Shock is identified according to its underlying cause.

LEARNING OUTCOME 2

Explain the medical management and nursing care of the client in shock.

Concepts for Lecture

1. Medical and nursing management of shock includes performing diagnostic tests and providing oxygen therapy, intravenous fluids, blood or blood products, cardiac support, and client support.
2. Shock must be fully resolved before a client can be discharged. Teaching the family to care for the client is needed to provide the client with a supportive and nurturing environment after discharge.

LEARNING OUTCOME 3

Explain nursing implications for administering fluids, blood products, and medications to clients with shock or trauma.

Concepts for Lecture

1. The main goal for clients with hypovolemic shock is to restore intravascular volume, with the type and amount of fluid chosen for replacement depending on the type of fluid lost.
2. Intravenous fluids are administered alone or in combination with colloids, blood, or blood products. Fluid replacements are given in a 3:1 ratio (300 mL fluid for every 100 mL of fluid loss).

 POWERPOINT SLIDES 22–54

Tables and/or Figures

- **Box 14-1** Types of Shock
- **Box 14-2** Manifestations Found in Each Stage of Shock
- **Box 14-3** Initial Manifestations of Hypovolemic Shock
- **Box 14-5** Manifestations of Anaphylactic Shock
- **Box 14-6** Manifestations of Cardiogenic Shock
- **Box 14-7** Manifestations of Septic Shock
- **Box 14-8** Manifestations of Neurogenic Shock
- **Figure 14-2** The Pathophysiology of Hypovolemic Shock

Nursing Care Plan: Client With Septic Shock

SUGGESTIONS FOR CLASSROOM ACTIVITIES

- Compare and contrast different types and causes of shock.

POWERPOINT SLIDES 55–56

SUGGESTIONS FOR CLINICAL ACTIVITIES

- Review manifestations of various types of shock in preconference. Assign students to make index cards with signs and symptoms of shock to be alert for while caring for clients.

Tables and/or Figures

- **Box 14-3** Initial Manifestations of Hypovolemic Shock
- **Box 14-4** Prehospital Emergency Care of the Client Experiencing Hemorrhage

Nursing Care Plan: Client With Septic Shock

 **POWERPOINT SLIDE 57**

SUGGESTIONS FOR CLASSROOM ACTIVITIES

- Invite an emergency room nurse or technician to class to discuss his or her experiences with treating clients experiencing shock and trauma.
- Divide students into groups. Give each group a case scenario of a different type of shock. Have them develop a plan of care or concept map for the case scenario and share these with the other groups.

 **SUGGESTIONS FOR CLINICAL ACTIVITIES**

- Arrange for students to have a clinical experience in the emergency department. Assist the students to view the trauma room and observe how supplies, equipment, and medications are arranged. Review the documentation forms

LEARNING OUTCOME 4

Use the nursing process to collect data, establish outcomes, provide individualized care, and evaluate responses for the client experiencing shock or trauma.

Concepts for Lecture

1. Nursing care of the client with a traumatic injury starts with primary assessment, includes collaborative interventions, and prepares the client and family for discharge.
2. Priorities of nursing care start with maintaining an adequate airway, breathing, and circulation and then focus on replacing fluid volume, restoring and maintaining tissue perfusion, preventing complications, and providing psychosocial support to the client and family.
3. The highest nursing diagnosis appropriate for the client with any type of shock is effective tissue perfusion.

LEARNING OUTCOME 5

Describe emergency management of clients with trauma, environmental injuries, or poisoning.

Concepts for Lecture

1. Clients experiencing a traumatic accident are assessed in the field and in the emergency department for airway, breathing, circulation, disability, and exposure. Traumatic injuries have serious consequences that must be treated rapidly.
2. Injuries that involve criminal activity require legal investigation, including forensic testing.

LEARNING OUTCOME 6

Describe the effects of a critical care unit on the client and the family.

Concepts for Lecture

1. The critical care unit is overwhelming to clients and families. The nurse plays an important role in reducing the psychosocial effects while caring for the acutely ill client.

used with trauma cases. If possible, have the students follow a client in shock or with a trauma through the admission and treatment procedure.

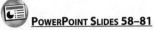 **POWERPOINT SLIDES 58–81**

Tables and/or Figures

- **Table 14-1** Giving Medications Safely: Colloid Solutions
- **Table 14-2** Blood and Blood Products
- **Table 14-3** Blood Group and Rh Types and Compatibilities
- **Table 14-4** Giving Medications Safely: Blood Transfusions

 **SUGGESTIONS FOR CLASSROOM ACTIVITIES**

- Assign groups of students to present on the following subjects: nursing implications for clients receiving colloid solutions and blood transfusions, and the types of blood and blood products.
- Discuss amount of fluid losses and have students calculate the amount of fluid replacement to administer based on fluid losses.

 **POWERPOINT SLIDES 82–85**

 **SUGGESTIONS FOR CLINICAL ACTIVITIES**

- Assign students to observe a client receiving a blood or blood product transfusion. Have them discuss the responsibilities of the nurse in administering blood and blood products. What are the different blood products that are transfused to clients? What is the procedure for obtaining blood from the blood bank? What are the steps to perform when the client has a reaction to the blood or blood product?

 **POWERPOINT SLIDES 86–89**

Tables and/or Figures

- **Box 14-5** Manifestations of Anaphylactic Shock
- **Box 14-6** Manifestations of Cardiogenic Shock
- **Box 14-7** Manifestations of Septic Shock
- **Box 14-8** Manifestations of Neurogenic Shock
- **Box 14-9** Focus on Older Adults: Geriatric Risks for Trauma
- **Box 14-11** Home Safety Tips
- **Box 14-12** Guidelines to Prevent Poisoning

Nursing Care Plan: Client With Septic Shock

SUGGESTIONS FOR CLASSROOM ACTIVITIES

- Assign groups of students to write and present to the class nursing care plans or case studies for clients experiencing each type of shock or trauma.

SUGGESTIONS FOR CLINICAL ACTIVITIES

- Using the nursing process, initiate a discussion on nursing care that students would expect to see on the unit for a client with septic shock or trauma.

LEARNING OUTCOME 7

Identify the nurse's role in the care of victims from natural or manmade disasters.

Concepts for Lecture

1. A variety of common injuries take place during each type of natural disaster.
2. Injuries that take place as a result of chemical and radiation weapons of mass destruction use are significant, and death may occur.
3. Disaster preparedness is a priority of the U.S. government and military.
4. Hospitals are the end point of a community response, and nurses should consider specific preparedness steps.
5. During a disaster, nurses assist in triage, provide physical care and emotional support to victims, and help to restore normal life routines.

GENERAL CHAPTER CONSIDERATIONS

1. Have students study and learn key terms listed at the beginning of the chapter.
2. Have students complete end of chapter exercises either in their book or on the MyNursingKit Website.
3. Use the Classroom Response Question PowerPoints to assess students prior to lecture.

- Ask the head nurse if one of the staff could talk to the students about procedures to be followed if one of their assigned clients experiences shock and what the role of the student would be.

Tables and/or Figures

- **Box 14-4** Prehospital Emergency Care of the Client Experiencing Hemorrhage
- **Table 14-5** Simple Triage System

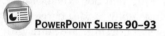 **POWERPOINT SLIDES 90–93**

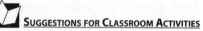 **SUGGESTIONS FOR CLASSROOM ACTIVITIES**

- Divide students into groups. Assign them to develop a plan of care for the prehospital emergency care of the client experiencing hemorrhage, loss of consciousness, impending respiratory or cardiac arrest, severe burn, or multiple fractures.
- Have students examine the crash cart and explain the use of the equipment and medications used to treat shock.

SUGGESTIONS FOR CLINICAL ACTIVITIES

- Arrange for students to spend time with an ambulance service. Have them compare the role of the emergency technician or paramedic with the role of the nurse in a prehospital emergency situation.
- Invite someone from EMS to talk with the students about the role of the emergency technician and/or paramedic and how they view the role of the nurse in the prehospital emergency situation.

SUGGESTIONS FOR CLASSROOM ACTIVITIES

- Discuss the psychosocial effects of the intensive care unit on the client and family. What interventions can the nurse provide to help alleviate these effects?

SUGGESTIONS FOR CLINICAL ACTIVITIES

- Have students interview clients or families about their intensive care unit experience and ask what the client or family feels could have made the experience less anxious for them.

Tables and/or Figures

- **Table 14-5** Simple Triage System
- **Figure 14-10** Form for Family Disaster Plan and Home Disaster Supply Kit
- **Figure 14-11** Basic Protection from Exposure to Unknown Biological Hazard

SUGGESTIONS FOR CLASSROOM ACTIVITIES

- Obtain disaster preparedness plans from local healthcare facilities. Have students review these in small groups and discuss the role of the nurse in these plans.

 SUGGESTIONS FOR CLINICAL ACTIVITIES

- Arrange for students to participate in a disaster drill.

- Clinical Reasoning Care Map

 MYNURSINGKIT
(www.mynursingkit.com)

- Websites
- NCLEX® Questions
- Case Studies
- Key Terms

 STUDENT WORKBOOK AND RESOURCE GUIDE

- Chapter 14 activities
- *Separate purchase*

PRENTICE HALL NURSE'S DRUG GUIDE

- *Separate purchase*

CLASSROOM RESPONSE QUESTION POWERPOINTS

TESTBANK

CHAPTER 15
THE CARDIOVASCULAR SYSTEM AND ASSESSMENT

LEARNING OUTCOME 1

Describe the structure and function of the heart and vascular systems.

Concepts for Lecture

1. The nurse needs to be knowledgeable about the structure of the heart and vascular systems.
2. The nurse needs to be knowledgeable about the function of the heart and vascular systems.

LEARNING OUTCOME 2

Discuss the mechanical and electrical properties of the heart.

Concepts for Lecture

1. The heart has both mechanical and electrical properties.
2. Cardiac muscle can generate an electrical impulse and contraction independent of stimulation by the nervous system.
3. The sinoatrial (SA) node located in the wall of the right atrium acts as the "pacemaker" of the heart.

LEARNING OUTCOME 3

Identify subjective and objective assessment data to collect for clients with cardiovascular disorders.

Concepts for Lecture

1. Assessment of clients with cardiovascular disorders contains both subjective and objective data.
2. Focused assessment begins by asking about current symptoms such as chest pain and its duration.

 **POWERPOINT SLIDES 21–29**

Tables and/or Figures

- **Figure 15-1** Location of the Heart Within the Chest Cavity
- **Figure 15-2** The Internal Anatomy of the Heart
- **Figure 15-3** Pulmonary and Systemic Circulation
- **Figure 15-4** The Coronary Arteries
- **Figure 15-7** Structure of Arteries, Veins, and Capillaries

 **SUGGESTIONS FOR CLASSROOM ACTIVITIES**

- Assign students to access the Website www.innerbody.com/image/cardov.html to review an interactive demonstration of the heart.

 **POWERPOINT SLIDES 30–36**

 SUGGESTIONS FOR CLINICAL ACTIVITIES

- Have students listen to the heart sounds of a client and analyze the quality of the heart sounds.

 REFERENCE

- InnerBody: Cardiovascular System. Available at www.innerbody.com/image/cardov.html

 **POWERPOINT SLIDES 37–38**

Tables and/or Figures

- **Figure 15-5** The Cardiac Conduction System
- **Figure 15-6** The Cardiac Cycle

 **SUGGESTIONS FOR CLASSROOM ACTIVITIES**

- Access the Website http://www.cardiovascular.cx/and view the video for more information on determining cardiac output.

 SUGGESTIONS FOR CLINICAL ACTIVITIES

- Collect information regarding a client's heart rate. Determine the client's cardiac output.

REFERENCE

- The Gross Physiology of the Cardiovascular System. Available at http://www.cardiovascular.cx/

LEARNING OUTCOME 4

Identify nursing responsibilities for common diagnostic tests and monitors for clients with cardiovascular disorders.

Concepts for Lecture

1. Nurses have responsibilities associated with common diagnostic tests and monitors for clients with cardiovascular disorders, including laboratory tests, electrocardiographic studies, and imaging studies.
2. The nurse must instruct the client undergoing laboratory tests concerning whether they should fast and whether alcohol is allowed. The nurse should also know what medications the client is taking because some medications can interfere with specific laboratory tests and need to be withheld.
3. The nurse provides teaching about the purpose of continuous or event cardiac monitoring and what the client's responsibilities are.
4. Some electrocardiographic and imaging studies require informed consent, and the nurse must ensure that this has been done.
5. The nurse must ask about specific allergies when the client is undergoing studies involving injection of a contrast dye.

GENERAL CHAPTER CONSIDERATIONS

1. Have students study and learn key terms listed at the beginning of the chapter.
2. Have students complete end of chapter exercises either in their book or on the MyNursingKit Website.
3. Use the Classroom Response Question PowerPoints to assess students prior to lecture.

 POWERPOINT SLIDES 39–41

Tables and/or Figures

- **Box 15-1** Focus on Diversity: Assessing Skin Color
- **Box 15-2** Documentation of Cardiovascular Assessment

 **SUGGESTIONS FOR CLASSROOM ACTIVITIES**

- Practice assessing the cardiovascular and peripheral vascular status of a classmate.

 SUGGESTIONS FOR CLINICAL ACTIVITIES

- Collect subjective and objective data for a client. Determine if the client is experiencing a cardiovascular or peripheral vascular disorder.

Tables and/or Figures

- **Table 15-1** Common Laboratory Tests for Cardiovascular Disease
- **Table 15-2** Diagnostic Electrocardiographic Studies
- **Table 15-3** Imaging Studies

 **SUGGESTIONS FOR CLASSROOM ACTIVITIES**

- Review the various types of diagnostic tests and monitors used to assess the cardiovascular and peripheral vascular systems. Practice applying the leads for an ECG on a classmate.

 SUGGESTIONS FOR CLINICAL

- Review the different diagnostic tests prescribed for a client with a cardiovascular or peripheral vascular disorder. Provide appropriate nursing care for the client undergoing diagnostic tests.

 **MYNURSINGKIT (www.mynursingkit.com)**

- Websites
- NCLEX® Questions
- Case Studies
- Key Terms

 STUDENT WORKBOOK AND RESOURCE GUIDE

- Chapter 15 activities
- *Separate purchase*

PRENTICE HALL NURSE'S DRUG GUIDE

- *Separate purchase*

CLASSROOM RESPONSE QUESTION POWERPOINTS

TESTBANK

Chapter 16
Caring for Clients With Coronary Heart Disease and Dysrhythmias

Learning Outcome 1

Describe the causes, pathophysiology, effects, and manifestations of coronary heart disease and heart rhythm disruptions.

Concepts for Lecture

1. Describe the causes, pathophysiology, effects, and manifestations of coronary artery disease.
2. Coronary heart disease (CHD) is caused by narrowing of the coronary arteries that supply blood to the heart muscle. Atherosclerosis is the primary cause of this narrowing and obstructed blood flow. The cause of atherosclerosis is unknown.
3. CHD tends to be symptom free until about 75% of the lumen of affected vessels is occluded.
4. Clients with CHD may present with no symptoms, episodic chest pain, or an acute event such as acute coronary syndromes or myocardial infarction.
5. Describe the causes, pathophysiology, effects, and manifestations of heart rhythm disruptions.

Learning Outcome 2

Differentiate among the effects of coronary heart disease: angina pectoris, acute coronary syndrome, and myocardial infarction.

Concepts for Lecture

1. The nurse should know the effects of coronary heart disease and how they differ among the following types of coronary heart disease: angina pectoris, acute coronary syndrome, and myocardial infarction.
2. In angina, myocardial ischemia develops with increased workload.
3. Angina often is a precursor to an acute cardiac event such as acute coronary syndrome or myocardial infarction.
4. Manifestations of angina include pain relieved by rest that may radiate to the neck, shoulder, and arms lasting 2 to 5 minutes. Other symptoms include indigestion, nausea, possible shortness of breath, and anxiety.
5. Whereas angina develops with increased workload, acute coronary syndrome often occurs at rest, and acute myocardial infarction begins abruptly unrelated to rest or exercise.

Learning Outcome 3

Discuss nursing implications for drugs commonly prescribed for clients with coronary heart disease or dysrhythmias.

Concepts for Lecture

1. Discuss the nursing implications for drugs prescribed for coronary artery disease or dysrhythmias.

 PowerPoint Slides 22–35

Tables and/or Figures

- **Table 16-1** Risk Factors for Coronary Heart Disease
- **Table 16-2** Classification of Cholesterol and LDL Levels
- **Table 16-5** Comparing Angina Pectoris, Acute Coronary Syndrome, and Acute Myocardial Infarction
- **Table 16-8** Characteristics, Causes, and Management of Selected Cardiac Rhythms
- **Box 16-1** Focus on Diversity: Coronary Heart Disease
- **Box 16-3** Manifestations of Angina
- **Box 16-6** Manifestations of Acute Myocardial Infarction
- **Box 16-7** Population Focus: Heart Disease in Women and Older Adults
- **Box 16-11** Focus on Older Adults: Dysrhythmias in Older Adults
- **Figure 16-12** Using an Automated External Defibrillator (AED)

SUGGESTIONS FOR CLASSROOM ACTIVITIES

- Invite three to four people with coronary heart disease and heart rhythm disruptions to speak to the class about their pathophysiology and the signs and symptoms they have experienced and to answer the students' questions. Have students write their questions before bringing in the speakers and select some of the questions to be answered.

 **PowerPoint Slides 36-37**

SUGGESTIONS FOR CLINICAL ACTIVITIES

- Assign students to clients with coronary heart disease and heart rhythm disruptions. Ask the students to present what they learned about the causes, pathophysiology, effects, and manifestations of coronary heart disease and heart rhythm disruptions from working with their assigned clients.

Tables and/or Figures

- **Box 16-3** Manifestations of Angina
- **Table 16-5** Comparing Angina Pectoris, Acute Coronary Syndrome, and Acute Myocardial Infarction
- **Table 16-7** Cardiac Marker Changes in Acute Myocardial Infarction

 **PowerPoint Slides 38–44**

LEARNING OUTCOME 4

Describe nursing care for clients undergoing invasive procedures or surgery of the heart.

Concepts for Lecture

1. Describe nursing care for invasive procedures or cardiac surgery.
2. The nurse must inform clients undergoing coronary angiography and percutaneous transluminal coronary angioplasty that they will remain awake during the procedure, which lasts 1 to 2 hours, and that they will be given sedation and a local anesthetic.
3. The nurse working with clients undergoing coronary angiography and percutaneous transluminal coronary angioplasty will document and report allergies to iodine, radiographic dyes, or seafood and will advise the clients that there will be a sensation of warmth and a metallic taste as the dye is inserted.
4. Postoperatively, the nursing care of clients undergoing coronary angiography and percutaneous transluminal coronary angioplasty includes close monitoring, the head of the bed elevated no more than 30 degrees, a pressure dressing in place over arterial access sites, a 5-pound sandbag over the access site for 6 hours or as ordered, and assessment for bleeding (if the access site is the groin, bleeding is assessed for under the buttocks).
5. Nursing care for the client undergoing a coronary artery bypass graft (CABG) includes routine preoperative care and teaching the client what to expect after surgery.
6. Postoperative care of the client undergoing CABG includes close monitoring of vital signs, heart sounds, respiratory status, peripheral pulses, LOC, arterial blood gasses, urine intake and output (hourly), chest tube intake and output (hourly), and continuous cardiac rhythm monitoring. The nurse rewarms the client as needed per orders or if the client temperature is below 96.8°F or 36°C.
7. The nurse working preoperatively with a client receiving a permanent pacemaker implant will position the ECG monitor electrodes away from potential incision sites.
8. Postoperative nursing care of clients receiving a permanent pacemaker implant includes monitoring pacemaker function and cardiac rhythm and reporting problems to the physician, such as failure to pace, hiccups, pulse rate 5 or more bpm slower than pacemaker rate, or signs of pacemaker malfunction: dizziness, fainting, fatigue, weakness, chest pain, or palpitations.

LEARNING OUTCOME 5

Use the nursing process to collect assessment data, contribute to care planning, and provide individualized nursing care for clients with coronary heart disease and dysrhythmias.

Concepts for Lecture

1. The nursing process is used to provide care for clients with coronary artery disease and dysrhythmias.
2. Maintaining adequate coronary blood flow and perfusion of the heart muscle is the highest priority of care for the client with CHD and angina.

SUGGESTIONS FOR CLASSROOM ACTIVITIES

- Have students work in small groups to make flashcards with questions on one side and answers on the other. The questions should be focused on comparing angina pectoris, acute coronary syndrome, and acute myocardial infarction.
- Invite a cardiologist to speak to the class. Ask the cardiologist to differentiate among the effects of coronary heart disease: angina pectoris, acute coronary syndrome, and myocardial infarction.

PowerPoint Slides 45–48

SUGGESTIONS FOR CLINICAL ACTIVITIES

- Assign students to work with clients with angina pectoris, acute coronary syndrome, and acute myocardial infarction.

Tables and/or Figures

- **Table 16-3** Giving Medications Safely: Cholesterol-Lowering Drugs
- **Table 16-4** Giving Medications Safely: Antianginal Drugs
- **Table 16-6** Giving Medications Safely: Antiplatelet Drugs
- **Table 16-9** Giving Medications Safely: Antidysrhythmic Drugs
- **Box 16-8** Nursing Care Checklist: Fibrinolytic Therapy

SUGGESTIONS FOR CLASSROOM ACTIVITIES

- Break students into small groups. Have each group develop and present a role play involving teaching about a drug assigned to the group from Tables 16-3, 16-4, or 16-6.
- Have students make drug cards or create a spreadsheet listing all of the medications used to treat coronary artery disease in order of priority of symptoms. Use the Website http://www.nlm.nih.gov/medlineplus/ency/article/001101.htm for more information.

SUGGESTIONS FOR CLINICAL ACTIVITIES

- Assign students to care for a client with coronary artery disease or a dysrhythmia. Have students assess the vital signs of the client. Students should give the rationale for assessing vital signs, know the normal parameters, and know what findings would need to be reported before holding or giving the medication. Students should prepare and administer medications safely for a client with coronary artery disease or a dysrhythmia.

PowerPoint Slides 49–69

Tables and/or Figures

- **Figure 16-3** Percutaneous Transluminal Coronary Angiography (PTCA) With Stent Placement

LEARNING OUTCOME 6

Provide and reinforce appropriate teaching for clients with coronary heart disease or dysrhythmias and their families.

Concepts for Lecture

1. Teaching to prevent coronary heart disease is a priority of nursing care to promote health for all clients.
2. Some risk factors for coronary heart disease cannot be changed, but lifestyle factors such as smoking, diet, and inactivity can be changed.

GENERAL CHAPTER CONSIDERATIONS

1. Have students study and learn key terms listed at the beginning of the chapter.
2. Have students complete end of chapter exercises either in their book or on the MyNursingKit Website.
3. Use the Classroom Response Question PowerPoints to assess students prior to lecture.

- **Figure 16-4** Coronary Artery Bypass Graft (CABG)
- **Figure 16-5** Open Heart Surgery
- **Figure 16-6** A Diagram of a Cardiopulmonary Bypass Pump
- **Box 16-4** Nursing Care Checklist: Coronary Angiography and Percutaneous Transluminal Coronary Angioplasty
- **Box 16-5** Nursing Care Checklist: Cardiac Surgery
- **Box 16-8** Nursing Care Checklist: Fibrinolytic Therapy
- **Box 16-12** Procedure Checklist: Initiating Cardiac Monitoring
- **Box 16-13** Nursing Care Checklist: Permanent Pacemaker Implantation

 **POWERPOINT SLIDES 70–74**

SUGGESTIONS FOR CLASSROOM ACTIVITIES

- Prepare a preoperative teaching plan for a client planning to undergo cardiovascular surgery.

SUGGESTIONS FOR CLINICAL ACTIVITIES

- Using the teaching plan created in class, provide instruction to a client planning to undergo cardiovascular surgery. Document the client's comprehension in the medical record.

 REFERENCES

- MedicineNet.com: Coronary artery bypass graft surgery. Available at http://www.medicinenet.com/coronary_artery_bypass_graft/article.htm
- National Heart, Lung, and Blood Institute. What is coronary artery bypass grafting? Available at http://www.nhlbi.nih.gov/health/dci/Diseases/cabg/cabg_whatis.html

Tables and/or Figures

- **Box 16-9** Assessment: Clients With Acute Myocardial Infarction
- **Table 16-8** Characteristics, Causes, and Management of Selected Cardiac Rhythms
- **Box 16-10** ECG Rhythm Analysis
- **Figure 16-2** ECG Changes During an Episode of Angina
- **Figure 16-7** ECG Changes With Acute Myocardial Infarction
- **Figure 16-11** Ventricular Pacing
- **Box 16-12** Procedure Checklist: Initiating Cardiac Monitoring

Nursing Care Plan: Client With Acute Myocardial Infarction

SUGGESTIONS FOR CLASSROOM ACTIVITIES

- Practice conducting a cardiovascular assessment on a classmate. Document the findings. Use the Website http://www.clevelandclinicmeded.com/diseasemanagement/cardiology/cad/cad.htm for more information or assistance.
- Provide EKG strips demonstrating rhythms of selected cardiac disorders and have students identify what the rhythms are.

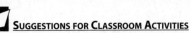

SUGGESTIONS FOR CLINICAL ACTIVITIES

- Assign students to conduct an assessment of a client with coronary artery disease or a dysrhythmia. Have students document their findings in the medical record.

SUGGESTIONS FOR CLASSROOM ACTIVITIES

- Have students make posters for teaching about risk factors for coronary heart disease and lifestyle changes that will reduce these risk factors.

SUGGESTIONS FOR CLINICAL ACTIVITIES

- Assign students to assess risk factors for coronary heart disease in their assigned clients and then to discuss lifestyle changes that will reduce risk factors found with their client(s).

- Clinical Reasoning Care Map

MYNURSINGKIT
(www.mynursingkit.com)

- Websites
- NCLEX® Questions
- Case Studies
- Key Terms

STUDENT WORKBOOK AND RESOURCE GUIDE

- Chapter 16 activities
- *Separate purchase*

PRENTICE HALL NURSE'S DRUG GUIDE

- *Separate purchase*

CLASSROOM RESPONSE QUESTION POWERPOINTS

TESTBANK

CHAPTER 17
CARING FOR CLIENTS WITH CARDIAC DISORDERS

LEARNING OUTCOME 1

Compare and contrast the causes, pathophysiology, effects, and manifestations of common cardiac disorders.

Concepts for Lecture

1. Compare and contrast the causes, pathophysiology, effects, and manifestations of common cardiac disorders including disorders of cardiac function, inflammatory cardiac disorders, and disorders of cardiac structure.

LEARNING OUTCOME 2

Discuss nursing implications for safe administration of drugs commonly prescribed for clients with heart disease.

Concepts for Lecture

1. Discuss nursing implications for providing medications safely to clients with heart disease.
2. Clients with heart failure typically receive multiple medications to reduce cardiac work and improve cardiac function.
3. The main drug classes used to treat heart failure are the angiotensin-converting enzyme (ACE) inhibitors, angiotensin II receptor blockers, beta-blockers, diuretics, inotropic drugs (which increase the strength of heart contractions), and direct vasodilators.

LEARNING OUTCOME 3

Describe nursing care for clients undergoing invasive procedures or surgery of the heart.

Concepts for Lecture

1. Heart transplant is the primary treatment for end-stage heart failure.
2. Ventricular assist devices (VADs), which are mechanical pumps, are often used as a bridge to transplantation.
3. Nursing care of the heart transplant client is similar to the care of any cardiac surgery client.
4. The major concern of the nurse in the early postoperative period after transplant is bleeding.
5. The nurse will monitor chest tube drainage, urinary output, heart rhythm, and hemodynamic parameters and be alert for signs of cardiac tamponade.
6. The nurse will carefully and gradually rewarm the client and prevent shivering.
7. The nurse must perform aggressive nursing care to prevent infection in the heart transplant client because infection and rejection of the transplanted organ are the leading causes of death.

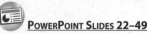
POWERPOINT SLIDES 22–49

Tables and/or Figures

- **Table 17-1** Selected Causes of Heart Failure
- **Table 17-2** Manifestations of Heart Failure
- **Figure 17-1** Left-Sided Heart Failure Causes Increased Pressure and Congestion
- **Figure 17-2** Edema of the Feet and Ankles of a Client With Heart Failure
- **Figure 17-3** Distended Neck Veins Reflecting the Backward Effects of Right-Sided and Biventricular Heart Failure
- **Box 17-1** Focus on Older Adults: Cardiac Function
- **Box 17-2** Heart Failure Classification
- **Box 17-6** Manifestations of Rheumatic Fever
- **Table 17-4** Classifications of Infective Endocarditis
- **Table 17-6** Characteristics of Common Heart Murmurs
- **Table 17-7** Classifications and Characteristics of Cardiomyopathy

POWERPOINT SLIDES 50–56

SUGGESTIONS FOR CLASSROOM ACTIVITIES

- Have students review the physiology of heart failure, explaining the difference between systolic and diastolic heart failure. Refer to the Website http://www.chfpatients.com/faq/dhf.htm

SUGGESTIONS FOR CLINICAL ACTIVITIES

- Assign students to clients with common cardiac disorders and have them identify current manifestations as well as earlier manifestations that have responded to treatment.

REFERENCES

- CHFpatients.com: Diastolic heart failure. Available at http://www.chfpatients.com/faq/dhf.htm
- MedlinePlus: Heart failure. Available at http://www.nlm.nih.gov/medlineplus/heartfailure.html

POWERPOINT SLIDES 57–68

Tables and/or Figures

- **Table 17-3** Giving Medications Safely: Heart Failure
- **Table 17-5** Indications for Antibiotic Prophylaxis to Prevent Endocarditis
- **Box 17-3** Complementary Therapies: Heart Failure

LEARNING OUTCOME 4

Use the nursing process to collect assessment data, contribute to care planning, and provide individualized nursing care for clients with disorders of the heart.

Concepts for Lecture

1. The nurse uses the nursing process to collect assessment data, contribute to care planning, and provide individualized nursing care for clients with disorders of the heart.
2. Reducing the oxygen demand of the heart is a major nursing goal and involves providing both physical and psychologic rest as well as administering and monitoring multiple drugs to reduce cardiac work, improve contractility, and manage symptoms.
3. Nursing care of the client in acute cardiac failure is directed toward measures that help reduce the workload of the heart.
4. The nurse needs to assess for and report increasing restlessness, anxiety, orthopnea, increased heart and respiratory rates, cough, and decreasing oxygen saturation levels because these may be early manifestations of pulmonary edema.
5. The client with severe chronic heart failure may develop liver failure as a result of chronic congestion of hepatic vessels, and kidney failure may develop due to impaired perfusion of renal vessels, so the nurse must monitor laboratory values including liver and renal function tests.
6. Impaired cerebral perfusion can lead to changes in mental status, so the nurse must monitor level of consciousness and cognition and report changes.
7. The nursing care focus for a client with rheumatic fever is on teaching to prevent long-term damage to heart valves and recurrence of the disorder.

LEARNING OUTCOME 5

Provide and reinforce appropriate teaching for clients with heart disorders and their families.

Concepts for Lecture

1. The nurse provides and reinforces appropriate teaching for clients with heart disorders and their families.
2. Client and family teaching for clients with heart disorders and their families focuses on self-care measures such as activity restrictions, dietary changes, and drugs used to reduce symptoms and/or prevent complications.
3. Client and family teaching also includes education about the disease process, its ultimate outcome, and treatment options.
4. The nurse provides teaching about the procedure to clients who are undergoing invasive procedures for diagnosis or treatment, including preparation and care following the procedure.
5. When heart transplant is an option, the nurse provides information about the procedure and initiates preoperative teaching.

SUGGESTIONS FOR CLASSROOM ACTIVITIES

- Have students prepare drug cards for medications in each category of medications used to treat heart disorders in preparation for caring for clients with cardiac disorders.

SUGGESTIONS FOR CLINICAL ACTIVITIES

- Assign students to clients who have a cardiac disorder and have them verbalize the purpose of the medication, nursing implications, and client teaching to be done before administering medications to their assigned client with a heart disorder.

REFERENCE

- National Heart, Lung, and Blood Institute. Heart attack signs. Available at http://www.nhlbi.nih.gov/actintime/

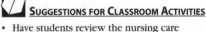

POWERPOINT SLIDES 69–84

Tables and/or Figures

- **Figure 17-6** Cardiac Transplantation
- **Box 17-8** Nursing Care Checklist: Pericardiocentesis

SUGGESTIONS FOR CLASSROOM ACTIVITIES

- Have students review the nursing care involved in various heart procedures. Refer to the Website http://www.ncbi.nlm.nih.gov/.
- Invite a nurse who works in a cardiac care unit to talk to the students about the nursing care for a client who is undergoing invasive procedures or surgery of the heart.

SUGGESTIONS FOR CLINICAL ACTIVITIES

- Assign students to assist with care needed for a client undergoing an invasive cardiac procedure.

POWERPOINT SLIDES 85–89

Tables and/or Figures

- **Box 17-3** Complimentary Therapies: Heart Failure
- **Box 17-5** Assessment: Clients With Heart Failure
- **Box 17-8** Nursing Care Checklist: Pericardiocentesis
- **Table 17-3** Giving Medications Safely: Heart Failure
- **Table 17-5** Indications for Antibiotic Prophylaxis to Prevent Endocarditis
- **Figure 17-10** Valvular Heart Disorders
- **Figure 17-11** Mitral Stenosis
- **Figure 17-12** Mitral Regurgitation
- **Figure 17-13** Aortic Stenosis
- **Figure 17-14** Aortic Regurgitation
- **Figure 17-15** Balloon Valvuloplasty
- **Figure 17-16** Prosthetic Heart Valves

Nursing Care Plan: Client With Heart Failure

GENERAL CHAPTER CONSIDERATIONS

1. Have students study and learn key terms listed at the beginning of the chapter.
2. Have students complete end of chapter exercises either in their book or on the MyNursingKit Website.
3. Use the Classroom Response Question PowerPoints to assess students prior to lecture.

Tables and/or Figures
- **Box 17-4** Client Teaching: Activity Guidelines for Clients With Heart Failure
- **Box 17-7** Client Teaching: Preventing Endocarditis

 SUGGESTIONS FOR CLASSROOM ACTIVITIES
- Ask students to each identify one heart disorder and create a discharge teaching plan for the disorder.

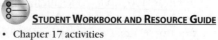 **SUGGESTIONS FOR CLINICAL ACTIVITIES**
- Ask students to implement the discharge teaching plan for a client with a heart disorder.

- Clinical Reasoning Care Map

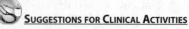 **MYNURSINGKIT**
(www.mynursingkit.com)
- Websites
- NCLEX® Questions
- Case Studies
- Key Terms

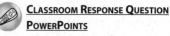 **STUDENT WORKBOOK AND RESOURCE GUIDE**
- Chapter 17 activities
- *Separate purchase*

PRENTICE HALL NURSE'S DRUG GUIDE
- *Separate purchase*

 CLASSROOM RESPONSE QUESTION POWERPOINTS

TESTBANK

CHAPTER 18
CARING FOR CLIENTS WITH PERIPHERAL VASCULAR DISORDERS

LEARNING OUTCOME 1

Relate physiology of the peripheral vascular system to common disorders affecting the peripheral vascular system.

Concepts for Lecture

1. Relate physiology of the peripheral vascular system to common disorders of the peripheral vascular system.
2. Several processes can affect blood vessels and interfere with peripheral blood flow: constriction, obstruction, inflammation, and spasm.
3. When conditions such as aneurysms and varicose veins occur, the structure of the vessel itself is altered.

LEARNING OUTCOME 2

Describe the pathophysiology and manifestations of common peripheral vascular disorders.

Concepts for Lecture

1. The nurse needs to be able to describe the pathophysiology and manifestations of common peripheral vascular disorders.
2. Peripheral vascular resistance is the primary factor in determining blood pressure.
3. Disruption of the physiologic mechanisms that regulate blood pressure is the underlying cause of hypertension.
4. Hypertension is usually advanced when symptoms develop.
5. In peripheral atherosclerosis, symptoms occur usually after 60% of the vessel is occluded.
6. Aneurysms often produce no symptoms and are discovered during a routine physical examination.
7. The signs and symptoms of Raynaud's disease occur intermittently, often following exposure to cold or work-related vibration.

LEARNING OUTCOME 3

Identify subjective and objective assessment data to collect for clients with peripheral vascular disorders.

Concepts for Lecture

1. The nurse assessing clients with peripheral vascular disorders will assess for both subjective and objective data.

 **POWERPOINT SLIDE 22**

Tables and/or Figures
- **Box 18-1** Focus on Older Adults: Hypertension
- **Box 18-2** Risk Factors for Hypertension
- **Box 18-6** Population Focus: Clients With Marfan Syndrome
- **Box 18-13** Risk Factors for Venous Thrombosis

 SUGGESTIONS FOR CLASSROOM ACTIVITIES
- Assign the students to small groups and have them select one disorder. Using the Internet, research the disorder and prepare a 10-minute presentation about the disorder for the rest of the class.

 **POWERPOINT SLIDES 23–37**

 SUGGESTIONS FOR CLINICAL ACTIVITIES
- Assign the students to a client with a peripheral vascular disorder. Have the students assess the client in an effort to identify any manifestations of the disorder.

 REFERENCES
- Mayo Clinical: High blood pressure. Available at http://www.mayoclinic.com/health/high-blood-pressure/DS00100
- MedlinePlus: Hypertension. Available at: http://www.nlm.nih.gov/medlineplus/ency/article/000468.htm

Tables and/or Figures
- **Table 18-1** Effects of Hypertension
- **Figure 18-2** Aortic Aneurysms
- **Figure 18-7** Venous Ulcer of the Ankle
- **Figure 18-9** A Varicose Vein in a Person's Leg
- **Table 18-4** Manifestations and Complications of Aortic Aneurysms
- **Figure 18-5** Hands of a Client With Raynaud's Phenomenon
- **Box 18-12** Manifestations of Arterial Thrombosis or Embolism
- **Box 18-14** Manifestation of Deep and Superficial Venous Thrombosis
- **Box 18-15** Manifestations of Varicose Veins

 **POWERPOINT SLIDES 38–60**

LEARNING OUTCOME 4

Explain the nursing implications of drugs used for clients with peripheral vascular disorders.

Concepts for Lecture

1. It is important that the nurse be knowledgeable about and be able to explain nursing implications of drugs used for clients with peripheral vascular disorders.
2. No one primary antihypertensive drug is used to treat hypertension, and nursing implications vary among the antihypertensive drugs.
3. When the client's average blood pressure is greater than 200/120, immediate treatment is vital with parenteral medications to reduce the blood pressure rapidly and prevent long-term consequences.
4. Nursing implications vary among the anticoagulant medications. In general, the client must avoid medications and activities that increase bleeding (e.g., avoid aspirin and NSAIDS, use electric razors, use soft toothbrushes, and limit foods rich in vitamin K).

LEARNING OUTCOME 5

Describe pre- and postoperative care for clients having vascular surgery.

Concepts for Lecture

1. The nurse must provide pre- and postoperative care for clients having vascular surgery.
2. When working preoperatively with a client with an aneurysm, the nurse will plan and implement measures to reduce the risk of aneurysm rupture and monitor for manifestations of impending rupture or other complications.
3. When working postoperatively with a client who had an aneurysm repaired, the nurse will assess frequently for bleeding, immediately report signs of graft leakage, and report evidence of complications.

LEARNING OUTCOME 6

Use the nursing process to provide individualized care to clients with peripheral vascular disorders.

Concepts for Lecture

1. The nurse uses the nursing process to provide individualized care to clients with hypertension.
2. The nurse uses the nursing process to provide care to clients with disorders of the aorta and its branches.
3. The nurse uses the nursing process to provide care to clients with peripheral arterial disorders.
4. The nurse uses the nursing process to provide care to clients with venous disorders.

SUGGESTIONS FOR CLASSROOM ACTIVITIES

- Break into small groups and have students discuss pathophysiology and manifestations of various peripheral vascular disorders. Students could list data they would gather about possible causes and manifestations.

POWERPOINT SLIDES 61–65

SUGGESTIONS FOR CLINICAL ACTIVITIES

- Assign students to clients with peripheral vascular disorders. Have students use the lists they made in class to gather information about pathophysiology and manifestations of the disorders their clients have.
- Do modified grand rounds with a client who has a peripheral vascular disorder and is willing to talk about his or her disorder with students. Use this as a postconference exercise.

REFERENCES

- Mayo Clinic: Raynaud's disease. Available at http://www.mayoclinic.com/health/raynauds-disease/DS00433
- MedlinePlus: Raynaud's phenomenon. Available at http://www.nlm.nih.gov/medlineplus/ency/article/000412.htm

POWERPOINT SLIDES 66–80

Tables and/or Figures

- **Box 18-5** Nursing Care Checklist: Accurate Blood Pressure Measurement
- **Box 18-10** Assessment: Assessing Clients With Peripheral Vascular Disease
- **Box 18-15**: Manifestations of Varicose Veins

SUGGESTIONS FOR CLASSROOM ACTIVITIES

- Have students prepare a list of assessment questions and measurements to be used to assess a client with a peripheral vascular disorder.

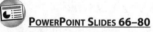

SUGGESTIONS FOR CLINICAL ACTIVITIES

- Have students use the assessment information prepared in class to assess a client with a peripheral vascular disorder.

REFERENCE

- PubMed: Peripheral vascular disorders. Available at http://www.ncbi.nlm.nih.gov/pubmed/2235633

POWERPOINT SLIDES 81–95

Tables and/or Figures

- **Table 18-3** Giving Medications Safely: Hypertension
- **Table 18-5** Giving Medications Safely: Anticoagulants
- **Figure 18-1** Sites and Mechanisms of Antihypertensive Drug Action

LEARNING OUTCOME 7

Reinforce client and family teaching to promote and maintain health in clients with common peripheral vascular disorders.

Concepts for Lecture

1. The nurse reinforces client and family teaching to promote and maintain health in clients with common peripheral vascular disorders.

GENERAL CHAPTER CONSIDERATIONS

1. Have students study and learn key terms listed at the beginning of the chapter.
2. Have students complete end of chapter exercises either in their book or on the MyNursingKit Website.
3. Use the Classroom Response Question PowerPoints to assess students prior to lecture.

 **SUGGESTIONS FOR CLASSROOM ACTIVITIES**

- Assign students to prepare medication provision cards/sheets for the major drug classifications of medications used to treat peripheral vascular disorders. Utilize any medication text for this information.
- Invite a professor from a local pharmacy school, a pharmD student, or a nurse practitioner to talk to the class about medications used to treat peripheral vascular disorders. Ask the speaker to include nursing implications in their presentation.

 POWERPOINT SLIDES 96–101

 SUGGESTIONS FOR CLINICAL ACTIVITIES

- Assign students to provide medications to a client with a peripheral vascular disease.

Tables and/or Figures

- **Figure 18-3** Repair of an Abdominal Aortic Aneurysm
- **Figure 18-8** A Vena Caval Filter to Trap Emboli
- **Box 18-7** Nursing Care Checklist: Surgery of the Aorta

 **SUGGESTIONS FOR CLASSROOM ACTIVITIES**

- Identify one surgical procedure used to treat a peripheral vascular disorder. Research the extent of surgery.

 SUGGESTIONS FOR CLINICAL ACTIVITIES

- Observe a surgical procedure for a client with a peripheral vascular disorder. Accompany this client into the recovery room.

Tables and/or Figures

- **Table 18-2** Recommended Follow-Up and Treatment for Hypertension
- **Box 18-3** The Dash Diet
- **Box 18-4** Complementary Therapies: Hypertension
- **Box 18-9** Complementary Therapies: Peripheral Vascular Disease
- **Figure 18-4** A Doppler (Ultrasound) Stethoscope

Nursing Care Plan: Client With Hypertension

 SUGGESTIONS FOR CLASSROOM ACTIVITIES

- Assign students to each prepare a plan of care for a client with a peripheral vascular disorder.

 SUGGESTIONS FOR CLINICAL ACTIVITIES

- Assign students to care for a client with a peripheral vascular disorder.

Tables and/or Figures

- **Box 18-8** Client Teaching: Leg and Foot Care for Clients With Peripheral Vascular Disease

 SUGGESTIONS FOR CLASSROOM ACTIVITIES

- Assign students to each create a teaching plan for a peripheral vascular disorder.

 SUGGESTIONS FOR CLINICAL ACTIVITIES

- Have students instruct an assigned client with a peripheral vascular disorder on the content placed in the teaching plan during the classroom activity.
- Ask the nurses on the clinical unit where students are assigned if one or more students can accompany them when they do some client teaching related to peripheral vascular disorders. Have students discuss their experience in postconference.

- Clinical Reasoning Care Map

 MYNURSINGKIT
(www.mynursingkit.com)

- Websites
- NCLEX® Questions
- Case Studies
- Key Terms

 **STUDENT WORKBOOK AND RESOURCE GUIDE**

- Chapter 18 activities
- *Separate purchase*

PRENTICE HALL NURSE'S DRUG GUIDE

- *Separate purchase*

CLASSROOM RESPONSE QUESTION POWERPOINTS

TESTBANK

CHAPTER 19
THE HEMATOLOGIC AND LYMPHATIC SYSTEMS AND ASSESSMENT

LEARNING OUTCOME 1

Describe the cells of the hematologic system and their function.

Concepts for Lecture

1. Blood is made up of plasma, a clear yellow, protein-rich fluid, and the cells suspended in it: red blood cells (erythrocytes), white blood cells (leukocytes), and platelets (thrombocytes).
2. Red blood cells (erythrocytes, RBCs) and the hemoglobin they contain are vital for transporting oxygen to body tissues and in helping carry carbon dioxide from the tissues to the lungs for excretion.
3. Red blood cells are shaped like biconcave disks. This shape maximizes the surface of the RBC for gas exchange and allows it to change shape as it moves through very small capillaries.
4. White blood cells (WBCs) are also called leukocytes and are part of the body's defense system against infection and disease.
5. Platelets are small fragments of cytoplasm without nuclei that contain many granules. They are an essential part of the body's clotting mechanism.

LEARNING OUTCOME 2

Identify and describe the structures and functions of the lymphatic system.

Concepts for Lecture

1. The lymphatic system structures include the lymphatic vessels, lymph nodes, and lymphoid organs such as the spleen, the thymus, and lymphoid tissue in the skin, respiratory system, and gastrointestinal system.
2. The lymphatic system has several functions; the lymph nodes assist the immune system by removing foreign matter, infectious organisms, and tumor cells from the lymph.
3. The spleen filters the blood, produces lymphocytes (a type of WBC), and stores blood and platelets.
4. The thymus and lymphoid tissue in the skin, respiratory, and gastrointestinal systems help protect the body from infection.

LEARNING OUTCOME 3

Collect subjective and objective assessment data related to the hematologic and lymphatic systems.

Concepts for Lecture

1. The nurse collects subjective and objective data related to the hematologic and lymphatic systems in the health history.
2. Physical assessment of the hematologic and lymphatic systems begins with an inspection of the color of the skin and mucous membranes.

 **POWERPOINT SLIDES 21–32**

Tables and/or Figures
- **Figure 19-1** The Formation of Different Types of Blood Cells From the Stem Cell
- **Figure 19-2** Top and Side Views of a Red Blood Cell
- **Figure 19-3** Fibrin Traps Red Blood Cells and Platelets to Form a Stable Clot
- **Figure 19-4** Pathways to Form a Stable Blood Clot
- **Table 19-1** Common Laboratory Tests for Hematologic and Lymphatic Disorders

 SUGGESTIONS FOR CLASSROOM ACTIVITIES

- Divide the students into two groups. Group 1 will focus on the RBCs. Group 2 will focus on the WBCs. Each group is to create a presentation that describes the creation, purpose, and life span of their respective cell type. Have the groups present the information to the entire class.

 SUGGESTIONS FOR CLINICAL ACTIVITIES

- On the clinical unit, collect laboratory data about a client's RBC and WBC status. Correlate the findings with the client's primary medical diagnosis.

 **POWERPOINT SLIDES 33–34**

Tables and/or Figures
- **Figure 19-5** The Lymphatic System

SUGGESTIONS FOR CLASSROOM ACTIVITIES

- Have students trace a drop of lymph fluid through the lymphatic tissue and structures. See the following Website: http://www.nlm .nih.gov/medlineplus/ency/article/002247 .htm.

 SUGGESTIONS FOR CLINICAL ACTIVITIES

- Have students assess an assigned client's lymphatic system.

3. The mucous membranes and the skin are also inspected for erythema, red streaks, or lesions such as petechiae, bruising, or purpura.
4. The nurse doing a physical assessment of the hematologic and lymphatic systems also palpates the skin for temperature, capillary refill, and edema of the extremities; the lymph nodes for swelling and tenderness; and the upper left quadrant of the abdomen for tenderness.

LEARNING OUTCOME 4

Provide appropriate nursing care for clients undergoing diagnostic tests to evaluate the hematologic and lymphatic systems.

Concepts for Lecture

1. Nursing care of the client undergoing diagnostic testing for a possible hematologic disorder is both educational (explain the purpose of tests and any special preparation or expected sensations during the test) and supportive.
2. There are a number of laboratory and diagnostic tests that can be done to identify disorders of the blood or lymph systems, and the nursing implications vary by test.
3. In many hematologic disorders, a bone marrow aspiration is done to analyze bone marrow to establish diagnosis. In addition to the usual preoperative care, the nurse will place the client in supine position if the sternum or anterior iliac crest will be used and in prone position if the posterior iliac crest will be used.
4. Postoperative nursing care of a client after bone marrow aspiration includes applying pressure to the puncture site for 5 to 10 minutes, applying a dressing to the site, and monitoring for bleeding and infection.
5. Teaching of the client and family focuses on an explanation of the procedure and instructions to take deep breaths to relieve pain and to stay still during the procedure, to expect soreness of the site for 3 to 4 days after aspiration, and to report excess drainage or bleeding.
6. For clients undergoing biopsy for suspected hematologic or lymphatic system malignancy, the nursing care is similar to that of client undergoing bone marrow aspiration, although the risk of bleeding and discomfort is generally less.
7. For clients undergoing a lymphangiogram, nursing care includes determining any allergies to iodine or seafood prior to the test and notifying physician if the client has any of these allergies.

GENERAL CHAPTER CONSIDERATIONS

1. Have students study and learn key terms listed at the beginning of the chapter.
2. Have students complete end of chapter exercises either in their book or on the MyNursingKit Website.
3. Use the Classroom Response Question PowerPoints to assess students prior to lecture.

 **POWERPOINT SLIDES 35–38**

Tables and/or Figures
- **Box 19-1** Documentation of Hematologic Assessment
- **Table 5-2** Characteristics Assessed by Palpation
- **Figure 5-5** Lymph Nodes of Head and Neck

SUGGESTIONS FOR CLASSROOM ACTIVITIES
- Ask students to create a guide sheet for the assessment of a client's hematologic and lymphatic systems.

SUGGESTIONS FOR CLINICAL ACTIVITIES
- Have students use the guide sheet prepared in class to assess a client's hematologic and lymphatic systems.

 **POWERPOINT SLIDES 39–46**

Tables and/or Figures
- **Table 19-1** Common Laboratory Tests for Hematologic and Lymphatic Disorders
- **Box 19-2** Nursing Care Checklist: Bone Marrow Aspiration

SUGGESTIONS FOR CLASSROOM ACTIVITIES
- Review the trays used for a bone marrow aspiration and/or lymph node biopsy, the care of the client, and the duties of a nurse assisting with these procedures.
- Have the students work in pairs or individually to develop a teaching plan for a client scheduled for a bone marrow biopsy.

SUGGESTIONS FOR CLINICAL ACTIVITIES
- Assign students whenever possible to accompany a client undergoing a bone marrow biopsy or lymph node tissue biopsy and to provide care and assist with the procedure if feasible.

 REFERENCE
- Mayo Clinic: Bone marrow biopsy and aspiration. Available at http://www.mayoclinic.com/health/bone-marrow-biopsy/MY00305

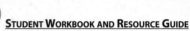

MYNURSINGKIT
(www.mynursingkit.com)

- Websites
- NCLEX® Questions
- Case Studies
- Key Terms

STUDENT WORKBOOK AND RESOURCE GUIDE

- Chapter 19 activities
- *Separate purchase*

PRENTICE HALL NURSE'S DRUG GUIDE

- *Separate purchase*

CLASSROOM RESPONSE QUESTION POWERPOINTS

TESTBANK

CHAPTER 20
CARING FOR CLIENTS WITH HEMATOLOGIC AND LYMPHATIC DISORDERS

LEARNING OUTCOME 1

Describe the pathophysiology and manifestations of common hematologic and lymphatic disorders.

Concepts for Lecture

1. Anemia, whether due to decreased RBCs or hemoglobin concentration, reduces the oxygen-carrying capacity of the blood, leading to tissue hypoxia.
2. Tissue hypoxia may cause angina, fatigue, dyspnea on exertion, and night cramps. Manifestations may include bone pain due to increased release of erythropoietin from the kidneys stimulating bone marrow, and headache, dizziness, and dim vision due to insufficient oxygen to the brain.
3. The severity of the manifestations of anemia depends on the cause and severity of the disorder; (e.g., rapid blood loss causes immediate symptoms, whereas slowly developing anemia may be asymptomatic until the condition is advanced).
4. Sickle cell anemia and thalassemia are inherited disorders. Sickled cells obstruct blood vessels causing tissue ischemia, and every organ of the body can be damaged. In thalassemia, the red blood cells are small and fragile, and stress on the bone marrow to produce RBCs can lead to thinning of bones and fractures.
5. Myelodysplastic syndrome (MDS) is a group of stem cell disorders characterized by abnormal-appearing bone marrow and ineffective blood cell production with risk factors involving exposure to environmental toxins. The client may be asymptomatic or complain of weakness, fatigue, dyspnea, and pallor, and some clients may have an enlarged spleen and/or skin lesions.
6. Polycythemia (erythrocytosis) is an abnormally high red blood cell count and high hematocrit, with secondary polycythemia being the most common form of the disorder developing as a result of chronic hypoxemia or excess production of erythropoietin. Primary polycythemia (*polycythemia vera*) involves increased production of all blood cells, and its cause is unknown.
7. Leukemia starts with the malignant transformation of a single stem cell; then, leukemic cells proliferate but do not become functional WBCs and cannot combat infection or maintain immune function, and they crowd out other cells, resulting in severe anemia and bleeding.
8. Malignant lymphomas are classified as Hodgkin lymphoma (Hodgkin disease) or non-Hodgkin lymphoma. Hodgkin disease involves painless enlargement of one or more lymph nodes and presence of Reed-Sternberg cells in the affected node, whereas non-Hodgkin lymphoma involves multiple lymph nodes and lymphoid tissue. Symptoms common to both types of lymphoma include night sweats, fatigue, and weight loss.
9. Multiple myeloma arises from one abnormal B-cell clone. As myeloma cells proliferate, they replace bone marrow and infiltrate the bone. The most common manifestations are bone and back pain, which become more severe as the disease progresses with pathologic fractures occurring.

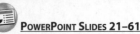

POWERPOINT SLIDES 21–61

Tables and/or Figures

- **Table 20-1** Selected Types and Causes of Anemia
- **Table 20-3** Major Classifications of Leukemia
- **Table 20-5** Comparison of Types of Hemophilia
- **Figure 20-1** Pallor of the Eyelid in a Client With Anemia
- **Figure 20-2** The Multisystem Effects of Anemia
- **Figure 20-3** Blood Smear Showing Normal RBCs and Sickle Cells
- **Figure 20-4** Pathophysiology Illustrated: Sickle Cell Anemia
- **Figure 20-5** The Multisystem Effects of Leukemia
- **Figure 20-7** Ecchymosis of Eyelid Associated With Minor Trauma in Client With Thrombocytopenia
- **Figure 20-8** Inheritance Pattern for Hemophilia A and B
- **Figure 20-9** Severe Lymphedema of the Lower Extremity
- **Box 20-1** Population Focus: Sickle Cell Disorders
- **Box 20-5** Manifestations of Malignant Lymphoma
- **Box 20-6** Risk Factors for DIC
- **Box 20-7** Manifestations of DIC

SUGGESTIONS FOR CLASSROOM ACTIVITIES

- Have students research one hematologic or lymphatic system disorder. Include in this research any recent studies or activities to aid in the diagnosis and treatment.
- Assign students to go to a library with holdings that include healthcare and nursing journals. Ask students to find a current journal article on a hematologic or lymphatic system disorder to bring to and share with the class. Ask the student to provide a copy for a notebook of current articles that students can read as desired.

SUGGESTIONS FOR CLINICAL ACTIVITIES

- Assign the students to a client with a hematologic or lymphatic disorder. Have the students list/identify the client's signs/symptoms that caused the client to seek medical attention/treatment.

REFERENCES

- Mayo Clinic: Anemia. Available at http://www.mayoclinic.com/health/anemia/DS00321
- MedlinePlus: Anemia. Available at http://www.nlm.nih.gov/medlineplus/ency/article/000560.htm

10. Neutropenia is a decrease in the number of circulating neutrophils that usually develops secondary to infection, hematologic disorders, a chronic disease, or chemotherapy. Symptoms include fatigue, weakness, sore throat, stomatitis, dysphagia, fever, and chills.

11. Disorders that interfere with effective clotting and lead to excessive bleeding are thrombocytopenia (lack of platelets), hemophilia (lack of one or more clotting factors interfering with clotting), and disseminated intravascular coagulation (abnormal clotting that depletes both platelets and clotting factors).

12. Disseminated intravascular coagulation results from activation of intrinsic and/or extrinsic clotting cascades in response to endothelial damage (i.e., it is a complication of other disorders). Both intravascular clotting and hemorrhaging occur. Bleeding is the most obvious manifestation; in addition, symptoms of tissue ischemia are present.

13. Lymphangitis is inflammation of the lymph vessels usually caused by a bacterial infection. Clients develop painful red streaks following the lymph vessels and extending up an arm or leg. Inflammation of lymph nodes is called *lymphadenitis*; the nodes may be swollen and tender, and the client may have fever, malaise, and chills.

14. Lymphedema is edema caused by obstruction of lymph vessels. Clients in the tropics may develop elephantiasis, which is a type of lymphedema caused by filaria, a nematode worm. Primary lymphedema may be congenital in origin, but the cause is unknown.

15. Infectious mononucleosis is an acute infectious disease caused by the Epstein-Barr virus that results in increased lymphocyte production and swelling of lymph glands with early manifestations of headache, malaise, and fatigue, followed by fever, sore throat, and enlargement and pain in the cervical lymph nodes.

LEARNING OUTCOME 2

Discuss interdisciplinary care of clients with hematologic or lymphatic disorders, including diagnostic tests and commonly prescribed medications.

Concepts for Lecture

1. A variety of diagnostic tests may be ordered when anemia is suspected, and each one tests for specific types of anemia.
2. A variety of medications are used to treat anemia depending on the type of anemia, and each drug has its own nursing implications and client teaching points.
3. The Z-track technique is used to administer iron by intramuscular (IM) injection; the skin is pulled laterally approximately 1 inch and held taut, the medication is administered, the needle is withdrawn, and the skin is released.
4. Interdisciplinary care and treatment of polycythemia focuses on reducing blood viscosity and volume and relieving symptoms, and this often involves phlebotomy, which is the removal of 300–500 mL of blood to keep blood volume and viscosity within normal limits. Chemotherapy may be used to suppress bone marrow in clients with polycythemia vera.
5. Diagnostic tests for leukemia include CBC with differential and platelet count and bone marrow examination.
6. Medications for clients with leukemia include chemotherapy drugs, colony-stimulating factors, and biologic agents such as interferon, interleukins, and monoclonal antibodies.
7. Diagnostic tests for lymphoma include chest x-ray and chest and abdominal computed tomography (CT) scans to identify enlarged

Tables and/or Figures
- **Table 20-2** Giving Medications Safely: Anemia
- **Table 20-4** Giving Medications Safely: Colony-Stimulating Factors
- **Figure 20-6** Areas of Radiation for Total Nodal Radiation Therapy
- **Box 20-2** Procedure Checklist: Z-Track Technique

SUGGESTIONS FOR CLASSROOM ACTIVITIES

- A variety of medications are available to treat hematologic and lymphatic disorders. Have the students research the most current medications available, including the route of administration and side effects.

SUGGESTIONS FOR CLINICAL ACTIVITIES

- Assign the students to a client with a hematologic or lymphatic disorder. Have the students either administer or observe the administration of the client's medications.
- Assign students to a client with a hematologic or lymphatic disorder. Ask the students to review the chart and interview the client to determine what diagnostic tests the client had and report on these tests at postconference.

REFERENCE

- University of Maryland Medical Center. Blood diseases. Available at http://www.umm.edu/blood/index.htm

POWERPOINT SLIDES 62–70

Tables and/or Figures
- **Box 20-3** Dietary Sources of Iron
- **Table 20-4** Giving Medications Safely: Colony-Stimulating Factors
- **Figure 20-6** Areas of Radiation for Total Nodal Radiation Therapy

SUGGESTIONS FOR CLASSROOM ACTIVITIES

- Have each student develop a teaching plan for a client with anemia including sources of iron.

SUGGESTIONS FOR CLINICAL ACTIVITIES

- Assign the students to observe activities in the organization's blood bank. Ideally, the students should begin with blood donation, processing, and preparation for infusion into a client.
- Assign students to clients with anemia, and have students use the teaching plan they developed in the classroom to inform the client about sources of iron.

lymph nodes. Positron emission tomography (PET) scans may be performed to diagnose malignant lymphomas or monitor disease progress.

8. Diagnostic tests for multiple myeloma include urine tests for Bence Jones protein, CBC for anemia, bone marrow studies for excessive immature plasma cells, and bone x-rays, which show punched out holes in the bone. Medications are for symptom relief because there is no cure.

9. The diagnostic test for neutropenia is the WBC count. Filgrastim (Neupogen) is a drug that may be given to stimulate the growth and development of WBCs in bone marrow.

10. Diagnostic tests for thrombocytopenia include CBC with platelet count, a bone marrow examination to evaluate platelet production, and ANA test to assess for autoimmunity. Serologic testing is done if heparin-induced thrombocytopenia is suspected. Corticosteroids and immunosuppressive drugs (e.g., cyclosporine) may be used.

11. Diagnostic tests for types of hemophilia include platelet count, coagulation studies, and clotting factor assays to identify specific clotting factor deficiencies. Treatment of hemophilia focuses on preventing and/or treating bleeding, primarily by replacing deficient clotting factors.

12. Diagnostic tests for DIC include CBC and platelet counts, the D-Dimer test, and evaluation of fibrin degradation products to confirm presence of fibrinolysis. Heparin may be given to interfere with the clotting cascade and prevent depletion of clotting factors due to uncontrolled clotting.

LEARNING OUTCOME 3

Relate the nursing implications for selected treatment measures for clients with hematologic or lymphatic disorders.

Concepts for Lecture

1. Dietary modifications may be ordered for nutritional deficiency anemias, such as iron deficiency anemia or folic acid deficiency anemia, and the nurse will do teaching on these modifications.

2. When anemia is due to a major acute blood loss, whole blood transfusions may be given to replace red blood cells. If the blood loss is chronic, packed red cells may be given.

3. Treatment of polycythemia focuses on reducing blood viscosity and volume and relieving symptoms. Phlebotomy and chemotherapy may be treatment measures.

4. The treatment of leukemia focuses on achieving remission/cure and relieving symptoms. Chemotherapy may be used to destroy leukemic cells and produce remission. Radiation therapy may be used to shrink lymph nodes.

5. Biologic therapy agents such as interferons, interleukins, and colony-stimulating factors, each with nursing implications, may be used to treat some leukemias.

6. There are two types of bone marrow transplants (BMT) that may be used to treat leukemia: allogenic BMT, which uses bone marrow of a healthy donor, and autologous BMT, which uses using the client's own bone marrow. In allogenic BMT, the nurse is concerned about the significant risk for infection and bleeding. In autologous BMT, the nurse is concerned about immunosuppression, malnutrition, infection, and bleeding.

7. Stem cell transplant is another treatment measure for clients with leukemias.

8. Treatment for the client with thrombocytopenia may include platelet transfusions, plasmapheresis, surgery, and/or splenectomy.

Tables and/or Figures
- **Box 20-3** Dietary Sources of Iron, Folic Acid, and Vitamin B$_{12}$
- **Box 20-4** Assessment: Clients With Leukemia

Nursing Care Plan: Client With Hodgkin Lymphoma

SUGGESTIONS FOR CLASSROOM ACTIVITIES

- Have the students prepare a plan of care for a client with a hematologic or lymphatic disorder. Ask students to address common problems such as nausea and pain. See http://www.umm.edu/blood/blooddis.htm.
- Invite a person with leukemia or Hodgkin lymphoma to speak to the class and talk about signs and symptoms that he or she experienced and his or her suggestions for data collection and working with clients with these disorders.
- Do modified grand rounds during postconference with a client who has a hematologic or lymphatic disorder. Gain the client's permission to do this; explain to the client what you want him or her to talk to the students about, and ask if the client is willing to answer the students' questions.

SUGGESTIONS FOR CLINICAL ACTIVITIES

- Assign the students to a client with a hematologic or lymphatic disorder. Implement the plan of care for nausea and pain.

POWERPOINT SLIDES 71–79

9. The treatment of lymphangitis includes relieving edema, maintaining skin integrity, and preventing/treating infection.
10. The treatment of lymphedema involves elevating the extremity, elastic stockings, skin care, bed rest, and sodium restriction.

LEARNING OUTCOME 4

Provide individualized nursing care for clients with hematologic or lymphatic disorders.

Concepts for Lecture

1. When anemia results from acute hemorrhage, restoring blood volume is the highest priority, but when anemia develops gradually, its effects on the client's ability to maintain normal and desired activities are a higher priority.
2. Teaching good eating habits to people of all ages is the primary nursing intervention to prevent anemia.
3. Nursing care of the client with leukemia focuses on the physical and psychosocial effects of the disease and its treatment.
4. Nursing care of the client with malignant lymphoma involves providing physical and emotional support throughout the course of treatment with consideration of the risk for infection and attention to nutritional status.
5. Nursing care of the client with multiple myeloma is similar to care of clients with leukemia, with pain and the risk for pathologic fractures being additional nursing care considerations.
6. Nursing care of the client with thrombocytopenia focuses on the risk for injury resulting from bleeding.
7. The priority for nursing care for the client with hemophilia is protection from injury and minimizing the risk for bleeding.
8. Because the client with DIC is critically ill, the priorities of nursing care include maintaining vital functions and tissue perfusion. The nurse also focuses on managing pain associated with widespread clotting and tissue ischemia, as well as measures to help relieve the client's and family's anxiety related to this critical illness.

GENERAL CHAPTER CONSIDERATIONS

1. Have students study and learn key terms listed at the beginning of the chapter.
2. Have students complete end of chapter exercises either in their book or on the MyNursingKit Website.
3. Use the Classroom Response Question PowerPoints to assess students prior to lecture.

 **POWERPOINT SLIDES 80–120**

- Clinical Reasoning Care Map

 MYNURSINGKIT
(www.mynursingkit.com)
- Websites
- NCLEX® Questions
- Case Studies
- Key Terms

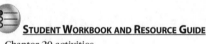 **STUDENT WORKBOOK AND RESOURCE GUIDE**
- Chapter 20 activities
- *Separate purchase*

PRENTICE HALL NURSE'S DRUG GUIDE
- *Separate purchase*

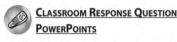 **CLASSROOM RESPONSE QUESTION POWERPOINTS**

 TESTBANK

LEARNING OUTCOME 1

Describe the structure and functions of the respiratory tract.

Concepts for Lecture

1. Structures of the upper respiratory tract include the nose and sinuses, pharynx, and larynx. The main function is to clean, humidify, and warm air. The upper respiratory tract is necessary for effective breathing.
2. Structures of the lower respiratory tract include the lungs, bronchi, alveoli, pulmonary arteries, and pulmonary veins.

LEARNING OUTCOME 2

Explain the mechanics of respiration.

Concepts for Lecture

1. Ventilation is the movement of air into and out of the lungs and has two phases: inspiration and expiration. These two phases make up a breath, which normally occurs 12–20 times per minute.
2. The phases of respiration are inspiration, during which air flows into the lungs, and expiration, during which gases flow out of the lungs.
3. Factors that affect respirations include the respiratory center in the brain, chemoreceptors in the brain, aortic arch, and carotid arteries. Receptors respond to changes in the amount of oxygen, carbon dioxide, and hydrogen ions in arterial blood. Other factors that affect ventilation and the work of breathing are airway resistance, compliance, elasticity, and surface tension on the walls of alveoli.
4. Aging commonly leads to structural and functional changes of the respiratory system.

LEARNING OUTCOME 3

Conduct a focused assessment of the upper and lower respiratory systems, identifying expected findings.

Concepts for Lecture

1. Assessment should include both subjective and objective information.
2. Assessment of respiratory function is important in all clients and vital in people with respiratory disorders.

LEARNING OUTCOME 4

Provide appropriate nursing care and teaching for clients undergoing diagnostic tests and procedures related to the respiratory system.

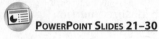

POWERPOINT SLIDES 21–30

Tables and/or Figures

- **Figure 21-1** Structures of the Upper Respiratory System and the Sinuses
- **Figure 21-2** The Lower Respiratory System, Showing the Lungs, Mediastinum, and Layers of the Visceral and Parietal Pleura
- **Figure 21-3** The Functional Tissue of the Lungs, Including the Respiratory Bronchioles and Alveoli
- **Figure 21-5** Changes in the Respiratory System Associated With Aging

POWERPOINT SLIDES 31–36

SUGGESTIONS FOR CLASSROOM ACTIVITIES

- Have the students identify the anatomy and physiology of the structures in the respiratory system.
- Have the students identify the position of the diaphragm and the difference in volumes and intrathoracic pressures during inspiration and expiration.

SUGGESTIONS FOR CLINICAL ACTIVITIES

- Assign students to complete a respiratory assessment on any of their clinical clients. Assessment findings should be submitted in writing.

POWERPOINT SLIDES 37–42

Tables and/or Figures

- **Figure 21-4** Inspiration and Expiration

POWERPOINT SLIDES 43–52

Concepts for Lecture

1. Diagnostic tests and procedures related to the respiratory tract include pulse oximetry, arterial blood gases, serum alpha$_1$-antitrypsin, sputum and tissue specimens, imaging studies, pulmonary function tests, and direct visualization (laryngoscopy and bronchoscopy).
2. Although specific responsibilities vary, depending on the procedure being performed, nursing care of the client undergoing diagnostic testing is both supportive and educational.
3. In some cases, such as a throat swab or sputum culture, the nurse is responsible for obtaining the specimen to be examined.

General Chapter Considerations

1. Have students study and learn key terms listed at the beginning of the chapter.
2. Have students complete end of chapter exercises either in their book or on the MyNursingKit Website.
3. Use the Classroom Response Question PowerPoints to assess students prior to lecture.

SUGGESTIONS FOR CLASSROOM ACTIVITIES

- Have the students measure their own oxygen saturation with a pulse oximeter. Have the students identify saturation variations with the probe at different body locations and when they hold their breath.
- In a laboratory setting, have students perform respiratory assessments and practice client interviews with one another. The students acting as clients should be told to give some answers that would indicate a possible respiratory system disorder. Findings and difficulties encountered while performing the assessments may be discussed by the class.

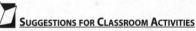

SUGGESTIONS FOR CLINICAL ACTIVITIES

- Assign students to perform a respiratory assessment on a client who smokes and one who does not smoke. The students should then compare and contrast their findings.

Tables and/or Figures

- **Figure 21-5** Changes in the Respiratory System Associated With Aging
- **Figure 21-6** Palpating for Equality of Chest Expansion
- **Figure 21-7** Sequence for Lung Auscultation on the Back
- **Figure 21-8** Placement of the Pulse Oximetry Sensor on a Finger to Measure Oxygen Saturation
- **Box 21-2** Procedure Checklist: Obtaining a Throat Swab
- **Box 21-3** Procedure Checklist: Obtaining a Sputum Specimen

SUGGESTIONS FOR CLASSROOM ACTIVITIES

- Assign students to review audiotapes of normal and abnormal breath sounds to become familiar with them.

SUGGESTIONS FOR CLINICAL ACTIVITIES

- Have students assess breath sounds in clients with no bronchial or lung pathology (normal sounds) and then assess breath sounds in clients with known bronchial and lung pathology.

Tables and/or Figures

- **Table 21-1** Common Laboratory Tests and Studies
- **Figure 21-9** The Relationship of Lung Volumes and Capacities
- **Figure 21-10** Fiberoptic Bronchoscopy
- **Box 21-4** Nursing Care Checklist: Bronchoscopy

SUGGESTIONS FOR CLASSROOM ACTIVITIES

- Review and practice sputum collection methods.

SUGGESTIONS FOR CLINICAL ACTIVITIES

- Assign students to perform a respiratory assessment on a young adult and an older adult. The clients chosen should have no history of respiratory abnormalities. Instruct the students to identify nonpathologic variations in the assessment.
- Assign students to perform a respiratory assessment on a client with a respiratory disorder. Have the students identify the abnormalities.

MYNURSINGKIT
(www.mynursingkit.com)

- Websites
- NCLEX® Questions
- Case Studies
- Key Terms

STUDENT WORKBOOK AND RESOURCE GUIDE

- Chapter 21 activities
- *Separate purchase*

PRENTICE HALL NURSE'S DRUG GUIDE

- *Separate purchase*

CLASSROOM RESPONSE QUESTION POWERPOINTS

TESTBANK

CHAPTER 22
CARING FOR CLIENTS WITH UPPER RESPIRATORY DISORDERS

LEARNING OUTCOME 1

Describe common disorders affecting the upper respiratory tract and their manifestations.

Concepts for Lecture

1. Upper respiratory infections may affect the nose, sinuses, pharynx, tonsils, and larynx.
2. Most upper respiratory infections (URIs) are minor illnesses; however, life-threatening complications can result, especially in the frail older adult.
3. Most URIs are caused by viruses or allergens that enter the airway, causing acute inflammation of the sinuses, pharynx, or larynx. Mucosa swells and secretes clear, yellow, or greenish exudates.
4. Bacterial infections may develop following a viral infection.
5. Rhinitis, inflammation of the nasal cavities, is the most common upper respiratory disorder. Acute viral rhinitis (the common cold) is highly contagious. More than 200 strains of viruses can cause the common cold.
6. Local manifestations of acute viral rhinitis include red, swollen, congested nasal mucosa; clear watery secretions with coryza (runny nose); and sneezing and coughing.
7. Systemic manifestations of acute viral rhinitis include low-grade fever, headache, malaise, and muscle ache.
8. Acute viral rhinitis lasts a few days to 2 weeks.
9. The local manifestations of allergic rhinitis are pale, swollen, and congested nasal mucosa; thin, watery nasal discharge; itchy, watery eyes; and sneezing. The systemic manifestation of allergic rhinitis is headache. Chronic congestion may cause snoring and postnasal drip. Allergic rhinitis occurs with exposure to allergens.
10. Respiratory syncytial virus (RSV) causes most respiratory illnesses in infants and young children. In adults, it usually presents as a common cold, but immunocompromised individuals and older adults may develop severe lower respiratory disease.
11. Influenza viruses are transmitted by airborne droplets and direct contact. The incubation period is short, and the manifestations develop rapidly.
12. The local manifestations of influenza are coryza; sore throat; dry, nonproductive cough that may become productive; and substernal burning.
13. The systemic manifestations of influenza include chills and fever; headache; malaise; muscle aches; and fatigue and weakness. The onset of influenza is abrupt.
14. Sinusitis is an inflammation of the mucous membranes of the sinuses, which may be caused by a viral or bacterial infection and often follows a URI.
15. Manifestations of sinusitis include tenderness across the affected sinuses, as well as headache, fever, and malaise. The pain usually increases with leaning forward. Pain may also be referred to the upper teeth. The nasal mucous membrane is red and swollen. The client may complain of nasal congestion, purulent nasal discharge, bad breath, fever, malaise, and fatigue.

POWERPOINT SLIDES 21–43

Tables and/or Figures

- **Table 22-1** Manifestations and Course of Rhinitis and Influenza
- **Box 22-1** Focus on Older Adults: Influenza in Older Adults
- **Figure 22-1** Tonsillitis
- **Box 22-2** Manifestations of Acute Pharyngitis
- **Figure 22-2** Epistaxis
- **Box 22-5** Manifestations of Nasal Fracture
- **Figure 22-5** Obstructive Sleep Apnea
- **Box 22-6** Population Focus: Laryngeal Cancer
- **Figure 22-6** Benign Tumor on Left Vocal Cord
- **Box 22-7** Manifestations of Laryngeal Cancer

SUGGESTIONS FOR CLASSROOM ACTIVITIES

- Have students discuss ways to prevent URIs and complications of URIs.
- Review Table 22-1 comparing rhinitis and influenza. Ask students to discuss the differences in methods of transmission, clinical manifestations, and nursing interventions for each disorder.
- Have students review signs of respiratory distress.

SUGGESTIONS FOR CLINICAL ACTIVITIES

- Assign students to care for older adult clients with upper respiratory infections. Have students identify possible life-threatening complications for the older adult.
- Have students monitor assigned clients with upper respiratory disorders for signs of respiratory distress.

REFERENCE

- MedlinePlus: Common cold. Available at http://www.nlm.nih.gov/medlineplus/ency/article/000678.htm

16. The symptoms of sinusitis often worsen after awakening and then become less severe in the afternoon or evening as secretions drain.

17. Pharyngitis or acute inflammation of the throat is common. It is usually viral but may be bacterial. Group A beta-hemolytic *Streptococcus* (strep throat) is the most common bacterial cause. Streptococcal infection also may cause tonsillitis. Pharyngitis and tonsillitis are contagious and are spread by droplet nuclei.

18. Pharyngitis causes pain and fever. Throat discomfort may vary from scratchiness to pain and dysphagia (difficulty swallowing). See Box 22-2 for manifestations of acute pharyngitis.

19. In tonsillitis, the tonsils are bright red and swollen with white exudate.

20. Acute epiglottitis (inflammation of the epiglottis) is uncommon. It is a medical emergency. Clients with epiglottis have difficulty swallowing food and have manifestations of pharyngitis. The epiglottis appears red, swollen, and edematous.

21. In laryngitis (inflammation of the larynx), the mucous membrane lining the larynx becomes inflamed, and the vocal cords may be swollen.

22. The primary manifestation of laryngitis is a change in the voice. Hoarseness or aphonia (complete loss of the voice) may occur. Clients complain of a sore, scratchy throat and may have a dry, harsh cough.

23. Pertussis, or whooping cough, is an acute, highly contagious upper respiratory infection. It is caused by infection with *Bordetella pertussis*, a gram-negative rod that is spread by respiratory droplets.

24. Pertussis starts with symptoms of upper respiratory infection beginning 7 to 10 days after exposure. Within 1 to 2 weeks, the cough increases with frequent paroxysms (bursts) of coughing that may end with an audible whoop of rapid inspiration. Coughing episodes may precipitate vomiting and can interfere with eating and sleeping.

25. Epistaxis, or nosebleed, may begin in many ways, including trauma (picking the nose or getting hit), drying of nasal mucous membranes, local or systemic infection, substance abuse, arteriosclerosis, hypertension, bleeding disorders, severe liver disease, or treatment with an anticoagulant or antiplatelet medication.

26. Nasal polyps are benign grapelike growths of the mucous membrane lining the nose. These benign tumors are usually bilateral and can interfere with air movement through nasal passages or obstruct sinus openings, leading to sinusitis. They usually affect people who have chronic allergic rhinitis or asthma. Polyps that develop during an acute upper respiratory infection may regress spontaneously when the infection resolves.

27. Polyps may be asymptomatic, although large polyps may cause nasal obstruction, rhinorrhea, and loss of sense of smell. Manifestations of sinusitis may develop. The voice may have a nasal tone.

28. A nasal fracture usually results from a sports injury or from trauma related to violence or motor vehicle crash. One or both sides of the nose may be broken.

29. See Box 22-5, Manifestations of Nasal Fracture. Manifestations of nasal fracture include epistaxis, deformity, crepitus, soft tissue trauma (local swelling, periorbital edema, bruising, and black eyes), and instability of the nasal bridge.

30. Laryngeal obstruction is a life-threatening emergency. The larynx can be partially or fully obstructed by aspirated food or foreign objects. Laryngospasm or laryngeal edema due to inflammation, injury, or anaphylaxis also can obstruct the larynx. Laryngospasm can be caused by repeated or traumatic attempts at intubation, chemical irritation of the airway, or hypocalcemia. An acute type I allergic response may cause anaphylaxis and severe laryngeal edema.

31. Manifestations of laryngeal obstruction include coughing, choking, gagging, obvious difficulty breathing with use of accessory muscles,

and inspiratory stridor. As the airway is obstructed, signs of asphyxia are seen. Respirations are labored and noisy with wheezing and stridor. The client may become cyanotic. Respiratory arrest and death may result without prompt intervention.

32. Obstructive sleep apnea, the temporary absence of breathing during sleep, is common. Risk factors for sleep apnea include obesity, a large neck, a large tongue, enlarged tonsils, and the use of alcohol or sedative before sleep.

33. During an apneic event, the person's oxygen saturation falls. Progressive asphyxia causes brief arousal from sleep, restoring airway patency and breathing. Sleep apnea leads to fragmented sleep and disruption of normal sleep events.

34. Common manifestations of sleep apnea include loud snoring, frequent nighttime waking, daytime sleepiness, headache, and irritability. Other problems may follow such as hypertension, morning headache, irritability, and impotence. Clients may show personality changes, impaired memory, and inability to concentrate.

35. Benign tumors of the larynx include papillomas, nodules, and polyps. Papillomas are thought to be viral in origin. Polyps and nodules result from voice overuse. Manifestations of vocal cord nodules include hoarseness and a breathy voice.

36. Laryngeal cancer may occur in any of the three areas of the larynx: the glottis, the supraglottis, and the subglottis.

37. The primary manifestation of cancer of the glottis is a change in the voice; the tumor prevents complete closure of the vocal cords during speech.

38. The tumor may be large before manifestations such as painful swallowing, a sore throat, or a feeling of a lump in the throat develop. As the tumor grows, the client may experience difficulty breathing, foul breath, a palpable lump in the neck, and pain that radiates to the ear.

39. Subglottic tumors (below the vocal cords) are the least common laryngeal cancers and often have no early symptoms. As the tumor enlarges, manifestations of airway obstruction develop. See Box 22-7 for common manifestations of laryngeal cancer.

LEARNING OUTCOME 2

Discuss the nursing implications for medications and treatments ordered for clients with upper respiratory disorders.

Concepts for Lecture

1. Most acute URIs are self-limiting. Medical management focuses on accurate diagnosis, providing symptomatic relief, and preventing complications.
2. Education is the primary nursing role in caring for most clients with acute or chronic URIs.
3. Clients need to be able to recognize the difference between acute, self-limiting disorders and those that require medical attention.
4. Yearly immunization influenza vaccine is the most important measure to reduce the risk of influenza.
5. Because influenza vaccine is produced in eggs, it should not be given to people with an allergy to eggs. The intranasal influenza vaccine, which contains live attenuated influenza virus, is not recommended for anyone who is immunosuppressed, has a chronic disease, or is pregnant.
6. Several drugs are available to prevent or shorten the duration of influenza in unvaccinated people who are exposed to the virus. Amantadine (Symmetrel) and rimantadine (Flumadine) also may be

 **POWERPOINT SLIDES 44–55**

Tables and/or Figures
- **Table 22-2** Giving Medications Safely: Upper Respiratory Infections
- **Box 22-4** Nursing Care Checklist: Administering Nose Drops
- **Box 23-6** Client Teaching: Breathing and Coughing Techniques
- **Figure 22-3** Posterior Nasal Packing
- **Figure 22-8** Permanent Tracheostomy; After a Total Laryngectomy, the Client Has No Connection Between Trachea and Esophagus
- **Figure 22-9** Tracheoesophageal Prosthesis

SUGGESTIONS FOR CLASSROOM ACTIVITIES
- Initiate a discussion on the use of pharmacologic/nonpharmacologic comfort measures in the treatment of upper respiratory disorders.
- Ask a Pharm-D student, pharmacist, or nurse practitioner to talk with the class about pharmacologic/nonpharmacologic comfort measures used in the treatment of upper respiratory disorders.

used to prevent influenza or decrease symptoms. Zanamivir (Relenza), oseltamivir (Tamiflu), and ribavirin (Virazole) reduce the severity and duration of influenza. These drugs attack the virus itself, reducing the spread in the body.

7. Although controversial, bacterial infections such as strep pharyngitis and tonsillitis often are treated with antibiotics. Treatment is continued for at least 10 days. The client is no longer considered contagious after 24 hours of antibiotic therapy.

8. Antibiotics also may be used to treat sinusitis when symptoms are severe or purulent discharge is noted in the pharynx. Antibiotic therapy is continued for a full 2 weeks; a longer course may be prescribed to prevent relapse. If the client's sinusitis does not improve, the client is referred to an otolaryngologist for further evaluation.

9. A number of drugs, many available without prescription, provide symptomatic relief of viral URIs. Mild decongestants may help relieve the manifestations of coryza and nasal congestion. Oral or topical (nasal spray) decongestants are also prescribed for clients with sinusitis to reduce mucosal edema and promote sinus drainage.

10. Topical nasal steroids may be used, although there is no evidence that they are more effective than placebo in relieving sinusitis symptoms.

11. To administer nose drips, tilt the client's head back and to the side in which the drops are to be instilled. Have the client remain in position for 5 minutes to allow the drops to reach the posterior nares.

12. Decongestant nasal sprays should be used for no more than 3 to 5 days. When used for a longer time, they can cause rebound congestion, which causes the client to use the spray more frequently and in larger doses.

13. Warm salt-water gargles, throat lozenges, or mild analgesics may be used for sore throats. Saline nasal irrigation is beneficial in relieving the manifestations of URI and sinusitis.

14. Over-the-counter analgesics such as aspirin, acetaminophen, or NSAIDs help relieve fever and muscle ache. Antitussives may decrease cough and promote rest. Systemic mucolytic agents such as guaifenesin help liquefy secretions and promote sinus drainage.

15. Complementary therapies and practices used to treat URIs include echinacea and garlic, which have antiviral and antibiotic effects. Taken at the first sign of infection, echinacea may reduce the duration and symptoms of a common cold or influenza.

16. Echinacea should not be used for longer than 2 weeks. It is contraindicated in women who are pregnant or lactating. Echinacea should not be used by people who have an autoimmune disease such as multiple sclerosis or rheumatoid arthritis.

17. Aromatherapy with essential oils such as basil, eucalyptus, frankincense, lavender, marjoram, peppermint, or rosemary can reduce congestion, enhance comfort, and promote recovery from a URI. The nurse needs to caution clients that these essential oils should be used only for inhalation and must not be taken internally.

18. See Table 22-2 for nursing implications for medications given for URIs.

19. When giving decongestants, the nurse assesses for contraindications such as high blood pressure or chronic heart disease because these drugs constrict blood vessels, increasing the blood pressure and heart rate. The nurse is cautioned not to give decongestants if the client is taking antihypertensive medications or a monoamine oxidase inhibitor.

20. Before giving or recommending antihistamines to a client, the nurse needs to ask about possible contraindications such as acute asthma or chronic respiratory disease; glaucoma; impaired gastrointestinal function or obstruction; an enlarged prostate gland or other urinary tract obstruction; and heart disease.

SUGGESTIONS FOR CLINICAL ACTIVITIES

- Assign students to care for clients with upper respiratory disorders. Supervise students in administering medications safely.
- Have students work with clients who need to cough effectively and have them teach the client how to do this.

REFERENCE

- Medscape: Upper respiratory tract infection. Available at http://emedicine.medscape.com/article/302460-treatment

21. Medication for epistaxis or nosebleed includes topical vasoconstrictors such as cocaine (0.5%), phenylephrine (Neo-Synephrine) (1:1,000), or adrenaline (1:1,000), which may be applied by nasal spray or on a cotton swab held against the bleeding site. The bleeding vessel may be cauterized using a chemical such as silver nitrate or Gelform.

22. If the bleeding cannot be controlled with pressure and local medications, quarter-inch petroleum gauze may be used to pack the nasal cavity.

23. Anterior nasal packs generally are left in place for 24 to 72 hours. Posterior nasal packing remains in place longer, up to 5 days, and is very uncomfortable for the client. It can interfere with respiration. Supplemental oxygen is given while posterior packing is in place. Discomfort is managed with narcotic analgesics.

LEARNING OUTCOME 3

Plan and provide appropriate individualized nursing care for clients with upper respiratory disorders.

Concepts for Lecture

1. Education is the primary nursing role in caring for most clients with acute or chronic URIs. Unless the problem is recurrent or a complication occurs, medical treatment is rarely required.

2. Nursing care for clients with significant manifestations or complications of URI focuses on maintaining airway clearance, breathing patterns, and adequate rest.

3. Subjective assessment data include presence of pain including location, character, timing, and aggravating factors as well as presence, timing, and productivity of a cough.

4. Assessment data include presence, amount, color, and odor of sputum and/or nasal drainage. The nurse notes complaints of shortness of breath, difficult or labored breathing, difficulty swallowing or smelling, or an altered sense of taste.

5. The nurse inquires about the client's past medical history, including known allergies, chronic respiratory problems, surgery or trauma of the upper respiratory tract, chronic diseases, the client's smoking history, and any known exposure to environmental pollutants or allergens.

6. The nurse obtains vital signs, including temperature and respiratory rate and depth. The nares and oropharynx are inspected for color, moisture, and the presence of swelling, exudate, or postnasal drainage. The nurse percusses over frontal and maxillary sinuses for tenderness and auscultates lung sounds.

7. The nurse assesses for and identifies potential complications of upper respiratory infections. Although most URIs are viral in origin, secondary bacterial infections may develop. The nurse needs to report manifestations such as a fever higher than 101°F or that continues for 5 or more days, cough productive of malodorous green or rust-colored sputum, shortness of breath, or dyspnea.

8. Localized pain, swelling, and symptoms such as a change in mental status, hearing, or the ability to swallow may indicate extension of an infection such as sinusitis or pharyngitis into adjacent tissues.

9. A possible nursing diagnosis for URIs is Ineffective Breathing Pattern, with a possible expected outcome that the client's respiratory rate and pattern will remain within normal or expected limits.

10. Nursing interventions for a nursing diagnosis of Ineffective Breathing Pattern include monitoring respiratory rate and pattern for changes from baseline; pacing activities to allow rest periods; and elevating the head of the bed to reduce the work of breathing and improve lung expansion.

 POWERPOINT SLIDES 56–68

Tables and/or Figures
- **Box 22-9** Procedure Checklist: Tracheostomy Care

Nursing Care Plan: Client With Upper Respiratory Infection

 **SUGGESTIONS FOR CLASSROOM ACTIVITIES**

- Have students work in pairs to develop a nursing care plan for a client with one of the upper respiratory disorders. The students can create their own client with medical problems and assessment data.

 **SUGGESTIONS FOR CLINICAL ACTIVITIES**

- Assign students to care for clients with upper respiratory disorders and to write an individualized care plan for their assigned clients.

11. Ineffective Airway Clearance is a nursing diagnosis used for upper respiratory infections. A possible expected outcome is that breath sounds will be clear on auscultation and client will develop no signs of respiratory distress.

12. Nursing interventions for Ineffective Airway Clearance include monitoring the effectiveness of the cough and the ability to remove airway secretions; following tonsillectomy, positioning the client with the head to the side for drainage of secretions from the mouth and pharynx; leaving the nasopharyngeal airway in place until the client can swallow and the gag reflex returns; applying an ice collar as ordered; immediately reporting excessive bleeding to the charge nurse and physician; maintaining adequate hydration; assessing mucous membrane moisture and skin turgor; increasing the humidity of inspired air with a bedside humidifier; teaching the client how to cough effectively; and administering analgesic medications as ordered.

13. Another nursing diagnosis for upper respiratory infections is Disturbed Sleep Pattern, with a possible expected outcome that the client will obtain adequate sleep.

14. Nursing interventions for Disturbed Sleep Pattern include assessing sleep using subjective and objective information, placing the client in a semi-Fowler's or Fowler's position to sleep; providing antipyretic and analgesic medications at bedtime or shortly before; and requesting a cough suppressant medication for nighttime use, if necessary.

15. Impaired Verbal Communication is a nursing diagnosis for some clients with upper respiratory infections. An expected outcome might be that the client will communicate needs effectively, minimizing voice use.

16. Nursing interventions for Impaired Verbal Communication include encouraging the client with laryngitis to rest the voice and to use alternate methods of communicating such as writing; instructing the client to use throat lozenges or sprays or to gargle with a warm antiseptic solution; and encouraging the client to quit smoking, if the client smokes.

17. Evaluating nursing care for a client with a URI involves collecting data such as the rate and ease of breathing, ability to manage symptoms, knowledge of appropriate medication use, and presence or absence of complications.

LEARNING OUTCOME 4

Provide care for clients having surgery involving the upper respiratory system.

Concepts for Lecture

1. Upper respiratory trauma or obstruction includes epistaxis, nasal trauma or deviated septum, nasal fractures, and laryngeal obstructions or trauma. Surgeries performed to correct these conditions include rhinoplasty, septoplasty, laryngectomy, and tracheostomy.

2. Severe epistaxis may be treated with nasal packing or surgery.

3. Tumors of the upper respiratory tract are relatively uncommon. However, they can obstruct the airway and interfere with breathing. The larynx is the upper airway structure most affected by tumors.

4. Tonsillectomy is done to treat recurrent or chronic infections, enlarged tonsils that may obstruct the airway, peritonsillar abscess, or malignancy. The most significant postoperative complication of tonsillectomy is hemorrhage. If hemorrhage develops, the client returns to surgery, where the bleeding vessel is ligated (tied off).

5. A peritonsillar abscess may be drained by needle aspiration or by incision and drainage (I&D) under local anesthesia. Tonsillectomy follows the I&D, either immediately or 6 weeks later.

POWERPOINT SLIDES 69–78

Tables and/or Figures

- **Figure 22-2** Epistaxis
- **Figure 22-3** Posterior Nasal Packing
- **Box 22-8** Nursing Care Checklist: Total Laryngectomy
- **Box 22-9** Procedure Checklist: Tracheostomy Care

SUGGESTIONS FOR CLASSROOM ACTIVITIES

- Assign students to find articles on nursing care of clients who are having surgery to correct upper respiratory trauma or obstruction (e.g., rhinoplasty, septoplasty, or laryngectomy).
- Practice tracheostomy care in the nursing lab.

6. Chemical or surgical cautery procedures may be used to seal bleeding vessels and, in the case of posterior epistaxis, as an alternative to nasal packing. The resulting scab must be left undisturbed until the mucosa has healed or further bleeding may occur. Some clients with posterior bleeding require surgery to tie off the bleeding artery. Following surgery, the client is carefully monitored for bleeding or respiratory complications.

7. Teaching about home care following polypectomy is a primary nursing responsibility when caring for the client with nasal polyps. The nurse provides postoperative care instructions and discusses measures to reduce the risk of bleeding.

8. The client post polypectomy is instructed to apply ice or cold compresses to the nose to decrease swelling, promote comfort, and prevent bleeding; avoid blowing the nose for 24 to 48 hours after nasal packing is removed; and avoid straining at stool, coughing vigorously, and engaging in strenuous exercise.

9. The nurse encourages the client post polypectomy to rest for 2 to 3 days after surgery to reduce the risk of bleeding. The client is instructed to increase fluid intake and clean the mouth frequently to reduce oral dryness associated with mouth breathing while nasal packing is in place.

10. Rhinoplasty (surgical reconstruction of the nose) is done to relieve airway obstruction and repair visible deformity of the nose following fracture. Using an intranasal incision, the framework of the nose is reshaped. Prosthetic implants may assist in reshaping the nose. Rhinoplasty is usually an outpatient procedure.

11. Following rhinoplasty, nasal packing is left in place for up to 72 hours to minimize bleeding and provide tissue support. A plastic splint molded to the shape of the nose is removed in 3 to 5 days.

12. Septoplasty or submucous resection may be done to correct septal deviation. The procedures are done using local anesthesia. The deviated portion of nasal cartilage is removed; bone also may be removed if necessary. Following the procedure, the nares on both sides are packed to prevent bleeding and provide support to the septum.

13. Surgical interventions for obstructive sleep apnea may include tonsillectomy and adenoidectomy to relieve upper airway obstruction. In a uvulopalatopharyngoplasty (UPPP), the uvula, soft palate, and pharynx are reconstructed to relieve obstruction. Clients with severe obstructive sleep apnea may require tracheostomy to maintain an open airway.

14. Nursing care for clients with sleep apnea focuses on teaching the client and family how to manage the disorder. The nurse discusses the relationship of obesity, alcohol, and sedatives to the syndrome and provides information about ways to promote weight loss. When positive pressure airway support is prescribed, the nurse collaborates with the respiratory therapist in teaching the client and family about its use and maintenance. The nurse suggests measures to promote comfort and rest and to eliminate airway dryness.

15. For pre- and postoperative nursing care of the client having a total laryngectomy, see Box 22-8, Nursing Care Checklist: Total Laryngectomy and Box 22-9, Procedure Checklist: Tracheostomy Care.

16. If cervical lymph nodes contain cancer cells, a modified or radical neck dissection may be done along with total laryngectomy. After surgery, the client may have difficulty lifting and turning the head because of muscle loss. The shoulder on the affected side drops. Postoperative neck exercises can help reduce shoulder drop and increase range of motion on the affected side.

SUGGESTIONS FOR CLINICAL ACTIVITIES

- Arrange for students to rotate through surgery to observe surgery for upper respiratory trauma or obstruction and to care for the client postoperatively.
- Assign students to care for clients who had laryngectomies and tracheostomies so they can use alternative methods of communication and do tracheostomy care.

REFERENCE

- Schiech L: Looking at laryngeal cancer. Available at http://journals.lww.com/nursing/Abstract/2007/05000/Looking_at_laryngeal_cancer.40.aspx

LEARNING OUTCOME 5

Identify nursing care needs for the client with a tracheostomy.

Concepts for Lecture

1. In a partial laryngectomy, a temporary tracheostomy (surgical opening into the trachea) may be inserted to maintain the airway in the early postoperative period. It is usually removed within a week postoperatively, and the stoma is allowed to heal.
2. In the total laryngectomy, a permanent tracheostomy is created. The tracheostomy tube inserted during surgery may be left in place for several weeks and then removed, leaving a natural stoma, or it may be left in place permanently.
3. Because the trachea and the esophagus are permanently separated, there is no risk of aspiration during swallowing.
4. See Box 22-9, Procedure Checklist: Tracheostomy Care.
5. When caring for a client with a tracheostomy, the nurse needs to assess the client's and family's resources and ability to provide home care following surgery, including activities of daily living, tracheostomy care, and manipulation of TEP or an electronic speech device (if the client had a laryngectomy).
6. The nurse needs to teach the client and family members how to care for the tracheostomy and provide the opportunity for redemonstration of care.
7. The client is taught to use clean technique rather than sterile technique in providing stoma care.
8. Once the stoma is fully healed, the tracheostomy tube may no longer be needed.
9. The nurse teaches the client the following: use a humidifier or vaporizer in the home to add humidity to inspired air; increase fluid intake to maintain mucosal moisture and loosen secretions; shield the stoma with a stoma guard to prevent particles from entering the lower respiratory tract; promptly remove secretions from skin surrounding the stoma to prevent irritation and skin breakdown; protect the stoma with a cupped hand or washcloth while showering or bathing; don't submerge the head or neck; and do not participate in water sports.
10. The client and family need emotional and motivational support, so referring them to local support groups is helpful.
11. The nurse encourages the client to discontinue the use of cigarettes and alcohol.
12. The nurse discusses with the client ways to achieve good nutrition.

GENERAL CHAPTER CONSIDERATIONS

1. Have students study and learn key terms listed at the beginning of the chapter.
2. Have students complete end of chapter exercises either in their book or on the MyNursingKit Website.
3. Use the Classroom Response Question PowerPoints to assess students prior to lecture.

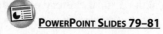

POWERPOINT SLIDES 79–81

Tables and/or Figures
- **Box 22-9** Procedure Checklist: Tracheostomy Care
- **Figure 22-9** Tracheoesophageal Prosthesis

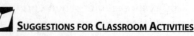

SUGGESTIONS FOR CLASSROOM ACTIVITIES

- Have students review tracheostomy care in class and discuss the needs of a client with a tracheostomy in class.

SUGGESTIONS FOR CLINICAL ACTIVITIES

- In a clinical lab setting, have students demonstrate tracheostomy care and suctioning.
- Assign students to care for clients with tracheostomies and to do tracheostomy care.
- In postconference, have the students describe the multiple needs of their clients who have tracheostomies. Discuss the nursing diagnoses, goals, and nursing interventions for the clients.

REFERENCE

- Bowers B, Scase C: Tracheostomy: facilitating successful discharge from hospital to home. Available at http://www.ncbi.nlm.nih.gov/pubmed/17551431

- Clinical Reasoning Care Map

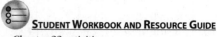

MYNURSINGKIT (www.mynursingkit.com)

- Websites
- NCLEX® Questions
- Case Studies
- Key Terms

STUDENT WORKBOOK AND RESOURCE GUIDE

- Chapter 22 activities
- *Separate purchase*

PRENTICE HALL NURSE'S DRUG GUIDE

- *Separate purchase*

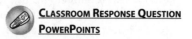

CLASSROOM RESPONSE QUESTION POWERPOINTS

TESTBANK

CHAPTER 23
CARING FOR CLIENTS WITH LOWER RESPIRATORY DISORDERS

LEARNING OUTCOME 1

Describe the pathophysiology of common lower respiratory system disorders.

Concepts for Lecture

1. Impairment of normal respiratory defenses increases risk for infection of the lower respiratory tract and can result in infection and inflammation of the bronchi or pneumonias that invade the alveoli of the lung.
2. Pneumonia can be infectious or noninfectious. Bacteria, viruses, fungi, protozoa, and other microbes can cause infectious pneumonia. Noninfectious causes include aspiration of gastric contents and inhalation of toxic or irritating gases.
3. Tuberculosis is caused by *Mycobacterium tuberculosis* and is transmitted by droplet nuclei, which are airborne droplets produced when an infected person coughs, sneezes, speaks, or sings.
4. Lung abscesses and empyema are potential complications of pneumonia and other respiratory infections. Aspiration pneumonia is the usual cause of lung abscess, whereas the major causes of empyema are bacterial pneumonia, rupture of a lung abscess, and infection due to lung trauma.
5. Severe acute respiratory syndrome (SARS) is caused by a newly identified virus called SARS-associated coronavirus (SARS-CoV) and is spread primarily by human contact. H1N1 (also called swine flu), though usually mild, may cause severe symptoms in high-risk individuals.
6. Asthma is triggered by a variety of factors such as allergens, environmental pollutants, respiratory infection, exercise in cold dry air, stress, and some drugs.
7. In chronic obstructive pulmonary disease (COPD), the airways are narrowed and gradually obstructed by inflammation, excess mucous production, and loss of elastic tissue and alveoli. Chronic bronchitis and emphysema can cause these airway and lung tissue changes. Alveolar ventilation and gas exchange between alveoli and the blood are impaired.
8. Cystic fibrosis is an inherited disorder of childhood that causes excess mucus secretion, with thick mucus plugging small airways and impairing normal airway clearing mechanisms, which leads to atelectasis, infection, bronchiectasis, and airway dilatation. Over time, COPD, pulmonary hypertension, and right-sided heart failure develop.
9. Atelectasis (partial or total lung collapse and airlessness), although usually caused by obstruction of the airway to affected area of lung, can also result from compression of the lung (e.g., by tumor) or an inability to keep the alveoli open.
10. Bronchiectasis (permanent dilation and destruction of large airways) is usually due to repeated respiratory infections. Inflammation and airway obstruction weaken and dilate bronchial walls causing secretions to pool.
11. Occupational lung diseases are directly related to inhaling noxious substances.
12. Lung cancer is 10–30 times more common in smokers than nonsmokers. In addition to smoking, other risk factors for lung cancer are exposure to secondhand smoke, radon, radiation, air pollution, and inhaled irritants, asbestos in particular.

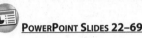

POWERPOINT SLIDES 22–69

Tables and/or Figures

- **Box 23-1** Focus on Older Adults: Lower Respiratory Tract Infections
- **Box 23-2** Focus on Diversity: Tuberculosis
- **Box 23-3** Focus on Older Adults: Tuberculosis
- **Table 23-6** Occupational Lung Diseases
- **Table 23-7** Lung Cancer Cell Types
- **Table 23-9** Types of Pneumothorax
- **Figure 23-1** Lobar Pneumonia With Consolidation of the Lower Lobes of the Lungs
- **Figure 23-7** Acute Asthma Attack
- **Figure 23-8** Chronic Bronchitis
- **Figure 23-9** Emphysema
- **Figure 23-12** A Thromboembolism Lodged in a Pulmonary Artery
- **Figure 23-13** Pleural Effusion
- **Figure 23-15** Pneumothorax
- **Figure 23-17** Flail Chest With Paradoxic Chest Wall Movement

SUGGESTIONS FOR CLASSROOM ACTIVITIES

- Invite someone from the county or state public health department tuberculosis unit to talk about the pathophysiology of tuberculosis.

SUGGESTIONS FOR CLINICAL ACTIVITIES

- Assign students to clients with pneumonia.
- Arrange for clinical experiences for students in the public health department unit working with clients with tuberculosis.

REFERENCES

- Knechel NA: Tuberculosis: Pathophysiology, clinical features, and diagnosis. Available at http://ccn.aacnjournals.org/cgi/content/full/29/2/34
- Manriquez DJ: Pathophysiology of pulmonary tuberculosis. Available at http://www.slideshare.net/davejaymanriquez/pathophysiology-of-pulmonary-tuberculosis

13. Most pulmonary emboli begin as clots in the deep veins of the legs or pelvis.
14. Pulmonary hypertension can develop with no obvious cause or may occur as a result of chronic lung disease or another problem.
15. Pleuritis (pleurisy) usually results from another process, such as a viral infection, pneumonia, or rib injury.
16. Pleural effusion results from respiratory disorders (e.g., pneumonia, lung cancer, or trauma) or from systemic diseases such as heart failure or kidney disease.
17. Pneumothorax involves accumulation of air in the pleural space, so pressure in the pleural space is no longer negative, and the lung on the affected side collapses.
18. Trauma or injury due to an external source, such as fractured ribs, flail chest, smoke inhalation, and near drowning, can affect the chest wall and the lung itself.

LEARNING OUTCOME 2

Relate manifestations of lower respiratory system disorders to the normal structure and function of the lungs and thoracic cage.

Concepts for Lecture

1. In pneumonia, the lower lobes are usually affected because of gravity.
2. The most common complication of pneumococcal pneumonia is pleuritis (pleurisy), which is painful inflammation of the adjacent pleura.
3. Diagnosis of tuberculosis is often asymptomatic and delayed for years.
4. In a severe asthma attack, use of accessory muscles, intercostal retractions, and distant breath sounds may be noted.
5. Infection from lung abscesses can spread to lungs and pleural tissue, and also via the blood, causing systemic sepsis.
6. By the time COPD is diagnosed, the client may have had a productive cough, dyspnea, and exercise intolerance for as long as 10 years.
7. In occupational lung disease, the work of breathing is difficult, so gas exchange is impaired, and the client develops hypoxemia.
8. Cancerous cells in lung tumors frequently spread via the lymph system to nodes and other organs, so symptoms are often related to the organs affected.

LEARNING OUTCOME 3

Discuss nursing implications for medications and treatments used for lower respiratory system disorders.

Concepts for Lecture

1. Antibiotics to treat pneumonia are initially based on clinical presentation; however, antibiotic therapy may be adjusted when culture and sensitivity results are available.
2. Oxygen therapy by a variety of delivery means may be ordered when pneumonia interferes with gas exchange.
3. Increasing fluid intake to 2,500 to 3,000 mL/day helps liquefy secretions, making them easier to cough up and expectorate.

 **PowerPoint Slides 70–99**

Tables and/or Figures

- **Box 23-1** Focus on Older Adults: Lower Respiratory Tract Infections
- **Table 23-1** Manifestations and Potential Complications of Pneumonia
- **Table 23-5** Manifestations of Chronic Bronchitis and Emphysema
- **Box 23-4** Manifestations of Acute Asthma
- **Box 23-7** Manifestations of Lung Cancer
- **Box 23-10** Manifestations of Pulmonary Embolism
- **Box 23-13** Manifestations of Carbon Monoxide Poisoning
- **Box 23-14** Manifestations of Respiratory Failure
- **Figure 23-9** Process of Emphysema
- **Figure 23-10** Favored Position of Clients With Emphysema
- **Figure 23-11** Clubbing of the Nails Caused by Chronic Hypoxia

 SUGGESTIONS FOR CLASSROOM ACTIVITIES

- Break students into small groups and assign each group a different disorder of the lower respiratory system. Have students discuss the manifestations of that disorder and relate the manifestations of that assigned lower respiratory system disorder to the normal structure and function of the lungs and thoracic cage.

 SUGGESTIONS FOR CLINICAL ACTIVITIES

- Assign students to care for clients with disorders of the lower respiratory system and have students present the manifestations that they identify for their clients. Discuss how these manifestations relate to the normal structure and function of the lungs and thoracic cage.

REFERENCES

- Mesothelioma & Lung Cancer: Lung cancer symptoms. Available at http://www.mesothelioma-lung-cancer.org/lung-cancer-sign-symptom.html?gclid=CNnc4IuNx50CFSDxDAodP20Msg
- National Prevention Information Network: Tuberculosis. Available at http://www.cdcnpin.org/scripts/tb/cdc.asp

4. When performing postural drainage on a client to remove secretions from a particular lung segment, the nurse positions the client with the lung area to be drained above the trachea or mainstem bronchus and does postural drainage before meals to avoid nausea and vomiting.

5. Clients with a recent skin test conversion from negative to positive for tuberculosis are started on daily isoniazid (INH) for 6–12 months to prevent active tuberculosis.

6. Because the tuberculosis bacillus readily becomes drug resistant when only one anti-infective agent is used, at least two antibacterial medications are used to treat active disease. Four antitubercular drugs may be used the first 2 months when active disease is present.

7. Because antitubercular drugs are often toxic to the liver, the nurse needs to warn the client on antitubercular medications to avoid alcohol and other liver toxins (e.g., acetaminophen) while taking these drugs.

8. Compliance with antitubercular drugs can be a problem, so medications are often given under direct supervision of the nurse.

9. Clients with asthma use daily medications for long-term control, including anti-inflammatory agents, long-acting bronchodilators, and leukitriene modifiers. Clients with asthma also have medications for quick relief of bronchoconstriction and airflow obstruction. These medications have their own individual nursing implications.

10. The client with COPD may be prescribed a combination of bronchodilators to manage symptoms, each with a variety of nursing implications. Corticosteroids may be given to reduce inflammation and edema of the airways.

11. The nurse can teach breathing and coughing techniques to help the client with obstructive lung disorders.

12. A thrombolytic drug (e.g., streptokinase, urokinase, or t-PA) may be given to disintegrate a large pulmonary embolus and restore pulmonary blood flow. The primary risk of thrombolytic therapy is bleeding, particularly intracranial bleeding, so the nurse must be alert to this possible complication.

LEARNING OUTCOME 4

Provide appropriate care for a client having thoracic surgery.

Concepts for Lecture

1. Surgery is the only real chance for a cure in most lung cancers, and in addition to routine preoperative preparation, the care of the client undergoing surgery for lung cancer includes reinforcing teaching of breathing and coughing techniques, allowing time to practice, and establishing a way to communicate if an endotracheal tube will be in place after surgery.

2. Postoperative care for the client having surgery for lung cancer includes frequently assessing respiratory status; assisting with coughing, postural drainage, and incentive spirometry; and suctioning as needed while intubated. The chest tube drainage system must also be maintained.

3. An umbrella-like filter may be inserted into the inferior vena cava of clients who have recurrent pulmonary emboli.

4. Chest tubes are inserted to restore negative pressure in the pleural space for clients with pneumothorax and hemothorax. Nursing care focuses on maintaining safety and promoting comfort and lung reexpansion.

POWERPOINT SLIDES 100–122

Tables and/or Figures

- **Figure 23-2** Oxygen Delivery Devices
- **Figure 23-3** Percussing the Upper Chest
- **Figure 23-4** Positions for Postural Drainage of Specific Areas of the Lungs
- **Figure 23-14** Thoracentesis
- **Table 23-2** Interpreting Tuberculin Test Results
- **Table 23-3** Giving Medications Safely: Antituberculosis Drugs
- **Table 23-4** Giving Medications Safely: Asthma Drugs
- **Box 23-5** Client Teaching: Using a Metered-Dose Inhaler or Dry-Powder Inhaler
- **Box 23-6** Client Teaching: Breathing and Coughing Techniques

SUGGESTIONS FOR CLASSROOM ACTIVITIES

- Have students break into small groups or pairs and practice teaching and doing coughing and breathing techniques such as pursed-lip breathing, diaphragmatic or abdominal breathing, controlled cough technique, and huff cough technique.

SUGGESTIONS FOR CLINICAL ACTIVITIES

- Assign students to clients with lower respiratory disorders who need help with coughing and breathing techniques and/or percussion and postural drainage.

POWERPOINT SLIDES 123–124

Tables and/or Figures

- **Table 23-8** Types of Lung Surgery
- **Box 23-8** Nursing Care Checklist: Lung Surgery

SUGGESTIONS FOR CLASSROOM ACTIVITIES

- Invite a nurse from the intensive care unit to talk to the class about care of the client who has undergone thoracic surgery.

SUGGESTIONS FOR CLINICAL ACTIVITIES

- Assign students to care for clients who have had thoracic surgery.

REFERENCE

- MedlinePlus: Lung surgery. Available at http://www.nlm.nih.gov/medlineplus/ency/article/002956.htm

LEARNING OUTCOME 5

Relate important concepts of caring for the client who requires airway support and mechanical ventilation.

Concepts for Lecture

1. Mechanical ventilation includes intubation with an endotracheal tube (ETT) or being placed on a ventilator, which is classified as either a negative-pressure or positive-pressure ventilator.
2. Negative-pressure ventilators are primarily used for clients with respiratory failure due to a neuromuscular disease (e.g., polio), whereas positive-pressure ventilators are used in acute respiratory failure.
3. Condensed moisture in ventilator tubing is drained toward the ventilator (away from the client) to reduce the risk of infection.
4. The nurse must work to facilitate communication when a client is on a mechanical ventilator.
5. Careful ventilator management is necessary to prevent complications of mechanical ventilation.
6. Clients who have been on prolonged mechanical ventilation require a gradual weaning off the ventilator. During the weaning period, vital signs, respiratory rate, dyspnea, oxygen saturation, and arterial blood gasses are frequently assessed.

LEARNING OUTCOME 6

Use the nursing process to assess, plan, and implement individualized care for clients with lower respiratory system disorders.

Concepts for Lecture

1. The hospitalized client with pneumonia is often quite ill, requiring careful monitoring and nursing interventions to support oxygenation and promote comfort.
2. Identifying populations vulnerable to tuberculosis and providing interventions and teaching to reduce the spread of tuberculosis are priorities of nursing care.
3. Nursing care for clients with lung abscesses and empyema involves maintaining a patent airway and adequate gas exchange, as well as emphasizing the importance of completing the prescribed antibiotic therapy.
4. The nurse needs to implement contact and airborne precautions in addition to Standard Precautions for clients with severe acute respiratory syndrome (SARS).
5. Nursing care priorities for a client experiencing an acute asthma attack focus on maintaining effective ventilation and gas exchange. After the attack subsides, the nursing focus is on teaching the client how to monitor disease status and prevent acute episodes.
6. In working with the client with COPD, maintaining clear airways is a high-priority nursing problem. Psychosocial issues are a priority concern because COPD affects all areas of life as it progresses.
7. Nursing care for clients with bronchiectasis and occupational lung diseases is similar to that for the client with COPD.
8. Nursing care for the client with cystic fibrosis is similar to that for the client with COPD; however, in addition, the genetic component and the client's age are important considerations.
9. Nursing care of the client with lung cancer focuses on maintaining effective breathing, airway clearance, and gas exchange. Because lung

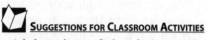

PowerPoint Slides 125–132

Tables and/or Figures

- **Table 23-10** Modes of Ventilator Operation
- **Figure 23-18** Nasal Endotracheal Intubation
- **Box 23-15** Nursing Care Checklist: Endotracheal Tube (ETT)
- **Box 23-16** Procedure Checklist: Endotracheal Suctioning

Nursing Care Plan: Client With COPD

Suggestions for Classroom Activities

- Ask the students to find articles in recent journals about caring for a client who is receiving mechanical ventilation by endotracheal tube or ventilator.

Suggestions for Clinical Activities

- Invite a critical care nurse and a respiratory therapist to talk to the class about mechanical ventilation and care of a client on a ventilator.

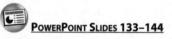

Reference

- Merck: Overview of mechanical ventilation. Available at http://www.merck.com/mmpe/sec06/ch065/ch065b.html

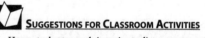

PowerPoint Slides 133–144

Nursing Care Plan: Client With COPD

Suggestions for Classroom Activities

- Have students work in pairs to list assessments they would do on a client with one of the more common lower respiratory disorders that they would likely see in the hospital.

Suggestions for Clinical Activities

- Assign students to work with a client with a lower respiratory disorder, and have the students conduct an assessment and present their findings in postconference.

cancer frequently cannot be cured, the psychologic and emotional effects on the client and family also are high priorities for nursing care.

10. Because pulmonary embolism can be a medical emergency, the nursing assessment is focused, asking about chest pain, shortness of breath, and risk factors, as well as collecting objective data.

11. Nursing care for clients with pulmonary hypertension is similar to COPD in assessment and interventions. The nurse discusses planned rest periods and the importance of not smoking.

12. Nursing care of the client with pleuritis focuses on promoting comfort; positioning and splinting the chest while coughing and wrapping the chest in wide elastic bandages may help relieve pain, but bandages must be loose enough to ensure that the lungs are fully ventilated.

13. Nursing care of the client with pleural effusion focuses on supporting respiratory function and assisting with procedures such as thoracentesis.

14. Restoring ventilation and gas exchange is the highest priority of care for the client with a pneumothorax. The nurse must immediately notify the physician if the trachea is displaced toward one side because this could indicate tension pneumothorax, which is a medical emergency.

15. Promoting effective airway clearance and gas exchange are the nursing care priorities for clients with chest and lung trauma.

LEARNING OUTCOME 7

Reinforce teaching and learning for clients with lower respiratory system disorders and their families.

Concepts for Lecture

1. For clients with acute bronchitis and those with pneumonia who are not hospitalized, nursing care focuses on teaching about increasing fluid intake, smoking cessation, and use and effects of ordered drugs, and explaining why antibiotics are not always appropriate.

2. Identifying populations vulnerable to tuberculosis and providing interventions and teaching to reduce the spread of tuberculosis are priorities of nursing care.

3. When teaching the client with lung abscess or empyema, the nurse stresses the importance of completing the prescribed antibiotic therapy, which may be continued for 1 month or more.

4. The nurse will teach the care-giving staff in community-based settings as well as clients with asthma how to monitor asthma effectively and how to use a metered-dose inhaler or dry-powder inhaler correctly.

5. The nurse will teach clients with asthma or COPD some breathing and coughing techniques (pursed-lip breathing, diaphragmatic or abdominal breathing, controlled cough technique, and huff cough technique).

6. Teaching for the client with cystic fibrosis includes reinforcing teaching for respiratory care techniques (percussion, postural drainage, and controlled cough techniques), stressing avoiding respiratory irritants and ways to prevent respiratory infection, and discussing the genetic transmission of cystic fibrosis.

7. Teaching for clients at risk for occupational lung disease focuses on how to reduce this risk (reducing dust in the work area, use of personal protective devices such as masks, etc.), how to avoid further lung damage, pulmonary hygiene measures, and the use and effects of any ordered medications.

 **POWERPOINT SLIDES 145–150**

Tables and/or Figures
- **Box 23-5** Client Teaching: Using a Metered-Dose Inhaler or Dry-Powder Inhaler
- **Box 23-6** Client Teaching: Breathing and Coughing Techniques
- **Box 23-9** Client Teaching: Cigarette Smoking

 **SUGGESTIONS FOR CLASSROOM ACTIVITIES**
- Provide a variety of metered-dose inhalers and dry-powder inhalers for the students to see and describe how they are used.
- Have students work in pairs or small groups to develop a teaching plan for one of the lower respiratory disorders. Have each pair or group present their teaching plan to the class.

SUGGESTIONS FOR CLINICAL ACTIVITIES
- Assign students to care for clients with lower respiratory disorders who have inhalers prescribed for their daily use, and have students administer prescribed medication via inhaler(s).
- Assign students to care for clients with lower respiratory disorders. Have students use the care plan they developed in class, if possible, and modify it for their client's individual needs.

 REFERENCES
- Mayo Clinic: Asthma inhalers: Which one is right for you? Available at http://www.mayoclinic .com/health/asthma-inhalers/HQ01081
- Mayo Clinic: How to use a dry powder disk inhaler. Available at http://www.mayoclinic .com/health/asthma/MM00405

8. Teaching for the client with lung cancer includes information about the harmfulness of cigarette smoke and nicotine and education to help the client to avoid smoking.

9. Additional teaching for the client with lung cancer includes providing information about planned treatments and ways to cope with noxious effects, the need to do coughing and deep-breathing exercises, symptoms to report to the doctor, information about medication use, and information about hospice and other support services.

10. Teach clients how to reduce the risk for deep vein thrombosis and pulmonary embolism. For clients with thrombosis or embolism, teach about prescribed anticoagulants, symptoms to report to the physician, mouth care, avoiding over-the-counter medications without the doctor's approval, and the importance of wearing a medical alert bracelet.

11. Teaching for clients with pulmonary hypertension includes manifestations to report to the physician and the importance of planned rest periods between activities and ways to conserve energy.

12. Teaching for clients with pleural effusion includes instructions on symptoms of recurrent effusion or complications after thoracentesis that should be reported to the physician.

13. The nurse will teach methods of prevention to prevent various chest trauma and lung injuries.

GENERAL CHAPTER CONSIDERATIONS

1. Have students study and learn key terms listed at the beginning of the chapter.

2. Have students complete end of chapter exercises either in their book or on the MyNursingKit Website.

3. Use the Classroom Response Question PowerPoints to assess students prior to lecture.

• Clinical Reasoning Care Map

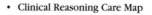

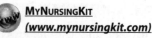 **MYNURSINGKIT**
(www.mynursingkit.com)
• Websites
• NCLEX® Questions
• Case Studies
• Key Terms

 STUDENT WORKBOOK AND RESOURCE GUIDE
• Chapter 23 activities
• *Separate purchase*

PRENTICE HALL NURSE'S DRUG GUIDE
• *Separate purchase*

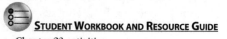 **CLASSROOM RESPONSE QUESTION POWERPOINTS**

 TESTBANK

CHAPTER 24
THE GASTROINTESTINAL SYSTEM AND ASSESSMENT

LEARNING OUTCOME 1

Describe the structure and function of the gastrointestinal (GI) tract and accessory organs of digestion (liver, gallbladder, and pancreas).

Concepts for Lecture

1. The mouth, the upper opening of the gastrointestinal tract, is lined with mucous membranes.
2. The stomach can expand to hold up to 4 liters.
3. The small intestine is about 20 feet long and 1 inch in diameter and hangs in coils in the abdomen suspended by folds of peritoneal membrane and surrounded by the large intestine.
4. The small intestine has three regions: the duodenum, the jejunum, and the ileum.
5. The duodenum begins at the pyloric sphincter and extends for about 10 inches.
6. The jejunum, the middle region, is about 8 feet long and connects with the ileum, the distal 12 feet of the small bowel, which meets the large intestine at the ileocecal valve.
7. Microvilli (tiny cell projections), villi (finger-like projections of the mucosa), and deep folds of the mucosal layers increase the surface area of the small intestine.
8. The large intestine, or colon, begins at the ileocecal valve and terminates at the anus. It is about 5 feet long. The first part of the large intestine is the cecum, which includes the appendix.
9. The colon is divided into ascending, transverse, and descending segments. The descending colon ends at the S-shaped sigmoid colon. The sigmoid colon terminates at the rectum.
10. The anorectal junction separates the rectum from the anal canal, which terminates at the anus.
11. The anus has an internal involuntary sphincter and an external voluntary sphincter. The sphincters are usually open only during defecation.
12. The function of the mouth is to form ingested food into a bolus, whereas the function of the stomach is to produce chyme.
13. The major function of the large intestine is to eliminate indigestible food residue (feces) from the body after the large intestine has absorbed water, salts, and vitamins from the semi-liquid chyme passing through the ileocecal valve.
14. The liver is the largest gland in the body (weight of approximately 3 pounds) and is located in the right side of the abdomen. It has four lobes: right (the largest), left, caudate, and quadrate. It is encased in a fibrous capsule and covered by a layer of peritoneum.
15. Each lobe of the liver contains many lobules, and within each lobule, plates of hepatocytes (liver cells) are arranged like the spokes of a wheel out from a central vein. The hepatocytes produce bile and perform many metabolic functions. Bile is necessary to emulsify and absorb fats.
16. Arterial and venous blood flows through enlarged capillaries (sinusoids) into the central vein where macrophages called Kupffer cells remove debris, such as bacteria and aged blood cells, from the blood.
17. The liver's primary functions are metabolic, hematologic, and digestive.

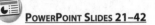 **POWERPOINT SLIDES 21–42**

Tables and/or Figures

- **Figure 24-1** The Gastrointestinal Tract and Accessory Organs of Digestion
- **Figure 24-2** Structures of the Stomach and Duodenum, Including the Common Bile Duct and Pancreatic Duct
- **Figure 24-3** A Cross-Section of the Small Intestine
- **Figure 24-4** Structure of the Rectum and Anus
- **Figure 24-6** A Liver Lobule

 **SUGGESTIONS FOR CLASSROOM ACTIVITIES**

- Have students study the anatomy and location of the organs of function. Provide a figure showing all the organs of function in their correct anatomic position, and have students label the organs without viewing their text. If students do not score 100, have them do this exercise the following week for mastery learning.
- Have students review auscultation of bowel sounds and how to chart their findings.

 SUGGESTIONS FOR CLINICAL ACTIVITIES

- Assign each student to at least one client to auscultate the client's bowel sounds and chart the findings.

REFERENCE

- National Digestive Diseases Information Clearinghouse: Your digestive system and how it works. Available at http://digestive.niddk.nih.gov/ddiseases/pubs/yrdd/

18. The gallbladder, a small sac on the inferior surface of the liver, concentrates and stores bile.
19. The pancreas is a gland located between the stomach and small intestine and produces enzymes necessary for digestion. The pancreas is actually two organs in one because it has both exocrine and endocrine structures and functions.

LEARNING OUTCOME 2

Describe the physiologic processes involved in ingestion, digestion, and elimination of foods and nutrients.

Concepts for Lecture

1. The teeth chew and grind food into smaller parts, while saliva produced by the salivary glands moistens food and enzymes in the saliva begin to break down food. The tongue mixes food with saliva, forms food into a bolus, and initiates swallowing.
2. The esophagus carries food to the stomach via peristalsis and enters the stomach through the cardiac or lower esophageal sphincter, which is normally closed except during swallowing to keep food in the stomach. The stomach can stretch to hold 4 liters.
3. Mechanical digestion continues in the stomach, where partially digested food is mixed with gastric juices to produce chyme. Four to 5 liters of gastric juices are produced by specialized cells in the stomach lining every day.
4. The pyloric sphincter controls emptying stomach contents into the duodenum. The stomach empties completely within 4–6 hours of eating a meal.
5. Pancreatic enzymes and bile from the liver enter the small intestine at the duodenum.
6. Food is chemically digested, and most of it is absorbed as it moves through the small intestine, where enzymes break down carbohydrates, proteins, and fats. Buffers produced by the pancreas neutralize the acid from the stomach.
7. Microvilli (tiny cell projections), villi (finger-like projections of the mucosa), and deep folds of the mucosal layers increase the surface area of the small intestine, and this aids reabsorption of nutrients.
8. Only indigestible fibers, some water, and bacteria enter the large intestine.
9. The rectum has transverse folds that help retain feces while allowing flatus to pass.
10. Feces are moved along the intestine by peristalsis, while goblet cells lining the large intestine secrete mucus that lubricates the feces, helping it move.
11. When feces enter the rectum and stretch the rectal wall, the defecation reflex causes the walls of the sigmoid colon to contract and the anal sphincters to relax, and defecation takes place.

LEARNING OUTCOME 3

Identify sources of various nutrients, including vitamins.

Concepts for Lecture

1. Carbohydrate sources include simple sugars, such as milk, sugar cane, sugar beets, honey, and fruits, and complex starches, including grains, legumes, and root vegetables.

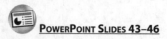

POWERPOINT SLIDES 43–46

Tables and/or Figures
- **Figure 24-3** Cross-Section of Small Intestine

SUGGESTIONS FOR CLASSROOM ACTIVITIES
- Track the process of food digestion, beginning with intake through the mouth and concluding with defecation.

SUGGESTIONS FOR CLINICAL ACTIVITIES
- Assign the students to a client with a digestive disorder. Have the students prepare a teaching plan to include the organs of ingestion, digestion, and defecation. Utilize this teaching plan for the client.

REFERENCE
- National Digestive Diseases Information Clearinghouse: Your digestive system and how it works. Available at http://digestive.niddk.nih.gov/ddiseases/pubs/yrdd/

Tables and/or Figures
- **Table 24-1** Nutrients, Food Sources, and Function

SUGGESTIONS FOR CLASSROOM ACTIVITIES
- Have each student keep a food journal for 3 days. After the third day, have the students complete a nutritional study of all of the foods in the journal.

SUGGESTIONS FOR CLINICAL ACTIVITIES
- Assign the students to a client, and have them conduct the classroom activity with the client.

POWERPOINT SLIDES 47–50

REFERENCES
- Lifeclinic: New in nutrition and fitness. Available at http://www.lifeclinic.com/focus/nutrition/
- Colorado State University: A guide for daily food choices. Available at http://www.ext.colostate.edu/pubs/foodnut/09306.html
- Lifeclinic: Food pyramid. Available at http://www.lifeclinic.com/focus/nutrition/nutritionview.asp?artID=1023

2. Protein sources include complete proteins, which contain all of the essential amino acids (e.g., eggs); other sources include milk, milk products, meat, fish, poultry, and plant or complementary proteins such as legumes, nuts, grains, cereals, and vegetables.

3. Fat sources consist of saturated fats and unsaturated fats. Essential fatty acids carry fat-soluble vitamins A, D, E, and K.

4. Vitamins (fat-soluble and water-soluble) and inorganic elements such as sodium, potassium, calcium, magnesium, chloride, and phosphorus are found in a variety of foods including fruits, vegetables, grains, and animal products.

LEARNING OUTCOME 4

Collect assessment data related to digestion, organ function, and nutritional status.

Concepts for Lecture

1. In the focused assessment of the abdomen and gastrointestinal (GI) tract, the nurse collects data about the client's nutritional status, the GI system, and its function.

2. When taking a health history, the nurse will ask about any current complaints related to food intake or tolerance, appetite, heartburn, nausea or vomiting, abdominal discomfort, diarrhea, or constipation.

3. The nurse will inquire about recent weight changes and any related factors, including the usual pattern and amount of daily food intake.

4. The nurse will ask about food allergies or intolerances and their effects.

5. The nurse will collect data about any dentures and associated problems, as well as any problems chewing or swallowing.

6. The nurse will ask the client to describe any abdominal pain or discomfort and about bowel habits and any recent changes in elimination.

7. The assessment will include listing current medications, including over-the-counter drugs.

8. The nurse will inquire about chronic diseases and any previous surgery of the GI tract or abdomen.

9. The physical assessment data includes general health status, skin color and condition, condition of hair and nails, height, weight, comparison of weight to the normal range for height, and body mass index.

10. Inspection of the mouth and teeth with a good light source is important.

11. The nurse inspects the abdomen for size and contour, visible vessels, striae or other skin or color changes, and visible peristalsis.

12. The assessment will include auscultatation for bowel sounds in all four quadrants, percussion, and light palpation of the abdomen in all four quadrants.

13. If the client has complained of abdominal pain, the nurse will palpate the affected quadrant or area last.

LEARNING OUTCOME 5

Discuss the nursing implications of diagnostic tests for clients with disorders of nutrition or affecting the GI tract or accessory organs.

Concepts for Lecture

1. Some diagnostic tests for clients with disorders of nutrition or affecting the GI tract or accessory organs require no special precautions or fasting (e.g., serum albumin and total protein, serologic *Helicobacter pylori* testing).

Tables and/or Figures

- **Box 24-1** Healthy Weights for Adults
- **Box 24-2** Documentation of Gastrointestinal and Nutritional Assessment
- **Figure 24-8** The Four Quadrants of the Abdomen, With the Organs Located Within Each Quadrant

- Have the students conduct a nutritional/digestion assessment on each other.

SUGGESTIONS FOR CLINICAL ACTIVITIES

- Have the students conduct a nutritional/digestion assessment on a client.

- United States Department of Agriculture: Dietary assessment. Available at http://fnic.nal.usda.gov/nal_display/index.php?info_center=4&tax_level=2&tax_subject=256&topic_id=1325
- United States Department of Agriculture: Dietary guidelines. Available at http://www.health.gov/dietaryguidelines/dga2005/recommendations.htm

Tables and/or Figures

- **Table 24-2** Common Laboratory Tests for Gastrointestinal Assessment
- **Table 24-3** Diagnostic Tests for Gastrointestinal Assessment

2. Stool specimen for occult blood requires a single random stool specimen, and the client may be advised to refrain from eating meats, poultry, and fish for 2–3 days before the test.

3. If collecting a stool specimen for fecal fat, the nurse will need to know whether it is a random one-time specimen or a 24- or 72-hour specimen, and sometimes the client is instructed to eat a high-fat diet for 3 days prior to testing.

4. There are a variety of liver function tests. Fasting is required for the bilirubin test, whereas other liver function studies may be performed without fasting.

5. When collecting urine for urobilinogen or pancreatic function tests, there is no food or fluid restriction, but the test may require a 2- or 24-hour specimen.

6. A gastric analysis test requires food, fluids, smoking, chewing gum, and some drugs to be withheld for 8–12 hours prior to the test. A nasogastric tube is inserted, and samples are collected. The nurse must explain the procedure and possible discomfort with tube insertion or length of procedure before the test. The nurse must be observant and take precautions to avoid aspiration.

7. For a urea breath test, the nurse must instruct the client to avoid antacids, bismuth sulfate, antibiotics, and omeprazole for 2 weeks before testing and withhold food and fluids for 4 hours prior to the test.

8. For an ambulatory pH monitoring test, the client needs instructions about caring for the electrode and data recorder.

9. The client getting tested for esophageal acidity and acid perfusion needs to have food and fluids withheld for 8–12 hours prior to the test and needs to be placed in high Fowler's position.

10. When a client is undergoing paracentesis, the nurse will explain that local anesthesia will be used so it should not be painful, but pressure will be felt when the needle is introduced. The nurse will obtain baseline weight and vital signs and instruct the client to void just before the test. Food and fluids are withheld as directed, and the client is positioned seated with feet supported. A dressing is placed over the wound, and wound drainage and vital signs are monitored after the procedure.

11. When a client is to have ultrasonography, the client is instructed to be NPO for 8 hours prior to the test. Cleansing enemas or bowel prep may be ordered.

12. When a client is undergoing radiologic studies, the nurse must inquire about possible pregnancy prior to the exam. If contrast is used, the nurse must inquire about allergies to iodine, seafood, or contrast media.

13. Flat plate of the abdomen requires no fasting or contrast media.

14. Upper GI series (barium swallow, upper GI with small bowel follow-through) requires restriction of food, fluids, and smoking for 8 hours prior to the exam. The nurse needs to instruct the client about the length of the test and advise the client to increase fluid intake for 24 to 48 hours after the test to promote barium elimination.

15. Barium enema (lower GI series) requires that the client be NPO for 8 hours prior to the test and for the client to take laxatives, suppositories, or enemas as ordered the evening before and the morning of the exam.

16. If a client is getting an oral cholecystogram, the nurse must assess for allergy to iodine, seafood, or other contrast media. Fat intake is restricted the evening before the test.

17. If a client is getting a CT scan, the nurse must inquire about allergies such as iodine and seafood and ensure the client is well hydrated to reduce the risk of kidney damage.

18. If getting an upper endoscopy (esophagoscopy, gastroscopy, or esophagogastroduodenoscopy), the client is instructed to fast for 8 hours. Dentures are removed, a check for loose teeth is made, and mouth

SUGGESTIONS FOR CLASSROOM ACTIVITIES

- Divide students into small groups. Have each group work on a teaching plan to explain and give instructions for two to three diagnostic tests associated with GI disorders that they may encounter in the clinical setting.

SUGGESTIONS FOR CLINICAL ACTIVITIES

- Assign the students to a client with a GI disorder. Have the student accompany the client to any diagnostic tests.

care is given. Because local anesthetic and conscious sedation are used, the nurse will withhold all food and fluids after the procedure until gag and cough reflexes have returned. The client is monitored for GI bleeding, pain, and difficulty swallowing or breathing.

19. When the client has a colonoscopy or sigmoidoscopy, there is a bowel preparation and limited food intake 24–48 hours prior to the exam. The client is asked to report any symptoms after the procedure. The client is instructed to avoid high-fiber foods for 1–2 days if a polyp is removed.

20. If a client is undergoing capsule endoscopy, a laxative may be ordered. Clear liquids may be allowed 2 hours after swallowing the capsule, and solid foods may be allowed 4 hours after swallowing the capsule. The procedure lasts about 8 hours or until the capsule is expelled during bowel movement. The camera does not need to be retrieved.

GENERAL CHAPTER CONSIDERATIONS

1. Have students study and learn key terms listed at the beginning of the chapter.
2. Have students complete end-of-chapter exercises either in their book or on the MyNursingKit Website.
3. Use the Classroom Response Question PowerPoints to assess students prior to lecture.

 MYNURSINGKIT
(www.mynursingkit.com)
- Websites
- NCLEX® Questions
- Case Studies
- Key Terms

 STUDENT WORKBOOK AND RESOURCE GUIDE
- Chapter 24 activities
- *Separate purchase*

PRENTICE HALL NURSE'S DRUG GUIDE
- *Separate purchase*

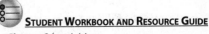 **CLASSROOM RESPONSE QUESTION POWERPOINTS**

 TESTBANK

CHAPTER 25
CARING FOR CLIENTS WITH NUTRITIONAL AND UPPER GASTROINTESTINAL DISORDERS

LEARNING OUTCOME 1

Describe the causes, pathophysiology, and manifestations of common nutritional and upper GI disorders.

Concepts for Lecture

1. Causes of common nutritional and upper GI disorders.
2. Pathophysiology of common nutritional and upper GI disorders.
3. Manifestations of common nutritional and upper GI disorders.

LEARNING OUTCOME 2

Recognize and take appropriate action for common complications of nutritional and upper GI disorders.

Concepts for Lecture

1. Discuss common complications of nutritional and upper GI disorders.
2. In most cases, anorexia, nausea, and vomiting are self-limited and require no treatment. If vomiting is severe or accompanied by other symptoms, nursing assessment is vital to determine the underlying problem that requires immediate care.
3. Treatment of obesity focuses on changing both eating and exercise habits.
4. In the obese client undergoing surgery, assessing for and preventing complications are nursing care priorities.
5. Approximately half of all hospitalized adults are malnourished or at risk for protein-calorie malnutrition, so the nurse must carefully assess a client's food and fluid intake and alert the charge nurse or physician when poor appetite, nausea, or NPO status interferes with intake.
6. Potential complications of malnutrition requiring nursing focus include increased risk for infection, deficient fluid volume, and skin breakdown.
7. If a hiatal hernia becomes trapped, impairing blood flow to the hernia, surgery may be necessary.
8. Gastrointestinal hemorrhage is a medical emergency requiring aggressive medical and nursing care.
9. When acute gastritis results from ingesting a poisonous or corrosive substance, this substance must immediately be diluted and removed. Vomiting is avoided because it might damage the esophagus and trachea.
10. When drug therapy and lifestyle management cannot control the symptoms or complications of PUD, surgery may be necessary, and if acute perforation or massive hemorrhage occurs, emergency surgery may be required.

 POWERPOINT SLIDES 21–79

Tables and/or Figures

- **Box 25-1** Population Focus: Obesity
- **Box 25-2** Problems Associated With Obesity
- **Box 25-4** Conditions Associated With Malnutrition
- **Table 25-2** Characteristics of Anorexia Nervosa and Bulimia
- **Figure 25-4** Oral Cancer
- **Box 25-9** Manifestations of Oral Cancer
- **Figure 25-6** Changes in the Mucosal Barrier With Peptic Ulcer
- **Box 25-11** Manifestations of Gastritis and Gastroenteritis
- **Table 25-4** Selected Causes and Characteristics of Gastroenteritis
- **Figure 25-8** A Cross-Section of a Peptic Ulcer Affecting the Stomach
- **Box 25-12** Manifestations of PUD and Its Complications
- **Box 25-13** Focus on Diversity: Stomach Cancer
- **Figure 25-9** Cancer of the Stomach

 SUGGESTIONS FOR CLASSROOM ACTIVITIES

- Have students each select one eating disorder or upper GI disorder and write about the pathophysiology and the manifestations of that disorder.
- Assign students to access the library and find one current article about an upper GI disorder and present briefly about the article in class.

SUGGESTIONS FOR CLINICAL ACTIVITIES

- Assign the students to clients with eating disorders or disorders of the upper GI tract and have the students conduct a health history for these clients.

REFERENCE

- Centers for Disease Control and Prevention. Ulcer facts. Available at http://www.cdc.gov/ulcer/

 **POWERPOINT SLIDES 80–94**

Tables and/or Figures

- **Box 25-1** Population Focus: Obesity
- **Box 25-2** Problems Associated With Obesity
- **Figure 25-3** Types of Surgical Procedures to Treat Obesity
- **Table 25-2** Characteristics of Anorexia Nervosa and Bulimia
- **Figure 25-9** Cancer of the Stomach

LEARNING OUTCOME 3

Contribute to assessing, planning, and evaluating care for clients with nutritional and upper GI disorders.

Concepts for Lecture

1. Care for clients with nutritional and upper GI disorders.
2. Assessing clients with nutritional and upper GI disorders.
3. Planning care for clients with nutritional and upper GI disorders.
4. Evaluating care for clients with nutritional and upper GI disorders.

LEARNING OUTCOME 4

Implement client-centered nursing care for clients with nutritional and upper GI disorders.

Concepts for Lecture

1. Implementation of care for clients with nutritional and upper GI disorders.

GENERAL CHAPTER CONSIDERATIONS

1. Have students study and learn key terms listed at the beginning of the chapter.
2. Have students complete end of chapter exercises either in their book or on the MyNursingKit Website.
3. Use the Classroom Response Question PowerPoints to assess students prior to lecture.

 POWERPOINT SLIDES 95–105

Tables and/or Figures

- **Figure 25-7** Sites Commonly Affected by Peptic Ulcer Disease
- **Figure 25-8** A Cross-Section of a Peptic Ulcer Affecting the Stomach
- **Box 25-12** Manifestations of PUD and Its Complications
- **Figure 25-10** Partial and Total Gastrectomy Procedures
- **Figure 25-11** Gastrostomy Tube Placement
- **Box 25-7** Nursing Care Checklist: Parenteral Nutrition
- **Box 25-10** Procedure Checklist: Gastric Lavage
- **Box 25-14** Nursing Care Checklist: Gastric Surgery

 POWERPOINT SLIDES 106–111

 SUGGESTIONS FOR CLASSROOM ACTIVITIES

- Select an eating disorder or upper GI disorder and research the long-term complications of this disorder. Create a teaching plan to aid a client with this eating disorder.

 SUGGESTIONS FOR CLINICAL ACTIVITIES

- Assign the students to clients with eating disorders or disorders of the small intestine. Have the students use the teaching plan created in class with their assigned clients.

Tables and/or Figures

- **Figure 25-1** Measuring Skinfold Thickness
- **Figure 25-2** USDA Food Guide Pyramid
- **Box 25-3** Client Teaching: Behavioral Strategies for Weight Loss
- **Box 24-1** Healthy Weights for Adults
- **Table 25-2** Characteristics of Anorexia Nervosa and Bulimia
- **Box 25-9** Manifestations of Oral Cancer
- **Box 25-11** Manifestations of Gastritis and Gastroenteritis
- **Table 25-4** Selected Causes and Characteristics of Gastroenteritis
- **Box 25-5** Procedure Checklist: Inserting a Nasogastric Tube
- **Box 25-6** Procedure Checklist: Enteral Feedings
- **Box 25-7** Nursing Care Checklist: Parenteral Nutrition
- **Box 25-14** Nursing Care Checklist: Gastric Surgery
- **Box 25-15** Nursing Care Checklist: Gastrostomy Tube

Nursing Care Plan: Client With Peptic Ulcer Disease

SUGGESTIONS FOR CLASSROOM ACTIVITIES

- Have the students select one nutritional disorder or disorder of the small intestine and create a plan to assess an individual with this disorder.

SUGGESTIONS FOR CLINICAL ACTIVITIES

- Assign the students to a client with a nutritional disorder or disorder of the small intestine that matches the disorder selected for the classroom activity. Have the students use the plan they created to assess this individual.
- Have students evaluate the plan of care they initiated and discuss their evaluation in post-conference.

Tables and/or Figures

- **Box 25-3** Client Teaching: Behavioral Strategies for Weight Loss
- **Box 25-8** Focus on Older Adults: Promoting Nutrition in the Older Adult
- **Table 25-1** Giving Medications Safely: Nausea and Vomiting
- **Table 25-5** Giving Medications Safely: GERD, Gastritis, and Peptic Ulcer Disease
- **Table 25-3** Giving Medications Safely: Stomatitis
- **Box 25-5** Procedure Checklist: Inserting a Nasogastric Tube
- **Box 25-6** Procedure Checklist: Enteral Feedings
- **Box 25-7** Nursing Care Checklist: Parenteral Nutrition

Nursing Care Plan: Client With Peptic Ulcer Disease

SUGGESTIONS FOR CLASSROOM ACTIVITIES

- Prepare a plan of care for a client with a nutritional disorder.

SUGGESTIONS FOR CLINICAL ACTIVITIES

- Assign the students to a client with a nutritional disorder or disorder of the small intestines. Have students provide care to this client using the plan of care created in class.

- Clinical Reasoning Care Map

MYNURSINGKIT
(www.mynursingkit.com)

- Websites
- NCLEX® Questions
- Case Studies
- Key Terms

STUDENT WORKBOOK AND RESOURCE GUIDE

- Chapter 25 activities
- *Separate purchase*

PRENTICE HALL NURSE'S DRUG GUIDE

- *Separate purchase*

CLASSROOM RESPONSE QUESTION POWERPOINTS

TESTBANK

CHAPTER 26
CARING FOR CLIENTS WITH BOWEL DISORDERS

LEARNING OUTCOME 1

Discuss the pathophysiology, manifestations, and management of bowel disorders.

Concepts for Lecture

1. Diarrhea can result from impaired water absorption or from increased water secretion into the bowel. Impaired water absorption occurs when the rate of peristalsis increases or when the absorptive surface of the bowel decreases. Increased water secretion may occur as a result of infection, unabsorbed fat, and some drugs.
2. Clients with diarrhea may have several large, watery stools per day or very frequent small stools containing blood, mucus, or pus.
3. Complications of diarrhea include water and electrolytes lost in the stool, dehydration that can lead to hypovolemic shock if the fluid losses are rapid, and acid–base imbalances.
4. Management of diarrhea includes identifying and treating the underlying cause, diagnostic tests, dietary management, medications, preventing complications, and preventing spread of the infection.
5. The term constipation is appropriate only when the client has two or fewer bowel movements weekly or defecation is excessively difficult or requires straining.
6. Constipation affects older adults more often than younger people; however, more significant factors contributing to constipation include general health, diet, medications, and activity levels. Use of narcotic analgesic medications is a significant risk factor.
7. Acute constipation may be due to an organic cause such as a tumor or partial bowel obstruction. Lifestyle and psychogenic factors (such as ignoring the urge to defecate on schedule) are the most frequent causes of chronic constipation. In older adults, habitual use of laxatives can lead to constipation when laxatives are withdrawn.
8. The client with significant constipation may develop a fecal impaction (hardened stool). Small amounts of watery mucus or liquid stool may pass around the impaction. The client has a full sensation in the rectal area and abdominal cramping. The abdomen may appear distended, and bowel sounds may be reduced.
9. Simple or chronic constipation is best treated with education and modification of diet and exercise routines. Foods with a high fiber content, such as fresh fruits and vegetables and whole-grain breads and cereals, are recommended.
10. Irritable bowel syndrome (IBS), a motility disorder characterized by alternating periods of constipation and diarrhea, involves some alteration of the central nervous system regulation of the motor and sensory functions of the bowel.
11. Motility of both the small and large intestine increases in response to stimulation by food intake, hormones, and physiologic and psychologic stress in clients with IBS. In addition, sensory responses to the movement of chyme through the bowel are exaggerated, and excess mucus may be secreted in the colon.
12. Stress may increase the manifestations of IBS but does not cause them.

POWERPOINT SLIDES 21–66

Tables and/or Figures

- **Table 26-1** Foods That May Aggravate Chronic Diarrhea
- **Table 26-2** Giving Medications Safely: Antidiarrheal Medications
- **Table 26-3** Common Causes of Constipation
- **Box 26-1** Focus on Older Adults: Constipation
- **Box 26-2** Manifestations of Irritable Bowel Syndrome
- **Box 26-3** Manifestations of Acute Appendicitis
- **Box 26-4** Manifestations of Peritonitis
- **Figure 26-2** Weighted Tip or Inflated Balloon at the End of an Intestinal Tube
- **Box 26-6** Focus on Diversity: Inflammatory Bowel Disease
- **Table 26-5** Manifestations and Complications of Inflammatory Bowel Disease
- **Figure 26-3** The Multisystem Effects of Inflammatory Bowel Disease
- **Table 26-6** Giving Medications Safely: Inflammatory Bowel Disease
- **Figure 26-8** The Distribution and Frequency of Cancers of the Colon and Rectum
- **Figure 26-12** An Inguinal Hernia
- **Figure 26-13** Selected Causes of Mechanical Bowel Obstruction
- **Box 26-11** Manifestations of Bowel Obstruction
- **Figure 26-14** Diverticula of the Colon
- **Table 26-8** High-Fiber, High-Residue Foods
- **Figure 26-15** Location of Internal Hemorrhoids and External Hemorrhoids

SUGGESTIONS FOR CLASSROOM ACTIVITIES

- Assign students to access Websites and journal articles and other resources and research one bowel disorder each. Ask the students to present their findings on the disorder they research to the class.

SUGGESTIONS FOR CLINICAL ACTIVITIES

- Assign students to care for clients with bowel disorders. Have the students review the diagnostic tests, treatments, and prescribed management for their clients and present what they have learned in postconference.

13. Management of IBS is directed toward relieving the symptoms and reducing or eliminating precipitating factors and includes stress reduction; exercises; counseling; regular use of bulk-forming laxatives to help reduce bowel spasm and reestablish a normal pattern of elimination; antidepressants, particularly selective serotonin reuptake inhibitors such as sertraline (Zoloft) and fluoxetine (Prozac), which may help relieve abdominal pain and spasm; reduced milk intake; restricting gas-forming foods; and adding fiber to the diet.

14. The appendix can become obstructed by a fecalith (hard mass of feces), a stone, inflammation, or parasites (e.g., pinworm). When obstructed, the appendix becomes distended with fluid, which increases pressure within the appendix and impairs its blood supply. The lack of blood supply leads to inflammation, edema, ulceration, and infection of the tissue. Within 24 to 36 hours, the appendix becomes necrotic and perforates if treatment is not initiated.

15. A manifestation of appendicitis is generalized or upper abdominal pain, which is often the initial symptom. The pain gradually intensifies and localizes in the right lower quadrant of the abdomen and is aggravated by moving, walking, or coughing. Localized and rebound tenderness are noted at McBurney's point. Extension of the right hip intensifies the pain. The client may have a low-grade fever, anorexia, nausea, and vomiting. Less acute pain in pregnant women and older adults may delay diagnosis.

16. Perforation is the major complication of acute appendicitis and is manifested by increased pain and a high fever. It can result in a small localized abscess, local peritonitis, or significant generalized peritonitis.

17. Appendicitis is managed by prompt diagnosis using WBC and an abdominal ultrasound to confirm the diagnosis if symptoms are atypical. Appendicitis is managed by surgery.

18. Peritonitis (inflammation of the peritoneum) may be due to perforation of a peptic ulcer, rupture of the appendix, or contamination of the abdominal cavity by bowel contents during surgery, allowing chemicals and bacteria from the GI tract to enter the normally sterile peritoneal cavity.

19. The inflammatory process from massive or continued contamination causes a fluid shift into the peritoneal space (third spacing), and peristalsis slows or stops (paralytic ileus) due to inflammation.

20. The client with peritonitis often presents with an acute abdomen including abrupt onset of severe pain, which is often accompanied by board-like abdominal muscle rigidity or guarding; distension; and diminished or absent bowel sounds.

21. Care of the client with peritonitis focuses on identifying and treating both the peritonitis and its cause.

22. Management of peritonitis includes intestinal decompression to relieve abdominal distention (nasogastric tube or long intestinal tube connected to continuous drainage). The client is NPO until peristalsis returns (bowel sounds heard and flatus passed). The client is placed on bed rest in Fowler's position to help localize the infection and make breathing easier. A broad-spectrum antibiotic is prescribed initially; however, when the organism is identified, a specific antibiotic directed at that organism is started.

23. Chronic inflammatory bowel disease (IBD) includes two closely related disorders, ulcerative colitis and Crohn's disease. These two conditions are similar in several ways, including the following: their cause is unknown, although infection, altered immune response, and lifestyle are thought to play a role; both are chronic and recurrent; diarrhea is a prominent symptom of both; and both may have associated manifestations, such as arthritis.

REFERENCES

- National Digestive Diseases Information Clearinghouse: What I need to know about irritable bowel syndrome. Available at http://digestive.niddk.nih.gov/ddiseases/pubs/ibs_ez/
- MedlinePlus: Appendectomy. Available at http://www.nlm.nih.gov/medlineplus/ency/article/002921.htm

24. Ulcerative colitis and Crohn's disease differ in some ways, including the following: ulcerative colitis tends to affect the mucosal layers of the colon and rectum in a continuous pattern and usually begins in the rectal area, whereas Crohn's disease primarily affects the small intestine in a patchy pattern.

25. In clients with ulcerative colitis, commonly there is a gradual onset of diarrhea with intermittent rectal bleeding and mucus. Attacks commonly last 1–3 months and occur at intervals of months to years with diarrhea being the chief symptom. Ulcerative colitis varies from mild to severe with the latter having more than 6–10 bloody stools per day with a risk for dehydration and malnutrition. Rectal inflammation causes fecal urgency and tenesmus (straining).

26. Crohn's disease causes inflammatory lesions of the bowel mucosa that may affect all layers of the bowel wall. Ulcers and deep fissures develop, and fistulas may form between loops of bowel or between the bowel and other organs. Inflammation and scarring cause the bowel to narrow and become partially or fully obstructed.

27. Manifestations of Crohn's disease include continuous or episodic diarrhea with liquid or semiformed stools that typically do not contain blood. Clients with Crohn's disease develop lesions of the rectum and anus, such as fissures, ulcers, fistulas, and abscesses. Clients may have fever, malaise, and fatigue.

28. Treatment of IBD is supportive, directed toward managing symptoms and controlling the disease process. Supportive care includes rest, stress reduction, drugs, and nutritional support.

29. Nearly all colon cancers begin as polyps (benign precancerous lesions of the large intestine). Colorectal cancer spreads by direct extension to involve the entire bowel wall and may extend into neighboring structures (liver or genitourinary tract). Cancerous cells may also spread through the lymphatic or circulatory system to the liver, lungs, brain, bones, and kidneys.

30. Manifestations of bowel tumors depend on the location and type of tumor, its size, and complications. Bleeding with defecation is often what leads clients to seek care. Other manifestations include change in bowel habits. In advanced disease, pain, anorexia, and weight loss occur, and a palpable abdominal or rectal mass may be present. Occasionally anemia from occult bleeding is found before other symptoms are noted.

31. The treatment of choice for colorectal cancer is surgical removal of the tumor.

32. Hernias are classified by their location, with most occurring in the groin and known as inguinal hernias. Inguinal hernias are usually caused by incomplete closure of the tract that develops as the testes descend into the scrotum before birth. These hernias often do not become apparent until increased intra-abdominal pressure causes abdominal contents to enter the channel in adulthood.

33. In older adults, weakness of the posterior inguinal wall can also lead to an inguinal hernia.

34. Inguinal hernias often cause no symptoms and are discovered during routine physical examination. A lump, swelling, or bulge in the groin may be noted with lifting or straining. The client may complain of pain that radiates into the scrotum.

35. Umbilical and ventral (incisional) hernias occur in the abdominal wall. Umbilical hernias may be congenital or acquired; pregnancy, obesity, and ascites are common risk factors.

36. Ventral hernias result from inadequate healing of a surgical incision.

37. If a hernia is reducible, contents of the sac return to the abdominal cavity when intra-abdominal pressure is reduced (with client lying down or with manual pressure).

38. A strangulated hernia occurs when the blood supply to tissue within the hernia is compromised. This can lead to infarction (necrosis) of affected bowel with severe pain and perforation.

39. When surgery is not an option for a client with a hernia, the client may be taught to reduce the hernia by lying down and gently pushing down against the mass.

40. A bowel obstruction may be either mechanical or functional. With a mechanical obstruction, the bowel is obstructed by a physical barrier like scar tissue, tumor, or twisted bowel or trapped loops of bowel within a hernia. Adhesions are the most common cause of mechanical bowel obstruction.

41. In a functional bowel obstruction (paralytic ileus), the bowel lumen remains patent, but peristalsis stops. It is associated with gastrointestinal surgery, peritoneal inflammation, and certain drugs such as narcotic analgesics.

42. Although manifestations of a small-bowel obstruction depend on how fast the obstruction develops and where it occurs, cramping or colicky abdominal pain that becomes progressively more severe is common. Vomiting is common, particularly with obstruction of the small intestine. Vomitus may smell like feces.

43. Initially, bowel sounds are hyperactive and loud (borborygmi) and may be high pitched, but as the obstructive process continues and with functional obstruction, few or no bowel sounds are heard.

44. Management of the client with a bowel obstruction focuses on relieving the obstruction and providing supportive care. Restoration and maintenance of fluid and electrolyte balance are vital to prevent complications.

45. Most partial and functional small-bowel obstructions are successfully treated with gastrointestinal decompression using a nasogastric tube or long intestinal tube.

46. In diverticular disease, clients have diverticula, which are acquired sac-like projections of bowel mucosa through the muscular layer of the colon. Diverticula occur most often in the sigmoid colon. Diverticula form when increased pressure within the bowel causes the mucosa to herniate through defects in the wall. Diverticulosis is the presence of diverticula.

47. Diverticulosis is usually asymptomatic; however, clients may experience episodic left lower quadrant pain, constipation, and diarrhea.

48. Diverticulitis is inflammation and perforation of a diverticulum. Pain is a common manifestation.

49. Management of diverticular disease ranges from no prescribed treatment to surgical resection of affected colon. A diet high in fiber is prescribed for clients with diverticulosis. The client is advised to avoid foods with small seeds. Bowel rest and antibiotic therapy are prescribed during acute episodes. The client may initially be NPO with intravenous feedings and parenteral feeding, with feeding resumed gradually.

50. Straining to defecate is the most common cause of hemorrhoids. Pregnancy is an important cause of hemorrhoids. Contributing factors include prolonged sitting, obesity, chronic constipation, and a low-fiber diet. Internal hemorrhoids develop above the mucocutaneous border or junction of the anus.

51. Internal hemorrhoids rarely cause pain and usually present with bright red bleeding unmixed with stool. The client may experience a feeling of incomplete stool evacuation. As hemorrhoids enlarge, they may prolapse or protrude through the anus.

52. With external hemorrhoids, bleeding is rare. Anal irritation, a feeling of pressure, and difficulty cleaning the anal region may be manifestations of external hemorrhoids.

53. Normal hemorrhoids are not painful. Thrombosed hemorrhoids cause extreme pain. Internal hemorrhoid associated with liver disease may rupture and bleed profusely.

54. Management of hemorrhoids is conservative unless complications occur. A high-fiber diet and increased water intake are effective for most clients with hemorrhoids.

55. Anorectal abscess is caused by bacterial invasion of tissue around the anus. The primary manifestation is pain aggravated by sitting or walking. Examination reveals swelling, redness, heat, and tenderness. If the abscess does not drain by itself, an incision and drainage are performed.

56. Anorectal fistula is a tunnel- or tube-like tract with one opening in the anal canal and the other usually in skin around the anus. A fistula may develop spontaneously or result from an anorectal abscess or Crohn's disease. The fistula may heal spontaneously, or a fistulotomy may be performed.

LEARNING OUTCOME 2

Provide appropriate nursing care and teaching related to measures used to manage bowel disorders.

Concepts for Lecture

1. The client's history and physical examination often provide enough information to identify the cause of the diarrhea.

2. Nursing care of the client with diarrhea is directed toward identifying the cause, relieving the symptoms, preventing complications, and (if infectious) preventing the spread of infection to others.

3. Client teaching for the client with diarrhea includes teaching the importance of hand washing, safe food handling, ensuring safe drinking water; and fluid intake to replace lost water and electrolytes.

4. The nurse working with an older client will teach about normal bowel elimination, expected changes with aging, and measures to promote regular elimination, including exercise, which may stimulate the urge to defecate.

5. The nurse will advise the client with constipation that most laxatives are appropriate only for short-term use. However, clients who require narcotic analgesics for chronic pain may regularly need both a stool softener and a stimulant laxative to manage associated constipation.

6. The nurse working with the client with irritable bowel syndrome will emphasize that symptoms are real, discuss the relationship between stress and manifestations, teach stress reduction techniques, and refer the client to a counselor for assistance in dealing with psychologic factors.

7. The nurse will do some teaching around diet. Although no specific diet is recommended for IBS, reducing milk intake helps some clients. The nurse discusses restricting gas-forming foods, fruits and berries, and caffeinated drinks; limiting sugar; adding fiber to the diet; and the use of complementary therapies.

8. The nurse teaches the client with IBS to avoid straining to defecate and stresses the importance of notifying the primary care provider if symptoms change, because the manifestations of IBS may mask an organic problem such as a tumor.

9. When working with clients with inflammatory bowel syndrome, the nurse will teach the client and family about the following: disease process, stress, treatment options, medications, complications including their manifestations and prevention, management of diarrhea, and diet.

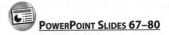

POWERPOINT SLIDES 67–80

Tables and/or Figures
- **Table 26-1** Foods That May Aggravate Chronic Diarrhea
- **Box 26-5** Assessing for Discharge: Peritonitis

SUGGESTIONS FOR CLASSROOM ACTIVITIES

- Assign clients to work in pairs or small groups and prepare a teaching plan for a client with a bowel disorder.

SUGGESTIONS FOR CLINICAL ACTIVITIES

- Assign students to clients with bowel disorders. Ask students to prepare a teaching plan for their assigned clients and discuss it in postconference, and have students critique care plans and give feedback to provide ideas for improving teaching.

REFERENCE

- National Digestive Diseases Information Clearinghouse: Crohn's disease. Available at http://digestive.niddk.nih.gov/ddiseases/pubs/crohns/

10. For the client who had an uncomplicated appendectomy, the nurse will teach wound or incision care and will instruct the client to report swelling, redness, drainage, bleeding, or warmth at the operative site, as well as any fever or increased abdominal pain.

11. There are activity restrictions after appendectomy. Heavy lifting may be restricted for up to 6 weeks.

12. For a client with peritonitis, teaching for home care will begin prior to discharge. Teaching includes verbal and written instructions for wound care, dressing changes, and irrigation procedures; where to obtain supplies; and referral to home health services.

13. Nursing care for the client with colorectal cancer is aimed at providing emotional support, teaching, and addressing the surgical client's needs.

14. Teaching for a client with colorectal cancer includes American Cancer Society dietary recommendations, the importance of regular examinations, information about tests and procedures, ostomy care, and pain and symptom management.

15. Most teaching related to hernias is done during routine health examinations. It includes what hernias are and risk factors for them, activity restrictions, what surgery involves, how to reduce hernias if necessary, and the importance of seeking immediate intervention if signs of strangulation or obstruction appear.

16. The nurse teaches clients with diverticulosis about the benefits of a high-fiber diet in preventing and reducing the incidence of complications of diverticulosis.

17. For the client with acute diverticulosis, the nurse will explain prescribed treatment and food and fluid restrictions and why dietary fiber is limited during acute inflammation but increased for chronic management.

18. Teaching for clients with hemorrhoids includes stressing the importance of dietary fiber, liberal fluid intake, and regular exercise to maintain stool bulk, softness, and regularity. The nurse also discusses signs of possible complications (e.g., bleeding, prolapse, and thrombosis) and does postoperative teaching if surgery occurs.

19. Teaching for the client with an anorectal lesion includes providing information about diet (e.g., adequate dietary fiber), fluids, preventing constipation, and postoperative care (e.g., sitz baths, symptoms to report to physician).

LEARNING OUTCOME 3

Effectively care for the client undergoing intestinal surgery.

Concepts for Lecture

1. Preoperative assessment of the client with suspected appendicitis focuses on describing the pain, as well as its onset, severity, and duration. The nurse asks about recent food or fluid intake and places the client on NPO because surgery is the treatment of choice. Laxatives and enemas or heat are not administered because these measures may cause perforation of the appendix.

2. The client with peritonitis may have a laparotomy in order to close a perforation, remove damaged and inflamed tissue, or remove an abscess. Peritoneal lavage may be done during surgery and continued for up to 3 days after surgery.

3. Supporting the client and managing responses to the acute inflammatory process are the priorities of nursing care for the client with peritonitis. Frequent focused assessment of clients with peritonitis is

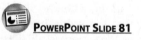

Tables and/or Figures

- **Figure 26-5** A Healthy-Appearing Stoma
- **Figure 26-6** Ileostomy Formed When Terminal Ileum and Entire Colon Are Removed
- **Figure 26-9** Location and Types of Colostomies
- **Figure 26-10** Transverse Colostomy
- **Figure 26-13** Selected Causes of Mechanical Bowel Obstruction
- **Table 26-7** Low-Residue Diet
- **Box 26-7** Nursing Care Checklist: Bowel Surgery
- **Box 26-10** Nursing Care Checklist: Ileostomy or Colostomy
- **Box 26-12** Nursing Care Checklist: Perianal Surgery (Postoperative)

vital. The focus is on monitoring the client's current status, monitoring the progress of recovery, and identifying possible complications.

4. Clients with ulcerative colitis may undergo a total colectomy (surgical removal of the colon) as a last resort.

5. The treatment of choice for colorectal cancer is surgical removal of the tumor, adjacent colon, and regional lymph nodes. Small, localized tumors may be removed by laser endoscopy, eliminating the need for abdominal surgery.

6. Most clients with colorectal cancer undergo a colectomy (removal of the affected part of the colon with anastomosis of remaining bowel). Whenever possible, the anal sphincter is preserved, and colostomy is avoided. Tumors of the rectum, however, usually require an abdominoperineal resection, in which the sigmoid colon, rectum, and anus are removed through both abdominal and perineal incisions. A permanent colostomy is created.

7. In a double-barrel colostomy, created to allow bowel healing, two separate stomas are created. The distal colon is not removed, but feces are diverted through the proximal stoma. A double-barrel colostomy usually is temporary.

8. Preoperative nursing care of the client undergoing ileostomy or colonoscopy includes discussing client concerns about surgery and the ostomy and referring the client to an ostomy support group as needed or desired.

9. After an ileostomy or colonoscopy, the nurse assesses the stoma location and appearance. The healthy stoma appears pink or red and moist and protrudes about 2 cm from the abdominal wall.

10. The nurse positions a collection bag or drainable pouch over the stoma and then monitors and records color and consistency of ostomy output. The nurse empties the drainable pouch or replaces the colostomy bag when it is more than one-third full.

11. The nurse assesses and cleanses skin surrounding the stoma and protects the skin with caulking agents, such as Stomahesive or karaya paste, and a skin barrier wafer as needed. The bag or pouch is changed if leakage occurs or the client complains of burning or itching skin.

12. A small needle hole high on the colostomy pouch will allow flatus to escape. To control odor, this hole may be closed with a Band-Aid and opened only while the client is in the bathroom.

13. The nurse will report any abnormal findings such as rash, purulent drainage, ulcerated skin, or bulging around the stoma to the charge nurse or physician.

14. Prior to discharge, the nurse teaches ostomy care, pouch management, skin care, and irrigation and allows time for practice.

15. The nurse emphasizes the importance of adequate fluid intake, particularly for clients with an ileostomy or proximal colostomy.

16. The nurse will discuss dietary concerns. A low-residue diet may initially be recommended. The client may be advised to avoid foods that may cause excessive odor or gas (e.g., cabbage, dried beans, beer, carbonated drinks, or dairy products). Foods that can cause a blockage are also avoided (e.g., corn, nuts, seeds, fresh tomatoes, and berries).

17. All types of hernias are surgically repaired (herniorrhaphy) unless specific contraindications to surgery exist. Heavy lifting and heavy manual labor are restricted for approximately 3 weeks after surgery.

18. Surgery may be required to relieve mechanical bowel obstruction. Prior to surgery, a nasogastric or intestinal tube is inserted to relieve vomiting and distention and to prevent aspiration. Intravenous fluids and electrolytes are administered prophylactically.

19. The client with diverticular disease may need surgery if an abscess or peritonitis develops.

REFERENCE

- Colonostomy http://digestive.niddk.nih.gov/ ddiseases/pubs/ileostomy/index.htm

20. When a hemorrhoidectomy is performed, anal packing may be left in place for 24 hours after surgery. The nurse needs to observe closely for bleeding when packing is removed. After hemorrhoidectomy, the nurse will provide pain relief as ordered because postoperative pain can be significant owing to rich innervation of the anal region and possible muscle spasms.

21. An incision and drainage may be performed for an anorectal abscess if the abscess does not drain spontaneously. A fistulotomy may be performed for an anorectal fistula if it does not heal spontaneously.

22. Pilonidal disease is treated with incision and drainage. The sinus tract and underlying cyst are excised and closed.

23. Following surgical treatment of hemorrhoids, anorectal abscess, anorectal fistula, and/or pilonidal disease, the nurse teaches the client to maintain a high-fiber diet and liberal fluid intake and stresses the importance of responding to the urge to defecate. The nurse instructs the client to keep the perineal region clean and dry and encourages sitz baths.

LEARNING OUTCOME 4

Discuss the care of clients with a colostomy or ileostomy.

Concepts for Lecture

1. Before colostomy or ileostomy, an enterostomal therapy nurse marks stoma placement and provides initial teaching about ostomy care and appliances.
2. After surgery, the nurse assesses the stomal location and appearance, positions a collection bag or drainable pouch over the stoma, and attends to the drainage from the collection bag or drainable pouch.
3. The nurse assesses and cares for the skin surrounding the stoma.
4. The nurse reports any abnormal findings (e.g., rash, purulent drainage, ulcerated skin, bulging around the stoma) to the physician.
5. Prior to discharge, the nurse teaches ostomy care, pouch management, skin care, and irrigation as indicated.
6. The nurse emphasizes the importance of adequate fluid intake and discusses the low-residue diet and any dietary concerns.

LEARNING OUTCOME 5

Contribute to assessment, planning, and evaluation of nursing care for clients with bowel disorders.

Concepts for Lecture

1. Assessment of the client with diarrhea includes asking about onset and duration of symptoms and any related events; frequency, character, and timing of stools; any related symptoms; any known chronic diseases; and all current medications.
2. The nurse obtains vital signs, including orthostatic blood pressure readings; notes general appearance; inspects mucous membranes; assesses the skin; observes the abdomen for shape and distention; auscultates bowel sounds; palpates the abdomen lightly for tenderness; and identifies any potential complications and reports them to the charge nurse or physician.
3. Interventions for the nursing diagnoses of diarrhea include monitoring and recording frequency and characteristics of bowel movements,

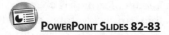

Tables and/or Figures
- **Figure 26-5** Healthy-Appearing Stoma
- **Table 26-7** Low-Residue Diet
- **Box 26-10** Nursing Care Checklist: Ileostomy or Colostomy

- Have students work in groups to research the different types of ostomies and, as a group, create a table or spreadsheet of the different types of ostomies. Students can use the following Website for one reference: http://ostomy .50megs.com/ostomies.html.
- Invite an enterostomal therapy nurse to come to the class and discuss the care he or she provides to clients.

REFERENCE

- Shaz's Ostomy Pages: Types of ostomies. Available at http://ostomy.50megs.com/ ostomies.html

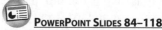

Tables and/or Figures
- **Figure 26-1** McBurney's Point
Nursing Care Plan: Client With Ulcerative Colitis

SUGGESTIONS FOR CLASSROOM ACTIVITIES

- Individually or in pairs, assign students to prepare a plan of care for a client with a bowel disorder and briefly present it to the class.

- Assign students to care for a client with a bowel disorder and to discuss their nursing care for this client in postconference.

measuring abdominal girth and auscultating bowel sounds every shift as indicated, administering antidiarrheal medication as prescribed, and limiting food intake for acute diarrhea, slowly re-introducing solid foods.

4. Risk for deficient fluid volume is a nursing diagnosis for a client experiencing diarrhea. Monitoring fluid volume status includes recording intake and output; weighing daily; assessing skin turgor, mucous membranes, and urine specific gravity every 8 hours; and monitoring orthostatic vital signs every 4–8 hours.

5. A drop in blood pressure of more than 10 mm Hg on moving from lying to sitting or from sitting to standing indicates orthostatic hypotension and possible fluid volume deficit. The pulse rate typically increases as well.

6. Diarrhea creates a risk for impaired skin integrity, so the nurse will provide good skin care, reposition frequently, protect pressure areas, assist with perianal care as needed, and apply proactive ointment or skin barrier cream.

7. The expected outcome for clients with the nursing diagnosis Constipation is that the client will resume normal or usual pattern of bowel elimination.

8. Interventions for clients with constipation include assessing and documenting pattern of defecation; assessing diet, fluid intake, and activity; and assessing abdominal shape and girth, bowel sounds, and tenderness. The nurse provides additional fluids to maintain an intake of at least 2,500 mL per day, encourages drinking a glass of warm water before and after breakfast, and provides time and privacy after breakfast for bowel elimination. Unless contraindicated, the nurse consults with the dietitian to increase dietary fiber, encourages activity, and if indicated, obtains an order for a stool softener, laxative, or enema.

9. Assessment of the client with suspected appendicitis focuses on describing the pain, as well as its onset, severity, and duration.

10. A nursing diagnosis for clients with appendicitis is Ineffective Tissue Perfusion (gastrointestinal) with an expected outcome that the client will remain free of signs of inflammation or infection.

11. For clients with a diagnosis of Ineffective Tissue Perfusion, the nurse will monitor for signs of perforation and peritonitis preoperatively, monitor vital signs, maintain intravenous fluids until the client is able to drink adequate fluids, and monitor wound, abdominal girth, and pain (postoperatively).

12. The assessment for a client with peritonitis focuses on monitoring the client's current status and progress of recovery and identifying possible complications.

13. Acute pain is a nursing diagnosis for a client with peritonitis with an expected outcome that the client will report pain at 3 or lower on a scale of 0–10.

14. Interventions for a client with acute pain include the following: place client in Fowler's position with knees and feet elevated; administer analgesics as ordered on a routine basis or using patient-controlled analgesia; promptly report a change in the location, severity, or character of pain; and teach and assist to use alternative pain management techniques along with analgesia.

15. Deficient Fluid Volume is a nursing diagnosis for a client with peritonitis. The nurse will record vital signs, intake and output, weight, and moisture of skin and mucous membranes as indicated. The nurse will monitor laboratory values, maintain intravenous fluids and electrolytes as ordered, and provide good skin care and frequent oral hygiene.

16. Ineffective Protection is a diagnosis for a client with peritonitis. The expected outcome is: will remain free of infection. The nurse will

monitor for signs of infection, obtain cultures of purulent drainage from any site, practice meticulous hand washing before and after providing care, and maintain fluid balance and adequate nutrition through either enteral or parenteral feedings as indicated.

17. Anxiety is a diagnosis for a client with peritonitis. The expected outcome is: will be able to rest when undisturbed and follow directions when necessary. The nurse will assess the client's and family's anxiety level and coping skills; present a calm, reassuring manner; minimize changes in caregiver assignments; explain all treatments, procedures, tests, and examinations; and teach and assist with relaxation techniques.

18. Assessment of a client with ulcerative colitis or Crohn's disease focuses on the client's current health status, presence of complications, and psychosocial factors related to the disease.

19. One nursing diagnosis for a client with ulcerative colitis or Crohn's disease is Diarrhea. The expected outcome is: will report decreasing number of daily stools; perineal skin will remain intact.

20. The nursing interventions for a client with ulcerative colitis or Crohn's disease include the following: monitor the appearance and frequency of bowel movements using a stool chart; administer anti-inflammatory and antidiarrheal medications as ordered; assess perianal area for irritated or denuded skin from the diarrhea; and use or provide gentle cleaning agents and zinc oxide–based cream for use after bowel movements.

21. Another nursing diagnosis for a client with ulcerative colitis or Crohn's disease is Risk for Deficient Fluid Volume. The expected outcome is: weight, urinary output, and vital signs will remain stable and within established range.

22. Nursing interventions for risk for fluid volume deficit include: maintain accurate intake and output records, including emesis and diarrheal stools; document vital signs every 4 hours; weigh daily; maintain fluid intake by mouth or intravenously as indicated; and provide good skin care.

23. One diagnosis for a client with ulcerative colitis or Crohn's disease is Imbalanced Nutrition: Less than Body Requirements, which may have an expected outcome of: will consume 100% of prescribed diet. The nurse carefully monitors food intake; provides a high-calorie, high-protein diet with nutritional supplements as ordered; provides parenteral nutrition as necessary; engages family members in dietary teaching; and monitors laboratory values.

24. Disturbed Body Image is another diagnosis that is often appropriate for a client with ulcerative colitis or Crohn's disease. The expected outcome might be: will acknowledge impact of IBD on personal roles, relationships, and responsibilities.

25. Nursing interventions for a nursing diagnosis of disturbed Body Image include encourage discussion about the effect of the disease on the client's feelings, self-perceptions, and relationships. The nurse will also discuss possible effects of treatment options openly and honestly; provide care in an accepting, nonjudgmental manner; and arrange for interaction with others who have IBD or ostomies.

26. Nursing assessment of the client with colorectal cancer focuses on the effects of the disease and its treatment on the client's ability to function and maintain ADLs.

27. One nursing diagnosis used with clients who have colorectal cancer is Acute Pain with an expected outcome of: will report pain as a 3 or lower of a scale of 0–10.

28. Nursing interventions for acute pain include frequently assessing the following: pain level, effectiveness of pain medications and adverse effects, the abdomen, the incision, and patency of catheters and tubes. The nurse also administers analgesics prior to an activity or procedure,

provides nonpharmacologic relief measures, and teaches the client to splint the incision with a pillow when coughing and deep breathing.

29. Grieving is a nursing diagnosis often used with clients who have colorectal cancer. The expected outcome is: will express fears, thoughts, and feelings about potential loss.

30. In working with clients who have a nursing diagnosis of Grieving, the nurse will work to develop a trusting relationship with the client and family and encourage expression of fears and concerns and discussion about the potential impact of loss on individual family members, as well as family structure and function. The nurse will help the client and family identify strengths, support systems, and successful coping mechanisms. Referral to cancer support groups, social services, or counseling, as appropriate, is an additional nursing intervention.

31. Risk for Sexual Dysfunction is often an appropriate nursing diagnosis for clients with colorectal cancer. The expected outcome is: will adapt modes of sexual expression to accommodate illness-related physical changes.

32. In working with clients who have a nursing diagnosis of Risk for Sexual Dysfunction, the nurse will provide opportunities for the client and family to express their feelings about the ostomy; provide consistent, secure colostomy care; and encourage expression of sexual concerns within the client's comfort zone. The nurse will also refer to social services or a family counselor for further interventions. Arranging for a visit by a member of the United Ostomy Association is also a possible intervention.

33. A nursing diagnosis often made for a client with a hernia is Risk for Ineffective Tissue Perfusion (gastrointestinal). The expected outcome is: will remain free of manifestations of bowel obstruction or strangulation.

34. Nursing interventions for a nursing diagnosis of Risk for Ineffective Tissue Perfusion (gastrointestinal) include assessing comfort and assessing bowel sound and abdominal distention at least every 8 hours. If signs of possible obstruction occur, the nurse will place the client in the supine position with hips elevated and knees slightly bent and keep the client NPO while beginning preparations for surgery.

35. The nurse assesses for bowel sounds and distention as well as for any complications in all clients who complain of abdominal pain or who stop eating in order to identify bowel obstructions early.

36. A nursing diagnosis often appropriate for a client with a bowel obstruction is Deficient Fluid Volume. The expected outcome is: vital signs, mental status, urine output, and weight will remain stable.

37. Nursing interventions for deficient fluid volume include monitoring vital signs and hemodynamic pressures hourly and measuring intake and output hourly and nasogastric output every 2–4 hours. The nurse will measure abdominal girth every 4–8 hours and notify the charge nurse or physician of changes in status.

38. Another nursing diagnosis for clients with a bowel obstruction is Ineffective Breathing Pattern. The expected outcome may be: will maintain clear, audible breath sounds throughout lung fields.

39. Nursing interventions for a nursing diagnosis of Ineffective Breathing Pattern include assessing respiratory rate, pattern, and lung sounds every 2–4 hours and monitoring pulse oximetry levels. The nurse will elevate the head of the bed and provide a pillow or folded bath blanket to use in splinting the abdomen while coughing. The nurse will maintain the patency of the nasogastric or intestinal suction and encourage use of incentive spirometry or other assistive devices. The nurse will contact the respiratory therapist as indicated and provide good oral care at least every 4 hours.

40. To evaluate the effectiveness of nursing interventions, the nurse can collect data to see if expected outcomes were met.

GENERAL CHAPTER CONSIDERATIONS

1. Have students study and learn key terms listed at the beginning of the chapter.
2. Have students complete end of chapter exercises either in their book or on the MyNursingKit Website.
3. Use the Classroom Response Question PowerPoints to assess students prior to lecture.

• Clinical Reasoning Care Map

MyNursingKit
(www.mynursingkit.com)

• Websites
• NCLEX® Questions
• Case Studies
• Key Terms

STUDENT WORKBOOK AND RESOURCE GUIDE

• Chapter 26 activities
• *Separate purchase*

PRENTICE HALL NURSE'S DRUG GUIDE

• *Separate purchase*

CLASSROOM RESPONSE QUESTION POWERPOINTS

TESTBANK

CHAPTER 27
CARING FOR CLIENTS WITH GALLBLADDER, LIVER, AND PANCREATIC DISORDERS

LEARNING OUTCOME 1

Describe the pathophysiology, manifestations and effects, and management of common disorders of the gallbladder, liver, and exocrine pancreas.

Concepts for Lecture

1. Most gallstones are formed in the gallbladder, prompted by the interaction of abnormal bile composition, ineffective bile flow, and inflammation of the gallbladder.
2. Risk factors for cholelithiasis (stones within the gallbladder or duct system that transports bile) include but are not limited to older age, female gender, obesity, family history, and use of oral contraceptives or estrogen therapy.
3. Cholelithiasis often is asymptomatic with early manifestations that are vague, including mild gastric distress after a large or fatty meal.
4. Cholecystitis is classified as either acute or chronic. Acute cholecystitis is characterized by severe epigastric or upper right quadrant pain radiating toward the back or right shoulder. Chronic cholecystitis often is asymptomatic or may cause mild nonspecific symptoms such as vague gastric upset or mid upper quadrant pain after eating.
5. Bile duct obstruction can lead to reflux of bile into the liver with resulting jaundice, pain, possible liver damage, and pancreatitis.
6. Management of gallstones includes surgery or lithotripsy (laparoscopic cholecystectomy, extracorporeal shock wave lithotripsy), oral bile acids to dissolve the stones, and dietary management (low-fat diet).
7. A complementary therapy for cholecystitis is goldenseal, an herb that stimulates bile and bilirubin secretion and inhibits growth of many of the bacteria known to infect the gallbladder. It should not be used during pregnancy due to possible stimulation of the uterus.
8. The liver is vulnerable to inflammation, damage, and tumors because it is constantly exposed to a large amount of blood that may contain pathogens, drugs, toxins, and possible malignant cells from elsewhere in the body.
9. More than 600 drugs, chemicals, herbal preparations, and other substances have been identified as damaging to the liver (hepatotoxic).
10. Many different disorders can affect liver function; however, the effects and manifestations of these disorders can be very similar and can be related to impaired cell function, impaired bilirubin excretion, and altered blood flow through the liver.
11. Hepatitis (inflammation of the liver) is usually caused by a virus but may be caused by alcohol, toxins (such as drugs), or gallbladder disease. Damage to liver cells resulting from hepatitis can lead to cirrhosis.
12. At least six different viruses can cause hepatitis. Hepatitis A, which is transmitted by fecal–oral route, and hepatitis B, which is transmitted by blood transfusion or contaminated needles, sexual contact, or from an infected mother to the fetus, are most common.
13. Hepatitis C is nearly always transmitted by blood and contaminated needles. It is the most common indication for liver transplant.
14. Hepatitis delta virus causes infection only in people who have active hepatitis B, causing more severe infection than hepatitis B alone.

POWERPOINT SLIDES 21–42

Tables and/or Figures

- **Box 27-1** Risk Factors for Gallstones
- **Figure 27-1** Gallstones Made Up of Cholesterol, Bile Pigments, and Calcium Salts
- **Figure 27-2** Common Locations of Gallstones
- **Box 27-2** Manifestations of Cholelithiasis and Cholecystitis
- **Box 27-3** High-Fat Foods to Avoid in Cholelithiasis
- **Box 27-6** Common Known Hepatotoxins
- **Box 27-7** Manifestations of Acute Viral Hepatitis
- **Table 27-1** Common Types of Viral Hepatitis
- **Box 27-8** Population Focus: People Who Should be Vaccinated for Hepatitis B
- **Box 27-9** Nursing Care Checklist: Liver Biopsy

Nursing Care Plan: Client With Cholelithiasis

SUGGESTIONS FOR CLASSROOM ACTIVITIES

- Ask students to interview a person in their family or community who has experienced a disorder of the gallbladder, liver, or pancreas. Have the students gather data on risk factors, manifestations, and management of the problem and compare their findings with the textbook descriptions.

SUGGESTIONS FOR CLINICAL ACTIVITIES

- Assign the students to conduct a health history for a client with a gallbladder, liver, or pancreas disorder.

REFERENCE

- Cedars-Sinai: Gallstones. Available at http://www.csmc.edu/5344.html

15. Hepatitis E is rare in the United States and is transmitted by water contaminated by feces.

16. Alcoholic hepatitis is acute or chronic inflammation of the liver caused by alcohol ingestion. It can lead to necrosis of liver cells and is the most common risk factor for cirrhosis.

17. There are three phases to alcoholic hepatitis: preicteric, icteric, and posticteric, or convalescent phase, each with manifestations.

18. There is no current cure for viral hepatitis. Treatment includes rest; nutrition; avoidance of strenuous activity, alcohol, and drugs toxic to the liver; interferon for hepatitis B or C; and possibly mild thistle or licorice root as complementary therapies.

19. Vaccines and immune globulin injections are available to prevent hepatitis A and B.

20. In cirrhosis, functional liver tissue is gradually destroyed and replaced with fibrous scar tissue. As hepatocytes and liver lobules are destroyed, the metabolic functions of the liver are lost.

21. Impaired blood flow through the liver increases pressure in the portal venous system, leading to portal hypertension.

22. Loss of functioning liver lobules ultimately leads to liver failure.

23. The manifestations and complications of cirrhosis result from impaired liver function and the altered blood flow through the portal venous system.

24. Various surgical procedures may be used to manage the effects and complications of cirrhosis including liver transplant, the only definitive treatment. Transplant is not appropriate for clients who continue to abuse alcohol.

25. Primary liver cancer is uncommon, but metastases to the liver from other primary sites are relatively frequent. Most primary liver cancers arise from the hepatocytes.

26. Manifestations of liver cancer include malaise, painful mass in the right upper quadrant, epigastric fullness, weight loss, anorexia, and fever. The client may have ascites, jaundice, or signs of liver failure.

27. Partial hepatectomy (resection and removal of a portion of the liver) is possible when the cancer is limited and has not spread beyond the liver. Radiation and chemotherapy may be used.

28. Pancreatitis can be either acute or chronic. Alcoholism is a primary risk factor for both acute and chronic pancreatitis. Acute pancreatitis occurs when the pancreas is damaged or its duct to the duodenum is blocked, allowing pancreatic enzymes to accumulate within the pancreas.

29. Chronic pancreatitis eventually destroys the pancreas and leads to pancreatic insufficiency. It may follow acute pancreatitis or have no known cause. Small ducts of the pancreas are block by calcified (stone-like) proteins.

30. The onset of acute pancreatitis is often sudden, with continuous severe epigastric and abdominal pain commonly radiating to the back and relieved somewhat by sitting up or leaning forward. There may be bruising to the flanks (Turner's sign) or around the umbilicus (Cullen's sign).

LEARNING OUTCOME 2

Discuss nursing implications for dietary and pharmacologic interventions related to the gallbladder, liver, and exocrine pancreas.

Concepts for Lecture

1. Nurses need to monitor blood levels of liver enzymes and watch for possible diarrhea in clients taking Ursodiol (Actigall) or chenodiol (Chenix) to treat small cholesterol gallstones.

 **POWERPOINT SLIDES 43–52**

Tables and/or Figures
- **Box 27-3** High-Fat Foods to Avoid in Cholecystitis
- **Box 27-8** Population Focus: People Who Should Be Vaccinated for Hepatitis B
- **Table 27-2** Giving Medications Safely: Cirrhosis
- **Table 27-4** Giving Medications Safely: Chronic Pancreatitis

2. The drug cholestyramine (Questran) is a drug that binds with bile salts to promote their excretion, and it may be given to clients with gallstones who have jaundice and resulting severe itching.

3. The nurse will advise the client that certain very low–calorie diets increase the risk for gallstones; however, the client needs to reduce dietary fat and calorie intake and increase intake of fresh fruits, vegetables, and whole grains.

4. All healthcare workers, including nurses, should be vaccinated for hepatitis B, along with other high-risk populations.

5. Nurses need to be aware that licorice root, used by herbalists to treat hepatitis because it has antiviral and anti-inflammatory effects, can lead to hypertension and affect fluid and electrolyte balance.

6. The nurse should refer clients interested in complementary therapies for hepatitis to a certified herbalist.

7. Clients with esophageal varices are at high risk for bleeding. The nurse will advise clients to avoid high-roughage foods (e.g., bacon), which can lead to hemorrhage of fragile vessels.

8. The nurse will advise clients with cirrhosis to avoid substances toxic to the liver, such as alcohol and acetaminophen, and drugs metabolized by the liver (e.g., barbiturates, sedatives, and hypnotics).

9. If serum ammonia levels are high or the client with cirrhosis has signs of portal systemic encephalopathy, dietary protein is restricted, but the client still needs adequate protein and calories.

10. Sodium intake is restricted to less than 2 grams per day to reduce edema in the client with cirrhosis.

11. Clients with cirrhosis particularly need to take thiamine, folate, and B_{12}, and the fat-soluble vitamins (A, D, and E) may need to be given in water-soluble form. Clients may also need a magnesium supplement.

12. When clients are taking spironolactone (Aldactone) or furosemide (Lasix), the nurse monitors vital signs and serum electrolytes and osmolality, weighs the client daily, monitors and records intake and output, and reports changes to the charge nurse or physician.

13. When clients with cirrhosis take neomycin sulfate, a gastrointestinal antibiotic used to destroy intestinal bacteria and decrease ammonia production in the bowel, the nurse needs to assess and monitor hearing and kidney and neurologic functions before and during treatment and also monitor the following: intake and output, blood urea nitrogen and creatinine levels, and digitalis levels as indicated.

14. Alcohol is forbidden in the diet of the client with pancreatitis because it may precipitate an attack.

15. Nursing implications for a client with pancreatitis taking pancrelipase (Lipancreatin), an enzyme supplement, include monitoring frequency and consistency of stools, weighing the client every other day and recording weights, giving the drug with meals, and monitoring side effects.

LEARNING OUTCOME 3

Provide appropriate nursing care for the client who has surgery of the gallbladder, liver, or pancreas.

Concepts for Lecture

1. Nursing care priorities for the client having surgery of the gallbladder, liver, or pancreas focus on helping the client maintain good nutritional status, reducing the risk for complications, managing symptoms, promoting comfort, and addressing psychosocial needs of the client and family.

2. Nursing care for clients undergoing cholecystectomy is similar to that of any abdominal surgery. Clients may require T-tube care.

SUGGESTIONS FOR CLASSROOM ACTIVITIES

- Individually or in small groups, have the students create a diet teaching plan for a client with a gallbladder, liver, or pancreas disorder.

SUGGESTIONS FOR CLINICAL ACTIVITIES

- Assign each student to care for a client with a gallbladder, liver, or pancreas disorder and to provide dietary instructions to the assigned client.

REFERENCE

- National Digestive Disease Information Clearinghouse: Homepage. Available at http://www.digestive.niddk.nih.gov/

POWERPOINT SLIDES 53–59

Tables and/or Figures

- **Figure 27-3** A T-Tube Placed in the Common Bile Duct
- **Figure 27-8** Transjugular Intrahepatic Portosystemic Shunt
- **Figure 27-10** Whipple's Procedure
- **Box 27-4** Nursing Care Checklist: Laparoscopic Cholecystectomy
- **Box 27-5** Nursing Care Checklist: T-Tube Care
- **Box 27-10** Nursing Care Checklist: Liver Transplant

Nursing Care Plan: Client With Cholelithiasis
Nursing Care Plan: Client With Alcoholic Cirrhosis

3. When caring for a client after laparoscopic cholecystectomy, the nurse needs to carefully assess the client's pain and provide adequate analgesia because the abdomen is inflated with carbon dioxide during surgery. The nurse needs to advise the client that the pain will be relieved as the gas is absorbed.

4. The client may have a T-tube after common bile duct exploration to keep the duct open and promote bile flow until edema decreases. Nursing care includes keeping the sterile collecting container and tubing below the level of the surgical wound, monitoring the drainage, placing the client in Fowler's position to facilitate drainage, inspecting the skin for bile leakage, and teaching the client how to manage the tubing and recognize signs of infection.

5. In caring preoperatively and postoperatively for the client having liver transplant, much of the care is similar to general surgery care. However, in addition, drugs are administered to prevent rejection (e.g., cyclosporine A, corticosteroids, azathioprine), and the client is carefully monitored for infection because these drugs suppress the immune response. The client is also monitored for signs of rejection.

6. Discharge teaching of the client who had a liver transplant includes how to recognize signs of infection and signs of rejection.

7. The nurse needs to secure and maintain the original position of the tube when a client has a Sengstaken-Blakemore or other multiple-lumen nasogastric tube to control bleeding esophageal varices. Soft restraints are used as needed. A syringe is kept at the bedside to deflate the balloon should the tube become displaced, because if the tube is dislodged while the balloon is inflated, the airway can become obstructed.

8. The nurse must observe the client closely for evidence of bleeds at the insertion site (jugular vein) or internally when caring for a client who has a transjugular intrahepatic portosystemic shunt (TIPS).

9. For clients who have a pancreatoduodenectomy (Whipple's procedure), postoperative nursing care is similar to that of the client undergoing intestinal surgery.

LEARNING OUTCOME 4

Use the nursing process to assess, plan, provide, and evaluate care for clients with disorders of the gallbladder, liver, or exocrine pancreas.

Concepts for Lecture

1. For most clients with gallbladder disease, the priority of nursing care is managing symptoms of the disorder and promoting comfort.

2. Focused assessment of clients with gallstones includes both subjective and objective data: asking about pain, relationship between food intake and pain as well as other symptoms, color of emesis and color and consistency of feces, color of skin and sclera, abdominal distention, and tenderness and guarding especially over the right upper quadrant.

3. The nurse must note any abrupt relief of pain in a client experiencing acute biliary colic or cholecystitis because this may signal perforation of the distended gallbladder.

4. The nurse must monitor for fever in the client with acute biliary colic or cholecystitis because continued fever may indicate infection or abscess formation.

5. The nurse will teach clients to avoid fats in their diet.

6. The nurse will teach the client to use Fowler's position because it decreases pressure on the inflamed area and helps relieve pain.

7. The nurse will assess any emesis and monitor complaints of nausea, administer antiemetics, remove noxious items and odor-producing

SUGGESTIONS FOR CLASSROOM ACTIVITIES

- Assign students to each research one of the surgical procedures involving the gallbladder, liver, and pancreas and provide a 10-minute report on the procedure for the class.
- Invite a surgical nurse or a surgeon to speak to the class about surgical procedures involving the gallbladder, liver, and pancreas.

SUGGESTIONS FOR CLINICAL ACTIVITIES

- Arrange for each student to observe a surgical procedure and postoperative care for a client with a gallbladder, liver, or pancreatic disorder.

POWERPOINT SLIDES 60–80

Tables and/or Figures

- **Box 27-2** Manifestations of Cholelithiasis and Cholecystitis
- **Box 27-3** High-Fat Foods to Avoid in Cholelithiasis
- **Box 27-7** Manifestations of Acute Viral Hepatitis
- **Box 27-11** Bleeding Precautions
- **Box 27-12** Assessment: Assessing for Discharge: Cirrhosis

Nursing Care Plan: Client With Cholelithiasis

SUGGESTIONS FOR CLASSROOM ACTIVITIES

- Assign the students to each create a teaching plan for a client with a disorder of the gallbladder, liver, or pancreas.

SUGGESTIONS FOR CLINICAL ACTIVITIES

- Assign students to provide care for a client with a disorder of the gallbladder, liver, or pancreas and to modify and use their teaching plan designed in the classroom.

substances, provide oral care, and hold the client NPO during episodes of nausea and vomiting.

8. The nurse caring for the client with gallbladder disease will collect data related to level of comfort, ability to consume ordered diet and fluids, respiratory status, and freedom from infection to evaluate the effectiveness of nursing interventions.

9. When working with clients suspected of having hepatitis, ask about known or possible exposure to hepatitis including recent travel, close contact with someone known to have hepatitis, occupational exposure, or high-risk behavior. Inquire about flu-like symptoms, appetite, discomfort, and any changes in skin or eye color or the color of feces and urine.

10. The nurse working with clients with hepatitis will use Standard Precautions and meticulous hand washing. If the client has hepatitis A, the nurse will use Standard Precautions and contact isolation if fecal incontinence is present.

11. The nurse will encourage clients at risk for hepatitis A or B or both to get immunized.

12. The nurse will promote and encourage rest as needed to relieve fatigue when caring for clients with hepatitis.

13. When working with clients with hepatitis, the nurse will use strategies to get the client to consume 100% of their prescribed or recommended meal (e.g., encourage smaller more frequent meals and eating when not nauseated).

14. To evaluate the effectiveness of nursing care for clients with hepatitis, the nurse will look at indicators such as household members free of infection and client knowledgeable about ways to prevent spread of infection.

15. The priority nursing care focus for clients with cirrhosis may vary depending on the stage of the disease, its effects on other body symptoms, and the presence of complications.

16. When caring for the client with cirrhosis, the nurse will weigh the client daily, assess for neck vein distention and peripheral edema, measure abdominal girth daily, provide a low-sodium diet, and restrict fluids as ordered.

17. The nurse will be aware that some medications can worsen manifestations of encephalopathy and will be aware of the need to avoid CNS depressant medication. The nurse will assess level of consciousness and mental status and monitor for changes in behavior, handwriting, speech, and asterixis (flapping of the hands).

18. The nurse will include family members in all teaching and will reinforce and repeat explanations as needed in regard to diet, fluid restrictions, medications, and when to contact the doctor.

19. In evaluating care, the nurse will look at outcomes related to nursing, especially looking at a client's behavior and mental status compared with normal for the client, any bleeding, respiratory status, and condition of skin.

20. The nurse working with a client with pancreatitis, who has acute pain, will assess onset of symptoms and risk factors for pancreatitis, verbal and nonverbal clues of pain, diet, previous attacks, alcohol use, food intake the day prior to onset of pain, and bowel sounds.

21. The nurse will administer pain medication on a regular schedule because unrelieved pain may increase secretion of pancreatic enzymes.

22. The nurse evaluating the effectiveness of nursing care for a client with acute pancreatitis will collect data on pain level, weight, ability to resume eating, and stability of cardiovascular and respiratory systems.

GENERAL CHAPTER CONSIDERATIONS

1. Have students study and learn key terms listed at the beginning of the chapter.
2. Have students complete end of chapter exercises either in their book or on the MyNursingKit Website.
3. Use the Classroom Response Question PowerPoints to assess students prior to lecture.

• Clinical Reasoning Care Map

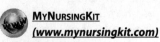 **MYNURSINGKIT**
(www.mynursingkit.com)

• Websites
• NCLEX® Questions
• Case Studies
• Key Terms

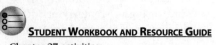 **STUDENT WORKBOOK AND RESOURCE GUIDE**

• Chapter 27 activities
• *Separate purchase*

PRENTICE HALL NURSE'S DRUG GUIDE

• *Separate purchase*

 CLASSROOM RESPONSE QUESTION
POWERPOINTS

 TESTBANK

CHAPTER 28
THE URINARY SYSTEM AND ASSESSMENT

LEARNING OUTCOME 1

Identify and describe the structures and functions of the renal and urinary system.

Concepts for Lecture

1. The urinary system is composed of two kidneys, two ureters, the bladder, and the urethra.
2. The kidney is composed of three distinct regions: cortex, medulla, and pelvis.
3. The outer region contains the glomeruli, which are small clusters of capillaries that are part of the nephron.
4. The nephron is the functional unit of the kidney and is responsible for making urine.
5. Different portions of the nephron are involved in the absorption of water and electrolytes, which concentrate urine.
6. Glomerular filtration is the process in which fluids and solutes pass through the nephron.
7. The urinary system plays a vital role in eliminating metabolic wastes and regulating fluid and electrolyte balance in the body. It also excretes or conserves water and solutes as needed.
8. The kidney helps regulate acid–base balance and is responsible for the regulation of blood pressure via the rennin–angiotensin–aldosterone system.
9. The renin–angiotensin–aldosterone system also regulates the sodium level in the body, which assists with fluid regulation.
10. The kidney secrets erythropoietin, which is responsible for the formation of RBCs.
11. Vitamin D is inactive when it enters the body and is activated in two steps by the liver and then the kidneys.
12. As adults age, nephrons are lost, resulting in a decrease in the glomerular filtration rate. This can affect medication tolerance.

LEARNING OUTCOME 2

Collect subjective information and physical assessment data related to the urinary system and kidney function.

Concepts for Lecture

1. A detailed health history is an important aspect of identifying disorders of the urinary system.
2. Various disease processes and past history may be the cause of present urinary disorders (e.g., diabetes, surgery). The nurse will ask about chronic diseases, pregnancy, and any family history of kidney disease or problems.
3. Vital signs and other objective findings change with urinary disorders.
4. The nurse will assess color, odor, and amount of urine; usual amount of fluid intake; normal pattern of urination and any recent changes;

 **POWERPOINT SLIDES 20–25**

Tables and/or Figures
- **Figure 28-1** The Kidneys, Ureters, and Bladder
- **Figure 28-2** An Illustration of the Internal Structures of the Kidney
- **Figure 28-3** Anatomy of the Urinary Bladder
- **Figure 28-4** The Structure of the Nephron and the Processes of Urine Formation
- **Table 28-2** Nursing Implications of Age-Related Changes in Kidney Function

 SUGGESTIONS FOR CLASSROOM ACTIVITIES
- Ask the students to trace the flow of urine through the kidney into the bladder.
- Have the students diagram the formation and concentration of urine.

 **SUGGESTIONS FOR CLINICAL ACTIVITIES**
- Assign students to care for older clients who are taking medication and ask the students to discuss in postconference how medication effects may change with aging and changing glomerular filtration rate.
- Assign students to each care for a client with a renal or urinary tract problem. Have the students assess their client's knowledge of the structure and function of the renal and urinary tract. Ask the students to supplement the client's knowledge as appropriate and needed.

 **REFERENCE**
- Adam.com: Urinary system. Available at http://www.besthealth.com/besthealth/bodyguide/reftext/html/urin_sys_fin.html

 **POWERPOINT SLIDES 26–28**

Tables and/or Figures
- **Figure 28-5** Percussing the Kidney
- **Figure 28-6** Inspecting the Urinary Meatus of the Male
- **Box 28-1** Nursing Care Checklist: Collecting a Midstream Clean-Catch Urine Specimen

and any pain or bleeding on urination. Normal urine is clear, pale yellow, and without blood, protein, WBCs, or nitrates.

5. The genital area and urinary meatus should be free of sores, lesions, discharge, redness, swelling, and tenderness.

6. The costovertebral angle is the area over the kidney; tenderness in this area may indicate a kidney infection.

7. Physical examination and assessment of the urinary system begins with obtaining a clean-catch urine specimen, which is inspected for color, odor, and clarity before sending it to the laboratory.

8. The nurse takes the vital signs, assesses skin color and condition looking for evidence of excessively dry skin or excoriations, ascultates bowel sounds, looks for evidence of edema, palpates the abdomen for tenderness, and percusses the kidneys for tenderness.

LEARNING OUTCOME 3

Provide appropriate nursing care for clients undergoing diagnostic tests to identify disorders of the urinary system or kidneys.

Concepts for Lecture

1. Diagnostic tests of the client with renal and urinary tract disorders and suspected disorders include blood studies, urine studies, and radiology studies.

2. Collecting urine specimens can involve midstream clean-catch technique to collect specimen in a sterile container or collecting a specimen from the drainage tubing using sterile technique (urinalysis, culture and sensitivity); specimens from first voiding of the day are used to measure the urine albumin to creatinine ratio.

3. A 24-hour urine test requires a specimen container with appropriate preservative if indicated, and the nurse must determine if the specimen needs refrigeration.

4. Radiologic testing may be done in the radiologic department, and some tests may require conscious sedation.

5. Radiology studies require the nurse to ask about and report allergies to seafood, iodine, or x-ray if a contrast media is used (intravenous pyelography, renal arteriogram, and renal scan).

6. Uroflowmetry implications for the nurse include instructing the client to drink fluids and avoid urination for several hours before the test.

7. When a client undergoes a cystometrogram, a measured amount of fluid is placed in the bladder, and the nurse measures pressures during filling and during voiding. The nurse instructs the client to identify when he or she feels the urge to void and when it is no longer possible to delay urination.

8. Nursing care for urinary studies usually includes client teaching, assessments, and client preparation.

GENERAL CHAPTER CONSIDERATIONS

1. Have students study and learn key terms listed at the beginning of the chapter.

2. Have students complete end of chapter exercises either in their book or on the MyNursingKit Website.

3. Use the Classroom Response Question PowerPoints to assess students prior to lecture.

 **POWERPOINT SLIDES 29–30**

Tables and/or Figures

- **Table 28-1** Characteristics of Normal Urine on Urinalysis
- **Table 28-4** Laboratory Tests Used to Evaluate Renal Function
- **Box 28-3** Nursing Care Checklist: 24-Hour Urine Specimen

SUGGESTIONS FOR CLASSROOM ACTIVITIES

- Assign each student one of the various diagnostic studies to research, write a report on, and present in class.

SUGGESTIONS FOR CLINICAL ACTIVITIES

- Assign the students to care for clients undergoing urinary diagnostic studies that they can research and possibly observe and/or discuss with personnel administering the studies.
- Assign students to the radiology department to observe diagnostic studies.
- Have students look at clients' blood and/or urine studies related to a urinary system problem and have the students identify abnormalities in the studies and discuss what these abnormalities mean to patient care.
- Have students perform client teaching for clients undergoing diagnostic studies.

 REFERENCES

- MedHelp: Uroflowmetry. Available at http://www.medhelp.org/medical-information/show/4528/Uroflowmetry
- MedlinePlus: Intravenous pyelogram. Available at http://www.nlm.nih.gov/medlineplus/ency/article/003782.htm

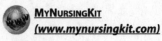 **MYNURSINGKIT**
(www.mynursingkit.com)

- Websites
- NCLEX® Questions
- Case Studies
- Key Terms

 STUDENT WORKBOOK AND RESOURCE GUIDE

- Chapter 28 activities
- *Separate purchase*

PRENTICE HALL NURSE'S DRUG GUIDE

- *Separate purchase*

CLASSROOM RESPONSE QUESTION POWERPOINTS

TESTBANK

CHAPTER 29
CARING FOR CLIENTS WITH RENAL AND URINARY TRACT DISORDERS

LEARNING OUTCOME 1

Describe the pathophysiology of common disorders of the kidneys and urinary tract.

Concepts for Lecture

1. Urinary continence requires a bladder that is able to expand and contract and sphincters that can maintain a higher pressure in the urethra than that in the bladder. When the pressure within the bladder is higher than urethral resistance, urine can escape.
2. Urinary incontinence has many causes and is not a normal part of the aging process.
3. Any condition that increases bladder pressures or reduces resistance within the urethra can cause incontinence. Pelvic muscle relaxation, impaired neural control, and bladder problems are common contributing factors.
4. Urinary incontinence (UI) is commonly categorized as stress incontinence, urge incontinence, overflow incontinence, reflex incontinence, and functional incontinence. A combination of stress and urge UI is common.
5. Urinary retention occurs when the bladder cannot empty and may be caused by obstruction to urine flow or by a functional problem.
6. Benign prostatic hypertrophy (BHP, or enlargement of the prostate) is one common cause of urinary retention.
7. Urinary tract infection is a common disorder due to a bacterial process. Women are more likely to experience a urinary tract infection (UTI) than men because women have a shorter straight urethra compared with a longer curved urethra in the male and because of the antibacterial effect of zinc in the prostatic fluid of men.
8. The proximity of the urinary meatus to the vagina and anus also contributes to more UTIs in females.
9. Cystitis is a lower urinary tract infection involving the bladder.
10. Pyelonephritis is an inflammatory disorder of the kidneys usually due to a bacterial process. *Escherichia coli* is responsible for most cases of acute pyelonephritis. The infection spreads from the renal pelvis to the cortex. The inflamed kidney becomes edematous. Local abscesses may form, and kidney tissue can be destroyed by the inflammatory process.
11. Glomerulonephritis is a disorder of the glomerulus that may be acute or chronic and may lead to renal failure.
12. Glomerulonephritis affects both the structure and function of the glomerulus. It damages the capillary membrane, allowing blood cells and proteins to escape from the vascular compartment into the filtrate. Loss of plasma proteins in the urine causes hypoalbuminemia, and edema develops. The decreasing glomerular filtration rate activates the renin–angiotensin–aldosterone system, leading to salt and water retention and hypertension.
13. Acute glomerulonephritis usually follows an infection with group A beta-hemolytic *Streptococcus*.
14. Nephrotic syndrome is a group of symptoms that result from damage to the glomerular membrane.

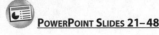
POWERPOINT SLIDES 21–48

Tables and/or Figures
- **Table 29-1** Types of Urinary Incontinence
- **Figure 29-2** Vesicoureteral Junction
- **Table 29-5** Causes of Acute Renal Failure
- **Box 29-6** Risk Factors for UTI
- **Figure 29-3** The Pathology of Glomerulonephritis
- **Figure 29-4** Pathophysiology Illustrated: Acute Glomerulonephritis
- **Figure 29-6** Potential Location of Stones Within the Urinary Tract
- **Box 29-15** Risk Factors for Cancer of the Urinary Tract

SUGGESTIONS FOR CLASSROOM ACTIVITIES

- Using case studies, have students describe the types of urinary incontinence. Students could also be assigned in groups to write a case study that involves one of the types of urinary incontinence.
- Have students find a journal article about the formation of urinary calculi and present their findings to the class.
- Assign students to research the causes of acute renal failure and present their findings to class.

SUGGESTIONS FOR CLINICAL ACTIVITIES

- Assign students to care for clients experiencing urinary incontinence. Have each student present his or her client and the type of incontinence and how it varies from other types.

REFERENCE

- Merck: Bacterial urinary tract infections. Available at http://www.merck.com/mmpe/sec17/ch231/ch231b.html

© 2011 Pearson Education, Inc.

15. Chronic glomerulonephritis usually is the result of kidney damage by a systemic disease such as diabetes. It can occur when no previous kidney disease or apparent cause can be identified. It is characterized by slow, progressive destruction of glomeruli and nephrons.

16. Urinary calculi are small stones that develop anywhere in the urinary system. They may cause blockage, pain, and hematuria.

17. Risk factors for kidney stones include personal or family history of urinary stones; dehydration; excess calcium, oxalate, or protein intake; gout; hyperparathyroidism; or urinary stasis.

18. Calculi are masses of crystals formed from materials normally excreted in the urine. Most are made of calcium.

19. Hydronephrosis is dilation of the renal pelvis and calyces. This dilation may damage the nephron.

20. Polycystic kidney disease is a hereditary disease characterized by cyst formation in the nephrons and kidney enlargement.

21. The kidneys are usually protected from trauma by the rib cage. Trauma to the kidneys may result in pain, hemorrhage, and possible shock due to the vascular nature of the kidney.

22. Both the bladder and the kidney may be affected by cancerous tumors. These tumors may lead to obstruction, renal failure, hemorrhage, and invasion of other surrounding tissues.

23. Bladder tumors begin as cell changes that develop into superficial or invasive lesions. Most are papillomas, with a polyp-like structure attached by a stalk to the bladder mucosa. When metastasis occurs, the pelvic lymph nodes, lungs, bones, and liver are most commonly involved. Kidney tumors can occur anywhere in the kidney and tend to invade the renal vein.

24. Acute renal failure is a rapid abrupt decline in renal function.

25. Acute renal failure may result from prerenal causes such as hypovolemia. Intrarenal causes include inflammation and vascular disorders such as hypertension. Acute tubular necrosis occurs from exposure to nephrotoxins.

26. Acute renal failure can last up to 1 year and is identified by various stages of renal decline.

27. Chronic renal failure is a slow process resulting in kidney destruction.

28. Chronic renal failure may go on for years prior to being recognized or the client having symptoms.

LEARNING OUTCOME 2

Compare and contrast the manifestations of common disorders of the kidneys and urinary tract.

Concepts for Lecture

1. Incontinence is categorized as stress, urge, overflow, reflex, and functional. Each has a different presentation, although all result in involuntary leakage of urine.

2. Urinary retention is the inability to empty the bladder completely. Assessment findings may include a firm, distended bladder that may be displaced. The client may complain of the sensation of needing to void or may not have any symptoms if the client is suffering from a neurologic cause.

3. Symptoms of urinary tract infection vary due to location. Cystitis may cause painful urination, urgency, and foul-smelling urine. Pyelonephritis may cause chills, fever, general malaise, and costovertebral tenderness.

4. Glomerulonephritis may cause few clinical symptoms, although edema may be seen. The client may exhibit urinary changes such as

 POWERPOINT SLIDES 49–65

Tables and/or Figures

- **Table 29-1** Types of Urinary Incontinence
- **Figure 29-3** The Pathophysiology of Glomerulonephritis
- **Figure 29-4** Pathophysiology Illustrated: Acute Glomerulonephritis
- **Figure 29-5** Severe Edema in a Client With Nephrotic Syndrome
- **Figure 29-10** A Polycystic Kidney and a Normal Kidney for Comparison
- **Figure 29-14** The Multisystem Effects of End-Stage Renal Disease and Uremia
- **Box 29-9** Manifestations of Acute Glomerulonephritis
- **Box 29-11** Manifestations of Urinary Stones
- **Box 29-13** Manifestations of Hydronephrosis
- **Box 29-15** Risk Factors for Cancer of the Urinary Tract
- **Box 29-18** Manifestations of End-Stage Renal Disease and Uremia

proteinuria and hematuria. There may be an increase in BUN and creatinine.

5. Acute glomerulonephritis may develop quickly in 10–14 days after initial injury or infection. Hypertension and edema may be seen.

6. Chronic glomerulonephritis may occur over time. Symptoms develop slowly and may not be recognized until renal failure is evident.

7. Urinary calculi may obstruct urine flow. This usually results in pain and hematuria and may cause symptoms of UTI such as pyelonephritis, depending on stone location.

8. Hydronephrosis may develop quickly and cause acute symptoms such as fever, colicky flank pain, hematuria, and nausea and vomiting. Hydronephrosis that develops over time may also cause hematuria and fever, but pain may be dull and intermittent.

9. Polycystic kidney disease occurs over time, and symptoms may not occur until the client is in his or her thirties or forties. Common symptoms usually include flank pain, hematuria, and proteinuria. Renal calculi may also develop, and most clients develop hypertension. The kidneys enlarge and may be palpable. Over time, signs of renal failure develop.

10. Kidney trauma may develop from a blunt or penetrating injury. Due to the vascular nature of the kidney, hemorrhage is common. Renal trauma may also include pain, hematuria, oliguria, or anuria.

11. Tumors of the urinary system cause symptoms based on their location. Bladder tumors may cause signs of obstruction or UTI.

12. Kidney tumors may disrupt urine formation, leading to proteinuria and hematuria. The client may exhibit flank pain and signs of pyelonephritis. The client may also exhibit fatigue, weight loss, and anemia.

13. Renal failure may be acute or chronic. Acute renal failure is manifested by oliguria. Acute renal failure involves three stages.

14. Chronic renal failure is a slow process and is often not identified until uremia develops. Clients may have early signs such as nausea, apathy, weakness, and fatigue. As the disease progresses, clients may experience vomiting, lethargy, and confusion. Uremic symptoms may develop and affect all systems.

LEARNING OUTCOME 3

Discuss the nursing implications of interdisciplinary care prescribed for clients with these disorders.

Concepts for Lecture

1. The focus of interdisciplinary care for urinary incontinence is to identify and correct the cause if possible. If the underlying problems cannot be corrected, techniques may be taught to manage urine output.

2. The nurse's role in interdisciplinary care for the client with urinary incontinence includes giving medications used to inhibit detrusor muscle contractions and increase bladder capacity. These may include tolterodine (Detrol) and oxybutynin (Ditropan). The nurse may need to do a postvoid residual volume. The nurse may need to teach pelvic floor (Kegel) exercises.

3. When working with a client who has urinary retention, the nurse may be administering cholinergic medications, which are useful in promoting bladder emptying. Common medications include bethanechol chloride (Urecholine). If bladder retention is due to an enlarged prostate, medications may be given to help decrease the size of the

SUGGESTIONS FOR CLASSROOM ACTIVITIES

• Using a game format, give students clinical manifestations and have them determine the origin of the problem(s).

SUGGESTIONS FOR CLINICAL ACTIVITIES

• Assign students to care for clients with urinary and kidney disorders. Working with the clients they are assigned to, have the students identify risk factors that their clients have for urinary and kidney disorders.
• Using laboratory studies, have students identify changes in urinary/kidney function.

REFERENCE

• National Kidney and Urologic Diseases Information Clearinghouse: Homepage. Available at http://kidney.niddk.nih.gov/

POWERPOINT SLIDES 66–81

Tables and/or Figures

• **Box 29-3** Client Teaching: Pelvic Floor (Kegel) Exercises
• **Table 29-2** Giving Medications Safely: UTI
• **Box 29-1** Nursing Care Checklist: Postvoid Residual Volume
• **Box 29-5** Nursing Care Checklist: Urinary Catheterization

Nursing Care Plan: Client With Acute Glomerulonephritis

prostate and maintain urine flow. Common medications include tamsulosin and finasteride.

4. The nurse working with a client who has urinary retention due to a neurogenic bladder may employ, or teach the client to employ, techniques to stimulate reflex voiding and promote complete bladder emptying. The nurse may also use the Credé method or have the client use the Valsalva maneuver to promote bladder emptying.

5. In caring for a client with a urinary tract infection (UTI), the nurse may be administering antibiotics that are effective against gram-negative bacilli. An uncomplicated UTI is treated with a 3–7 to 10-day course of medications such as sulfonamides, trimethoprim–sulfamethoxazole (TMP-SMZ, Bactrim, Septra), nitrofurantoin (Macrobid), and fluoroquinolones (ciprofloxacin, Cipro). Treatment is often started before urine cultures are obtained.

6. The nurse, working with a client with a UTI, may need to obtain urine specimens from a client with an indwelling urinary catheter by briefly (15 minutes or less) clamping the proximal drainage tubing and then withdrawing urine directly from the port using sterile technique.

7. Care of the client with acute or chronic glomerulonephritis focuses on identifying and treating the underlying disease process and preserving kidney function. In most cases, there are no specific medications available for treating glomerulonephritis.

8. It is important that nurses and nursing students recognize the side effects of steroids on other body systems. Penicillin or other antibiotics may be used in clients with poststreptococcal glomerulonephritis to kill any remaining bacteria. The nurse working with clients who have acute or chronic glomerulonephritis may be giving prescribed antihypertensives and diuretics to lower blood pressure and reduce edema.

9. The nurse may be working with the client who has acute or chronic glomerulonephritis to restrict sodium intake and increase dietary proteins if they are being lost in the urine. However, if azotemia is present, dietary protein is restricted. When proteins are restricted, those included should be complete proteins such as meat, fish, eggs, soy, or poultry because these supply all the essential amino acids for growth and tissue maintenance.

10. The nurse administering medications to clients with renal calculi will find that medications prescribed for these clients are mainly for pain relief. Narcotic analgesics prescribed are mainly for pain relief. Narcotic analgesics provide analgesia and relieve urethral spasms. Often analgesics are administered intravenously for rapid pain relief. Respiratory rate and depth and level of consciousness are important assessment parameters when administering IV narcotics.

11. When working with clients who have polycystic kidney disease, the nurse may be administering medications given to control symptoms associated with the disease (e.g., ACE inhibitors and other antihypertensive agents). The nurse will teach about polycystic kidney disease and how to maintain good kidney function. The nurse will instruct the client to drink about 2,500 mL of fluid per day and maintain good hygiene measures.

12. When working with clients who have tumors of the kidney or bladder, the tumors may be malignant and need chemotherapeutic agents to treat the tumor. Some agents may be instilled in the bladder for local action. Other medications the nurse may administer or do teaching about include BCG Live, which causes a local inflammatory action to reduce superficial tumors.

13. During acute renal failure, all nephrotoxic medications are avoided or used with great caution. All drug dosages need to be adjusted due to

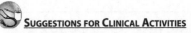

SUGGESTIONS FOR CLASSROOM ACTIVITIES

- Assign students to work in small groups. Give each group of students the names of various medications used to target symptoms of urinary and renal disorders. Have the students discuss the major side effects of the medications.
- Invite a nurse who works in hemodialysis to talk to the students about the effect of various medications during hemodialysis. Ask the nurse to talk about any medication that should be withheld during hemodialysis.

SUGGESTIONS FOR CLINICAL ACTIVITIES

- Using assigned clients with urinary and renal disorders, have the students identify potential nephrotoxic medications.
- Have students discuss medications their clients are taking and determine their use in urinary and kidney disorders.
- Identify common side effects of medications that clients may be taking for urinary or kidney disease.
- Assign students to observe in a renal dialysis unit or go with a nurse working with home hemodialysis clients. Ask the students to pay attention to medications withheld prior to hemodialysis and medications, if any, given during hemodialysis.

slowed excretion and prolonged half-life. The same is true with chronic renal failure.

14. Often in chronic renal failure, diuretics such as furosemide (Lasix) are used to reduce fluid volume. The nurse will weigh the client daily and measure intake and output each shift to assist in monitoring fluid status. The physician may order other antihypertensive agents, particularly ACE inhibitors, to lower blood pressure.

15. The nurse needs to know the type of dialysis the client with chronic renal failure is having. Many medications are excreted during the dialysis treatment, and their doses need to be adjusted when the client is receiving dialysis.

LEARNING OUTCOME 4

Provide appropriate nursing care for the client having surgery of the kidneys or urinary tract.

Concepts for Lecture

1. Urinary incontinence is commonly not treated with surgery. If the incontinence is due to a cystocele or urethrocele or is due to an enlarged prostate gland, surgery may be performed. A bladder neck suspension is used to treat urethrocele. If urinary incontinence or retention is due to an enlarged prostate, a prostatectomy may be performed.

2. Nursing care of a client having bladder neck suspension includes routine preoperative care and teaching and providing instruction to avoid straining and the Valsalva maneuver postoperatively. The nurse provides routine postoperative care, frequently assesses vaginal drainage and dressing, and notifies the charge nurse or physician of bright red bleeding on dressing or from the vagina or in the urine. The nurse monitors and records quantity, color, and clarity of urine and tapes urinary catheters in position. Activity and ambulation are encouraged. Urine output is monitored following catheter removal. If a urethral or suprapubic catheter is in place at discharge, the nurse teaches appropriate care. The importance of keeping scheduled appointments and contacting the physician if signs of a urinary tract infection or other complication develop is stressed.

3. The client with glomerulonephritis may undergo a kidney biopsy to determine the extent of kidney damage and to identify any causative factors. The client will need to sign informed consent and will need adequate teaching and NPO status 8 hours prior to the procedure.

4. Following a renal biopsy, close assessment of the site for bleeding is important for the first 24 hours. Frequent vital signs and assessment of hemoglobin and hematocrit are important. Urine output is monitored, and initial hematuria is common. The nurse positions the client in a supine position to maintain pressure on the biopsy site. Manifestations the nurse needs to report to the charge nurse or physician include flank or back pain, shoulder pain, pallor, light-headedness, abdominal pain, guarding, and decreased bowel sounds.

5. Client and family teaching for a renal biopsy includes describing what the procedure will involve, advising the client to avoid coughing for 24 hours after the procedure, avoiding strenuous activity for about 2 weeks, and what symptoms to report.

6. Urinary calculi may require surgical intervention if the stones are too large to pass spontaneously. Lithotripsy, which is the crushing of renal calculi with sound or shock waves, is commonly used. For the client undergoing lithotripsy, adequate preprocedure teaching is needed.

 **POWERPOINT SLIDES 82–84**

Tables and/or Figures

- **Table 29-4** Bladder Cancer Surgeries
- **Box 29-2** Nursing Care Checklist: Bladder Neck Suspension
- **Box 29-10** Nursing Care Checklist: Kidney Biopsy
- **Box 29-12** Nursing Care Checklist: Lithotripsy
- **Box 29-14** Nursing Care Checklist: Ureteral Stent
- **Box 29-16** Nursing Care Checklist: Cystectomy and Urinary Diversion
- **Box 29-17** Nursing Care Checklist: Nephrectomy
- **Box 29-21** Nursing Care Checklist: Kidney Transplant

SUGGESTIONS FOR CLASSROOM ACTIVITIES

- Divide the students into small groups. Have each group develop a teaching plan for a client undergoing various surgical procedures. Have each group present to the class.
- Invite a urologist who does surgical procedures to talk to the class about the variety of surgical procedures for disorders of the renal and urinary system.

SUGGESTIONS FOR CLINICAL ACTIVITIES

- Make arrangements for students to observe surgical procedures for disorders of the renal and urinary system.
- Assign students to access a postoperative client who has had a surgical procedure for problems of the renal and urinary system.
- Assign students to care for clients undergoing surgical procedures of the urinary system.

Following the procedure, frequent vital sign monitoring is needed. The urine output is monitored for amount, color, and clarity.

7. Hydronephrosis may develop from renal calculi. To assist in keeping the ureters open, a ureteral stent may be placed. These stents may be temporary or permanent and are placed during cystoscopy or during a surgical incision. When caring for a client with a ureteral stent, the nurse labels all drainage tubes and stents for easy identification and secures positions, attaches each catheter and stent to a separate closed drainage system, monitors for infection or bleeding, and encourages fluids (especially those that acidify urine). If the stent is indwelling, the nurse teaches follow-up care and prevention of complications.

8. Cystoscopy is used to visualize and possibly remove calculi from the urinary bladder and distal ureters.

9. Kidney trauma may necessitate surgical intervention to stop bleeding and/or remove a damaged kidney. Ensuring the client is hemodynamically stable postoperatively is essential. Adequate monitoring of vital signs, hemoglobin and hematocrit, and intake and output is essential to ensure adequate circulation and prevent complications. As with other surgical procedures, the surgical site is monitored for bleeding and drainage.

10. A cystoscopy is done to visualize and biopsy a bladder lesion. Tumor of the kidney and urinary tract may necessitate surgical intervention. Surgical procedures may range from simple resection of the tumor to removal of the bladder and surrounding structures.

11. Radical nephrectomy (removal of affected kidney and surrounding tissue) is done when cancer affects the kidney. Nursing care of the client having a nephrectomy includes routine pre- and postoperative care. The nurse also assesses urine output hourly for the first 24 hours; labels and secures all catheters, stents, and nephrostomy tubes or drains; irrigates only as ordered by the physician; and supports the grieving process and adjustment to the loss of a kidney.

12. The client with chronic renal failure will need a dialysis access. This involves the creation of an arteriovenous fistula. Preoperative teaching is similar to other surgical procedures. Postoperatively, assessment of vital signs, laboratory studies, and patency of the graph is essential. The graph is assessed for a palpable bruit or thrill and an audible bruit to assure functioning.

LEARNING OUTCOME 5

Use the nursing process as a framework for providing individualized care to clients with disorders of the kidneys or urinary tract.

Concepts for Lecture

1. Applying the nursing process to clients with disorders of the kidneys or urinary tract is similar for many of the disorders.
2. Client-centered goals assist in providing direction for care to clients with kidney and urinary disorders. Goals may be short term or long term depending on the disease process. Goals assist in planning nursing care.
3. Many nursing interventions are common for clients with kidney and urinary disorders. Interventions are numerous and expand to include all systems.
4. Evaluation of the client's progress in meeting goals includes ensuring the client remains free of discomfort and that the client exhibits

PowerPoint Slides 85–95

Nursing Care Plan: Client With Bladder Cancer

SUGGESTIONS FOR CLASSROOM ACTIVITIES

- Using a case study approach, have students develop a plan of care and a teaching plan for a client with a renal or urinary disorder.
- Give students various containers of liquids (e.g., carton of milk, glass of water, popsicle, etc.) that a case study would have consumed on an 8-hour shift and have them determine the amount of intake in millimeters, and then have the students chart the intake.
- Give students the fluid restriction orders for theoretical clients and have the students figure out what amounts of liquids the clients can have at each meal and in between meals.
- Have students develop goals for clients with urinary disorders.

normal vital signs, stable weight, and normal laboratory studies for the client and his or her disease process. The client being free of signs of infection is also part of the evaluation process.

GENERAL CHAPTER CONSIDERATIONS

1. Have students study and learn key terms listed at the beginning of the chapter.
2. Have students complete end of chapter exercises either in their book or on the MyNursingKit Website.
3. Use the Classroom Response Question PowerPoints to assess students prior to lecture.

 SUGGESTIONS FOR CLINICAL ACTIVITIES

- Have students care for clients with kidney and urinary disorders and develop a plan of care for assigned clients.
- Allow students to access clients with arteriovenous fistulas in the clinical setting.
- If feasible, have students observe hemodialysis.
- Have students participate in client/family teaching for clients with renal disorders.
- Have students participate in intake and output and fluid restrictions.
- Assign students to clients who need daily weights. Have students assess fluid status based on weight changes.

- Clinical Reasoning Care Map

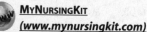 **MYNURSINGKIT**
(www.mynursingkit.com)

- Websites
- NCLEX® Questions
- Case Studies
- Key Terms

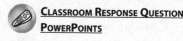 **STUDENT WORKBOOK AND RESOURCE GUIDE**

- Chapter 29 activities
- *Separate purchase*

PRENTICE HALL NURSE'S DRUG GUIDE

- *Separate purchase*

 CLASSROOM RESPONSE QUESTION POWERPOINTS

TESTBANK

CHAPTER 30
THE REPRODUCTIVE SYSTEM AND ASSESSMENT

LEARNING OUTCOME 1

Identify the major structures and functions of the male reproductive system.

Concepts for Lecture

1. The structures of the male reproductive system include the paired testes, scrotum, ducts, glands, and penis.
2. The testes produce sperm and testosterone, with sperm produced in the seminiferous tubules of the testes and Leydig's cells within the testes producing testosterone.
3. The process of spermatogenesis (sperm production) begins with puberty and continues throughout a man's life.
4. Testosterone, the primary male sex hormone, is essential to develop male secondary sex characteristics and to develop and maintain sexual function. It promotes metabolism, muscle and bone growth, and libido.
5. Sperm mature and are stored in the epididymis, a long coiled tube that lies over the outer surface of each testis. When a man is sexually excited, the epididymis contracts to push the sperm through the vas deferens to mix with seminal fluid.
6. Seminal fluid nourishes the sperm, provides volume to the semen, and increases its alkalinity. An alkaline pH is essential to mobilize the sperm and ensure fertilization of the ovum.
7. The prostate gland, about the size of a walnut, encircles the urethra just below the urinary bladder.
8. Secretions of the prostate gland make up approximately one-third of the volume of the semen. These secretions enter the urethra through several ducts during ejaculation. It is the contraction of the muscular prostate that causes the semen to be ejaculated.
9. The penis is composed of a shaft and a tip called the glans, which is covered by the foreskin (or prepuce). The shaft contains three columns of erectile tissue, with the two lateral columns called the corpora cavernosa and the central mass called the corpus spongiosum.
10. Erection of the penis occurs when a reflex triggers the parasympathetic nervous system to stimulate arteriolar vasodilation, filling erectile tissue with blood. The erection reflex may be initiated by touch, pressure, sights, sounds, smells, or thoughts of a sexual encounter. After ejaculation, the arterioles constrict, and the penis becomes flaccid.

LEARNING OUTCOME 2

Identify the major structures and functions of the female reproductive system.

Concepts for Lecture

1. The female reproductive system includes the paired ovaries and fallopian tubes, uterus, vagina, external genitalia, and breasts.
2. The ovaries produce estrogens, progesterone, and androgens in a cyclic pattern and store immature ova called oocytes.

 **POWERPOINT SLIDES 21–22**

Tables and/or Figures
- **Figure 30-1** The Male Reproductive System

 **SUGGESTIONS FOR CLASSROOM ACTIVITIES**

- Have students work individually or in groups to complete a project that creatively teaches the structure and function of the male reproductive system. Projects could be posters, comic book characters telling the story, a PowerPoint presentation, or other type of project.

SUGGESTIONS FOR CLINICAL ACTIVITIES

- Assign students to care for clients with disorders of the male reproductive system. Have students assess the client's knowledge of structure and function of the male reproductive system and to do teaching to supplement the client's knowledge as appropriate.

REFERENCE

- MedlinePlus: Aging changes in the male reproductive system. Available at http://www.nlm.nih.gov/medlineplus/ency/article/004017.htm

 POWERPOINT SLIDES 23–28

Tables and/or Figures
- **Figure 30-2** The Internal Organs of the Female Reproductive System
- **Figure 30-3** (A) Changes in Ovarian Follicles During the 28-Day Ovarian Cycle; (B) Corresponding Changes in the Endometrium During the Menstrual Cycle
- **Figure 30-4** The Female External Genitalia
- **Figure 30-5** Structure of the Female Breast

3. Estrogens are steroid hormones essential to development and maintenance of female secondary sex characteristic. Estrogens along with other hormones help prepare the female reproductive organs for growth of a fetus. They also help maintain skin, bone, and blood vessel structure; affect serum cholesterol and high-density lipoprotein levels; enhance blood clotting; and affect sodium and water balance.

4. Progesterone primarily affects breast glandular tissue and the endometrium. During pregnancy, progesterone relaxes smooth muscle to decrease uterine contractions

5. The ovarian cycle has three phases lasting about 28 days: the follicular phase (days 1–10), the ovulatory phase (days 11–14), and the luteal phase (days 14–28).

6. Each ovary contains many small structures called ovarian follicles. Each follicle contains an immature ovum, called an oocyte. Each month, several follicles mature, stimulated by follicle-stimulating hormone (FSH) and luteinizing hormone (LH). The mature follicles (graafian follicles) produce estrogen, which stimulates development of the endometrium. When the estrogen level is high enough to stimulate the anterior pituitary gland, a surge of LH is produced, which stimulates development of the oocyte into a mature ovum and causes the ovarian follicle to rupture, releasing the ovum. The ruptured follicle becomes a corpus luteum, which produces estrogen and progesterone to support the endometrium until conception occurs or the cycle begins again.

7. The fallopian tubes are thin tubes about 4 inches long and 1 cm in diameter. They are attached to the uterus on one end and open on the distal end with projections called fimbriae that drape over the ovary. The fimbriae pick up the ovum after it is released from the ovary.

8. The fallopian tubes are made of smooth muscle and lined with cilia. Movement of the cilia and smooth muscle contractions move the ovum through the tubes toward the uterus. Fertilization of the ovum by sperm usually occurs in the outer portion of one of the fallopian tubes.

9. The uterus is a thick-walled, pear-shaped muscular organ located between the bladder and rectum. Its function is to receive the fertilized ovum and provide a site for growth and development of the fetus.

10. The uterus has three parts: the fundus, the body, and the cervix. The uterus is a firm structure that softens during pregnancy.

11. The cervix projects into the vagina. The uterine opening of the cervix is called the internal os, and the vaginal opening is called the external os. The endocervical canal between the openings allows discharge of menstrual fluid and entrance of sperm.

12. The vagina is a fibromuscular tube about 3–4 inches long located between the bladder and urethra and the rectum. The upper end contains the cervix in an area called the fornix. The mucous membrane walls of the vagina form folds, called rugae. It has an acid pH that is maintained by estrogen and normal vaginal flora.

13. The vagina is the birth canal, allows excretion of menstrual fluid, and is an organ of sexual response.

14. The external genitalia include the mons pubis, the labia, the clitoris, the vagina, urethral openings, and glands.

15. The labiae are divided into two structures: the labia majora and the labia minora. The labia minora contain some erectile tissue.

16. The area between the labiae is called the vestibule, which contains the openings of the vagina and urethra, as well as Bartholin's glands, which secrete lubricating fluid during sexual stimulation. Skene's glands open onto the vestibule on each side of the urethra and produce fluid to moisten the vestibule.

17. The clitoris is an erectile organ, similar to the penis in the male. It is highly sensitive and distends with blood during sexual arousal.

SUGGESTIONS FOR CLASSROOM ACTIVITIES

- Have students work individually or in groups to complete a project that creatively teaches the structure and function of the female reproductive system. Projects could be posters, comic book characters telling the story, a PowerPoint presentation, or other type of project.

SUGGESTIONS FOR CLINICAL ACTIVITIES

- Assign students to care for clients with disorders of the female reproductive system. Have students assess the client's knowledge of structure and function of the female reproductive system and to do teaching to supplement the client's knowledge as appropriate.

REFERENCE

- MedicineNet: Your guide to the female reproductive system. Available at http://www.medicinenet.com/female_reproductive_system/article.htm

18. The vaginal opening, called the introitus, is surrounded by a connective tissue membrane called the hymen.
19. The breasts (or mammary glands) are supported by the pectoral muscles and are richly supplied with nerves, blood, and lymph. The primary purpose of the breasts is to supply nourishment for the infant.

LEARNING OUTCOME 3

Describe normal age-related changes in male and female reproductive system structure and function.

Concepts for Lecture

1. With aging, the secretion of androgens, estrogens, and gonadotropic hormones declines.
2. Reduced hormone levels lead to changes in secondary sex characteristics of both men and women.
3. In women, lower estrogen levels lead to atrophy of the ovaries, uterus, and vaginal tissues. Subcutaneous fat is lost from perineal tissues, and pelvic floor muscles weaken, increasing the risk for stress incontinence. Vaginal secretions diminish and become more alkaline. The breasts and nipples decrease in size. Fibrosis and calcification may develop in the ducts of the breasts.
4. The sperm count of older men is reduced, and the testes become firmer. The size of the penis may diminish, but the ability to achieve erection is maintained. The prostate enlarges in older men and may interfere with urinary elimination.

LEARNING OUTCOME 4

Collect subjective and objective assessment data related to the reproductive system.

Concepts for Lecture

1. Assessment of the reproductive system includes both subjective and objective data that can be obtained through a health history, physical examination, and diagnostic tests.
2. Assessment of reproductive function often is left until the latter part of an interview and examination to allow development of trust and comfort between the client and the nurse.
3. In conducting a health history, it is important to use familiar terms, to ask questions in a nonthreatening manner, and to avoid judging the client's responses moving from more general questions to problems such as sexually transmitted infections or difficulty maintaining an erection.
4. It is advisable to first ask about the presenting problem. Identify its onset, manifestations, and effect on ADL (e.g., difficulty urinating or dribbling or excessive menstrual flow). Ask about possible contributing factors and associated symptoms (e.g., fever or pain).
5. Because the urinary and reproductive systems are so closely linked in men, ask about problems with the urinary system.
6. Ask males about any urethral discharge or any rash or sores on the penis.
7. In women, ask about color, amount, and character of vaginal bleeding and its relationship to the menstrual cycle as well as inquiring about any vaginal discharge, including onset, color, character, odor, and any itching or rashes.

 POWERPOINT SLIDES 29–32

SUGGESTIONS FOR CLASSROOM ACTIVITIES

- Assign students to find journal articles related to normal age-related changes in male and female reproductive system structure and function (e.g., female incontinence and treatments for female incontinence due to changes as a result of aging; enlarged prostate and treatments for this condition). Ask students to bring the articles to class and to talk briefly about the contents.
- Ask a gynecologist to speak to the class about normal age-related changes in male and female reproductive system structure and functioning and any treatments that might be helpful for any of these conditions.

SUGGESTIONS FOR CLINICAL ACTIVITIES

- Assign students to care for clients with prostate enlargement and clients with urinary stress incontinence. Ask students to share their plan of care in postconference.

REFERENCE

- MedlinePlus: Aging changes in the male reproductive system. Available at http://www.nlm.nih.gov/medlineplus/ency/article/004017.htm

 **POWERPOINT SLIDES 33–36**

Tables and/or Figures

- **Figure 30-6** Palpating the Male Inguinal Area for Bulges
- **Figure 32-9** Teaching Breast Self-Examination
- **Box 30-1** Documenting Assessment of the Reproductive System

8. Obtain a history of any chronic diseases such as diabetes, heart disease, multiple sclerosis, or spinal cord problems.

9. Ask about a family history of cancer and any possible intrauterine exposure to diethylstilbestrol because it is linked to urinary tract deformity and sterility in men and cervical and vaginal cancer in women.

10. Determine what medications the client is taking.

11. Ask about physical or psychosocial stressors that may contribute to sexual problems.

12. The nurse will explore the client's lifestyle, specifically asking about use of alcohol, cigarettes, or street drugs.

13. Inquire about sexual history and history of specific sexual problems or sexual trauma, use of erectile-enhancing drugs or contraceptives, and current sexual satisfaction.

14. The physical examination of the male includes inspection and palpation of the breasts, including the areola and nipple; inspection and palpation (using a gloved hand) of the inguinal area and groin for bulges; and inspection of the penis, retracting the foreskin in the uncircumcised client and inspecting the urinary meatus looking for skin irritation, sores, or drainage from the meatus.

15. After replacing the foreskin, the nurse inspects the skin around the base of the penis and palpates the shaft of the penis and also inspects the scrotum, palpating each of the testes and epididymis.

16. The physical examination of the female includes inspecting both breasts with the client seated. Inspection begins with the arms at the sides, then overhead, followed by the hands pressed on hips, and then learning forward. The nurse observes size, symmetry, contour, skin color, texture, venous patterns, and any lesions.

17. With the client supine and a small pillow under the shoulder and an arm over head, the nurse palpates each breast, axilla, and supraclavicular area, palpating all areas of the breast including the axillary tail.

18. The nipples are palpated and compressed between the thumb and index finger noting any discharge and its color and consistency.

19. The nurse places the client in lithotomy position and, wearing gloves, inspects and palpates the labia majora for excoriation, rashes, lesions, or bulging. The nurse separates the labia minora and inspects and palpates it. The nurse inspects the clitoris, vaginal opening, and perineum and asks the client to strain or "bear down," looking for bulging of the vagina wall, protrusion of the cervix or uterus, or urinary incontinence.

LEARNING OUTCOME 5

Provide appropriate nursing care for clients undergoing diagnostic tests related to the reproductive system.

Concepts for Lecture

1. A variety of diagnostic tests may be used to identify disorders affecting the reproductive system, including diagnostic examinations, laboratory testing, imaging studies, and special procedures.

2. Pre-exam nursing responsibilities in caring for the client having a pelvic examination include: obtaining equipment, having the client empty the bladder, obtaining a clean-catch urine specimen if indicated, explaining the procedure, answering any questions, remaining in the room if the physician is male, asking the client to remove all clothing and put on a gown, and providing a sheet for draping.

3. During a pelvic examination, the nurse will place the client in lithotomy position with knees flexed and separated; position the light

POWERPOINT SLIDES 37–38

Tables and/or Figures

- **Table 30-1** Diagnostic Laboratory Tests
- **Table 30-2** Diagnostic Ultrasound Studies
- **Box 30-2** Nursing Care Checklist: Pelvic Examination
- **Box 30-3** Nursing Care Checklist: Laparoscopy

SUGGESTIONS FOR CLASSROOM ACTIVITIES

- Have students review nursing care for clients having diagnostic tests related to the reproductive system in preparation for caring for clients experiencing disorders of the male or female reproductive system.

source to illuminate the pelvic area; assist the physician, nurse practitioner, or other caregiver as needed; and provide continuing support for the client.

4. After the pelvic examination, the nurse will provide tissues and towelettes for cleaning lubricant from the perineal area; provide a minipad to protect garments; allow privacy while the client dresses; prepare requisitions and slides for laboratory testing as indicated; provide information about when to expect test results and follow-up appointments; and answer any further questions.

5. Laboratory tests related to the reproductive system include progesterone and serum estradiol. The nursing care involves noting sex, age, and day of last menstrual period or trimester of pregnancy on the lab requisition and scheduling tests before or at least 7 days after nuclear medicine scans.

6. Follicle-stimulating hormone (FSH), luteinizing hormone (LH), and serum testosterone are tests related to the reproductive system.

7. A Papanicolaou (Pap) smear requires scheduling when the client is not menstruating and instructing the client to avoid sexual intercourse, douching, or vaginal medications for 48 hours prior to the exam. The nurse asks the client to void before the exam.

8. The nurse will schedule testing of the tumor marker human chorionic gonadotropin (hCG) either before or at least 7 days after a nuclear scan because radioisotopes interfere with results. The nurse will note on the requisition the age, sex, and date of last menstrual period.

9. When the client is scheduled for a prostate-specific antigen (PSA) test, the nurse schedules the test before or at least 2 weeks after any manipulation of the prostate (DRE, biopsy, etc.). The nurse instructs the client to not eat for 8 hours prior to the exam.

10. For clients being tested for cancer antigen 125 (CA 125), the nurse schedules the test before or at least 7 days after any nuclear scans.

11. For any syphilis serology, the nurse instructs the client to avoid alcohol intake for 14 hours prior to the test and to avoid food intake for 8 hours before the test. The client is also instructed to abstain from sexual contact until the test results are known. Positive results are reported to the state health department. If the test is positive, the nurse instructs the client to refrain from sexual contact until effectively treated and to notify all sexual partners of the test results.

12. For genital culture, the nurse instructs men to avoid urinating for at least an hour prior to the test to reduce the number of organisms present. Women are instructed to avoid douching for 25 hours prior to the exam. The specimen is to be obtained before antibiotic therapy is started.

13. A number of ultrasonography examinations may be used to detect reproductive system problems. Breast ultrasound and abdominal ultrasound require no special preparation.

14. The nurse will instruct the client having pelvic ultrasound to increase fluids and not void before the procedure to ensure a full bladder.

15. For males having transrectal ultrasonography, the nurse instructs the clients to use a disposable phosphate enema the evening or early morning before the procedure and have the client void before the procedure.

16. Several endoscopy procedures are used to evaluate the reproductive system. Abdominal laparoscopy is done using local anesthesia and conscious sedation, and it may be combined with laparoscopic ultrasound.

17. In men, cystoscopy may be used to evaluate the size of the prostate gland and obtain tissue for biopsy.

18. Colposcopy is used to examine tissue of the vagina and cervix using a brightly lighted microscope. It can identify early premalignant changes in cervical tissue and is performed when Pap test results are abnormal. This test is often done with an endocervical curettage to obtain cell samples for biopsy.

SUGGESTIONS FOR CLINICAL ACTIVITIES

- Assign students to care for clients experiencing disorders of the male or female reproductive system and, when possible, to provide instructions to these clients prior to diagnostic tests related to the reproductive system and to accompany clients during the tests and provide care during and after the tests as appropriate.

REFERENCE

- About.com: What is a colposcopy? Available at http://womenshealth.about.com/cs/cevicalconditions/a/colposcopy.htm

19. Colposcopy should be scheduled between days 8 and 12 of the client's menstrual cycle. The nurse provides psychologic support during the procedure and instructs the client to refrain from sexual intercourse or insertion of anything into the vagina until the cervix is healed, which takes approximately 7–10 days.

GENERAL CHAPTER CONSIDERATIONS

1. Have students study and learn key terms listed at the beginning of the chapter.
2. Have students complete end of chapter exercises either in their book or on the MyNursingKit Website.
3. Use the Classroom Response Question PowerPoints to assess students prior to lecture.

MYNURSINGKIT
(www.mynursingkit.com)

- Websites
- NCLEX® Questions
- Case Studies
- Key Terms

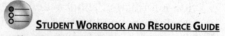

STUDENT WORKBOOK AND RESOURCE GUIDE

- Chapter 30 activities
- *Separate purchase*

PRENTICE HALL NURSE'S DRUG GUIDE

- *Separate purchase*

CLASSROOM RESPONSE QUESTION POWERPOINTS

TESTBANK

CHAPTER 31
CARING FOR MALE CLIENTS WITH REPRODUCTIVE SYSTEM DISORDERS

LEARNING OUTCOME 1

Describe the pathophysiology and manifestations of common disorders of the male reproductive system.

Concepts for Lecture

1. Benign prostatic hyperplasia (BPH) develops in men with testes. Testosterone, the primary androgen produced mainly in the testes, is converted to dihydrotestosterone (DHT) in the prostate gland. DHT stimulates growth of the prostate. Testosterone levels decrease with aging, but estrogen levels increase. Estrogen appears to make the prostate more responsive to DHT, promoting its growth. Increases in estrogen levels in relation to testosterone levels may contribute to BPH.

2. BPH develops as small nodules that form and grow in the central and transition zones of the prostate, next to the urethra. The expanding prostate compresses surrounding tissue, narrowing the urethra.

3. Symptoms of BPH include weak urinary stream, difficulty initiating urine flow, dribbling, and urinary retention. Nocturia is an early symptom.

4. If BPH is not treated, increased pressure in the bladder causes urine reflux (backflow) into the ureters. This can eventually lead to hydronephrosis, which can affect kidney function.

5. Prostate cancer is usually an adenocarcinoma, arising from glandular epithelial cells. It usually begins in the peripheral, posterior tissue of the gland. As the tumor grows larger, it may compress the urethra, obstructing urine flow. The tumor may spread locally to involve the seminal vesicles or bladder. The pelvic lymph nodes are most frequently involved in metastasis. The tumor may spread to distal areas.

6. In the early stages, prostate cancer usually causes no symptoms. Manifestations of prostate cancer include dysuria, hesitancy, reduced urinary stream, nocturia, hematuria, erectile dysfunction, hard enlarged prostate on DRE, bone or joint pain, back pain, lower extremity weakness, bladder or bowel dysfunction, weight loss, anemia, and fatigue.

7. Acute bacterial prostatitis is often associated with lower urinary tract infections. The infecting organism is usually *Escherichia coli*, but other pathogens may also invade the prostate. Infected urine may reflux into the prostatic ducts, or organisms may ascend the urinary tract. There is evidence that contamination of the urinary meatus during vaginal or anal sexual intercourse may play a role in ascending infections.

8. Nonbacterial prostatitis may be caused by organisms such as chlamydiae, mycoplasmas, and viruses, but its exact cause is unknown. Nonbacterial prostatitis may be a type of sexually transmitted disease or an autoimmune disorder.

9. Manifestations of prostatitis include burning on urination; frequency; urgency; chills; fever; low back, perineal, or genital pain; pain after ejaculation; and obstructed urine flow.

10. Cryptorchidism is the failure of one or both testes to descend through the inguinal ring into the scrotum. In most cases, the testes descend without intervention in the first year of life. Cryptorchidism is primarily a childhood problem, although on rare occasion, it is missed and discovered later in adolescent or adult life. If the disorder continues

POWERPOINT SLIDES 21–49

Tables and/or Figures
- **Figure 31-1** Benign Prostatic Hyperplasia (BPH)
- **Box 31-1** Manifestations of Benign Prostatic Hyperplasia
- **Box 31-5** Manifestations of Prostate Cancer
- **Box 31-7** Manifestations of Prostatitis
- **Box 31-9** Risk Factors for Priapism
- **Figure 31-4** Common Scrotal Masses

SUGGESTIONS FOR CLASSROOM ACTIVITIES

- Have students work in pairs or small groups to identify questions they would ask to determine what manifestations a client with BPH has experienced or is still experiencing. Ask students to think about how they would word the questions and what communication techniques they would use to get the desired information.
- Divide students into small groups and ask each group to design and do a role play involving a nurse and a client with one of the male reproductive disorders. The nurse is to elicit the symptoms the client has with the disorder.

SUGGESTIONS FOR CLINICAL ACTIVITIES

- Assign the students to care for male clients with BPH and determine what manifestation they have experienced or are still experiencing.

REFERENCES

- Johns Hopkins Medicine: BPH symptoms. Available at http://www .johnshopkinshealthalerts.com/alerts_index/ prostate_disorders/991-1.html
- Mayo Clinic: Prostate gland enlargement. Available at http://www.mayoclinic.com/ health/prostate-gland-enlargement/DS00027

into adolescence and adulthood, there is an increased risk for testicular cancer and problems of fertility.

11. Epididymitis is inflammation of the epididymis. It is usually caused by an infection spread from the bladder, urethra, prostate gland, or seminal vesicles. In younger men, the cause is often a sexually transmitted organism such as *Chlamydia trachomatis* or *Neisseria gonorrhoeae*. In older men, epididymitis usually is associated with a urinary tract infection or prostatitis.

12. Early manifestations of epididymitis include pain and local swelling; the scrotum may swell to the extent that it interferes with walking. Fever and general malaise may develop. Sterility is a potential complication of epididymitis.

13. Orchitis is inflammation of the testicle. It is commonly caused by an infection from other parts of the genitourinary track. Other causes include the mumps virus being excreted in the urine, especially in adult men, and trauma including vasectomy and other scrotal surgeries.

14. Manifestations of orchitis include severe testicular pain and swelling. Possible complications include hydrocele and abscess, which can lead to infertility or impotence.

15. Infertility is the inability to conceive a child during a year or more of unprotected intercourse. When the sperm count drops below 20 million/mL, the client is likely to be infertile. Male infertility usually results from a testicular disorder, such as cryptorchidism or orchitis. Less often, it may be caused by a systemic disease, hormonal disorder, or obstructed outflow of sperm from the testes. In many cases, no specific cause can be found for the infertility.

16. A hydrocele is a collection of fluid in the sac that encloses the testes. The cause is not always identifiable, but it may follow epididymitis, orchitis, injury, or a tumor.

17. Scrotal enlargement may be the only manifestation of hydrocele, although it may cause pain or a tight sensation in the scrotum.

18. A spermatocele is a mobile, usually painless mass in the epididymis that contains dead sperm cells. The cause is thought to be leakage of sperm due to trauma or infection.

19. A varicocele is an abnormal dilation of the spermatic veins above the testis. It is caused by incompetent or absent valves in the veins and almost always occurs on the left side. The dilated veins form a soft mass (often described as a "bag of worms") that can cause dull pain in the scrotum. This condition can decrease the sperm count and cause atrophy of the testicle, resulting in infertility.

20. Scrotal trauma is usually minor, resulting in temporary hematomas caused by minor crushing or straddle-type injuries. More severe crush injuries can rupture the testicles. Occasionally, the client's clothing and scrotal skin can be trapped in moving machinery, resulting in avulsion injuries. The skin can be torn away from the penis and scrotum, sometimes releasing scrotal contents. Penetrating injuries can also occur.

21. Testicular cancer grows within the testicle, eventually replacing most of the normal issue. Usually only one testicle is affected. This cancer can spread rapidly through blood and lymph vessels to other organs. The classic presenting symptom of testicular cancer is a painless hard nodule. Occasionally, the client may have a dull ache in the pelvis or scrotum. Acute pain is rare.

22. Phimosis is constriction of the foreskin so that it cannot be pushed back over the glans penis. It may be congenital or may follow infection or injury. Phimosis increases the risk of secondary infections, scarring, and perhaps cancer of the penis.

23. Peyronie's disease causes a hard fibrous layer of plaque (similar to scar tissue) to develop under the skin on one side of the penis. When

the penis is erect, the scar tissue is less flexible than the rest of the penile skin and causes the penis to curve. The plaque is caused by thickened layers of tissue and is benign. The condition can cause pain and can cause sexual intercourse to be difficult.

24. Priapism is a sustained, painful erection that is not associated with sexual arousal. It is caused by impaired blood flow in the corpora cavernosa of the penis. Priapism may be idiopathic or be secondary to certain conditions or drugs. The sustained erection of priapism often is painful and harder than normal. If the condition continues, there is a risk of tissue damage and impotence.

25. Squamous cell carcinoma accounts for 95% of all penile cancers. The tumor usually develops as a nodular or wart-like growth or a red velvety lesion on the glans or foreskin. Penile cancer can spread to regional lymph nodes and, very late in the disease, may spread to the bone, liver, or lungs. Manifestations include a mass or persistent sore or ulcer at the distal end of the penis involving the glans or foreskin. Most of these lesions are painless; however, they may ulcerate and bleed. Purulent, foul-smelling discharge may be noted under the foreskin.

26. Erectile dysfunction (ED) or impotence may involve total inability to achieve erection, an inconsistent ability to achieve erection, or the ability to sustain only brief erections. Causes include chronic diseases such as diabetes and atherosclerosis and many drugs. In most men, the cause of ED is primarily physiologic. Psychologic factors also contribute and are believed to cause 10–20% of cases of ED. For an erection to occur, the blood supply to the penis must be adequate, normal nervous system and hormonal actions are necessary, and appropriate psychologic and social responses need to occur. Interruption of any of these factors and certain drugs can lead to impotence.

27. There are many types of ejaculatory dysfunction: premature ejaculation, delayed ejaculation, and retrograde ejaculation. Premature ejaculation is often caused by psychologic factors; diabetes can also be a cause. Delayed ejaculation can be related to aging changes such as decreased penile sensation or decreased libido. Ejaculation can be affected by drugs to treat hypertension, depression, and anxiety and narcotic medications. Retrograde ejaculation (semen discharged into the bladder) is usually related to treatment of prostate disorders or testicular cancer.

LEARNING OUTCOME 2

Discuss nursing implications for medications used to treat disorders of the male reproductive system.

Concepts for Lecture

1. Several drugs may be used to shrink the enlarged prostate and reduce the manifestations of BPH. Finasteride (Proscar) inhibits the conversion of testosterone to DHT in the prostate, causing the gland to shrink. The nurse needs to be aware that this drug affects libido and can cause impotence.

2. Alpha-blockers such as terazosin (Hytrin), doxazosin (Cardura), and tamsulosin (Flomax) relax smooth muscle in the prostate, urethra, and bladder neck. Smooth muscle relaxation reduces urethral obstruction and improves urinary flow and symptoms of BPH.

3. Saw palmetto is an herbal therapy with effects similar to those of finasteride, although its mechanism of action is unknown. Nurses need to be aware of the usual dose, which is 640 mg, and the side effects, which include constipation, diarrhea, headache, and urinary retention. It should not be taken by pregnant women.

**POWERPOINT SLIDES 50–53**

Tables and/or Figures

- **Table 31-2** Giving Medications Safely: Drugs for Erectile Dysfunction

SUGGESTIONS FOR CLASSROOM ACTIVITIES

- Assign students to work in pairs and design a role play involving a nurse teaching a client about one or more medications used in treating disorders of the male reproductive system.
- Assign students to research and present in class on one of the medications used in treating disorders of the male reproductive system.

4. Hormone therapy is used to treat advanced prostate cancer. Hormone therapy can be accomplished by removing the testes or by using drugs that block the effects of testosterone and other androgens, thus inhibiting tumor growth but not curing prostate cancer. The nurse needs to be aware of the side effects of hormone therapy, which include loss of libido, erectile dysfunction or impotence, hot flashes, and gynecomastia. Body image problems may occur in the client who undergoes an orchiectomy. Silicone testicle prostheses may help with body image, and they prevent shrinkage of the scrotum.

5. When working with a client with prostatitis, the nurse needs to stress the importance of finishing any ordered course of antibiotic therapy to effectively treat the infection.

6. Stage III testicular cancer is treated with a combination of surgery and chemotherapy.

7. Erectile dysfunction can be treated with drugs that work in a variety of ways. The nurse needs to teach clients taking sildenafil and related drugs that these drugs can cause a dangerous drop in blood pressure when used together with nitrates. The nurse will advise men who use nitrates to prevent or treat angina and/or who have cardiovascular disease to talk to their cardiologist before taking erectile dysfunction drugs. The nurse needs to instruct all men using erectile dysfunction drugs to avoid use of recreational nitrates. The client will be warned that sildenafil and related drugs can cause priapism.

LEARNING OUTCOME 3

Use the nursing process to provide care for clients with disorders of the male reproductive system.

Concepts for Lecture

1. Educating the client and monitoring for adverse effects of the disorder and its treatment are priority nursing responsibilities when working with a client with BPH.

2. Assessment for BPH includes asking older men about difficulty starting and stopping the flow of urine, size of urinary stream, and any symptoms such as burning, frequency, urgency, or nocturia. Urine output needs to be monitored, including amount (total and per voiding), color, clarity, and odor.

3. A nursing diagnosis for BPH is ineffective therapeutic regimen management. One possible expected outcome is: will explain the disease process of BPH and list two self-care strategies for affected men.

4. The nurse provides the client with information about BPH and its treatment. The client is advised to drink 2–3 liters of fluids daily to prevent UTIs and reduce dysuria, unless contraindicated by other medical conditions. The client is advised to restrict alcohol intake, especially late at night, to minimize problems with nocturia.

5. When working with a client with prostate cancer who is having transrectal ultrasound-guided biopsy of the prostate, the nurse reinforces teaching about what to expect during the procedure and instructs the client to avoid aspirin products and NSAIDs for a week before biopsy. Before the procedure, an enema is often given, and a signed consent is obtained. Postoperatively, the nurse monitors vital signs and urine output for an hour and instructs the client to expect hematuria and some bloody streaks in the stool for up to 48 hours and that ejaculate may contain blood for up to 2 weeks. The client is instructed to report unusual bleeding and signs of infection.

SUGGESTIONS FOR CLINICAL ACTIVITIES

- Have students do medication cards on drugs used in treatment of disorders of the male reproductive system with a focus on nursing implications.
- Assign students to administer and then document giving medications to one to two clients with disorders of the male reproductive system.

REFERENCE

- Johns Hopkins Medicine: New treatments for BPH. Available at http://www .johnshopkinshealthalerts.com/reports/ prostate_disorders/1683-1.html

POWERPOINT SLIDES 54–71

Tables and/or Figures

- **Box 31-8** Testicular Self-Examination

Nursing Care Plan: Client With Erectile Dysfunction

SUGGESTIONS FOR CLASSROOM ACTIVITIES

- Divide the class into small groups. Assign each group to one of the following scenarios. Ask each group to use the nursing process to present a case study and a teaching plan for their scenario.
- Scenario A: A 26-year-old male with nonbacterial prostatitis
- Scenario B: A 62-year-old male postoperative suprapubic prostatectomy
- Scenario C: A 14-year-old male with testicular torsion
- Scenario D: A 35-year-old male who is thinking about having a vasectomy
- Scenario E: A 30-year-old male who is experiencing testicular cancer

SUGGESTIONS FOR CLINICAL ACTIVITIES

- Assign students to care for clients experiencing disorders of the male reproductive system. Have them discuss their observations in postconference. Ask the students to list nursing diagnoses and outcomes for the clients, and have an open discussion on the nursing interventions needed to meet the expected outcomes.

© 2011 Pearson Education, Inc.

6. Impaired urinary elimination (risk for incontinence) is one nursing diagnosis for clients with prostate cancer. A possible expected outcome is: will maintain urinary continence after treatment for prostate cancer.

7. Interventions for impaired urinary elimination include the following: assess the degree of incontinence and its impact on lifestyle, teach Kegel exercises, refer to physical therapy or a continence specialist, teach methods to control dampness and odor, explore options such as external collection device, and encourage expression of feelings about impact of incontinence on quality of life.

8. Sexual dysfunction is another nursing diagnosis for clients with prostate cancer. A possible expected outcome is: will discuss feelings about sexual function and options for treatment if indicated after prostate surgery.

9. Nursing interventions for a diagnosis of sexual dysfunction include encouraging discussion of sexual function between the client, his partner, and his physician; discussing various treatment options and their effects on sexual function; and encouraging the client to discuss concerns about sexuality with a counselor or therapist.

10. Acute pain is a possible nursing diagnosis for a client with prostate cancer. The nurse will assess the intensity, location, and quality of pain and teach pain control methods, including pharmacologic and nonpharmacologic measures.

11. Nursing care of clients with prostatitis includes encouraging clients to increase fluid intake to about 3 liters daily, to void often, and to maintain regular bowel habits. Local heat, such as sitz baths, may help relieve pain and irritation. The nurse will stress the importance of finishing a course of antibiotics. The nurse will advise the client with nonbacterial prostatitis that frequent ejaculation may help decrease congestion of the gland.

12. Nursing care for clients with structural and inflammatory disorders of the testes and scrotum includes asking about the onset, duration, and severity of symptoms and inspecting the scrotum for swelling, redness, and bruising or discoloration. The nurse palpates each testes and epididymis with a gloved hand, checking for warmth, tenderness, or masses. The nurse will teach the client about the disorder and its treatments.

13. Nurses can be instrumental in identifying testicular cancer at an early, treatable age. The nurse asks the client if there is any change in the size of the testicles. The nurse palpates the scrotum and testicles, noting any differences in size or changes from the normal, and promptly reports to the physician a testicle that is hard, irregular in shape, or fixed within the scrotum.

14. Nursing diagnoses for clients with testicular cancer may include deficient knowledge and risk for sexual dysfunction.

15. The nurse working with a client with phimosis will teach the client about the importance of hygiene measures to prevent infection and how to perform self-examinations for cancer of the penis.

16. Nurses may be able to help clients with Peyronie's disease by talking with them about body image issues.

17. Nursing care of the client with priapism includes analgesics, sedation, fluids, and ice packs to the perineum. The penis is inspected for the degree of erection and palpated for firmness and degree of rigidity. Urine output is monitored. The nurse reports oliguria or signs of acute urinary retention. The nurse addresses the client's anxiety about the condition, pain, treatment, and threat to sexual function and reassures the client that the erection is not within his control.

18. The nurse observes the penis for any visible lesions during routine care and reports any lesions noted to the physician. After surgery for cancer of the penis, the nurse will monitor the surgical site for healing and any signs of infection, monitor intake and output, and provide

REFERENCE

• About.com: Priapism. Available at http://menshealth.about.com/od/diseasesconditions/a/priapism.htm

routine postoperative care. The client will be advised that dribbling after voiding may occur for several weeks after surgery. The nurse teaches perineal care to reduce the risk of skin irritation and breakdown. Sitz baths may help relieve pain and promote healing. The nurse listens to the client's concerns, being aware of the effect of penectomy on body image, self-concept, and sexuality.

19. Nursing care of the client with erectile dysfunction includes asking about chronic diseases that may be responsible for the dysfunction, exploring psychosocial stressors, asking about sexual function, providing information about treatment, and referring the client and his partner for counseling.

LEARNING OUTCOME 4

Contribute to the plan of care for male clients undergoing surgery for reproductive system disorders.

Concepts for Lecture

1. Clients with BPH may need surgery to relieve urinary obstruction. Transurethral incision of the prostate (TUIP) and transurethral resection of the prostate (TURP) are the most common procedures used. Nursing care for a client having a TURP includes routine preoperative care and teaching and advising the client that he will return from surgery with a urinary catheter in place.

2. Postoperatively, the nurse provides routine care and assesses and manages pain, including urethral discomfort, bladder spasms, and abdominal cramping due to gas. The nurse uses aseptic technique when managing urinary drainage and irrigation. Intake and output is maintained, accounting for amounts of irrigating solution used or subtracting from output depending on hospital protocol. The nurse encourages intake when allowed, assesses catheter for patency, and records color and character of urine. The urine should gradually clear of clots and become light pink to yellow after 24–48 hours.

3. Prostatectomy, surgical removal of the prostate gland, may be done to treat prostate cancer. In a simple prostatectomy, only the prostate tissue is removed. A radical prostatectomy involves removal of the prostate, prostatic capsule, seminal vesicles, and a portion of the bladder neck. Prostatectomy may be done by several different approaches, each with nursing implications.

4. In a retropubic prostatectomy, the prostate is removed through an abdominal incision; the bladder left intact. The nurse assesses the abdominal incision for urine drainage (none should be present) and signs of infection.

5. In a suprapubic prostatectomy, the prostate gland is removed through an abdominal incision into the bladder. The nurse assesses the urine output from suprapubic and urethral catheters and assesses the abdominal dressing for urine drainage. A skin care specialist may be consulted. When the urethral catheter is removed, the nurse clamps the suprapubic catheter as ordered and encourages voiding. After voiding, the nurse assesses residual urine by unclamping the catheter and measuring the output.

6. In a perineal prostatectomy, the prostate gland is removed through a perineal incision between the scrotum and the anus. The nurse assesses the perineal incision for drainage and evidence of infection, avoids rectal temperatures or enemas, and applies a T-binder or padded scrotal support to hold dressings in place. After the dressing is removed, heat lamps or sitz baths may be used to promote comfort

POWERPOINT SLIDES 72–76

Tables and/or Figures

- **Table 31-1** Approaches to Prostatectomy
- **Box 31-3** Client Teaching: Prostate Surgery
- **Figure 31-5** Vasectomy
- **Figure 31-6** Types of Penile Implants
- **Box 31-2** Nursing Care Checklist: Transurethral Resection of the Prostate (TURP)
- **Box 31-6** Nursing Care Checklist: Transrectal Ultrasound-Guided Biopsy of the Prostate

Nursing Care Plan: Client With Erectile Dysfunction

SUGGESTIONS FOR CLASSROOM ACTIVITIES

- Assign students to find articles on care of the client having surgery for a male reproductive disorder and have students bring the articles to class for other students to read. Post the articles on the bulletin board or put them in a place where students can read them. Allow time for students to break into small groups and discuss one or more articles.

SUGGESTIONS FOR CLINICAL ACTIVITIES

- Make arrangements for students to observe surgery for male reproductive disorders and report on their observations in postconference.
- Assign students to care for clients who will have or have had surgery for male reproductive disorders.

REFERENCES

- MedlinePlus: Radical prostatectomy. Available at http://www.nlm.nih.gov/medlineplus/ency/article/007300.htm

and healing. The nurse teaches perineal irrigation as ordered and after bowel movements.

7. Cryosurgery is a possible treatment option for a client with cancer of the prostate. Guided by ultrasound, a cryoprobe is inserted into the tumor. Prostate tissue is destroyed by intermittent freezing and thawing. The nurse needs to be aware that this surgical treatment is associated with a risk of bladder outlet injury, urinary incontinence, impotence, and rectal damage.

8. The most common surgery of the scrotum is vasectomy, a sterilization procedure in which a portion of the spermatic cord is removed. Some clients develop scar tissue that causes chronic pain.

9. For the client undergoing scrotal surgery, the nurse teaches the client about the disorder and its treatment and discusses the following: client's fears about the surgery, pain management, and measures to reduce bleeding. Postoperatively, the nurse reports excessive swelling or discoloration to the physician because this would indicate excessive bleeding. The nurse will discuss the possible effects of surgery on fertility and actively listen to the client's concerns.

GENERAL CHAPTER CONSIDERATIONS

1. Have students study and learn key terms listed at the beginning of the chapter.
2. Have students complete end of chapter exercises either in their book or on the MyNursingKit Website.
3. Use the Classroom Response Question PowerPoints to assess students prior to lecture.

- Clinical Reasoning Care Map

MYNURSINGKIT
(www.mynursingkit.com)

- Websites
- NCLEX® Questions
- Case Studies
- Key Terms

STUDENT WORKBOOK AND RESOURCE GUIDE

- Chapter 31 activities
- *Separate purchase*

PRENTICE HALL NURSE'S DRUG GUIDE

- *Separate purchase*

CLASSROOM RESPONSE QUESTION POWERPOINTS

TESTBANK

CHAPTER 32
CARING FOR FEMALE CLIENTS WITH REPRODUCTIVE SYSTEM DISORDERS

LEARNING OUTCOME 1

Describe the pathophysiology of commonly occurring disorders and changes of the breast and female reproductive system.

Concepts for Lecture

1. The pathology of premenstrual syndrome (PMS) is not clearly understood. Hormonal changes such as altered estrogen–progesterone ratios, increased prolactin levels, and rising aldosterone levels during the luteal phase of the menstrual cycle are thought to contribute to the problem. Increased aldosterone levels cause salt and water retention and edema. Neurotransmitters such as monoamine oxidase and serotonin affect emotions and probably play a role in PMS.
2. Premenstrual dysphoric disorder is a severe form of PMS. The etiology is genetic, hormonal, psychological, environmental, and social.
3. Dysmenorrhea is pain associated with menstruation. In primary dysmenorrhea, no disease process is identified. Prostaglandins stimulate muscles in the uterus to contract. These contractions can cause mild cramping to severe muscle spasms. As the muscles contract, blood flow to the uterus is restricted, causing ischemia and pain.
4. Dysfunctional uterine bleeding is vaginal bleeding that is abnormal in amount, duration, or time of occurrence. Hormonal imbalance, particularly progesterone deficiency with relative estrogen excess, causes endometrial tissue to proliferate. Unless this tissue is supported by adequate progesterone, sloughing occurs. Depending on ovarian function and the hormone imbalance, irregular, prolonged, or profuse vaginal bleeding may occur.
5. Amenorrhea is the absence of menstruation. It is usually caused by hormone imbalance.
6. Metrorrhagia, bleeding between menstrual periods, may be a sign of cervical or uterine cancer. Mid-cycle spotting associated with ovulation is not considered metrorrhagia.
7. Postmenopausal bleeding may be caused by endometrial polyps, endometrial hyperplasia, uterine or cervical cancer, and vaginal tissue atrophy or hormone replacement therapy. The possibility of cancer makes early evaluation and treatment essential.
8. Menopause (or the climacteric) is the period during which menstruation permanently ceases. It is a normal physiologic process. Perimenopause includes the 4 or 5 years surrounding menopause, during which estrogen production declines and the menses permanently cease due to loss of ovarian function. It extends for 1 year after the final menstrual period. At this point, a woman is said to be postmenopausal.
9. During menopause, the number of ovarian follicles declines significantly, and the follicles that remain are less sensitive to follicle-stimulating hormone (FSH) and luteinizing hormone (LH). As follicles cease to develop, ovarian estrogen production ceases. The ovaries continue to produce androgens, and small amounts of a less active form of estrogen are produced by the adrenal glands. This remaining estrogen is insufficient to maintain the female secondary sexual characteristics, which causes a loss of breast tissue, body hair, and subcutaneous fat.

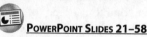

POWERPOINT SLIDES 21–58

Tables and/or Figures

- **Figure 32-2** Sites of Uterine Fibroid Tumors
- **Figure 32-5** (A) Anteversion and (B) Retroversion (C) Anteflexion (D) Retroflexion
- **Figure 32-6** Complete Uterine Prolapse With Inversion of the Vagina
- **Figure 32-7** Fibrocystic Breast Changes
- **Table 32-3** Vaginal Infections
- **Table 32-5** Breast Cancer Risk Factors

SUGGESTIONS FOR CLASSROOM ACTIVITIES

- Invite a gynecologist or urologist to talk about cystocele, urethrocele, rectocele, and uterine prolapse to the class. Have the class prepare questions ahead of time and hand them in. Select questions to be answered by the guest speaker or give the speaker the questions so he or she can choose some pertinent ones to answer.

SUGGESTIONS FOR CLINICAL ACTIVITIES

- Assign students to care for clients with reproductive system disorders. Have the students identify the pathology associated with the disorder their client has and discuss the pathology in postconference.

REFERENCE

- National Kidney and Urologic Diseases Information Clearinghouse: Cystocele. Available at http://kidney.niddk.nih.gov/kudiseases/pubs/cystocele/

10. Endometriosis is a condition in which endometrial tissue is found outside the uterus (e.g., on the ovary and other pelvic organs or tissues). The cause of endometriosis is unknown. It may be caused by backflow of menstrual blood carrying endometrial cells through the fallopian tubes into the abdomen. Cells that can develop into endometrium may be implanted during embryonic development, or be spread through the blood or lymph. Inflammation or immune responses may contribute to endometriosis.

11. A cyst is a fluid-filled sac. Cysts can develop in the vulva, endometrium, or ovaries.

12. Ovarian cysts may be either follicular cysts or corpus luteum cysts. Follicular cysts develop when a mature follicle does not rupture or when the fluid in an immature follicle does not reabsorb after ovulation. Corpus luteum cysts occur when the corpus luteum remains enlarged after ovulation. Most cysts regress spontaneously within two or three menstrual cycles.

13. Polycystic ovary syndrome (PCOS) is characterized by numerous follicular cysts. It is an endocrine disorder in which LH, estrogen, and androgen hormone levels are higher than normal and FSH levels are low.

14. Fibroid tumors or uterine leiomyomas are benign tumors of the uterus or cervix. They are common among all women of childbearing age and are a leading reason for hysterectomy. They are classified by their location in the wall of the uterus: Intramural (within the uterine wall), subserous (beneath the outer layer of the uterus), or submucous (beneath the endometrial lining of the uterus). The cause of fibroid tumors is not clear, but they are probably related to estrogen secretion.

15. Vaginitis, inflammation or infection of the vagina, is common. Vaginal infections are classified by cause and may be fungal (candidiasis), protozoan (trichomoniasis), or bacterial (*Gardnerella*) infections.

16. The low pH of vaginal secretions, normal vaginal flora, and estrogen normally protect against vaginal infections. An infection is more likely to develop when any or all of these factors are disrupted. When conditions are favorable, microorganisms invade the vulva and vagina.

17. Candidiasis organisms are part of the normal vaginal environment, causing problems only when they multiply rapidly. When increased estrogen levels, antibiotics, fecal contamination, or other factors alter the normal vaginal flora, *Candida* organisms multiply, causing a yeast infection.

18. Trichomoniasis, a protozoan infection, is a sexually transmitted infection. This organism frequently is carried asymptomatically by the male partner.

19. Pelvic inflammatory disease (PID) is an infection of the pelvic organs (fallopian tubes, ovaries, uterus, and cervix). PID is usually caused by infection with *Neisseria gonorrhoeae* and/or *Chlamydia trachomatis*. Clients are often infected with more than one organism.

20. In PID, infectious organisms can enter the vagina and travel to the uterus during intercourse or other sexual activity. They can also enter during childbirth, abortion, or reproductive tract surgery. The infection then spreads through the fallopian tubes, leading to inflammation and obstruction due to scar tissue. It settles on the ovary and also may enter the lymphatic system or bloodstream, leading to systemic infection.

21. Toxic shock syndrome (TSS) is a rare but acute illness caused by virulent strains of *Staphylococcus aureus* that enter the bloodstream through open blood vessels during the menses, the placental site after childbirth, or other open wound. Once inside the body, the organism produces toxins that cause vasodilation, hemodynamic instability, and shock. TSS can be fatal.

22. Most cervical cancers begin as changes in squamous cells of the cervix. These changes are called cervical intraepithelial neoplasia (CIN). Over a number of years, these cells become more abnormal, and the number

of affected cells increases, developing into carcinoma in situ. Untreated, carcinoma in situ becomes invasive, spreading into surrounding tissues, as well as metastasizing to the pelvis and other organs.

23. Endometrial cancers tend to be associated with estrogen excess and begin with endometrial hyperplasia. The endometrial tumor usually begins in the fundus of the uterus, invades the muscle of the uterus, and spreads throughout the female reproductive tract. Metastasis occurs by the lymphatic system and bloodstream, as well as through the fallopian tubes to the peritoneal cavity.

24. Ovarian cancer is the most lethal of the gynecologic cancers. Because the ovaries contain several different tissue types, there are different types of ovarian cancers that grow and spread at different rates. The most common type is an epithelial tumor. Malignant tumors usually present as solid masses with areas of necrosis and hemorrhage.

25. Ovarian cancer spreads by shedding cancer cells into the peritoneal cavity and by direct invasion of the bowel and bladder. Tumor cells also spread through lymph and blood to lymph nodes and organs such as the liver and lungs.

26. Cancer of the vulva usually arises in epithelial cells. The primary site is usually the labia majora, but it can also be found on the labia minora, clitoris, vestibule, and other perineal tissues. It spreads by direct extension into surrounding tissues, as well as through the lymph system to regional and pelvic lymph nodes. In younger women, cancer of the vulva is strongly associated with sexually transmitted infections, particularly human papillomavirus (HPV). Herpes simplex virus type 2 infection also is a risk factor for vulvar cancer.

27. Uterine displacement can be congenital or acquired. Childbirth or inflammation and scarring within the pelvic cavity can lead to displacement of the uterus. An anteverted uterus is tilted toward the bladder, whereas a retroverted uterus is tilted toward the rectum.

28. A cystocele is a prolapse of the urinary bladder into the vagina. It develops as the ligaments that support the bladder are stretched. Thinning of the vaginal wall commonly occurs during menopause, increasing the risk of cystocele. Cystocele is often accompanied by a urethrocele or prolapse of the urethra into the vagina.

29. Rectocele is a protrusion of the anterior rectal wall into the vagina. It may be caused by trauma during childbirth or chronic constipation with straining to defecate.

30. Uterine prolapse may vary from mild to complete prolapse outside the body. Uterine prolapse is caused by stretching of the ligaments that normally support the uterus within the pelvis. Increased pressure within the abdomen also can lead to uterine prolapse.

31. A fistula is an abnormal opening or passage between two organs or spaces that are normally separated. A vaginal fistula may develop between the vagina and the urinary bladder or between the vagina and the rectum. The fistula may be a complication of childbirth, surgery, or radiation therapy. Bladder cancer may lead to vaginal fistula. Urine or stool and flatus enter the vagina through this abnormal opening causing complaints of involuntary leakage of urine or gas.

32. Fibrocystic breast changes are noncancerous changes in breast tissue, causing swelling, pain, tenderness, and lumpiness. They are thought to be caused by an excessive response to cyclic hormone changes.

33. Fibrocystic changes are classified as nonproliferative or proliferative changes. Nonproliferative fibrocystic changes involve fibrosis of connective tissue, cyst formation, and inflammation. These changes do not increase the risk of breast cancer.

34. Proliferative fibrocystic changes involve cell growth, with an increase in cell numbers, especially of epithelial gland cells. The risk for cancer

is higher in clients with proliferative breast changes. Both forms of fibrocystic changes may be present.

35. Mastitis is inflammation that causes tenderness, swelling, and redness of the breast. Mastitis usually affects lactating women, caused by organisms from the infant's nose and throat.

36. Several problems are associated with breast augmentation: scarring may occur around the implant, causing excessive firmness and distortion of the breast; or the implant may rupture or bleed silicone gel through the capsule, causing local inflammation.

37. Breast cancer is unregulated growth of abnormal cells in breast tissue. It begins as a single transformed cell, which then multiplies. Breast cancer is hormone dependent. It does not develop in women without functioning ovaries who have never received estrogen replacement therapy.

38. Most tumors occur in the ductal areas of the breast. Breast tumors are classified as noninvasive (in situ) or invasive.

39. Most breast cancers are invasive, arising from the intermediate ducts of the breast. These tumors can be differentiated by cell type. Invasive breast cancers spread to involve surrounding breast tissue, lymph, and blood vessels. The cancer can metastasize to distant sites through blood or lymph.

40. Although rare, inflammatory breast cancer is the most malignant form of breast cancer.

41. Paget's disease is a rare breast cancer that involves the nipple ducts.

LEARNING OUTCOME 2

Compare and contrast the manifestations of benign and malignant disorders of the breast and female reproductive system.

Concepts for Lecture

1. Manifestations of PMS include irritability, depression, edema, and breast tenderness preceding menses. These manifestations generally occur 7–10 days before onset of the menstrual flow and are relieved when the menstrual flow begins.

2. The manifestations of dysmenorrhea include mild cramping to severe muscle spasm, ischemia and abdominal pain, headache, nausea, vomiting, diarrhea, fatigue, and breast tenderness.

3. In dysfunctional uterine bleeding, there is vaginal bleeding that is abnormal in amount, duration, or time of occurrence.

4. The manifestations of menopause include cessation of menses; loss of breast tissue, body hair, and subcutaneous fat; loss of elasticity of the skin and atrophy of the vaginal and perineal tissues; and a decrease in vaginal lubrication. Other manifestations include possible irritability, anxiety, insomnia, difficulty concentrating, and depression.

5. The manifestations of endometriosis occur just before and during the menses. They include dysmenorrhea with backache and cramps, painful defecation, dysuria, dyspareunia, and infertility.

6. Ovarian cysts are often asymptomatic, although the pain associated with cyst rupture may be confused with the pain of appendicitis.

7. Manifestations of polycystic ovary syndrome (PCOS), an endocrine disease, include LH, estrogen, and androgen hormone levels that are higher than normal with FSH levels that are low, irregular menstrual periods, hirsutism, acne, obesity, infertility, and possibly insulin resistance developing early in adulthood. With PCOS, there is increased risk of endometrial cancer, hypertension, and abnormal cholesterol levels.

8. Uterine fibroid tumors, or uterine leiomyomas, are benign tumors of the uterus or cervix. Small fibroid tumors may be asymptomatic. Large

POWERPOINT SLIDES 59–71

Tables and/or Figures

- **Box 32-4** Focus On Diversity: Uterine Fibroid Tumors in African American Women
- **Figure 32-2** Sites of Uterine Fibroid Tumors
- **Table 32-3** Vaginal Infections
- **Box 32-5** Manifestations of Toxic Shock Syndrome
- **Box 32-9** Manifestations of Breast Cancer

SUGGESTIONS FOR CLASSROOM ACTIVITIES

- Ask students to find articles in the library or on the Internet that discuss manifestations of one of the disorders of the female reproductive system. Have students write a brief report on the key concepts of the article including the manifestations. Have students put their reports in a binder or on a bulletin board to share them with peers. Students may also be asked to do a brief presentation on their article in class.

SUGGESTIONS FOR CLINICAL ACTIVITIES

- Assign students to clients who have reproductive system disorders. Ask the students to review their assigned client's charts and talk with the client about early manifestations and later manifestations of their disorder.

fibroids can crowd other organs, causing pelvic pressure, pain, dysmenorrhea, menorrhagia, and fatigue. Depending on tumor location, constipation and urinary urgency and frequency are common. The uterus is enlarged. Excessive bleeding often causes anemia.

9. Vaginitis, inflammation or infection of the vagina, is common. See Table 32-3 for specific manifestations of vaginal infections.

10. Pelvic inflammatory disease (PID) is an infection of the pelvic organs usually caused by infection with *Neisseria gonorrhoeae* and/or *Chlamydia trachomatis*. Manifestations of PID include high fever, vaginal discharge, severe lower abdominal pain, nausea, malaise, and dysuria.

11. Toxic shock syndrome (TSS) is a rare but acute illness caused by *Staphylococcus aureus* infection. Manifestations of TSS include high fever, nausea, vomiting, abdominal pain, diarrhea, muscle pain, sore throat, headache, dizziness, low blood pressure, diffuse red rash, conjunctivitis, peeling skin on palms and soles, and altered mental state.

12. Early cervical cancer causes no symptoms. Invasive cancer produces bleeding and leukorrhea (whitish discharge from the vagina), which increase as the cancer progresses. Other manifestations include pain in the back or thighs, hematuria, bloody stools, anemia, and weight loss.

13. Most endometrial cancers are slow to grow and metastasize. Abnormal uterine bleeding after menopause is the most common manifestation of endometrial cancer. This bleeding is usually painless but may be moderate to large in amount. Vaginal discharge is another sign of endometrial cancer. On pelvic examination, the uterus often is enlarged.

14. Ovarian cancer is the most lethal of the gynecologic cancers because it is often asymptomatic until it is advanced. When manifestations do develop, they are often vague and mild, such as indigestion, urinary frequency, abdominal bloating, and constipation. Pelvic pain sometimes occurs. An enlarged abdomen with ascites is a late manifestation of ovarian cancer.

15. Cancer of the vulva often causes no symptoms, and lesions are discovered on routine examination or self-examination. The lesion may appear as a white macular patch, a small raised lump, ulceration, or a red painless sore. Persistent pruritus and irritation of the vulva is the most common symptom. Perineal pain and bleeding occur with advanced disease.

16. Clients with uterine displacement may experience painful menses, discomfort during intercourse, and backache. The client may have difficulty conceiving a child.

17. The client with a cystocele often develops stress incontinence. Other manifestations include urinary frequency and urgency and difficulty emptying the bladder. Frequent bladder infections may develop due to urinary retention.

18. The client with a rectocele may have a sense of pelvic pressure and difficulty defecating.

19. The client with a uterine prolapse experiences a heavy or dragging sensation in the groin and lower back that is relieved by lying flat. The client may notice a mass protruding from the vagina, especially after bearing down or with heavy lifting. Constipation, urinary incontinence, and painful intercourse are common.

20. A client with a vaginal fistula will complain of involuntary leakage of urine or gas.

21. Fibrocystic breast changes cause bilateral or unilateral breast pain or tenderness and a sense of fullness that increases just prior to menstruation. Lumps may be felt in the breasts, and discharge from the nipple may be noted. Multiple, mobile cysts can form, usually in both breasts. Fluid may be aspirated from these cysts.

22. Mastitis is inflammation that causes tenderness, swelling, and redness of the breast.

REFERENCES

- Park S, Shatsky JB, Pawel BR, Wells L: Atraumatic compartment syndrome. Available at http://www.ejbjs.org/cgi/content/extract/89/6/1337
- MedlinePlus: Uterine cancer. Available at http://www.nlm.nih.gov/medlineplus/uterinecancer.html

23. Breast implants may have problems such as scarring around the implant, causing excessive firmness and distortion of the breast, and local inflammation from implant rupture or leaking of silicone gel through the capsule.

24. Noninvasive cancers of the breast are usually diagnosed by mammography rather than a palpable breast mass or nipple discharge.

25. Most breast tumors are discovered by the client as small, hard, and painless lumps or masses usually found in the upper outer quadrant of the breast. See Box 32-9 for other manifestations of breast cancer.

26. Inflammatory carcinoma is rare but the most malignant form of breast cancer. The client presents with a diffuse redness, warmth, and edema of the breast. A discrete mass may not be palpable.

LEARNING OUTCOME 3

Provide appropriate preoperative and postoperative nursing care for the client having gynecologic surgery.

Concepts for Lecture

1. Dysfunctional uterine blooding (DUB) is the leading cause of hysterectomy. The least invasive intervention that proves effective is preferred, beginning with a therapeutic dilation and curettage (D&C), then endometrial ablation, uterine balloon heart therapy, and, finally, hysterectomy.

2. In a therapeutic D&C, the cervical canal is dilated, and the uterine wall is scraped. D&C is used to diagnose and treat DUB and certain other disorders. D&C is contraindicated for any woman taking anticoagulant drugs.

3. Box 32-1 describes nursing care of the client having a D&C.

4. Hysterectomy may be done using an abdominal or a vaginal approach or a vaginal approach with laparoscopic visualization of the pelvic cavity. Presurgical care of a client having an abdominal or vaginal hysterectomy includes: (1) asking about the client's understanding and reinforcing teaching as needed; (2) providing emotional support; (3) instructing the client to cleanse abdominal and perineal areas as ordered; (4) if ordered, administering a small cleaning enema and having the client empty their bladder; and (5) providing routine preoperative care as ordered.

5. Postoperative care of a client having an abdominal or vaginal hysterectomy includes: (1) providing routine postoperative care; (2) reporting excessive bleeding; (3) monitoring for potential complications such as infection, ileus, venous thrombosis, and pulmonary embolus; (4) assessing vaginal drainage; (5) teaching perineal care; and (6) advising the client to restrict physical activity for 4-6 weeks (3-4 weeks for the vaginal procedure) and avoid heavy lifting, stair climbing, douching, tampons, and sexual intercourse.

6. Additional postoperative care nursing duties include: (7) instructing the client to shower, avoiding tub baths, until bleeding has stopped; (8) instructing the client to report to the physician any temperature greater than 100°F, vaginal bleeding greater than a typical menstrual period or that is bright red, urinary incontinence, urgency, burning, frequency, or severe pain; (8) encouraging expression of feelings and concern; (9) if appropriate, providing information about hormone replacement therapy; and (10) reinforcing the importance of regular gynecologic examinations even after hysterectomy.

7. See Box 32-7, Nursing Care Checklist: Cervical Biopsy for pre- and postoperative care of the client having a cervical biopsy.

POWERPOINT SLIDES 72–84

Tables and/or Figures
- **Figure 32-3** Conization, Removal of a Cone-Shaped Section of the Uterus
- **Figure 32-4** Vulvectomy for Cancer of the Vulva
- **Figure 32-10** Types of Breast Biopsy
- **Figure 32-11** Surgery for Breast Cancer
- **Figure 32-12** Breast Reconstruction Surgeries
- **Box 32-1** Nursing Care Checklist: Dilation and Curettage (D&C)
- **Box 32-2** Nursing Care Checklist: Abdominal or Vaginal Hysterectomy
- **Box 32-7** Nursing Care Checklist: Cervical Biopsy
- **Box 32-11** Nursing Care Checklist: Breast Biopsy
- **Box 32-12** Nursing Care Checklist: Mastectomy

SUGGESTIONS FOR CLASSROOM ACTIVITIES
- Have students research and write about female gynecological surgical procedures giving details of the procedures and the preoperative and postoperative nursing care. Ask students to write their questions that they will ask surgical staff.

SUGGESTIONS FOR CLINICAL ACTIVITIES
- Arrange for students to observe D&Cs and hysterectomies at outpatient surgical centers or hospital surgeries.
- Assign students to care for clients having a D&C and/or hysterectomy.

REFERENCE
- eMedicineHealth: Dilation and curettage. Available at http://www.emedicinehealth .com/dilation_and_curettage_dandc/ article_em.htm

8. See Box 32-11, Nursing Care Checklist: Breast Biopsy for pre- and post-operative care of the client having a breast biopsy.

9. See Box 32-12, Nursing Care Checklist: Mastectomy for pre- and post-operative care of the client having a mastectomy.

LEARNING OUTCOME 4

Use the nursing process when providing nursing care for female clients with perimenopausal changes and disorders of the breast and reproductive system.

Concepts for Lecture

1. Nursing care for the client with premenstrual dysphoric disorder (PMDD), a severe form of PMS, focuses on teaching the client to manage manifestations of the disorder.

2. A nursing diagnosis for PMS or PMDD is Effective Therapeutic Regimen Management, with a possible expected outcome that the client will explore self-care and coping mechanisms for PMS or PMDD. Nursing interventions include: (1) encouraging the client to keep a journal of her menstrual cycle, physical symptoms, and mood changes; (2) reviewing symptoms, relating them to diet, activity, and stress levels; (3) exploring self-care measures that have helped the client cope with mood alterations in the past; (4) encouraging coping strategies such as relaxation techniques and exercise; (5) reviewing daily activities and suggesting ways to balance rest periods and activity; (6) exploring ways to rearrange or reschedule activities during PMS symptoms; and (7) teaching self-care measures to relieve pain, such as heat application, relaxation techniques, and exercise.

3. To evaluate the effectiveness of nursing care, the client's level of understanding about PMS and symptom management is assessed.

4. Nursing assessment of a client with dysfunctional uterine bleeding focuses on subjective data related to the onset of symptoms, timing and amount of menstrual flow (pads per day and duration of period), and associated symptoms such as pain or cramping, weakness, or excessive fatigue.

5. A nursing diagnosis for dysfunctional uterine bleeding (DUB) is Ineffective Coping, with a possible expected outcome that the client will describe her psychosocial support system and state how she will manage the stress of DUB and its treatment. Nursing interventions for Ineffective Coping include discussing results of diagnostic tests and examinations with the client face to face; providing information about causes, treatment, risks, long-term effects, and prognosis; evaluating coping strategies and psychosocial support systems; and teaching appropriate coping strategies if indicated.

6. Another nursing diagnosis for a client with DUB is Sexual Dysfunction, with a possible expected outcome that the client will discuss her feelings about sexuality as they relate to DUB. Nursing interventions include: (1) discussing sexual intercourse during menstruation; (2) explaining that orgasm may help relieve symptoms, but that it is necessary to use contraception to prevent pregnancy even during menstruation; (3) providing an opportunity to express concerns related to effect of DUB on lifestyle and sexual functioning; (4) encouraging frequent rest periods; and (5) providing information about alternative methods of sexual expression.

7. Evaluation of effective nursing care for a client with DUB includes collecting data related to the client verbalizing ability to cope with

POWERPOINT SLIDES 85–102

Nursing Care Plan: Client With Cervical Cancer

SUGGESTIONS FOR CLASSROOM ACTIVITIES

- Divide students into small groups and have the groups select a disorder of the female reproductive system and write a care plan for a client with that disorder. Have students from two groups join together so there are half as many groups. Ask the students to critique the care plans and improve them.

SUGGESTIONS FOR CLINICAL ACTIVITIES

- Assign students to care for clients with disorders of the female reproductive system. Ask students to collect data using information from the text to suggest data to be gathered. Have students review the chart to see what additional data the nurses assigned to the client have gathered.
- Have students review the chart for their assigned client to see the plan of care for the client. Ask students to write their own plan of care.

symptoms and treatment of the disorder, and the client discussing acceptable and satisfying sexual practices with partner.

8. Assessing a client who is menopausal involves collecting subjective assessment data about the date of the last menstrual period, timing and regularity of the menstrual cycle, and duration and amount of menstrual flow; checking with the client to see if she could be pregnant; and inquiring about menopausal symptoms and measures taken to relieve the symptoms.

9. Nursing diagnoses for clients who are menopausal include Deficient Knowledge (Menopause), Sexual Dysfunction, and Risk for Situational Low Self-Esteem.

10. Evaluation of the effectiveness of nursing care for the client who is menopausal includes assessing the client's level of understanding about the perimenopausal period and measures to reduce unpleasant effects and discussing the effects of menopause on sexuality and self-esteem with the client to evaluate coping.

11. Nursing care of the client with endometriosis focuses on helping the client to deal with the manifestations and potential complications of endometriosis.

12. Nursing diagnoses for a client with endometriosis include Acute Pain as this is often the primary manifestation of endometriosis. Anxiety is another nursing diagnosis used for a client with endometriosis.

13. Nursing care of a client with ovarian cysts focuses on education unless surgery is performed.

14. Nursing care of the client with a uterine fibroid tumor focuses on teaching if surgery is deferred. If surgery is chosen, nursing care involves emphasizing pain control techniques and doing preoperative and postoperative teaching. Nursing care also involves teaching dietary modifications to increase iron intake, prevent constipation, and promote healing.

15. Nursing care of the client with vaginitis focuses on teaching the client and, if necessary, her sexual partner to comply with the treatment regimen, use safer sex practices, and prevent future transmission of the infection.

16. Nursing diagnoses for a client with vaginitis include Deficient Knowledge (Prevention of Vaginitis) and Acute Pain. Evaluation of the effectiveness of interventions for these diagnoses includes collecting data related to the client's and her partner's understanding of the treatment and prevention of vaginitis, as well as the client's level of comfort.

17. Nursing care of the client with pelvic inflammatory disease (PID) focuses on promoting prompt and effective treatment of PID and compliance with the prescribed treatment.

18. Nursing diagnoses for a client with PID may include Risk for Injury, with an expected outcome that the client will not experience complications of PID, and Deficient Knowledge (Sexually Transmitted Infection [STI] Prevention), with an expected outcome that the client will state how to use safer sex practices.

19. To evaluate the effectiveness of nursing care for a client with PID, the nurse collects data related to manifestations of the disease and its complications, as well as the client's and her partner's understanding of and willingness to use measures to prevent future infections.

20. The focus in caring for clients with toxic shock syndrome (TSS) is to provide teaching, both about causes and potential consequences of the infection and about the importance of completing the course of treatment.

21. Nursing diagnoses for a client with TSS may include Ineffective Tissue Perfusion and Decreased Cardiac Output.

22. Evaluation of the effectiveness of nursing care for the client with TSS involves collecting data about the client's vital signs and fluid volume status.

23. Nursing care of the client with cervical cancer involves helping the client deal with the physical and psychological effects of cancer, providing information needed to make informed decisions, and minimizing the adverse effects of treatment.

24. Nursing diagnoses for a client with cervical cancer may include Impaired Tissue Integrity, Fear, and Disturbed Body Image.

25. Evaluating the effectiveness of nursing interventions for the client with cervical cancer involves collecting data related to skin integrity and absence of infection and how well the client and family are coping with the diagnosis and treatment.

26. Nursing care of the client with endometrial cancer involves helping the client deal with the physical and psychological effects of endometrial cancer, make informed decisions, and minimize the adverse effects of therapy.

27. A nursing diagnosis for clients who have endometrial cancer is Disturbed Body Image.

28. Nursing care of the client with ovarian cancer is similar to the nursing care for clients with other gynecologic cancers.

29. Nursing care of the client with cancer of the vulva focuses on the disruption of perineal tissues, sexuality, and body image.

30. Nursing care of the client with pelvic organ prolapse includes teaching the client how to perform Kegel exercises, discussing hormone replacement therapy with postmenopausal women, teaching appropriate perineal care measures, and suggesting that the client reduce or eliminate caffeine intake and minimize consumption of diet sodas because caffeine and artificial sweeteners can aggravate urinary incontinence.

31. Nursing care of the client with a vaginal fistula is similar to that provided for any client undergoing pelvic surgery.

32. The nursing care for women with fibrocystic breast changes is primarily educational. The nurse provides preoperative teaching and psychological support before breast biopsy. After the procedure, the nurse discusses home care and possible complications that should be reported to the physician. The nurse reinforces teachings about measures to promote comfort and suggests eliminating caffeine or taking vitamin E to relieve discomfort.

33. Nursing care of the client with breast cancer focuses on supporting the client's decision-making and grieving processes, as well as promoting rehabilitation following treatment.

34. Nursing diagnoses that may be used with clients who have breast cancer include Decisional Conflict (Treatment Options) with a possible expected outcome that the client will state treatment options for breast cancer, including their advantages and disadvantages. Other nursing diagnoses for a client with breast cancer include Grieving, with an expected outcome that the client will discuss feelings and concerns about having breast cancer, and Risk for Infection, with an expected outcome that the client will not experience infection in the surgical area. Risk for Injury and Risk for Disturbed Body Image are often applicable to the client with breast cancer.

GENERAL CHAPTER CONSIDERATIONS

1. Have students study and learn key terms listed at the beginning of the chapter.

2. Have students complete end of chapter exercises either in their book or on the MyNursingKit Website.

3. Use the Classroom Response Question PowerPoints to assess students prior to lecture.

- Clinical Reasoning Care Map

MYNURSINGKIT
(www.mynursingkit.com)
- Websites
- NCLEX® Questions
- Case Studies
- Key Terms

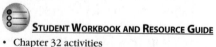
STUDENT WORKBOOK AND RESOURCE GUIDE
- Chapter 32 activities
- *Separate purchase*

PRENTICE HALL NURSE'S DRUG GUIDE
- *Separate purchase*

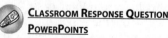
CLASSROOM RESPONSE QUESTION POWERPOINTS

TESTBANK

CHAPTER 33
CARING FOR CLIENTS WITH SEXUALLY TRANSMITTED INFECTIONS

LEARNING OUTCOME 1

Describe the pathophysiology of the most common sexually transmitted infections (STIs).

Concepts for Lecture

1. Chlamydial infections are thought to be the most common STIs in the United States and the leading cause of pelvic inflammatory disease (PID).
2. *Chlamydia trachomatis* is a bacterium that behaves like a virus, reproducing only within the host cell. It is spread by sexual contact and to the neonate by passage through the birth canal of an infected mother.
3. The incubation period for *Chlamydia trachomatis* is from 1–3 weeks.
4. Genital herpes is caused by HSV-2, which is closely related to HSV-1, which commonly causes fever blisters or cold sores. Genital herpes is spread by vaginal, anal, or oral–genital contact. Its incubation period is 3–7 days.
5. The first outbreak of herpes lesions is called the first episode infection. Subsequent episodes or recurrent infections are usually less severe and last for a briefer period. The period between episodes is called latency. Even without symptoms present, the person is infectious. During latency, the virus withdraws into the nerve fibers that lead from the infected site to the lower spine, remaining dormant until recurrence.
6. Genital warts, also known as condylomata acuminata or venereal warts, are caused by human papillomavirus (HPV). HPV is a common virus with over 40 types that can cause STIs in humans. Some strains have been linked to cervical cancer. HPV is transmitted by all types of sexual contact. The incubation period for genital warts is about 3 months.
7. Potential complications of genital warts include destruction of normal tissue or destruction of the urethra. The virus can also be transmitted to the fetus.
8. Gonorrhea (GC, clap) is caused by *Neisseria gonorrhoeae*, a gram-negative diplococcus. It is transmitted by direct sexual contact and during delivery as the neonate passes through the birth canal. The incubation period is 2–8 days. The organism initially targets the cervix and the male urethra. Without treatment, the disease spreads to other organs.
9. Syphilis is caused by a spirochete, *Treponema pallidum*, which may infect almost any body tissue or organ. It is transmitted from open lesions during any sexual contact (genital, oral–genital, or anal–genital).
10. *Treponema pallidum* can survive for days in fluids. It may be transmitted by infected blood or other body fluids such as saliva. The average incubation period is 20–30 days. Once it has entered the system, *T. pallidum* spreads through the blood and lymphatic system. Congenital syphilis is transferred to the fetus through the placental circulation.

 POWERPOINT SLIDES 21–31

Tables and/or Figures
- **Box 33-2** Risk Factors for STIs

 **SUGGESTIONS FOR CLASSROOM ACTIVITIES**

- Describe the pathophysiology of the most common sexually transmitted infections (STIs).
- Assign students to each research one of the sexually transmitted infections focusing on pathophysiology, and have the students each present the results of their research in class.

 SUGGESTIONS FOR CLINICAL ACTIVITIES

- Assign students to work in small groups and to create a pamphlet about STIs and include the pathophysiology of the infections in the pamphlet.

REFERENCE

- HealthGuidance: Pathology of syphilis. Available at http://www.healthguidance.org/entry/6784/1/Chapter-II—Pathophysiology-of-Syphilis.html

LEARNING OUTCOME 2

Identify laboratory and diagnostic tests used for STIs.

Concepts for Lecture

1. Chlamydial infection can be diagnosed in several ways. Infected tissue can be cultured to identify the presence of the bacteria. More often, the diagnosis is made based on detection of chlamydial antigens or nucleic acid or by detecting antibodies to *Chlamydia* in the blood or local secretions.
2. Genital herpes is usually diagnosed by the history (including lesion characteristics and patterns of recurrence) and physical exam.
3. Genital and anal warts are diagnosed primarily by their clinical appearance. HPV also may be diagnosed by examination of cervical cells taken during a Pap smear or cervical biopsy.
4. In men, the diagnosis of gonorrhea can usually be confirmed by obtaining a smear of urethral discharge. Cultures are not necessary unless Gram stains of smears are negative despite typical clinical symptoms of gonorrhea.
5. In women, cultures of cervical discharge are necessary to confirm the diagnosis of gonorrhea. Because cultures require 24–48 hours for confirmation, treatment is usually begun on a presumptive diagnosis.
6. Tests widely used to diagnose syphilis include VDRL and RPR, which become positive about 4–6 weeks after infection. Because these tests are not specific, additional tests may be necessary.
7. Another test used to diagnose syphilis is the FTA-ABC test, which is specific for *T. pallidum* and can be used to confirm VDRL and RPR findings. Immunofluorescent staining or dark-field microscopy can be used to identify the presence of *T. pallidum* in a specimen obtained from a chancre or by aspirating a lymph node.

LEARNING OUTCOME 3

Identify general measures to prevent and treat common STIs.

Concepts for Lecture

1. STIs are directly related to lifestyle. The nurse needs to teach all clients to use safer sexual practices such as abstinence, mutual monogamy with an uninfected partner, and barrier protection during sexual relations.
2. Most STIs can be prevented by the use of latex condoms. Education of the general populace, especially high-risk groups, is essential in preventing transmission of STIs.
3. High-risk groups for STIs include young people under 25. Two-thirds of all STIs occur in people under 25. People with multiple partners have the highest risk of acquiring an STI. People of color in urban settings with lower socioeconomic status and less education have a high incidence of STIs.
4. For treatment of STIs to be effective, sexual partners of the infected person must also be screened and treated to prevent reinfection.
5. Clients who are infected with STIs need to be encouraged to follow the plan of treatment to prevent reinfection and complications.
6. All states require reporting of syphilis, gonorrhea, and AIDS to state and federal agencies. Chlamydia is reportable in some states. The CDC recommends screening asymptomatic women who are at high risk for chlamydia.

 **POWERPOINT SLIDES 32–35**

 SUGGESTIONS FOR CLASSROOM ACTIVITIES

- Identify and discuss the nursing implications for laboratory and diagnostic tests used for STIs.
- Invite a laboratory technician who runs tests for STIs to come and talk with the class about the tests for STIs.

SUGGESTIONS FOR CLINICAL ACTIVITIES

- Assign students to community health centers where STIs are treated. Have students spend part of their time focusing on tests used to diagnose STIs in the clients. Ask students to report on what they learned about laboratory and diagnostic tests for STIs.

REFERENCE

- Agency for Healthcare Research and Quality: Screening for gonorrhea. Available at http://www.ahrq.gov/Clinic/uspstf05/gonorrhea/gonrs.htm

 **POWERPOINT SLIDES 36–38**

Tables and/or Figures

- **Box 33-1** Population Focus: Syphilis in Men Who Have Sex With Men
- **Box 33-2** Risk Factors for STIs

SUGGESTIONS FOR CLASSROOM ACTIVITIES

- Invite a public health nurse to talk about the current statistics on STIs and public awareness information that is available. Ask the nurse to talk about education for prevention as well as treatment for STIs.
- Initiate a discussion on general measures to prevent and treat STIs.
- Ask students to volunteer to play the roles of a community health nurse and a client. Have them present a skit of the client asking questions regarding a particular STI and the nurse providing client teaching. The skit should include preventative measures, methods of transmission, and medications.

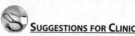 **SUGGESTIONS FOR CLINICAL ACTIVITIES**

- Assign students to observe a public health setting where clients are screened for STIs and where teaching for prevention and treatment for clients testing positive takes place. Ask students to write a report on their experiences.

7. Some STIs can be cured with appropriate antibiotic treatment. Some infections like genital herpes and genital warts are chronic conditions that can be managed but not cured.

8. Gardasil is a relatively new vaccine that immunizes women against several types of HPV that cause genital warts and cervical cancer. The nurse shares with parents that this vaccine is recommended for girls age 11 and 12 years old and for girls and women age 13–26 if they did not receive the vaccine when they were younger. There are three injections. The second and third injections are given 2 and 6 months after the first dose.

LEARNING OUTCOME 4

List the signs and symptoms of the most common STIs.

Concepts for Lecture

1. Chlamydial infections are asymptomatic in most women until *Chlamydia trachomatis* has invaded the uterus and fallopian tubes. Early manifestations, when present, include dysuria, urinary frequency, and vaginal discharge.

2. Nearly a third of men with chlamydia are asymptomatic. Manifestations of the infection in men include dysuria, urethral discharge (white or clear), and possible testicular pain.

3. Although a man may be asymptomatic with chlamydia, he is still potentially infectious.

4. Manifestations of genital herpes include single or multiple small painful papules that become vesicles on an erythematous base on the genitals with associated pruritus, followed by painful ulcers. In men, the lesions usually occur on the glans or shaft of the penis. In women, the lesions often occur on the labia, vagina, and cervix. Anal intercourse may result in lesions in and around the anus.

5. After the papules appear, they form small painful vesicles (blisters) filled with clear fluid containing the virus particles. The skin around the vesicles is red and painful. The blisters break, shedding the virus and creating painful ulcers that last 6 weeks or longer.

6. Warning signs of herpes outbreaks (prodromal symptoms) include burning, itching, tingling, or throbbing at the sites where lesions commonly appear. There may be pain radiating to the legs, thighs, groin, or buttocks.

7. Recurrent infections have symptoms of herpetic lesions, general malaise or headache, fever, dysuria and urinary retention, and vaginal or urethral discharge.

8. Most people who carry HPV have no symptoms, whereas others develop single or multiple painless, cauliflower-like growths on the vulvovaginal area, perineum, penis, urethra, or anus. In women, the growth may appear in the vagina or on the cervix and be apparent only during a pelvic examination. Several subtypes of HPV are strongly associated with cervical dysplasia and an increased risk of cancer.

9. In men, gonorrhea can cause acute, painful inflammation of the prostate, epididymis, and periurethral glands and can lead to sterility. In women, gonorrhea can cause PID, endometritis, salpingitis, and pelvic peritonitis. In the neonate, gonorrhea can infect the eyes, nose, or anorectal region.

10. The primary stage of syphilis is characterized by the appearance of a painless ulcer called a chancre at the site of inoculation (genitals, anus, mouth, breast, or finger). Regional lymph nodes may be swollen. The chancre appears 3–4 weeks after the infectious contact.

REFERENCE

- American Social Health Association: STD/STI prevention tips. Available at http://www.ashastd.org/learn/learn_prevention.cfm

POWERPOINT SLIDES 39–46

Tables and/or Figures

- **Figure 33-3** Genital Herpes Blisters on the Penis
- **Figure 33-4** Genital Warts on the Penis
- **Figure 33-5** Chancre of Primary Syphilis on the Penis
- **Figure 33-6** Palmar Rash of Secondary Syphilis
- **Table 33-1** Selected STIs, Manifestations, Treatment, and Complications

SUGGESTIONS FOR CLASSROOM ACTIVITIES

- Ask students to research for articles on STIs that discuss the manifestations of one or more STIs as well as pictures of manifestations of STIs. Have students display their findings on bulletin boards or in a notebook. Ask students to do a brief presentation in class.

SUGGESTIONS FOR CLINICAL ACTIVITIES

- Assign students to areas where clients are screened and treated for STIs. Have students look for opportunities to observe manifestations of STIs or ask clients to describe their signs and symptoms.

REFERENCE

- Palo Alto Medical Foundation: Sexually transmitted infection. Available at http://www.pamf.org/teen/sex/std/gensymp.html

11. In women, a genital chancre may go unnoticed, disappearing within 4–6 weeks.

12. Manifestations of secondary syphilis may appear any time from 2 weeks to 6 months after the initial chancre disappears and include skin rash, especially on the palms of the hands or soles of the feet; mucous patches in the oral cavity; sore throat; generalized lymphadenopathy; condyloma lata (flat broad-based papules, unlike the pedunculated structure of genital warts) on the labia, anus, or corner of the mouth; flulike symptoms; and alopecia in random spots on the scalp. These manifestations generally disappear in 2–6 weeks.

13. Tertiary syphilis may be manifested as benign late syphilis, characterized by localized infiltrating tumors (gummas) in skin, bones, and liver. This form of tertiary syphilis generally responds promptly to treatment.

14. Another manifestation of tertiary syphilis is a diffuse inflammatory response that involves the central nervous system and the cardiovascular system and has a more insidious onset. The disease can still be treated at this stage, but much of the cardiovascular and central nervous system damage is irreversible.

LEARNING OUTCOME 5

Discuss nursing implications for medications prescribed for clients with STIs.

Concepts for Lecture

1. The nurse working with a client taking medication for treatment of STIs needs to stress completing prescribed medication regimens as ordered and to keep all recommended follow-up appointments because incomplete treatment may result in continued infection and organisms that are resistant to antibiotic therapy.

2. Medications for chlamydia include doxycycline for 7 days or azithromycin PO once. Erythromycin PO is an alternative for pregnant women.

3. The nurse will advise the client that, at present, there is no cure for genital herpes. The nurse will encourage the client to use antiviral drugs such as acyclovir (Zovirax) or famciclovir (Famvir) to help reduce the length and severity of the first episode and decrease the frequency of recurrent episodes. For severe episodes, acyclovir can be given intravenously. The nurse can suggest using sterile Vaseline, docosanol cream (Abreva), or aloe vera gel to protect painful lesions.

4. The nurse will teach parents and young women about Gardasil, a relatively new vaccine that immunizes women against several types of HPV.

5. Genital warts may be treated in the physician's office with a topical agent (podophyllin resin) applied directly to the warts. The nurse will emphasize the need for the client and infected partners to return for regular treatment, abstinence from sexual relations until lesions have resolved, and the use of condoms to prevent reinfection.

6. Treatment for gonorrhea includes cephalosporins in a single injection plus azithromycin PO in a single dose or doxycycline PO for 7 days to treat possible coexisting chlamydia.

7. The client with syphilis is treated with penicillin G IM in a single injection or with doxycycline PO for 14 days. Syphilis of unclear or more than 1 year in duration is treated with penicillin G IM weekly for 3 weeks or doxycycline PO for 28 days.

POWERPOINT SLIDES 47–48

Tables and/or Figures

- **Table 33-1** Selected STIs, Manifestations, Treatment, and Complications

SUGGESTIONS FOR CLASSROOM ACTIVITIES

- Discuss the nursing implications of the medications prescribed for clients with STIs.

SUGGESTIONS FOR CLINICAL ACTIVITIES

- Assign students to care for clients who have sexually transmitted diseases. Have students give medications for sexually transmitted diseases, and if none are ordered, the students can interview the clients about what medications they have taken for sexually transmitted diseases.

REFERENCE

- Mayo Clinic: Genital warts. Available at http://www.mayoclinic.com/health/genitalwarts/DS00087/DSECTION=treatments-and-drugs

LEARNING OUTCOME 6

Use the nursing process to provide individualized care for clients with STIs.

Concepts for Lecture

1. Teaching about the infection, its treatment, and potential effects on reproductive health for the client and his or her partners is the priority for nursing care of the client with chlamydia.

2. Nursing care focuses on identifying the infection, eradicating it, preventing future infections, and managing any complications.

3. Clients are assessed for current symptoms, general health, past medical history, sexual activity, possibility of pregnancy, and social habits such as tobacco, alcohol, or other drug use, frequency, and amount (subjective data).

4. The client's vital signs are obtained, the entire skin is inspected, and bowel sounds are auscultated. The abdomen and suprapubic region are palpated for tenderness, and the inguinal lymph nodes and perineal tissues are palpated for tenderness or swelling (objective).

5. A nursing diagnosis considered when planning and delivering care for a client with an STI is Ineffective Health Maintenance. Interventions include teaching client about infection, safe sex practices, treatment, and potential effects on reproductive health of client and partners.

6. Impaired Skin Integrity is a nursing diagnosis often used in caring for a client with an STI. A possible expected outcome is: will do own perineal hygiene to keep area clean and dry, and will have intact skin. Interventions include teaching client to keep perineal area clean and dry, advising cleansing from front to back after urinating and defecating, and advising the client to wear cotton underwear and loose clothing.

7. Risk for Injury is a nursing diagnosis used in caring for clients with STIs. A possible expected outcome is: will state the importance of taking all medications and adhering to therapeutic regimen, including ways to prevent future infection. Interventions include stressing importance of taking prescribed medications; instructing to abstain from sexual contact until client and partners are cured and to use condoms; and providing information about signs and symptoms of reinfection and other STIs.

8. Anxiety is another nursing diagnosis appropriate for clients with STIs. Interventions include emphasizing that most STIs can be effectively treated to prevent complication and transmission to infants and that cesarean delivery can prevent transmission of infection to the neonate.

9. Situational Low Self-esteem is a nursing diagnosis used in caring for clients with STIs. Interventions include creating an environment where client feels respected and safe to discuss concerns about the disease and its effect on the client's life; providing privacy and confidentiality; and communicating caring for the client.

10. Sexual Dysfunction is a nursing diagnosis used in caring for clients with STIs. The nurse will help the client to understand that the STI is a consequence of sexual behavior and not a punishment.

11. Acute Pain is a nursing diagnosis used in caring for clients with STIs. An important intervention is to keep blisters clean and dry.

 POWERPOINT SLIDES 49–53

Tables and/or Figures

- **Box 33-3** Assessment: Clients With an STI
- **Box 33-4** Client Teaching: Preventing STIs: A Checklist for Clients

Nursing Care Plan: Client With Gonorrhea

 SUGGESTIONS FOR CLASSROOM ACTIVITIES

- Have students break into small groups and design a care plan for a client with one of the sexually transmitted infections.

 **SUGGESTIONS FOR CLINICAL ACTIVITIES**

- Assign students to care for clients with sexually transmitted diseases and to develop a plan of care for assigned clients.

GENERAL CHAPTER CONSIDERATIONS

1. Have students study and learn key terms listed at the beginning of the chapter.
2. Have students complete end of chapter exercises either in their book or on the MyNursingKit Website.
3. Use the Classroom Response Question PowerPoints to assess students prior to lecture.

• Clinical Reasoning Care Map

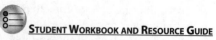

MyNursingKit
(www.mynursingkit.com)

• Websites
• NCLEX® Questions
• Case Studies
• Key Terms

STUDENT WORKBOOK AND RESOURCE GUIDE

• Chapter 33 activities
• *Separate purchase*

PRENTICE HALL NURSE'S DRUG GUIDE

• *Separate purchase*

CLASSROOM RESPONSE QUESTION POWERPOINTS

TESTBANK

CHAPTER 34
THE ENDOCRINE SYSTEM AND ASSESSMENT

LEARNING OUTCOME 1

Describe the structure and function of the organs of the endocrine system, including the pancreas, and the actions of hormones secreted by the endocrine glands.

Concepts for Lecture

1. The primary function of the endocrine system is to regulate the body's internal environment.
2. The major organs of the endocrine system are the hypothalamus, pituitary gland, thyroid gland, parathyroid glands, thymus, adrenal glands, pancreas, and gonads.
3. The hypothalamus is located in the brain between the cerebrum and the brainstem, with the pituitary gland and the hypothalamus physically attached.
4. The pituitary gland controls anterior pituitary function by regulating temperature, fluid volume, and growth. It also responds to pain, pleasure, hunger, and thirst stimuli.
5. The pituitary gland is located in the skull beneath the hypothalamus.
6. The pituitary gland is often called the "master gland" because its hormones regulate many different body functions.
7. The pituitary gland has two parts: the anterior lobe (adenohypophysis) and the posterior lobe (neurohypophysis).
8. The anterior lobe of the pituitary gland secretes six different hormones.
9. The posterior lobe of the pituitary gland releases antidiuretic hormone (ADH) and oxytocin.
10. The thyroid gland is shaped like a butterfly and sits on either side of the trachea. This gland has two lobes connected by a structure called the isthmus.
11. The thyroid gland needs an adequate supply of iodine in order to secrete thyroid hormone (thyroxine, T_4) and triiodothyronine (T_3), which increases metabolism.
12. The thyroid gland also secretes calcitonin, a hormone that decreases excess calcium levels in the blood.
13. The parathyroid glands (usually four to six) are embedded on the posterior lobes of the thyroid gland. They secrete parathyroid hormone (PTH, or parathormone).
14. PTH secretion increases when calcium levels in the plasma fall, and it decreases phosphorus levels. Normal levels of vitamin D are necessary for PTH to apply this effect on bone and kidneys.
15. The two adrenal glands are pyramid-shaped organs that sit on top of the kidneys. Each gland consists of two parts, an outer cortex and an inner medulla.
16. The adrenal cortex secretes several different hormones called corticosteroids, which are classified into two groups, glucocorticoids and mineralocorticoids. These hormones are essential to life.
17. Cortisol, a glucocorticoid, affects carbohydrate metabolism. Glucocorticoids also have an anti-inflammatory response and affect emotions.
18. The primary mineralocorticoid, aldosterone, maintains normal salt and water balance through its action on the kidneys. It is released

POWERPOINT SLIDES 21–43

Tables and/or Figures
- **Figure 34-1** Location of the Major Endocrine Glands
- **Figure 34-2** Actions of the Major Hormones of the Anterior Pituitary
- **Figure 34-3** Action of Insulin and Glucagon on Blood Glucose Levels
- **Table 34-1** Endocrine Organs, Hormones, and Functions

SUGGESTIONS FOR CLASSROOM ACTIVITIES

- Provide the students with a schematic drawing of the cerebrum and ask them to identify the location of the pituitary gland. Once identified, ask the students to list disease processes that might adversely affect the function of this gland.

SUGGESTIONS FOR CLINICAL ACTIVITIES

- Ask the hospital pathologist at a hospital where you have clinical affiliation contracts if students could observe an autopsy on a volunteer basis; the autopsy should be one in which the pituitary and other endocrine glands will be identified. If permission can be obtained, have the pathologist notify you of such autopsies and make a list of students who want to be notified when there is opportunity to view an autopsy.
- Assign students to care for clients with endocrine disorders. Have students assess their assigned client's thyroid gland.

REFERENCE

- National Institute of Child Health and Development: adrenal gland disorders. Available at http://www.nichd.nih.gov/health/topics/Adrenal_Gland_Disorders.cfm

when blood volume or blood pressure falls below normal levels and acts to save sodium and water, which in turn raises blood volume and pressure.

19. The adrenal cortex also releases small amounts of androgens (sex hormones).

20. The adrenal medulla produces two hormones (catecholamines): epinephrine (also called adrenaline) and norepinephrine (or noradrenaline). Both catecholamines increase heart rate and the force of heart contractions and constrict blood vessels.

21. Epinephrine and norepinephrine are released during times of stress and initiate the fight-or-flight response.

22. The pancreas is located behind the stomach between the spleen and the duodenum.

23. The pancreas serves two major functions: Acini cells secrete digestive enzymes into the duodenum, and the islets of Langerhans release insulin and glucagons into the bloodstream. These hormones must be in balance to prevent hyperglycemia or hypoglycemia.

LEARNING OUTCOME 2

Identify subjective and objective assessment data to collect for clients with endocrine disorders.

Concepts for Lecture

1. The health interview focuses on subjective data. The nurse asks the client about changes in energy level and fatigue and how these changes affect the client's activities of daily living (ADL). The nurse asks if the client has become more sensitive to heat or cold. Additional questions are asked about weight loss or gain, diarrhea or constipation, appetite, urination, thirst, and salt cravings.

2. During the health interview, the nurse asks about high blood pressure, abnormally fast or slow heart rate, palpitations, or shortness of breath. The nurse asks about vision changes, excessive tearing, or swelling around the eyes. The nurse asks if the client has any numbness or tingling in lips or extremities; nervousness; hand tremors; changes in memory, mood, or sleep pattern; thinning or loss of hair; dry or moist skin; brittle nails; easy bruising; or slow wound healing.

3. The nurse obtains a past medical history regarding any hormone replacement therapy or previous surgery, chemotherapy, or radiation, especially of the neck area, as well as brain surgery or a head injury. The nurse asks about a family history of diabetes mellitus, diabetes insipidus, goiter, obesity, Addison's disease, or infertility.

4. The nurse obtains a sexual history regarding changes in sexual function or secondary sex characteristics and asks women about changes in menstruation or menopause.

5. During the physical examination, the nurse begins by assessing the client's general appearance and obtaining and documenting vital signs, height, and weight. Note extremely short or tall height.

6. The nurse assesses skin color, temperature, texture, and moisture. The nurse observes for rough, dry, or smooth, flushed skin, noting any bronze color over knuckles, purple striae over the abdomen, and any bruising. The lower extremities are inspected for lesions and any signs of healing. The nurse assesses the texture and condition of the hair and nails. The nurse observes for thinning and loss of hair as well as thick or brittle nails and excessive hair growth on face, chest, or abdomen.

POWERPOINT SLIDES 44–49

Tables and/or Figures
- **Figure 34-4** Palpating the Thyroid Gland
- **Figure 7-16** Positive Chvostek's Sign and Positive Trousseau's Sign

SUGGESTIONS FOR CLASSROOM ACTIVITIES
- Have the students work in small groups to create a template to use for collecting subjective and objective data on a client with an endocrine disorder history.

SUGGESTIONS FOR CLINICAL ACTIVITIES
- Assign students to care for clients with a diagnosis of an endocrine disorder. Have the students complete a subjective and objective assessment for their assigned client.

7. The nurse assesses for increased size of hands and feet, trunk obesity, and thin extremities. Men are inspected for gynecomastia. Muscle strength and deep tendon reflexes are assessed. Chvostek's sign and Trousseau's sign are assessed. The client is assessed for the ability to sense touch, hot/cold, and vibration in the extremities.

8. The lungs are auscultated for adventitious sounds, and the heart is auscultated for extra heart sounds. The hands and feet are palpated for edema.

9. The relationship between aging and endocrine function is unclear. Aging causes fibrosis of the thyroid gland and decreases production of T_3 (triiodothyronine), reducing the older adult's metabolic rate and contributing to weight gain. The adrenal cortex decreases in weight, but the overall level of cortisol remains the same.

10. The most common endocrine disorders in older adults include thyroid abnormalities and an increased risk for diabetes mellitus.

LEARNING OUTCOME 3

Recognize abnormal findings of common tests used to diagnose endocrine disorders.

Concepts for Lecture

1. Growth hormone (GH) normal findings are less than 5 ng/mL for men and less than 10 ng/mL in women. Anything outside these ranges is abnormal.

2. The normal findings for a water deprivation test are 1–5 pg/mL. Anything outside this range is abnormal.

3. The normal range of findings for thyroid-stimulating hormone (TSH) is 0.35–5.5 mcg/mL, the normal range for T_3 is 80–200 ng/dL, and the normal range for T_4 is 4.5–11.5 mcg/dL. Anything outside these ranges is abnormal.

4. The normal findings for a serum calcium test is 9–11 mg/dL. The normal findings for a serum phosphate test are 2.5–4.5 mg/dL. These tests are used to assess parathyroid functioning.

5. Two cortisol readings are done and normal lab findings are as follows: 8:00–10:00 am = 5–23 mcg/dL and 4:00–6:00 pm = 3–13 mcg/dL.

6. The normal range of findings for aldosterone levels is 4–30 ng/dL in sitting position and less than 16 ng/dL in supine position.

7. The normal range of urinary 17-ketosteroids (17-KS) is 5–15 mg/24 hours for men and 5–25 mg/24 hours for women. 17-KS are metabolites of testosterone that are released from the adrenal cortex. Levels increase with Cushing's syndrome and decrease in Addison's disease.

8. The normal range for fasting blood glucose is 70–110 mg/dL.

9. The normal range for glycosylated hemoglobin (HbA1c) is 5.5%–7%.

10. The normal range for 2-hour oral glucose tolerance is less than 125 mg/dL. In diabetics, the level is higher than 200 mg/dL.

11. The results of a urine glucose test should be negative. A positive result is abnormal.

12. Urine ketones should be negative. Positive results mean lack of insulin or diabetic ketoacidosis.

13. The normal range for the urine test for microalbumin is 0.2–1.9 mg/dL. Microalbumin is the earliest indicator for development of diabetic neuropathy.

14. An imaging study to detect tumors of the pituitary gland and hypothalamus is magnetic resonance imaging (MRI).

15. Abdominal computed tomography (CT) scan is used to detect tumors of the adrenal gland and pancreas.

 POWERPOINT SLIDES 50–52

Tables and/or Figures
- **Table 34-2** Common Laboratory Tests for Endocrine Disorders
- **Table 34-3** Imaging Studies

 **SUGGESTIONS FOR CLASSROOM ACTIVITIES**
- Have the students create a grid/table that identifies the endocrine organ, hormone secreted, condition that develops with either hypo- or hypersecretion, the laboratory test(s) or imaging test(s) that could help confirm a diagnosis of hypo- or hypersecretion, and the normal range or report of these tests.

 **SUGGESTIONS FOR CLINICAL ACTIVITIES**
- Assign the students to clients with an endocrine disorder. Have the students accompany the client to any scheduled diagnostic tests. Have the students identify laboratory tests on the medical record that were done to aid in the diagnosis of the disorder and interview the client about diagnostic tests that they have undergone.

 REFERENCE
- National Endocrine and Metabolic Disease Information Service: Adrenal insufficiency and Addison's disease. Available at http://endocrine.niddk.nih.gov/pubs/addison/addison.htm

16. The thyroid scan is used to detect thyroid malignancy. Cold spots that do not take up the I-125 indicate malignancy.
17. The radioactive iodine (RAI) uptake test is used to detect Graves' disease and hypothyroidism. Increased uptake indicates Graves' disease; decreased uptake means hypothyroidism.

LEARNING OUTCOME 4

Identify nursing responsibilities for common diagnostic tests for clients with endocrine disorders.

Concepts for Lecture

1. Nursing implications for test for growth hormone include ensuring that the client is fasting, well rested, and not physically or emotionally stressed.
2. The water deprivation test requires that the nurse tell the client to fast for 12 hours and to withhold fluids and smoking at midnight.
3. The thyroid-stimulating hormone test does not require fluid restriction. The nurse instructs the client to avoid shellfish for several days prior to the test.
4. Serum calcium and serum phosphate do not require the nurse to have the client fast; however, the tests are part of a chemistry panel that requires fasting.
5. The client who is getting a cortisol test needs to be advised by the nurse to rest in bed for 2 hours before blood is drawn. The nurse needs to explain that two blood samples are drawn—one at 8:00 to 10:00 am and the other at 4:00 to 6:00 pm.
6. The nurse will ask the client to be in a supine position for 1 hour prior to a laboratory test for aldosterone.
7. When a client is to collect urine for urinary 17-ketosteroids, the nurse will instruct the client about 24-hour urine collection, which must be iced or refrigerated during collection.
8. The nurse will instruct the client about fasting for a fasting blood glucose test.
9. No fasting or other instructions are required for a glycosylated hemoglobin (HbA1c) test.
10. When a client is scheduled for a 2-hour oral glucose tolerance test, the nurse instructs the client to be NPO for 12 hours before the test. The client must be instructed to drink the entire 100 g of glucose and not eat anything else until his or her blood is drawn.
11. When a urine glucose is ordered for a client, the nurse will collect a fresh specimen because stagnant urine may alter the test results.
12. The nurse needs to know that some drugs may interfere with both positive and negative results of a laboratory test for urine ketones.
13. The nurse must collect a fresh urine sample for a urine test for microalbumin.
14. When an MRI is ordered for a client, the nurse must assess for presence of metallic implants because clients with metal implants cannot have an MRI. The nurse also informs clients having an MRI to lie motionless during the test and makes sure all metal objects are removed from the client.
15. When a client is scheduled for a CT scan with contrast dye, the nurse must ask the client about allergies to iodine and seafood. The nurse instructs the client that he or she must lie still during the procedure.
16. When a client is scheduled for a thyroid scan, the nurse asks about allergies to iodine and seafood. The client may need to withhold thyroid

POWERPOINT SLIDES 53–57

Tables and/or Figures
- **Table 34-2** Common Laboratory Tests for Endocrine Disorders
- **Table 34-3** Imaging Studies

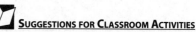

SUGGESTIONS FOR CLASSROOM ACTIVITIES

- Have students work in small groups. Have each group write a script about a client who is to get a laboratory test or imaging test for an endocrine disorder. In the skit, the students are to have the client ask questions that the nurse answers as well as gives instructions for the test.

SUGGESTIONS FOR CLINICAL ACTIVITIES

- Assign students to care for clients who have laboratory or imaging studies ordered for endocrine disorders or suspected endocrine disorders. Make arrangements with the staff nurse assigned to the client to have the student be present when instructions are given to the client about the testing or to have the student give the instructions.

REFERENCE

- MedlinePlus: Glucose tolerance test. Available at http://www.nlm.nih.gov/medlineplus/ency/article/003466.htm

drugs or medications containing iodine for weeks before the study. No fasting is required.

17. When a client is scheduled for a radioactive iodine uptake test, the nurse ensures that the client fasts for 8 hours before the test. The client can eat 1 hour after the radioiodine capsule or liquid has been taken. Thyroid drugs containing iodine are held for weeks before the study.

GENERAL CHAPTER CONSIDERATIONS

1. Have students study and learn key terms listed at the beginning of the chapter.
2. Have students complete end of chapter exercises either in their book or on the MyNursingKit Website.
3. Use the Classroom Response Question PowerPoints to assess students prior to lecture.

MYNURSINGKIT
(www.mynursingkit.com)

- Websites
- NCLEX® Questions
- Case Studies
- Key Terms

STUDENT WORKBOOK AND RESOURCE GUIDE

- Chapter 34 activities
- *Separate purchase*

PRENTICE HALL NURSE'S DRUG GUIDE

- *Separate purchase*

CLASSROOM RESPONSE QUESTION POWERPOINTS

TESTBANK

CHAPTER 35
CARING FOR CLIENTS WITH ENDOCRINE DISORDERS

LEARNING OUTCOME 1

Describe the pathophysiology of the common disorders of the pituitary, thyroid, parathyroid, and adrenal glands.

Concepts for Lecture

1. Growth hormone (GH), produced by the anterior lobe of the pituitary gland, stimulates the growth of the epiphyseal plates of the long bones and is necessary for skeletal and muscle growth. Excess secretion of GH before puberty and the closure of the epiphyseal plates results in gigantism.
2. Dwarfism occurs from inadequate production of GH during childhood.
3. Acromegaly (enlargement of bones and connective tissue) develops during adulthood from hypersecretion of GH. Usually, a benign, slow-growing tumor (pituitary adenoma) stimulates the hypersecretion.
4. Disorders of the posterior pituitary are caused by too much or too little antidiuretic hormone (ADH). ADH regulates total body water by acting on the kidney to retain or release water. Receptors in the hypothalamus control the release of ADH in response to serum osmolarity (concentration of particles in the blood). When serum osmolarity increases, ADH secretion increases, and renal water is reabsorbed, which decreases urine output. Hyposmolarity suppresses the release of ADH, so urine output increases.
5. Diabetes insipidus (DI) is a condition that results from ADH insufficiency. There are two types: neurogenic and nephrogenic. Neurogenic DI can result from damage to the pituitary gland following head injury or cranial injury. Nephrogenic DI occurs when the kidneys fail to respond to ADH secretion. This condition may be due to renal failure.
6. Syndrome of inappropriate ADH secretion (SIADH) is a condition that results from excess production of ADH. This disorder may be caused by lung tumors, head injury, pituitary surgery, or the use of barbiturates, anesthetics, or diuretics.
7. Hyperthyroidism (thyrotoxicosis) involves an excess production of thyroid hormone. Hyperthyroidism is caused by an autoimmune response, by excessive doses of thyroid medication, or by excess secretion of thyroid-stimulating hormone from the pituitary gland.
8. Graves' disease, the most common cause of hyperthyroidism, is an autoimmune disorder.
9. Thyroid crisis (thyroid storm) is an extreme state of hyperthyroidism but is rare today. This disorder may result from untreated hyperthyroidism along with a stressor such as an infection, untreated diabetic ketoacidosis, physical or emotional trauma, or thyroid surgery. Thyroid crisis is a life-threatening condition and requires immediate medical attention.
10. The underlying problem in hypothyroidism is a failure of the thyroid gland. Hypothyroidism occurs when the thyroid gland produces an

POWERPOINT SLIDES 22–31

Tables and/or Figures
- **Figure 35-2** Individual With Enlargement of the Thyroid Gland

SUGGESTIONS FOR CLASSROOM ACTIVITIES
- Have the students create a grid/table that identifies the endocrine organ, hormone secreted, and condition that develops with either hypo- or hypersecretion.

SUGGESTIONS FOR CLINICAL ACTIVITIES
- Assign the students to care for a client with an endocrine disorder. Ask the students to interview the client and the client's physician, if possible, to learn about the pathophysiology involved in the client's disorder.
- Have students discuss the pathophysiology of their assigned client's disorder in postconference.

REFERENCE
- Department of Health and Human Services: Hashimoto's thyroiditis. Available at http://www.womenshealth.gov/faq/hashimoto-thyroiditis.cfm

insufficient amount of thyroid hormone. Thyroid deficiency may be caused by congenital defects in the gland, antithyroid medication, and surgical removal of the gland or iodine deficiency. The main disorders are goiter, Hashimoto's thyroiditis, and myxedema coma. Certain drugs (lithium carbonate, which blocks thyroid hormone [TH] synthesis, and amiodarone, which has high iodine content) can lead to hypothyroidism.

11. When TH production decreases, the thyroid gland enlarges in an attempt to produce more hormone. The enlargement is called a goiter.

12. The most common cause of primary hypothyroidism is Hashimoto's thyroiditis. It is an autoimmune disorder in which antibodies destroy thyroid tissue.

13. Myxedema coma is a life-threatening form of hypothyroidism requiring immediate medical attention. It may be brought on by exposure to cold temperatures, infection, surgery, trauma, or use of central nervous system depressants (especially narcotics and tranquilizers). This crisis occurs most often in winter months.

14. Hyperparathyroidism results from increased secretion of parathyroid hormone (PTH), which regulates normal serum levels of calcium. It is classified as either primary or secondary. Primary hyperparathyroidism is the most common and usually results from an adenoma (tumor) in one of the parathyroid glands. Secondary hyperparathyroidism may result from chronic renal failure. The increase in PTH causes calcium to leave the bones and enter the blood, resulting in hypercalcemia. Excess PTH also causes excretion of phosphate, leading to hypophosphatemia.

15. Hypoparathyroidism results from inadequate secretion of PTH. The usual cause is accidental damage to or removal of the parathyroid glands during a thyroidectomy. The lack of circulating PTH causes hypocalcemia and an elevated blood phosphate level. The reduced PTH levels impair kidney regulation of calcium and phosphate. Decreased activation of vitamin D leads to lower calcium absorption by the intestines. The low calcium levels increase neuromuscular activity, especially the peripheral motor and sensory nerves.

16. Cushing's syndrome is a chronic disorder in which the adrenal cortex produces excessive amounts of the hormone cortisol. Several factors may lead to Cushing's syndrome: (1) adrenal tumors causing an increased production of cortisol; (2) a tumor of the pituitary gland increases adrenocorticotropic hormone (ACTH) release, which stimulates the adrenal cortex to produce cortisol; (3) chronic glucocorticoid therapy; and (4) increased release of ACTH from lung or pancreatic tumors.

17. Addison's disease is primary adrenal cortex hypofunction. In primary Addison's disease, an autoimmune response destroys the client's own adrenal cortex. This leads to reduced levels of glucocorticoids, mineralocorticoids, and androgens.

18. Addisonian crisis is a serious life-threatening response to acute adrenal insufficiency. Major stressors such as surgery, trauma, or severe infections usually precipitate this condition. Addisonian crisis may also occur in clients who are abruptly withdrawn from corticosteroid medication.

19. Pheochromocytoma is a benign tumor of the adrenal medulla. The tumor erratically produces excessive amounts of catecholamines (epinephrine or norepinephrine), which stimulate the sympathetic nervous system. This leads to a dramatic rise in the systolic blood pressure of 200–300 mm Hg and a diastolic pressure greater than 150 mm Hg.

Learning Outcome 2

Contrast the manifestations resulting from hypersecretion and hyposecretion of hormones from the pituitary, thyroid, parathyroid, and adrenal glands.

Concepts for Lecture

1. In the oversecretion of growth hormone, as a child, a person becomes abnormally tall, often over 7 feet, with normal body proportions. In the undersecretion of growth hormone, as a child, the person has short stature and usually has normal body proportions and intelligence. Hypersecretion of GH as an adult results in bones other than the long bones and connective tissue growing at a very slow rate, causing an enlarged forehead and protruding jaw. With overgrowth of tissue in the hands and feet, clients require larger shoes, gloves, and rings. If untreated, complications such as hypertension, diabetes mellitus, cardiac enlargement, and cardiac failure can result.

2. Diabetes insipidus (ADH insufficiency) causes a urinary output of 5 to 15 liters per day. The client develops polydipsia (excessive thirst). If unable to replace the water loss, the client becomes dehydrated and is at risk for hypernatremia. The client has very pale urine, weakness, and poor skin turgor. Clients with inappropriate ADH secretion have excess production of ADH. This condition leads to water retention, hyponatremia, and serum hyposmolarity. There is decreased urine output and concentrated urine.

3. In hyperthyroidism, there is an excess production of thyroid hormone (TH) and an increase in metabolic rate, whereas in hypothyroidism, an insufficient amount of thyroid hormone is produced, and the metabolic rate is slowed. Increased TH rate results in exophthalmos, where the sclera is often visible above the iris and the person has a characteristic unblinking stare. The person with excess secretion of TH can also go into life-threatening thyroid crisis in which the metabolic rate rises suddenly; the client has a high fever, tachycardia, and hypertension. Restlessness and tremors are common, progressing to confusion, delirium, coma, and seizures. In hypothyroidism, most of the body systems slow down. Many of the manifestations are opposite those of hyperthyroidism.

4. In myxedema coma, a life-threatening form of hypothyroidism, the client presents with seizures, lethargy quickly progressing to coma, and hypothermia. The respiratory and cardiovascular systems shut down, causing bradycardia and decreased respiratory rate.

5. In hyperparathyroidism, the increase in parathyroid hormone (PTH) causes calcium to leave the bones and enter the blood, resulting in hypercalcemia and hypophosphatemia. Many clients are asymptomatic. Eventually, symptoms can include possible pathologic fractures, muscle weakness and atrophy, polyuria, and renal calculi.

6. In hypoparathyroidism, there is inadequate secretion of PTH, which causes hypocalcemia and an elevated blood phosphate level. Clients may be asymptomatic. With more acute disease, neuromuscular manifestations result. Tetany (a continuous spasm of muscles) is the primary symptom. In severe cases, bronchospasm, laryngeal spasms, convulsions, and even death may occur.

7. Cushing's syndrome, in which the adrenal cortex produces excessive amounts of cortisol, has the following manifestations: fat deposits in the abdomen, fat pads under the clavicle, a "buffalo hump" over the upper back, and a round "moon face." There is muscle weakness and wasting in the extremities as well as poor wound

PowerPoint Slides 32–44

Tables and/or Figures

- **Box 35-1** Manifestations of Diabetes Insipidus
- **Box 35-2** Manifestation of Syndrome of Inappropriate ADH (SIADH)
- **Figure 35-1** Multisystem Effects of Hyperthyroidism
- **Figure 35-2** Individual With Enlargement of the Thyroid Gland
- **Figure 35-3** Exophthalmos in a Client With Graves' Disease
- **Figure 35-4** Multisystem Effects of Hypothyroidism
- **Figure 35-5** A Woman Before and After Developing Cushing's Syndrome
- **Figure 35-6** Major Clinical Manifestations of Cushing's Syndrome
- **Box 35-6** Manifestations of Hyperparathyroidism
- **Box 35-7** Manifestations of Hypoparathyroidism
- **Box 35-9** Manifestations of Addison's Disease

Suggestions for Classroom Activities

- Review the grids created for the hypo- and hypersecreted hormones. Add a column for manifestations for each of the disorders.
- Present the students with an outline of a person and ask them to write in the manifestations, drawing arrows to the part of the body affected by each manifestation.

Suggestions for Clinical Activities

- Assign the students to care for a client with an endocrine disorder. Have the students identify the manifestations of the disorder with supporting evidence.

References

- National Endocrine and Metabolic Diseases Information Service: Adrenal insufficiency and Addison's disease. Available at http://endocrine.niddk.nih.gov/pubs/addison/addison.htm
- National Endocrine and Metabolic Diseases Information Service: Cushing's syndrome. Available at http://endocrine.niddk.nih.gov/pubs/cushings/cushings.htm#causes

healing. Additional symptoms include osteoporosis, compression fractures of the vertebrae, sodium and water retention, potassium loss, hypertension, greater risk of infection, hirsutism in women, and emotional instability.

8. In Addison's disease, there are reduced amounts of glucocorticoids, mineralocorticoids, and androgens. Manifestations develop when more than 90% of the gland is destroyed. Manifestations result from elevated ACTH levels and decreased aldosterone and cortisol. The manifestations of Addisonian crisis, a life-threatening condition that occurs when clients are abruptly withdrawn from corticosteroid medications, include hypotension; rapid, weak pulse; extreme weakness; and confusion resulting from circulatory collapse and shock. Potassium levels can reach dangerously high levels, leading to cardiac dysrhythmias.

9. In pheochromocytoma, excessive amounts of catecholamines are produced, which stimulates the sympathetic nervous system leading to a dramatic rise in systolic blood pressure of 200–300 mm Hg and a diastolic pressure greater than 150 mm Hg. Additional symptoms include pounding headache, tachycardia, profuse sweating, flushing, and palpitations.

LEARNING OUTCOME 3

Identify laboratory and diagnostic tests used to diagnose endocrine disorders.

Concepts for Lecture

1. Diagnosis of disorders of the anterior pituitary gland is confirmed by magnetic resonance imaging (MRI) and computed tomography (CT) scans. Serum growth hormone levels are also used in diagnosis of hyperpituitarism and hypopituitarism.

2. Diagnosis of SIADH or diabetes insipidus is based in part on the results of the water deprivation test (see Chapter 34, Table 34-2).

3. The diagnosis of hyperthyroidism is often confirmed by elevated serum T_3 and T_4 levels, decreased TSH levels, and increased radioactive iodine uptake.

4. Laboratory tests for hypothyroidism include T_4, which is decreased in hypothyroidism.

5. Elevated levels of serum calcium, PTH, and alkaline phosphatase confirm a diagnosis of hyperparathyroidism. Once the diagnosis is confirmed, bone density studies are conducted to determine whether bone loss has occurred.

6. Hypoparathyroidism is diagnosed by low serum calcium levels and high phosphorous levels in the absence of renal failure, an absorption disorder, or a nutritional disorder.

7. Diagnosis of Cushing's syndrome is confirmed by an increased plasma cortisol level and an elevated 24-hour urine test for 17-ketosteroids and 17-hydroxycorticosteroids. Plasma ACTH levels are elevated when Cushing's syndrome is caused by a pituitary gland tumor. Serum sodium and glucose levels are also elevated in Cushing's syndrome.

8. Addison's disease is diagnosed through findings of decreased serum levels of cortisol and aldosterone and urinary 17-ketosteroids. Potassium is increased and blood glucose and sodium levels are decreased. CT scan and MRI may identify atrophy of the adrenal glands.

9. Pheochromocytoma is diagnosed by increased catecholamine levels in the blood or urine, CT scan, and MRI.

LEARNING OUTCOME 4

Discuss the nursing implications for medications and treatment ordered for clients with endocrine disorders.

Concepts for Lecture

1. The nurse teaches clients with hypopituitarism about the need for lifelong hormone replacement therapy. For the client with hyperpituitarism taking octreotide (Sandostatin), the nurse conveys that the drug decreases growth hormone production but does not reduce the tumor size.

2. Clients with SIADH (diabetes insipidus) may be given ADH replacement therapy with desmopressin (DDAVP) or vasopressin (Pitressin). The nurse needs to teach the client with DI about how to administer DDAVP intranasally and about the manifestations of water excess from an overdosage of DDAVP. Sodium restriction and thiazide diuretics may be ordered for clients with nephrogenic DI. Demeclocycline (Declomycin), a tetracycline antibiotic, is used to promote urine production.

3. The client in thyroid crisis may be given antithyroid medication such as propylthiouracil (Propyl-Thyracil) to reduce thyroid hormone production. The nurse monitors cardiovascular and respiratory status throughout treatment.

4. Medications given for hyperthyroidism include the antithyroid drugs methimazole (Tapazole) and propylthiouracil (Propyl-Thyracil). Nursing implications include the need to give the drug at the same time each day to maintain stable blood levels. The client is monitored for itching, rash, fever, nausea, loss of taste, and agranulocytosis. The client is also monitored for hypothyroidism, bradycardia, fatigue, and weight gain.

5. When the client with hyperthyroidism is given potassium iodide, saturated solution (SSKI) or strong iodine solution (Lugol's solution), the nurse must ask about allergies to shellfish and monitor for bleeding if the client takes anticoagulants.

6. When the client with hyperthyroidism is given propranolol (Inderal), the nurse must be aware that the drug is not to be given to clients with asthma or heart disease. The nurse will monitor for side effects of bradycardia, fatigue, and weakness.

7. Clients with hyperthyroidism may be given radioactive iodine (I-131) to destroy thyroid cells so they produce less thyroid hormone. The client may experience mouth and throat dryness for 2–3 days, and the nurse instructs the client to take frequent sips of water or ice chips.

8. Hypothyroidism is treated with thyroid hormone replacement. Drug therapy is started with small doses that are gradually increased. When giving thyroid replacement such as levothyroxine sodium (Synthroid, Levothroid) and liothyronine sodium (Cytomel), the nurse will give the drug 1 hour before breakfast and check the client's pulse. If the resting pulse is greater than 100, the nurse will call the physician. The nurse monitors for side effects of nervousness and weight loss, monitors for bleeding if taking anticoagulants, and checks blood glucose levels closely in diabetics.

9. For clients with hypothyroidism who develop large goiters that cause breathing or swallowing problems and for pregnant women who cannot be exposed to radiation therapy, a subtotal thyroidectomy may be indicated. This surgery leaves enough gland tissue to produce an adequate amount of thyroid hormone.

POWERPOINT SLIDES 52–62

Tables and/or Figures

- **Table 35-1** Giving Medications Safely: Hyperthyroidism
- **Table 35-2** Giving Medications Safely: Hypothyroidism
- **Table 35-3** Giving Medications Safely: Addison's Disease

SUGGESTIONS FOR CLASSROOM ACTIVITIES

- Have the students prepare medication cards for each of the medications used to treat endocrine disorders.

SUGGESTIONS FOR CLINICAL ACTIVITIES

- Assign the students to a client with an endocrine disorder. Have the students research the medications and treatments prescribed to treat the disorder.

REFERENCE

- RxList: Pitressin. Available at http://www.rxlist.com/pitressin-drug.htm

10. Clients with thyroid cancer may have a subtotal thyroidectomy and not need thyroid replacement therapy, or the client may have a total thyroidectomy and then require lifelong thyroid hormone replacement.

11. Treatment of hyperparathyroidism focuses on decreasing the serum calcium levels. Those with acute hyperparathyroidism are given bisphosphonates such as alendronate (Fosamax) or pamidronate (Aredia) to inhibit bone resorption.

12. The first priority for clients with hypoparathyroidism is to increase calcium levels. The client may receive intravenous calcium gluconate immediately to reduce tetany. The client could develop respiratory distress, so the nurse ensures a patent airway. The conscious client is asked to breathe in and out of a paper bag. Long-term therapy includes supplemental calcium with oral calcium salts. The client needs a diet high in calcium but low in phosphate. Vitamin D therapy is given to increase GI absorption of calcium.

13. The treatment of Cushing's syndrome includes surgery, radiotherapy, or medications. Medications include mitotane (Lysodren) and metyrapone and aminoglutethimide (Cytadren).

14. When an adrenal cortex tumor causes Cushing's syndrome, an adrenalectomy may be done. Clients with inoperable tumor may receive radioactive isotopes implanted into the pituitary gland.

15. The client in Addisonian crisis will likely receive IV fluids, glucose, sodium, and glucocorticoids in intensive care. During the crisis, the nurse will keep the client warm and quiet, monitor potassium levels, and monitor for hypotension.

16. The client with Addison's disease will likely receive hydrocortisone orally to replace cortisol and fludrocortisones (Florinef) to replace mineralocorticoids. Nursing implications include giving oral forms of cortisol with food to reduce ulcers and checking stools for occult blood and urine for glycosuria. The nurse will report increased blood pressure, edema, or weight gain; bruising; or weakness and assess for impaired wound healing.

17. Surgical removal of the tumor(s) by laparoscopic adrenalectomy is the treatment of choice for pheochromocytoma. The nursing implications include stabilizing the client's blood pressure during the attack and prior to surgery. Following surgery, the client may require adrenal hormone replacement therapy and monitoring of blood pressure.

LEARNING OUTCOME 5

Identify the preoperative and postoperative nursing care for a client undergoing either a subtotal thyroidectomy or an adrenalectomy.

Concepts for Lecture

1. For the client undergoing a subtotal thyroidectomy, the nurse will preoperatively give ordered antithyroid medications and iodine preparations as ordered.

2. Postoperatively, the nurse will place the client in a semi-Fowler's position and support the client's head and neck with pillows. The nurse will monitor and report the following complications to the physician: hemorrhage, respiratory distress, laryngeal nerve damage, tetany, and thyroid storm.

3. To assess hemorrhage, the nurse assesses the dressing and the back of the neck for bleeding, assesses tightness of the dressing, and monitors blood pressure and pulse for symptoms of hypovolemic shock.

4. To assess respiratory distress, the nurse assesses respiratory rate, rhythm, depth, and effort. The nurse provides humidification and has

 POWERPOINT SLIDES 63–65

Tables and/or Figures
- **Box 35-3** Nursing Care Checklist: Care of the Client Having a Subtotal Thyroidectomy

 **SUGGESTIONS FOR CLASSROOM ACTIVITIES**
- Have the students prepare a plan of care for a client undergoing a subtotal thyroidectomy.

 **SUGGESTIONS FOR CLINICAL ACTIVITIES**
- Assign the students to care for clients with a thyroid disorder either preoperative or postoperative. If possible, assign the students to care for clients both preoperatively and postoperatively. If the client is going to surgery, make arrangements for the student to observe the surgery, if possible.

ready for immediate use the following equipment: suction, oxygen, and a tracheostomy set.

5. The nurse assesses laryngeal nerve damage by assessing the ability to speak aloud and hoarseness.

6. Usually, only one adrenal gland is involved in an adrenalectomy. Following an adrenalectomy, the client is cared for in the intensive care unit because of the risk for Addisonian crisis, also known as adrenal crisis.

LEARNING OUTCOME 6

Use the nursing process to care for clients with disorders of the pituitary, thyroid, parathyroid, and adrenal glands.

Concepts for Lecture

1. Nursing care of clients with anterior pituitary disorders focuses on helping them cope with body image changes and with anxiety about an unknown future following surgery.

2. Nursing care for the client with diabetes insipidus focuses on managing fluid and electrolyte problems and replacing ADH. Nursing diagnoses include: Deficient Fluid Volume related to deficiency of ADH.

3. A nursing diagnosis for SIADH is Excess Fluid Volume related to excess production of ADH.

4. When working with a client with hyperthyroidism, the nurse must consider the multisystem effects of the disorder when planning nursing care for the client. Although each client has different needs, the priority problems include altered cardiovascular function, imbalanced nutrition, fatigue, visual deficits, and body image disturbance.

5. Nursing diagnoses for a client with hyperthyroidism may include Risk for Decreased Cardiac Output, Risk for Imbalanced Nutrition: Less than Body Requirements, Fatigue, Risk for Injury, corneal abrasion, and Disturbed Body Image.

6. When planning care for the client with hypothyroidism, the nurse takes into account that the disorder has a multisystem effect. The highest priority client problems include cardiovascular function, imbalanced nutrition, constipation, and activity level. Nursing diagnoses may include Decreased Cardiac Output, Imbalanced Nutrition: More than Body Requirements, Constipation, and Activity Intolerance.

7. Care of the client with hyperparathyroidism focuses on interventions related to impaired physical mobility and risk for injury due to the client's muscle weakness and altered mentation. It is important for the nurse to monitor for manifestations of urinary tract infection. The client may need additional interventions to decrease chronic pain and promote sound nutrition intake.

8. The most common problems the nurse will identify when caring for a client with Cushing's disease are related to fluid and electrolyte balance, injury, infection, and body image. Nursing diagnoses may include Excess Fluid Volume, Risk for Injury, Risk for Infection, and Disturbed Body Image.

9. Nursing care of the client with Addison's disease focuses on restoring fluid and electrolyte balance and increasing nutritional intake. Nursing diagnoses include Deficient Fluid Volume, Activity Intolerance, and Imbalanced Nutrition: Less than Body Requirements.

10. When caring for a client with pheochromocytoma, the nursing care during the acute attack and prior to surgery focuses on stabilizing the blood pressure. The client is often admitted to the intensive care unit where constant hemodynamic monitoring and intravenous antihypertensive medications are instituted. After surgery, the client may require adrenal hormone replacement therapy and monitoring of blood pressure.

POWERPOINT SLIDES 66–76

Nursing Care Plan: Client With Graves' Disease

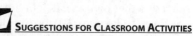

SUGGESTIONS FOR CLASSROOM ACTIVITIES

- Divide the students into groups. Have them prepare a plan of care for a client with a specified endocrine disorder.

SUGGESTIONS FOR CLINICAL ACTIVITIES

- Assign the students to a client with an endocrine disorder. Have each student discuss their plan of care in postconference.
- Find a client in the clinical area who has a diagnosis of endocrine disorder and who is willing to be part of a grand rounds presentation where the client tells his or her history and allows the students to ask questions.

REFERENCE

- Daub KF: Pheochromocytoma: challenges in diagnosis and nursing care. Available at http://www.ncbi.nlm.nih.gov/pubmed/17270594

LEARNING OUTCOME 7

Reinforce teaching guidelines for clients receiving long-term hormonal replacement therapy.

Concepts for Lecture

1. Clients with hypothyroidism or postoperative total thyroidectomy will be prescribed long-term thyroid replacement therapy.
2. The nurse, working with a client who is prescribed long-term thyroid replacement therapy, will teach the client to take his or her pulse before taking the medicine, which includes levothyroxine sodium (Synthroid, Levothroid) or liothyronine sodium (Cytomel), and to call the physician if the resting pulse is greater than 100. The client is instructed to take the medicine at the same time every day 1 hour before breakfast. The client is also taught not to take the medicine with antacids or iron preparation, to take the medicine for the rest of the client's life, and to report unusual weight loss, nervousness, bleeding, or chest pain. The client is instructed to check blood glucose levels closely if diabetic because thyroid dugs alter insulin action.
3. Clients with Addison's disease will be prescribed long-term corticosteroids, which include cortisone (Cortone), hydrocortisone (Cortef, Solu-Cortef), prednisone (Deltasone), dexamethasone (Decadron), prednisolone (Delta-Cortef), and methylprednisolone (Solu-Medrol).
4. Teaching for clients taking cortisol replacements includes instruction to take the medication with food to reduce ulcers, report any gastric distress or dark stool, never stop the medication abruptly, take medication for the rest of the client's life, eat a diet high in potassium and low in sodium, and weigh daily and report weight gain or edema.

GENERAL CHAPTER CONSIDERATIONS

1. Have students study and learn key terms listed at the beginning of the chapter.
2. Have students complete end of chapter exercises either in their book or on the MyNursingKit Website.
3. Use the Classroom Response Question PowerPoints to assess students prior to lecture.

POWERPOINT SLIDES 77–81

Tables and/or Figures

- **Table 35-2** Giving Medications Safely: Hypothyroidism
- **Table 35-3** Giving Medications Safely: Addison's Disease

SUGGESTIONS FOR CLASSROOM ACTIVITIES

- Assign the students to research hormone replacement medications in current use, including older and new medications, and to prepare a 10-minute presentation to be shared in class.

SUGGESTIONS FOR CLINICAL ACTIVITIES

- Assign the students to care for a client with an endocrine disorder. Ensure that the student comprehends the medications prescribed for this disorder. Supervise the students giving medications to clients with endocrine disorders whenever possible.

REFERENCE

- Alt.Support.Thyroid: Hypothyroidism medication. Available at http://www.altsupportthyroid.org/treatment/hypomed.php

- Clinical Reasoning Care Map

MYNURSINGKIT
(www.mynursingkit.com)

- Websites
- NCLEX® Questions
- Case Studies
- Key Terms

STUDENT WORKBOOK AND RESOURCE GUIDE

- Chapter 35 activities
- *Separate purchase*

PRENTICE HALL NURSE'S DRUG GUIDE

- *Separate purchase*

CLASSROOM RESPONSE QUESTION
POWERPOINTS

TESTBANK

CHAPTER 36
CARING FOR CLIENTS WITH DIABETES MELLITUS

LEARNING OUTCOME 1

Differentiate risk factors, pathophysiology, and clinical manifestations between type 1 and type 2 diabetes mellitus.

Concepts for Lecture

1. Type 1 diabetes mellitus is caused by autoimmune destruction of beta cells of the islets of Langerhans. This destruction leads to a state of absolute insulin deficiency, whereas in type 2 diabetes, there is a state of sufficient insulin to prevent ketoacidosis but insufficient to lower blood glucose levels.
2. Type 1 diabetes usually occurs in childhood and adolescence but may occur at any age, whereas type 2 diabetes usually occurs after age 30.
3. The client with type 1 diabetes is prone to developing ketoacidosis and is insulin dependent, and if the client does not receive insulin, he or she will die. Clients with type 2 diabetes may become insulin requiring but not insulin dependent. If the client with type 2 diabetes does not receive insulin, he or she will become ill but will not die.
4. In both type 1 and type 2 diabetes, clients have polyuria, polydipsia, fatigue, and blurred vision. In type 2 diabetes, the client has recurrent infections and paresthesias. Malaise occurs with type 1 diabetes. In type 1 diabetes, there is weight loss, whereas in type 2, the client is often overweight.
5. Risk factors for type 1 include heredity and environmental factors. Viral infections including mumps, rubella, or Coxsackie 4 have been linked to type 1 diabetes. Risk factors for type 2 diabetes include heredity, obesity, physical inactivity, illnesses, increasing age, and belonging to a high-risk ethnic group.

LEARNING OUTCOME 2

Identify the diagnostic tests used to diagnose and monitor self-management of diabetes mellitus.

Concepts for Lecture

1. Three laboratory tests are used to screen for the presence of diabetes mellitus: plasma glucose (PG) level, fasting blood glucose (FBG), and an oral glucose tolerance test (OGTT).
2. In the clinical setting, the FBG is preferred because it is easier to administer, more convenient, and more economical than the other two.
3. Routine screening tests should be done if the client meets any of the following criteria: is obese, has first-degree relative with diabetes mellitus (DM), is in a high-risk ethnic population (e.g., African American, Hispanic American, Native American, Asian American, Pacific Islander), has delivered a baby weighing more than 9 pounds or has been diagnosed with gestational diabetes mellitus, is hypertensive, has a high-density lipoprotein cholesterol level of less than 35 mg/dL, has triglycerides greater than 250 mg/dL, or has had impaired glucose tolerance or fasting glucose in the past.

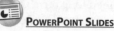

POWERPOINT SLIDES

Tables and/or Figures

- **Table 36-1** Classification and Characteristics of Diabetes
- **Box 36-1** Manifestations of Type 1 and Type 2 Diabetes Mellitus

SUGGESTIONS FOR CLASSROOM ACTIVITIES

- Diagram the pathophysiology of type 1 and type 2 diabetes, and based on this diagram, have the students identify the cause of the signs and symptoms of the disease.

SUGGESTIONS FOR CLINICAL ACTIVITIES

- Assign the students to each care for a client with either type 1 or type 2 diabetes mellitus. Have the students ask the client about when the client was diagnosed, the presenting signs and symptoms at diagnosis, and the current manifestations of the disease.

REFERENCE

- MedlinePlus: Type 2 diabetes risk factors. Available at http://www.nlm.nih.gov/medlineplus/ency/article/002072.htm

POWERPOINT SLIDES

SUGGESTIONS FOR CLASSROOM ACTIVITIES

- Provide a variety of self-monitoring blood glucose meters. Have the students check a partner's blood glucose, or they can check their own blood glucose on a voluntary basis. If students object to participating voluntarily, have them verbalize the procedure for checking blood glucose.

SUGGESTIONS FOR CLINICAL ACTIVITIES

- Assign the students to clients with diabetes. Have the students measure their assigned client's blood glucose level with a glucometer. Have the student measure the client's urine ketones and glucose with either the tablets or strips. Have the students document their findings.

4. The most common diagnostic tests to monitor diabetes management are fasting blood glucose (FBG), glycosylated hemoglobin (A1c), urine glucose and ketone levels, and serum cholesterol and triglyceride levels.

5. The ADA recommends that Hgb A1c levels be measured twice per year and kept at 7% or below. The ADA recommends raising HDL cholesterol to greater than 45 mg/dL, lowering LDL cholesterol to less than 100 mg/dL, and lowering triglycerides to less than 150 mg/dL (ADA, 2008).

6. People with diabetes can self-monitor their blood glucose and achieve metabolic control.

7. Self-monitoring is useful when the person is ill or pregnant or has symptoms of hypoglycemia or hyperglycemia.

8. Self-monitoring of blood glucose (SMBG) should be done three or more times per day for clients with type 1 diabetes; for clients with type 2 diabetes, the testing should be sufficient to help them reach glucose goals.

9. Equipment needed for SMBG includes some type of lancet to perform a finger stick to get a drop of blood, a blood glucose measuring machine, and test strips. The manufacturer's specific operating instructions must be followed closely.

10. A new insulin pump receives information from a continuous glucose monitor (CGM) worn on the skin. The CGM has a sensor that is inserted under the skin, just like the insulin pump. This sensor sends data to the insulin pump screen, warning of high or low glucose levels.

11. Urine testing for ketones and glucose was once the only available method for evaluating diabetic management. It has unpredictable results.

12. Urine testing should be done in people with type 1 DM who have unexplained hyperglycemia during illness or pregnancy to monitor for hyperglycemia and ketoacidosis.

13. Urine testing for ketones can be done with either acid test tablets or ketostix.

14. The normal result of a test for ketones is negative for ketones.

LEARNING OUTCOME 3

Discuss the nursing implications for insulin and oral antidiabetic agents ordered for clients with diabetes mellitus.

Concepts for Lecture

1. The pharmacologic treatment for DM depends on the type of diabetes. People with type 1 DM must have insulin; those with type 2 are usually able to control glucose levels with oral antidiabetic medication, but they may require insulin when control is inadequate.

2. Insulin is derived from pork pancreas or made synthetically in the laboratory.

3. Insulins are available in rapid-acting, short-acting, intermediate-acting, and long-acting preparations.

4. The common insulins and times of onset, peak, and duration of actions are listed in Table 36-2.

5. Insulin is dispensed as 100 Units/mL (U-100 insulin) and 500 Units/mL (U-500 insulin) with the standard concentration being 100 Units/mL. U-500 insulin is used only in rare cases of insulin resistance when very large doses are needed.

6. Insulin is given in sterile, single-use, disposable insulin syringes, marked in units per milliliter.

7. Common syringe sizes are either 0.5 (50 U) or 1.0 mL (100 U). The advantage of the 0.5-mL size is that the distance between unit markings is greater so that it is easier to measure the dose accurately.

REFERENCE

• Karter AJ, Ackerson LM, Darbinian JA, D'Agostino RB Jr, Ferrara A, Liu J, Selby JV: Self-monitoring of blood glucose levels and glycemic control: the Northern California Kaiser Permanente Diabetes registry. Available at http://www.ncbi.nlm.nih.gov/pubmed/11448654

POWERPOINT SLIDES

Tables and/or Figures

• **Table 36-2** Action of Insulin Preparations
• **Figure 36-1** Using an Insulin Pen
• **Figure 36-2** Sites of Insulin Injection
• **Box 36-2** Techniques to Minimize Painful Injections
• **Table 36-3** Giving Medications Safely: Insulin and Client Teaching
• **Table 36-4** Insulin Regimens
• **Table 36-5** Giving Medications Safely: Oral Antidiabetic Agents
• **Box 36-2** Procedure Checklist: Techniques to Minimize Painful Injections
• **Box 36-3** Procedure Checklist: Mixing Insulins: 10 Units of Regular and 20 Units of NPH

8. Regular insulin may be given by either subcutaneous or intravenous routes. All other insulins are given only subcutaneously.

9. Special injection products (alternative delivery methods) include insulin pens and jet spray injectors, as well as continuous subcutaneous infusion pump.

10. Clients who use the insulin pen dial the appropriate dose before injection. These pens are useful for people who are visually impaired or traveling.

11. Jet injectors shoot insulin through the skin into the subcutaneous tissue. High cost and bruising limit their use.

12. The continuous subcutaneous insulin infusion (CSII) delivers a constant amount of programmed regular or rapid-acting insulin throughout each 24-hour period. It delivers a bolus of insulin when programmed manually (e.g., before meals).

13. The advantages of CSII include more normal glucose control and greater lifestyle flexibility.

14. Disadvantages of CSII are an increased risk of ketoacidosis from a malfunctioning pump and infection at the needle insertion site. The needle is changed every 3 days.

15. To administer insulin, the nurse or client gently pinches a fold of skin and injects the needle at a 90-degree angle. If the person is very thin, a 45-degree angle may be required to avoid injecting into muscle.

16. The nurse does not massage the injection site after injecting and will advise clients giving insulin not to massage the injection site.

17. Techniques to minimize painful injections are to be used by the nurse and taught to clients. These techniques are summarized in Box 36-2.

18. The recommended injection sites are the upper arm, the abdomen except for a 2-inch circle around the umbilicus, the anterior lateral part of the thigh, and the buttocks (Figure 36-2). The distance between injection sites should be about 1 inch. Rotation of injection sites is recommended to give more consistent blood glucose levels and to prevent lipodystrophy.

19. Problems with insulin injections include lipodystrophy (hypertrophy of subcutaneous tissue) and lipoatrophy (atrophy of subcutaneous tissue). Lipodystrophy and lipoatrophy may occur if the same injection sites are used repeatedly. The use of refrigerated synthetic or pork insulin may trigger the development of tissue hypertrophy or atrophy.

20. People who require more than one type of insulin must mix their insulins to avoid multiple injections per dose. Instructions for mixing insulin are provided in Box 36-3.

21. Clients who have difficulty mixing insulin because of poor eyesight or impaired manual dexterity can use premixed insulins such as 70% NPH and 30% regular insulin.

22. Mix only NPH with regular, lispro, aspart, and glulisine insulins.

23. Do not mix insulin glargine (Lantus) with any other types of insulin.

24. Do not mix human and pork insulins because they will inactivate each other.

25. Nursing implications for giving insulin safely and teaching clients and family include discarding vials of insulin whose expiration date has passed or vials of insulin that are discolored or contain clumps, granules, or solid deposits on the sides of the vial and how to properly store insulin.

26. When drawing up an insulin dose, the nurse always checks type and dose with another nurse.

27. The client's blood glucose level is checked 30 minutes before giving an insulin injection. If the client's meal is delayed, the nurse holds administration of rapid-acting insulin.

28. The nurse will notify the physician when the client eats an inadequate diet.

SUGGESTIONS FOR CLASSROOM ACTIVITIES

- Provide students with a variety of insulin vials, insulin syringes with needles, and doctors' order forms with orders for insulin to be given to a mock client. Have students practice drawing up insulin according to the order sheet they are given and mock administering the insulin (e.g., to an orange).
- Have students practice locating anatomic areas for insulin injection.
- Have students divide into small groups, and have each group prepare a skit in which a nurse teaches a client to self-administer insulin.

SUGGESTIONS FOR CLINICAL ACTIVITIES

- Assign the students to each care for a client with diabetes mellitus. Have the students prepare and study medication administration cards for different types of insulin and for antidiabetic medications. Have the students prepare and administer the insulin or antidiabetic medication, as ordered, under your supervision.

29. The nurse will inspect injection sites for signs of lipodystrophy and will monitor client for signs and symptoms of hypo- and hyperglycemia.

30. The nurse will teach the client and family about safe use of insulin, as described in Table 36-3. The nurse will also teach clients how to monitor for hyperglycemia and hypoglycemia.

31. The client is taught to keep a regular vial of insulin available for emergencies. The client is also taught to keep a candy or sugar source available to treat hypoglycemia.

32. Insulin regimens are individualized. See Table 36-4.

33. Sliding scale insulin provides subcutaneous regular insulin injections that are adjusted according to capillary blood glucose levels. Blood glucose levels are measured every 6 hours or at specified times such as before meals and at bedtime as ordered. Sliding scale insulin allows for tighter control of blood glucose levels, especially during hospitalization or times of infection, acute illness, surgery, altered caloric intake, or physical and/or emotional stress.

34. Oral antidiabetic agents are used to treat people with type 2 DM.

35. All clients taking oral antidiabetic drugs must be taught to monitor their blood glucose levels at least two to three times per week. Testing may be more frequent when a client has trouble meeting his or her glucose goals.

36. Two new injectable drugs, exenatide (Byetta) and pramlintide (Symlin), are being used to manage glucose control better.

37. Nursing implications and client teaching for oral antidiabetic agents are provided in Table 36-5. Client teaching is important because of the potential interactions of oral antidiabetic drugs with other medications.

LEARNING OUTCOME 4

Compare and contrast the causes, manifestations, and interdisciplinary care of diabetic ketoacidosis (DKA), hyperosmolar hyperglycemic state (HHS), and hypoglycemia.

Concepts for Lecture

1. Diabetic ketoacidosis (DKA) is a life-threatening illness occurring in type 1 diabetes. It is characterized by hyperglycemia, dehydration, and coma. It often develops in a client with undiagnosed and untreated diabetes or in an individual who is sick, has an infection, omits insulin, or has excessive physical or emotional stress.

2. In DKA, without insulin, glucose cannot enter the cell, which stimulates the liver to increase glucose production, leading to hyperglycemia. The excess glucose acts as an osmotic diuretic, pulling fluid from extracellular space and causing polyuria and eventually dehydration and sodium and potassium loss.

3. In DKA, because glucose cannot be used for energy, the fat stores break down, resulting in continued hyperglycemia and burning of fatty acids. This causes the formation of ketones.

4. When more ketones are produced than the cells can use and the kidneys can excrete, ketoacidosis develops.

5. Increased buildup of ketones depresses the central nervous system (CNS), leading to coma and death if left untreated.

6. To compensate for the acidic state produced by DKA, the respiratory center increases the rate and depth of breathing. This is known as Kussmaul respiration.

7. Hyperosmolar hyperglycemic state (HHS) differs from DKA in several ways. One way is that DKA affects type 1 diabetics, whereas HHS occurs in people with type 2 DM. Ketoacidosis does not occur in HHS

like it does in DKA because the type 2 diabetic has enough insulin. Like DKA, HHS can be triggered by several factors including infection and surgery. Dialysis can also trigger HHS.

8. In both DKA and HHS, there are elevated blood glucose levels. The level in DKA will be greater than 250 mg/dL, and the level in HHS will be greater than 600 mg/dL.

9. HHS is characterized by severely elevated blood glucose levels, extreme dehydration, and an altered level of consciousness. HHS has a higher mortality rate than DKA.

10. The manifestations of DKA and HHS are compared and contrasted in Box 36-5.

11. Treatment of DKA and HHS includes fluids, insulin, and correction of electrolyte imbalances.

12. Hypoglycemia occurs in both type 1 and type 2 DM. It may be caused by too much insulin intake, overdose of oral antidiabetic agents, too little food, or excess physical activity. The onset is sudden, and the blood glucose is usually less than 50 mg/dL.

13. The brain requires a constant supply of glucose, so a hypoglycemic episode alters brain function. The manifestations of hypoglycemia result from activation of the autonomic nervous system (ANS) and from impaired cerebral function. Severe hypoglycemia, if untreated, may lead to death.

14. Manifestations of hypoglycemia caused by responses of the ANS include hunger, nausea, anxiety, sweating, shakiness, irritability, rapid pulse, hypotension, and pale, cool skin.

15. Manifestations of hypoglycemia caused by impaired cerebral function include strange or unusual feelings, headache, difficulty in thinking, inability to concentrate, changes in emotional behavior, slurred speech, blurred vision, decreasing levels of consciousness, seizures, and coma.

16. The elderly may not experience the manifestations caused by the autonomic nervous system because, as the body ages, the ANS becomes less responsive.

17. Some people with long-standing type 1 diabetes may develop hypoglycemia unawareness because the mechanisms that should raise blood glucose levels fail.

18. Mild hypoglycemia (blood glucose 60–70 mg/dL) requires immediate treatment with about 15 g of a rapid-acting sugar (e.g., three glucose tablets, ½ cup of fruit juice or regular soda, 8 oz of skim milk, 3 tsp of sugar or honey).

19. Diabetic clients with severe hypoglycemia (blood glucose less than 60 mg/dL) are often hospitalized. If the client is alert and conscious, 15 g of oral carbohydrate may be given.

20. If the client is unconscious, 25 to 50 mL of 50% dextrose is given intravenously, followed by intravenous infusion of 5% dextrose in water. When IV glucose is unavailable, glucagon 1 mg may be given by the subcutaneous or intramuscular route to stimulate the release of glycogen.

21. Because glucagon has a short action period, a carbohydrate snack is given to prevent a recurrence of hypoglycemia.

LEARNING OUTCOME 5

Explain the interdisciplinary care of chronic complications for clients with type 1 and type 2 diabetes mellitus.

Concepts for Lecture

1. Chronic complications of diabetes mellitus result from consistently high glucose levels in the body.

REFERENCES

- MedlinePlus: Diabetic ketoacidosis. Available at http://www.nlm.nih.gov/medlineplus/ency/article/000320.htm
- MedlinePlus: Diabetic hyperglycemic hyperosmolar syndrome. Available at http://www.nlm.nih.gov/medlineplus/ency/article/000304.htm

POWERPOINT SLIDES

Tables and/or Figures

- **Box 36-7** Manifestations of Peripheral Vascular Disease

2. The complications are categorized as macrovascular disease and microvascular disease.

3. The macrocirculation (the large blood vessels) in people with diabetes undergoes changes due to atherosclerosis, which has an increased incidence and earlier age of onset in people with diabetes.

4. Macrovascular complications include coronary artery disease, stroke, and peripheral vascular disease.

5. Coronary heart disease and high lipid levels are major risk factors in the development of myocardial infarction in people with diabetes, especially older people with type 2 DM.

6. Coronary heart disease is the most common cause of death in people with diabetes. Persons who have a myocardial infarction are more prone to develop heart failure as a complication of the infarction. They are less likely to survive in the period immediately following the infarction than people without diabetes.

7. Stroke is two to six times more likely to occur in the type 2 diabetic. Although the exact cause is unknown, hypertension plays a major role in its development. The manifestations of impaired cerebral circulation are often similar to hypoglycemia or HHS and warrant immediate medical attention.

8. Peripheral vascular disease of the lower extremities accompanies both types of DM, but the incidence is greater in type 2 DM.

9. Atherosclerosis of the lower legs is usually bilateral, develops at an earlier age, progresses more rapidly, and develops equally in men and women with type 2 DM.

10. Occlusions can form in the large vessels below the knee, causing impaired peripheral circulation. Decreased arterial circulation can lead to lower leg ulcers and gangrene.

11. Gangrene from diabetes is the most common cause of nontraumatic amputations of the lower leg.

12. Microvascular complications involve alterations in the microcirculation (the smaller blood vessels and capillaries) especially the eyes, kidneys, and nerves. Microvascular disease is sometimes called microangiopathy.

13. Diabetic retinopathy is the collective name for the destructive retinal changes that occur in the person with diabetes. Changes in the retinal capillaries cause decreased blood flow to the retina, leading to retinal ischemia and possible retinal hemorrhage or detachment. After 20 years of diabetes, most type 1 and 70% of type 2 diabetics have some degree of retinopathy.

14. All diabetics have a greater risk for developing cataracts as a result of increased glucose levels within the lens.

15. Yearly eye exams by an ophthalmologist are recommended because laser photocoagulation surgery can help to prevent loss of vision.

16. Diabetic nephropathy is a disease of the kidneys characterized by the presence of albumin in the urine, hypertension, edema, and progressive renal insufficiency. This disorder is the most common cause of renal failure requiring dialysis or transplantation in the United States.

17. Nephropathy occurs in 30% to 40% of type 1 diabetics in contrast to 15% to 20% of type 2 diabetics.

18. Changes in the glomerular capillaries in the kidney result in glomerulosclerosis. This condition severely impairs the filtering function of the glomerulus so that albumin is lost in the urine.

19. The first indication of nephropathy is microalbuminuria. With the presence of microalbuminuria, usually the client progresses to end-stage renal disease or renal failure.

20. Because hypertension increases the progression of nephropathy, clients are treated with angiotensin-converting enzyme (ACE) inhibiting drugs such as captopril (Capoten).

SUGGESTIONS FOR CLASSROOM ACTIVITIES

- Have the students divide into small groups. Assign each group a long-term complication. Have each group create a presentation about the complication that includes presenting signs and symptoms and care of the client with the assigned complication.

SUGGESTIONS FOR CLINICAL ACTIVITIES

- Assign each of the students to a client with diabetes. Have the students complete an assessment for the presence of any long-term complications or risk of complications. Ask the students to share their findings in postconference.

REFERENCE

- National Institute of Diabetes and Digestive and Kidney Diseases: Complications of diabetes. Available at http://www2.niddk.nih .gov/Research/ScientificAreas/Diabetes/ Complications/

21. Diabetic neuropathy involves disorders of the peripheral nerves and the autonomic nervous system, and these disorders cause one or more of the following problems: sensory and motor impairment, postural hypotension, delayed gastric emptying, diarrhea, and impaired genitourinary function.

22. Neuropathies result from thickening of the capillary membrane and destruction of myelin sheath, which impairs nerve conduction.

23. Peripheral neuropathies are bilateral, appearing first in the toes and feet and progressing upward to involve the fingers and hands. Initial manifestations of peripheral neuropathies include distal paresthesias (feeling of numbness or tingling); pain described as aching, burning, or shooting; and a feeling of cold feet. People experience reduced feeling, touch, and position sense, increasing their risk for falls. Foot injuries are common due to impaired temperature and pain sensation.

24. There is no specific treatment for peripheral neuropathy. Collaborative management focuses on controlling the neuropathic pain with tricyclic antidepressants, anticonvulsants such as gabapentin (Neurontin), or topicals like capsaicin (Zostrix) or a lidocaine patch.

25. Autonomic neuropathies involve numerous organ systems, including cardiovascular with fixed, slightly rapid heart rate and postural hypotension; gastrointestinal with delayed gastric emptying, resulting in irregular blood glucose control, constipation, and diarrhea; and genitourinary with neurogenic bladder (inability to empty the bladder completely) leading to urinary retention and an increased risk of urinary tract infections and sexual dysfunction in men and women.

Learning Outcome 6

Reinforce teaching guidelines to clients with diabetes mellitus regarding self-management of medications, diet, exercise, and foot care.

Concepts for Lecture

1. The client taking insulin needs teaching, and reinforcement of teaching, about manifestations of diabetes mellitus; how to store insulin vials in a cool place, avoiding exposure to extreme temperatures; the need to refrigerate unopened extra insulin vials and not freeze them; and bringing insulin to room temperature before using it.

2. The nurse needs to teach the client about self-administration of insulin and have the client demonstrate this procedure. The nurse needs to reinforce teaching about how to mix two kinds of insulin; the need to discard outdated or discolored insulin; keeping a regular insulin vial available for emergencies; the need to check blood glucose before meals, at bedtime, and as prescribed; and the need to delay giving rapid-acting insulin if a meal is delayed.

3. The nurse needs to provide information on the signs of hypoglycemia and hyperglycemia, precautions to take, and correct procedures for administering insulin and for rotating injection sites.

4. The nurse teaches the client specific information related to the drug taken for diabetes (Tables 36-3 and 36-5).

5. Diabetes management requires a careful balance between nutrient intake, daily expenditure of energy, and the dose and timing of insulin or oral antidiabetic agents.

6. Persons with diabetes must eat a more structured diet in order to prevent hyperglycemia. Early in the diagnosis of diabetes, clients should be referred to a certified diabetic educator and registered dietitian for meal planning and teaching.

7. The standard ADA diet is no longer recommended by the American Diabetes Association. Meal planning may be based on the Food

 **PowerPoint Slides**

Tables and/or Figures
- **Figure 36-5** Ulceration Following Trauma to the Foot of a Person With Diabetes
- **Table 36-6** Nutrient Recommendations for Adults With Diabetes
- **Box 36-4** Population Focus: Exercise Guidelines for Clients With Type 1 and Type 2 DM
- **Box 36-9** Client Teaching: Sample Foot Care Teaching Session
- **Box 36-10** Client Teaching: Teaching for Client Self-Management of Diabetes

Suggestions for Classroom Activities
- Have the students create a teaching plan for self-management of medications, diet, exercise, or foot care.

Suggestions for Clinical Activities
- Assign each student to care for a client with diabetes. Ask the students to assess their client in regard to a need for instruction in self-management in medications, diet, exercise, or foot care. Ask the students to provide instruction to the client in one aspect of self-management where the client indicates they have the most need for more information.

 Reference
- MedlinePlus: Diabetic foot. Available at http://www.nlm.nih.gov/medlineplus/diabeticfoot.html

Pyramid, carbohydrate counting, the consistent-carbohydrate diabetes meal plan, or exchange lists.

8. The American Diabetes Association recommends daily dietary intake of carbohydrates, proteins, and fats (Table 36-6).

9. Carbohydrates have the greatest effect on postprandial (after-meal) blood glucose levels. Clients can be taught to count carbohydrates so they can administer a prescribed amount of regular insulin or lispro insulin for every 10–15 grams of carbohydrate eaten in a meal. Carbohydrate counting provides better glucose control than the traditional exchange list plan and is, therefore, replacing it.

10. An obese older adult with type 2 DM may need a diet, exercise, and weight reduction program.

11. To improve compliance with the diet plan, the nurse should consider dietary likes and dislikes, eating habits, person preparing the meals, age-related changes in taste and smell and dental health, and age-related decline in calorie needs and reduced physical activity. The nurse must consider that many older adults live on a fixed income, limiting their diet to canned foods.

12. Coexisting illnesses and the use of multiple medications decrease appetite and reduce the client's energy to plan, cook, or eat.

13. Exercise is extremely important for diabetic clients because it reduces blood glucose levels by increasing glucose use by the muscles. This potentially decreases the need for insulin.

14. Exercise also decreases cholesterol and triglycerides, reducing the risk of cardiovascular disorders. People with diabetes should consult their primary healthcare provider before beginning or changing an exercise program. Clients with type 1 and type 2 diabetes over age 35 should have an exercise-stress electrocardiogram prior to beginning an exercise program.

15. The nurse should assess the client's lifestyle before determining the type of exercise program. The nurse should consider the following lifestyle factors: client's usual exercise habits, living environment, and community programs.

16. Clients with diabetes should follow the recommendations of the American Diabetes Association when exercising: use proper footwear, inspect the feet daily and after exercise, avoid exercise in extreme heat or cold, and avoid exercise during periods of poor glucose control.

17. People with diabetes mellitus experience more problems with their feet and subsequent amputations because of macrovascular disease, neuropathy, and infection.

18. Common sources of foot trauma are cracks and fissures caused by dry skin or infections such as such as athlete's foot, blisters from ill-fitting socks and shoes, ingrown toenails, and direct trauma (cuts, bruises, or burns). Foot lesions usually begin as a superficial injury and then progress into an ulceration. In time, the ulcer extends deeper into muscles and bone and can lead to abscess or osteomyelitis. Infections commonly occur in the traumatized or ulcerated area.

19. Dry gangrene is manifested by cold, dry, shriveled, and black tissue of the toes and feet. Treatment of dry gangrene consists of bed rest, antibiotics, and debridement. If untreated, the whole foot eventually becomes gangrenous and requires amputation.

20. The nurse can teach the client the following about buying and wearing shoes and stockings: shoes that allow ½ to ¾ inch of toe room and have smooth inside stitching and lining with a soft insole are best; the heel should fit snugly; and the shoe should have good arch support. The nurse advises the client to buy shoes late in the afternoon, when feet are at their largest, and to buy shoes that feel comfortable.

21. Shoes should not have open toes. Shoes made of natural fibers (leather, canvas) allow perspiration to escape.

22. Box 36-9 describes a client teaching session about foot care.

23. The content of a teaching plan for a client with DM includes information about how diabetes changes body metabolism; the dietary plan; the importance of exercise; how to monitor glucose levels; and what to do for high or low blood glucose.

24. The plan also includes information about oral agents; factors causing DKA or HHS, manifestations of each, and what to do when they occur; safety precautions (carrying ID card and rapid-acting glucose, carrying insulin and glucagon kit, and having a contact to notify in case of emergency); hygiene measures; vision exams; what to do about food, fluids, and medications on sick days; and communication and follow-up in regard to what to report and to whom and when, the importance of follow-up appointments, and resources (Box 36-10).

LEARNING OUTCOME 7

Use the nursing process to collect data, establish outcomes, provide individualized care, and evaluate responses for the client with diabetes mellitus.

Concepts for Lecture

1. Assessment data collected by the nurse can determine the extent to which DM is affecting the client's life, identify risk factors for complications, and suggest guidelines for medical treatment or self-care.

2. Subjective and objective data to collect are described in Box 36-8.

3. The nurse will palpate peripheral pulses, note color and temperature of lower extremities and any edema, and monitor and report blood glucose levels above or below expected range.

4. Diagnoses for clients with DM include Imbalanced Nutrition: More than Body Requirements, with one possible expected outcome: maintain balance of nutrition, activity, and blood glucose levels. Interventions include monitoring blood glucose levels regularly, monitoring what the client eats, identifying food preferences, providing meals and snacks on time, giving insulin and/or oral antidiabetic agents as orders, and encouraging the client to include physical exercise into daily routines.

5. Another diagnosis for clients with DM is Impaired Skin Integrity with a possible expected outcome being: remain free from areas of skin breakdown. Interventions include teaching foot care; using devices to prevent skin breakdown; encouraging fluid intake of at least 2,500 mL/day unless contraindicated; discussing the importance of not smoking; notifying the physician immediately if boils, pimples, or skin breakdowns occur; rotating insulin sites; teaching foot care; and discussing importance of maintaining blood glucose levels as near normal as possible.

6. Risk for Infection is another nursing diagnosis for clients with DM. A possible outcome is: remains free of signs of infection. Interventions include assessing for manifestations of infection, obtaining specimens and sending for culture and sensitivity test as ordered, using and teaching meticulous hand washing, keeping skin clean and dry, providing catheter and perineal care, using meticulous sterile technique with wound care, encouraging adequate nutrition and fluid intake, assisting clients with oral hygiene, and teaching female diabetics the symptoms and preventative measures of vaginitis caused by *Candida albicans*.

 **POWERPOINT SLIDES**

Tables and/or Figures
- **Box 36-8** Assessment: Diabetes Mellitus

Nursing Care Plan: Client With Type 1 Diabetes

SUGGESTIONS FOR CLASSROOM ACTIVITIES
- Have the students break into small groups and create plans of care for theoretical clients with type 1 and type 2 diabetes.

SUGGESTIONS FOR CLINICAL ACTIVITIES
- Assign the students to care for clients with a diagnosis of diabetes. Have the students work with the primary nurse for their client and ask the primary nurse to share the plan of care in place for that client. Assign the students to write their own individualized care plan for their clients based on their data collection.

GENERAL CHAPTER CONSIDERATIONS

1. Have students study and learn key terms listed at the beginning of the chapter.
2. Have students complete end of chapter exercises either in their book or on the MyNursingKit Website.
3. Use the Classroom Response Question PowerPoints to assess students prior to lecture.

• Clinical Reasoning Care Map

MYNURSINGKIT
(www.mynursingkit.com)

• Websites
• NCLEX® Questions
• Case Studies
• Key Terms

STUDENT WORKBOOK AND RESOURCE GUIDE

• Chapter 36 activities
• *Separate purchase*

PRENTICE HALL NURSE'S DRUG GUIDE

• *Separate purchase*

CLASSROOM RESPONSE QUESTION POWERPOINTS

TESTBANK

CHAPTER 37
THE NERVOUS SYSTEM AND ASSESSMENT

LEARNING OUTCOME 1

Describe the structure and functions of the central and peripheral nervous systems, the eye, and the ear.

Concepts for Lecture

1. The nervous system consists of the brain, spinal cord, and peripheral nerves. It controls all motor, sensory, and autonomic activities of the body.
2. The visual system includes internal and external structures, which are important for visual function.
3. The auditory system functions to receive and perceive sounds as well as maintain position sense and balance.
4. The nervous system is divided into the central nervous system (CNS) and the peripheral nervous system (PNS). The brain and spinal cord make up the CNS. The PNS consists of the cranial nerves, the spinal nerves, and the autonomic nervous system.
5. The neuron is the basic cell of the nervous system. It is made up of a dendrite, a cell body, and an axon. Dendrites are short, branch-like extensions on the cell body.
6. Dendrites carry impulses to the cell body from other cells. The cell body controls the function of the neuron. At the other end of the neuron is a single, long projection known as the axon, which carries impulses away from the cell body. Many axons are protected and insulated by a white fatty substance called myelin sheath.
7. Neurons are responsible for neurotransmission. Neurons move from one neuron to another across a synapse. A chemical neurotransmitter such as acetylcholine either helps the impulse cross the synapse or stops it.
8. Sensory (or efferent) neurons carry impulses from the skin and muscles to the CNS. Motor (or efferent) neurons carry impulses from the CNS to the muscles for contraction and to glands in order to release secretions.
9. The brain is the control center of the nervous system. A rigid bony skull protects the brain from external injury.
10. Beneath the skull are three protective membranes or meninges: (1) dura mater, the outer layer; (2) arachnoid, the middle layer; and (3) pia mater; the inner layer directly attached to the brain.
11. Arterial blood vessels are located in the epidural space between the skull and dura mater. Cerebrospinal fluid (CSF) is found in the subarachnoid space between the arachnoid and the pia mater.
12. There are four major regions of the brain: cerebrum, diencephalon, brainstem, and cerebellum.
13. The cerebrum is the largest area of the brain and is divided into a right and left hemisphere. Deep grooves called fissures separate the hemispheres and separate the cerebrum from the cerebellum. The two hemispheres are connected by a thick band of nerve fibers called the corpus callosum, which lies deep in the brain and allows communication between the hemispheres.
14. The left hemisphere is responsible for speech, problem solving, reasoning, and calculations. The right hemisphere controls visual-spatial information such as art, music, and the surrounding physical environment.

POWERPOINT SLIDES

Tables and/or Figures
- **Figure 37-1** A Neuron
- **Figure 37-2** The Four Major Regions of the Brain
- **Figure 37-3** Cerebral Lobes With Their Functions
- **Figure 37-4** Distribution of Spinal Nerves
- **Figure 37-5** A Reflex Arc of the Spinal Nerve
- **Figure 37-6** Autonomic Nervous System and the Organs It Affects
- **Figure 37-7** The External and Accessory Structures of the Eye
- **Figure 37-8** The Internal Structures of the Eye
- **Figure 37-9** The Visual Fields of the Eyes and the Optic Pathways
- **Figure 37-10** Structures of the External, Middle, and Inner Ear
- **Table 37-1** The Cranial Nerves

SUGGESTIONS FOR CLASSROOM ACTIVITIES
- Prior to class, divide students into 12 groups. Preassign each group a cranial nerve. Instruct student groups to prepare a 2–3 minute presentation on the function of their assigned nerve, as well as deficits that might be seen indicating impairment.
- Have students practice in pairs testing the functioning of the 12 cranial nerves.
- Present students with a detailed figure of the brain and ask them to label major structures of the brain.

SUGGESTIONS FOR CLINICAL ACTIVITIES
- Have students work in small groups to present an in service on the structure and functions of the central and peripheral nervous systems, the eye, and the ear. The students can divide up the work and can issue invitations to the nursing staff to attend a review of this material.
- Arrange for students to observe a nurse practitioner doing an assessment of the function of the 12 cranial nerves.

15. Each cerebral hemisphere is divided into four lobes: frontal, parietal, temporal, and occipital, each separated by fissures.

16. The diencephalon contains the thalamus and hypothalamus. The thalamus relates all sensory information to the cortex. The hypothalamus regulates temperature, fluid balance, thirst, appetite, emotions, and the sleep/wake cycle.

17. The brainstem consists of the midbrain, pons, and medulla oblongata.

18. The midbrain is the center for auditory and visual reflexes and serves as a nerve pathway between the cerebral hemispheres and lower brain. The pons controls respiration. The medulla oblongata, found at the base of the brainstem, controls heart rate, blood pressure, respirations, coughing, swallowing, and vomiting.

19. The cerebellum has two hemispheres and controls involuntary muscle activity and fine motor movements as well as balance and posture.

20. Four ventricles within the brain make and circulate CSF in the subarachnoid space of the brain and spinal cord. This liquid protects the brain and spinal cord from trauma and provides a place for nutrient exchange and waste removal.

21. The brain cannot store oxygen or glucose so it needs a constant supply of both. The internal carotid arteries and the vertebral arteries supply blood to the brain.

22. The blood–brain barrier is composed of astrocytes that are joined by tight junctions. This decreases permeability so harmful substances in the blood cannot enter the brain. Brain injury may cause a local breakdown of the barrier.

23. The spinal cord exits the skull through the foramen magnum and extends to the first or second lumbar vertebra where it ends in the cauda equina. It is surrounded and protected by the vertebral column.

24. There are 31 pairs of spinal nerves named in reference to the corresponding vertebrae of the spine: cervical (8 pairs, C1–C8), thoracic (12 pairs, T1–T12), lumbar (5 pairs, L1–L5), and sacral (5 pairs, S1–S5).

25. The inside of the spinal cord is H shaped and consists of gray matter surrounded by white matter.

26. The white matter of the spinal cord forms ascending and descending pathways known as spinal tracts, which carry messages to and from the brain: ascending sensory pathways and descending motor pathways.

27. On exiting the brain, motor and sensory nerve fibers cross to the opposite side of the spinal cord. This is why a stroke in the left hemisphere affects motor and sensory function on the right side of the body.

28. The peripheral nervous system links the CNS with the rest of the body. It receives and conducts information from the external environment and transmits signals to muscles and organs of the body. Spinal nerves, cranial nerves, and ganglia make up the PNS, which is divided into the somatic and autonomic nervous systems.

29. The somatic system connects the skin and muscles to the CNS. The autonomic nervous system controls visceral organs and some glands.

30. Each spinal nerve has sensory and motor fibers. The dorsal and ventral root of each spinal nerve attaches it to the spinal cord. Sensory fibers are in the dorsal root and motor fibers in the ventral root. Damage to the dorsal root causes loss of sensation, whereas damage to the ventral root results in flaccid paralysis.

31. An area of skin supplied by a single spinal nerve is called a dermatome. The dorsal roots of the spinal nerves carry sensations from specific dermatomes. Dermatomes are useful for locating pain sites and neurologic lesions.

32. There are 12 pairs of cranial nerves beginning in the brain or brainstem. They have sensory or motor functions or both. The vagus nerve

extends into the thorax and abdominal areas, but the other 11 cranial nerves innervate only head and neck regions.

33. Cranial nerves I (olfactory), II (optic), and VIII (vestibulocochlear) control sensory function only.

34. The autonomic nervous system (ANS) is part of the peripheral nervous system. It is responsible for maintaining the body's internal homeostasis. The ANS regulates respiration, heart rate, digestion, urinary excretions, body temperature, and sexual function.

35. There are two divisions of the autonomic nervous system: the sympathetic nervous system (SNS) and the parasympathetic nervous system (PNS). Fibers from both systems can affect the same structures. Generally, when one system increases an action, the other system decreases the action to keep the body in balance.

36. The SNS prepares the body to handle stress. The parasympathetic nervous system operates during nonstressful situations, conserving the body's energy by regulating digestion, elimination, and other activities.

37. Functions of the cranial nerves are as follows: I, olfactory = smell; II, optic = vision; III, oculomotor = pupil constriction, eyeball movement, raising of upper eyelid; IV, trochlear = eyeball movement; V, trigeminal = sensation of the scalp, nose, mouth, and cornea and chewing; VI, abducens = lateral movement of the eyeball; VII, facial = movement of facial muscles, secretions from lacrimal and salivary glands, taste in anterior two-thirds of tongue; VIII, vestibulocochlear = sense of hearing and equilibrium; IX, glossopharyngeal = taste in posterior one-third of tongue, sensation of pharynx and tongue, gag reflex, swallowing, secretions of parotid gland; X, vagus = swallowing; XI, accessory = neck and shoulder movement; and XII, hypoglossal = tongue movement.

38. The eyes are complex structures. The primary function of the eye is to convert patterns of light from the environment into a message that is transmitted via the optic nerve to the brain. The brain allows us to make sense of what we see.

39. The eye is supported and protected by the accessory structures: eyelids and eyelashes, conjunctiva, lacrimal apparatus, and eye muscles.

40. The wall of the eyeball has three layers. The outermost layer consists of the white, fibrous sclera and the transparent cornea. The sclera protects and gives shape to the eyeball. The border between the sclera and the cornea is called the limbus. The cornea is a transparent window that allows light to enter the eye.

41. The middle layer of the eyeball is the uvea, which is very vascular. It includes the iris, the ciliary body, and the choroid.

42. The iris is the colored part of the eye, and it regulates light entering the eye by controlling the size of the pupil. The pupil constricts in bright light and dilates in dim light or darkness.

43. The ciliary body encircles the lens. It controls the shape of the lens to focus light on the retina. The lens is a transparent structure behind the pupil that can change shape to focus light onto the retina. The retina is the innermost lining of the eyeball containing millions of light receptors called rods and cones. Rods are very light sensitive and allow us to see in dim light. Cones allow us to see in color and provide a sharper image than rods. Most cones are in the macula, the area where light passing through the pupil and lens focuses on the retina.

44. The eyeball is divided into two interior cavities. The larger posterior cavity behind the lens contains the clear gelatinous vitreous body, which shapes and supports the eye. The anterior chamber is further divided into the anterior chamber and the posterior chamber.

45. Aqueous humor circulates through the anterior cavity nourishing the lens and cornea. Aqueous humor is constantly formed and drained to

maintain a relatively constant pressure within the eye. The canal of Schlemm at the junction of the sclera and the cornea allows aqueous humor to flow between the anterior and posterior chambers.

46. As light enters the eye, it is bent (refraction) to focus on the retina. The cornea, aqueous humor, lens, and vitreous body bend light rays to focus the image. To change the point of focus from far to near, the lens changes shape, the pupil constricts, and the eyes converge. This is called accommodation.

47. The optic nerves are cranial nerves that meet at the optic chiasma. Nerve fibers from the medial half of each retina cross to the opposite side to join nerve fibers from the lateral half of the other eye. Impulses generated in the retina travel to the visual cortex in the occipital lobe of the brain. The brain translates the impulses into the image we see.

48. The visual fields of each eye overlap, and each eye sees a slightly different view, which allows for depth perception, the ability to identify differences in distance between objects.

49. The ear has two primary functions: hearing and maintaining balance.

50. The ear is divided into three areas: the external ear, the middle ear, and the inner ear. The inner ear also helps maintain balance.

51. The external ear includes the auricle (or pinna), the auditory canal, and the tympanic membrane (eardrum).

52. The auricles direct sound waves into the ear. The auditory canal focuses sound waves on the eardrum.

53. The tympanic membrane (eardrum) separates the external and the middle ear. Glands in the canal secrete cerumen (earwax), which traps dirt and debris, protecting the tympanic membrane and middle ear from infection.

54. The middle ear contains the auditory ossicles (bones): the malleus, the incus, and the stapes. These bones transmit vibrations from the tympanic membrane to the oval window of the inner ear.

55. The middle ear is filled with air. It opens into the eustachian tube, which connects it with the nasopharynx. This proximity to the nasopharynx increases the likelihood for middle ear infections associated with upper respiratory infections.

56. The eustachian tube helps equalize the pressure in the middle ear with atmospheric pressure.

57. The inner ear (labyrinth) is a maze of bony, fluid-filled chambers. The labyrinth has three regions: the vestibule, the semicircular canals, and the cochlea.

58. The vestibule contains the oval window and joins the cochlea and the semicircular canals. Receptors in the vestibule respond to changes in gravity and head position, helping maintain balance.

59. The three semicircular canals also contain receptors that respond to head movements.

60. The cochlea contains the organ of Corti, the receptor for hearing. The organ of Corti is the set of sensory hair cells innervated by cranial nerve VIII, the vestibulocochlear nerve.

61. Hearing is the perception and interpretation of sound. Sound waves enter the external auditory canal causing the eardrum to vibrate. The ossicles transmit this vibration to the oval window, setting fluid within the vestibule into motion. The fluid movement stimulates receptors in the organ of Corti, which sends signals to the brain via CN VIII.

62. Nerve fibers from each ear cross, so the auditory centers on each side of the brain receive impulses from both ears. The brain can receive and interpret a wide variety of sounds and localize the source of the sound.

63. The inner ear provides information to the brain about head position, and this information is used to coordinate body movements so that equilibrium and balance are maintained.

LEARNING OUTCOME 2

Identify subjective and objective assessment data to collect for clients with neurologic or sensory disorders.

Concepts for Lecture

1. Focused assessment of a client with a neurologic disorder begins with identifying the client's level of consciousness (LOC).
2. The nurse inquires about numbness, tingling, sensations, tremors, problems with coordination or balance, loss of movement in any part of the body, or difficulty walking or using the hands.
3. The nurse determines which symptoms the client experienced first and if they are constant or intermittent.
4. If the client is experiencing pain, the nurse asks if coughing, sneezing, or walking increases the pain.
5. The nurse determines whether the client has difficulty with speaking, seeing, hearing, tasting, or detecting odors.
6. The nurse inquires about memory, feelings of anxiety or depression, recent changes in sleep patterns, ability to perform activities of daily living, sexual activity, and weight.
7. The client's prescription and over-the-counter medications including herbal remedies are noted, and the nurse asks about the purpose, frequency, and duration of use and any side effects.
8. The past medical history, focusing on previous incidents of seizures, fainting, dizziness, headaches, any trauma, surgery, or tumors of the brain, spinal cord, or nerves, is obtained and documented. The nurse asks about any illnesses that may cause neurologic manifestations and asks about any presence of or a family history of diabetes, high blood pressure, stroke, seizures, or mental health problems. The nurse inquires about any problems with short- or long-term memory.
9. The nurse asks about occupational exposure to toxic chemicals or materials, use of protective headgear, and the amount of time doing repetitive motion tasks such as data entry and assembly work.
10. The nurse determines the diet and use of alcohol, tobacco, or recreational drugs. In addition, the nurse asks if the client wears a helmet during bicycle or motorcycle riding or when participating in contact sports.
11. If the client presents with a problem related to one or both eyes, the nurse asks about the onset of the problem, symptoms, and precipitating and relieving factors. The nurse determines if the client notices rings of color around streetlights at night or has difficulty reading the paper.
12. The nurse observes the client for squinting or abnormal eye movements that indicate problems with eye function. The nurse asks about watery or irritated eyes, changes in vision, the use of eye medications, corrective eyewear, and care of eyeglasses or contact lenses.
13. The nurse asks about a personal or family history of glaucoma, cataracts, diabetes, high blood pressure, thyroid disorders, and eye infections. The nurse questions whether there is a history of nearsightedness or farsightedness, cancer of the retina, or color blindness. Information is collected about environmental or work exposure to chemicals or participation in sports or hobbies that increase the risk of eye injury.
14. Exploration of changes in hearing such as difficulty hearing high-pitched or low-pitched sounds, ringing in the ears (tinnitus), ear pain, drainage from the ears, or use of hearing aids is carried out.
15. The nurse asks about trauma, surgery, or ear infections as well as infectious diseases such as meningitis or mumps. The nurse determines the use of medications that may affect hearing such as aminoglycoside

PowerPoint Slides

Tables and/or Figures

- **Box 37-1** Documentation of Neurologic Assessment
- **Table 37-1** The Cranial Nerves
- **Figure 37-11** Testing Vision Using a Rosenbaum Eye Chart
- **Figure 37-12** Ptosis

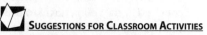

Suggestions for Classroom Activities

- Discuss the implications of an altered LOC on the validity of a neurologic exam.
- Discuss in further detail the various techniques/exams used when assessing sensory motor, eye, and ear functioning (Romberg, shoulder shrug, etc.).
- Divide students into small workgroups. Have students practice a neurologic assessment in total or in part on a partner.
- Show examples of Snellen and Rosenbaum charts.
- Using a student volunteer, demonstrate a focused neurologic exam.

Suggestions for Clinical Activities

- Assign students to clients having neurologic deficits/diseases. Have students perform a focused neurologic exam.
- Have students share in postconference the differences in practicing a neurologic exam on a well classmate in lab versus completing an actual neurologic exam on a client.

Reference

- National Center for Biotechnology Information: The nervous system. Available at http://www.ncbi.nlm.nih.gov/bookshelf/br.fcgi?book=gnd&part=A75

antibiotics and obtains the client's family history of hearing loss or ear problems and the date of the last ear examination.

16. The focused physical examination begins by assessing the client's posture, movement, and appearance and identifying orientation and mental and emotional state. The client is assessed to determine if he or she can see, hear, and feel the nurse's touch.

17. The client's dress, hygiene, and grooming, as well as gait and posture, are assessed along with the client's actions and affect. The LOC is assessed along with content and quality of speech, mood swings, personality changes, and orientation to time, place, and person. Memory and perceptual deficits are assessed.

18. The client's blood pressure in both arms is obtained (unless contraindicated) along with pulse, respiratory rate, and temperature.

19. The nurse observes for any abnormal breathing patterns such as Cheyne-Stokes. The pupils are checked for response to light, and the client is observed for ptosis and nystagmus.

20. The ability of the client to swallow a small drink of water is observed looking for presence of dysphagia.

21. The client is asked to shrug his or her shoulders and to stick out the tongue. The tongue should be in the midline, and there should be no facial droop. The nurse has the client turn his or her head side to side against resistance and performs the Romberg test.

22. The upper and lower extremities are assessed for weakness, atrophy, and tremors, as well as for decreased muscle tone (flaccidity) or increased muscle tone (spasticity). The client's gait and ability to stand on one foot and walk heel to toe are assessed. Deep tendon reflexes (DTRs) are assessed.

23. The client's distance vision is assessed using the Snellen chart. Near vision is tested using a Rosenbaum chart. To assess for extraocular movements, the nurse asks the client to follow a pen or a finger while keeping the head stationary. The eyelids are inspected for unusual redness or discharge. The nurse checks for abnormal wideness of the lids, which may be due to exophthalmos. The cornea and iris are inspected for cloudiness or irregularities, and the sclera is checked for redness or yellow discoloration.

24. The nurse assesses for hearing loss by performing the whisper test and the Rinne and Weber tests. The auricle is inspected for redness, drainage, scales, or skin lesions. The auricles and area over the mastoid process are palpated for tenderness, swelling, or nodules.

POWERPOINT SLIDES

Tables and/or Figures
- **Figure 37-12** Ptosis
- **Table 37-2** Age-Related Changes in the Eye and Vision

LEARNING OUTCOME 3

Explain changes in neurologic function, vision, and hearing that occur with aging.

Concepts for Lecture

1. Some changes in neurologic function can be expected as a result of aging.

2. It is imperative that healthcare professionals not make the assumption that neurologic deficits found in the elderly are expected, normal signs of aging. They often indicate neurologic or chronic physiologic problems that may be treated.

3. In the older adult, the brain atrophies, causing slower movement and reflexes as well as a degree of forgetfulness.

4. Significant short- and long-term memory loss, mental status changes, altered coordination, loss of motor skills, and altered speech signal a need for further assessment.

SUGGESTIONS FOR CLASSROOM ACTIVITIES

- Have students share personal or clinical experiences with the elderly. Facilitate discussion related to normal and abnormal changes of aging.
- Encourage students to discuss their personal feelings and expectations related to aging.
- Elaborate on the physiologic causes of neurologic changes such as confusion. Discuss the consequences of making assumptions about neurologic changes in the elderly in terms of poor client outcomes.
- Invite a panel of "well elders" to speak with students. The panel should consist of three or four persons aged 75 or above who are living independently and caring for themselves. Invite the panel to share the experiences/factors in their lives that have enabled them to "age well."

5. Older adults often experience sleep disorders and reduced pain perception, which may result from chronic diseases and medication use or more serious neurologic dysfunction.
6. Depression, delirium, and dementia develop in many older adults, which usually signals underlying disease.
7. Confusion, memory loss, and depression are not associated with normal aging.
8. Changes in the eye and vision occur with aging and include the lens becoming less elastic, affecting near vision (presbyopia).
9. Eyelid muscles may lose tone causing the lower lid to turn out (ectropion) or the upper lid to droop (ptosis). The lid margin may turn inward (entropion) causing the lashes to irritate the eye. Tears are decreased, so the eyes may feel dry and scratchy.
10. Hearing difficulties may be mechanical or natural. Inability to hear high-frequency sounds may develop from degeneration in the cochlea or the loss of small hairs in the ears. Increased accumulation of cerumen or earwax can reduce hearing ability.

LEARNING OUTCOME 4

Identify nursing responsibilities for common diagnostic tests and monitor the results for clients with neurologic or sensory disorders.

Concepts for Lecture

1. Several nonspecific laboratory tests are done to rule out other causes of neurologic dysfunction, including blood glucose to identify hypoglycemia and serum sodium and osmolarity to identify low sodium levels or increased or decreased osmolarity, which may cause a coma. Arterial blood gases are used to rule out low oxygen or high carbon dioxide levels and other causes of altered LOC. A CBC with differential and cultures from blood, urine, throat, and nose are done to identify infectious diseases.
2. Elevated serum creatinine and BUN, which reflect decreased kidney function, can decrease LOC. Liver studies such as ALT, AST, and serum ammonia are elevated in liver failure, which can affect LOC. Blood and urine toxicology screenings are useful in identifying drug or alcohol toxicity.
3. Radiography is used to identify neurologic abnormalities (e.g., lesions and tumors). Combined with contrast medium, radiography is used to study blood flow through vessels. If contrast is used, the nurse inquires about allergies to iodine and seafood before the exam. The nurse ensures good hydration before and after the exam to reduce the risk of kidney damage. Women of childbearing age are asked about possibility of pregnancy before the exam.
4. Skull and spine x-rays are used to identify fractures, bone erosion, and calcifications. The nurse needs to explain to the client any different positions needed.
5. Computed tomography (CT) scans produce images with more detail than standard x-rays.
6. Magnetic resonance imaging (MRI) is used to identify stroke, tumor, trauma, multiple sclerosis, and seizures. The nurse needs to assess for metal implants such as pacemaker, defibrillator, or body piercing and provide teaching because the experience can be frightening.
7. Cerebral angiography is an invasive procedure combining x-ray and fluoroscopy with injection of contrast. It is used to detect brain cancer, Alzheimer's disease, epilepsy, and Parkinson's disease. The nurse will withhold the meal prior to the test. The nurse will explain that the client

SUGGESTIONS FOR CLINICAL ACTIVITIES

• Assign students to care for elderly clients experiencing neurologic changes related to physiologic alterations (medication toxicities, electrolyte imbalances, etc.). Ask students to identify changes that are expected with aging and abnormal changes and to discuss the changes in postconference.

REFERENCE

• MedlinePlus: Aging changes in the nervous system. Available at http://www.nlm.nih.gov/medlineplus/ency/article/004023.htm

POWERPOINT SLIDES

Tables and/or Figures

• **Table 37-3** Imaging Techniques
• **Table 37-4** Electrographic Studies
• **Table 37-5** Diagnostic Tests for Visual and Auditory Systems

SUGGESTIONS FOR CLASSROOM ACTIVITIES

• Discuss in further detail the purposes of each diagnostic test and what neurologic disease would be identified by its use.
• Discuss the importance of client teaching to alleviate client fears about diagnostics.
• Discuss the challenges nurses face in preparing a client with neurologic impairments for certain diagnostic tests. Elicit from students strategies to facilitate the completion of testing for these clients.

SUGGESTIONS FOR CLINICAL ACTIVITIES

• Assign students to clients who are due to have any of the neurologic diagnostic tests completed during the clinical day. Have the students accompany the client to the testing area. Have students participate in both pre- and postprocedure care.
• Assign students to develop client teaching brochures for designated neurologic diagnostic tests.
• If permitted, assign individual students to observe in diagnostic areas such as radiology for 2- to 4-hour blocks. Have students share observations in postconference.
• Invite personnel from various neurologic diagnostic areas to speak with students at postconference.

will have a hot flush of the head and neck when contrast is injected and will encourage oral fluids to aid in the removal of the radioisotope.

8. Carotid duplex study involves sound waves used to identify blood flow velocity. The nurse explains the study to the client.

9. Electroencephalography (EEG) involves placing electrodes on the scalp to record brain electrical activity. The nurse will assist the client to wash electrode paste out of his or her hair. The nurse will closely monitor neurologic and vital signs and maintain a pressure dressing and ice to the injection site. The nurse will report any bleeding or swelling.

10. Myelography involves x-ray of the spinal cord and canal after injection of contrast media. This test identifies spinal cord tumors, herniated intervertebral disks, and arthritic bone spurs. The nurse will closely monitor neurologic and vital signs and immediately report leakage or bleeding from the lumbar puncture site.

11. Positron emission tomography (PET) involves having a radioactive agent injected, and computed tomography measures metabolic activity of the brain. The nurse withholds food and fluids 4 hours before the exam and explains that an IV line will be inserted. After the test, encourage oral fluids to aid removal of radioisotope.

12. EMG involves needles inserted into muscles to record electrical activity. The nurse will explain there is discomfort when the needles are inserted and tell the client to avoid caffeine or nicotine for 3 hours before the test.

13. Evoked potentials involve visual or auditory stimulus to evoke electrical activity related to nerve conduction along sensory pathways. The nurse will instruct the client to wash his or her hair before the exam.

14. Fluorescein stain involves injection of fluorescein dye onto the cornea, and the cornea is viewed with a slit lamp. The nurse explains that the dye may sting slightly when inserted and it will wash away with tears.

15. A visual field testing involves a semicircular bowl-like instrument that shows light in different parts of the bowl to map the field of vision. The nurse needs to explain that the procedure does not cause pain but may tire the client.

16. Facial x-rays and CT scan are used to identify orbital fractures or the presence of foreign bodies in the eye. The nurse needs to explain the procedure to the client.

17. Ultrasonography is used to measure for lens implant after cataract removal and to diagnose retinal detachment. The nurse will explain to the client that the cornea is anesthetized before the procedure.

18. Audiometry involves the client wearing earphones through which sounds are presented to determine the hearing range. The nurse explains that the test is done by an audiologist.

19. X-ray and CT scan are used to evaluate the auditory canal for diagnosing Ménière's disease. The nurse will explain the procedure to the client.

20. Caloric testing (electronystagmography) involves injection of cold or warm water into the semicircular canals. The client is observed for symptoms indicating labyrinth disease. The nurse ensures client safety by observing for vomiting and assisting as necessary to prevent aspiration.

GENERAL CHAPTER CONSIDERATIONS

1. Have students study and learn key terms listed at the beginning of the chapter.
2. Have students complete end of chapter exercises either in their book or on the MyNursingKit Website.
3. Use the Classroom Response Question PowerPoints to assess students prior to lecture.

REFERENCES

- MedlinePlus: Cerebral angiography. Available at http://www.nlm.nih.gov/medlineplus/ency/article/003799.htm
- MedlinePlus: Caloric stimulation. Available at http://www.nlm.nih.gov/medlineplus/ency/article/003429.htm

MYNURSINGKIT (www.mynursingkit.com)

- Websites
- NCLEX® Questions
- Case Studies
- Key Terms

STUDENT WORKBOOK AND RESOURCE GUIDE

- Chapter 37 activities
- *Separate purchase*

PRENTICE HALL NURSE'S DRUG GUIDE

- *Separate purchase*

CLASSROOM RESPONSE QUESTION POWERPOINTS

TESTBANK

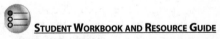

CHAPTER 38
CARING FOR CLIENTS WITH INTRACRANIAL DISORDERS

LEARNING OUTCOME 1

Identify common manifestations and neurologic effects of head injuries, increased intracranial pressure, tumors, cerebrovascular accident, seizures, brain infections, and headaches.

Concepts for Lecture

1. Traumatic brain injury (TBI) is the most serious form of head injury. It is a leading cause of death and disability in the United States. Major vehicle accidents (MVAs) and falls are the major causes of head injuries, followed by violent assaults and sports injuries.

2. Brain damage results from either direct trauma to the tissue or from cerebral edema and increased intracranial pressure (pressure exerted within the cranium by the brain, blood, and cerebrospinal fluid).

3. Head injuries include scalp lacerations, skull fractures, concussions, contusions, and hematomas. There are four types of skull fractures: linear, comminuted (crushed in small pieces), depressed (bone fragments may be pushed into the brain), and basilar (occurs at the base of the skull and may extend to the paranasal sinus of the frontal bone or the middle ear found in the temporal bone).

4. The basilar fracture can cause blood or cerebrospinal fluid (CSF) to leak from the nose or the ears. Other manifestations include Battles's sign (bruising over the mastoid process) and periorbital ecchymosis, sometimes called "raccoon eyes." If CSF leakage is present, the risk for infection is high.

5. Brain damage in a head injury may result from open or closed head injuries. Open injuries occur in two ways. Severe blunt trauma can create an opening through the scalp, skull, and dura to expose the brain, as seen in a depressed skull fracture. An object such as a bullet or knife can penetrate the skull and damage the brain.

6. Clients with open injuries have a higher risk of meningitis.

7. Closed head injuries usually result from an acceleration–deceleration injury, also called the coup-contrecoup phenomenon (Figure 38-1). An example is when the head hits an object and the brain bounces forward (acceleration) and then rapidly rebounds and hits the back of the skull (deceleration).

8. Another type of closed head injury is a concussion, caused by violent shaking of the brain. The manifestations include immediate loss of consciousness for less than 5 minutes, drowsiness, confusion, dizziness, headache, and blurred or double vision.

9. Contusion is bruising of brain tissue occurring when the brain strikes the inner skull such as in coup-contrecoup injury. Contusion can cause cerebral edema and increased intracranial pressure (IICP). The manifestations vary with the size and location of the injury but include initial loss of consciousness. If the level of consciousness (LOC) remains altered, the client may become combative. Full consciousness is regained very slowly, and some residual effects may persist.

10. Epidural hematoma involves a severe blow to the brain causing bleeding that collects between the skull and dura mater. This can be caused by skull fractures or contusion. The manifestations include a brief loss of consciousness followed by a short period of alertness. Next there is

POWERPOINT SLIDES

Tables and/or Figures

- **Figure 38-1** Coup-Contrecoup Head Injuries
- **Figure 38-2** Three Types of Hematomas: Epidural, Subdural, and Intracerebral
- **Table 38-1** Common Brain Injuries With Pathophysiology and Manifestations
- **Table 38-2** Manifestations of Increased Intracranial Pressure
- **Table 38-3** Glasgow Coma Scale
- **Table 38-6** Manifestations and Complications of Cerebrovascular Accident
- **Box 38-4** Manifestations of Brain Tumors
- **Box 38-7** Right-Hemisphere Versus Left-Hemisphere Cerebrovascular Accident
- **Figure 38-6** Types of Paralysis
- **Figure 38-7** Homonymous Hemianopia
- **Box 38-13** Manifestations of Meningitis
- **Table 38-9** Types of Headaches

Nursing Care Plan: Caring for a Client After Cerebrovascular Accident

SUGGESTIONS FOR CLASSROOM ACTIVITIES

- Discuss the concept of the cranium as a closed space. Use transparencies that depict the percentage of the cranium occupied by the three main components.
- Point out to students how increased intracranial pressure (IICP) is a common manifestation/complication of many intracranial disorders. Have students list all the disorders of which IICP can be a manifestation or complication.
- Have an intensive care nurse come to class and talk to the students about IICP.

SUGGESTIONS FOR CLINICAL ACTIVITIES

- Assign students to care for clients who have been hospitalized with intracranial disorders. Ask students to write a paper about the manifestations their assigned client has demonstrated and to compare each of these manifestations to those described in the textbook.
- Get permission for students to rotate one by one through the ICU and see equipment in use to monitor intracranial pressure.

REFERENCE

- MedlinePlus: Increased intracranial pressure. Available at http://www.nlm.nih.gov/medlineplus/ency/article/000793.htm

a rapid deterioration to a coma, contralateral (opposite side) hemiparesis, ipsilateral (same side) fixed pupil dilation, and seizures.

11. Subdural hematoma is a closed head injury causing venous blood to collect between the dura mater and the subarachnoid layer.

12. There are three types of subdural hematomas.

13. In the acute type, there is rapid deterioration from drowsiness and confusion to coma, ipsilateral pupil dilation, and contralateral hemiparesis. In the subacute type, the manifestations appear 48 hours to 2 weeks later. The alert period is followed by slow progression to coma. The chronic type occurs most often in elderly, alcoholics, and those taking anticoagulants.

14. The manifestations of subdural hematomas include slowed thinking, confusion, and drowsiness developing weeks to months after initial injury.

15. Intracerebral hematoma involves bleeding into the brain tissue caused by gunshot wound or a depressed skull fracture. Manifestations include a decreasing level of consciousness to coma, pupil changes, and motor deficits.

16. The cranium has three compartments: (1) the brain (80%), (2) blood (10%), and (3) cerebrospinal fluid (10%). Intracranial pressure (ICP) is the pressure exerted within the cranium by these contents. If the volume of one component increases, the volume of the other components must decrease to keep the pressure within its normal range. When this does not occur, increased intracranial pressure (IICP) develops.

17. Cerebral blood flow is vital to deliver the required oxygen and glucose. For the brain to function properly, an adequate blood supply must travel to the brain.

18. When ICP increases, cerebral vasoconstriction occurs, which reduces cerebral blood flow and causes ischemia. If ischemia lasts longer than 5 minutes, the result is irreversible brain damage.

19. Increased carbon dioxide levels and/or decreased oxygen levels cause vasodilatation of the cerebral arteries. Either of these conditions will increase intracranial pressure.

20. Any increase in ICP causes changes in the client's LOC, pupil response, speech, motor function, and vital signs. The changes become more dramatic as ICP increases.

21. Manifestations of IICP may be labeled as early or late and develop slowly or rapidly. Not all manifestations occur in all clients. The location and cause of IICP will determine the symptoms (Table 38-2).

22. Cerebral edema increases the amount of extracellular or intracellular brain tissue volume. As the brain swells within the rigid skull, intracranial pressure increases.

23. Brain injury, intracranial surgery, tumors, hemorrhage, and infections can cause cerebral edema. Edema rises to its highest level within 48 to 72 hours after the assault to the brain and then gradually subsides.

24. Head injuries severe enough to cause IICP can lead to altered LOC, brain herniation, and brain death.

25. The Glasgow Coma Scale provides a guide for assessing LOC. It measures how well the client responds with eye opening and verbal and motor responses. The lower the score is, the worse the client's condition (Table 38-3).

26. Intracranial tumors are classified as benign or malignant, based on tissue type and cell characteristics. The term benign can be misleading. The tumor may be inaccessible by surgery, and as it grows, it presses on vital centers; if this continues, it can lead to disability and death.

27. Brain tumors are also categorized as primary or secondary, with primary tumors developing from cells and structures within the brain. Secondary brain tumors develop in areas outside of the brain and metastasize to the brain (see Table 38-4 for the most common brain tumors).

28. As the tumor grows, it disrupts the normal balance of brain tissue, blood, and CSF within the skull. When the brain fails to compensate for the increase in volume, increased intracranial pressure develops and leads to typical manifestations of IICP. If untreated, the result is brain herniation and death.

29. Manifestations of brain tumors are either local or generalized. Local manifestations relate to the location and function of that specific site (Box 38-4).

30. Tumors can press on cerebral blood vessels, decreasing their blood supply and causing dizziness. Common generalized manifestations include headache, seizures, vomiting, and changes in memory, communication, and concentration.

31. Headache, a prominent early symptom of brain tumor, is usually intermittent, worse in the morning, and associated with nausea and vomiting.

32. A cerebrovascular accident (CVA) is also called brain attack or stroke. It leads to neurologic deficits from decreased blood supply to a local area of the brain.

33. A transient ischemic attack (TIA) is a brief episode of reversible neurologic deficits, lasting from a few minutes to less than 24 hours. It results from a temporary reduction of blood flow to a specific area of the brain. TIA is often a warning signal of a future CVA.

34. Manifestations of a TIA include dizziness; visual loss in one eye; one-sided numbness or weakness of the fingers, arms, or legs; and aphasia.

35. A CVA is a sudden loss of neurologic function with three causes: thrombus, embolus, and hemorrhage. Any one of these causes can partially or completely reduce blood flow to cerebral tissues. This decreases oxygen to the area of the brain supplied by the involved blood vessels. Initially, the brain cells are ischemic but quickly die, resulting in a cerebral infarction. If the brain experiences anoxia for more than 10 minutes, irreversible brain damage occurs.

36. The signs and symptoms of a CVA vary depending on the area of the brain involved, the size of the area, and collateral blood flow. Typical manifestations alter movement, sensation, thought, memory, behavior, or speech.

37. The effects of a CVA are not limited to the nervous system. Complications can affect respiration, elimination, and muscle function.

38. Manifestations of CVAs include hemiparesis, hemiplegia, facial droop, expressive aphasia, receptive aphasia, global aphasia, dysarthria, diplopia, homonymous hemianopia, agnosia, apraxia, neglect syndrome (client ignores the affected side of the body), memory loss, short attention span, poor judgment, poor problem-solving ability, emotional lability, and depression (Table 38-6).

39. Strokes usually occur in one hemisphere. A comparison of right and left hemisphere strokes is provided in Box 38-7 (e.g., a right hemisphere CVA results in left hemiplegia and left visual field deficits, whereas a left-hemisphere CVA results in right hemiplegia and right visual field deficits).

40. Speech deficits usually result from a CVA affecting the dominant hemisphere. The left hemisphere is dominant in all right-handed people and most left-handed people.

41. Strokes cause many speech and language problems, including expressive aphasia, receptive aphasia, global aphasia, and dysarthria.

42. When a CVA damages the parietal and temporal lobes, vision is impaired. The client may experience diplopia or homonymous hemianopia (the loss of vision in half of the eye). The visual loss is opposite of the side affected by the stroke. The client sees only one-half of the normal vision and must turn the head to see the environment (Figure 38-7).

43. When the stroke damages only one hemisphere, bladder and bowel problems are usually short term. Initially, the client may experience

urinary frequency, urgency, or incontinence. Constipation develops as a complication of immobility. A stroke can impair the ability to swallow. Dysphagia may result in choking, drooling, aspiration, or regurgitation.

44. A cerebral aneurysm is an abnormal outpouching or dilation of a cerebral artery. It occurs at the point where the arterial wall is the weakest. The weakness is related to atherosclerosis, hypertension, or a congenital defect. Cerebral aneurysms usually develop in the circle of Willis.

45. At first, the weakened portion of the artery enlarges and presses on nearby cranial nerves. Unless it affects cranial nerve function, the person is asymptomatic. As the aneurysm enlarges, it may periodically leak blood into the brain. The person complains of headache, nausea, vomiting, and pain in the neck and back. If the leak can spontaneously seal itself with a clot, the client again becomes asymptomatic. If the aneurysm keeps expanding, it is likely to rupture, forcing blood into the subarachnoid space at the base of brain, which causes meningeal irritation.

46. Manifestations of a subarachnoid hemorrhage include (1) sudden explosive headache; (2) stiff neck (nuchal rigidity); (3) changes in consciousness; (4) photophobia; (5) nausea and vomiting; and (6) cranial nerve deficits. The major complications are rebleeding and vasospasms.

47. A *seizure* is a brief disruption of brain function caused by abnormal electrical activity in the nerve cells of the brain. A *convulsion* is involuntary muscle contraction and relaxation that involves the entire body.

48. Simple partial seizures cause uncontrolled jerking movements of the finger, hand, foot, leg, or face. This motor seizure may spread to other areas of the body and is known as a jacksonian march. Sometimes simple partial seizures involve the sensory part of the brain.

49. Symptoms of simple partial seizures include flashing lights, tingling sensations, or hallucinations. The seizure activity usually lasts 20–30 seconds, and the client does not lose consciousness.

50. Complete partial seizures, also known as psychomotor seizures, usually begin in the temporal lobe. Manifestations include repetitive, nonpurposeful actions, lip smacking, aimless walking, or picking at clothing. These behaviors are called automatisms and last less than 1 minute. During the seizure, the person has an altered level of consciousness.

51. After the seizure, the client may be confused or not remember the seizure. The seizure can be preceded by an aura such as an unusual smell, a sense of déjà vu, or a sudden intense emotion.

52. Generalized seizures involve both hemispheres of the brain and result in loss of consciousness. There are two forms of generalized seizures. Absence seizures occur more frequently in children. They are characterized by a brief change in consciousness such as a blank stare, blinking of the eyes, eyelid fluttering, and lip smacking. All motor activity is stopped during the seizure, which lasts only 5–10 seconds. The client may be unaware of it.

53. In a tonic-clonic seizure, the most common seizure disorder in adults and children, the muscles are rigid, with the arms and legs extended and jaws clenched. Pupils become fixed and dilated. Breathing stops briefly, and cyanosis develops.

54. During clonic contractions, movements are jerky as the muscles alternately contract and relax. The eyes roll back; tongue and cheek biting and frothing from the mouth may occur. Urinary and bowel incontinence are common. The entire seizure lasts about 1 to 2 minutes.

55. In the postictal phase, the client is unconscious for up to 30 minutes. The client regains consciousness slowly and may be confused and disoriented on waking.

56. Individuals often experience headache, muscle aches, and fatigue following a generalized seizure. Many people sleep for several hours afterwards. Amnesia of the events prior to the seizure is normal.

57. Status epilepticus is a continuous period of tonic-clonic seizures usually lasting 5 minutes or more in which the client does not regain consciousness. It causes physical exhaustion and respiratory distress. This is a life-threatening emergency.

58. Brain infections include meningitis, encephalitis, and brain abscesses.

59. Manifestations of meningitis include severe headache; high fever; photophobia; diplopia; signs of meningeal irritation, including nuchal rigidity (stiff neck), positive Brudzinski's sign, and positive Kernig's sign; restlessness; irritability; confusion; altered LOC; signs of IICP, including elevated blood pressure, bradycardia, changes in respiratory pattern, decreased LOC, and vomiting; seizures; and petechial rash (in meningococcal meningitis) (Box 38-13).

60. Encephalitis is an acute inflammation of the white and gray matter of the brain and spinal cord. Manifestations of encephalitis are similar to those of meningitis, including high fever, headache, stiff neck, seizures, confusion, and disorientation. As the disease progresses, the LOC deteriorates, and the client becomes comatose.

61. A brain abscess is a collection of purulent material within the brain. The microorganisms in the brain tissue cause local inflammation. As the white blood cells destroy the organisms, pus forms. A capsule forms around the pus. Unless the abscess is treated, the capsule enlarges and compresses nerves and brain tissues. Chronic inflammation can lead to edema and IICP. Initially, the client complains of a headache, fever, chills, and malaise. As the abscess expands, nausea, vomiting, drowsiness, confusion, weakness on one side, and seizures develop.

62. Clinical manifestations of headaches vary according to the cause and type of the headache. The most common types of headaches are migraine, cluster, and tension headaches.

63. Migraine headaches may or may not be preceded by an aura. Manifestations include pulsating or throbbing headache on one side of the head, accompanied by nausea, vomiting, and sensitivity to light and sound.

64. The manifestations of cluster headaches include unilateral pain located around or behind the eye that can wake the client as well as nasal congestion, tearing, and facial flushing.

65. The manifestations of tension headaches include bilateral pain, tightness, pressure, or vise-like feeling; pain is most common on waking (Table 38-9).

LEARNING OUTCOME 2

Identify laboratory and diagnostic tests used to diagnose intracranial disorders.

Concepts for Lecture

1. Laboratory tests ordered to determine the cause of the client's altered LOC include blood glucose when hypoglycemia is suspected; arterial blood gases to monitor pH and levels of oxygen and carbon dioxide; toxicology screening of blood and urine to identify alcohol or drug toxicity; serum creatinine and BUN when renal failure is suspected; and liver function tests to evaluate liver function.

2. Tests ordered to determine the cause of IICP include computed tomography (CT) scan or magnetic resonance imaging (MRI) to detect hemorrhage, edema, hematomas, or tumor; cerebral angiography to obtain x-ray views of cerebral blood flow to determine if client has had a stroke; and lumbar puncture to obtain a sample of CSF to analyze for possible meningitis.

 **POWERPOINT SLIDES**

Tables and/or Figures
- **Box 38-2** Nursing Care Checklist: Lumbar Puncture

 **SUGGESTIONS FOR CLASSROOM ACTIVITIES**
- Use clinical examples of alterations in lab results that would indicate a metabolic cause of altered LOC.

 **SUGGESTIONS FOR CLINICAL ACTIVITIES**
- Assign students to care for clients with intracranial or suspected intracranial disorders. Ask the students to find examples of abnormal lab results in their clients' charts and bring these examples to postconference for discussion.
- Have students ask permission to be present when the physician explains the results of tests to their assigned clients.

3. The National Institutes of Health Stroke Scale is a clinical evaluation tool used to assess neurologic outcome and the degree of recovery for a client who has had a stroke.

4. Tests used to detect the potential for a stroke or to identify physiologic changes once the CVA has occurred include CT scan to identify the size and location of the CVA and to differentiate between an infarction and hemorrhage; MRI, which detects areas of infarction earlier than a CT scan; cerebral arteriography to identify vessel abnormalities such as an angiogram; Doppler ultrasound studies to evaluate the flow of blood through the carotid arteries and identify if a vessel is partially or completely occluded; positron emission tomography (PET) to identify the amount of tissue damage following a CVA; and lumbar puncture to obtain cerebrospinal fluid for examination. Blood in the CSF indicates a hemorrhagic CVA.

5. Diagnosis of a cerebral aneurysm is made by a CT scan, angiography, and lumbar puncture. The CT scan shows the location and size of the aneurysm. Cerebral angiography is done to view the cerebral arteries, locate the aneurysm, and identify a vasospasm. The presence of blood in the cerebrospinal fluid during a lumbar puncture confirms a subarachnoid hemorrhage.

6. Diagnostic tests for seizures include an EEG to determine the type of seizure and locate the seizure focus; skull x-rays to identify possible skull fractures; CT scan or MRI to detect a tumor, CVA, or hemorrhage; and blood studies to assess CBC, electrolytes, BUN, and blood glucose levels.

7. The diagnosis of bacterial or viral meningitis or encephalitis is based on clinical manifestations. Diagnosis of brain abscess is more difficult because there are unclear symptoms.

8. Diagnostic tests that may be ordered when bacterial or viral meningitis or encephalitis is suspected include lumbar puncture; culture and sensitivity and Gram stain of the CSF to identify the virus or bacteria causing meningitis or encephalitis; cultures from the blood, urine, throat, and nose to identify the bacterial source of infection; and CT scan, MRI, or skull x-rays to identify the infection source causing a brain abscess.

9. The lumbar puncture findings that indicate a positive diagnosis of bacterial meningitis are as follows: (1) cloudy CSF ; (2) elevated protein level and WBC count; (3) decreased glucose level; and (4) elevated CSF pressure.

10. Diagnostic tests for clients with complaint of headache include brain scan, MRI, x-ray studies of the skull and cervical spine, EEG, and lumbar puncture for CSF to rule out other neurologic problems. Serum metabolic screens and hypersensitivity testing may be performed if systemic problems are suspected.

LEARNING OUTCOME 3

Describe the interdisciplinary care required for managing clients with increased intracranial pressure.

Concepts for Lecture

1. It is important to identify and prevent IICP in any client with a neurologic problem.
2. Medications are given immediately to lower ICP.
3. Clients with severe brain injuries need their ICP monitored.
4. Uncontrolled intracranial bleeding requires immediate surgery.

REFERENCE

- MedlinePlus: Cerebral spinal fluid collection. Available at http://www.nlm.nih.gov/medlineplus/ency/article/003428.htm

POWERPOINT SLIDES

Tables and/or Figures

- **Box 38-3** Assessment: Clients With Increased Intracranial Pressure

SUGGESTIONS FOR CLASSROOM ACTIVITIES

- Invite an ICU nurse who does monitoring of ICP to come to class and discuss ICP monitoring.

SUGGESTIONS FOR CLINICAL ACTIVITIES

- Assign students to rotate through ICU to observe monitoring of ICP whenever possible and to discuss their observations in postconference.

LEARNING OUTCOME 4

Discuss the nursing implications for medications ordered for clients with intracranial disorders.

Concepts for Lecture

1. Frequently ordered medications to manage clients with IICP are osmotic diuretics, loop diuretics, anticonvulsants, antipyretics, and histamine antagonists or proton pump inhibitors.

2. Intravenous fluids are used to maintain the client's fluid and electrolyte balance and to prevent hypotension. Only 0.9% normal saline and lactated Ringer's solution are given because they do not cross the blood–brain barrier and increase cerebral edema. They are infused at low rates such as 50 to 75 mL/hr. All IV solutions must be given using an intravenous pump to prevent volume overload.

3. The nurse must closely monitor the client who is receiving diuretics for dehydration and electrolyte losses, especially sodium and potassium. Osmotic diuretics (e.g., mannitol) draw water out of the edematous brain tissue to be excreted by the kidneys. Large or frequent doses of mannitol cause dehydration and electrolyte losses. Loop diuretics decrease cerebral edema but cause less fluid and electrolyte losses.

4. A histamine H_2-receptor antagonist like ranitidine (Zantac) or a proton pump inhibitor such as pantoprazole (Protonix) is given to prevent gastric irritation and ulcers. Antiemetics are used to prevent vomiting and the risk for aspiration.

5. Anticonvulsants are ordered to treat seizure activity associated with a head injury. The most commonly ordered anticonvulsant is phenytoin (Dilantin).

6. Acetaminophen is used alone or with a hypothermia blanket to treat hyperthermia. Hyperthermia raises cerebral metabolism and increases ICP.

7. Clients with severe traumatic brain injury (TBI) and continually elevated ICP may be given barbiturates, which place the client in a coma, reducing metabolism of the injured brain and allowing the brain time to heal. During this therapy, the client is closely monitored in the critical care unit.

8. Clients with brain tumors may receive mannitol, an osmotic diuretic, to open the blood–brain barrier, enabling chemotherapy to reach the tumor. Tumors in the meninges may be treated with chemotherapy through an Ommaya reservoir, which is surgically implanted into the lateral ventricle of the brain (Figure 38-4).

9. Time-release, biodegradable chemotherapy wafers can be placed directly into the tumor cavity after the tumor is removed by surgery.

10. Medications are given to prevent a CVA in clients with TIAs or a previous CVA. Antiplatelet medications are most frequently ordered. Daily use of low-dose aspirin effectively reduces clot formation. Other antiplatelet medications include dipyridamole (Persantine), ticlopidine (Ticlid), and clopidogrel (Plavix).

11. If a thrombotic or embolic stroke is suspected, the client is given a thrombolytic drug, recombinant tissue plasminogen alteplase (Activase rt-PA). This drug dissolves blood clots, increases blood flow, and prevents damage to the brain cells. To be effective, it must be given intravenously within the first 3 hours after symptoms appear. It is not given when intracerebral bleeding is present.

12. Thrombotic strokes are treated with anticoagulant therapy. They do not dissolve an existing clot but prevent new clots from

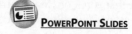

POWERPOINT SLIDES

Tables and/or Figures
- **Figure 38-4** Ommaya Reservoir for Medication Administration
- **Table 38-7** Giving Medications Safely: Anticonvulsant Drugs

SUGGESTIONS FOR CLASSROOM ACTIVITIES
- Assign students to research various medications given to clients with intracranial disorders and to present in class on their selected medications. Instruct students to include and focus on nursing implications of these medications.
- Invite a pharmacist or a pharmacy student to come to class and discuss medications given to clients with intracranial disorders.

SUGGESTIONS FOR CLINICAL ACTIVITIES
- Assign students to care for clients who have intracranial disorders. Supervise the students in administering medications after quizzing them about the nursing implications.
- Have students discuss, in postconference, the medications given to their clients. Compare medications given to those mentioned in this chapter.

REFERENCE
- MedlinePlus: Cluster headache. Available at http://www.nlm.nih.gov/medlineplus/ency/article/000786.htm

forming. Anticoagulants are never given to a client who is bleeding within the brain. The most common anticoagulants are heparin, warfarin (Coumadin), and low-molecular-weight heparin such as Lovenox.

13. Antiplatelet medications or heparin are started 24 hours after thrombolytic therapy.

14. During the acute phase, the client may receive antihypertensive drugs to control blood pressure. Hypertension can increase the area of infarction.

15. If the client has IICP, mannitol (an osmotic diuretic) or furosemide (a loop diuretic) is used to decrease cerebral edema.

16. An anticonvulsant such as phenytoin is given to prevent or control seizures.

17. The client with a cerebral aneurysm may be given medications to avoid rebleeding and vasospasm until surgery is possible. Calcium channel blockers, such as nimodipine (Nimotop), decrease vasospasm.

18. The client with a cerebral aneurysm is given anticonvulsants to prevent seizures. Stool softeners prevent unnecessary straining that can increase intracranial pressure. Acetaminophen or codeine is used for pain control.

19. For nursing implications of anticonvulsant drugs, see Table 38-7.

20. In cases of bacterial meningitis, high doses of intravenous third-generation cephalosporins or vancomycin (Vancocin) are started immediately.

21. The specific antibiotic is chosen after the culture and sensitivity report identifies the causative organism. Antibiotic therapy is given in high doses so that it will cross the blood–brain barrier and reach the CSF. Drug therapy is continued from 7 to 21 days.

22. The CDC recommends that isolation for bacterial meningitis be continued for 24 hours after antibiotic therapy is started.

23. Antibiotics are also used to treat brain abscesses.

24. Anyone exposed to meningococcal meningitis is started on prophylactic antibiotic therapy immediately. The drugs of choice are rifampin (Rifadin) and vancomycin (Vancocin). All cases of meningitis must be reported to the local public health department.

25. Treatment for encephalitis consists of antiviral drugs such as vidarabine (Vira-A) and acyclovir (Zovirax). They are most effective if used before the client becomes comatose.

26. Medications are given to relieve symptoms and to prevent complications from any one of the intracranial infections. Anticonvulsant medication may be given to control seizures, and antipyretics may be given to reduce fever. Analgesics such as acetaminophen are given to relieve headache and neck pain. Osmotic diuretics and corticosteroids may decrease cerebral edema. Antiemetics may be given to control nausea and vomiting. Intravenous fluids may be necessary to prevent dehydration until the client is able to take oral fluids.

27. The choice of medications for managing headaches depends on the specific type of headache. To reduce the frequency and severity of migraines, several prophylactic medications are ordered.

28. Propranolol (Inderal) prevents dilation of cerebral blood vessels, and verapamil (Calan) controls cerebral vasospasms. Amitriptyline (Elavil) blocks the uptake of serotonin and catecholamines. Methysergide maleate (Sansert) decreases serotonin action; however, it can produce severe side effects and must be used cautiously.

29. Topiramate (Topamax), an anticonvulsant, may be effective in preventing migraines, but abrupt discontinuation can cause seizures.

30. Before a migraine becomes severe, ergotamine with caffeine (Cafergot) is given by oral, sublingual, rectal, or intranasal route. When

given at the first sign of an attack, ergotamine is effective in controlling up to 70% of acute attacks.

31. Two serotonin agonists, sumatriptan (Imitrex) and zolmitriptan (Zomig), act rapidly to stop migraines. Sumatriptan is available for oral, subcutaneous, or intranasal use.

32. Once a migraine attack is in progress, narcotic analgesics such as codeine or meperidine (Demerol) may be needed. Antiemetics such as promethazine (Phenergan) or metoclopramide (Reglan) may be given to control nausea and vomiting.

33. Many of the same medications used for migraines may treat cluster headaches. Some clients gain relief from a cluster headache by inhaling 100% oxygen at 7 to 9 L/min for 15 minutes. Ergotamine tartrate may be given in suppository form at bedtime to prevent cluster headaches.

34. Nonnarcotic analgesics such as aspirin or acetaminophen may be effective in relieving tension headaches. For prophylaxis, amitriptyline (Elavil) may be given at bedtime.

LEARNING OUTCOME 5

Identify the preoperative and postoperative care for clients undergoing neurosurgery.

Concepts for Lecture

1. Preoperative care of a client having a craniotomy includes (1) providing routine preoperative care (see Chapter 10), (2) assessing the client's understanding and level of anxiety of the planned surgery, and (3) preparing the family for how the client will appear after surgery (e.g., a large dressing covering the head; possible swollen, bruised eyelids; and an endotracheal tube).

2. Postoperative care for clients undergoing neurosurgery includes (1) providing routine postoperative care (see Chapter 10), (2) reviewing nursing care intervention for IICP, (3) monitoring respiratory status every 1 to 2 hours and assessing airway patency, (4) monitoring oxygen saturation levels as needed, (5) positioning on the nonoperative side if a bone flap or large mass was removed to decrease venous collection and pressure on the surgical incision, (6) applying cool cloth over client's eyes, (7) reducing noise and bright lights in the room, (8) using acetaminophen with codeine for pain, (9) assessing and reporting CSF leak from ears, nose, or wound (a leak might indicate an opening in the dura that could allow bacteria into the brain), and (10) providing interventions to prevent infection.

3. Postoperative care also includes the following: (11) use strict aseptic technique when changing dressings and caring for wound drains and ICP monitor lines; (12) monitor for any purulent drainage; (13) administer prescribed antibiotics; (14) assess for manifestations of meningitis; (15) after the head dressing is removed (usually 3 days after surgery), clean the incision with half-strength hydrogen peroxide to remove dried blood; (16) if CSF leak is present, place a sterile dressing over the drainage area and change when damp; (17) if CSF leaks from the nose, elevate head of bed 20 degrees unless contraindicated; (18) do not suction nasally, do not clean the nose, and tell client not to put fingers in the nose; (19) if CSF leaks from the ear, position client on side of leakage unless contraindicated; (20) do not clean the ear, and tell the client not to put fingers in the ear; and (21) monitor for seizures and maintain seizure precautions.

POWERPOINT SLIDES

Tables and/or Figures
- **Box 38-5** Nursing Care Checklist: Clients Having a Craniotomy

SUGGESTIONS FOR CLASSROOM ACTIVITIES
- Have students break into small groups or pairs to discuss the nursing care checklist for a client having a craniotomy. Ask the students if they can add anything else to the checklist or if they have any questions about items on the checklist.

SUGGESTIONS FOR CLINICAL ACTIVITIES
- Assign students to assist with the care for a client before and/or after a craniotomy or to observe the care.

LEARNING OUTCOME 6

Use the nursing process to collect data, establish outcomes, provide individualized care, and evaluate nursing responses for the client with an intracranial disorder.

Concepts for Lecture

1. Clients with traumatic brain injury need frequent nursing assessments to prevent IICP. The nurse observes and reports immediately to the physician any sudden change in neurologic function.

2. Subjective data collected from clients with increased intracranial pressure include noting when the change in LOC or memory first occurred and whether the onset was slow or rapid. The nurse assesses for the Babinski reflex, the corneal reflex, and the gag reflex; assesses for abnormal posturing; and monitors and reports diagnostic test results beyond expected range. See Box 38-3 Assessment: Clients With Increased Intracranial Pressure.

3. One nursing diagnosis for a client with increased intracranial pressure is Ineffective Cerebral Tissue Perfusion. A possible outcome is that the client maintains adequate tissue perfusion.

4. Interventions for the nursing diagnosis of Ineffective Cerebral Tissue Perfusion include elevating the head of the bed 30 degrees and keeping the head in a midline position, giving oxygen as ordered and using pulse oximetry to measure oxygen levels, and keeping PaO_2 levels above 94% and $PaCO_2$ levels between 35 and 45.

5. Additional interventions for a nursing diagnosis of Ineffective Cerebral Tissue Perfusion include avoiding hip flexion and abdominal distention, monitoring patency of the nasogastric tube, and monitoring the temperature every 2 hours for hyperthermia; if possible, avoid taking rectal temperatures (taking a rectal temperature can increase ICP).

6. Nursing interventions also include keeping the client quiet, reducing noise and lights in the room, spacing nursing activities over the shift, speaking softly and calmly, turning the client slowly and gently with a turn sheet, limiting fluid over a 24-hour period, and avoiding restraints if the client is combative.

7. Another nursing diagnosis possible for brain injury or increased intracranial pressure is Ineffective Breathing Pattern with a possible expected outcome that the client will maintain an effective breathing pattern.

8. Nursing interventions for ineffective breathing pattern include monitoring respiratory rate, depth, and rhythm for changes and assessing the client's ability to clear secretions. The nurse inserts an oral airway as needed to prevent the tongue from obstructing the airway and turns the client from side to side every 2 hours to prevent the pooling of secretions in one area of the lung. Side position prevents the tongue from obstructing the airway.

9. If the client is unconscious, the nurse keeps the client NPO and provides oral hygiene.

10. Another nursing diagnosis for the client with a head injury or increased intracranial pressure is Risk for Imbalanced Nutrition: Less than Body Requirements with a possible expected outcome that the client will maintain weight within range for height and age.

11. Nursing interventions for a nursing diagnosis of Risk for Imbalanced Nutrition: Less than Body Requirement could include giving tube feedings or administering total parenteral nutrition as ordered. Before each tube feeding, the nurse checks the gastric residual. The nurse monitors daily weights.

POWERPOINT SLIDES

Tables and/or Figures
- **Figure 38-9** Positioning the Client With Hemiplegia to Prevent Deformity of the Affected Extremities
- **Box 38-12** Assessment: Clients With Seizure Disorders
- **Box 38-15** Assessment: Clients With Headaches

Nursing Care Plan: Client With Increased Intracranial Pressure and Altered Level of Consciousness

SUGGESTIONS FOR CLASSROOM ACTIVITIES
- Divide students into small groups to develop a nursing care plan for a client for one of the intracranial disorders. Students can revise and expand on nursing interventions.

12. Additional nursing diagnoses for brain injury or increased intracranial pressure include Risk for Impaired Skin Integrity, Impaired Physical Mobility, and Risk for Infection.

13. Evaluation of the effectiveness of nursing care for a client with IICP includes monitoring vital signs, assessing level of alertness and orientation, assessing strength of hand grip, assessing extremity movement and gait, and looking for the absence of diplopia, tinnitus, dizziness, nausea, vomiting, or abnormal pupil response.

14. In the unconscious client, the nurse evaluates effectiveness of care by collecting data about breathing pattern, reflex response, posturing, and skin integrity.

15. The nurse assessing the client with a brain tumor gathers information about the client's history and performs a basic neurologic examination. Assessment data can identify how the brain tumor is interfering with the client's life. See Box 38-6 (Assessment: Clients With Brain Tumors).

16. If the client with a brain tumor is confused or has difficulty answering questions, the family should be included in the interview.

17. Nursing diagnoses for the client with a brain tumor include Anxiety with an expected outcome that the client will verbalize that anxiety has decreased. Nursing interventions include explaining diagnostic procedures and treatment methods to the client and family and repeating information as needed; encouraging the client and family to express their feelings; and providing emotional support by listening and staying with the client or, if the client prefers, arranging for a member of the clergy to visit.

18. Another nursing diagnosis for the client with a brain tumor is Disturbed Body Image with a possible expected outcome that the client verbalizes positive and negative feelings. Nursing interventions include assessing for signs and symptoms of a negative body image and providing or arranging for a client to have a surgical cap, scarf, or turban; assisting the client to obtain a wig or hairpiece; and reinforcing the fact that the hair will grow back.

19. The nurse evaluating the effectiveness of nursing interventions for the client following a craniotomy will look at neurologic deficits, IICP, bleeding, signs of infection, level of anxiety, pain, and knowledge of follow-up care at home. The nurse will evaluate the client's ability to accept the long-term consequences of a brain tumor and side effects of the treatments.

20. On admission to the hospital, the client with a suspected TIA or CVA is assessed for any neurologic deficits. If the client's condition is unstable, respiratory and cardiac statuses are closely monitored. See Box 38-10 for assessment of subjective and objective data.

21. A nursing diagnosis for a client with CVA is Ineffective Cerebral Tissue Perfusion with an expected outcome that the client will demonstrate stable or improved cerebral perfusion. ICP is monitored closely.

22. Another nursing diagnosis for a client with a CVA is Risk for Ineffective Airway Clearance with expected outcome that the client maintains a patent airway. Nursing interventions include suctioning the airway as necessary, placing the client in a side-lying position to prevent aspiration, monitoring respiratory status, and giving oxygen as ordered.

23. A third possible nursing diagnosis for a client with a CVA is Impaired Physical Mobility. A possible expected outcome is that the client demonstrates ability to move and increased muscle strength. Interventions include turning the client from side to side every 2 hours around the clock, keeping the body aligned, and placing extremities in proper position with pillow. Interventions are also aimed at reducing the risk of other complications resulting from

immobility and include monitoring calves each shift for symptoms of thrombophlebitis, not using a footboard, and performing active ROM exercises on unaffected extremities and passive ROM exercises on affected extremities every 4 hours.

24. Another possible nursing diagnosis for a client with a CVA is Impaired Verbal Communication with a possible expected outcome that the client uses oral and other communication techniques as able. Nursing interventions include speaking to the client as an adult in a normal voice, allowing adequate time for the client to answer, facing the client and talking slowly, letting the client know if you cannot understand the client's speech, using short simple statements and "yes" and "no" questions, instructing clients to nod their head or blink their eyes if they cannot speak, and providing techniques to help the client communicate (e.g., pad and pencil, magic slate, flash cards, computerized talking board, and/or picture board).

25. Additional nursing diagnoses for a client with a CVA include Disturbed Sensory Perception, Impaired Urinary Elimination and Constipation, Self-Care Deficit, and Impaired Swallowing.

26. Evaluation of the effectiveness of nursing care of a client with CVA involves assessing the airway patency; ability to swallow, communicate, move extremities, and provide self-care or with assistance; and urinary and bowel patterns. The nurse evaluates by collecting data on the client's coping ability, willingness to participate in rehabilitation, and knowledge of medications and home care.

27. The nurse working with a client with a seizure disorder collects subjective assessment data to determine the extent to which the seizure activity is interfering with the client's life and the type of medical intervention needed. Objective observations are made before, during, and after a seizure (Box 38-12).

28. A nursing diagnosis for a client with a seizure disorder is Risk for Ineffective Airway Clearance with a possible expected outcome that the client maintains a patent airway. Nursing interventions include loosening clothing around the neck, turning the client on the side, not forcing anything into the client's mouth, giving oxygen by mask as needed, and providing suction at the bedside.

29. Another nursing diagnosis for a client with a seizure disorder is Risk for Injury with an expected outcome that the client will remain free from injury during seizure activity. Nursing interventions include maintaining the bed in a low position and keeping the side rails up; placing blankets or protective pads over the side rails; if the client is sitting or standing when the seizure begins, gently lowering the client to the floor and placing a folded towel or pillow under the client's head; not restraining the client during a seizure; and clearing the area of objects that could cause harm.

30. A third nursing diagnosis for a client with a seizure disorder is Anxiety with a possible expected outcome that the client verbalizes that anxiety is reduced. Nursing interventions include encouraging the client to identify potential concerns and misconceptions, providing information about community support groups, and referring the client to any local and state agencies for information about driving or operating dangerous machinery.

31. Evaluation of the effectiveness of nursing care for the client with a seizure disorder involves collecting data regarding the type and number of seizures, any occurrence of injury during a seizure, and knowledge of medications, as well as the client's level of anxiety to manage a potential chronic disorder.

32. Assessing a client with an intracranial infection involves obtaining a careful history and identifying subjective and objective data (Box 38-14).

33. A nursing diagnosis for a client with an intracranial infection is Risk for Ineffective Cerebral Tissue Perfusion with a possible expected outcome that the client maintains adequate cerebral perfusion. A nursing intervention is monitoring for altered neurologic function.

34. Hyperthermia is another possible nursing diagnosis for a client with an intracranial infection. A possible expected outcome would be that the client's temperature would return to normal parameters. Nursing interventions include monitoring body temperature at least every 4 hours; removing unnecessary clothing and bed linen from the client; giving antipyretic medications or tepid sponge baths or using a cooling blanket, as ordered; monitoring for signs and symptoms of dehydration noting skin turgor, mucous membranes, and daily body weight; and measuring and comparing intake and output every 2 to 4 hours.

35. A third nursing diagnosis for a client with an intracranial infection is Acute Pain with an expected outcome that the client's pain is absent or decreases to tolerable levels. Nursing interventions include reducing environmental stimuli, keeping the room quiet and dimming bright lights, providing gentle ROM exercises to reduce joint stiffness and promote circulation, placing the client in a position of comfort, placing a cool cloth over the client's eyes, and giving a mild analgesic such as acetaminophen or codeine.

36. Evaluation of the effectiveness of nursing care for a client with an intracranial infection begins by collecting data showing the temperature within normal range, absence of headache and neurologic irritation, absence of signs of IICP, and knowledge of anti-infective therapy.

37. When working with a client experiencing headaches, the nursing care begins by obtaining a history and description of the headache. It is important to identify the effects of recurring headaches on the client's daily life. Nursing interventions focus on controlling the pain and discomfort of the headache. See Box 38-15 for a list of assessment data to collect.

38. A nursing diagnosis for a client with headaches would be Acute Pain, with a possible expected outcome that the client's pain is absent or decreased to tolerable levels. Nursing interventions include asking the client to rate his or her pain on a scale of 0 to 10, with 10 being the worst pain, or providing a visual analog scale of faces that show different levels of discomfort; minimizing light, noise, and activity; providing rest in a quiet, nonstimulating environment when the headache is present; encouraging the client to use deep breathing or relaxation techniques; applying cold or warm cloth to the head and neck as ordered; and offering a back massage.

39. The nurse can collect information to evaluate the effectiveness of providing care to the client with headaches. This information includes decreased or absence of pain, understanding of medications, and modification of lifestyle to reduce headaches.

LEARNING OUTCOME 7

Discuss home care teaching guidelines for clients with altered neurologic function.

Concepts for Lecture

1. If clients with a mild head injury are not hospitalized, they must be closely monitored at home.
2. If a client has a linear skull fracture, the family is taught to wake and observe the client every 2 hours during the first 8 hours after the accident.

POWERPOINT SLIDES

Tables and/or Figures

- **Box 38-5** Nursing Care Checklist: Clients Having a Craniotomy

SUGGESTIONS FOR CLASSROOM ACTIVITIES

- Invite an emergency room nurse to come and talk to the class about home care teaching done in the emergency room with the client who has altered neurologic function.

3. The client and family are taught that they should return to the emergency department if the client develops increasing drowsiness, confusion, or slurred speech; if there is difficulty waking the client; if the client is vomiting or has blurred vision with one or both pupils dilated; or if the client has prolonged headache, blood or clear fluid leaking from the nose or ears, weakness in arm or leg, or seizures.

4. Clients and their families should receive a copy of the home care instructions that were reviewed in the emergency department.

5. Clients with severe head injuries usually require extensive rehabilitation either as inpatients or outpatients. The client and family need teaching about medications, exercises and positioning, skin care, diet, use of assistive devices, and potential complications.

6. If a client with a brain tumor has chemotherapy or radiation therapy ordered, the following information should be given to the client and family: importance of keeping appointments for chemotherapy or radiation therapy, adverse effects of chemotherapy or radiation, skin care with radiation therapy, ways to manage nausea or vomiting, and nutritional support.

7. The client with a brain tumor and their family may need information about support groups and community resources.

8. Before the client with a brain tumor is discharged home, the nurse should provide verbal and written information on the following: the use and side effects of anticonvulsant and anti-inflammatory medications; wound care; if postoperative, not to shampoo hair until the incision is healed and then patting the incision after shampooing and avoiding a curling iron or hair dryer on hot setting until hair has grown back; wearing a hat outside to prevent sunburn; and protecting the head until the wound is healed.

9. The client with a brain tumor and the family are taught what signs and symptoms to report, such as swelling at incision site; bloody, yellow, or clear drainage from ears, nose, or incision; increased drowsiness; changes in behavior; stiff neck, severe headache, and elevated temperature; new sensory or motor deficits, vision changes, or seizures; and safety precautions for motor deficits, sensory deficits, lack of coordination, seizures, and cognitive deficits.

10. The client and family are taught the importance of follow-up visits.

11. Discharge planning for the client with a CVA includes assessing the client's and family's ability to care for the client. The following topics should be addressed with the client and family before the client is sent home: the physician's name and emergency numbers; complications such as aspiration, pneumonia, UTI, blood clots, and skin breakdown; medication use, dose, and side effects; equipment modifications in the home; safety measures to prevent falls; demonstration of feeding techniques and use of assistive devices; demonstration of ROM exercises and the use of any splints; physical care (ADLs, transfer techniques, skin care); psychologic support for client and family; respite care for the caregiver; and information on community resources.

12. Discharge teaching following a subarachnoid hemorrhage is similar to that for a CVA. Clients with significant neurologic deficits are referred for rehabilitation services. The client and family need to follow postoperative craniotomy guidelines (Box 38-5).

13. The client experiencing seizures needs to be taught ways to reduce the incidence of seizure activity and promote safety. Safety teaching includes not smoking in bed or when alone, installing grab bars in the shower, taking a shower rather than a bath, and keeping bedroom and bathroom doors unlocked in case of an emergency.

14. The nurse working with a client experiencing seizures and the client's family emphasizes the importance of follow-up care, keeping

SUGGESTIONS FOR CLINICAL ACTIVITIES

- Assign students to shadow a nurse in the emergency room. Have the students note any teaching done with clients who have had altered neurologic function and their family members.
- Assign students to accompany home health nurses on visits to clients who are receiving or following teaching regarding dealing with altered neurologic function.

appointments with the physician and laboratory, and taking prescribed anticonvulsant medications even when no seizure activity occurs. The nurse teaches about medication use, side effects, and the need to take medications at prescribed intervals.

15. The nurse teaches the family and client to record any seizure activity and medications taken daily.

16. The client experiencing seizures is taught to avoid activities that require alertness and coordination until medication levels are stable.

17. The client is instructed to wear an ID bracelet identifying seizure condition and medications.

18. The nurse reviews any state laws that apply to people with seizure disorders and instructs the client to avoid factors that may trigger a seizure, such as fasting, caffeine, excess alcohol intake, fatigue, flashing and blinking lights, and sleep loss. The nurse teaches family members first aid for a seizure and when to call for medical assistance.

19. The nurse teaches the care and observations necessary before, during, and after a seizure.

20. Following the acute phase of an intracranial infection, the client requires several weeks of convalescence. The client and family need to understand home management.

21. After assessing the client's and family's abilities and resources to provide care after discharge, the nurse includes the following topics in the teaching session: medications; use, dose, and side effects; and the importance of taking all antibiotic or antiviral medication until completely gone. The nurse emphasizes the importance of reporting fever, headache, or neck stiffness in people who have had close contact with the client with meningitis. The nurse encourages adequate rest and sleep and a well-balanced diet, advises the client to increase physical activity gradually, and stresses the importance of reporting any signs or symptoms of ear infection, sore throat, or upper respiratory infection. For infections transmitted by mosquitoes, the client and family need to know how to destroy breeding sites of insect larvae and to avoid mosquito and tick bites by wearing protective clothing and insect repellants.

22. The nurse working with a client who has long-term or migraine headaches will teach the client about medication use, dosage, and side effects. The nurse will teach clients on ergotamine to report any side effects; to eliminate caffeine, cured meats, monosodium glutamate (MSG), and foods containing tyramine; and to avoid smoking.

23. The nurse working with a client with headaches will teach the client to participate in regular moderate exercise; to avoid fasting, fatigue, and irregular sleep patterns; to keep a headache diary, and to identify comfort measures during a headache (e.g., darkened, quiet room, and applying a cool cloth to the forehead).

GENERAL CHAPTER CONSIDERATIONS

1. Have students study and learn key terms listed at the beginning of the chapter.

2. Have students complete end of chapter exercises either in their book or on the MyNursingKit Website.

3. Use the Classroom Response Question PowerPoints to assess students prior to lecture.

- Clinical Reasoning Care Map

MYNURSINGKIT
(www.mynursingkit.com)

- Websites
- NCLEX® Questions
- Case Studies
- Key Terms

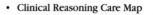

STUDENT WORKBOOK AND RESOURCE GUIDE

- Chapter 38 activities
- *Separate purchase*

PRENTICE HALL NURSE'S DRUG GUIDE

- *Separate purchase*

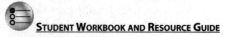

CLASSROOM RESPONSE QUESTION
POWERPOINTS

TESTBANK

CHAPTER 39
CARING FOR CLIENTS WITH DEGENERATIVE NEUROLOGIC AND SPINAL CORD DISORDERS

LEARNING OUTCOME 1

Describe the causes, pathophysiology, and manifestations of common degenerative neurologic disorders and spinal cord injuries.

Concepts for Lecture

1. Multiple sclerosis (MS) is a chronic, degenerative disease that damages the myelin sheath surrounding the axons of the CNS.
2. MS is marked by periods of exacerbation followed by periods of remission.
3. The exact cause of MS is unknown.
4. MS affects Caucasian females (age 20–50) more frequently, with a peak age of 30.
5. Family history of MS and living in the cold, damp, northern part of the United States increase the risk of MS.
6. Viral infections seem to trigger an autoimmune response. Emotional stress, fatigue, pregnancy, and acute respiratory infections tend to occur before the onset of MS.
7. Myelin sheaths make up what is known as white matter in the CNS. Multiple sclerosis destroys the myelin sheath of the spinal cord, brain, and optic nerve and replaces it with plaque. This process is called demyelination. When the myelin is destroyed, nerve impulse conduction slows.
8. Manifestations vary according to the area of the nervous system affected.
9. As the disease progresses, exacerbations last longer and occur more often. When the nerve cells are finally destroyed, the manifestations become permanent.
10. Fatigue is a symptom that affects almost all clients with MS, and it is often ignored. Other symptoms include diplopia, weakness, and tingling and numbness in the extremities. Motor symptoms worsen after a hot shower or exercise.
11. Parkinson's disease (PD) is a chronic, progressive, degenerative neurologic disease that alters motor coordination.
12. Most people with PD are diagnosed after the age of 65, but PD can develop in those under age 65. It affects Caucasian men more than women.
13. The cause of primary Parkinson's disease in unknown. Secondary parkinsonism may be caused by repeated head trauma, encephalitis, or exposure to carbon monoxide or cyanide poisoning. Drugs such as haloperidol (Haldol) and methyldopa (Aldomet) may induce parkinsonism. The symptoms disappear when the drug is stopped.
14. Parkinson's disease results from a deficiency of dopamine. In PD, neurons in the cerebral cortex atrophy, and the number of dopamine receptors decreases. The balance of dopamine (inhibitory neurotransmitter) and acetylcholine (excitatory neurotransmitter) is upset. Acetylcholine causes constant excitement of the motor neurons, which is the basis of the manifestations of PD.
15. Manifestations of PD are subtle and may be mistaken as signs of normal aging. The three cardinal signs of PD are (1) tremor, (2) rigidity, and (3) bradykinesia (slowed voluntary movements and speech).

POWERPOINT SLIDES

Tables and/or Figures

- **Figure 39-1** Multisystem Effects of Multiple Sclerosis
- **Figure 39-2** Subtle Changes in Facial Expression and Movement Occur in Parkinson's Disease
- **Box 39-2** Manifestations of Parkinson's Disease
- **Figure 39-3** Sensory and Motor Branches of the Trigeminal Nerve: Ophthalmic, Maxillary, and Mandibular
- **Figure 39-4** Typical Drooping of One Side of the Face in a Client With Bell's Palsy
- **Figure 39-5** Spinal Cord Injury Mechanisms
- **Table 39-3** Functional Abilities by Level of Spinal Cord Injuries
- **Figure 39-8** A Herniated Intervertebral Disk
- **Box 39-7** Manifestations of Herniated Intervertebral Disk
- **Box 39-10** Assessment: Clients With Herniated Intervertebral Disk

SUGGESTIONS FOR CLASSROOM ACTIVITIES

- Break students into small groups or pairs to work on comparing and contrasting the degenerative neurologic diseases.
- Tape large pieces of paper or poster board on the walls, one for each disease discussed in this chapter. Have students write on each board one of the devastating effects the disease could have on the client/family/friends in terms of family process and loss of functioning as a family member and friend.

SUGGESTIONS FOR CLINICAL ACTIVITY

These clinical activities would be especially applicable in a long-term care facility or in a home health clinical rotation.

- Assign students to a client with Parkinson's disease. Have students complete a neurologic exam for this client.
- Assign students to develop an art or music activity for the client with Parkinson's disease and to implement the activity. Students can share the resulting behavior of their client in postconference.

REFERENCE

- MedlinePlus: Herniated disk. Available at http://www.nlm.nih.gov/medlineplus/herniateddisk.html

16. The classic "pill-rolling tremor" occurs when the thumb and fingers move like they are rolling a pill. Tremors disappear during sleep and movement. Tremors may move from one arm to both arms and may involve lips, jaw, head, and lower extremities.

17. Extremities may move in a jerky movement, called cog wheeling. The client may have stooped posture and shuffling gait.

18. Bradykinesia may include inability to initiate voluntary movements, slurred speech, low amplitude, decreased blinking, and mask-like, expressionless face.

19. The client with PD may have drooling, postural hypotension, depression, memory loss, and skin problems such as excessive sweating of face and neck and excessively oily skin.

20. Myasthenia gravis is a chronic autoimmune disorder affecting women most often between the ages of 20 and 30.

21. Clients with myasthenia gravis experience periods of exacerbations and remissions. Stress, pregnancy, and secondary infections may trigger an acute onset.

22. For an unknown reason, in myasthenia gravis, the thymus gland produces antibodies that block or reduce the number of acetylcholine receptors at each neuromuscular junction.

23. In myasthenia gravis, the nerve impulses cannot be sent to the cranial nerves that control muscles of the face, lips, tongue, neck, and throat. This causes weakness of the facial, speech, and chewing muscles.

24. Characteristic manifestations of myasthenia gravis include eyelid ptosis, diplopia, slurred speech, nasal voice, difficulty chewing and swallowing, and fatigue. A smile appears as a snarl or grimace.

25. In myasthenia gravis, there is progressive difficulty in performing fine motor tasks such as writing and progressive weakness of the respiratory muscles. The onset is gradual, and manifestations may vary each day.

26. Huntington's disease (HD) is a progressive, inherited neurologic disease. It is transmitted as an autosomal-dominant genetic trait. Each child of a parent with HD has a 50% chance of inheriting the disease. There is no cure for this disease.

27. Men and women are affected with HD equally between the ages of 30 and 50.

28. HD involves a lack of the neurotransmitter gamma-aminobutyric acid (GABA). This lack causes acetylcholine levels to drop and dopamine levels to rise. The excess of dopamine causes uncontrolled movements. Without GABA, there is premature death of basal ganglia and cerebral cortex cells.

29. All of the changes in neurotransmitter levels and resulting effects develop slowly, affecting (1) personality, (2) intellectual function, and (3) movement.

30. Emotional lability in HD ranges from irritability and anger to depression. Delusions and hallucinations are not unusual. Memory and intellectual function decline to the point of dementia.

31. Chorea (constant, jerky, uncontrolled movements of the body) is a characteristic manifestation. The client exhibits mild fidgeting or writhing and twisting of the entire body.

32. Motor symptoms in HD are worse with emotional stress but decrease during sleep.

33. Facial grimaces and tics affect speech, chewing, and swallowing, leading to choking and malnutrition. Bowel and bladder control are lost. As the chorea increases, the client is confined to bed. Prognosis is poor, with inevitable total dependence.

34. Amyotrophic lateral sclerosis (ALS), also called Lou Gehrig's disease, is a rapidly progressive, fatal neurologic disease. The exact cause is not known.

35. ALS affects men more and typically appears between the ages of 40 and 70.

36. ALS involves loss of motor neurons in the spinal cord and brainstem. When electrical impulses cannot be sent from the brain to the voluntary muscles, they lose strength and atrophy. Although body function decreases in ALS, the person remains mentally alert.

37. ALS is characterized by muscle weakness, fasciculations (involuntary contractions of the voluntary muscles, or twitching), and muscle wasting of the arms, legs, and trunk.

38. In ALS, brainstem involvement causes speech and swallowing difficulties. Toward the end, clients develop breathing problems, and death is from aspiration pneumonia or respiratory failure.

39. About 50% of clients die within 2–5 years of diagnosis. Diagnosis is based on the client's symptoms.

40. Guillain-Barré syndrome (GBS) is an acute, progressive inflammation of the peripheral nervous system (PNS).

41. The cause of GBS is unknown but most often follows a recent respiratory or gastrointestinal (GI) infection, viral vaccination, or surgery. Infection with *Campylobacter jejuni* causes about 60% of Guillain-Barré cases.

42. In GBS, a cell-mediated immune system reaction destroys the myelin sheath covering the peripheral nerves. Without myelin, impulses are poorly conducted to the sensory and motor nerves. This causes rapid muscle weakness, loss of reflexes, and paralysis.

43. Manifestations of GBS start in the lower extremities and move upward. The first symptoms are bilateral weakness and numbness and tingling in the legs. Within 24–72 hours, weakness extends to the arms and respiratory muscles and then progresses to paralysis. Cranial nerve involvement causes chewing, swallowing, and talking problems.

44. If the autonomic nervous system is affected, blood pressure and pulse changes develop.

45. Throughout the process of developing GBS, the person remains alert and oriented.

46. Trigeminal neuralgia (tic douloureux) involves two branches of the trigeminal nerve; the maxillary and the mandibular. The disease causes pain along one or both of these branches.

47. Trigeminal neuralgia usually affects middle-aged and older adult women more often than men.

48. The actual cause of trigeminal neuralgia is unknown, but it may be from dental or surgical procedures, facial trauma, infection, or pressure on the nerve by a tumor.

49. Trigeminal neuralgia is characterized by periodic, severe, one-sided facial pain lasting a few seconds to a few minutes. The pain is stabbing or burning in the forehead, along the nose, lips, or checks. Attacks occur for several weeks and then suddenly disappear.

50. The client may remain pain free for days to years. With age, remissions become shorter.

51. Trigger zones on the face initiate an attack when they are stimulated. Actions such as shaving, chewing, brushing the teeth, or washing the face, can set off an attack, as can wind or a change in temperature. An attack may cause wincing, grimacing, or tearing of the eye. To control pain, the clients may refuse to wash, shave, eat, or talk.

52. Bell's palsy (facial paralysis) is associated with the herpes simplex virus. Inflammation causes edema and pressure on the facial nerve, resulting in necrosis. Edema and pressure lead to sudden weakness and paralysis on one side of the face. Paralysis distorts the affected side causing ptosis of the eyelid, tearing, mouth drooping, drooling, inability to smile, and difficulty chewing. The pain is around or behind the ear.

53. Most clients with Bell's palsy improve within a few weeks or months, although some are left with residual paralysis.

54. Rabies is a viral infection of the CNS caused by an animal bite. The virus spreads from the wound to the peripheral nerves and eventually travels to the CNS. Incubation of rabies varies from 14 days to 3 months.

55. Clinical manifestations of rabies occur in three stages. In stage 1, the wound is painful, with a tingling sensation. The client experiences malaise, fever, headache, and sensitivity to light and loud noises.

56. Stage 2 of rabies develops within 24 to 72 hours. Any attempt at swallowing causes forceful spasms of the larynx. The person refuses to drink (hydrophobia). Swallowing problems lead to frothy drooling. Eventually, the sight or sound of water triggers the muscle spasms and excessive salivation.

57. In stage 3 of rabies, the client will die in about 7 days if untreated. Death occurs from cardiopulmonary arrest.

58. Tetanus, or lockjaw, is a disorder of the nervous system caused by *Clostridium tetani*. This anaerobic bacillus produces spores that live in the soil and enter the body through open wounds contaminated with dirt, street dust, or feces.

59. Most cases of tetanus occur after age 50 when the tetanus booster is older than 10 years.

60. When *Clostridium tetani* spores enter an open wound, two exotoxins are absorbed by the peripheral nerves and carried to the spinal cord. They interfere with the transmission of neuromuscular impulses, leading to uncontrolled muscle spasms.

61. Initially the person with tetanus exhibits pain at the wound site, stiffness of the jaw and neck, mild spasms, and difficulty swallowing.

62. As tetanus advances, the person has difficulty opening the jaw (trismus). Spasms of facial muscles give the person a grinning expression. Painful seizures cause the back to arch. The client remains alert and oriented.

63. The mortality rate with tetanus is high, and death is usually due to asphyxia from spasms of the glottis and respiratory muscles.

64. Creutzfeldt-Jakob disease (CJD) is a rare, progressive neurologic disease causing brain degeneration. The disease is transmissible and fatal within 6–12 months after diagnosis. CJD primarily affects adults over 60 with more cases in England, Chile, and Italy.

65. CJD destroys the brain's gray matter. On autopsy, the brain has numerous tiny holes resembling a sponge (called spongiform encephalopathy).

66. The underlying cause of CJD seems to be an infective protein pathogen called a prion. It is resistant to normal chemical and physical sterilization methods. A few cases have been transmitted through corneal transplants and human growth hormone from cadavers.

67. Early manifestations of CJD include memory loss and personality and visual changes. Then the person rapidly develops dementia, muscle contractions, speech problems, and ataxia. Clients in the terminal stage are comatose until death.

68. Spinal cord injury (SCI) is usually due to trauma of various types. Most injuries occur in the lumbar and cervical regions, where the vertebrae are not protected by other parts of the skeleton such as the rib cage or pelvis.

69. Spinal cord injuries are classified according to the level of injury and the amount of cord damage (e.g., an injury at the sixth cervical vertebra is called a C6 SCI). Cord damage is described as complete or incomplete.

70. A complete SCI results in total loss of motor and sensory function below the level of injury. Incomplete injury causes varying degrees of function below the level of injury. The client may have deficits in movement, sensation, and reflex activity.

71. The level of a spinal cord injury determines whether the client develops paraplegia or tetraplegia. Damage at the thoracic level causes paraplegia (paralysis of the lower part of the body). High cervical injuries result in tetraplegia, formerly called quadriplegia, which is paralysis of the arms, trunk, legs, and pelvic organs.

72. Spinal shock is a temporary loss of reflex activity below the level of SCI. It typically occurs 30–60 minutes after a complete SCI. Manifestations include loss of motor function, sensation, spinal reflexes, and autonomic function; bradycardia; hypotension; loss of sweating and temperature control below the level of injury; bowel and bladder dysfunction; flaccid paralysis; and loss of the ability to perspire.

73. Autonomic dysreflexia is an exaggerated sympathetic response in clients with SCIs at or above the T6 level; this is because impulses from the ANS are blocked by the SCI. Stimuli such as a full bladder or fecal impaction trigger a hypertensive crisis.

74. With autonomic dysreflexia, the client develops pounding headache; flushed diaphoretic skin above the lesion, and pale, cold, and dry skin below it; goose bumps; and anxiety. If untreated, seizures, CVA, or death can occur.

75. A herniated intervertebral disk, also called ruptured or slipped disk, usually is more common in middle age when age-related changes occur. Disk injury can develop from trauma, lifting incorrectly, sudden twisting of the spine, or degenerative changes due to arthritis.

76. The intervertebral disks are located between the vertebrae of the spinal column. They are made of an inner nucleus pulposus and an outer fibrous ring, the annulus fibrosus. The disks allow the spine to absorb compression by acting as shock absorbers. A herniated intervertebral disk occurs when the nucleus pulposus protrudes through a weakened or torn annulus fibrosus. When the disk herniates, or "slips," it compresses the nearby spinal nerve root and causes motor and sensory changes, pain, and altered reflexes.

77. The classic manifestation of a ruptured lumbar disk is recurrent low back pain. Pain can also follow along the sciatic nerve (sciatica). It is usually unilateral and radiates down the hip to the ankle and ranges from mild to excruciating. Manifestations of a herniated disk in the lumbar-sacral area also include muscle spasms, numbness and tingling of the leg and foot, and decreased or absent knee and/or ankle reflexes.

78. The manifestations of a herniated disk in the cervical area are neck stiffness and pain radiating from the shoulder down the arm to the hand; numbness and tingling of neck, shoulder, arm, and possibly hand; decreased arm strength; and decreased triceps reflex (Box 39-7).

79. Spinal cord tumors may be benign or malignant and primary or secondary. Primary tumors develop from a part of the cord. Secondary tumors start from lung, breast, or other cancer sites, and then spread to the spinal cord. Spinal cord tumors are also classified as intramedullary (within the spinal cord) or extramedullary (outside the spinal cord).

80. Slow-growing tumors allow the cord to adapt to the compression, and symptoms do not appear until the tumor is quite involved.

81. Metastatic tumors grow quickly, so symptoms appear sooner. Pain is often the first sign and is described as localized or radiating. There are also motor and sensory deficits on one side of the body. Motor deficits include weakness and clumsiness. Sensory deficits consist of numbness, tingling, and coldness in an extremity. Bladder involvement causes urinary frequency, urgency, and difficulty voiding.

LEARNING OUTCOME 2

Discuss the nursing implications for medications and treatments ordered for clients experiencing degenerative neurologic disorders.

Concepts for Lecture

1. During an exacerbation of multiple sclerosis (MS), medications such as corticosteroids and ACTH are used to decrease inflammation, which in turn limits manifestations and increases periods of remission.

2. Immunomodulators seem to slow MS progress and reduce the number of attacks. These drugs include interferon beta-1a (Avonex), interferon beta-1b (Betaseron), and glatiramer (Copaxone).

3. Clients with advanced MS are being treated with mitoxantrone (Novantrone), but use is limited because of its cardiotoxicity.

4. A monoclonal antibody, natalizumab (Tysabri) significantly reduces the frequency of attacks in people with relapsing MS, but it can only be given by trained physicians.

5. Muscle spasms may be reduced with baclofen (Lioresal) and dantrolene (Dantrium). For severe spasms, the client may receive the baclofen by intrathecal route. Fatigue is controlled with amantadine (Symmetrel) and CNS stimulants such as pemoline (Cylert). Clients with urinary retention and frequency are given bethanechol (Urecholine) and propantheline (Pro-Banthine). Depression is managed with antidepressants.

6. Physical therapists teach the client ways to maintain balance (e.g., standing with feet slightly apart to give a wider base of support). The client with ataxia is taught to use a walker or cane. Spasticity is managed with stretching exercises, gait training, and the use of braces or splints. Surgery is used as a last resort to treat spasticity and uncontrolled pain.

7. Plasmapheresis or plasma exchange is a procedure that removes plasma from whole blood in order to remove T lymphocytes that cause inflammation. There is some success with plasmapheresis causing a remission for clients with MS.

8. Medications for Parkinson's disease are not a cure but a way to control symptoms. Four different classes of drugs are used: dopaminergics, dopamine agonists, anticholinergics, and monoamine oxidase inhibitors (MAOIs). Nursing implications for these medications are found in Table 39-1.

9. Selected nursing implications for these drugs include checking for drug interactions before giving; not giving dopaminergics to clients with angle-closure glaucoma; monitoring the client for nausea, hypotension, confusion, and dyskinesia; assessing for "on-off" effect (symptoms appearing or disappearing suddenly); holding Sinemet to avoid toxicity; and monitoring for adverse reactions.

10. Selected nursing implications for giving anticholinergics include not giving these medications to clients with glaucoma, cardiac dysfunction, and prostatic hypertrophy; tapering off drugs slowly to avoid parkinsonism; checking for drug interactions; and monitoring for side effects of dry mouth, blurred vision, constipation, urinary retention, and confusion.

11. Nursing implications for giving MAOI inhibitors include monitoring for ataxia, insomnia, dizziness, or postural hypotension.

12. Nursing implications for giving anticholinesterase drugs to clients with myasthenia gravis include assessing the client's ability to swallow, giving the medication on a regular schedule at the exact time, monitoring for myasthenic crisis, and notifying physician immediately

POWERPOINT SLIDES

Tables and/or Figures

- **Table 39-1** Giving Medications Safely: Parkinson's Disease
- **Table 39-2** Giving Medications Safely: Myasthenia Gravis
- **Table 39-4** Giving Medications Safely: Antispasmodics in Spinal Cord Injury
- **Box 39-9** Nursing Care Checklist: Laminectomy

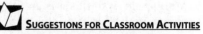

SUGGESTIONS FOR CLASSROOM ACTIVITIES

- Have students break into small groups to discuss medications given in specific degenerative neurologic and spinal cord disorders. Provide the students with questions to answer in regard to the medications.

SUGGESTIONS FOR CLINICAL ACTIVITIES

- Assign the students to care for clients with degenerative neurologic and spinal cord disorders. Ask the students to note each medication and treatment the client is receiving and compare this information with what was learned in class. Have the students present on medications and treatments for their clients in postconference.

REFERENCE

- National Institute of Neurological Disorders and Stroke: Myasthenia gravis fact sheet. Available at http://www.ninds.nih.gov/disorders/myasthenia_gravis/detail_myasthenia_gravis.htm

if the client has severe muscle weakness or difficulty breathing, swallowing, or speaking. The nurse also monitors for cholinergic crisis (excess salivation and sweating, bradycardia, nausea, and vomiting).

13. Medications are given to control the symptoms of Huntington's disease. The chorea movements may be modified by haloperidol (Haldol) or diazepam (Valium). Antidepressants and antipsychotics are prescribed in the early stages of the disease.

14. Only one medication, riluzole (Repute), seems to slow the destruction of motor neurons in amyotrophic lateral sclerosis. Other medications include baclofen and diazepam to relieve muscle spasms.

15. Medical management of Guillain-Barré syndrome includes plasmapheresis and intravenous immune globulin. Plasmapheresis removes the antibodies that caused GBS. It is beneficial if used within the first 2 weeks. Clients typically have five exchanges over 8 to 10 days. The action of intravenous immune globulin is unclear, but the effects are similar to plasmapheresis. Antibiotics are prescribed for urinary tract or respiratory infections. Anticoagulants are given to prevent DVT and pulmonary embolism. Morphine is given to control muscle pain.

16. The drug most useful in controlling the pain of trigeminal neuralgia is carbamazepine (Tegretol). When this drug is ineffective, other medications such as phenytoin (Dilantin) and baclofen (Lioresal) are added. If drug therapy fails, biofeedback and nerve blocks with local anesthetics are tried. Another option is a rhizotomy (severing of a nerve root to control pain). Only the sensory nerve root is destroyed. Nursing care focuses on teaching self-care strategies including medications and potential side effects.

17. Clients with Bell's palsy have a loss of blinking, which increases the risk for corneal drying. The nurse needs to demonstrate how to instill artificial tears four times a day and how to apply an eye patch at night.

18. The person who is bitten by an animal is taken to the emergency department to receive rabies immune globulin (RIG) as soon as possible after the bite. This is followed by five doses of inactivated human diploid cell rabies vaccine (HDCV). The nurse needs to know that RIG and HDCV are never put in the same syringe or administered at the same site.

19. Clients who develop tetanus are cared for in a critical care unit with minimal stimulation. They are given antibiotics to destroy the organism and anticonvulsants to stop any seizures. Paralytic agents are used when the muscle spasms and seizures are severe. Airway obstruction is managed by mechanical ventilation.

20. No specific treatment exists for Creutzfeldt-Jakob disease. Standard precautions are followed when handling all blood and body fluids.

21. When a client with a spinal cord injury develops autonomic dysreflexia, the blood pressure readings may be severely elevated. Raising the head of the bed 45 degrees may lower the blood pressure. If it does not, antihypertensives are given.

22. Following a spinal cord injury, corticosteroids are given for 1 to 2 weeks to decrease or control edema of the cord. Muscle spasms are treated with antispasmodics such as baclofen (Lioresal). Proton pump inhibitors (e.g., pantoprazole, Protonix) are used to prevent stress-related gastric ulcers. Thrombophlebitis is prevented with anticoagulants. Stool softeners may be given as part of a bowel training program.

23. When giving baclofen (Lioresal), diazepam (Valium), or dantrolene (Dantrium), the nursing implications include assessing the client's spasticity and involuntary movements, giving with food to decrease gastrointestinal symptoms, and monitoring for drowsiness, dizziness, and therapeutic effect.

24. Surgery is necessary when bone fragment or a hematoma compresses the spine.

25. Spinal cord tumors are treated by surgical excision and radiation therapy. Severe pain is managed by inserting an epidural catheter for continuous narcotic analgesic administration. Corticosteroids are given to control edema of the cord.

26. Medications for a client with a herniated intravertebral disk include nonsteroidal anti-inflammatory drugs for pain. Short-term opioids are used for acute pain but are discontinued with chronic pain because of the risk of dependency. Muscle spasms are treated with muscle relaxants. Transcutaneous electrical stimulation (TENS) may be used to relieve uncontrolled pain. Corticosteroids may be effective in relieving acute pain and decreasing inflammation.

27. The client with a herniated intervertebral disk may get physical therapy. Warm moist compresses to the neck may help relieve muscle spasms. The client may get surgery when conservative measures fail or there are serious neurologic deficits. Surgery procedures that may be used include diskectomy, laminectomy, spinal fusion, or microdiskectomy.

28. The most common surgical procedure for herniated intervertebral disk is laminectomy (removal of the vertebral lamina to relieve pressure on the nerves). See Box 39-9.

29. The nurse caring for a client before laminectomy will provide routine preoperative care and teach logrolling technique.

30. Postoperatively after a cervical laminectomy, the nurse will place a small pillow under the client's neck and keep the cervical collar in place. The nurse will assess sensation and movement of arms and hands and assess for difficulty swallowing, hoarseness, increased swelling at neck, or labored breathing.

31. After a lumbar laminectomy, the nurse will keep the bed flat or elevate the head of the bed slightly and place a small pillow under the head and a pillow under the knees. The nurse will assess sensation and movement of lower extremities and feet and report any impairment immediately.

32. For both cervical and lumbar laminectomy, the nurse will logroll the client every 2 hours, inspect the dressing for drainage with halo sign and test for glucose, palpate the operative site for a hematoma, maintain wound suction and patency of drains, assess for urinary retention, and ensure the client voids within 8 hours after surgery.

LEARNING OUTCOME 3

Describe the client's functional ability according to the level of damage to the spinal cord.

Concepts for Lecture

1. If the spinal cord damage is at the level of C_1–C_3, there is no movement or sensation below the neck. The client is ventilator-dependent. For ADLs and elimination, the client is dependent. Mobility is by voice- or sip-n-puff–controlled electric wheelchair.

2. If the spinal cord damage is at the level of C_4, the client has movement and sensation of head and neck and some partial function of the diaphragm. The client is dependent for ADL and elimination and can be mobile with a chin-operated electric wheelchair.

3. If the spinal cord injury is at the level of C_5, the client can control the head, neck, and shoulders and flex the elbows. The client can perform activities of daily living with assistance but is dependent for elimination. Mobility for this client is the electric wheelchair.

4. If the client has a spinal cord injury at the level of C_6, the client can use the shoulders and extend the wrists and is independent or can attend to ADL and elimination with assistance.

POWERPOINT SLIDES

Tables and/or Figures

- **Table 39-3** Functional Abilities by Level of Spinal Cord Injury

SUGGESTIONS FOR CLASSROOM ACTIVITIES

- Using a medical model of a skeleton, review the three different regions of the spinal cord by referring to the associated vertebrae.
- Discuss in detail the functions that remain following injury according to the level of injury.
- Begin discussion of how the amount of nursing care provided will correspond to the degree of function that is lost.
- Compare and contrast tetraplegia with paraplegia.
- Invite someone who had a spinal cord injury and has some loss of function but can get around in a wheelchair to come and talk with the class.

5. If the client has a spinal cord injury at the level of C_7–C_8, the client can extend the elbows and flex the wrist and has some use of the fingers. The client is independent for ADL and elimination. This client can use a manual wheelchair.

6. If the client has a spinal cord injury at the level of T_1–T_5, the client has full hand and finger control and full use of thoracic muscles. This client is independent for ADLs and elimination and can use a manual wheelchair.

7. If the spinal cord injury is at the level of T_6–T_{10}, the client controls the abdominal muscles, has good balance, and is independent for ADL and elimination. This client can use a manual wheelchair.

8. If the spinal cord injury is at the level of T_{11}–L_5, the client flexes and abducts the hips, flexes and extends the knees, is independent for ADL and elimination, and ambulates with leg braces, short braces, or canes.

9. If the spinal cord injury is at the level of S_1–S_5, the client has full control of legs and has progressive bowel, bladder, and sexual function. The client ambulates with leg braces, short braces, or canes.

LEARNING OUTCOME 4

Describe the interdisciplinary care required for clients with quadriplegia and other spinal cord disorders.

Concepts for Lecture

1. Emergency care of the client with an SCI begins at the crash scene. Clients are not moved unless there is a life-threatening danger, such as being burned, crushed, or drowned.

2. At the crash scene, the client's airway, breathing, and circulation are immediately assessed.

3. The client is next assessed for complaints of neck pain or changes in movement or sensation.

4. The neck and spine are then immobilized by rolled towels or blankets and keeping the client in the supine position until emergency personnel arrive and apply a rigid cervical collar and place the client on a spinal backboard in a neutral position.

5. Oxygen needs are assessed, and intravenous fluids are given to prevent shock.

6. In the emergency department, the client is assessed for other injuries, respiratory distress, and neurologic defects.

7. Until the client's condition is stable, the client is closely monitored for respiratory, cardiac, urinary, and GI complications.

8. High-dose methylprednisolone (Solu-Medrol), a corticosteroid, is started immediately to prevent secondary spinal cord damage from edema and ischemia.

9. Diagnostic studies used to diagnose SCIs include cervical spine x-rays, which show fracture or displacement of the vertebrae; CT scan or MRI, which shows damage to the vertebrae, spinal cord, and tissues around the cord; and arterial blood gasses, which determine baseline or identify any respiratory insufficiency.

10. Medications for spinal cord injuries include corticosteroids given for 1–2 weeks to decrease or control edema of the cord, antispasmodics to control muscle spasms, and proton pump inhibitors to prevent stress-related gastric ulcers.

11. Early management includes stabilizing and immobilizing the spinal cord. Thoracic and lumbar injuries are immobilized with braces or body casts.

 SUGGESTIONS FOR CLINICAL ACTIVITIES

- If possible, assign students to clients who have experienced differing levels of spinal cord injury. Have students share their assessment findings in terms of functional abilities.
- Have students discuss how the nursing plan for care changes depending on the client's functional ability.
- Assign students to a rehabilitation department. Have them participate in the rehabilitation plan of care for the client with an SCI.

 **REFERENCE**

- National Institute for Neurological Disorders and Stroke: NINDS spinal cord injury information page. Available at http://www.ninds.nih.gov/disorders/sci/sci.htm

 POWERPOINT SLIDES

Tables and/or Figures

- **Figure 39-6** Gardner–Wells Tongs
- **Box 39-5** Nursing Care Checklist: Clients in Halo Vests

 **SUGGESTIONS FOR CLASSROOM ACTIVITIES**

- Invite someone from the emergency medical service and/or paramedic rescue team to discuss specific examples of emergent care of the client with spinal cord injury.
- Invite a radiologist or neurosurgeon to speak to the class, and if possible, have him or her bring x-ray films to demonstrate views of anatomic damage from spinal cord injuries.
- Divide the students into small work groups. Assign each work group a class of drugs used in the treatment of spinal cord injury. Have students report on the nursing responsibilities for each class of drug.
- Using transparencies or other photos, discuss the various devices used to stabilize the spinal cord.

SUGGESTIONS FOR CLINICAL ACTIVITIES

- Assign students on a clinical day on a rotating basis to the emergency room and to the radiology department. Have students observe for clients undergoing treatment for spinal cord injuries in the emergency room and receiving radiologic exams for spinal cord injury. Ask students to share their experiences in postconference.

12. Cervical injuries are treated with tongs or a halo vest. The tongs are inserted into the skull and attached to weights to keep the spine in correct alignment. Tongs are less frequently used today. If the traction is interrupted, the client faces additional spinal cord damage. The halo vest is used for stable cervical or thoracic fractures without cord damage. It allows for greater mobility, self-care, and participation in a rehabilitation program. Those with a halo vest can be placed in a regular bed.

13. Nursing care of a client in a halo vest includes inspecting pins and traction bars for tightness and reporting loose pins to the physician; checking for access to the front of the vest for emergency intervention; taping an appropriate wrench to the head of the bed; remembering to never use the halo ring to lift or reposition the client; assessing the pin sites for redness, edema, and drainage; cleaning the pin sites daily; and inspecting the skin under the vest for pressure areas. To provide skin care, the nurse will loosen the sides of the vest, wash and thoroughly dry the skin, and prevent the lining of the vest from becoming wet. The nurse will change the sheepskin lining when it is soiled or weekly, turn the client every 2 hours, and provide a mild analgesic for headache, as ordered (Box 39-5).

14. Surgery can be used to remove bone fragments or hematomas and to stabilize and support the spine. Different spinal surgeries can be performed such as a spinal fusion, decompression laminectomy, or insertion of metal rods.

LEARNING OUTCOME 5

Reinforce teaching to clients with a degenerative neurologic disorder.

Concepts for Lecture

1. It is important for the nurse to ensure that the client understands how to prevent fatigue and exacerbations of MS. The client should be taught to avoid stress, extremes of cold and heat, high humidity, and physical overexertion. The nurse needs to discuss with the client preventative measures to avoid urinary and respiratory infections. The nurse will advise women considering pregnancy to consult with their healthcare provider because pregnancy can increase manifestations.

2. Clients with Parkinson's disease need reinforcement of discussion about avoiding stress and fatigue. It is also important to teach preventative measures because these clients are at risk for developing malnutrition, falls, constipation, skin breakdown from incontinence, and joint fractures. Clients also need to be taught ways to prevent postural hypotension when changing positions. The nurse will talk with clients about safety issues when taking their medications.

3. The nurse needs to provide information about PD, its management, and strategies for coping with tremors, dysphagia, and speech problems. The nurse needs to explain the purpose, side effects, and directions for each medication. The nurse will reinforce gait training, ROM exercises, and proper posture. The nurse will explain the importance of follow-up meetings with speech therapy, physical therapy, and occupational therapy.

4. Clients with myasthenia gravis and their families need information to help them understand the disease and ways to cope with the physical and psychosocial problems. The nurse needs to make sure the family knows cardiopulmonary resuscitation (CPR) and demonstrate how to insert an airway, suction, and use an Ambu bag. Teaching should emphasize medication actions, side effects, scheduling, and symptoms of myasthenic and cholinergic crisis. The nurse will stress the importance of

 **POWERPOINT SLIDES**

Tables and/or Figures
- **Box 39-8** Nursing Care Checklist: Myelography

SUGGESTIONS FOR CLASSROOM ACTIVITIES
- Have the students work in small groups to develop a teaching plan for a client with one of the degenerative neurologic disorders. Have the students prepare a skit in which a nurse reinforces teaching to a client with a degenerative neurologic disorder.

SUGGESTIONS FOR CLINICAL ACTIVITIES
- Assign students to care for clients with degenerative neurologic and/or spinal cord disorders. Ask the students to assess the client's teaching needs and to reinforce teaching with their assigned clients.

taking medications on an exact schedule. The client will be advised to wear a MedicAlert bracelet.

5. Many families become overwhelmed with the physical and psychologic debilitation that Huntington's disease brings. The nurse can refer them to local support groups, the Huntington's Disease Foundation, or a psychologist. Eventually, skilled long-term care is needed.

6. When working with the client who has trigeminal neuralgia, the nursing care focuses on teaching self-care strategies including medications and potential side effects. The nurse discusses with the client ways to avoid trigger points, such as room temperature water and soft cotton pads to wash the face. The nurse encourages a soft high-protein and high-calorie diet if the client refuses to eat. After surgery, the client with trigeminal neuralgia may lose sensation and corneal reflexes on the involved side. The nurse teaches the client to chew on the unaffected side, to avoid hot foods or liquids, and to brush the teeth and check for food pockets between gums and cheek after every meal. The nurse advises men to use an electric razor to shave. The nurse advises clients to protect the face from very cold or windy conditions and, if necessary, to wear a protective eye shield.

7. The nurse working with a client with Bell's palsy demonstrates how to instill artificial tears four times a day and how to apply an eye patch at night. The nurse makes certain the client understands how to inspect the eye each day and to report eye pain, redness, swelling, or discharge. The nurse recommends wearing dark glasses or goggles when outside or working in dusty conditions.

8. Discharge responsibilities of the nurse working with a client with a spinal cord injury include teaching the client and family how to provide medications, ADL, exercises, bowel and bladder programs such as urinary catheterization, and skin care. The nurse also discusses ways to prevent potential complications and emphasizes indications for notifying the physician.

9. Nursing care of the client with a herniated intervertebral disk includes preparing clients for diagnostic tests (e.g., myelography).

10. The nurse provides teaching about the importance of doing the prescribed physical therapy exercise and does discharge teaching for the client with a herniated intervertebral disk.

11. The nurse advises the client with a herniated intervertebral disk to sleep on a firm mattress and that warm compresses to the neck are useful to relieve muscle spasm.

LEARNING OUTCOME 6

Use the nursing process to assess, plan, and implement individualized care for the client with degenerative neurologic and spinal cord disorders.

Concepts for Lecture

1. The nurse will collect subjective data on the client with multiple sclerosis. The data collected will include extreme fatigue; diplopia or blurred vision; mood swings (depression to euphoria); muscle weakness or ataxia; numbness and tingling in extremities; urinary frequency, retention, or incontinence; constipation; difficulty chewing or swallowing; weight loss; past history of viral infections; living in northern United States; physical or emotional stress; pregnancy; and use of steroid or immunosuppressant medications.

2. The nurse will collect objective data on the client with multiple sclerosis. The data collected will include observation of the client for inattentiveness, difficulty finding the right word, poor coordination, muscle

 **POWERPOINT SLIDES**

Tables and/or Figures
- **Box 39-1** Assessment: Clients With Multiple Sclerosis
- **Box 39-3** Assessment: Clients With Parkinson's Disease
- **Box 39-6** Assessment: Clients With Spinal Cord Injury
- **Box 39-10** Assessment: Clients With Herniated Intervertebral Disk

Nursing Care Plan: Client With Multiple Sclerosis

weakness, ataxia, tremors, any disheveled appearance or signs of incontinence, slurred speech, or hesitating speech pattern. The nurse will auscultate for bowel tones; decreased bowel tones indicate slowed peristalsis (Box 39-1).

3. One nursing diagnosis for a client with multiple sclerosis is Fatigue. A possible expected outcome would be that the client verbalizes ways to conserve energy. Interventions will include planning daily activities to include rest periods, encouraging the client to perform tasks in the morning hours, and advising the client to avoid extremes of temperature to reduce exacerbations of the disorder.

4. Another nursing diagnosis for a client with multiple sclerosis is Self-Care Deficits. An expected outcome could be that the client performs ADL to the extent possible. Interventions could include encouraging the client to perform as much self-care as possible, allowing adequate time to perform tasks, and providing adaptive devices as needed (braces, long-handled combs, modified clothing, shower chair, or raised toilet seat).

5. A third possible nursing diagnosis for a client with multiple sclerosis is Ineffective Coping. An expected outcome could be that the client uses effective coping strategies. Interventions include encouraging the client to state his or her feelings and consult with a counselor or psychiatrist and referring the client to a support group and state vocational rehabilitation agency as needed. Evaluation of nursing care involves collecting data to determine to what extent the expected outcomes were met.

6. The assessment of a client with Parkinson's disease should identify the client's symptoms and the extent to which the disease is affecting the client's daily life (Box 39-3).

7. One possible nursing diagnosis for a client with Parkinson's disease is Impaired Physical Mobility. A possible expected outcome could be that the client maintains mobility without injury. Interventions could include performing ROM exercises at least twice a day, assisting with ambulation at least four times a day, using assistive devices as needed, and consulting with a physical therapist.

8. A second possible nursing diagnosis is Impaired Verbal Communication with a possible expected outcome that the client communicates orally or with assistive devices. Nursing interventions include teaching the client to face the listener and speak in short sentences; providing the client with a write-on, wipe-off slate and flash cards with common phrases; asking the client to point to objects; suggesting possible referral to a speech therapist; and trying to anticipate the client's needs.

9. A third possible nursing diagnosis for a client with Parkinson's disease is Imbalanced Nutrition: Less than Body Requirements. A possible outcome could be that the client maintains normal weight without difficulty swallowing. Nursing interventions could include placing the client in upright positions at meals, keeping suction equipment at the bedside, cutting food in small pieces, reducing distractions during mealtime, using modified utensils that are easier for the client to grasp, and increasing daily fluid intake and fiber.

10. The nurse working with a client with a diagnosis of myasthenia gravis collects data about the client's muscle weakness; speech, chewing, or swallowing difficulties; and changes in vision. Nursing care focuses on decreasing or preventing respiratory and swallowing problems as well as reducing fatigue. The nursing diagnoses and interventions are similar to those presented for the client with MS or PD.

11. Nursing care of a client with Guillain-Barré syndrome focuses on preventing immobility problems; promoting adequate hydration, nutrition, and respiratory function; and providing psychosocial support.

SUGGESTIONS FOR CLASSROOM ACTIVITIES

- Discuss assessment findings that would alert the nurse to the client's need for ventilatory assistance.
- Discuss the assessment techniques used to assess sensation.
- Review the technique of palpating for bladder fullness.
- Divide the students into small groups to discuss the nursing diagnoses listed in the text and the interventions for these diagnoses. Ask the students to critique the interventions and list any questions they may have about the diagnoses. Direct the students to add interventions that are appropriate.

SUGGESTIONS FOR CLINICAL ACTIVITIES

- Assign students to care for clients with spinal cord injuries of varying degrees. Assist the students to complete head-to-toe assessments of their clients, focusing on their level of functioning. Have students compare assessments in postconference.
- Have students develop an individualized nursing plan of care for their assigned client based on their assessment findings.

12. Nursing care of a client with rabies focuses on airway maintenance and seizure control. Standard Precautions are essential because the rabies virus is present in the saliva of the client.

13. Nursing care of a client with Creutzfeldt-Jakob disease focuses on providing support and comfort. Standard precautions are followed when handling all blood and body fluids.

14. The client with a spinal cord injury is assessed from head to toe on arrival at the hospital (Box 39-6). One nursing diagnosis is Ineffective Breathing Pattern with a possible outcome that the client will maintain normal breathing patterns and respiratory rate. Nursing interventions include monitoring pulse oximetry levels, turning the client at least every 2 hours, having the client cough and deep breathe, and suctioning the client PRN. The nurse will administer supplemental oxygen as ordered and increase fluids to 2,000 mL/day.

15. A second nursing diagnosis is Impaired Physical Mobility with possible expected outcome that the client will be free from immobility complications such as skin breakdown, DVT, and contractions. Nursing interventions include performing passive ROM exercises to all extremities twice a day; using splints, trochanter rolls, and high-top tennis shoes to prevent wrist drop, foot drop, and external rotation of the hips; inspecting skin at least once per shift for pressure ulcers and turning client every 2 hours; providing a diet high in protein, carbohydrate, and calories; and assessing the lower extremities each shift for thrombophlebitis. The nurse will apply antiembolic stockings (TEDs) and remove for 30–60 minutes each shift.

16. A third nursing diagnosis for the client with a spinal cord disorder is Impaired Urinary Elimination and Constipation with a possible expected outcome that the client will remain free from UTIs and constipation. Interventions include inserting a Foley catheter or performing intermittent catheterization during spinal shock. After spinal shock, the nurse can initiate a bladder training program. The client can be taught to use trigger-voiding techniques (e.g., stroking inner thigh, pulling the pubic hair, etc.). The nurse will place the client on a bedside commode if possible; monitor for cloudy, foul-smelling urine and increased fluid intake; and begin a bowel training program.

17. Another nursing diagnosis for a client with a spinal cord disorder is Situational Low Self-Esteem with a possible expected outcome that the client will demonstrate positive self-perception given physical abilities. Nursing interventions include allowing the client time to grieve or express denial, depression, and anger over lifestyle changes; providing accurate information based on the physician's prognosis; including the family and significant others to treat the client as normally as possible; and referring the family and significant others to support groups.

18. Nursing care for the client with a herniated disk focuses on managing pain and preventing any further injury. The client is assessed for the degree to which a herniated intervertebral disk affects the client's daily life (Box 39-10). A common nursing diagnosis for a client with a herniated intervertebral disk is Acute Pain. Interventions include maintaining bed rest as prescribed, teaching client logrolling when changing positions, using a firm mattress or a board under the mattress, elevating the client's head and placing a small pillow under the knees, giving muscle relaxant and analgesic medications as ordered on a regular basis around the clock, applying moist heat as ordered, avoiding calling the client an addict, and referring the client to a pain management clinic when pain is unrelieved.

19. To evaluate the effectiveness of nursing care for a client with a herniated disk, the nurse collects data related to absence of pain, muscle spasms, numbness, tingling, and neurologic deficits. After surgery, the nurse evaluates the client's understanding of home care.

20. Assessments and interventions for the client with a spinal cord tumor are similar to those described for clients with an SCI or surgery for a herniated intervertebral disk. Care is different depending on whether the client has a benign or a metastatic tumor.

GENERAL CHAPTER CONSIDERATIONS

1. Have students study and learn key terms listed at the beginning of the chapter.
2. Have students complete end of chapter exercises either in their book or on the MyNursingKit Website.
3. Use the Classroom Response Question PowerPoints to assess students prior to lecture.

• Clinical Reasoning Care Map

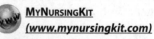
(www.mynursingkit.com)

• Websites
• NCLEX® Questions
• Case Studies
• Key Terms

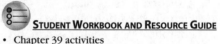

• Chapter 39 activities
• *Separate purchase*

PRENTICE HALL NURSE'S DRUG GUIDE

• *Separate purchase*

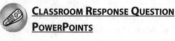

CHAPTER 40
CARING FOR CLIENTS WITH EYE AND EAR DISORDERS

LEARNING OUTCOME 1

Describe the pathophysiology and manifestations of common eye and ear disorders.

Concepts for Lecture

1. Blepharitis, inflammation of the eyelid, may be caused by an infection or by dermatitis. The eyelid is irritated and itchy. The eyelid margins are red, crusted, and scaly.
2. A hordeolum (sty) is an infection of the sebaceous glands of the eyelid, usually caused by *Staphylococcus aureus* (Figure 40-1A). A sty is red and painful. It may affect either the external or internal lid margin.
3. A chalazion is a painless cyst or nodule of the eyelid.
4. Conjunctivitis (inflammation of the conjunctiva) is usually caused by a bacterial or viral infection spread by direct contact (e.g., from hands, tissues, or towels). Acute conjunctivitis (pink eye) is usually mild, with redness, itching, tearing, and discharge of the eye (Figure 40-2).
5. Keratitis is inflammation of the cornea, usually caused by infection, lack of tears, or trauma.
6. Inflammation of the cornea causes discomfort, tearing, discharge, and photophobia (extreme sensitivity to light). Blepharospasm (spasm of the eyelid and inability to open the eye) may develop. Sudden severe eye pain may indicate corneal perforation.
7. Corneal ulcers may be caused by infection, trauma, or misuse of contact lens. Herpes viruses such as herpes zoster (shingles) can cause corneal ulcers, which can be superficial or deep. Scarring may occur, clouding the cornea. If the cornea is perforated, infection of the internal eye and vision loss may result.
8. Uveitis is inflammation of the middle vascular layer of the eye.
9. With iritis (inflammation of the iris), the client complains of severe eye pain, photophobia, and blurred vision. The pupil is constricted, and the limbus (where the cornea meets the conjunctiva) is red.
10. Common refractive errors include myopia (nearsightedness), hyperopia (farsightedness), and astigmatism.
11. Myopia is caused by an abnormally long eyeball. Light rays focus in front of the retina. Distant objects are unclear. Focus improves as object is closer to the eye.
12. Hyperopia (farsightedness) is caused by an abnormally short eyeball; light focuses behind the retina.
13. Presbyopia is caused by impaired accommodation of the lens caused by aging. Close objects are unclear. The client can focus on distant objects through accommodation.
14. Astigmatism is caused by irregularities in the curvature of the cornea and lens. In astigmatism, the light rays are imperfectly focused on the retina.
15. A cataract is clouding of the lens of the eye that impairs vision. Risk factors for cataracts include exposure to sunlight (UV-B rays), cigarette smoking, heavy alcohol consumption, congenital conditions, eye trauma, diabetes mellitus, and drugs such as corticosteroids and chlorpromazine (Thorazine).
16. Most cataracts are senile cataracts, caused by aging. As the lens ages, its cells become less clear. First, this usually affects the edges of the

POWERPOINT SLIDES

Tables and/or Figures

- **Figure 40-1** (A) Hordeolum (sty); (B) Chalazion
- **Figure 40-2** An Eye With Acute Conjunctivitis
- **Figure 40-3** Corneal Ulcers
- **Figure 40-5** Blurring of Near and Distant Vision With a Cataract
- **Table 40-1** Common Refractive Errors
- **Box 40-3** Population Focus: Glaucoma
- **Box 40-4** Manifestations of Glaucoma
- **Figure 40-10** Detached Retina
- **Figure 40-7** Types of Glaucoma
- **Figure 40-8** Narrowing of the Visual Field With Glaucoma
- **Figure 40-11** Blurred Central Vision Occurs in Age-Related Macular Degeneration
- **Figure 40-12** A Red, Bulging Tympanic Membrane of Otitis Media

SUGGESTIONS FOR CLASSROOM ACTIVITIES

- Using a medical model, review the anatomic structures of the eye.
- Have students break into small groups to discuss manifestations of one or two eye and ear disorders. The instructor could place names of the disorders on small pieces of paper folded up and have the groups draw for disorders to discuss.

SUGGESTIONS FOR CLINICAL ACTIVITIES

- Assign students to rotate through the offices of medical specialists serving people with disorders of the eye and ear for an observational experience. Have students keep a log of disorders they observe being treated and the manifestations of those disorders.
- Arrange for students to talk with clients who have disorders of the eye or ear. This can be accomplished in the experience described above or by bringing people with disorders of the eye or ear to come to class and describe their experiences with the disorder, including manifestations experienced.

REFERENCES

- MedlinePlus: Glaucoma. Available at http://www.nlm.nih.gov/medlineplus/ency/article/001620.htm
- National Institute on Deafness and Other Communication Disorders: Otitis media. Available at http://www.nidcd.nih.gov/health/hearing/otitism.asp

lens, gradually spreading toward the center. Eventually, the entire lens may be clouded. When only a portion of the lens is affected, the cataract is called immature. A mature cataract involves the entire lens.

17. As a cataract matures, both near and distance vision are affected. Details become obscured. The clouded lens scatters light rays, causing problems with glare and difficulty adjusting between light and dark environments. With a mature cataract, the pupil appears cloudy gray or white rather than black.

18. Glaucoma is a disease characterized by increased intraocular pressure and gradual loss of vision. Peripheral vision is lost so slowly that it often is not noticed until late in the disease. This vision loss is permanent.

19. In open-angle glaucoma, aqueous humor drainage through the trabecular meshwork into the canal of Schlemm is obstructed. The amount of fluid in the eye increases, and as a result, intraocular pressure increases. The increased pressure damages retinal neurons and the optic nerve. Peripheral vision is gradually lost, and the visual field narrows. Both eyes are usually affected. Untreated glaucoma eventually leads to blindness.

20. Manifestations of open-angle glaucoma include painlessness, gradual loss of peripheral vision, difficulty adapting from light to dark, blurred vision, halos around lights, and difficulty focusing on near objects.

21. In angle-closure glaucoma (a medical emergency), the angle between the cornea and iris closes, completely blocking drainage of aqueous humor from the eye. The intraocular pressure rises abruptly, damaging the retina and the optic nerve.

22. Manifestations of angle-closure glaucoma include acute severe eye pain, blurred or cloudy vision, nausea and vomiting, halos around lights, affected eye red, cornea clouded, and fixed (nonreactive) pupil.

23. A detached retina is separation of the retina from the choroids, the vascular layer of the eye. Retinal detachment can occur spontaneously or result from trauma. The vitreous humor shrinks with aging, increasing the risk for detached retina. The retina can remain intact but separate from the choroids or tear and fold back on itself.

24. A break or tear in the retina allows fluid to seep between the retina and choroid, separating these layers. If the layers remain separated, the neurons of the retina become ischemic and die, causing permanent vision loss. Retinal detachment is a medical emergency.

25. A detached retina is painless. The client may sense that a curtain or veil is being drawn across the vision. The affected area of vision relates to the area of detachment. Because light rays cross as they pass through the lens, a detachment in the upper part of the eye affects vision in the lower part of the visual field.

26. Common manifestations of a detached retina include floaters and flashes of light.

27. Macular degeneration is a common cause of blindness in adults over 65.

28. When the macula is damaged, central vision becomes blurred and distorted, but peripheral vision remains intact. Distortion of vision in one eye is a common early symptom. Straight lines become wavy or distorted. Macular degeneration particularly affects activities that require close central vision such as reading and sewing.

29. Diabetic retinopathy is a disorder affecting the capillaries of the retina. The capillaries are no longer able to transport blood and oxygen to the retina. Retinopathy develops about 15 years after being diagnosed with either type 1 or type 2 diabetes mellitus.

30. Manifestations of diabetic retinopathy include changes in vision, including blurring; black spots (floaters), cobwebs, or flashing lights in the visual field; or a sudden loss of vision in one or both eyes.

31. External otitis (swimmer's ear) is inflammation of the ear canal. It usually is caused by bacteria. Swimmers, divers, and surfers are particularly prone to external otitis. Wearing a hearing aid or earplugs, which

holds moisture in the ear canal, also is a risk factor. Cerumen is water repellent and has an antibacterial effect. Removal of earwax can increase the risk of infection.

32. External otitis causes ear pain, which may be severe, and a feeling of fullness in the ear. Manipulating the outer ear increases the pain. Drainage may be present. The ear canal appears inflamed and swollen.

33. The ear canal can become obstructed by earwax or foreign objects such as insects. As earwax dries, it moves out of the ear canal. In some people, however, the earwax accumulates and the earwax can become impacted. Older adults are at risk for impaction because, with aging, earwax becomes harder and dryer.

34. Ear canal obstruction interferes with sound conduction and hearing. The client reports a sensation of fullness and tinnitus (ringing) in the ear.

35. Otitis media, inflammation or infection of the middle ear, is the most common middle ear disorder. It usually affects infants and young children but can occur in adults.

36. Organisms can enter the middle ear from the nose and throat through the eustachian tube. Upper respiratory infection and eustachian tube dysfunction are risk factors for otitis media.

37. Serous otitis media occurs when the eustachian tube is obstructed for a long time. Air in the middle ear is gradually absorbed, causing negative pressure in the middle ear. The negative pressure draws serous fluid from the capillaries into the space.

38. Manifestations of serous otitis media include decreased hearing and a "snapping" or popping sensation in the affected ear. The eardrum moves less freely and may appear retracted ("sucked in") or bulging. Fluid or air bubbles may be seen behind the drum.

39. Changes in atmospheric pressure can cause acute pain, bleeding into the middle ear, rupture of the eardrum, or rupture of the round window.

40. Acute otitis media usually follows URI. Swelling of the eustachian tube impairs drainage of the middle ear. Mucus and serous fluid collect in the middle ear. Bacteria enter from the nasopharynx, growing and multiplying in this fluid. The infections cause an immune response, and pus forms in the middle ear. The pus increases pressure in the middle ear and can rupture the ear drum.

41. Acute otitis media causes pain, often severe, in the affected ear. The client may have a fever and complain of hearing loss, dizziness, vertigo, and tinnitus. The eardrum is red and inflamed or dull and bulging. It does not move normally and may rupture, causing purulent drainage.

42. Otosclerosis is a hereditary disorder that usually affects white females. In otosclerosis, abnormal bone forms, immobilizing the stapes and causing a conductive hearing loss. Hearing loss usually begins in adolescence or early adulthood. Both ears are affected. Air conduction of sound is lost, but sound is conducted through bone, so the client may be able to use a telephone but have difficulty conversing in person. In addition to hearing loss, the client may experience tinnitus.

43. Labyrinthitis is inflammation of the inner ear. It may be caused by bacteria or viruses. Manifestations include severe vertigo, hearing loss, and nystagmus (rapid involuntary eye movements); nausea and vomiting often accompany the vertigo.

44. Ménière's disease is a chronic inner ear disorder caused by excess fluid and pressure in the labyrinth of the inner ear. Onset may be gradual or sudden. Manifestations include recurring attacks of vertigo with tinnitus and gradual hearing loss, which usually affects one ear, although the other ear may be affected. Attacks of severe vertigo occur abruptly and are unpredictable, lasting from minutes to hours.

45. Hearing loss is classified as conductive, sensorineural, or mixed depending on what portion of the auditory system is affected. A hearing deficit can be partial or total and congenital or acquired. It can

affect one or both ears. Some types of hearing loss affect the ability to hear specific frequencies of sound.

46. Anything that affects sound transmission from the external opening of the ear to the inner ear causes a conductive hearing loss. Obstruction of the ear canal by impacted cerumen is the most common cause. Other causes of conductive loss include perforated eardrum, damage to the ossicles of the middle ear, fluid, scarring, or tumors of the middle ear.

47. Disorders that affect the inner ear or the auditory pathways of the brain may cause a sensorineural hearing loss. Trauma, infection, diseases such as Ménière's disease, ototoxic medications, and prenatal exposure to rubella can lead to sensory hearing loss. Noise exposure is the major cause of sensorineural hearing loss in the United States. Ototoxic drugs such as aspirin, furosemide, vancomycin, streptomycin, aminoglycoside antibiotics, antimalarial drugs, and chemotherapy such as cisplatin (Platinol) also damage the hair cells of the organ of Corti.

48. Sensory hearing losses usually affect the ability to hear high-frequency sounds more than low-frequency sounds.

49. Presbycusis is a type of sensorineural loss. With aging, the hair cells of the cochlea degenerate, causing progressive hearing loss. Presbycusis causes loss of high-frequency tones and understanding of consonants such as *t*, *p*, or *s*. Talking louder does not help the client hear or understand speech better.

LEARNING OUTCOME 2

Describe nursing implications for drugs prescribed for clients with eye and ear disorders.

Concepts for Lecture

1. Topical anti-infectives applied as eye drops or ointments often are ordered to treat eye infections. Antihistamines or corticosteroids may be prescribed when the eye is inflamed but no infection is present. Clients with uveitis may be given eye drops to keep the pupil dilated and reduce discomfort.

2. Mydriatics (drugs that dilate pupils) such as atropine must be avoided in clients with angle-closure glaucoma.

3. Adrenergic agonists are avoided in clients with angle-closure glaucoma, cardiac arrhythmias, or coronary artery disease.

4. The nurse reports to the physician any lid edema or discharge from the eyes. The nurse instructs the client to report immediately to the physician any change in vision or eye pain that may indicate acute angle-closure glaucoma.

5. When giving beta-blockers, which decrease intraocular pressure, the nurse must report contraindications such as asthma, COPD, heart block, and heart failure.

6. The nurse holds pressure over the bridge of the client's nose after instilling drops to prevent systemic absorption. The nurse also reports side effects such as bradycardia, hypotension, and difficulty breathing.

7. When giving prostaglandin analogs (latanoprost, Xalatan), the nurse administers the drug once daily at bedtime and reports side effects such as burning, stinging, or redness of the eye.

8. When giving the carbonic anhydrase inhibitor dorzolamide, the nurse instills the drug 10 minutes apart from other topical ophthalmic drugs. The nurse reports adverse or allergic effects such as conjunctivitis or redness and itching of the lid.

 **POWERPOINT SLIDES**

Tables and/or Figures
- **Table 40-2** Giving Medications Safely: Glaucoma
- **Box 40-7** Nursing Care Checklist: Instilling Eardrops

SUGGESTIONS FOR CLASSROOM ACTIVITIES
- Review with students the correct technique for drop instillation and ointment application in the eye and ear.
- Divide students into small work groups. Assign each group a class of drugs used in the treatment of glaucoma. Have students list the nursing responsibilities for each drug used.

SUGGESTIONS FOR CLINICAL ACTIVITIES
- Assign students to care for clients who have drugs prescribed for either eye disorders or ear disorders. Assign the students to research the medications their client is to receive and to write down the nursing implications for each drug. Ask students about the nursing implications and other pertinent information they need to know before administering the medications under supervision.

9. When giving the carbonic anhydrase inhibitor acetazolamide, the nurse monitors the client's weight daily, as well as intake and output and vital signs, and reports serum electrolyte values to the physician.

10. When instilling eardrops, the nurse washes his or her hands, warms the drops by holding the bottle or putting it in a pocket for about 5 minutes before instilling, places the client on the unaffected side or tilts the head toward the unaffected side, partially fills the ear dropper with medication, straightens the ear canal by pulling the pinna of the ear up and back using the nondominant hand, instills the prescribed number of drops into the ear canal, keeps the client on the side for about 5 minutes after putting in the drops, and loosely places a small piece of cotton in the opening to the ear canal for 15–20 minutes (Box 40-7).

11. Mineral oil or topical lidocaine drops are used to immobilize or kill insects before they are removed from the ear canal.

12. Decongestants are used to improve eustachian tube function but show minimal effectiveness in treating serous otitis media.

13. Acute otitis media is treated with antibiotics for 5–10 days often combined with decongestants. Mild analgesics such as acetaminophen are recommended to relieve pain and reduce fever.

14. Acute mastoiditis needs aggressive treatment with intravenous antibiotics and possibly myringotomy.

15. Drugs such as meclizine (Antivert), prochlorperazine (Compazine), or hydroxyzine (Vistaril) are given to relieve vertigo and nausea for the client with Ménière's disease.

LEARNING OUTCOME 3

Provide appropriate nursing care for a client having eye or ear surgery.

Concepts for Lecture

1. Prior to eye surgery, the nurse will provide routine preoperative care as indicated; assess understanding of the procedure; clarify information as needed; and orient the client to the environment.

2. The nurse will also assess vision in the unaffected eye before surgery and reinforce teaching about postoperative restrictions to prevent increased intraocular pressure, including avoiding vomiting, straining at stool, coughing, sneezing, lifting more than 5 lb, and bending over at the waist.

3. The nurse will remove all eye makeup and contact lenses or glasses and store them in a safe place and administer preoperative medications and eye drops or ointments as ordered before eye surgery.

4. After eye surgery, the nurse assesses and documents vital signs, level of consciousness, comfort, and status of the eye dressing, and the nurse maintains the eye patch and shield as ordered.

5. The nurse places the client in semi-Fowler's or Fowler's position or as ordered and approaches the client on their unaffected side after surgery.

6. The nurse will intervene as necessary to prevent vomiting, coughing, sneezing, or straining and will immediately report sudden, sharp eye pain to the physician.

7. After surgery, the nurse will place all the client's personal articles and call bell within easy reach, assist with ambulation when allowed, and administer eye drops and other medications as ordered.

8. After surgery, the nurse will teach the client and family (1) how to instill eye drops and provide information about ordered medications; (2) how and when to apply eye patch and eye shield; (3) to avoid scratching, rubbing, touching, or squeezing the affected eye; (4) how to prevent constipation and straining and about activity limitations;

REFERENCE

- Scribd: Timoptic eye drops. Available at http://www.scribd.com/doc/19540133/Drug-Timoptic-Eye-Drops

POWERPOINT SLIDES

Tables and/or Figures

- **Box 40-2** Nursing Care Checklist: Eye Surgery

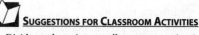

SUGGESTIONS FOR CLASSROOM ACTIVITIES

- Divide students into small groups or pairs. Ask the students to develop a skit about a nurse giving a client preoperative, postoperative, or discharge instructions to a client having eye or ear surgery.

SUGGESTIONS FOR CLINICAL ACTIVITIES

- Assign students to care for clients before and after eye or ear surgery. Have the students observe a primary nurse giving a client pre- and postoperative instructions. Ask the students to discuss how they communicated with clients having eye or ear surgery and how caring for these clients differed from care of other clients.

(5) symptoms that should be reported to the physician, including eye pain or pressure, redness or cloudiness, drainage, decreased vision, floaters or flashes of light, or halos around bright objects; (6) to wear sunglasses with side shields when outdoors; and (7) to make and keep recommended follow-up appointments.

9. The nurse arranges or refers the client for assistance with other healthcare needs (Box 40-2).

10. Postoperative care of a client who has an eye removed by a procedure known as enucleation includes teaching, psychological support, and observing for potential complications. The client may be instructed to apply warm compresses and instill antibiotic ointment or drops postoperatively.

11. Preoperative nursing care of a client undergoing ear surgery includes providing routine preoperative care as ordered; assessing hearing or verifying that hearing has been assessed before surgery; discussing postoperative communication strategies; and explaining postoperative restrictions such as avoiding blowing the nose, coughing, and sneezing. The nurse will instruct the client to leave the mouth open if coughing or sneezing is necessary.

12. Postoperatively, the nurse provides routine postoperative care as ordered for the client who has had ear surgery.

13. After surgery, the nurse will assess the client who has had ear surgery for bleeding or drainage from the affected ear, noting color, character, and amount of any drainage. In addition, the nurse assesses the client for nausea and administers antiemetics as ordered to prevent vomiting.

14. After surgery, the nurse elevates the head of the client's bed and positions the client on the unaffected side.

15. The nurse assesses the postsurgical client for vertigo or dizziness, especially with movement; avoids unnecessary movements such as turning; and ensures safety during ambulation. The nurse assesses hearing.

16. The nurse stands on the client's unaffected side to communicate and uses alternative strategies such as writing when needed.

17. The client is reminded by the nurse to avoid coughing, sneezing, or blowing the nose.

18. The nurse provides the client with instructions for home care including avoiding showers, shampooing, and immersing the head until approved by the physician. The nurse also instructs the client to keep the outer earplug clean and dry, changing it as needed and not removing the inner ear dressing until ordered by the physician.

19. The client is advised not to swim, dive, or travel by air until allowed by the physician.

20. The nurse advises the client in the instructions for home care that the client may need to take an antiemetic/antihistamine drug for up to 1 month after surgery.

21. The nurse instructs the client to notify the physician if he or she develops a fever, bleeding, increased drainage, or increased dizziness.

LEARNING OUTCOME 4

Use the nursing process to provide individualized care for clients with problems that affect vision or hearing.

Concepts for Lecture

1. Assessment of a client with a corneal transplant includes the client's description of their symptoms and the onset of symptoms, any relationship between the symptoms and an injury or exposure to an infection or allergen, and the effect of symptoms on vision.

 **POWERPOINT SLIDES**

Tables and/or Figures
- **Box 40-1** Assessment: The Cardinal Fields of Vision
- **Box 40-5** Assessment: Visual Fields by Confrontation

Nursing Care Plan: Client With Glaucoma and Cataracts

2. During assessment, the nurse inquires about associated symptoms such as chills or fever. The date of the client's most recent eye examination is noted, and the nurse asks about corrective lens use, including type of lenses.

3. The nurse gathers information on past medical history, especially any chronic diseases, previous eye problems, and current medication use.

4. As part of the assessment, the nurse tests the client's vision (with the client wearing corrective lenses if normally worn) with a Snellen chart or Rosenbaum chart.

5. During the assessment of the client with an eye disorder, the nurse inspects the eye, including the conjunctiva, lids, and surrounding tissues. The pupil is checked for size and response to light and accommodation.

6. A possible nursing diagnosis for a client with a corneal transplant is Risk for Disturbed Sensory Perception (Visual) with a possible expected outcome that the client remains free from visual deficits.

7. Nursing interventions for a nursing diagnosis of Risk for Disturbed Sensory Perception (Visual) could include instructing the client to wash his or her hands thoroughly before inserting or removing contact lenses or instilling any eye medications and teaching the client to avoid touching or rubbing the eyes. Note, hand washing is the single most important measure to prevent transmission of infection to the eye.

8. The nurse emphasizes the importance of proper contact lens care, including periodic lens removal and cleaning.

9. If the cornea perforates, the nurse places the client in the supine position, closes the eye and covers it with a dry, sterile dressing, and notifies the physician immediately.

10. A second possible nursing diagnosis for a client with a corneal transplant is Acute Pain, with an expected outcome that the client states pain is absent or at a tolerable level.

11. Possible nursing interventions for a nursing diagnosis of Acute Pain include administering analgesics routinely in the first 12 to 24 hours after corneal surgery; patching both eyes if necessary; teaching the client to apply warm compresses for 15 minutes three to four times a day; instructing the client to wear dark sunglasses with ultraviolet protection when out of doors, even on cloudy days; and advising the client to avoid excessive reading or other close tasks.

12. Another possible nursing diagnosis for a client with a corneal transplant is Risk for Injury, with a possible expected outcome that the client will remain free from injury.

13. Nursing interventions for Risk for Injury include discussing the effect of an eye patch on depth perception and peripheral vision; teaching the client to scan from side to side and to be careful when judging distances or speed; instructing the client not to rub or scratch the eye; and teaching the client how to apply an eye shield at night, and to use eye protection during activities that can damage the eye.

14. Evaluation of the effectiveness of nursing care involves collecting data about the appearance of the eye and vision (using a chart to measure visual acuity). The nurse needs to determine whether the client demonstrates proper contact lens care and uses appropriate technique to instill eye drops.

15. A possible nursing diagnosis for a client with cataracts is Deficient Knowledge (Cataracts), with a possible expected outcome that the client will state knowledge of postoperative care.

16. Nursing interventions for a nursing diagnosis of Deficient Knowledge (Cataracts) include providing information about cataracts and their surgical removal, explaining that cataracts usually are removed only when they interfere with vision and ADL, and demonstrating a caring, understanding attitude toward concerns about vision to promote trust and reduce anxiety.

SUGGESTIONS FOR CLASSROOM ACTIVITIES

• Using the nursing diagnoses provided on the PowerPoint slides, discuss in detail the nursing interventions for clients with glaucoma and/or other selected eye and ear disorders. Students can be instructed to list and discuss additional nursing interventions.

SUGGESTIONS FOR CLINICAL ACTIVITIES

• Assign students to a nurse preceptor in the clinic setting. Have students observe and/or assist with gathering assessment data related to glaucoma and/or other eye and ear disorders.

17. Nursing assessment related to glaucoma focuses on identifying clients at risk. The nurse asks about vision, including recent changes, difficulty seeing at night, halos around lights, family history of glaucoma or any previous episodes of angle-closure glaucoma, and the date of the most recent eye examination.

18. The nurse inspects the eye for possible redness or clouding of the cornea. The nurse assesses vision (with correctives if worn) using a standard eye chart. The nurse assesses pupil response to light and evaluates peripheral vision.

19. When the nurse assesses visual fields by confrontation, the nurse faces the client, seated about 2 feet apart, and instructs the client to cover the right eye and focus on the nurse's face. The nurse covers his or her left eye and focuses on the client's face. Midway between the client and the nurse, the nurse brings a light-colored object into the field of vision from the side and asks the client to indicate when the object is seen. The nurse checks all visual fields of both eyes in this way. See Box 40-5.

20. A possible nursing diagnosis for a client with glaucoma is Deficient Knowledge (Ocular care), with a possible expected outcome that the client will verbalize understanding of glaucoma and demonstrate appropriate eye care.

21. Interventions for Deficient Knowledge (Ocular Care) may include providing detailed verbal and written instructions about the ordered drugs; teaching the client how to instill eye drops and having the client return the demonstration; ensuring that the client can identify all the medications he or she is taking; and emphasizing the importance of keeping all follow-up appointments.

22. Another possible nursing diagnosis for a client with glaucoma is Risk for Injury, with a possible expected outcome that the client remains free from injury. Nursing interventions could include assessing client's ability to provide self-care and providing assistance as needed; alerting caregivers and housekeepers not to move items in the client's room; raising the side rails on the bed with the client's permission; and keeping traffic area free of clutter.

23. A third possible nursing diagnosis for a client with glaucoma is Anxiety, with a possible expected outcome that the client will report less anxiety. Nursing interventions for a nursing diagnosis of Anxiety could include assessing for evidence of anxiety and discussing the effects of glaucoma and possible vision loss on lifestyle and roles.

24. Evaluating the effectiveness of nursing care for the client with glaucoma includes identifying any visual deficits and determining whether the client can safely perform ADL and instill eye drops as ordered. The nurse can also identify the client's knowledge about taking ophthalmic medications, the importance of follow-up care, and the date of the next vision exam.

25. Early identification and treatment of a detached retina are vital to preserve sight. Retinal detachment is painless.

26. A possible nursing diagnosis for a client with a detached retina is Ineffective Tissue Perfusion (Retinal), with a possible expected outcome that the client reports no visual loss in the affected eye.

27. A nursing intervention for a nursing diagnosis of Ineffective Tissue Perfusion (Retinal) could be positioning the client so that the area of detachment is dependent. For instance, if vision is lost in the upper outer portion of the left eye, indicating an inferior medial retinal detachment of the left eye, place the client on the right side in a supine position.

28. Another nursing diagnosis for a client with a detached retina could be Anxiety, with an expected outcome that the client will report less anxiety. Nursing interventions for a nursing diagnosis of Anxiety

could include maintaining a calm, confident attitude while providing priority care; reassuring the client that a detached retina is treatable, usually on an outpatient basis; explaining all procedures fully, including the reason for positioning; and allowing supportive family members or friends to remain with the client as much as possible.

29. The nurse can evaluate the effectiveness of nursing care by collecting data on the extent of any visual deficits before and after treatment. There should be an absence of floaters or flashes of light. The nurse can identify the degree to which anxiety has been controlled or decreased.

30. Assessment of a client with external otitis includes asking about ear cleaning practices and participation in water sports or activities. The assessment also includes obtaining the client's description of the ear pain, including its character, timing, aggravating factors, and relieving factors.

31. Hearing is assessed in both ears, using the whisper test or an audiometer.

32. The nurse inspects the external ear for drainage, redness, or evidence of trauma.

33. Using an otoscope, the nurse inserts the speculum just inside (no more than 1 cm) into the canal to inspect for redness, swelling, drainage, or trauma.

34. A possible nursing diagnosis for a client with external otitis is Impaired Tissue Integrity, with a possible expected outcome that the client's tissue integrity returns to normal. Nursing interventions include teaching the client not to clear the ear canal with a toothpick, cotton-tipped applicator, or other tool; teaching the client how to instill prescribed eardrops; and instructing the client to avoid getting water in the affected ear until it is fully healed. Cotton balls may be used while showering to prevent water from entering the ear canal.

35. To evaluate the effectiveness of teaching related to external otitis, the nurse can have the client demonstrate instilling eardrops and review knowledge and willingness to avoid water sports until healing is complete. The nurse can have the client describe measures to prevent future episodes of external otitis.

36. Assessment of the client with otitis media includes collecting data about the onset and duration of symptoms, including pain, popping, or snapping sensations in the ear and any drainage from the ear. The nurse also asks about any recent URIs.

37. During assessment the nurse moves the auricle of the ear, asking how movement affects the pain. The pain of otitis media usually does not change with manipulation of the external ear.

38. The nurse inspects the client's throat for redness, swelling, or drainage; obtains the client's temperature; assesses hearing in both ears, using the whisper test or an audiometer; and inspects and palpates the mastoid process for tenderness. If trained, the nurse uses an otoscope to inspect the ear canal and eardrum.

39. A possible nursing diagnosis for a client with otitis media is Acute Pain, with a possible outcome that the client states the pain is absent or at a tolerable level. Interventions may include advising the client to use a mild analgesic every 4 hours as needed to relieve pain and fever; advising the client to apply heat to the affected side of the face and head unless contraindicated; and instructing the client to report abrupt pain relief to the physician because it may mean that the eardrum has ruptured.

40. Another nursing diagnosis for a client with otitis media is Deficient Knowledge (Otitis Media), with a possible expected outcome that the client verbalizes treatment and prevention of otitis media. Nursing interventions include (1) stressing the importance of completing the full course of antibiotic therapy; (2) discussing the desired and potential adverse effects of the prescribed antibiotic; (3) informing the client that the antibiotic may cause diarrhea, vaginitis, or thrush; (4) unless

contraindicated, instructing the client to eat 8 oz. of yogurt with live bacterial cultures daily during antibiotic therapy; (5) stressing the importance of keeping follow-up appointments; (6) instructing the client with ventilation tubes to avoid water sports and submerging the head while bathing; (7) instructing the client to avoid air travel, rapid changes in elevation, or diving; and (8) encouraging the client to rest, increase fluid intake, and eat a nutritious diet.

41. The nurse can evaluate the effectiveness of care by collecting data on the presence of any hearing deficits, ear pain, and drainage. The nurse can identify the client's understanding of the treatment plan and symptoms to report to the primary care provider. The nurse also determines knowledge about follow-up visits and compliance with prescribed treatment.

42. Assessment of clients with inner ear disorders includes assessing the effects of the disorder on balance and the ability to safely ambulate, assessing hearing, using the whisper test, and inquiring about tinnitus, including pitch, tone, quality, and duration. The nurse refers the client for a complete hearing and ear examination if this has not been done. The nurse assesses for nystagmus by having the client follow an object through the six cardinal fields of vision (Box 40-1). The nurse asks about usual food and fluid intake and assesses height and weight, skin color and condition, and other signs of nutritional status. The nurse discusses the effect of the disorder on the client's life because unpredictable attacks of vertigo, tinnitus, and hearing loss can affect lifestyle, employment, sleep, rest, and the ability to cope.

43. A possible nursing diagnosis for a client with an inner ear disorder is Risk for Injury, with a possible expected outcome that the client remains free from injury.

44. Nursing interventions for Risk for Injury may include (1) asking the client not to get up without assistance during acute attacks of vertigo; (2) teaching the client to avoid sudden head movements or position changes; (3) administering drugs as ordered including antiemetics, diuretics, and sedatives; (4) teaching the client who senses an oncoming attack to take the prescribed medication and lie down in a quiet darkened room; (5) instructing the client to pull to the side of the road and wait for the symptoms to subside if an attack occurs while driving; (6) discussing the importance of wearing a Medic-Alert bracelet or necklace; (7) discussing the effect of one-sided hearing loss on the ability to identify sound direction; and (8) encouraging the client to use other senses as well, for example, when crossing the street.

45. Another nursing diagnosis that may be used for a client with an inner ear disorder is Sleep Deprivation, with a possible expected outcome that the client reports relief from symptoms of sleep deprivation. Nursing interventions include discussing options for masking tinnitus (e.g., ambient noise, white-noise machine, a hearing aid that produces a tone, a hearing aid that amplifies ambient sound) and suggesting that the client discuss possible medications to treat tinnitus with the doctor.

46. The nurse can evaluate the effectiveness of nursing care for the client with an inner ear disorder by assessing for the presence of symptoms of inner ear problems, determining the client's ability to remain safe during periods of vertigo, discussing the client's understanding of the disease and measures to reduce the frequency and severity of attacks, and discussing coping strategies the client can use to manage the effects of the disorder on lifestyle.

47. Assessing the client with a hearing loss, the nurse finds that caregivers often can recognize signs of the hearing loss; for example, the client's voice volume frequently increases, and the client positions the head with the better ear toward the speaker.

48. In assessing the client with a hearing loss, the nurse is alert for signs of impaired hearing such as cupping an ear, difficulty understanding

verbal communication when the person cannot see the speaker's face, difficulty following conversation in a large group, and withdrawal from social activities. The client may appear unsociable or paranoid.

49. The nurse needs to inspect the external ear canal and eardrum using an otoscope and perform the whisper test and Rinne and Weber tests to evaluate hearing. The nurse recommends an audiologist for further evaluation if indicated.

50. A possible nursing diagnosis for a client with a hearing loss is Disturbed Sensory Perception (Auditory), with a possible expected outcome that the client demonstrates understanding by verbal, written, or signed response. Nursing interventions include (1) encouraging the client to talk about the hearing loss and its effect on ADL; (2) providing information about hearing loss and available services to the client and family; (3) replacing batteries in hearing aids on a regular and as-needed basis; and (4) making sure the hearing aid toggle switch for microphone telephones is in the appropriate position if applicable.

51. Another nursing diagnosis for a client who is hard of hearing is Impaired Verbal Communication, with a possible expected outcome that the client uses effective communication techniques. Nursing interventions include (1) using a wave of the hand or tap on the shoulder to get the client's attention before beginning to speak; (2) facing the client and keeping the hands away from the face when speaking to the client; (3) using a low voice pitch with normal loudness when speaking to the client; (4) speaking at a normal rate without overarticulating; (5) using nonverbal and written communication as needed; (6) rephrasing sentences as necessary; (7) asking the client to repeat important information; and (8) telling other staff about the client's hearing loss and effective communication strategies.

52. A third nursing diagnosis for clients with a hearing loss is Social Isolation, with a possible expected outcome that the client interacts with others and participates in activities. Nursing interventions may include (1) helping the client identify the extent and cause of social isolation; (2) encouraging interaction with friends and family on a one-to-one basis in quiet settings; (3) treating the client with dignity; (4) reminding friends and family that hearing loss does not mean loss of mental faculties; (5) involving the client in activities that do not require acute hearing such as checkers and chess; (6) obtaining a pocket talker or encouraging the client or family to do so; (7) referring the client to an audiologist for evaluation and possible hearing-aid fitting; and (8) referring the client to resources such as support groups and senior citizen centers.

53. The nurse can evaluate the effectiveness of nursing interventions by listening to the client's responses and observing behavior, interactions with others, and signs of anxiety or stress.

LEARNING OUTCOME 5

Describe appropriate teaching content for the client with eye or ear disorders.

Concepts for Lecture

1. The nurse needs to teach all clients about hand washing and proper eye care. Instruction includes advising clients to use a new, clean cotton-tipped swab or cotton ball for each eye when cleaning eyelids.
2. The client is to be taught how to instill eye drops and ointments.
3. If an eye patch is ordered, the nurse must be sure the client or a family member knows how to apply it and where to obtain necessary supplies.

 **POWERPOINT SLIDES**

Tables and/or Figures
- **Box 40-2** Nursing Care Checklist: Eye Surgery
- **Box 40-6** Client Teaching: Tips to Prevent External Otitis
- **Box 40-9** Nursing Care Checklist: Ear Surgery

SUGGESTIONS FOR CLASSROOM ACTIVITIES
- Assign students to select an eye or ear disorder and develop a teaching tool for prevention of that disorder or dealing with manifestations of that disorder. Students can develop a hand out, a comic book, or a skit on video, or come up with some innovative way to get teaching points across to clients.

4. The nurse needs to teach contact lens users how to care for and clean the lenses and stress the importance of periodically removing lenses, even extended-wear lenses. In general, lenses should be removed at night.

5. The nurse stresses the importance of follow-up appointments after a corneal transplant.

6. The nurse reinforces teaching about how to prevent increased intraocular pressure (e.g., avoiding straining, vomiting, coughing, and lifting).

7. The nurse instructs the client and family to promptly report inflammation, graft cloudiness, or increased pain after a corneal transplant.

8. It is an important nursing responsibility to teach people how to prevent eye injuries. The nurse can teach employees and people participating in high-risk sports when and how to use eye protectors.

9. The nurse teaches clients to flush the eye immediately with copious amounts of water if a chemical splash occurs.

10. The nurse can teach that loose, visible foreign bodies can be removed from the eye using a clean, moistened cotton-tipped swab and that the client should never try to remove objects that penetrate the eye.

11. If an abrasion or penetrating or blunt injury is suspected, it is advisable to cover the eye loosely with sterile gauze and seek medical attention immediately. Both eyes should be patched until medical help is obtained.

12. Following an injury, it is necessary to reinforce teaching about follow-up treatment. Discuss the ordered medications, and instruct on how to instill eye drops and ointments; how to apply the eye pad or shield, if ordered; not to rub or scratch the eye; and if ordered, to avoid activities that increase intraocular pressure to prevent further eye damage.

13. It is important for the nurse to educate the public about risk factors for glaucoma such as increased age and higher incidence in African Americans, Mexican Americans, and Asians. The public is advised that eye examinations should be done in people over 40 every 2 to 4 years, and anyone with a family history of glaucoma or over age 65 should be examined every 1 to 2 years. Early vision screening can reduce the severity and potentially damaging, permanent effects of glaucoma.

14. Following treatment for a detached retina, the nurse stresses the importance of positioning as ordered. The client may be instructed to maintain a position with the affected area of the eye inferior to maintain contact between the retina and the choroid.

15. A client who has had a spontaneous retinal detachment has an increased risk of future detachments. The nurse discusses early symptoms and emphasizes the importance of seeking immediate treatment if they occur. The nurse emphasizes the need to maintain follow-up treatment with the ophthalmologist. If the retina remains detached, the nurse discusses safety measures to accommodate the loss of vision and changes in depth perception.

16. Nursing care focus for diabetic retinopathy is on education. The nurse stresses the importance of regular eye examinations for all clients with diabetes and teaches the client to report promptly any change in vision, including blurring; black spots (floaters), cobwebs, or flashing lights in the visual field; or a sudden loss of vision in one or both eyes.

17. The nurse emphasizes that controlling blood glucose levels and maintaining blood pressure within normal limits will help limit diabetic retinopathy or slow its progress.

18. Client teaching tips to prevent future episodes of external otitis in a client with otitis externa (Box 40-6) include advising the client to stay out of the water for 7 to 10 days or until completely healed and, when resuming water activities, to use earplugs, a tight-fitting swim cap, or a wetsuit hood to keep water out of the ears or protect the ear from cold water temperatures.

SUGGESTIONS FOR CLINICAL ACTIVITIES

• Assign students to care for clients who have ear or eye disorders. Have the students assess the learning needs of their clients in regard to their disorders and develop a teaching tool to use with their assigned client. If appropriate, they can modify and use one of the teaching tools developed in class.

19. Additional tips to prevent external otitis include using a hair dryer on the lowest setting to dry ear canals after swimming and not inserting cotton swabs or any other object into the ear canals.

20. The nurse needs to provide verbal and written instructions for prescribed medications for external otitis. The nurse needs to inform all clients that ear canals rarely need cleaning beyond washing the external opening with soap and water and to teach clients of all ages not to clean the ear canals with any implement.

21. The client with otitis externa is instructed to report any increase in pain, swelling, or redness around the ear, fever, malaise, or increased fatigue to the primary care provider.

22. Teaching is important to prevent obstruction of the ear canal with earwax. Advise the client with impacted cerumen to use mineral oil or commercial products to soften wax and remove it by irrigating the canal with water. The nurse stresses the risk of impacting cerumen against the eardrum if cotton-tipped swabs are used to clean the ear canal. The swab may break and lodge in the canal.

23. The nurse teaches the client and family how to instill eardrops if they have been prescribed.

24. The client is taught to seek immediate medical attention when severe ear pain with or without drainage exists, and this is especially important when these manifestations accompany a URI.

25. The nurse providing instruction to a client with otitis media will teach about otitis media, its causes and prevention, and any specific treatment. The nurse will provide verbal and written instructions about the ordered antibiotic, its effects, recommended timing (with or without food, doses evenly spaced throughout the day), and possible side effects. The nurse will discuss the symptoms of allergic or adverse reactions that should be reported to the physician and will stress the importance of completing the full course of therapy.

26. If surgery has been performed for otitis media, the nurse will teach the client and family members about postoperative care. The nurse will discuss postoperative precautions such as avoiding water in the ear canals and sudden changes in air pressure.

27. Safety is a primary focus of teaching for home care for the client with labyrinthitis. The nurse teaches the client to change positions slowly, especially when ambulating. Turning the whole body rather than just the head helps to prevent vertigo.

28. Because attacks of vertigo are unpredictable, the client should not ambulate alone unless in a safe environment.

29. The nurse teaches the client with vertigo about prescribed medications, providing both verbal and written instructions about their use, desired effects, possible adverse effects, and precautions.

30. The nurse suggests resources such as the Better Hearing Institute and Self-Help for Hard of Hearing People.

31. If the client with vertigo has had surgery, the nurse provides information about postoperative care and follow-up. The nurse teaches techniques to minimize postoperative vertigo and associated nausea. Since surgery may cause permanent hearing loss in the affected ear, the nurse discusses safety and communication strategies.

32. Education is vital to help prevent hearing loss. The nurse needs to promote environmental noise control and ear protection. The Occupational Health and Safety Administration requires ear protection in workplaces that exceed 85 decibels.

33. It is essential for the nurse to teach about care of ears and ear canals, including cleaning and treatment of ear infections; use of earplugs when swimming or diving; use of ear protectors when operating loud equipment, shooting firearms, or when exposed to loud noise; and never placing hard objects into the ear canal.

General Chapter Considerations

1. Have students study and learn key terms listed at the beginning of the chapter.
2. Have students complete end of chapter exercises either in their book or on the MyNursingKit Website.
3. Use the Classroom Response Question PowerPoints to assess students prior to lecture.

• Clinical Reasoning Care Map

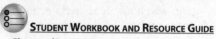

MyNursingKit
(www.mynursingkit.com)
• Websites
• NCLEX® Questions
• Case Studies
• Key Terms

Student Workbook and Resource Guide
• Chapter 40 activities
• *Separate purchase*

Prentice Hall Nurse's Drug Guide
• *Separate purchase*

Classroom Response Question PowerPoints

Testbank

CHAPTER 41
THE MUSCULOSKELETAL SYSTEM AND ASSESSMENT

LEARNING OUTCOME 1

Describe the structure and function of the musculoskeletal system.

Concepts for Lecture

1. The musculoskeletal system includes bones and joints of the skeleton, connective tissues such as tendons and ligaments, and the skeletal muscles.
2. The musculoskeletal system allows us to remain upright and to move and protect our organs.
3. The human skeleton has 206 bones. Bones provide structure and support soft tissue. They protect vital organs from injury.
4. Bones are classified by shape. Long bones, like those in the arms and legs, have a shaft, called a diaphysis, and two broad ends, called epiphyses.
5. Short bones include those of the wrist and ankle.
6. Flat bones, including skull bones, the sternum, and the ribs, are thin and flat, and most are curved.
7. Irregular bones vary in size and shape. They include the vertebrae, the scapulae, and the bones of the pelvis.
8. Bone cells include osteoblasts (cells that form bone), osteocytes (cells that maintain bone), and osteoclasts (cells that resorb bone).
9. Bones contain collagen (a type of connective tissue) and minerals (primarily calcium and phosphate). Bones are covered with periosteum, a double-layered connective tissue that contains blood vessels and nerves.
10. There are two types of bone: compact bone is smooth and dense, whereas spongy bone contains spaces. Both types are found in almost all bones of the body. Compact bone forms the shaft of long bones and the outside layer in other types of bones. The spongy sections of bones contain bone marrow.
11. Red bone marrow, found mostly in flat bones such as the sternum, ribs, and ileum, makes blood cells and hemoglobin. Yellow bone marrow, found in the shaft of long bones, primarily contains fat and connective tissue.
12. Bones being used and subjected to stress are constantly remodeled. Bone remodeling is regulated by hormones, the effects of gravity, and mechanical stress from the pull of muscles. Without activity and stress on the bones, more bone is resorbed, and less new bone is formed.
13. Joints, also called articulations, are where two or more bones meet. Joints hold the skeleton together.
14. Three primary types of joints are synarthrosis (immovable joints, e.g., skull sutures), amphiarthrosis (slightly movable joints, e.g., vertebral joints), and diarthrosis or synovial (freely movable joints, e.g., joints of the limbs).
15. Synovial joints are found at all limb articulations. The surfaces of these joints are covered by cartilage, and the joint cavity is enclosed by a tough, fibrous capsule. This cavity is lined with synovial membrane and filled with synovial fluid, which lubricates the joint, facilitating smooth movement of the articulating bones. Synovial joints allow many different kinds of movements (Table 41-1).

 POWERPOINT SLIDES

Tables and/or Figures
- **Figure 41-1** Bones of the Human Skeleton
- **Table 41-1** Movement of Synovial Joints

 **SUGGESTIONS FOR CLASSROOM ACTIVITIES**

- Review the structure of the musculoskeletal system using an anatomic model that illustrates bones, joints, and attachment of muscles, ligaments, and tendons.
- Have students prepare index cards with information they can use to teach a client about the structure and function of bones, joints, muscles, ligaments, and tendons.
- Have students break into small groups and prepare a skit in which a nurse explains to a client some part of the structure and function of bones, joints, muscles, ligaments, and/or tendons.

 SUGGESTIONS FOR CLINICAL ACTIVITIES

- Assign students to care for clients who have alterations in structure or function of the musculoskeletal system. Have students use one or more of their teaching cards prepared in class to teach the client about the musculoskeletal system structure and function or to assess what the client knows about this system and reinforce it.

16. Ligaments are bands of connective tissue that connect bones to bones. Ligaments limit or enhance movement, provide joint stability, and enhance joint strength.

17. Tendons are fibrous connective tissue bands that connect muscles to bones and enable the bones to move when skeletal muscles contract.

18. Bursae are small sacs of synovial fluid that cushion and protect bony areas that are at high risk for friction, such as the knee and the shoulder.

19. There are three types of muscle tissue: skeletal muscle, smooth muscle, and cardiac muscle. Skeletal muscle, also known as voluntary muscle, allows voluntary movement. Both smooth muscle and cardiac muscle are involuntary; their movement is controlled by internal mechanisms.

20. Skeletal muscles are thick bundles of parallel fibers. Each muscle fiber is a bundle of smaller structures called myofibrils. These myofibrils are strands of smaller repeating units called sarcomeres, which allow the muscle to contract.

21. The cells of skeletal muscle are excitable, meaning they can receive and respond to a stimulus. Skeletal muscle contracts when motor neurons release acetylcholine, a neurotransmitter. This produces an action potential (electrical impulse) that spreads through the muscle fiber, causing it to contract. The more fibers that contract, the stronger the muscle contraction is. Muscle fibers extend when they relax.

22. Skeletal muscles can be moved through conscious, voluntary control or by reflex activity. Muscle fibers return to their resting length after shortening or lengthening in response to stimuli. There are approximately 600 skeletal muscles in the body.

23. Nerve impulses maintain muscle tone. Lack of use causes muscle atrophy, whereas regular exercise increases the size and strength of muscles. Prolonged strenuous activity can cause a buildup of lactic acid and muscle fatigue.

LEARNING OUTCOME 2

Identify age-related changes in the musculoskeletal system.

Concepts for Lecture

1. Aging commonly affects the musculoskeletal system. Although some musculoskeletal system changes appear to relate to the aging process itself, others result from decreased activity, lifestyle factors, or pathophysiologic processes.

2. Older adults, women in particular, tend to lose bone mass with aging.

3. Disk and joint cartilage dehydrate and lose flexibility. These changes contribute to a loss of height (an average of about 1.5 to 2 inches) and a stooped posture.

4. With aging, the hips and knees are somewhat flexed, and the head is tilted slightly backward to maintain eye contact, which changes the older adult's center of gravity, increasing the risk of falls.

5. Dehydration of joint cartilage contributes to degenerative joint disease (osteoarthritis) in older adults. Affected joints tend to stiffen and lose range of motion. Cartilage deteriorates and pieces of cartilage may be loose in the joint space, contributing to joint pain and stiffness.

6. Ligaments and tendons lose flexibility with aging, increasing the risk of tears and joint instability.

7. Reduced activity levels, decreased muscle cell innervation, and endocrine changes associated with aging contribute to skeletal muscle atrophy in the older adult.

8. Muscle tone decreases with aging, as do muscle strength and stamina.

 **POWERPOINT SLIDES**

SUGGESTIONS FOR CLASSROOM ACTIVITIES

- Have students interview several older people each, inquiring about the amount of exercise they do, whether they have a diagnosis of osteoarthritis, and whether they experience joint pain. Have the students discuss their findings to determine if they think there is any correlation between exercise and healthier joints.

- Have students ask older people if they have lost any inches in height. Have students observe the posture of older adults. Do their observations match the textbook description of the posture of older adults? Have students discuss these findings in small groups or in class.

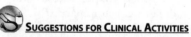 **SUGGESTIONS FOR CLINICAL ACTIVITIES**

- Assign students to care for older adults in clinical. Have students talk with their clients about any musculoskeletal problems the clients may have.

LEARNING OUTCOME 3

Perform and document focused assessment of the musculoskeletal system.

Concepts for Lecture

1. Pain and limited mobility are the primary manifestations of musculoskeletal trauma and disorders.
2. In gathering a health history, the nurse will explore the client's chief complaint, inquiring about the onset of the problem, its duration and specific manifestations, and the effect of the problem on function and ability to maintain activities of daily living (ADL).
3. The nurse will ask about any precipitating events for the complaints, such as trauma, stressors, or other associated events.
4. The nurse will determine the location and any radiation of pain; its character (sharp, dull, constant, or intermittent), duration, and timing; factors that aggravate or relieve the pain; and the effect on function.
5. The nurse will inquire about associated complaints such as fever, fatigue, weight changes, rash, or swelling.
6. The health history also includes exploring past injuries or related or similar problems and treatment measures and their effectiveness.
7. In conducting a physical examination, the nurse assesses the client's posture, gait, ability to walk and change directions with or without assistive devices, ability to sit in and arise from a chair, and ability to feed, clothe, and dress self, as well as other ADL.
8. The physical examination includes inspecting general muscle mass and symmetry and equality of limb length. The muscle strength can be graded from 0–5, with 5 being full range of motion against resistance. Various muscle groups can be evaluated (Tables 41-2 and 41-3).
9. The nurse inspects and palpates bones and joints for obvious deformity, tenderness or pain, swelling, warmth, and ROM. Joint ROM often is assessed only when a musculoskeletal problem is present. When ROM is assessed, it is important to assess and compare corresponding joints on both sides of the body. *Clinical alert:* Never attempt to move a joint past its normal range of motion for the client or past the point at which pain is experienced.
10. Joints such as the shoulders and knees are palpated for crepitus, a grating sound or sensation during ROM (Table 41-4).
11. Several special physical assessment maneuvers may be performed with additional training and as indicated, including the bulge sign and ballottement, which are used to assess for fluid in the knee joint.
12. The Thomas test may be performed when a hip flexion contracture is suspected.

LEARNING OUTCOME 4

Recognize alterations in musculoskeletal structure and/or function.

Concepts for Lecture

1. With aging, several changes bring a loss in height, a stooped posture, and joints that tend to stiffen and lose range of motion.
2. Anything less than a grade of 5 when grading muscle strength on a scale of 0–5 (Table 41-2) is an alteration in musculoskeletal structure or function. Any inability to follow instructions of the nurse evaluating muscle strength (Table 41-3) is an alteration in musculoskeletal structure or function.

POWERPOINT SLIDES

Tables and/or Figures

- **Table 41-2** Grading Muscle Strength
- **Table 41-3** Instructions to Evaluate Muscle Strength
- **Table 41-4** Instructions for Assessing Range of Motion

SUGGESTIONS FOR CLASSROOM ACTIVITIES

- Ask students to practice physical examination of the musculoskeletal system on each other under supervision and then to practice on relatives and friends. Students could videotape their examinations and have peers critique them, or these videotapes could be turned in for instructor critique.

SUGGESTIONS FOR CLINICAL ACTIVITIES

- Assign the students to care for clients with musculoskeletal problems. Have the students do partial or complete assessments on their assigned clients, under supervision.

POWERPOINT SLIDES

Tables and/or Figures

- **Table 41-5** Laboratory Test to Evaluate Musculoskeletal Disorders
- **Table 41-6** Diagnostic Tests to Evaluate Musculoskeletal Disorders
- **Figure 41-4** Checking for the Bulge Sign
- **Figure 41-5** Checking for Ballottement

3. Any failure to follow the nurse's instructions in assessing range of motion (Table 41-4) is an alteration in musculoskeletal structure or function.

4. When checking for a bulge sign, with the client supine, the nurse milks upward on the medial side of the knee, then taps the lateral side of the patella while observing for a fluid bulge. If there is a fluid bulge, this is an alteration in musculoskeletal structure or function (Figure 41-4).

5. The nurse doing ballottement applies pressure with one hand placed just above the knee. With the other hand, the nurse taps the patella. Any fluid in the knee causes the patella to rebound against the fingers (Figure 41-5). Any rebound of the patella is an alteration in musculoskeletal structure or function.

6. When a hip flexion contracture is suspected, the reclining client is asked to bring one knee up to the chest while keeping the other leg straight. With a hip flexion contracture, the extended leg rises off the examining table (Thomas test).

7. Any deviation from the normal value range of laboratory tests to evaluate musculoskeletal disorders (Table 41-5) or abnormal findings on imaging studies and other diagnostic procedures commonly used for clients with suspected musculoskeletal trauma or disorders may indicate an alteration in musculoskeletal structure or function and may need further attention (Tables 41-5 and 41-6).

SUGGESTIONS FOR CLASSROOM ACTIVITIES

- Have students break into small groups to discuss possible alterations in musculoskeletal structure and/or function.

SUGGESTIONS FOR CLINICAL ACTIVITIES

- Assign students to rotate through the office of a physician who specializes in musculoskeletal problems. Have students keep a log of their experiences and of the alterations in musculoskeletal structure and/or function that they have observed in this rotation. Ask students to share what they observed and learned about alterations in musculoskeletal structure and/or function.

LEARNING OUTCOME 5

Provide nursing care for clients undergoing diagnostic tests for musculoskeletal system disorders.

Concepts for Lecture

1. X-ray is used to evaluate bone density and structure and joint structure. The computed tomography (CT) scan produces computer-generated images with significantly more detail than standard x-ray. Contrast medium may be injected to help visualize specific features.

2. There is no special preparation for the x-ray or CT scan. The nurse needs to inquire if the female client of childbearing age could be pregnant, and if so, the nurse needs to alert the physician and radiologic technician. If contrast will be used, the nurse needs to assess for allergies to iodine, shellfish, or contrast medium used previously and notify the physician or radiologist if present.

3. Magnetic resonance imaging (MRI) produces a detailed image of bone and muscle structures and may be used to evaluate soft tissue injuries, degenerative disk changes in the spine, and joint inflammation and injuries.

4. When the client gets an MRI, the nurse must ask about the presence of a pacemaker, prosthetic device (e.g., hip joint prosthesis), or other metallic objects.

5. A bone density scan (bone densitometry) is used to diagnose osteoporosis by measuring bone mineral density. This scan helps predict fracture risk by comparing the individual's bone mass to that of a healthy 25- to 35-year-old person. No special preparation is needed for this test.

6. Ultrasound procedures may be used to evaluate overall bone density by estimating bone density over the heel or kneecap. No special preparation is needed for this test.

7. When a client gets a bone scan, the scan evaluates the amount of an injected radioactive isotope taken up by bones to reveal "hot spots"

POWERPOINT SLIDES

Tables and/or Figures
- **Table 41-6** Diagnostic Tests to Evaluate Musculoskeletal Disorders

SUGGESTIONS FOR CLASSROOM ACTIVITIES

- Invite someone who does CT scans, MRIs, and bone scans to talk to the class about preparation for these tests and why these preparations are important in getting an accurate set of data.
- Invite a physician who does arthrocentesis or arthroscopy to talk to the class about these procedures, and invite a nurse working with the physician to talk about nursing responsibilities.

SUGGESTIONS FOR CLINICAL ACTIVITIES

- Assign students to care for clients who have musculoskeletal problems and to learn about nursing implications for any tests they may be receiving to evaluate their disorders.

where uptake is increased due to infection or malignancies or "cold spots" where uptake is reduced (e.g., an area of bone that has decreased flow).

8. The nurse needs to have the client give informed consent prior to a bone scan. The nurse needs to notify the physician if the client is or might be pregnant. Instructions are given to increase fluid intake after the scan to promote excretion of the radioactive isotope. Warm compresses may be applied if the injection site is red or swollen.

9. Arthrocentesis is the insertion of a needle into the joint capsule to withdraw joint fluid for examination, for culture and sensitivity if an infection is suspected, or to remove excess fluid.

10. Nursing responsibilities for an arthrocentesis include assisting with positioning the extremity as needed and applying a pressure dressing to the site following aspiration to prevent bleeding into the tissues. The nurse also instructs the client to apply a cold pack, maintain the pressure dressing, and elevate the extremity for 8 to 24 hours as indicated. The nurse instructs the client to rest the affected joint for 2 to 3 days following the procedure.

11. Arthroscopy uses a flexible fiberoptic endoscope to view joint structures and tissues. This procedure is used to identify torn tendons or ligaments, an injured meniscus, inflammatory joint changes, and damaged cartilage.

12. The nurse will ensure that informed consent is obtained for an arthroscopy and that the client fasts for 8 hours prior to the procedure if general anesthesia is to be used.

13. Additional nursing responsibilities when working with a client having arthroscopy include frequently assessing neurovascular status of the distal extremity and comparing findings with the unaffected side. The nurse also monitors pain and provides analgesics as ordered; assesses for bleeding, excessive swelling, or constriction of the extremity; and instructs the client to elevate the extremity for 24 to 48 hours, applying ice to the affected area for the first 24 hours.

14. When working with a client who is getting knee arthroscopy, the nurse will teach the client how to use crutches to avoid weight bearing on the joint for the first 24 hours following the procedure.

15. If the client is getting shoulder arthroscopy, the nurse places the affected arm in a sling and provides instructions as directed by the physician. The nurse provides instructions for ROM exercises or referral to physical therapy as directed.

16. The electromyelogram (EMG) uses electrodes inserted into skeletal muscle to measure electrical activity at rest and during contraction. It is useful for diagnosing neuromuscular disorders.

17. When working with a client getting an EMG, the nurse instructs the client to avoid fluids containing caffeine and not to smoke for 3 hours before the test. The client is also instructed not to take any medicine before the test unless specifically directed by the physician to do so.

GENERAL CHAPTER CONSIDERATIONS

1. Have students study and learn key terms listed at the beginning of the chapter.
2. Have students complete end of chapter exercises either in their book or on the MyNursingKit Website.
3. Use the Classroom Response Question PowerPoints to assess students prior to lecture.

REFERENCE

- American Academy of Orthopaedic Surgeons: Arthroscopy. Available at http://orthoinfo. aaos.org/ topic.cfm?topic=A00109

- Clinical Reasoning Care Map

MYNURSINGKIT
(www.mynursingkit.com)

- Websites
- NCLEX® Questions
- Case Studies
- Key Terms

STUDENT WORKBOOK AND RESOURCE GUIDE

- Chapter 41 activities
- *Separate purchase*

PRENTICE HALL NURSE'S DRUG GUIDE

- *Separate purchase*

CLASSROOM RESPONSE QUESTION
POWERPOINTS

TESTBANK

CHAPTER 42
CARING FOR CLIENTS WITH MUSCULOSKELETAL TRAUMA

LEARNING OUTCOME 1

Discuss risk factors for and mechanisms of musculoskeletal trauma.

Concepts for Lecture

1. Older clients are at higher risk for musculoskeletal trauma due to falls, so the home needs to be assessed for potential hazards such as poorly lighted stairs or no hand railings. Throw rugs and clutter need to be removed from travel areas. The nurse needs to discuss using bath mats, installing grab bars in bathrooms, and wearing shoes with good treads to decrease the risk of slipping.
2. High-risk activities for musculoskeletal trauma include contact sports, roller blading, and skateboarding. The nurse needs to teach and encourage clients to use appropriate equipment and safety devices such as helmets, pads, and braces when engaging in these activities and other high-risk activities.
3. Musculoskeletal trauma occurs when tissues are subjected to more force than they are able to absorb.
4. The severity of trauma depends on both the amount of force and the location of impact because different parts of the body can withstand different amounts of force (e.g., small bones in the hand cannot absorb as much energy as the femur).
5. Many external sources can cause trauma, and the force can vary in severity (e.g., a step off the curb, a fall, being tackled in a football game, or a car crash).
6. Musculoskeletal trauma ranges from mild to severe, for example, soft tissue injury, fracture, or complete amputation.
7. Musculoskeletal trauma often affects surrounding tissues. A bone fracture can affect the function of muscles, tendons, and ligaments that attach to it.
8. A contusion, the simplest musculoskeletal injury, is bleeding into soft tissue resulting from blunt force. With significant bleeding, a hematoma forms. A contusion causes swelling and discoloration (a bruise), which initially appears purple or blue. As blood cells break down and are absorbed, the mark becomes brown, then yellow, and finally disappears.
9. Sprain, strains, and soft tissue damage are common injuries. A sprain is a ligament injury. Sprains are caused by a twisting motion that overstretches or tears the ligament.
10. Sprains are graded by the extent of the damage. Grade I is overstretching with mild bleeding and inflammation; grade II is severe stretching and some tearing with inflammation and hematoma; grade III is complete tearing of the ligament; and grade IV means that the bony attachment of the ligament is broken away.
11. A strain is a microscopic tear in the muscle that causes bleeding into the tissues. A strain or "pulled muscle" occurs when a muscle is forced to extend past its elasticity. Strains may be caused by inappropriate lifting or a sudden acceleration–deceleration injury such as a motor vehicle crash.

 **POWERPOINT SLIDES**

Tables and/or Figures
- **Box 42-1** Characteristics of Sprains and Strains

 SUGGESTIONS FOR CLASSROOM ACTIVITIES
- Have students research state laws on seat belts, helmets, and other protective equipment.
- Have students do an assessment of their home and the safety risks for injury.

SUGGESTIONS FOR CLINICAL ACTIVITIES
- Discuss risks of the elderly for musculoskeletal trauma in a post clinical conference.
- Talk with assigned clinical clients about risks for injury in the clinical area and how to prevent them.
- Have students prepare a teaching plan for their elderly clients on home safety to prevent musculoskeletal trauma.
- Discuss in preconference how nurses can prevent injuring themselves in the clinical setting.

LEARNING OUTCOME 2

Safely and appropriately assess clients with musculoskeletal trauma.

Concepts for Lecture

1. To assess soft tissue injury, the nurse collects both subjective and objective data.
2. Assessment of soft tissue injury includes asking about the mechanism of injury and when it occurred; asking about any protective devices that were being used at the time of injury (e.g., seat belt or air bag); and obtaining specific information about pain, including location, character, intensity, and aggravating and relieving factors.
3. The assessment of soft tissue injury includes asking about the effect of the injury or pain on use of the extremity and ability to bear weight as well as asking about movement and sensation distal to the injury, especially numbness, tingling, or inability to move.
4. The nurse assessing a soft tissue injury also inquires about previous injuries and self-care measures that have been used for this injury (e.g., analgesics, ice or heat, wrapping or rest).
5. The nurse assessing a soft tissue injury inspects the injured area for redness, swelling, or deformity and assesses active range of motion of affected joints. The nurse palpates for swelling, warmth, tenderness, deformity, and crepitus (a grating sensation or sound) and checks for capillary refill, pulses, movement, and sensation distal to the injury.
6. The nurse promptly reports complaints of numbness, tingling, weakness, or inability to move distal to the injury as these may be signs of nerve damage. Circulation may be impaired if the extremity is cool or pale. The nurse must check capillary refill and peripheral pulses and report these assessment findings immediately.

LEARNING OUTCOME 3

Describe how fractures are classified.

Concepts for Lecture

1. Fractures are classified in a number of different ways (see Table 42-1).
2. A closed or simple fracture is the most common fracture. In this type of fracture, the skin over the fracture remains intact.
3. An open or compound fracture disrupts the skin over the fracture, allowing bacteria to enter the wound. Broken bone protrudes through the skin. This increases the risk of complications such as infection or nerve damage.
4. A complete fracture involves the entire width of the bone, whereas incomplete fractures do not involve the entire width of the bone.
5. In a comminuted fracture, the bone fragments into many pieces.
6. In a compression fracture, the bone is crushed.
7. In an impacted fracture, the broken ends of bone are forced together.
8. Broken bone is pressed inward (e.g., the skull) in a depressed fracture.
9. With a spiral fracture, a jagged break occurs due to twisting force.
10. A greenstick fracture means there is an incomplete break occurring along the length of the bone.

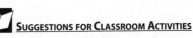 **POWERPOINT SLIDES**

Tables and/or Figures
- **Box 42-1** Characteristics of Sprains and Strains

 **SUGGESTIONS FOR CLASSROOM ACTIVITIES**

- Have students work in pairs to practice assessing a soft tissue injury. The students should verbalize what they are assessing for, such as palpating for swelling, warmth, tenderness, and so on; find out the client's complaints (numbness, tingling, etc.); and describe how they would check circulation and what they would expect to find.

 **SUGGESTIONS FOR CLINICAL ACTIVITIES**

- Assign students to rotate through the emergency department of a hospital and/or the office of an orthopedic specialist to observe and assist with assessment of clients with musculoskeletal trauma.

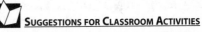 **POWERPOINT SLIDES**

Tables and/or Figures
- **Table 42-1** Types of Fractures

 **SUGGESTIONS FOR CLASSROOM ACTIVITIES**

- Provide pictures of various types of fractures and have students label the picture with the type of fracture depicted. This could be a collection of small pictures on one or two pages that the students could label in individual work, or it could be larger pictures for the class to identify as a group. The students could also be divided into two teams and the teams could each decide on the correct labels for the pictures as a contest to see which team can get the most correctly labeled pictures of fractures.

SUGGESTIONS FOR CLINICAL ACTIVITIES

- Talk with the supervisor in outpatient surgery and the emergency room and ask to be notified when people with various types of fractures are being admitted and ask for permission for students to be allowed to see the fracture x-rays and, if possible, to observe the actual fracture and talk with the client.
- Have a radiologist talk with the students about different types of fractures and provide x-rays of the various types of fractures.

LEARNING OUTCOME 4

Discuss interdisciplinary care for clients who have experienced musculoskeletal trauma.

Concepts for Lecture

1. When a client has a soft tissue injury, an x-ray may be done to rule out fracture. If further examination is necessary, an MRI may be done.
2. Soft tissue trauma is treated with measures to decrease swelling, alleviate pain, and encourage rest and healing.
3. The client with soft tissue trauma is instructed to avoid using the injured area. A splint may be applied.
4. Ice is applied for the first 48 hours after a soft tissue injury. After 48 hours, heat can be applied.
5. A compression dressing, such as an Ace bandage, may be applied to a soft tissue injury. The injured extremity should be elevated to the level of the heart to increase venous return and decrease swelling.
6. If the lower extremity is injured, crutches are provided. A knee injury requires a knee immobilizer. If the upper extremity is injured, a sling is provided.
7. Nonsteroidal anti-inflammatory drugs (NSAIDs) and analgesics, including narcotics, may be ordered to manage pain and reduce the inflammatory response.
8. A fracture requires prompt treatment. The fracture is reduced and immobilized as soon as possible. When a fracture is suspected, the extremity or affected body part is immobilized before the client is moved. The neck and back are immobilized using a rigid cervical collar and backboard if a vertebral fracture is suspected.
9. The joints above and below a suspected extremity fracture are immobilized.
10. Pulses, color, movement, and sensation of the extremity are checked both before and after splinting. Open wounds and fractures are covered with a sterile dressing.
11. On arrival in the healthcare setting, x-rays of the affected body part are usually obtained to confirm the diagnosis of a fracture.
12. A hip fracture usually is diagnosed by history, physical examination, and an x-ray of the affected hip. When a person has a hip fracture, Buck's traction may be applied to reduce muscle spasm until surgery can be done.
13. An ORIF or hip replacement procedure is performed to promote mobility, decrease pain, and prevent complications. Fixation is accomplished by securing the femur with pins, screws, nails, or plates (Figure 42-9A).
14. ORIF works well for fractures in the trochanteric area. If the femoral head or neck is fractured, prosthesis is inserted to replace the femoral head (Figure 42-9B). This procedure is called an orthoplasty.
15. If both the femoral head and the hip socket (the acetabulum) must be replaced, a total hip replacement or arthroplasty is performed.
16. Following amputation, the wound may be open (guillotine) or closed (flap). Open amputations are done when an infection is present. The end of the stump (remaining portion of the limb) is left open to drain. Continuous skin traction is applied to the limb. When the infection has cleared, the wound is closed.
17. In a closed amputation, a flap of skin is formed to cover the end of the wound. A compression dressing is applied to the stump after amputation to reduce edema, prevent infection, and promote healing.
18. The compression dressing applied to the stump helps mold the stump to fit the prosthesis and helps prevent edema.

POWERPOINT SLIDES

Tables and/or Figures

- **Figure 42-2** Emergency Medical Technicians Apply a Traction Splint to Immobilize the Lower Leg
- **Figure 42-9A** Procedure to Repair a Hip Fracture: ORIF
- **Figure 42-9B** Procedure to Repair a Hip Fracture: Hip Prosthesis

SUGGESTIONS FOR CLASSROOM ACTIVITIES

- Have someone from EMS talk about care of a person with suspected fracture and demonstrate immobilization of a person with a suspected fracture.

SUGGESTIONS FOR CLINICAL ACTIVITIES

- Assign students to help put a client in Buck's traction when the opportunity arises. If there are no opportunities to put a client in Buck's traction or to care for a client in Buck's traction, have a hospital staff member work with the clinical group in postconference to find where the equipment is located and discuss how the equipment is set up for the client.

19. The client with a closed amputation may return from surgery with a temporary prosthesis.
20. Limited weight bearing may be allowed within a week or two after surgery.
21. The client with an amputation will be referred to a prosthetist who discusses available prosthetic options. The prosthesis is custom made and fitted to the client.
22. Some clients may have several prostheses made for different functions, depending on their age, occupation, and activity level.

LEARNING OUTCOME 5

Discuss common complications of fractures, their manifestations, and nursing strategies to prevent them.

Concepts for Lecture

1. Common manifestations of fractures include deformity, swelling, ecchymosis (bruising), pain, tenderness, guarding, immobility, numbness, crepitus, and muscle spasms (see Box 42-2, Manifestations of Fractures).
2. While most fractures are uncomplicated, serious complications can develop.
3. A fractured pelvis or femur may cause significant bleeding and hypovolemic shock. Up to 4.5 liters of blood can be lost with a pelvic fracture.
4. Open fractures can be complicated by infection. Significant tissue trauma may accompany open fractures.
5. The fractured bone may damage peripheral nerves, affecting movement and/or sensation distal to the fracture.
6. Blood flow to a portion of fractured bone may be disrupted, causing necrosis.
7. Blood vessel damage and immobility increase the risk for developing deep venous thrombosis (DVT).
8. A compartment is a space enclosed by a fibrous membrane or fascia. Compartments within the limbs may enclose and support bones, nerves, and blood vessels. Compartment syndrome occurs when excess pressure restricts blood vessels and nerves within a compartment.
9. Compartment syndrome may be caused by bleeding or edema within the compartment or by external compression of the limb by a too-tight cast. In compartment syndrome, nerve damage occurs within 30 minutes. Unless properly relieved, compartment syndrome may lead to loss of the limb and sepsis.
10. Compartment syndrome usually develops within the first 48 hours of injury, when edema is at its peak.
11. Manifestations of compartment syndrome include the "5 Ps:" (1) pain unrelieved by narcotic analgesics; (2) pallor and decreased capillary refill; (3) paresthesias (numbness and tingling); (4) paresis (weakness), or paralysis; and (5) pulselessness (pulse may be normal early on).
12. If compartment syndrome develops, pressure is relieved by removing the tightly fitting cast or performing a fasciotomy, a surgical procedure to relieve pressure within the compartment.
13. Complex regional pain syndrome (CRPS) is a complication of musculoskeletal injury leading to severe, diffuse, and burning extremity pain. The cause of CRPS is unclear; it may be due to nervous system damage or a disrupted healing or immune process.

POWERPOINT SLIDES

Tables and/or Figures
- **Box 42-2** Manifestations of Fractures
- **Box 42-3** Manifestations of Compartment Syndrome

SUGGESTIONS FOR CLASSROOM ACTIVITIES

- Assign students to each find an article about one or more common complications of fractures, their manifestations, and nursing strategies to prevent them. Have students each do a brief presentation on the pertinent information in their article.

SUGGESTIONS FOR CLINICAL ACTIVITIES

- Assign students to care for clients with musculoskeletal disorders. Have the students write about possible complications their client might experience, what to look for in assessing for these complications, and nursing strategies to prevent the complications. Discuss this information in preconference.

REFERENCE

- MedlinePlus: Compartment syndrome. Available at http://www.nlm.nih.gov/medlineplus/ency/article/001224.htm

14. In CRPS, pain increases with movement, is more severe than would be expected for the injury, and is accompanied by vasomotor changes that affect skin color and temperature.

15. The affected extremity in CRPS initially is red, warm, and edematous, later becoming cool and cyanotic. Over time, muscle wasting and skin and nail changes may occur.

16. When a bone breaks, fat globules can leave the bone marrow and enter the bloodstream. In the bloodstream, fat globules combine with platelets and travel to the brain, lungs, kidneys, and other organs, blocking small vessels and causing tissue ischemia.

17. Fat emboli occur when fat globules lodge in a pulmonary vessel or the peripheral circulation. Fracture of a long bone, the femur in particular, is the primary risk factor for fat emboli.

18. Manifestations of fat emboli usually develop within a few hours to a week after injury. The symptoms result from impaired blood flow to the tissues and from fatty acids in the circulation. Altered cerebral perfusion causes confusion and changes in level of consciousness. If pulmonary circulation is affected, chest pain and acute shortness of breath develop.

19. Manifestations of pulmonary edema and acute respiratory distress syndrome may occur. Normal clotting is disrupted, and petechiae develop on the skin and mucous membranes.

20. Deep venous thrombosis (DVT) is formation of a blood clot within a large vein. Risk factors for DVT include (1) venous stasis (decreased blood flow), (2) damage to blood vessels, and (3) altered blood clotting.

21. DVT usually affects vessels of the legs or pelvis. Clients who are immobilized for an extended time after a fracture are at particular risk for developing DVT.

22. The manifestations of DVT include swelling, leg pain, tenderness, or cramping; however, not all clients have symptoms. Clots can break loose, becoming emboli, which usually lodge in pulmonary blood vessels (pulmonary emboli) and cause chest pain and respiratory distress.

23. Delayed union is prolonged healing of bones beyond the expected time. Bone healing may be impaired by factors such as delayed fracture reduction, inadequate immobilization, infection, and age.

24. Delayed union may lead to nonunion with persistent pain and movement at the fracture site.

LEARNING OUTCOME 6

Discuss psychologic effects unique to amputation.

Concepts for Lecture

1. Regardless of the cause, amputation is devastating to the client.
2. The loss of a limb has significant physical and psychosocial effects on the client and family. Adapting to amputation may take a long time and significant effort.
3. Most amputees experience phantom limb sensations after surgery. These sensations include tingling, numbness, or itching of the amputated limb.
4. When phantom limb sensations are painful, they are called phantom limb pain.
5. Although the cause is unknown, phantom limb pain may be caused by trauma to the nerves serving the amputated part. The missing extremity feels crushed, trapped, twisted, or burning.

 **POWERPOINT SLIDES**

Tables and/or Figures
- **Box 42-10** Focus on Older Adults: Amputation

 **SUGGESTIONS FOR CLASSROOM ACTIVITIES**

- Invite two or three persons who have had amputations to come and speak to the class about their experiences with amputation, especially their experiences dealing with psychologic effects of amputation.

SUGGESTIONS FOR CLINICAL ACTIVITIES

- Assign students to work with clients in rehabilitation after amputation and to use therapeutic communication to find out about psychologic effects the clients are experiencing.

6. Management of phantom pain is challenging, often requiring referral to a pain clinic and a comprehensive pain management program.
7. The client with an amputation may experience grief over the loss of the amputated part.

LEARNING OUTCOME 7

Provide individualized nursing care for clients who have experienced musculoskeletal trauma.

Concepts for Lecture

1. Teaching measures to promote comfort, prevent further injury, and allow healing are the priorities for nursing care for the client with soft tissue trauma.
2. To assess soft tissue injury, the nurse collects both subjective and objective data. See Learning Objective 2 for assessment information.
3. A possible nursing diagnosis for soft tissue trauma is Acute Pain with a possible expected outcome that the client will use analgesic and nonanalgesic measures appropriate to manage comfort.
4. Nursing interventions for pain include instructing the client to rest the injured extremity; applying ice to the injury; maintaining compression dressing, such as an Ace bandage; elevating the extremity 1 inch above the heart; teaching the acronym RICE to remember when dealing with acute injury care (**r**est, **i**ce, **c**ompression, and **e**levation); if the pain continues after several days, instructing the client to apply heat; advising the client to take aspirin or NSAIDs on a regular basis with food; and instructing the client to use over-the-counter or prescribed analgesics to maintain comfort, preventing pain from becoming severe.
5. Another possible nursing diagnosis for a client with soft tissue injury is Impaired Physical Mobility. A possible expected outcome is that the client will demonstrate correct use of assistive devices.
6. Nursing interventions for Impaired Physical Mobility may include teaching correct use of crutches, canes, or slings if prescribed; reminding the client to rest the injured extremity; and encouraging follow-up with the primary care provider.
7. Evaluation of the effectiveness of nursing care for the client with soft tissue trauma involves assessing pain, safety when ambulating, and knowledge of home care.
8. Assessing the client who has a fracture involves obtaining information about the circumstances of the injury.
9. The nurse assesses pain in the injured extremity using a standard pain scale and the effectiveness of analgesia in relieving pain.
10. The nurse compares the quality of pulses in the affected limb to those of the unaffected limb and assesses sensations proximal and distal to the fracture. The nurse checks skin color and temperature in the extremity and assesses motion distal to the fracture site.
11. For nursing implications for specific fractures, see Table 42-2.
12. A nursing diagnosis for a client with a fracture is Acute Pain with a possible expected outcome that the client will report pain at a level of 3 or lower on a standard 0–10 pain scale.
13. Possible nursing interventions for a nursing diagnosis of Acute Pain for a client with a fracture include administering analgesics and NSAIDs, as ordered, on a regular basis to prevent intense pain; splinting and supporting the injured area; elevating the injured extremity above the heart; applying ice; moving gently and slowly; and

encouraging distraction and other adjunctive pain relief measures such as meditation and visualization.

14. A second nursing diagnosis for a client with a fracture is Impaired Physical Mobility, with a possible expected outcome that the client demonstrates correct use of exercises and assistive devices prior to discharge.

15. Nursing interventions for a nursing diagnosis of Impaired Physical Mobility may include assisting the client with active ROM exercises of the unaffected limbs and joints, teaching the client isometric exercises, and encouraging the exercises every 4 hours.

16. Interventions may also include encouraging ambulation when able, providing assistance as needed, reinforcing teaching and observing use of assistive devices, encouraging flexion and extension exercises of the lower extremities, turning the client on bed rest every 2 hours, and if in traction, teaching the client to shift weight hourly. The nurse also encourages frequent use of the incentive spirometer, deep breathing, and coughing.

17. Another nursing diagnosis for a client with a fracture is Risk for Ineffective Peripheral Tissue Perfusion, with a possible expected outcome that circulation will remain effective, as evidenced by normal temperature, color, and sensation of extremities.

18. Nursing interventions for a nursing diagnosis of Risk for Ineffective Peripheral Tissue Perfusion include performing CMS checks and assessing for the "5 Ps" (pain, pallor, pulse, paresthesias, and paresis) every 1 to 2 hours.

19. Nursing interventions also include assessing the cast for tightness and, if the cast is too tight, preparing to assist with bivalving; elevating the injured extremity above the heart; administering anticoagulants as ordered; and applying antiembolism stockings or pneumatic compression boots.

20. Evaluating the effectiveness of nursing care involves collecting data related to pain and the effectiveness of analgesia, safety and mobility, and tissue perfusion. The nurse also assesses learning and ability to safely use assistive devices as ordered.

21. Assessing a client with a hip fracture involves assessment before and after surgery.

22. The nurse monitors vital signs frequently and reports changes from baseline. The nurse assesses color, temperature, capillary refill, pulses, and movement and sensation of affected leg, comparing findings with the unaffected leg.

23. After surgery, the nurse assesses the wound for healing, drainage, and signs of infection or inflammation. The nurse promptly reports shortening and internal rotation of the affected leg, which could indicate dislocation of the affected hip.

24. A nursing diagnosis appropriate for a client with a hip fracture is Acute Pain, with a possible expected outcome that the client reports pain at a level of 3 or lower on a standard pain scale.

25. Nursing interventions include asking about location and nature of pain; asking the client to rate the pain using a standardized pain scale before and after any interventions; applying Buck's traction as ordered; administering analgesics as ordered; moving the client gently and slowly; and encouraging distraction, deep breathing, relaxation, and other adjunctive pain relief measures.

26. Another nursing diagnosis for a client with a hip fracture is Impaired Physical Mobility, with a possible expected outcome that the client demonstrates appropriate use of assistive devices with supervision.

27. Interventions for a nursing diagnosis of Impaired Physical Mobility include turning clients on bed rest at least every 2 hours; placing a

pillow or abductor splint between the legs when in bed and during turning; encouraging isometric exercises and flexion and extension exercises of the feet, ankles, elbows, shoulders, and knees every 4 hours; working with physical therapy to promote activities as allowed; assisting to a hip chair (reclining wheelchair) at the bedside; assisting and encouraging ambulation per physician's orders; applying antiembolism (TED) hose or pneumatic compression devices (PCDs) as ordered; administering anticoagulants as ordered; and monitoring for adverse effects (bleeding).

28. A third nursing diagnosis for a client with a hip fracture is Risk for Infection, with a possible expected outcome that the client remains free of infection.

29. Nursing interventions for a nursing diagnosis of Risk for Infection include using sterile technique for dressing changes; assessing wound color, healing, and the presence of any drainage; administering antibiotics as ordered; and promptly reporting any temperature elevation, tachycardia, or signs of wound infection to the physician.

30. Evaluation of the effectiveness of nursing care, for the client with a fractured hip, involves collecting data regarding level of pain and pain relief, ability to resume physical mobility, wound healing, and skin integrity.

31. Assessment of joint injuries involves inquiring about known trauma, circumstances of injury, or participation in at-risk activities; inquiring about pain, including location, character, timing, and activities or movements that aggravate or relieve the discomfort; and inquiring about any measures used to relieve pain and swelling.

32. The nurse examines the affected joint for tenderness, crepitus, temperature, and swelling. The nurse instructs or assists the client to move the joint through its normal range of motion, stopping and noting where pain is experienced. When a joint dislocation is suspected, the nurse assesses color, temperature, pulses, movement, and sensation of the limb distal to the affected joint.

33. A possible nursing diagnosis for joint pain is Acute Pain, with a possible expected outcome that the client will use analgesic and nonanalgesic measures appropriately to promote comfort and healing.

34. Nursing interventions for a nursing diagnosis of Acute Pain include teaching the client safe application of ice or heat to the affected joint as indicated; instructing the client about using NSAIDs as ordered; teaching the use of assistive devices such as a sling, crutches, or cane to reduce stress on the affected joint or minimize weight bearing; and instructing the client not to discontinue treatment abruptly.

35. Impaired Physical Mobility is another nursing diagnosis appropriate for the client with joint trauma, with an expected outcome that the client verbalizes an understanding of potential benefits of physical or occupational therapy.

36. Nursing interventions for a nursing diagnosis of Impaired Physical Mobility include referring the client to physical therapy for appropriate exercises and suggesting occupational therapy.

37. Evaluation of the effectiveness of nursing care for clients with joint injuries involves assessing their knowledge and understanding of the disorder and its treatment.

38. Assessing a client who has or will have an amputation includes asking about the mechanism of injury (as appropriate), current health status, and chronic diseases. The nurse inquires about pain, all current medications, and any known allergies.

39. When a nonemergent amputation is planned, the nurse explores the client's understanding of and responses to the planned procedure and its outcome.

40. The nurse assessing a client who has or will have an amputation obtains objective assessment data, focusing on cardiopulmonary status (vital signs, heart sounds, cardiac rhythm, and lung sounds), peripheral circulation (pulses, warmth, and capillary refill of extremities), and movement and sensation of extremities.

41. The nurse identifies any potential complications. Any significant change in vital signs is reported to the charge nurse or physician. Temperature is monitored every 4 hours. The nurse reports an output of less than 30 mL/hour and any pain unrelieved by analgesics or pain changes in location or character.

42. The nurse assesses wound and dressing, reporting excessive or bright red drainage that could indicate hemorrhage. The wound is monitored for healing, redness, swelling, purulent drainage, or evidence of a hematoma.

43. A nursing diagnosis for a client who has an amputation is Acute Pain, with a possible outcome that the client reports pain at a level of 3 or lower on a standard pain scale.

44. Nursing interventions for a nursing diagnosis of Acute Pain include administering analgesics as ordered; splinting and supporting injured areas; unless contraindicated, elevating the stump for 24 hours; frequently repositioning and turning the client slowly and gently; and encouraging distraction, meditation, deep breathing, and relaxation exercises.

45. A second nursing diagnosis for a client who has amputation is Risk for Infection, with an expected outcome that the client will remain free from signs of infection.

46. Nursing interventions for a nursing diagnosis of Risk for Infection include changing the wound dressing as ordered using aseptic technique; protecting the wound and dressing from contamination by urine or feces; administering antibiotics as ordered; teaching stump wrapping techniques; and reporting elevated WBC count.

47. Another possible nursing diagnosis for a client with amputation is Grieving, with a possible expected outcome that the client will express thoughts and feelings about loss of the limb and its function.

48. Interventions for a diagnosis of Grieving include encouraging verbalization of feelings, asking open-ended questions; maintaining eye contact and actively listening; reflecting on the client's feelings; and allowing unlimited visiting hours, if possible.

49. Another nursing diagnosis for a client with amputation is Disturbed Body Image, with a possible expected outcome that the client will acknowledge change in appearance and body function.

50. Interventions for a nursing diagnosis of Disturbed Body Image include allowing the client to wear clothing from home; encouraging the client to look at the stump; encouraging participation in stump care; offering visitation by another amputee; and encouraging active participation in rehabilitation.

51. Another nursing diagnosis for a client with amputation is Impaired Physical Mobility, with an expected outcome that the client will demonstrate correct use of prescribed exercises and assistive devices.

52. Nursing interventions for a diagnosis of Impaired Physical Mobility include performing ROM exercises on all joints; maintaining postoperative dress (rigid or compression); frequently turning and repositioning the client; and placing the client with a lower extremity amputation in the prone position every 4 hours.

53. To evaluate the effectiveness of nursing care for the client with an amputation, the nurse assesses pain and the effectiveness of relief measures. The nurse notes the presence or absence of wound infection or a complication such as pneumonia. The evaluation also

includes noting the client's and family's response to the wound and the loss of a body part. The nurse assesses physical mobility and participation in physical therapy.

General Chapter Considerations

1. Have students study and learn key terms listed at the beginning of the chapter.
2. Have students complete end of chapter exercises either in their book or on the MyNursingKit Website.
3. Use the Classroom Response Question PowerPoints to assess students prior to lecture.

• Clinical Reasoning Care Map

MyNursingKit (www.mynursingkit.com)

• Websites
• NCLEX® Questions
• Case Studies
• Key Terms

Student Workbook and Resource Guide

• Chapter 42 activities
• *Separate purchase*

Prentice Hall Nurse's Drug Guide

• *Separate purchase*

Classroom Response Question PowerPoints

Testbank

CHAPTER 43
CARING FOR CLIENTS WITH MUSCULOSKELETAL DISORDERS

LEARNING OUTCOME 1

Relate the effects of common musculoskeletal disorders to the normal structure and function of the musculoskeletal system.

Concepts for Lecture

1. Osteoporosis is a bone disorder in which bone mass is lost, which weakens its structure, increasing the risk of fracture. Bone loss affects primarily spongy bone, so clients with osteoporosis are at particular risk for fractures of the spine and the neck of the femur.
2. Paget's disease is a progressive disorder characterized by fragile mis-shapen bones. In Paget's disease the activity of osteoclasts (cells that break down and resorb bone) increases in one or more bones, stimulating activity in osteoblasts (cells that make new bone) to replace lost bone. The new bone formed is structurally abnormal, so it is soft, weak, and prone to fractures.
3. In osteomalacia, insufficient amounts of calcium or phosphate are available, so the bone does not harden normally, is deformed, and is unable to bear weight. Pathologic fractures occur.
4. Osteomyelitis is an infection of the bone. In the infection-fighting process, eventually there is necrosis of bone tissue. Instead of normal weight bearing, there is now limited weight bearing. A surgical wound or fracture that does not heal may be the initial sign of osteomyelitis.
5. Primary tumors cause bone breakdown (osteolysis), which weakens the bone, resulting in fractures.
6. Malignant bone tumors invade and destroy adjacent bone tissue. Benign bone tumors, unlike malignant ones, have a symmetric, controlled growth pattern. As they grow, they push against neighboring bone tissue, weakening the bone's structure.
7. Hallux valgus and hammertoe are common foot disorders that cause pain or difficulty walking.
8. In hallux valgus, the toe bends away from the midline of the body, the metatarsophalangeal (MTP) joint becomes enlarged, and calluses develop over the joint.
9. Hammertoe may affect any toe, but the second toe is usually affected. The flexed proximal interphalangeal (PIP) joint rubs against the shoe, causing painful corns to develop (Figure 43-3B).
10. Osteoarthritis (OA) is a degenerative joint disease characterized by progressive loss of joint cartilage to synovial joints. OA affects the entire joint: the cartilage, bone, synovial membrane, and the ligaments, muscles, and tendons that surround the joint.
11. The joint cartilage loses its strength and elasticity and is gradually destroyed. As the cartilage erodes and ulcerates, the underlying bone is exposed. The bone thickens in exposed areas, and cysts develop.
12. Cartilage-coated osteophytes (bony outgrowths) change the anatomy of the joint. As these spurs or projections enlarge, small pieces may break off, leading to mild inflammation of the joint.
13. Rheumatoid arthritis (RA) is a chronic systemic inflammatory disorder that primarily affects the joints. Inflammation affects the joints and surrounding tissues.

POWERPOINT SLIDES

Tables and/or Figures
- **Figure 43-2** Osteomyelitis
- **Table 43-3** Primary Bone Tumors
- **Figure 43-3A** Hallux Valgus
- **Figure 43-3B** Hammertoe
- **Figure 43-7** Joint Inflammation and Destruction in Rheumatoid Arthritis

SUGGESTIONS FOR CLASSROOM ACTIVITIES
- Show pictures/illustrations of normal feet/toes and contrasting pictures of hallux valgus and hammertoe.
- Show pictures/illustrations of normal skin and a contrasting picture of erythema migrans.

SUGGESTIONS FOR CLINICAL ACTIVITIES
- Assign students to care for two clients, one with a musculoskeletal disorder and one without, in order to contrast the manifestations of a musculoskeletal disorder against the normal structure and function. Have students discuss their observations and data collection in postconference.

REFERENCES
- National Institute of Arthritis and Musculoskeletal and Skin Disorders: Osteoporosis overview. Available at http://www.niams.nih.gov/Health_Info/Bone/Osteoporosis/default.asp
- National Institute of Arthritis and Musculoskeletal and Skin Disorders: Osteoporosis in men. Available at http://www.niams.nih.gov/Health_Info/Bone/Osteoporosis/men.asp
- National Institute of Arthritis and Musculoskeletal and Skin Disorders: Paget's bone disease. Available at http://www.niams.nih.gov/Health_Info/Bone/Pagets/default.asp

14. In systemic lupus erythematosus (SLE), there is an inflammatory response that damages the tissues. There can be damage to the kidneys, musculoskeletal system, brain, heart, spleen, lung, GI tract, skin, and peritoneum.

15. Gout is a metabolic disorder that involves the accumulation of urate crystals in joints and surrounding tissues.

16. Uric acid is the breakdown product of purine metabolism. Crystals tend to form in peripheral tissues of the body. Unless treated, gout may progress from asymptomatic hyperuricemia, with high serum uric acid levels but no symptoms, to acute gouty arthritis.

17. Lyme disease is an inflammatory disorder usually spread by ticks. It may spread via lymph or blood to other skin sites, nodes, or organs. As Lyme disease spreads, secondary skin lesions develop, as do migratory musculoskeletal symptoms. If untreated, the client may develop chronic arthritis, myocarditis, meningitis, encephalitis, and other neurologic manifestations.

18. Ankylosing spondylitis is a chronic inflammatory arthritis that primarily affects the spine, causing pain and progressive stiffening.

19. Fibromyalgia is a common rheumatic syndrome of musculoskeletal pain, stiffness, and tenderness. The pain of fibromyalgia may be localized or involve the entire body.

20. In general, there are five types of low back pain: (1) local pain often caused by fractures, strains, or sprains or tumors pressing on pain-sensitive structures; (2) referred pain caused by disorders of organs in the abdomen or pelvis; (3) pain of spinal origin associated with pathology of the spine; (4) radicular back pain radiating from the back to the leg along a nerve root; and (5) muscle spasm pain associated with many spine disorders.

LEARNING OUTCOME 2

Identify manifestations of impaired musculoskeletal function.

Concepts for Lecture

1. Osteoporosis is often asymptomatic. When present, its usual manifestations are loss of height, progressive curvature of the spine, low back pain, and fractures.

2. Height is lost in osteoporosis as vertebral bodies collapse. Characteristic dorsal kyphosis and cervical lordosis develop, causing the "dowager's hump" often associated with aging. The abdomen tends to protrude, and knees and hips flex as the body attempts to maintain its center of gravity.

3. A fracture may be the first obvious sign of osteoporosis. Some fractures are spontaneous. Others may result from everyday activities. These are known as pathologic fractures, fractures that occur with minimal or no trauma.

4. The manifestations of Paget's disease include bone pain, deformity, pathologic fractures, chalk-stick fractures of lower extremities, compression fractures, kyphosis, and loss of height.

5. The manifestations of osteomalacia include bone pain, difficulty changing positions (lying to sitting and sitting to standing), muscle weakness, waddling gait, dorsal kyphosis, and pathologic fractures.

6. Manifestations of osteomyelitis include chills and fever; general malaise; fatigue; pain in the affected limb; limited weight bearing in extremity; redness, swelling, heat, and tenderness over site; purulent wound drainage; and slowed healing.

7. Manifestations of bone tumors include deep bone pain that is worse at night and at rest; redness, warmth, and swelling over the affected

POWERPOINT SLIDES

Tables and/or Figures
- **Box 43-4** Manifestations of Paget's Disease and Osteomalacia
- **Box 43-6** Manifestations of Osteomyelitis
- **Box 43-7** Manifestations of Bone Tumors
- **Box 43-8** Manifestations of Osteoarthritis
- **Box 43-11** Manifestations of Rheumatoid Arthritis
- **Figure 43-9** Butterfly Rash of Systemic Lupus Erythematosus
- **Figure 43-10** The Multisystem Effects of Systemic Lupus Erythematosus

Nursing Care Plan: Client With Rheumatoid Arthritis

SUGGESTIONS FOR CLASSROOM ACTIVITIES
- Develop a matching practice quiz of manifestations to match with disorders of the musculoskeletal system.

SUGGESTIONS FOR CLINICAL ACTIVITIES
- Assign students to work with clients who have various disorders of the musculoskeletal system. Ask students to take a history from the clients of their symptomatology and to gather data on their client's current manifestations. Ask students to compare their client's

bone; enlarging mass over affected bone; muscle weakness or atrophy; and fever.

8. Manifestations of hallux valgus are complaint of pain and difficulty fitting into shoes.

9. The manifestations of hammertoe include painful corns.

10. The onset of osteoarthritis (OA) is usually gradual and insidious, and the course is slowly progressive.

11. Localized deep aching joint pain (arthralgia) is the most common symptom of OA. Pain is aggravated by use and relieved by rest. Following periods of immobility (e.g., on awakening in the morning or after an automobile ride), involved joints may stiffen. Range of motion of the joint decreases as the disease progresses, and grating or crepitus may be noted during movement.

12. Bony overgrowth in OA may cause joint enlargement. Enlarged joints are characteristically bony hard and cool on palpation.

13. Manifestations of osteoarthritis include Heberden's nodes on distal interphalangeal (DIP) joints and Bouchard's nodes on PIP joints.

14. Manifestations of rheumatoid arthritis include swelling, warmth, tenderness, and pain usually affecting PIP and metacarpophalangeal (MCP) joints of fingers, wrists, knees, ankles, and toes; limited range of motion; morning stiffness lasting more than 1 hour; and joint destruction and deformity including swan-neck deformity, boutonniere deformity, ulnar deviation and subluxation of MCP joints, carpal tunnel syndrome, and hallux valgus and hammertoe deformities of the foot.

15. Systemic manifestations of rheumatoid arthritis include fatigue, weakness, anorexia, weight loss, low-grade fever, anemia, and rheumatoid nodules.

16. Early in the disease, the manifestations of systemic lupus erythematosus (SLE) mimic those of rheumatoid arthritis, including fever, anorexia, malaise, weight loss, and joint pain, inflammation, and stiffness. Skin manifestations in SLE include the characteristic red butterfly rash across the cheeks and the bridge of the nose. Many clients with SLE are photosensitive. A diffuse rash on the skin exposed to the sun is common. Because SLE affects many body systems, its manifestations can be diverse.

17. The course of SLE is mild and chronic in most clients, with periods of remission and exacerbations. The number and severity of exacerbations tend to decrease with time. Clients tend to have difficulty carrying a pregnancy to term and an increased risk for infections.

18. Unless treated, gout may progress from asymptomatic hyperuricemia, with high serum uric acid levels but no symptoms, to acute gouty arthritis. The acute attack in gout, usually affecting a single joint, occurs unexpectedly, often beginning at night. About half of initial attacks are in the joint of the great toe. The affected joint becomes red, hot, swollen, and exquisitely painful and tender. The client with gout may have fever, chills, and general malaise last days to weeks.

19. In chronic tophaceous gout, deposits of urate crystals known as tophi develop in cartilage, synovial membranes, tendons, and soft tissues. Tophi may be seen in the helix of the ear and on the extremities. The skin over tophi may ulcerate.

20. In Lyme disease, there is an incubation period of up to 30 days after the tick bite. After this period, the lesion migrates outward in the skin, forming a characteristic lesion called erythema migrans, which may spread via lymph or blood to other skin sites, nodes, or organs. The erythema migrans is the initial manifestation of Lyme disease. This flat or slightly raised red lesion at the site of the tick bite expands over several days (up to a diameter of 50 cm) with the central area clearing as it expands.

21. Systemic symptoms of Lyme disease such as fatigue, malaise, fever, chills, and muscle pain often accompany the initial lesion. As the disease

manifestations with the manifestations described in the textbook. Provide the students with a two-column form with columns labeled "Textbook Picture" and "My Client." Have students present their work in postconference or in class.

- Collect work from all the students as described above and put it in a notebook for sharing or put the work on display on a bulletin board.

REFERENCE

- MedlinePlus: Ankylosing spondylitis. Available at http://www.nlm.nih.gov/medlineplus/ency/article/000420.htm

spreads, secondary skin lesions develop, as do migratory musculoskeletal symptoms, including muscle and joint pain and tendonitis. Headache and stiff neck are common.

22. The onset of ankylosing spondylitis is usually insidious. Clients may complain of persistent or intermittent bouts of low back pain. The pain is worse at night, followed by morning stiffness that is relieved by activity. Pain may radiate to the buttocks, hips, or down the legs.

23. As the disease of ankylosing spondylitis progresses, back motion is limited, the lumbar curve is lost, and the thoracic curvature is accentuated. In severe cases, the entire spine is fused, preventing any motion. Clients with ankylosing spondylitis may also develop arthritis in other joints, primarily the hip, shoulders, and knees.

24. Systemic manifestations of ankylosing spondylitis include anorexia, weight loss, fever, and fatigue. Many clients develop uveitis, inflammation of the iris and the middle vascular layer of the eye.

25. Fibromyalgia typically has a gradual onset of chronic, achy muscle pain. The pain may be localized or involve the entire body. The neck, shoulders, lower back, and hips are often affected. Tenderness is present, usually in small localized trigger points. Local tightness or muscle spasm may also occur.

26. Systemic manifestations of fibromyalgia include fatigue, sleep disruptions, headaches, and an irritable bowel. Pain and fatigue are aggravated by exertion.

27. Low back pain varies with the type of pain associated with the cause of the pain. It is often caused by fractures, strains, or sprains or tumors pressing on sensitive structures.

28. Referred pain is caused by disorders of various organs in other locations in the body.

29. Pain of spinal origin is associated with pathology of the spine.

30. Radicular back pain radiates from the back to the leg along a nerve root. It is sharp pain that may be aggravated by movement, such as coughing, sneezing, or sitting.

31. Muscle spasm pain is associated with many spine disorders. This type of pain is dull and may be accompanied by abnormal posture and taut spinal muscles.

32. Low back pain may range from mild discomfort lasting a few hours to chronic, debilitating pain.

LEARNING OUTCOME 3

Describe the pathophysiology of common musculoskeletal disorders.

Concepts for Lecture

1. Osteoporosis, literally defined as "porous bones," is a bone disorder in which bone mass is lost. Bone is constantly being remodeled over a person's lifetime, with old bone being replaced by new bone. In osteoporosis, more bone is lost than is gained, and bone mass is lost. In women, bone loss accelerates during menopause, slowing after age 60. Men also lose bone mass with aging, although the rate of loss is slower than it is in women. Bone loss affects primarily spongy bones.

2. In Paget's disease, the activity of osteoclasts (which break down and resorb bone) increases in one or more bones, stimulating activity in osteoblasts (cells that form new bone) to replace lost bone. The new bone formed is fragile, misshapen, soft, weak, and prone to fractures.

3. Paget's disease commonly affects the femur, tibia, pelvis, vertebrae, and skull, although any bone can be affected. Involved bones enlarge and become deformed.

POWERPOINT SLIDES

Tables and/or Figures
- **Figure 43-3A** Hallux Valgus
- **Figure 43-3B** Hammertoe

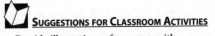

SUGGESTIONS FOR CLASSROOM ACTIVITIES
- Provide illustrations of a person with advanced osteoporosis and one without osteoporosis so students can see the differences.
- Have students interview elderly people about their diet, calcium supplements, history of bone density testing, and any loss of height they have experienced. Have students report their findings.
- Encourage students to discuss how knowing about the pathology of osteoporosis might affect their own health behaviors (e.g., will they get bone density testing or will they start taking calcium supplements with vitamin D).

4. Osteomalacia (adult rickets) results from inadequate mineralization of bone. When insufficient amounts of calcium or phosphate are available, the bone does not harden normally and is unable to bear weight. The weight-bearing bones are deformed, and pathologic fractures can occur.

5. Osteomalacia is commonly caused by a lack of vitamin D. Vitamin D, obtained from certain foods and ultraviolet radiation from the sun, is necessary to maintain calcium and phosphate levels in the body. Inadequate intake and/or impaired absorption (e.g., related to gastrectomy) are risk factors for osteomalacia, as are chronic kidney or liver disease.

6. Osteomyelitis is an infection of the bone. Pathogens usually enter the bone through an open wound, such as an open fracture or a gunshot or puncture wound. Bacteria also may spread to the bone from a local tissue infection. After entry, bacteria lodge and multiply in the bone, causing an inflammatory and immune system response. Phagocytes attempt to contain the infection. In the process, they release enzymes that destroy bone tissue; however, pus forms, followed by edema and vascular congestion.

7. Canals in the marrow cavity of the bone allow the infection to spread to other parts of the bone. If the infection reaches the outer margin of the bone (Figure 43-2), it raises the periosteum of the bone and spreads along the surface. Pus and edema disrupt the blood supply to the bone, leading to ischemia and, eventually, necrosis of the bone. Blood and antibiotics cannot reach the bone tissue, making it difficult to treat the infection. The diagnosis of osteomyelitis often is not made until the infection has become chronic.

8. Primary bone tumors are classified by the tissue from which they arise: bone (osteogenic), cartilage (chondrogenic), collagen (collagenic), and bone marrow (myelogenic).

9. Primary tumors cause bone breakdown (osteolysis), which weakens the bone, resulting in fractures.

10. Malignant bone tumors invade and destroy adjacent bone tissue by producing substances that promote bone resorption or by interfering with a bone's blood supply.

11. Benign bone tumors grow in a symmetric, controlled pattern. As they grow, they push against neighboring bone tissue. This weakens the bone's structure until it is unable to withstand the stress of ordinary use and frequently causes pathologic fracture.

12. Hallux valgus, or bunion, is enlargement and lateral displacement of the great toe (Figure 43-3A), which develops due to chronic pressure against the great toe. The toe bends away from the midline of the body, and the metatarsophalangeal (MTP) joint becomes enlarged. Calluses develop over the joint.

13. Heredity and joint disorders contribute to hallux valgus, as does wearing pointed, narrow-toed shoes or high heels.

14. Hammertoe (claw toe)—a deformity of the toe characterized by flexion of the proximal interphalangeal (PIP) joint with hyperextension of the middle interphalangeal (MIP) and distal interphalangeal (DIP) joints—may affect any toe, but the second toe is usually affected. The flexed PIP joint rubs against the shoe, causing painful corns to develop (Figure 43-3B).

15. Osteoarthritis (OA) is a degenerative joint disease characterized by progressive loss of joint cartilage to synovial joints. OA affects the entire joint: the cartilage, bone, synovial membrane, and ligaments, muscles, and tendons that surround the joint.

16. In OA, the joint cartilage loses its strength and elasticity and is gradually destroyed. As the cartilage erodes and ulcerates, the underlying bone is exposed. The bone thickens in exposed areas, and cysts develop. Cartilage-coated osteophytes (bony outgrowths) change the

SUGGESTIONS FOR CLINICAL ACTIVITIES

• Assign students to work with clients who have osteoporosis so they can gather data on the pathologic changes and compare their client's experience with the information in the textbook about osteoporosis.

anatomy of the joint. As these spurs or projections enlarge, small pieces may break off, leading to mild inflammation of the joint.

17. In rheumatoid arthritis, an abnormal immune response is initiated by an unknown trigger. Genetic factors are known to contribute.

18. In the abnormal immune response of RA, IgG, an immunoglobin, is produced. The body sees this as a foreign substance and produces antibodies to the IgG. These autoantibodies, known as rheumatoid factors, bind with the IgG to form immune complexes.

19. Compliment and other immune factors are activated in RA, and a variety of white blood cells are attracted to the area. These cells phagocytize (destroy) immune complexes. In the process, they release enzymes that destroy joint tissue. The resulting inflammation affects the joints and surrounding tissues. Joint tissue is destroyed by an extensive network of new blood vessels (vascular tissue known as pannus) in the synovial membrane. Pannus erodes the cartilage and bone of affected joints and invades surrounding tissues, including ligaments and tendons (Figure 43-7).

20. In systemic lupus erythematosus (SLE), autoantibodies are produced that target normal body cells and cell components such as DNA, blood cells, and proteins involved in normal coagulation. These autoantibodies react with their antigens to form immune complexes. These complexes are then deposited in the connective tissue of blood vessels, lymphatic vessels, and other tissues. This causes an inflammatory response that damages the tissues.

21. In SLE, immune complexes frequently are deposited in and damage the kidneys. Other affected tissues include the musculoskeletal system, brain, heart, spleen, lung, GI tract, skin, and peritoneum.

22. Gout is a metabolic disorder that involves the accumulation of urate crystals in joints and surrounding tissues. Uric acid is the breakdown product of purine metabolism. Normally uric acid production and excretion are balanced, with most of what is produced each day excreted via the kidneys and the rest in the feces. The serum uric acid level is normally between 3.5 and 8.0 mg/dL.

23. At levels greater than 8.0 mg/dL, urate crystals may form, often in peripheral tissues of the body, where lower temperatures exist.

24. Unless treated, gout may progress from asymptomatic hyperuricemia to acute gouty arthritis. The acute attack of gout usually affects a single joint and occurs unexpectedly often at night. About half the initial attacks are in the joint of the great toe. Attacks last from days to several weeks and typically subside spontaneously. The interval between acute attacks is called the intercritical period. It may last years, although most people have another acute attack within 1 year.

25. In chronic tophaceous gout, deposits of urate crystals known as tophi develop in cartilage, synovial membranes, tendons, and soft tissues. Tophi may be seen in the helix of the ear and on the extremities. The skin over tophi may ulcerate. Tophi can also develop in the tissues of the heart and spinal epidural. In some cases, uric acid stones may form in the kidney.

26. Lyme disease is an inflammatory disorder caused by a spirochete, *Borrelia burgdorferi*, which is usually spread by ticks. *Borrelia burgdorferi* incubates for up to 30 days, then migrates outward in the skin, forming a characteristic lesion called erythema migrans (bullseye) that may reach 50 cm in diameter, clearing from the center as it expands. It may spread via lymph or blood to other skin sites, nodes, or organs, with secondary skin lesions developing along with migratory musculoskeletal symptoms. If untreated, the client may develop chronic arthritis, myocarditis, meningitis, encephalitis, and other neurologic manifestations.

27. Ankylosing spondylitis is a chronic inflammatory arthritis that primarily affects the spine, causing pain and progressive stiffening.

The cause of ankylosing spondylitis is unknown. Heredity plays a role in its development.

28. Fibromyalgia is a common rheumatic syndrome of musculoskeletal pain, stiffness, and tenderness. It may be precipitated or aggravated by stress, sleep disorders, trauma, or depression. The pain of fibromyalgia may be localized or involve the entire body. This disorder may resolve spontaneously or become chronic and recurrent.

29. Acute or chronic low back pain usually is due to strains in the muscles and tendons of the back caused by abdominal stress or overuse.

30. In general, there are five types of back pain: local pain often caused by fractures, strains, or sprains or tumors pressing on pain sensitive structures; referred pain caused by disorders of organs in the abdomen or pelvis; pain of spinal origin associated with pathology of the spine; radicular back pain radiating from the back to the leg along a nerve root; and muscle spasm pain associated with many spine disorders.

LEARNING OUTCOME 4

Discuss interdisciplinary care for clients with musculoskeletal disorders

Concepts for Lecture

1. The care of the client with osteoporosis focuses on stopping or slowing the process, relieving the symptoms, and preventing complications. Proper nutrition and exercise are important components of treatment for osteoporosis.

2. Bone mineral density (BMD) measurements can help predict the risk for fracture. X-rays may not show osteoporotic changes until more than 30% of the bone is lost. All women age 65 and older and men age 70 and older should undergo BMD testing. Testing should be done earlier if the client has risk factors such as a family history of osteoporosis, low body weight, or a prior fracture with minimal trauma.

3. Treatment goals for clients with Paget's disease are to manage and minimize symptoms, improve function, and slow the disease progress to limit disability. Diagnostic testing involves obtaining serum alkaline phosphatase levels, x-rays of involved bones, and a bone scan.

4. Bisphosphonates are prescribed for clients with Paget's disease to suppress bone resorption and prevent fractures. Calcitonin may be ordered for clients who are unable to tolerate bisphosphonates. Acetaminophen or an NSAID is often used to help relieve bone pain. Some clients with Paget's disease may eventually need surgery to repair fractures or replace affected joints.

5. Bone x-rays and laboratory tests are used to diagnose osteomalacia. X-ray shows the effects of bone demineralization. Serum calcium levels may be low or normal; alkaline phosphatase usually is elevated.

6. Treatment focuses on correcting the underlying cause and ensuring adequate vitamin D, calcium, and phosphate intake. Clients with osteomalacia often are placed on vitamin D supplements. Calcium and phosphate supplements also may be ordered. Drugs such as bisphosphonates and calcitonin are used along with calcium supplements for clients with osteomalacia.

7. Early diagnosis and treatment of osteomyelitis with antibiotic therapy are important to prevent bone necrosis. Diagnostic tests used in diagnosis of osteomyelitis include WBC and erythrocyte sedimentation rate, which are elevated in osteomyelitis; blood and tissue cultures to identify the infecting organism; magnetic resonance imaging (MRI),

POWERPOINT SLIDES

Tables and/or Figures
- **Box 43-9** Complementary Therapies: Osteoarthritis

SUGGESTIONS FOR CLASSROOM ACTIVITIES
- Invite professionals from the x-ray department, lab, surgery, and physical therapy to talk with the class about interdisciplinary care of clients with musculoskeletal disorders.

SUGGESTIONS FOR CLINICAL ACTIVITIES
- Assign students to care for clients with musculoskeletal disorders. Ask students to observe and make note of all the disciplines that care for the client and what roles various disciplines play in the care of the client.

computed tomography (CT) scan, or ultrasound to identify the infection site; and a bone scan to identify active infection.

8. In diagnosing tumors, the diagnosis may be delayed because symptoms are vague. Laboratory testing often shows elevated serum alkaline phosphatase and calcium levels, as well as a high red blood cell count. Diagnostic tests to identify the tumor location and extent of bone and surrounding tissue involvement include x-rays, CT, and MRI scans. A biopsy is performed to identify the type of tumor cells.

9. Malignant bone tumors are treated with a combination of surgery, chemotherapy, and radiation therapy. Whenever possible, surgery is performed to remove the tumor. The tumor may be excised, or the affected limb may be amputated. To avoid amputation, a bone graft from a cadaver or metal prostheses often is used to replace missing bone.

10. Chemotherapeutic drugs are given to shrink the tumor before surgery, to prevent recurrence after surgery, or to treat tumor metastasis. Radiation therapy may be used in combination with chemotherapy. After surgery, it is used to eradicate any remaining tumor cells. Radiation therapy also is frequently used to control pain in metastatic bone lesions.

11. Corrective shoes are often ordered for clients with foot disorders. Orthopedic devices that cushion and stretch the affected joints may be placed within shoes or between the toes.

12. Analgesics may be ordered or corticosteroid drugs may be injected into the affected joints of people with foot disorders to relieve acute inflammation.

13. A bunionectomy may be done to treat hallux valgus. Surgery may be done to correct hammertoe.

14. The diagnosis of OA is based on the history and on physical and x-ray examination of affected joints. Initially, the joint space narrows. As the disease progresses, bone density increases, osteophytes are seen at the joint periphery, and bone cysts may be noted.

15. Clients with OA are encouraged to lose weight if obese and to remain physically active. Exercise helps maintain muscle tone and joint support and promotes weight loss. Exercise in water (non–weight bearing) may help clients with OA of the knees or hips.

16. Heat applied locally to affected joints can relieve discomfort (see Box 43-9 for complementary therapies that may be beneficial for clients with OA).

17. The diagnosis of rheumatoid arthritis is based on the history, physical exam, and diagnostic tests. Diagnostic tests for RA include rheumatoid factors, which are present in most people with RA; ESR, which is typically elevated, often markedly so; analysis of synovial fluid aspirated from inflamed joints; and x-ray of affected joints, which shows characteristic joint changes as the disease progresses.

18. There currently is no cure for RA. Treatment goals are to relieve symptoms, stop or reduce joint destruction, and maintain function.

19. A multidisciplinary approach to treatment of RA is used, with a balance of rest, exercise, physical therapy, and treatments to modify the disease process. For the older client, less emphasis may be placed on preventing joint deformity and more emphasis on maintaining function.

20. The diagnosis of systemic lupus erythematosus (SLE) is based on history and physical examination.

21. Diagnostic tests for SLE include anti-DNA antibody testing, which may not be positive in many clients with SLE; C-reactive protein (CRP) levels, which are elevated during acute exacerbations; erythrocyte sedimentation rate (ESR), which is often elevated in SLE; and CBC, which shows anemia and low RBC, WBC, and platelet counts. Urinalysis and renal function studies such as serum creatinine and blood urea nitrogen may be ordered to assess for kidney damage.

22. The classic presentation of acute gout is so distinctive that the diagnosis often is based on the laboratory and physical exam. Serum uric acid is nearly always elevated, usually about 8.5 mg/dL. Fluid aspirated from the inflamed joint shows typical needle-shaped urate crystals.

23. A number of antibiotics may be used to treat Lyme disease. Treatment may be continued for up to 1 month to ensure that the organism has been eradicated. Aspirin or another NSAID may be prescribed to relieve arthritic symptoms of Lyme disease. The affected joint may be splinted to rest the joint. When the knee is involved, weight bearing may be restricted and the client instructed to use crutches.

24. In ankylosing spondylitis, physical therapy and daily exercises are important to maintain posture and joint range of motion. NSAIDs relieve pain and stiffness and allow the client to perform necessary exercises.

25. Low back pain usually is diagnosed by the history and physical examination. X-rays, CT scan, and MRI are ordered only when a potentially serious underlying condition is suspected.

26. Most clients with acute low back pain need only short-term treatment. Ice packs or ice massage can be applied or rubbed over the painful area for 15 minutes every hour or more. Moist warm towels or a heating pad can be used as an alternative to ice therapy.

27. Prolonged rest is not recommended for low back pain. Increased activity helps to restore function and may increase endorphin levels. Exercise is initiated and increased gradually. Physical therapy frequently is used in combination with exercise. Diathermy (deep heat therapy), ultrasonography, hydrotherapy, and transcutaneous electrical nerve stimulation (TENS) units may be used to reduce the muscle spasm and relieve pain. Other treatments for low back pain include chiropractic manipulation of the spine to reduce spasms and pain.

28. Low back pain often can be managed with NSAIDs and analgesics. Muscle relaxants may be ordered. For intense intractable pain, a steroid solution may be injected into the epidermal space. This helps decrease the swelling and inflammation of the spinal nerves.

LEARNING OUTCOME 5

Provide individualized nursing care for clients with musculoskeletal disorders.

Concepts for Lecture

1. When assessing the client with osteoporosis, ask about known risk factors for osteoporosis, age of menopause, usual activity level, and history of previous fractures or back pain. Measure the client's height, compare the height with the height in early adulthood, and observe for spinal curvature.

2. A possible nursing diagnosis for a client with osteoporosis is Imbalanced Nutrition: Less than Body Requirements, with a possible expected outcome that the client verbalizes ways to increase calcium intake to recommended levels. Nursing interventions may include teaching the client about the recommended calcium intake for their age (Table 43-1); providing a list of foods high in calcium (Box 43-3) and helping identify ways to include these foods in the diet; and teaching clients using calcium supplements to take calcium carbonate supplement 30–60 minutes before meals to prevent GI distress.

3. Another possible nursing diagnosis for the client with osteoporosis is Risk for Injury, with a possible outcome that the client will remain free of injury. Nursing interventions for Risk for Injury include assessing the environment for safety hazards; advising the client to use the

POWERPOINT SLIDES

Tables and/or Figures
- **Table 43-1** Recommended Daily Calcium Intake
- **Box 43-3** Foods High in Calcium

SUGGESTIONS FOR CLASSROOM ACTIVITIES
- Have students break into small groups to discuss care of clients with one or more of the musculoskeletal disorders. Students can design a care plan addressing what they would assess and creating a hypothetical client and a hypothetical set of data. Based on their findings, they can write nursing diagnoses, expected outcomes, and nursing interventions and describe what they would evaluate.

SUGGESTIONS FOR CLINICAL ACTIVITIES
- Assign students to care for a client with a musculoskeletal disorder and have the students write an individualized care plan for their client.

handrail on stairways and to take precautions when walking on slippery surfaces; keeping the bed in low position and using side rails if indicated to prevent the client from getting up alone; avoiding restraints if at all possible; encouraging weight-bearing exercises for 30–40 minutes at least four times a week; encouraging older adults to use assistive devices as needed; teaching older clients about safety and fall precautions; evaluating medication regimen for drugs that may increase the risk of falling (some antihypertensives, antianxiety agents, antihistamines, or sedatives); and teaching about the safe use of prescribed medications.

4. Clients with osteoporosis may also have a nursing diagnosis of Pain, with an expected outcome that the client reports pain at a level of 3 or lower on a standard 0–10 pain scale. Nursing interventions may include assessing acute or new complaints of pain; giving acetaminophen or anti-inflammatory drugs as indicated for pain; applying heat to the painful area, being careful to avoid burning the client; and assisting physical therapy to plan an exercise regimen.

5. Evaluating the nursing care of a client with osteoporosis includes evaluating the client's knowledge and understanding of fall and injury prevention measures; having the client verbalize about incorporating calcium-rich foods into the diet; and asking the client to restate drug safety measures and adverse effects to be reported to the physician.

6. The nurse's role in caring for a client with Paget's disease includes teaching about the disorder, managing chronic pain, teaching how to take NSAIDs, and discussing measures to maintain mobility and safety, including use of assistive devices as recommended.

7. Nursing care for clients with osteomalacia is similar to that provided for clients with osteoporosis. It is important to teach older adults how to get enough calcium, vitamin D, and exercise and how to prevent falls.

8. Priorities of nursing for the client with osteomyelitis focus on preventing further infection, maintaining comfort, limiting immobility, and addressing emotional responses to the disease.

9. One nursing diagnosis for a client with osteomyelitis is Risk for Infection, with a possible expected outcome that the infection remains limited to affected bone, with no evidence of extension. Nursing interventions include using sterile technique when caring for the dressing and irrigation setup, assessing for manifestations of further infection, administering prescribed antibiotics at specified times, and maintaining optimal calorie and protein intake.

10. Another nursing diagnosis for a client with osteomyelitis is Pain, with a possible expected outcome that the client reports pain at a level of 3 or lower on a standard pain scale of 0–10. Nursing interventions for pain include frequently assessing level of pain using a standard pain scale; assessing effectiveness of prescribed analgesics; reporting pain that is not adequately relieved or that changes in character or location; providing analgesics on a scheduled basis over 24 hours rather than as needed; offering analgesics 20 to 30 minutes prior to tests, procedures, or exercises; splinting or immobilizing the affected extremity; using adjunctive strategies (e.g., distraction, relaxation) for pain management; providing assistive devices; and handling the affected area gently.

11. Another nursing diagnosis for a client with osteomyelitis is Hyperthermia, with a possible expected outcome that the client will report early signs of elevated temperature. Nursing interventions for Hyperthermia include monitoring temperature every 4 hours and during periods of chilling, and reporting fever to the charge nurse or physician.

12. Impaired Physical Mobility is a nursing diagnosis for osteomyelitis. A possible expected outcome is that the client will use assistive devices as needed to prevent further injury to affected extremity.

Nursing interventions for Impaired Physical Mobility include keeping the affected limb in a functional position when immobilized; having the client maintain rest; avoid weight bearing on the affected extremity; and assisting with active or passive ROM every 4 hours.

13. Nursing care needs for the client with a bone tumor focus on both the physical aspects of care and the psychosocial effects of the diagnosis and its treatment.

14. Pain related to the tumor is a priority for nursing intervention. For a nursing diagnosis of Acute Pain, the expected outcome could be that the client will report pain at a level of 3 or lower on a standard pain scale of 1–10. Nursing interventions include: (1) assessing pain, including location, intensity, quality or type, aggravating and relieving factors, and duration; (2) developing strategies for controlling acute pain (from surgery, fracture, or inflammation or malignant pain from tumor growth and spread); (3) providing assistive devices (e.g., canes, walkers, crutches) when ambulating; (4) and providing regular rest periods between scheduled treatments.

15. A second nursing diagnosis for a client with a bone tumor could be Impaired Physical Mobility, with an expected outcome that the client will demonstrate correct use of assistive devices and exercises. Nursing interventions include teaching correct use of the trapeze; beginning muscle-strengthening and active and passive ROM exercises immediately after surgery; assisting the client who has leg surgery or amputation with exercises to strengthen the triceps muscles of the arms and to do quadriceps and gluteal sitting exercises and leg raises; and referring the client to physical or occupational therapy for fitting of and teaching about assistive devices such as a cane, crutches, or a walker.

16. Another nursing diagnosis for a client with a bone tumor would be Disturbed Body Image, with a possible expected outcome that the client will acknowledge impact of loss on current roles and relationships. Nursing interventions for this nursing diagnosis include listening to and supporting the client who is coping with loss of a limb or other changes such as hair loss associated with treatment, and allowing time for open discussions of feelings about changes in body image and potential changes in social and personal life.

17. Another nursing diagnosis for a client with a bone tumor is Grieving, with a possible expected outcome that the client will express thoughts, feelings, fears, and spiritual beliefs about loss. Nursing interventions include listening actively and encouraging verbalization of feelings and concerns about the diagnosis and treatment; presenting information in a matter-of-fact manner, taking time to listen to and address concerns; and referring the client to a counselor, the clergy, or, as appropriate, to hospice.

18. Nursing care of the client with a foot disorder focuses on managing discomfort associated with the disorder and teaching measures to maintain mobility.

19. Nursing assessment of the client with osteoarthritis focuses on the effects of the disease on activities of daily living (ADL). The nurse inquires about pain; its timing, location, and effect on sleep and rest; and measures used for relief. The nurse asks about limitations on mobility and ADL related to stiffness and pain. The nurse observes the client's gait, ability to sit and rise from sitting, and ability to perform various ADL. The nurse assesses joints for swelling, tenderness, warmth, and redness and assesses ROM, noting limitations and the presence of crepitus or complaints of pain with movement.

20. A nursing diagnosis for osteoarthritis is Chronic Pain, with a possible expected outcome that the client will verbalize and use appropriate ways to manage pain. Interventions for Chronic Pain include: (1) administering analgesic or anti-inflammatory medication as needed or on a

regular schedule as ordered; (2) teaching use of splints or other devices on affected joints as needed; (3) applying heat to painful joints using the shower, a tub or sitz bath, warm packs, hot wax drips, heated gloves, or diathermy; (4) emphasizing the importance of proper posture and good body mechanics for walking, sitting, lifting, and moving; (5) encouraging the overweight client to lose weight; and (6) encouraging the use of nonpharmacologic pain-relief measures such as progressive relaxation, meditation, visualization, and distraction.

21. Another nursing diagnosis for a client with osteoarthritis is Impaired Physical Mobility, with a possible expected outcome that the client will appropriately use exercise and assistive devices to maintain mobility. Nursing interventions include: (1) teaching active and passive ROM exercises and isometric, progressive resistance exercises; (2) encouraging participation in low-impact aerobic exercises; (3) providing analgesics or other pain-relief measures prior to exercise or ambulation; (4) teaching good body mechanics and encouraging to avoid heavy lifting; (5) encouraging planned rest periods during the day; and (6) teaching use of ambulatory aids such as a cane or walker as ordered.

22. Another nursing diagnosis for a client with osteoarthritis is Self-Care Deficit, with a possible expected outcome that the client will identify and use techniques and assistive devices to maintain ADL. Nursing interventions include assisting the client with ADL as needed; referring client to an occupational therapist for exercises and assistive devices; and helping the client obtain assistive devices such as long-handled shoehorns, zipper grabbers, and others.

23. Evaluation of the effectiveness of nursing care involves collecting data regarding ability to manage pain, maintain mobility, and perform ADL.

24. Assessment of the client with rheumatoid arthritis (RA) focuses on the progress of the disease and its effect on functional abilities. Assessment includes collecting data on pain level; number of affected joints; duration of morning stiffness, redness, heat, and swelling of affected joints; and other symptoms such as fatigue, weakness, anorexia, and fever.

25. A nursing diagnosis for rheumatoid arthritis is Chronic Pain, with a possible expected outcome that the client will verbalize an understanding of measures to promote comfort and relieve pain. Nursing interventions include: (1) encouraging the client to adjust activities according to pain level; (2) teaching the use of heat or cold for pain relief; (3) discussing the importance of taking anti-inflammatory medications as ordered and the relationship between inflammation and pain; and (4) encouraging use of other nonpharmacologic pain-relief measures such as visualization, distraction, meditation, and progressive relaxation techniques.

26. Another nursing diagnosis for a client with rheumatoid arthritis is Fatigue, with a possible expected outcome that the client will plan activities to reduce fatigue while maintaining desired roles and responsibilities. Interventions include: (1) encouraging a balance of activity with periods of rest; (2) stressing the importance of planned rest periods during the day; (3) assisting the client to prioritize activities, scheduling the most important ones early in the day; (4) encouraging the client to engage in regular physical activity in addition to ordered ROM exercises; and (5) helping identify tasks that can be delegated to others.

27. Another nursing diagnosis for a client with rheumatoid arthritis is Ineffective Role Performance, with a possible expected outcome that the client will verbalize ways to manage life roles and responsibilities within limitations of the disease. Nursing interventions include: (1) discussing effects of the disease on career and other life roles; (2) encouraging discussion of feelings about the disease and its effect on client and family roles; (3) listening actively to concerns and acknowledging their validity; (4) helping identify strengths to use in coping with role changes; (5) encouraging client to make decisions

and assume personal responsibility for disease management; (6) encouraging client to maintain life roles to the extent possible; and (7) referring client to counseling or support groups.

28. Another nursing diagnosis for a client with rheumatoid arthritis is Disturbed Body Image, with a possible expected outcome that the client will acknowledge actual changes in appearance and function. Nursing interventions for Disturbed Body Image include: (1) demonstrating a caring, accepting attitude; (2) encouraging discussion about the effects of RA, both physical and psychosocial; (3) involving client in decision making and provide choices whenever possible; (4) discussing clothing and adaptive devices that promote independence; (5) providing positive feedback for self-care activities and adaptive strategies; and (6) referring client to self-help groups, support groups, the Arthritis Foundation, and other agencies for assistive devices and literature.

29. To evaluate the effectiveness of nursing care for a client with RA, you will need to collect data such as quality and quantity of rest; effective use of NSAIDs and analgesics; ability to maintain ADL and usual roles; and statements about body image and coping with disease effects.

30. A nursing diagnosis for a client with SLE is Impaired Skin Integrity, with a possible expected outcome that the client will demonstrate an understanding of optimal skin and wound care. Nursing interventions include discussing the relationship between sun exposure and disease activity, both dermatologic and systematic; helping identify strategies to limit sun exposure; keeping skin clean and dry; and applying therapeutic creams or ointments to lesions as ordered.

31. Another nursing diagnosis for SLE is Risk for Infection, with a possible expected outcome that the client remains free of infection. Nursing interventions include: (1) washing hands on entering room and before providing direct care; (2) using strict sterile techniques for intravenous lines and indwelling urinary catheters or when performing any wound care; (3) monitoring temperature and vital signs every 4 hours; (4) reporting signs of infection, including tenderness, redness, swelling, and warmth; (5) reporting abnormal laboratory values; (6) if necessary, using protective isolation; (7) instructing family members and visitors to avoid direct contact with the client when the client is ill; (8) helping to ensure adequate food intake, offering supplementary feedings as indicated or maintaining parenteral nutrition if necessary; (9) teaching the importance of good hand washing after using the bathroom and before eating; and (10) providing good mouth care.

32. A nursing diagnosis for gout is Acute Pain, with a possible expected outcome that the client reports pain at a level of 3 or lower on a standard scale of 0–10. Nursing interventions include: (1) positioning the client for comfort; (2) elevating the joint or extremity (usually the great toe) on a pillow, maintaining alignment; (3) protecting the affected joint from pressure; (4) using a foot cradle to keep covers off the foot; (5) administering prescribed anti-inflammatory and antigout medications as ordered (in the initial period, colchicines may be given hourly); (6) administering analgesics as prescribed; (7) monitoring for desired and adverse effects of medications; (8) reporting adverse effects to the physician; and (9) maintaining bed rest.

33. Nursing care for clients with fibromyalgia is supportive and educational and provided in community settings such as clinics and other primary care settings. It is important to validate concerns and reassure clients that their symptoms are not "all in the head."

34. Nursing care of the client with fibromyalgia includes teaching about the disorder; providing written and verbal instructions about management strategies; instructing the client to take prescribed medications at bedtime because they may cause drowsiness; and cautioning about driving while taking the medication.

35. A nursing diagnosis for a client with low back pain is Ineffective Health Maintenance with a possible expected outcome that the client will develop and use strategies to prevent future episodes of back pain. Nursing interventions include: (1) teaching appropriate body mechanics in lifting and reaching, instructing the client to plan the lift, keep the object being lifted close to the body and avoid twisting when lifting; (2) encouraging the client to obtain help when lifting; (3) encouraging the client to avoid prolonged standing or sitting, lying prone, and wearing high heels; (4) encouraging an exercise program to strengthen abdominal and back muscles; (5) teaching or referring for teaching about exercises such as partial sit-ups with the knees bent and knee-chest exercises to stretch hamstrings and spinal muscles; (6) instructing the client to do each exercise five times, gradually increasing to 10 repetitions; (7) advising the client to stop any exercise that increases pain and to seek professional advice before continuing; (8) suggesting workplace or environmental modifications to minimize stress on the lower back; (9) encouraging obese clients to lose weight; and (10) encouraging the client to stop smoking.

36. Another nursing diagnosis for a client with low back pain is Acute Pain, with a possible expected outcome that the client will identify and use strategies to effectively manage pain. Nursing interventions include: (1) assessing the quality, severity, and location of pain and factors that tend to aggravate or relieve it; (2) instructing the client to take NSAIDs or analgesics on a routine schedule rather than as needed; (3) instructing the client on bed rest to assume a side-lying position with the hips and knees flexed with a pillow under or between the knees; (4) instructing the client to use a footstool when seated to support the weight of the feet; and (5) teaching the client about the "rebound phenomenon" of prolonged heat or ice therapy (ice remaining on the skin longer than 15 minutes or heat remaining on the skin more than 30 minutes will cause the reverse effect and can increase inflammation and pain).

LEARNING OUTCOME 6

Care for clients undergoing musculoskeletal surgery.

Concepts for Lecture

1. Surgery for the client with osteomyelitis may be done to obtain a specimen for culture. It may also be done to debride the area.
2. During surgery to debride the area, the area may be irrigated, and drainage tubes may be connected to an irrigation system inserted to keep the cavity clean. After surgery, the nurse is responsible for instilling and removing dilute antibiotic solutions through the drainage tubes. Use strict sterile technique when caring for a wound irrigation to prevent additional contamination of the infected bone.
3. When caring for a client who is having a total joint replacement, the nurse provides care before and after surgery.
4. Before surgery, nursing care includes providing routine preoperative care and teaching; reinforcing teaching about postoperative activity restrictions and exercises as indicated; teaching use of the overhead trapeze for changing positions; teaching postoperative pain management, including use of patient-controlled analgesia (PCA) or other anticipated analgesic delivery systems, stressing the importance of reporting unrelieved or increasing pain; teaching or providing ordered skin preparation; and administering preoperative medications as ordered.
5. After surgery, the nurse provides routine postoperative care: (1) monitors vital signs, pain status, and LOC every 4 hours or more frequently

POWERPOINT SLIDES

Tables and/or Figures
- **Box 43-10** Nursing Care Checklist: Total Joint Replacement

SUGGESTIONS FOR CLASSROOM ACTIVITIES
- Invite a prosthesis representative to talk to the class about joint replacements.
- Arrange for students to see a continuous passive range-of-motion (CPM) device and to become familiar with operating it.

SUGGESTIONS FOR CLINICAL ACTIVITIES
- Make arrangements for students to observe joint replacement surgery.
- Assign students to care for clients who have recently had joint replacement surgery.
- Have students do a clinical rotation in a rehabilitation department or hospital.

as indicated and reports any significant changes to the charge nurse or physician; (2) assesses neurovascular status (color, temperature, pulses, and capillary refill, movement, and sensation) of the affected limb hourly for the first 12 to 24 hours and then every 2 to 4 hours, reporting abnormal findings immediately; (3) frequently assesses for bleeding; (4) empties and records wound suction drainage every 4 hours; (5) reinforces the dressing as needed, reporting significant bleeding to the charge nurse or physician; (6) maintains intravenous infusion(s) as ordered; (7) monitors intake and output during the initial 48 to 72 hours as indicated; (8) reports urine output of less than 30 mL/hr for 2 or more hours; and (9) maintains extremity position using sling, abduction splint, brace, immobilizer or other ordered device.

6. Additional postoperative nursing care includes: (10) helping the client to shift position at least every 2 hours while on bed rest; (11) encouraging frequent use of incentive spirometer, deep breathing, and coughing; (12) assisting the client out of bed as soon as allowed; (13) reinforcing teaching about avoiding weight bearing on affected extremity; (14) using overhead trapeze, pivot turning, and toe touch; (15) initiating physical therapy and exercises as prescribed; and (16) using sequential compression devices or antiembolism stockings as ordered.

7. When caring for a client postoperatively who had a total hip replacement, take measures to prevent hip flexion greater than 90 degrees and adduction of the affected leg; provide a seat riser for toilet or commode; and report signs of hip prosthesis dislocation, including pain or shortening and internal rotation of the affected leg.

8. When caring for a client postoperatively who had a total knee replacement, use a continuous passive motion (CPM) device or range-of-motion exercises as prescribed.

9. When CPM is ordered, set the prescribed degree of flexion and extension and speed of movement per instructions. With the CPM machine in extension, pad the CPM with sheepskin before placing the extremity in the CPM. Adjust the frame length and foot plate to the extremity and align the joints with the frame joints. Disable the electric bed controls as indicated to maintain alignment of the extremity with the CPM and elevate the head of the bed up to 20 degrees if allowed.

10. Start CPM, observing rate, degree of flexion, and client responses. Maintain CPM as ordered, frequently assessing comfort, incision, skin condition, and neurovascular status.

11. Reinforce teaching about postdischarge exercises and activity restrictions and emphasize the importance of scheduled follow-up physician visits.

12. For clients requiring addition nursing care and rehabilitation after discharge, assist with transfer to a long-term rehabilitation facility and provide complete and accurate data to the nursing staff of the receiving facility.

13. Make referrals as needed to home health agencies and physical therapy.

REFERENCES

- National Institute of Arthritis and Musculoskeletal and Skin Disorders: Joint replacement surgery and you. Available at http://www.niams.nih.gov/Health_Info/Joint_Replacement/default.asp#7
- National Institute of Arthritis and Musculoskeletal and Skin Disorders: Arthritis. Available at http://www.niams.nih.gov/Health_Info/Joint_Replacement/default.asp

LEARNING OUTCOME 7

Provide teaching and home care for clients with musculoskeletal disorders.

Concepts for Lecture

1. To prevent osteoporosis, stress the importance of maintaining an adequate calcium intake. Milk and milk products provide the best calcium sources (see Box 43-3 for additional sources). When a calcium supplement is used, recommend one that also contains vitamin D to help the body absorb and use calcium.

POWERPOINT SLIDES

Tables and/or Figures

- **Box 43-13** Client Teaching: Preventing Lyme Disease

© 2011 Pearson Education, Inc.

2. When teaching the client who has osteoporosis, stress the importance of regular physical activity that includes weight bearing to prevent bone loss. One suggestion is to walk for 20 minutes or more at least four times per week.

3. Teach postmenopausal women about hormone replacement therapy to prevent bone loss. Discuss with the client with osteoporosis the importance of not smoking, avoiding excess alcohol intake, and limiting caffeine intake to prevent osteoporosis. Recommend that the client with a significant risk for osteoporosis talk to his or her primary care provider about bone-density testing.

4. Discuss safety and fall prevention with the client who has osteoporosis and with caregivers, advising them to remove scatter rugs and clutter from walkways in the house and to use a night light or graduated light from the bedroom to the bathroom to reduce the risk of nighttime falls. Also discuss placing grab bars in strategic locations such as the shower and next to the toilet to reduce the risk of falling.

5. Provide the client who has osteoporosis and his caregivers with a list of local and national resources and refer the client to a healthcare provider, social services, or occupational therapy, as indicated, for bone-density testing, home care services, or rehabilitation.

6. When working with a client with Paget's disease, teach the client about the disease and about prescribed medication, precautions for safe use of medications, and adverse effects to report to the physician. Teach the client to take NSAIDs on a regular basis to maintain their anti-inflammatory and analgesic effect. Discuss measures to maintain mobility and safety, including use of assistive devices as recommended.

7. Nursing care for clients with osteomalacia is similar to that provided for clients with osteoporosis. Teach older adults about the importance of taking calcium with vitamin D supplements if they are unable to get adequate amounts in their diet and the importance of taking safety measures to prevent falls. Advise clients with bone pain and muscle weakness to use assistive devices when ambulating. Encourage the client to participate in a supervised exercise program or to discuss physical therapy with their primary care provider.

8. When working with a client with osteomyelitis, reinforce teaching about medications and wound management at home. Emphasize the importance of taking all antibiotics as prescribed. Instruct the client to use pain medications as needed to prevent pain from becoming severe. Discuss possible drug side effects and provide information about managing these effects (e.g., increasing fluid and fiber intake to prevent constipation caused by many analgesics and consuming 8 ounces of live-culture yogurt to prevent diarrhea and yeast infections often caused by prolonged antibiotic therapy).

9. Teach wound care as needed to the client with osteomyelitis and refer the client for home health services as appropriate. Teach the client the general principles of infection control, including the importance of good hand washing, especially after toileting or contact with wound drainage. Also provide instruction about rest or limited weight bearing as ordered by the physician. Teach the client how to avoid complications of immobility and the importance of good nutrition. Stress the need to keep all follow-up appointments.

10. When working with a client with a bone tumor, teach the client about the disease, its potential consequences, treatment options, and how to minimize treatment side effects. Depending on the location of the tumor and planned treatment, modification of the home environment may be necessary. Discuss potential barriers to

SUGGESTIONS FOR CLASSROOM ACTIVITIES

- Have students work in small groups to develop a teaching tool for teaching clients who have one of the musculoskeletal disorders. The students could design a poster, do a PowerPoint presentation, develop a handout, or come up with another means of teaching key points.

SUGGESTIONS FOR CLINICAL ACTIVITIES

- Assign students to care for clients with musculoskeletal disorders. Have students assess the client's learning needs and provide teaching for the client based on their needs.

mobility, such as stairs or lack of access to transportation. Help identify a network of support people who can assist with coping care and treatment as needed.

11. If surgery has been performed on the client with a bone tumor, teach wound care, demonstrating dressing changes and stump care if amputation has occurred. Additional home care and teaching include providing a list of local resources for obtaining supplies, discussing activity and weight-bearing restrictions, referring to physical therapy for teaching about ambulation and appropriate muscle group–strengthening exercises, and ensuring referral to a prosthetic specialist for the client who has experienced an amputation. If the client has a metastatic disease, the nurse discusses hospice services and support groups for clients with cancer.

12. Instruct the client with a foot disorder about the importance of wearing supportive and nonrestrictive or corrective footwear at all times. Discuss with women in particular the long-term effects of wearing high-heeled shoes with constricting toes. Suggest shoes, such as running or walking shoes that provide arch support and ample toe room. Suggest protective pads to wear over bunions, calluses/corns, and the ball of the foot.

13. Advise the client to remove pads and inspect feet every other day. Suggest that the client use a mirror or a helper to inspect areas that are difficult to see. Teach the client proper foot care (Box 36-9). Discuss the possible effects of bunions on balance, and talk about safety measures to prevent falls and injuries.

14. The client with osteoarthritis often can remain home and independent with environmental modifications and assistive devices. Assess the home for hazards to mobility, such as scatter rugs. Identify the need for assistive devices such as handrails, grab bars, walk-in shower stall, or shower chair and handheld shower head.

15. Teach the client ways to help maintain joint function and mobility such as advising the client to exercise (e.g., walking as an effective low-impact exercise), not overuse or stress affected joints, balance exercise with rest of affected joints, sit in a straight chair without slumping, avoid soft chairs or recliners, and sleep on a firm mattress or use a bed board.

16. Teach the client with osteoarthritis about prescribed or over-the-counter medications for osteoarthritis. Discuss nonpharmacologic pain relief measures such as heat, rest, massage, relaxation, and medication.

17. If arthroplasty was done on the client with osteoarthritis, reinforce teaching about activity and weight bearing; teach the use of splints, braces, slings, or other devices to maintain the desired limb position during healing. Discuss assistive devices such as overhead trapeze for getting out of bed, elevated toilet seats, and chairs to use and avoid when sitting. Encourage practice of prescribed exercises and observe and reinforce teaching as needed for using crutches or a walker.

18. Discuss possible complications, including signs of infection or dislocation, and instruct the client to notify the physician promptly if these occur. Refer the client for home care, physical or occupational therapy, or other community resources as indicated.

19. Teach the client with rheumatoid arthritis about the disease and its systemic effects. Stress the importance of following all aspects of the treatment plan and encourage active involvement in planning care. Help the client identify strategies to balance rest and exercise. Instruct the client to reduce exercise and increase rest if pain and stiffness increase. Teach the client to use heat and cold to promote comfort and activity.

20. Teach the client with systemic lupus erythematosus (SLE) about SLE and its potential effects, the impact of the disease, community and social service resources, and local support groups. Refer the client and family to counseling as needed. Discuss the importance of skin care and avoiding irritating soaps, shampoos, or chemicals to prevent excessive drying of the skin. Encourage use of hypoallergenic products and stress the importance of using an appropriate sunscreen, wearing long sleeves and wide-brimmed hats, and limiting sun exposure, particularly between 10:00 a.m. and 3:00 p.m. For clients with hair loss, discuss using wigs, turbans, or other head coverings, and remind the client that the hair will regrow during remission.

21. Teach the client with SLE about the treatment plan, including rest and exercise, medications, and follow-up appointments, and to contact the physician promptly if symptoms of an exacerbation develop. Stress the importance of avoiding exposure to infection. Encourage the client to wear a Medic-Alert bracelet or tag.

22. Discuss family planning. Oral contraceptives may be contraindicated. Pregnancy is not contraindicated, but the client is instructed to tell her women's healthcare practitioner about her SLE and to notify the primary care physician of any pregnancy.

23. For the client with gout, teaching is done about the disease and its manifestations. The client is advised that initial attacks cause no permanent damage but recurrent attacks can lead to permanent damage and joint destruction. Potential effects of continued hyperuricemia include tophaceous deposits in subcutaneous and other connective tissues and risk for kidney damage and stones.

24. Teach the client about prescribed medications, including the need to continue medications until discontinued by the physician, even if there are no symptoms. Discuss potential side effects of the drugs and their management. Instruct the client to drink about 3 quarts of fluid per day and to avoid using alcohol. Teach the client not to use over-the-counter medications without talking to the physician. Encourage the client to keep follow-up appointments.

25. See Box 43-13 for client teaching for preventing Lyme disease.

26. When working with a client with ankylosing spondylitis, provide supportive care and education. Encourage the client to maintain a fluid intake of 2,500 mL or more per day. Performing exercises in the shower is suggested because warm, moist heat promotes mobility. The client is provided indirect lighting and a darkened room for photophobia.

27. If the client's vision is significantly impaired, the nurse orients the client to the surroundings and does not move furniture or place objects in usual pathways. Introduce yourself verbally when entering the room, and tell the client what you are doing during procedures. Assist the client during ambulation by holding onto the nurse's elbow.

28. The client with fibromyalgia is taught about the disorder and provided verbal and written instructions about management strategies. Instruct the client to take prescribed medications at bedtimes, because they may cause drowsiness. The client is cautioned about driving while taking the medication.

29. Teach the client with low back pain about health practices to prevent back pain. Teach safe lifting, bending, and turning during physical activity. Stress the importance of using large muscle groups of the leg to lift rather than bending and lifting with the smaller muscles of the back. Teach other aspects of good body management. Discuss the positive effect of maintaining optimal body weight and good physical fitness.

GENERAL CHAPTER CONSIDERATIONS

1. Have students study and learn key terms listed at the beginning of the chapter.
2. Have students complete end of chapter exercises either in their book or on the MyNursingKit Website.
3. Use the Classroom Response Question PowerPoints to assess students prior to lecture.

• Clinical Reasoning Care Map

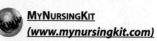 **MyNursingKit**
(www.mynursingkit.com)

• Websites
• NCLEX® Questions
• Case Studies
• Key Terms

 Student Workbook and Resource Guide

• Chapter 43 activities
• *Separate purchase*

Prentice Hall Nurse's Drug Guide

• *Separate purchase*

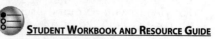 **Classroom Response Question PowerPoints**

 Testbank

CHAPTER 44
THE INTEGUMENTARY SYSTEM AND ASSESSMENT

LEARNING OUTCOME 1

Identify the structure and functions of the skin and its appendages.

Concepts for Lecture

1. The skin, glands, hair, and nails make up the integumentary system.
2. The skin provides an external covering for the body, separating the body's organs and tissues from the external environment.
3. The skin contains receptors for touch and sensation, helps regulate body temperature, and assists in fluid and electrolyte balance.
4. The skin provides cues to racial and ethnic background, conveys emotional responses, and helps determine self-concept, roles, and relationships.
5. The skin is composed of two regions: the epidermis and the dermis.
6. The epidermis (surface part) is made up of several layers of epithelial cells. There are about 20–30 sheets of dead cells filled with keratin fragments arranged in "shingles" that flake off as dry skin.
7. The deepest layer of the epidermis contains cells that produce melanin and keratin. Melanin forms a shield to protect nerve endings in the dermis from the damaging effects of ultraviolet light. Keratin is a fibrous, water-repellent protein that makes the epidermis tough and protective.
8. The epidermis protects tissues from physical, chemical, and biologic damage; prevents water loss; and serves as a water-repellent layer. The dermis also converts cholesterol molecules to vitamin D when exposed to sunlight. The dermis contains phagocytes, which prevent bacteria from penetrating the skin.
9. The dermis, the second layer of the skin, is made up of a flexible connective tissue. This layer is richly supplied with blood cells, nerve fibers, and lymphatic vessels.
10. The dermis regulates body temperature by dilating and constricting capillaries. The dermis also transmits messages via nerve endings to the central nervous system. Most of the hair follicles, sebaceous glands, and sweat glands are located in the dermis.
11. The sebaceous (oil) glands secrete sebum, which lubricates skin and hair and plays a role in killing bacteria.
12. The eccrine sweat glands regulate body heat by excretion of perspiration, and the apocrine glands have unknown function.
13. The hair cushions the scalp. Eyelashes and cilia protect the body from foreign particles and provide insulation in cold weather.
14. The nails protect the fingers and toes, aid in grasping, and allow for various other activities such as scratching the skin, picking up small items, peeling an orange, and so on.

 **POWERPOINT SLIDES**

Tables and/or Figures
- **Table 44-1** Functions of the Skin and Its Appendages
- **Figure 44-1** Anatomy of the Skin

 SUGGESTIONS FOR CLASSROOM ACTIVITIES

- Have students work in small groups to draw a picture of a person on large sheets of paper or poster board and label the skin and appendages with information about structure and function.
- Have students work in pairs or small groups to design a teaching tool to use to explain the structure and function of the integumentary system to clients and interested others (e.g., a booklet with drawings or a paper on the subject).

 SUGGESTIONS FOR CLINICAL ACTIVITIES

- Assign students to care for clients who have disorders of the integumentary system. Have students use their teaching tool to explain the structure and function of the skin and its appendages to their clients.

LEARNING OUTCOME 2

Describe factors that influence skin color.

Concepts for Lecture

1. The color of the skin is the result of varying levels of pigmentation. Melanin, a yellow-to-brown pigment, is darker and is produced in greater amounts in persons with dark skin color than in those with light skin.
2. Exposure to sun causes a buildup of melanin and a darkening of the skin in people with light skin.
3. Carotene (a yellow-to-orange pigment) is more abundant in the skins of persons of Asian ancestry and, together with melanin, accounts for their golden skin tone.
4. The epidermis in Caucasian skin has very little melanin and is almost transparent. The color of their red blood cells shows through, lending Caucasians a pinkish skin tone.
5. Skin color is influenced by emotions and illnesses.
6. Erythema (a reddening of the skin) may occur with embarrassment such as blushing, fever, hypertension, or inflammation. It may also result from a drug reaction, sunburn, or other factors.
7. Cyanosis (bluish discoloration of the skin and mucous membranes) results from poor oxygenation of hemoglobin or lack of adequate hemoglobin or RBCs.
8. Pallor, or paleness of skin, may occur with shock, fear, or anger, or in anemia and hypoxia.
9. Jaundice is a yellow-to-orange color visible in the skin and mucous membranes; it most often results from a liver disorder.

POWERPOINT SLIDES

SUGGESTIONS FOR CLASSROOM ACTIVITIES

- Ask students to observe people in their family or their friends and note differences in skin color. Have the students identify factors influencing the skin color of family members and friends and report on their observations.

SUGGESTIONS FOR CLINICAL ACTIVITIES

- Assign students to care for clients who have cyanosis or jaundice so students can observe these conditions

REFERENCE

- MedlinePlus: Skin pigmentation disorders. Available at http://www.nlm.nih.gov/medlineplus/skinpigmentationdisorders.html

---

LEARNING OUTCOME 3

Identify subjective and objective assessment data to collect for clients with integumentary disorders.

Concepts for Lecture

1. If the client has a skin problem, identify its onset, characteristics, course, and severity. Note any precipitating and relieving factors and whether symptoms are associated with specific circumstances.
2. Ask about any change in health, skin color changes, dryness or oiliness, growth of or changes in warts or moles, the presence of lesions, and delayed wound healing.
3. Determine whether the client takes hormones, vitamins, steroids, or antibiotics, which may cause skin side effects.
4. For obese clients, inquire about any chafing in areas where moisture accumulates such as overlapping skin folds.
5. When the client complains about itching, ask the client to describe the type of itching. Inquire about precipitating causes such as medications, soaps, shampoos, cosmetics, skin care products, pets, travel, stress, or diet changes. Ask about skin reactions to insect bites and stings.
6. In assessing the client's hair, ask about problems with thinning or baldness, excessive hair loss, change in distribution of hair, use of hair-care products, diet, and dieting.
7. When assessing nail problems, ask about nail splitting or breakage, discoloration, infection, diet, and exposure to chemicals.
8. Obtain the client's past medical history, focusing on previous problems, allergies, surgery, and lesions. Skin problems may be symptoms of other health disorders, such as cardiovascular disorders, diabetes mellitus, thyroid disease, liver disease, and hematologic disorders.

POWERPOINT SLIDES

Tables and/or Figures
- **Figure 44-2** Tenting in an Elderly Client
- **Figure 23-11** Clubbing of the Nails Caused by Chronic Hypoxia

SUGGESTIONS FOR CLASSROOM ACTIVITIES

- Have students work in pairs and design flash cards to test material from this learning objective.
- Have students work in small groups. Ask the students to discuss the importance of history in the diagnosis of skin problems.

SUGGESTIONS FOR CLINICAL ACTIVITIES

- Assign students to care for clients who have skin disorders. Assist the students to collect subjective and objective assessment data about the client's integumentary system.
- Ask the primary nurses on the clinical area if they have any clients with clubbing of the fingers or any other abnormal assessment findings. Ask permission for the students to observe these abnormal findings.

9. Occupational and social history may provide clues to skin problems; ask the client about exposure to chemicals at work, travel, use of alcohol, and responses to stress.

10. Assess the presence of risk factors for skin cancer carefully. These factors include male gender; age over 50; family history of skin cancer; light-colored hair and eyes; extended exposure to sunlight; tendency to sunburn; history of sunburn or other skin trauma; living in high altitudes or near equator; exposure to radiation, x-rays, coal, tar, or petroleum products; and the use of sun-protection products.

11. Explore the risk factors for malignant melanoma. These factors include a large number of moles, the presence of atypical moles, a family history of melanoma, prior melanoma, repeated severe sunburns, ease of freckling and sun burning, or inability to tan.

12. During the physical examination, areas to be examined include inspecting the skin for pallor, cyanosis, or jaundice. Take special care when assessing the skin color in people with dark skin, including Caucasians with deep suntans.

13. In dark-skinned clients, paleness is seen as dull color. The skin may appear dull and darker when cyanosis is present. Jaundice is best assessed on the palms of the hands or sclera of the eyes.

14. Assess for redness, swelling, and pain related to various rashes, inflammation, infections, and burns. First-degree burns cause painful erythema and swelling. Red painful blisters occur in second-degree burns, and white or blackened areas appear in third-degree burns.

15. Check for vitiligo, an abnormal, patchy loss of melanin, over the face, hands, and groin.

16. Assess for petechiae, which are small, reddish-purple pinpoint spots over the abdomen and buttocks.

17. Inspect the skin for primary and secondary lesions (Table 44-2). Look for raised bluish or yellowish bruises. Note bruises that are in varying stages of healing. Assess for lesions that appear in circles, groups, or along the sensory nerves.

18. Palpate skin temperature, texture, moisture, and turgor. Note any warmth and redness associated with inflammation and coolness related to decreased blood flow.

19. Observe for rough, dry or smooth, oily skin, as well as excessive perspiration, and inspect for tenting of the skin. Tenting is a common finding in the elderly.

20. Note any decreased skin turgor as seen in dehydration.

21. Assess for edema by depressing the client's skin over the ankle.

22. Inspect the distribution and quality of hair. Look for hirsuitism (excessive hair) or alopecia (hair loss). Palpate the hair for coarseness or fineness.

23. Inspect the scalp for lesions such as pustules or scales. Look for nits (eggs) seen with head lice adhering to the base of the hair shaft. Note excessive greasy flakes rather than mild dandruff.

24. Inspect the nails for clubbing (angle of nail base greater than 180 degrees; Figure 23-11).

25. Observe nail surface for inflammation, separation from the nail bed, grooves, pitting, or spoon shape. Inspect for yellowish-colored, bluish-green, or dark nails.

26. Look at the nails for red splinter hemorrhages and pigmented bands, which are normal in 90% of African Americans.

LEARNING OUTCOME 4

Describe skin changes in the older adult.

Concepts for Lecture

1. A variety of normal skin changes are seen in the older adult, including loss of subcutaneous tissue, dermal thinning, and decreased elasticity, which may cause wrinkles and sagging of the skin.
2. The skin in older adults is thinner especially over bony prominences and dorsal surfaces of the hands and feet, and turgor is decreased.
3. Older adults are unable to respond to heat or cold quickly, increasing their risk for heat stroke and hypothermia.
4. In older adults, dry, itchy skin may result from the reduced number of sweat and oil glands.
5. Overall production of melanocytes decreases, while abnormal localized hyperpigmentation may lead to the development of senile lentigines, commonly called "liver spots." These senile lentigines are flat brown macules commonly appearing on the arms and hands in areas of sun exposure.
6. Keratoses also result from hyperpigmentation. Seborrheic keratoses are dark, raised lesions and are benign. Actinic keratoses are reddish, raised plaques on areas of high sun exposure, which may become malignant.
7. Skin tags, small flaps of excess skin, are normal in aging skin.
8. Both hair and nail growth decrease with aging. Older men may develop coarse hair in the ears and nose and over the eyebrows.
9. Decreased estrogen levels may cause postmenopausal women to develop dark facial hair over the upper lip and under the chin.
10. Hair becomes gray due to a reduction of melanocytes.
11. With aging, nails may thicken, yellow, and peel.

 **POWERPOINT SLIDES**

Tables and/or Figures
- **Figure 44-2** Tenting in an Elderly Client

 SUGGESTIONS FOR CLASSROOM ACTIVITIES
- Ask students to find articles on aging and integumentary changes and to bring these articles to class to share.

SUGGESTIONS FOR CLINICAL ACTIVITIES
- Assign students to care for older clients who have skin changes associated with aging. In postconference, ask students to share their observations of these changes in their client.

REFERENCE
- MedlinePlus: Aging changes in hair and nails. Available at http://www.nlm.nih.gov/medlineplus/ency/article/004005.htm

---

LEARNING OUTCOME 5

Identify nursing responsibilities for common diagnostic tests and monitors for clients with integumentary disorders.

Concepts for Lecture

1. The most common diagnostic test is the skin biopsy. Other tests include stains and cultures to identify bacterial, fungal, and viral infections. Photographs may be taken to document wound healing or to record wounds in suspected abuse cases.
2. For a biopsy or a cutaneous immunofluorescence biopsy, the nursing implications include ensuring a consent form is signed, assisting with getting supplies the physician will need, applying dressing, giving follow-up instructions, and sending the specimen to the laboratory.
3. For the following tests, the nursing implications are teaching the client about the purpose of the test and sending a specimen to the laboratory: potassium hydroxide, culture and sensitivity, Tzanck test, skin scraping, patch test, and Wood's lamp.

 **POWERPOINT SLIDES**

Tables and/or Figures
- **Table 44-3** Common Diagnostic Tests for Integumentary Disorders

SUGGESTIONS FOR CLASSROOM ACTIVITIES
- Have someone who does the lab tests mentioned in the Concepts for Lecture come to class and discuss these tests.
- Have students research the various tests mentioned in the Concepts for Lecture.

 **SUGGESTIONS FOR CLINICAL ACTIVITIES**
- Assign students to care for clients receiving laboratory tests for skin disorders. Ask permission for the student to observe the test or tests.

GENERAL CHAPTER CONSIDERATIONS

1. Have students study and learn key terms listed at the beginning of the chapter.
2. Have students complete end of chapter exercises either in their book or on the MyNursingKit Website.
3. Use the Classroom Response Question PowerPoints to assess students prior to lecture.

- Clinical Reasoning Care Map

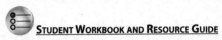

MyNursingKit
(www.mynursingkit.com)

- Websites
- NCLEX® Questions
- Case Studies
- Key Terms

STUDENT WORKBOOK AND RESOURCE GUIDE

- Chapter 44 activities
- *Separate purchase*

PRENTICE HALL NURSE'S DRUG GUIDE

- *Separate purchase*

CLASSROOM RESPONSE QUESTION POWERPOINTS

TESTBANK

CHAPTER 45
CARING FOR CLIENTS WITH SKIN DISORDERS

LEARNING OUTCOME 1

Relate skin changes in the older adult to an increased risk for dry skin, pruritus, skin cancer, and pressure ulcers.

Concepts for Lecture

1. Dry skin is the most common skin disorder seen in the elderly due to the decreased activity of sebaceous and sweat glands. The primary manifestation of dry skin is pruritus.
2. The incidence of skin cancers occurs most frequently in adults between the ages of 30 and 60 years. The incidence increases with excess exposure to the sun.
3. Pressure ulcers are a risk for the older adult because of the high incidence of limited mobility, paralysis, and critical illnesses or other conditions that affect mobility.
4. Incontinence, poor nutrition, and chronic illness create an increased risk for skin breakdown in the older adult.

LEARNING OUTCOME 2

Compare and contrast the pathophysiology, manifestations, and interdisciplinary care of clients with common skin disorders, infections and infestations of the skin, malignant skin disorders, and pressure ulcers.

Concepts for Lecture

1. Pruritus is a subjective itching sensation that produces an urge to scratch. Pruritus is not a disorder itself but a manifestation of an underlying irritation or condition. Almost anything in the internal or external environment can cause pruritus. Pruritus may occur as a secondary manifestation of systemic disorders. Pruritus is initiated by a stimulation or irritation of receptors in the junction between the epidermis and dermis.
2. The secondary effects of pruritus include skin excoriation, erythema, wheals, changes in pigmentation, and infections. Pruritus may interrupt sleep patterns because the itching is more intense at night.
3. Dry skin may occur at any age as a result of exposure to environmental heat and low humidity, sunlight, excessive bathing, and a decreased intake of liquids. The primary manifestation is pruritus. Other manifestations include visible flaking of surface skin and observable pattern of fine lines over the area. If dry skin and pruritus persist for a long period, the client may have secondary skin lesions and lichenification (thickening).
4. The actual cause of psoriasis is unknown, but evidence suggests it is an autoimmune disorder. Psoriasis is characterized by raised, reddened, round circumscribed plaques of varied size, covered by silvery white scales. The plaques shed thick gray scales. The lesions may appear anywhere on the body but are most common on the scalp, extensor surfaces of the arms and legs, elbows, knees, sacrum, and around the nails. Sunlight, stress, seasonal changes, hormone fluctuations, steroid withdrawal, and certain drugs (such as beta-blockers,

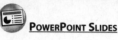

SUGGESTIONS FOR CLASSROOM ACTIVITIES

- Assign students to research journal articles about older adults and skin changes that these older adults may experience. Ask the students to bring these articles to class and share them.

SUGGESTIONS FOR CLINICAL ACTIVITIES

- Assign students to care for older clients with skin changes. Have students look at these skin changes and, when appropriate, relate them to increased risk for dry skin, pruritus, skin cancer, and pressure ulcers. Have students report in postconference the skin changes they observed in their clients.

REFERENCE

- MedlinePlus: Aging changes in skin. Available at http://www.nlm.nih.gov/medlineplus/ency/article/004014.htm

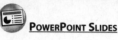

POWERPOINT SLIDES

Tables and/or Figures

- **Figure 45-1** Characteristic Lesions of Psoriasis
- **Figure 45-2** Atopic Dermatitis or Eczema
- **Figure 45-3** Inflammatory Acne Lesions
- **Figure 45-4** Cellulitis
- **Figure 45-5** Lesions of Herpes Zoster
- **Figure 45-6** Head Lice Crawling Through Hair
- **Figure 45-7** Squamous Cell Carcinoma
- **Figure 45-8** Malignant Melanoma

SUGGESTIONS FOR CLASSROOM ACTIVITIES

- Prepare pictures of the different common skin disorders. Ask students to match the name of the disorder with the picture.
- Prepare a matching quiz for students to identify whether the infection/infestation is bacterial, viral, fungal, or parasitic.
- Ask students to do an online search for articles that discuss risks of skin cancer.
- Ask students to read an article on pressure ulcers that discusses prevention and intervention techniques.

corticosteroids, lithium, and chloroquine) appear to make the disorder worse. About one-third of clients have a family history of psoriasis. Trauma to the skin from surgery, sunburn, or excoriation may also precipitate psoriasis. The skin manifestations may disappear and recur throughout life.

5. Various agents or illnesses cause the inflammatory response of the skin in dermatitis. Initial skin responses include erythema, formation of vesicles and scales, and pruritus. Later, irritation from scratching promotes edema, a serous discharge, and crusting. Long-term irritation in chronic dermatitis causes the skin to become thickened, leathery, and darker in color.

6. Contact dermatitis is caused by a hypersensitivity response or chemical irritation. Major sources known to cause contact dermatitis are dyes, perfumes, poison plants (ivy, oak, sumac), chemicals, and metals. Latex dermatitis is a contact dermatitis that is common in the health field.

7. Atopic dermatitis is also called eczema. The exact cause is unknown but related factors include depressed cell-mediated immunity, elevated immunoglobulin E (IgE) levels, and increased histamine sensitivity. Clients with atopic dermatitis have a family history of hypersensitivity reactions, such as eczema, asthma, and allergic rhinitis.

8. Characteristic lesions of atopic dermatitis include chronic lichenification, erythema, and scaling, the result of pruritus and scratching. The lesions are usually found on the hands, feet, or flexor surfaces of the arms and legs. Scratching and excoriation increase the risk of secondary infections, as well as invasion of the skin by viruses such as herpes simplex.

9. The cause of seborrheic dermatitis is unknown. This disorder is seen in all ages, from the very young (called "cradle cap") to the very old. This chronic inflammatory disorder involves the scalp, eyebrows, eyelids, ear canals, nasolabial folds, axillae, and trunk. Clients taking methyldopa for hypertension occasionally develop this disorder, and it is a component of Parkinson's disease. Seborrheic dermatitis is frequently seen in clients with AIDS.

10. The lesions of seborrheic dermatitis are yellow or white plaques with scales and crusts. The scales are often yellow or orange and have a greasy appearance. Mild pruritus is also present.

11. A preexisting skin disorder such as psoriasis, atopic dermatitis, contact dermatitis, or seborrheic dermatitis may be present in exfoliative dermatitis, which is also associated with leukemia and lymphoma.

12. Systemic manifestations of exfoliative dermatitis include weakness, malaise, fever, chills, and weight loss. Scaling, erythema, and pruritus may be localized or involve the entire body. In addition to peeling of skin, the client may lose the hair and nails.

13. Acne is a disorder of the sebaceous glands. Acne lesions are primarily comedones (pimples, whiteheads, and blackheads). Inflammatory acne lesions include comedones, erythematous pustules, and cysts.

14. Acne vulgaris is common in adolescents and young to middle-aged adults. Many factors once thought to cause acne vulgaris, including high-fat diets, chocolate, infections, and cosmetics, have been disproved.

15. Acne rosacea, chronic facial acne, occurs more often in middle-aged and older adults. The lesions begin with erythema over the cheeks and nose. Over years, the skin color changes to dark red, and the pores over the area become enlarged.

16. Pruritus, dry skin, psoriasis, dermatitis, and acne are most often treated at home. Treatment focuses on identifying and eliminating or modifying any precipitating factors, providing relief from itching and pain, and reducing the risk of further damage to the skin.

17. Bacterial infections of the skin arise from the hair follicle, where bacteria can accumulate and grow and cause a localized infection. If the bacteria invade deeper tissues, they can cause a systemic infection, a potentially

SUGGESTIONS FOR CLINICAL ACTIVITIES

- Arrange for students to have clinical experiences in a dermatology clinic or a dermatologist's office.
- Arrange for clinical experiences in the rapid treatment section of the emergency department where clients with minor illnesses are seen.
- Find a client in the clinical area who has stage III and/or stage IV pressure ulcers. Use this as a case study presentation in a postconference.

REFERENCE

- American Academy of Family Physicians: Recognizing neoplastic skin lesions. Available at http://www.aafp.org/afp/980915ap/rose.html

life-threatening disorder. Hospital-acquired (nosocomial) infections of wounds or open lesions often result from bacterial infections, especially by methicillin-resistant *Staphylococcus aureus* (MRSA).

18. Folliculitis is most often caused by *Staphylococcus aureus*. The infection begins at the skin surface and extends down into the hair follicle. The bacteria release enzymes and chemical agents that cause an inflammation.

19. In folliculitis, the lesions appear as pustules surrounded by an area of erythema on the surface of the skin. Folliculitis is found most often on the scalp and extremities, on the face of bearded men, on the legs of women who shave, and on the eyelids (called a stye). Contributing factors for folliculitis include poor hygiene, poor nutrition, prolonged skin moisture, and trauma to the skin. Folliculitis may develop in an abscess.

20. A furuncle ("boil") is also an infection of the hair follicle. A group of infected hair follicles is called a carbuncle. It often begins as folliculitis, but the infection spreads down the hair shaft, through the wall of the follicle, and into the dermis. The causative organism is commonly *Staphylococcus aureus*. Contributing factors to the development of a furuncle include poor hygiene, trauma to the skin, areas of excessive moisture including perspiration, and systemic disease, such as diabetes mellitus.

21. A furuncle is initially a deep, firm, red, painful nodule from 1–5 cm in diameter. After a few days, the nodule changes into a large, tender cystic nodule. The cysts may contain purulent drainage. Carbuncles have multiple openings onto the skin and may cause fever, chills, and malaise.

22. Cellulitis, a localized infection of the dermis and subcutaneous tissue, can occur following a wound or skin ulcer or as extension of furuncles or carbuncles. The infection spreads as a result of a substance called spreading factor or hyaluronidase, which is produced by the causative organism. Hyaluronidase breaks down the fibrin network and other barriers that normally localize the infection in the skin.

23. The area of cellulitis is red, swollen, and painful. In some cases, vesicles may form over the area of cellulitis. The client with cellulitis may experience fever, chills, malaise, headache, and swollen lymph glands.

24. Superficial fungal infections of the skin are often referred to as ringworm or tinea. Fungal disorders are also called mycoses. The fungi that cause superficial skin infections are called dermatophytes.

25. In humans, the dermatophytes live on keratin in the stratum corneum, hair, and nails. The fungal organism may be transmitted by direct contact with animals or other infected persons or by inanimate objects. Factors that increase the risk of a fungal infection include the use of broad-spectrum antibiotics that kill off normal flora and allow the fungi to grow, diabetes mellitus, immunodeficiencies, nutritional deficiencies, pregnancy, increasing age, and iron deficiency.

26. Tinea pedis (athlete's foot) affects the soles of the feet, the space between the toes, and the toenail. The lesions vary from mild scaliness to painful fissures with drainage, and they are usually accompanied by pruritus and a foul odor.

27. Tinea cruris is an infection of the groin that may extend to the inner thighs and buttocks. It is also called "jock itch," is often associated with tinea pedis, and is more common in people who are physically active, obese, and/or wear tight underclothing.

28. Candidiasis infections are caused by *Candida albicans*, a yeast-like fungus. This fungus is normally found on mucous membranes, on the skin, in the vagina, and in the gastrointestinal tract. *Candida albicans* becomes a pathogen when certain conditions encourage its growth, such as an environment of moisture, warmth, or altered skin integrity; systemic antibiotics; pregnancy; birth control pills; poor nutrition;

immunosuppression; diabetes mellitus; Cushing's disease; or other chronic debilitating illnesses.

29. Candidiasis occurs in the mouth, vagina, uncircumcised penis, nails, and deep skin folds. The first sign of infection is a pustule that often burns and itches. As the infection spreads, a white to yellow curd-like substance covers the infected area.

30. Viral infections are caused by viruses that are pathogens consisting of a ribonucleic acid (RNA) or DNA core surrounded by a protein coat. They depend on live cells for reproduction. Viruses that cause skin lesions either increase cellular growth or cause cellular death. Viral skin disorders may have a variety of causes including drugs such as birth control medications, corticosteroids, and antibiotics.

31. Warts (verrucae) are lesions caused by the human papillomavirus (HPV). Warts may be found on skin and mucous membranes. Nongenital warts are benign lesions. Genital warts may be precancerous. Warts are transmitted through skin contact. Warts may be flat, fusiform, or round, but most are round and raised and have a rough gray surface. Warts resolve spontaneously when immunity to the virus develops. This response may take up to 4 years.

32. There are many types of HPV including common warts and plantar warts, which occur at pressure points on the soles of the feet. Plantar warts tend to extend deeper beneath the skin surface and are often painful. Condylomata acuminata (venereal warts) occur in moist areas, along the glans of the penis, in the anal region, and on the vulva. They are usually cauliflower-like in appearance and have a pink or purple color.

33. Herpes simplex ("fever blister," "cold sore") infections are caused by two types of herpes virus: HSV I and HSV II. Most infections above the waist are caused by HSV I, whereas genital herpes infections can result from either HSV I or II. The virus can be transmitted by physical contact, oral sex, or kissing. The virus lives in nerve ganglia and may cause recurrent lesions in response to sunlight, menstruation, injury, or stress.

34. Herpes simplex infection begins with a burning or tingling sensation, followed by the development of erythema, vesicle formation, and pain. The vesicles progress through pustules, ulcers, and crusting until healing occurs in 10-14 days. The initial infection of herpes simplex is often severe and accompanied by systemic manifestations, such as fever and sore throat. Recurrences are more localized and less severe.

35. Herpes zoster ("shingles") is a viral infection of the skin caused by varicella zoster, the same herpesvirus that causes chickenpox. The varicella virus remains dormant in the sensory dorsal ganglia. Years after the initial chickenpox infection, the virus becomes reactivated. This often occurs when the client is immunocompromised. Clients with Hodgkin disease, certain types of leukemia, and lymphomas are more susceptible to an outbreak of herpes zoster. Once the virus is reactivated, inflammation and painful vesicles develop in the skin area connected to the same sensory dorsal ganglia.

36. The herpes zoster lesions are vesicles with an erythematous base usually appearing unilaterally on the face, trunk, and/or thorax. The vesicles continue to erupt for 3-5 days and then crust and dry. Recovery occurs in 4-6 weeks.

37. The older adult is especially sensitive to the pain and often experiences more severe outbreaks of herpes zoster. Complications include postherpetic neuralgia (a sharp, spasmodic pain along the course of one or more nerves) and vision loss. The neuralgia results from inflammation of the root ganglia. Vision loss may follow occurrence of lesions arising from the ophthalmic division of the trigeminal nerve.

38. Pediculosis is an infestation with lice, parasites that ingest the blood of an animal or human host. Pediculosis is often found in overcrowded living conditions or in people who do not have access to

bathing and clothes-washing facilities. Children tend to contract head lice while attending day care or school. Infestation occurs through contact with an infected person or contact with clothing and linen infested with the parasites.

39. Three types of lice live on human hosts. Pediculosis corporis is an infestation with body lice. These lice live in clothing fibers and are transmitted primarily by contact with infested clothes and bed linens. The louse bites cause a macule, followed by wheals and papules. Itching is common.

40. Pediculosis capitis is an infestation with head lice. The lice are often found behind the ears and nape of the neck but may spread to other hairy areas of the body. Transmission is by contact with an infected person or object such as a comb. The infestation causes itching, scratching, and erythema.

41. Pediculosis pubis is an infestation with pubic lice ("crabs"). The lice are spread through sexual activity or contact with infested clothing or linens. The infestation causes skin irritation and intense itching.

42. Scabies is an infestation caused by the female mite. It is spread by skin-to-skin contact, but the mite can live for 2 days on clothing and bedding. Scabies is found between the fingers, inner surfaces of the wrist and elbow, the axillae, the female nipple, the penis, the belt line, and the gluteal crease. Lesions appear about 4 weeks after contact with an infected person. The lesions are small red-brown burrows, about 2 mm in length, sometimes covered by vesicles that appear as a rash. Pruritus is common, especially at night. Excoriations from scratching predispose the person to secondary bacterial infections.

43. Interdisciplinary care for infections and infestations of the skin and mucous membranes are usually diagnosed and treated by a primary healthcare provider and then by self-care at home. Treatment is focused on identifying the causative agent, administering medications to kill the bacteria or eradicate the organism, and preventing secondary infections.

44. Two types of nonmelanoma skin cancers are basal cell carcinoma and squamous cell carcinoma. The factors involved in the development of nonmelanoma skin cancer include ultraviolet radiation (UVR), chemicals, skin pigmentation, and preexisting pigmented skin lesions. UVR from the sun is believed to be the cause of most nonmelanoma skin cancers. Sun rays are thought to either alter DNA or suppress T-cell and B-cell immunity. Exposure to ultraviolet radiation in tanning booths has also been implicated in nonmelanoma skin cancer development.

45. Human papillomavirus is implicated in the development of squamous cell carcinoma, as is damage to the skin from burns.

46. Squamous cell carcinoma begins as a firm, flesh-colored or erythematous papule. The tumor may be crusted. As it grows, it may ulcerate, bleed, and become painful. As the tumor extends into the surrounding tissue and becomes a nodule, the area around the nodule becomes indurated. Recurrent squamous cell carcinoma can be invasive, increasing the person's risk of metastasis.

47. Melanoma (cutaneous or malignant melanoma) is a skin cancer arising from melanocytes, the cells that produce melanin. The lesions, confined to the epidermis, are flat and relatively benign. When these cells penetrate the dermis, they mingle with blood and lymph vessels and are capable of metastasizing. At this latter stage, the tumors develop a raised or nodular appearance and often have smaller nodules, called satellite lesions, around the periphery.

48. The incidence of melanoma is higher in Caucasians who have had severe, blistering sunburns during childhood or live in sunny climates, clients who burn easily, and clients who visit tanning parlors. Precursor lesions for the development of melanoma are dysplastic nevi (moles), congenital nevi, and lentigo maligna.

49. Treatment of all skin cancers focuses on removal of malignant tissue using such methods as surgery, curettage and electrodessication, cryotherapy, or radiotherapy. The management of melanoma begins with identification, diagnosis, and tumor staging. Melanoma is also treated with chemotherapy, immunotherapy, radiation therapy, and biologic therapies (interleukin-2, interferon, monoclonal antibodies, or therapeutic vaccines containing melanoma antigens).

50. Pressure ulcers (decubitus ulcers) are ischemic lesions of the skin and underlying tissue caused by external pressure that impairs the flow of blood and lymph. The ischemia causes tissue necrosis and eventual ulceration. Pressure ulcers tend to develop over a bony prominence, but they may appear on any part of the body subjected to external pressure, friction, or shearing forces.

51. When a person lies or sits in one position for an extended length of time, without moving, pressure on the tissue between a bony prominence and the external surface of the body distorts capillaries and interferes with normal blood flow. If the pressure is not relieved, platelets clump in the endothelial cells surrounding the capillaries and form microthrombi, which impede blood flow, resulting in ischemia and hypoxia of tissues. Eventually, the cells and tissue of the immediate area and of the surrounding area die and become necrotic. The necrotic tissue elicits an inflammatory response.

52. The client with a pressure ulcer and inflammatory response may experience fever and pain and an increased white blood cell count. Secondary bacterial invasion is common. Enzymes from bacteria and macrophages dissolve necrotic tissue, resulting in a foul-smelling drainage.

53. People most at risk for pressure ulcers are older adults with limited mobility, people with quadriplegia, and clients in the critical care setting. Others at risk are clients with fractures of large bones and those who have undergone orthopedic surgery or sustained spinal cord injury. Incontinence, nutritional deficiency, and chronic illnesses create increased risk.

54. Laboratory tests are conducted to determine the presence of a secondary infection and to differentiate the cause of the ulcer. If an ulcer is deep or appears infected, drainage or biopsied tissue is cultured to determine the causative organism.

LEARNING OUTCOME 3

Use the nursing process to collect data and provide interventions for clients with common skin disorders, infections and infestations of the skin, malignant skin disorders, and pressure ulcers.

Concepts for Lecture

1. Assessment data, collected by the nurse working with clients who have common skin problems, include data to determine the degree of discomfort, the extent to which the skin condition is interfering with the client's activities of daily living and usual lifestyle, and the risk factors for complications (Box 45-2).

2. A common diagnosis for clients with common skin problems is Impaired Skin Integrity. A possible nursing implication includes advising the client to (1) use warm water because hot water dries the skin and increases itching, (2) trim the nails short, (3) keep environmental temperatures slightly cool, and (4) wear loose clothing, (5) rub the pruritic area rather than scratching, (6) use pressure or cold to relieve pruritus, and (7) wear cotton gloves at night. These measures relieve pruritus and decrease the risk of infection.

 POWERPOINT SLIDES

Tables and/or Figures
- **Box 45-2** Assessment: Clients With Common Skin Problems
- **Box 45-4** Assessment: Clients With Skin Cancer
- **Box 45-5** Pressure Ulcer Staging

Nursing Care Plan: Client With Malignant Melanoma

SUGGESTIONS FOR CLASSROOM ACTIVITIES
- Invite a wound care nursing specialist to discuss nursing care of pressure ulcers.
- Contact skin care product representatives to speak to the class about skin care and use of various products, beds, and supportive devices to treat skin conditions.
- Invite a school nurse to discuss processes for preventing spread of parasitic infections to school children.

3. Additionally the client is advised to use distraction or relaxation techniques; use mild detergent and rinse twice; avoid using fabric softeners, perfumes, and lotions containing alcohol; and apply skin lubricants after a bath to retain moisture.

4. Additional strategies to relieve itching and prevent excoriation include demonstrating methods of taking therapeutic baths or treatments, including using a soft washcloth in a circular motion; drying the skin with a soft towel using a blotting or patting motion; and teaching the client and family to watch for and report any complications of treatment (e.g., excoriation, increased redness, skin peeling, or blister formation).

5. A second possible nursing diagnosis for clients with common skin problems is Disturbed Body Image. Nursing interventions may include establishing a trusting nurse–client relationship; encouraging talking about self-perception and asking questions about the disease and the treatment; encouraging interactions with others through family involvement in care, referral to support groups, and referral to organizations (e.g., National Psoriasis Foundation).

6. Deficient Knowledge (Medication Administration) is another possible nursing diagnosis for a client with common skin problems. A nursing intervention is teaching the client general guidelines for applying topical medication. The nurse will teach clients using oral corticosteroids never to stop taking the medication abruptly.

7. Evaluation includes collecting data to determine the client's knowledge of medications and their use, the client's degree of comfort, and any changes in the level of skin integrity or involvement.

8. The nurse caring for clients with skin infections and skin infestations will collect subjective and objective assessment data to identify the manifestations and to determine the degree to which the client is at risk for complications.

9. One possible nursing diagnosis for a client with a skin infection or a skin infestation is Acute Pain. Nursing interventions include assessing and monitoring the location, duration, and intensity of the pain; administering prescribed medications regularly and evaluating their effectiveness; and using measures to relieve pruritus.

10. Another nursing diagnosis for clients with skin infections and skin infestations is Sleep Deprivation. Nursing interventions include providing interventions to relieve pain and pruritus, maintaining a cool environment, and avoiding heavy bed covers.

11. A third nursing diagnosis for clients with skin infections and skin infestations is Risk for Infection. Nursing interventions may include taking and recording vital signs every 4 hours, using interventions to decrease the itch-scratch-itch cycle, and instituting infection control procedures.

12. Evaluation of the effectiveness of nursing care for clients with a skin infection or infestation involves collecting assessment data, evaluating for changes in skin integrity and the need for additional measures to protect skin and underlying tissues from injury, and determining the client's understanding of medications and their use and of how to prevent transmission of the infection or infestation.

13. The nurse gathers data to determine factors in the client's history that may have increased the risk for skin cancer and to identify skin lesions (Box 45-4).

14. One nursing diagnosis for clients with skin cancers is Anxiety. Nursing interventions include providing reassurance; supporting the client's coping mechanisms; using short sentences; providing accurate information to the client and family about the illness, treatment, and expected length of recovery; encouraging discussion of expected physical changes and ways to minimize disfigurement through cosmetics and clothing; and providing the client with strategies for participating in the recovery process.

SUGGESTIONS FOR CLINICAL ACTIVITIES

- Have students spend a day with the wound/ostomy skin care nursing specialist.
- Invite the director of nursing or head nurse of the unit at the clinical agency to talk to the students about measures in the agency to prevent the occurrence of pressure ulcers.
- Arrange for clinical experiences at a wound clinic.

REFERENCE

- MedlinePlus: Pressure ulcers. Available at http://www.nlm.nih.gov/medlineplus/ency/article/007071.htm

15. Another nursing diagnosis for a client with skin cancer is Impaired Skin Integrity. Intervention includes monitoring the client every 4 hours for fever, tachycardia, and malaise, as well as for incisional erythema, swelling, pain, or drainage that increases or becomes purulent. The nurse also keeps the incision line clean and dry, follows principles of medical and surgical asepsis when caring for a client's incision, and encourages and maintains adequate calories and protein intake in the client's diet.

16. A third nursing diagnosis for a client with skin cancer is Hopelessness. Nursing interventions include using active listening, open-ended questions, and reflection on the client's statements; providing opportunities for the client to express hope, faith, a sense of purpose, and the will to live; exploring the client's perceptions; and encouraging the client to identify support systems and to participate in self-care, mutual decision making, and goal setting. The nurse encourages the client to focus not only on the present but also on the future.

17. Evaluating the effectiveness of nursing care for the client with skin cancer requires ongoing assessment and collection of data about effectiveness of treatment measures, client's understanding of and compliance with treatments, and effectiveness of medications.

18. Pressure ulcers are staged as stage I through stage IV. Stage I involves nonblanchable erythema of intact skin. Stage II is partial-thickness skin loss involving epidermis and/or dermis. The ulcer is superficial and presents clinically as an abrasion, blister, or shallow crater. Stage III is full-thickness skin loss involving damage or necrosis of subcutaneous tissue that may extend down to, but not through, underlying fascia. The ulcer presents clinically as a deep crater with or without undermining of adjacent tissue. Stage IV involves full-thickness skin loss with extensive destruction; tissue necrosis; or damage to muscle, bone, or supporting structures (e.g., tendon or joint capsule).

19. Nursing diagnoses for pressure ulcers include risk for Impaired Skin Integrity and impaired skin integrity. Nursing interventions include identifying at-risk individuals and the factors that place them at risk; minimizing skin exposure to moisture from body fluids; minimizing friction and shearing forces; ensuring adequate dietary intake of protein or calories; maintaining the clients' current level of activity, mobility, and range of motion; and teaching clients who can do so to shift their weight every 15 minutes.

LEARNING OUTCOME 4

Provide client and family teaching appropriate for prevention and self-care of disorders of the skin.

Concepts for Lecture

1. Because clients with disorders of the skin usually care for themselves at home, nursing interventions are primarily educational.

2. The nurse teaches clients taking tretinoin (Retin-A) for acne to apply it to clean dry skin and to expect redness and peeling of skin. If the client is taking isotretinoin (Acutane), the nurse teaches the client to take the pills with food, not to take vitamin A supplement or drink alcohol while using this drug, and to use sunscreen and protective clothing when outside. The client is to use a reliable contraceptive for 1 month before, during, and 1 month after therapy. If visual disturbances, nausea, vomiting, and headache occur, the client is to stop the drug at once and report manifestations to the physician (Table 45-1).

3. The nurse does health promotion stressing the importance of avoiding overexposure to ultraviolet rays, chemical irritants, and radiation;

 **POWERPOINT SLIDES**

Tables and/or Figures
- **Table 45-1** Giving Medications Safely: Acne
- **Table 45-2** Giving Medications Safely: Fungal Infections
- **Box 45-3** Client Teaching: Preventing Skin Cancer

SUGGESTIONS FOR CLASSROOM ACTIVITIES
- Have students prepare and present a teaching plan to parents on the treatment of head lice.
- Discuss the various OTC skin products that people use and the recommended value of these products. Ask students to reflect on how they would incorporate this information when teaching clients and their families.

eating a well-balanced diet and getting adequate sleep to promote healthy skin, hair, and nails; getting exercise; and bathing often enough to remove excess oil and perspiration.

4. The nurse teaches clients to use warm, not hot, water because hot water dries the skin and increases itching.

5. The nurse advises clients to trim their nails short, keep the environment cool, and wear loose clothing.

6. The nurse teaches clients to wash their clothing in a mild detergent, to rinse clothes twice, and not to use fabric softeners.

7. The nurse teaches clients taking antifungal agents to complete the full prescription; to avoid alcohol and exposure to sunlight; to take griseofulvin with meals; and if taking ketoconazole (Nizoral) or miconazole (Monistat), to continue vaginal applications through the menses and either refrain from sexual intercourse or have the partner wear a condom. If a client is taking nystatin (Mycostatin), the sexual partner must be treated at the same time or the infection will be passed back and forth (Table 45-2).

8. One of the most effective methods of reducing the spread of infection in any setting is careful hand washing. Healthcare providers must wash their hands with soap and water before and after every client contact, even if gloves are worn. All clients, family members, and visitors should be taught how to wash their hands effectively, and the importance of this procedure should be stressed.

9. The incidence of skin infections and infestations should be reduced with good hygiene practices and avoidance of shared clothing, linens, or towels. The nurse stresses the importance of wearing clean clothes and avoiding walking barefoot in gyms or pools.

10. The nurse teaches the client with a fungal infection that fungal infections are contagious. The nurse teaches the client not to share linens or personal items with others and to use a clean towel and washcloth each day; to carefully dry all skin folds; to not wear the same pair of shoes every day; to wear cotton socks or hose with cotton feet; to not wear rubber- or plastic-soled shoes; and to use talcum powder or an antifungal powder twice a day.

11. The nurse teaches the woman with a vaginal yeast infection to avoid tight jeans and pantyhose, to wear cotton or cotton-crotch panties, to bathe more frequently and dry the genital area well, and to have the sexual partner treated at the same time.

12. The nurse teaches the client with a viral infection that the disease is usually self-limiting.

13. The nurse advises the client with herpes zoster to not have contact with children or pregnant women until crusts have formed over the blister.

14. Teaching for clients with parasitic infestations and their family includes teaching to prevent the spread of the infestation and to dispel the myth that only dirty people have lice. The nurse teaches the client and family to wash clothing and linens in soap and hot water, iron clothing to kill lice eggs, boil personal care items, treat all family members and sexual partners, and not use combs, brushes, or hats of others.

15. Increased incidence of skin cancer requires that nurses be involved in early detection and in teaching preventive behaviors in all settings (Box 45-3).

16. The nurse teaches the client or family who is at risk for, or has been diagnosed with, skin cancer how to conduct self-examination of the skin on the same day of the month each month.

17. The nurse teaches prevention of pressure ulcers in clients cared for at home. The nurse teaches caregivers about the definition, description, and common location of pressure ulcers; risk factors for the development of pressure ulcers; skin care; ways to avoid injury; and diet. The nurse stresses eliminating pressure, friction, and shearing forces.

SUGGESTIONS FOR CLINICAL ACTIVITIES

- Assign students to care for clients with skin disorders. In postconference, have the students discuss how the families of their clients could be involved in the care of the clients and what teaching they would need.

18. Depending on the stage of the pressure ulcer, the nurse teaches the client or caregiver how to care for ulcers that are already present, including how to change wet-to-dry dressings, apply skin barriers, and avoid injury and infection.

GENERAL CHAPTER CONSIDERATIONS

1. Have students study and learn key terms listed at the beginning of the chapter.
2. Have students complete end of chapter exercises either in their book or on the MyNursingKit Website.
3. Use the Classroom Response Question PowerPoints to assess students prior to lecture.

- Clinical Reasoning Care Map

 MYNURSINGKIT *(www.mynursingkit.com)*
- Websites
- NCLEX® Questions
- Case Studies
- Key Terms

 STUDENT WORKBOOK AND RESOURCE GUIDE
- Chapter 45 activities
- *Separate purchase*

PRENTICE HALL NURSE'S DRUG GUIDE
- *Separate purchase*

 CLASSROOM RESPONSE QUESTION POWERPOINTS

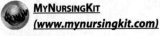 **TESTBANK**

CHAPTER 46
CARING FOR CLIENTS WITH BURNS

LEARNING OUTCOME 1

Discuss types, classification, extent estimation, and stages of treatment for burns.

Concepts for Lecture

1. A burn is an injury in which a transfer of energy from a heat source to the human body results in tissue loss, damage, or irreversible destruction. Burns may be the result of thermal, chemical, electrical, or radiation damage. The causative agents and priority treatment measures are unique to each type.

2. Thermal burns result from exposure to dry heat (flames) or moist heat (steam and hot liquids). Thermal burns are the most common type of burns and occur mostly in children and older adults.

3. Chemical burns are caused by direct skin contact with either acid or alkaline agents.

4. The severity of electrical burns depends on the type and duration of current and amount of voltage.

5. Radiation burns are usually associated with sunburn or radiation treatment for cancer. This type of burn tends to be superficial, involving only the outermost layers of the epidermis.

6. Tissue damage from a burn is determined primarily by the extent of the burn (the percentage of body surface area involved) and the depth of burn. See Table 46-1 for characteristics of burns by depth (superficial, partial-thickness, and full-thickness burns).

7. A superficial burn involves only loss of the epidermal skin layer. The skin is pink to red and dry. There may be local edema. Skin function is present. Pain sensation is present. Manifestations at the burn site are pain and local edema. The treatment is regular cleaning, topical agent of choice, and mild analgesics; scarring is none; outer layer peels; and the time to heal is 3 to 6 days.

8. In a partial-thickness burn, the skin layers lost are the epidermis and the dermis. Partial-thickness burns are subdivided into superficial or deep, depending on the depth of the burn. A superficial partial-thickness burn involves the entire dermis. A deep partial-thickness burn involves the entire dermis plus hair follicles, but sebaceous glands and epidermal sweat glands remain intact. The skin appearance is fluid-filled blister, and the skin is bright pink or red with edema. The skin function and pain sensation are absent. Manifestations at the burn site include severe pain, edema, and weeping of fluid. The treatment is regular cleaning and topical agent of choice, and the client may require skin grafting of deep partial-thickness burns. Scarring may occur in deep burns. The time to heal is 14 days to greater than 21 days.

9. In a full-thickness burn, the skin layers lost include the epidermis, dermis, and underlying tissue. The skin appearance over the burn is waxy white, dry, leathery, and charred. The skin function and pain sensation are absent. The manifestations at the burn site include little pain and some edema. The treatment for full-thickness burns is regular cleaning, topical agent of choice, skin substitutes, excision of eschar, and skin grafting. There is scarring of grafted area. The time for healing requires the skin graft to heal.

POWERPOINT SLIDES

Tables and/or Figures
- **Table 46-1** Characteristics of Burns by Depth
- **Figure 46-1** Burn Injury Classification According to the Depth of the Burn
- **Figure 46-2** Partial-Thickness Burn Injury
- **Figure 46-4** The "Rule of Nines"

SUGGESTIONS FOR CLASSROOM ACTIVITIES

- Ask a nurse from a burn unit to talk to the class about types, classification, extent estimation, and stages of treatment for burns. Ask the speaker to present some case illustrations. Have the students prepare questions in writing for the speaker and give them to the speaker prior to the presentation to the class.

SUGGESTIONS FOR CLINICAL ACTIVITIES

- Arrange for students to visit a regional burn center if clients with burns are not treated in your clinical agency. If clients with burns are treated in your clinical agency, arrange to have students rotate through the burn unit.
- If possible, have students assigned to care for clients with burns at the various stages of treatment. Have the students present these cases for group discussion in a postclinical conference.

REFERENCE

- EMS responder: Burn injuries. Available at http://www.emsresponder.com/print/ EMS-Magazine/Burning-Issues/1$10592

10. The "rule of nines" (see Figure 46-4) is a rapid method of estimating the extent of partial- and full-thickness burns. The head, trunk, arms, legs, and perineum are assigned percentages. The "rule of nines" is used during prehospital and emergency care phases. On admission to a facility, more accurate methods for estimating the extent of injury are employed.

11. The emergent or resuscitative stage lasts from the onset of injury through successful fluid resuscitation. It includes estimating the extent of the burn, instituting initial first-aid measures, and implementing fluid resuscitation therapies. The client is assessed for shock and respiratory distress. Physicians determine whether the client is to be transported to a burn center.

12. The acute stage begins with the start of diuresis and ends with closure of the burn wound. Hydrotherapy and excision and grafting of full-thickness wounds are done as soon as possible. Enteral and parenteral nutritional interventions are started early to address caloric needs. Topical and systemic antimicrobial agents are given to the client to combat infection. Narcotic agents must be administered before all invasive procedures to maximize client comfort and to reduce the anxieties associated with wound debridement and intensive physical therapy.

13. The rehabilitative stage begins with wound closure and ends when the client returns to the highest level of health, which may take years. The primary focus is biopsychosocial adjustment: the prevention of contractures and scars, and the client's successful resumption of work, family, and social roles through physical, vocational, occupational, and psychosocial rehabilitation.

LEARNING OUTCOME 2

Describe the pathophysiology of a major burn.

Concepts for Lecture

1. The pathophysiologic changes associated with major burns involve all body systems.
2. The burn injury impairs the normal physiologic functions of the skin that prevent evaporative water loss and bacteria entry and that maintain body warmth.
3. If the microcirculation of the skin remains intact during burning, it cools and protects the deeper portions of the skin and cools the outer surface once the heat source is removed. With extensive burn injury, however, the microcirculation is lost, and the burning process continues even after the heat source is removed.
4. The thickness of the dermis and epidermis varies considerably from one area of the body to another. A temperature that damages the medial aspect of the forearm may not cause damage to the skin covering the same person's back.
5. Major burns affect the cardiovascular system by causing hypovolemic shock, cardiac dysrhythmias, cardiac arrest, and vascular compromise.
6. Within minutes of the burn, cell wall integrity at the injury site and in the capillary bed is lost. This causes a massive amount of fluid to shift from the intracellular space into the interstitial space. The capillary walls become more permeable so that fluid leaks from the capillaries at the burn wound site and throughout the body, decreasing intravascular fluid volume. Without adequate fluids in the intracellular and intravascular spaces, the client becomes hypovolemic. Plasma proteins and sodium escape, further increasing edema formation. Blood pressure falls as cardiac output diminishes. The net result is hypovolemic shock, which is called burn shock.

SUGGESTIONS FOR CLASSROOM ACTIVITIES

• Divide the students into small groups to discuss the pathophysiology of major burns. Ask the students to diagram the physiologic changes occurring in a major burn.

SUGGESTIONS FOR CLINICAL ACTIVITIES

• Have students look at lab values for clients with burns, identifying electrolyte changes, changes in CBC values, changes in protein levels, and changes in blood gases. Ask students to discuss the abnormal values and what they might represent in terms of pathologic changes in specific body systems.

7. The loss of intravascular volume causes an increase in blood viscosity that increases the risk for blood clots. As the vascular system attempts to compensate for fluid loss, vasoconstriction occurs. Abnormal platelet aggregation and WBC accumulation result in ischemia and eventual thrombosis in the deeper tissue below the burn.

8. RBCs are hemolyzed due to direct damage from the burn. Because plasma fluid is lost rather than RBCs, hemoconcentration develops, which is seen as an elevated hematocrit.

9. Neutrophils accumulate at the burn site, producing an elevated leukocyte count.

10. The leakage of fluid into the interstitial spaces compromises the lymphatic system, resulting in intravascular hypovolemia and edema at the burn wound site. Edema impairs peripheral circulation and results in necrosis of the underlying tissue.

11. Potassium ions leave the cells due to burn injury and RBC hemolysis. Without adequate potassium to maintain normal cardiac rhythms, the client is at an increased risk of developing cardiac dysrhythmias.

12. Burn shock reverses when fluid is absorbed from the interstitium into the intravascular space. The blood pressure rises as cardiac output increases and urinary output improves. Diuresis continues from several days to 2 weeks post burn. During this phase, the extra cardiac workload may predispose the older client or the client with cardiovascular disease to fluid volume overload. Even after capillary integrity is restored, fluid losses continue until the burn wound is closed.

13. Circumferential burns to the extremities may damage blood vessels, which decreases circulation. Damaged tissue may become edematous, causing further reduction in circulation. When circumferential burns and edema occur together, compartment syndrome may result.

14. Inhalation injury is a complication that may range from mild respiratory inflammation to massive pulmonary failure. Exposure to toxic chemicals that can cause asphyxia, smoke, and heat initiates the pathophysiologic processes.

15. Curling's ulcer is an acute ulceration of the stomach or duodenum that may form following a burn injury. Paralytic ileus may occur secondary to burn trauma. Lack of intestinal motility leads to gastric distention, nausea, vomiting, and hematemesis.

16. Massive fluid losses occur during the early stages of the burn injury, leading to dehydration, hemoconcentration, and decreased urinary output. Dark brown concentrated urine may indicate hemoglobinuria, which is the result of the release of large amounts of dead or damaged erythrocytes after a major burn. The pigments can occlude the renal tubules and cause renal failure, especially when dehydration, acidosis, or shock is also present.

17. Capillary leakage impairs the active components of both the cell-mediated and humeral immune systems. Serum levels of all immunoglobulins are significantly reduced. Serum protein levels remain persistently low until wound closure occurs. These changes in the immune system create a state of acquired immunodeficiency, which places the burn client at risk for infection for up to 4 weeks following the injury.

18. Cortisol is released due to the stress of the burn injury, which depresses the immune system and increases the risk of infection.

19. Two metabolic phases occur as the body responds to the burn injury. In the first 3 days of the injury, the ebb phase takes place. During this phase, there is decreased oxygen consumption, fluid imbalance, shock, and inadequate circulating volume. These responses protect the body from the initial impact of the injury.

20. The flow phase occurs when adequate burn resuscitation has been accomplished. Now there is increased cellular activity and protein catabolism, lipolysis, and gluconeogenesis.

21. The basal metabolic rate (BMR) reaches twice the normal rate, causing the body weight and heat to drop dramatically. Hypermetabolism continues until after wound closure and may reappear if complications occur.

LEARNING OUTCOME 3

Identify the interdisciplinary care necessary for the client with a major burn, including diagnostic tests; medications; fluid resuscitation; respiratory management; nutritional support; wound management; surgery; biologic and biosynthetic dressings; scar, keloid, and contracture prevention; and wound dressings.

Concepts for Lecture

1. After stabilization in the emergency department, the client is transferred to the critical care unit or a specialized burn center. In both settings, continuous monitoring of laboratory tests, administration of fluids and pharmaceutical agents, pain control, wound management, and nutrition support therapies are the focus of care.

2. Urinalysis is done to evaluate renal perfusion and nutritional status. In catabolic states, nitrogen is excreted in large amounts into the urine. Nitrogen loss is measured through 24-hour urine collections for total nitrogen, urea nitrogen, and amino acid nitrogen. Loss of plasma protein and dehydration lead to proteinuria and elevated urine specific gravity.

3. The complete blood count reveals hematocrit elevated secondary to hemoconcentration and fluid shifts from the intravascular compartment during the emergent phase. Hemoglobin is decreased secondary to hemolysis. White blood cells (WBCs) are elevated in the presence of infection. Sodium levels are decreased secondary to massive fluid shifts into the interstitium. Potassium levels initially are increased, but decrease after burn shock resolves, as fluid shifts back to intracellular and intravascular compartments.

4. Total protein and albumin indicate nutritional status during the rehabilitative state. Arterial blood gases are used to monitor oxygen status and acid–base disturbances. The burn-injured client may have elevated or lowered pH, decreased PCO_2, decreased PO_2, and low-normal bicarbonate levels.

5. Pulse oximetry allows continuous assessment of oxygen saturation levels. The burn-injured client may have oxygen saturation below 95%.

6. Chest x-ray studies document changes within the first 24 to 72 hours that may reflect the presence of atelectasis, pulmonary edema, or acute respiratory distress. If an upper airway injury is manifested, a flexible bronchoscopy permits direct visualization.

7. Electrocardiograms (ECGs) are necessary to monitor the development of dysrhythmias, especially those associated with hypokalemia and hyperkalemia.

8. Burns often cause excruciating pain. In the emergent stages of care, intravenously administered narcotics such as morphine, hydromorphone, or fentanyl are the best means of managing pain, with morphine being the drug of choice.

9. Once the client is stabilized, it is appropriate to administer narcotic agents prior to wound care or intensive exercising routines. Since burn treatments can cause high levels of anxiety, anxiolytics such as midazolam and lorazepam are effective when given an hour before wound care.

POWERPOINT SLIDES

Tables and/or Figures

- **Table 46-2** Giving Medications Safely: Topical Antimicrobial Agents
- **Figure 46-5** Escharotomy
- **Figure 46-7** Wound Vacuum
- **Figure 46-8** Burn Contracture
- **Figure 46-9** Closed Method of Dressing a Burn
- **Figure 46-10** Custom-Made Elastic Pressure Garment

SUGGESTIONS FOR CLASSROOM ACTIVITIES

- Arrange for a dietitian who works with clients who have burns to come and talk to the class about nutritional support for the client who has major burns.
- Invite a wound care specialist as a guest speaker to discuss wound management for clients with major burns.

SUGGESTIONS FOR CLINICAL ACTIVITIES

- Assign students to assist primary nurses with the care of clients with major burns. If this is not possible, arrange for students to observe the care of clients with major burns. Have students review the client's charts and observe care, making note of the interdisciplinary care necessary for the client with a major burn.

REFERENCE

- Levenson SM, Kan D, Gruber C, Crowley LV, Lent R, Watford A, Seifter E: Chemical debridement of burns. Available at http://www.ncbi.nlm.nih.gov/pmc/articles/instance/1344165/

10. See Table 46-2, Giving Medication Safely: Topical Antimicrobial Agents. Antimicrobial agents that are effective against gram-negative and gram-positive organisms and are used to prevent burn wound infections include mafenide acetate (Sulfamylon), a synthetic antibiotic; silver nitrate, a bacteriostatic agent used in a 0.5% solution in distilled water to prevent burn wound infections; and silver sulfadiazine (Silvadene), a cream that acts on bacterial cell membranes as a bactericidal.

11. Fluid resuscitation is the administration of intravenous fluids to restore the circulating blood volume during the acute period when capillary permeability is increased. To counter the effects of burn shock, fluid resuscitation guidelines are used to replace the extensive fluid and electrolyte losses associated with major burn injuries. Fluid replacement is necessary in all burn wounds that involve more than 20% of the total body surface area (TBSA).

12. Colloids, crystalloids, blood, and blood products are used for fluid resuscitation and maintenance. Warmed lactated Ringer's solution is the intravenous fluid of choice during the first 24 hours after burn injury because it most closely approximates the body's extracellular fluid composition.

13. Hourly urine output is an indicator of effective fluid resuscitation, with 30 to 50 mL/hr considered adequate.

14. A pulmonary artery catheter monitors cardiac output, cardiac index, and pulmonary wedge pressures. All measurements must be maintained within normal limits to attain adequate fluid resuscitation.

15. The client's head needs to be elevated to 30 degrees or more to maximize respiratory efforts.

16. The airway passages must be kept clear with frequent suctioning, encouraging the client to use incentive spirometry, and helping the client cough and deep breathe every 2 hours.

17. If airway obstruction occurs, the client will require intubation. Oxygen flow rate is based on arterial blood gas results. The client may be placed on a face mask, steam collar, T-piece, mechanical ventilation with positive end-expiratory pressure (PEEP), pressure support ventilation, or high-frequency jet ventilation.

18. The goal of all therapies is to maintain adequate tissue oxygenation with the least amount of inspired oxygen flow necessary.

19. Oral intake can seldom meet the caloric requirements necessary to reverse the excessive protein breakdown and to begin the healing process. Calorie needs may be as great as 4,000 to 6,000 kcal/day.

20. Enteral feedings are started within 24 to 38 hours of the burn injury to offset hypermetabolism, improve nitrogen balance, and decrease length of hospital stay. A gastrointestinal feeding tube is inserted with the tip extending past the pylorus to prevent reflux and aspiration.

21. Enteral feeding is contraindicated in Curling's ulcer, bowel obstruction, feeding intolerance, pancreatitis, or septic ileus. When the enteral route cannot be used, a central venous catheter is inserted via the subclavian or jugular vein for the administration of total parenteral nutrition.

22. Wound management includes cleaning and debriding of necrotic tissue and blisters to promote healing and prevent prolonged inflammation. Wound management also includes cleaning the wound with a mild, nonperfumed antimicrobial soap or wound cleanser solution to remove dead skin and separate eschar. The solution is rinsed with warm saline or tap water. Body hair is shaved close to the burn wound before debridement to decrease the risk of infection. Intravenous narcotics and anxiolytics are administered during debridement to control pain and anxiety.

23. Mechanical debridement is performed during hydrotherapy. In this procedure, loose necrotic tissue is gently washed with a washcloth or gauze pad to remove dead skin and eschar. Blistered skin is grasped

with a dry gauze and gently removed. The edges of blisters or eschar are trimmed with blunt scissors.

24. Hydrotherapy measures include showering, using a spray table, or immersion in a tub of water. Prolonged immersion in a tub is used less often because it can lead to chilling after the bath and can increase risk of wound infection.

25. Enzymatic debridement involves the use of a topical agent to dissolve and remove necrotic tissue. Following hydrotherapy, an enzyme of choice is applied in a thin layer directly to the wound and covered with one layer of fine mesh gauze. A topical antimicrobial agent is applied and covered with a bulky wet dressing, and the wound is immobilized with expandable mesh gauze.

26. Various surgical procedures are performed to treat the burn wound, including surgical debridement, which is the process of excising tissue from the burn wound to the level of viable tissue. The most common technique is electrocautery. Debridement may also be performed by using a dermatome to slice off thin layers of damaged skin.

27. Escharotomy is performed by the physician with a scalpel or electro-cautery. A sterile surgical incision is made longitudinally along the extremity or the truck to prevent constriction, impaired circulation, and possibly gangrene.

28. Autografting is used to effect permanent skin coverage of the wound. Skin is removed from healthy tissue of the burn-injured client and applied to the burn wound. After the autograft is applied, the grafted area is immobilized.

29. Cultured epithelial autografting is a technique in which skin cells are removed from unburned sites on the client's body, minced, and placed in a culture medium for growth. Enough skin can be grown over a period of 3 to 4 weeks to cover an entire human body. The cells are prepared in sheets and attached to petroleum jelly gauze backing, which is applied to the burn wound site.

30. Biologic dressing and biosynthetic dressing refer to any temporary material that rapidly adheres to the wound bed, promotes healing, or prepares the burn wound for permanent autograft coverage. The dress-ings are applied as soon as possible. They help eliminate the loss of water through evaporation, reduce infection, and promote wound heal-ing. Biologic and biosynthetic dressings that are currently in use include Biobrane, Dermagraft, Integra, AlloDerm, TransCyte, and Apligraf.

31. One of the newer treatment methods is the vacuum-assisted closure (VAC) device. VAC consists of a sponge placed over the wound with tubing that connects the sponge to a pump. An occlusive, adhesive dressing covers the wound and tubing, sealing the wound to create negative pressure. VAC aids in reducing wound edema, removing exu-date, and improving healing in partial-thickness burns.

32. When a burn extends into the dermal layer of skin, the skin is repaired through scar formation. Two types of excessive scar may develop: (1) a hypertrophic scar is an overgrowth of dermal tissue that remains within the boundaries of the wound; (2) a keloid is a scar that extends beyond the boundaries of the original wound. People with darker skin are at greater risk for the formation of hyper-trophic scars and keloids.

33. During the healing process, the burn scar shrinks and becomes fixed and inelastic, resulting in contracture of the wound (permanent short-ening of connective tissue). Once a contracture forms, the tissue resists being stretched, and its inelasticity limits body movement. Positioning, splinting, exercise, and constant pressure application help prevent contractures from forming.

34. After the wound has been cleaned and debrided, it may be dressed by the open or closed method.

35. In the open method, the burn wound remains open to air, covered only by a topical antimicrobial agent. This method allows easy wound assessment. It can be used only when strict isolation precautions are followed. Topical agents must be reapplied frequently because they tend to rub off onto the bedding.

36. In the closed method, a topical antimicrobial agent is applied to the wound site, which is covered with gauze or a nonadherent dressing and then gently wrapped with a gauze roll bandage. With the closed method, burns are usually dressed twice daily and as needed. With wet to dry dressings, thick gauze is applied to maintain moisture and is soaked every 2 hours with the ordered solution.

37. Splints are used to immobilize body parts and prevent contractures of the joints. The splints are applied and removed according to a schedule established by the physical therapist who also prescribes range of motion exercises. The exercises are performed during hydrotherapy and every 2 hours at bedside.

38. Applying uniform pressure can prevent or reduce hypertrophic scarring. Tubular support bandages are applied 5 to 7 days after graft. They maintain a tension ranging from 10 to 20 mm Hg to control scarring. The client wears custom-made elastic pressure garments such as a Jobst garment for 6 months to a year postgraft.

LEARNING OUTCOME 4

Use the nursing process to collect data and provide interventions for clients with major burns.

Concepts for Lecture

1. The client with a burn injury may require care ranging from education for self-care at home to complex care planning involving the multidisciplinary team. The client and family will experience a wide range of psychologic and emotional responses. Part of the nurse's role is to support them and to address their concerns.

2. In the emergent stage of burn injury care, nursing priorities are fluid resuscitation, maintenance of patent airway, pain, anxiety, and nutrition.

3. In the acute stage, nursing care priorities are on wound care including skin grafting as needed, pain, prevention of infection, physical and occupational therapy, and nutrition.

4. In the rehabilitative stage, care focuses on assisting the client to resume a functional role in society. Continuous psychosocial support is essential for the client and family throughout all stages.

5. The nurse initially assesses all body systems of the client with a major burn to identify abnormal findings and potential problems that may occur as a result of the injury. See Box 46-1 for assessment data to collect. These data are necessary to determine fluid resuscitation, causative agent, any on-the-scene treatment, health history, and age. Body weight on admission is necessary to monitor nutritional status during treatment.

6. A nursing diagnosis for a client with a burn is Impaired Skin Integrity, with a possible outcome that the client remains free of edema and impaired circulation. Nursing interventions include; (1) monitoring appearance of the burn wound, amount and type of drainage, body temperature, and WBC count; (2) reporting changes from usual condition; (3) assisting with daily wound care, including debridement and hydrotherapy; (4) applying topical antimicrobial agents as prescribed and reapplying as necessary; (5) providing special skin care to sensitive body areas; (6) cleaning burns involving the eyes with normal

POWERPOINT SLIDES

Tables and/or Figures
- **Box 46-1** Initial Focused Assessment of the Client With a Major Burn

Nursing Care Plan: Client With a Major Burn

SUGGESTIONS FOR CLASSROOM ACTIVITIES
- Discuss the role of the nurse in each of the stages of care of a client with a major burn. Illustrate how the nursing process is used in the emergency department and critical care unit, through the rehabilitative stages.
- Prepare a list of potential client problems that may occur in a client with a major burn. Ask students to work in groups of two or three students. Give each group a problem. Ask the students in the group to identify data they could collect about the problem, determine what care would be appropriate to resolve the problem, and how they would evaluate the effectiveness of care.

SUGGESTIONS FOR CLINICAL ACTIVITIES
- Have the students care for clients with burns in the clinical setting. Assign students to create a client problem list along with nursing care interventions.
- Have students present an actual case study of a client with major burns that illustrates the powerlessness that a client with major burns may experience. Ask students to express how they would feel in the same circumstances.

saline or sterile water; and (7) if contractures of the eyelid develop, applying eye drops or ointment to the eye to prevent corneal abrasion.

7. Nursing interventions for Impaired Skin Integrity also include: (8) gently wiping burns of the lips with saline-soaked pads; (9) applying an antibiotic ointment as ordered; (10) assessing the mouth frequently and performing mouth care routinely; (11) repositioning the oral endotracheal tube (if one is in place) often to prevent pressure sore formation; (12) positioning nasogastric and nasotracheal tubes to prevent excessive pressure; (13) not covering the ears with dressing and not using pillows (a foam donut is used to reduce pressure to the ears); (14) cleaning burns of the perineum during hydrotherapy; (15) assessing the area for evidence of infection and rinsing thoroughly after toileting; and (16) changing dressings as prescribed.

8. When the open method of dressing is used, follow strict sterile technique. If the closed method is used, apply in a distal-to-proximal manner. Wrap all fingers and toes separately, elevate burned or newly skin-grafted extremities at or above the heart level, and immobilize skin graft sites for 3 to 5 days.

9. Deficient Fluid Volume is another nursing diagnosis for clients with major burns. A possible expected outcome is that the client maintains adequate circulating volume. Nursing interventions for Deficient Fluid Volume include assessing vital signs frequently; following prescribed orders for administering intravenous fluids; monitoring intake and output hourly; weighing daily; and testing all stools and emesis for the presence of blood. The nurse needs to monitor the client for fluid volume overload (assess breath sounds, pulse, and blood pressure).

10. Risk for Infection is another nursing diagnosis for a client with major burns. A possible expected outcome is that the client remains free of signs of infection. Nursing interventions for Risk for Infection include: (1) monitoring and recording body temperature every 1 to 2 hours; (2) documenting and reporting increased body temperature; (3) monitoring WBC counts; (4) determining tetanus immunization status; (5) maintaining an aseptic environment; and (6) monitoring for the presence of urgency, frequency, dysuria, bacteria in the urine, and fever. If the client has an indwelling catheter, the nurse needs to assess the urine for cloudiness and a foul odor and obtain urine and culture sensitivity at least weekly.

11. Another nursing diagnosis for a client with major burns is Impaired Physical Mobility, with an expected outcome that the client will maintain mobility to the level possible without contractures. Interventions include performing active or passive range of motion exercises to all joints every 2 hours and ambulating the client when stable; applying splints as prescribed; maintaining antideformity positions and repositioning hourly; and maintaining limbs in functional alignment. The nurse needs to assess all clients, especially the older adult, for signs of pressure ulcer formation under a splint.

12. Imbalanced Nutrition: Less than Body Requirements is another nursing diagnosis for a client with major burns. A possible expected outcome is that the client maintains weight within normal limits. Nursing interventions include maintaining nasogastric/nasointestinal tube placement; maintaining enteral/parenteral nutritional support as prescribed; observing and reporting any evidence of feeding intolerance; and weighing daily.

13. Acute Pain is a nursing diagnosis for clients with major burns. A possible expected outcome is that the client verbalizes a level of acceptable pain. Nursing interventions for Acute Pain include assessing level of pain; anticipating the need for prophylactic analgesia; explaining all procedures and expected levels of discomfort; and using nonnarcotic pain control along with medications for pain.

14. Powerlessness is a nursing diagnosis for clients with major burns. A possible expected outcome is that the client expresses a sense of control. Nursing interventions for Powerlessness include allowing as much control over the surroundings and daily routine as possible, such as choosing times for dressing changes; keeping needed items within reach, such as a call light, urinal, water pitcher, and tissues; encouraging expression of feelings; helping set short-term realistic goals; and helping access support systems.

15. To evaluate the effectiveness of nursing care, the nurse collects data about wound healing, fluid and electrolyte status, patency of airway, absence of infection, adequate nutrition, pain relief, and absence of complications. The nurse also needs to assess the client's perceptions of ability to control the outcomes of treatment and care. As the burn heals, the nurse will need to evaluate effectiveness of exercises and splinting in preventing contractures.

LEARNING OUTCOME 5

Provide client and family teaching for care of the burn after discharge.

Concepts for Lecture

1. Client and family teaching is an important component of all phases of burn care. As treatment progresses, encourage family members to assume more responsibility in providing care; from admission to discharge, teach family members to assess all findings, implement therapies, and evaluate progress.

2. Early in the plan of care, explain to the client and family the long-term goals of rehabilitation care: to prevent soft tissue deformity, protect skin grafts, maintain physiologic function, manage scars, and return the client to his or her optimal level of independence.

3. The teaching plan focuses on helping the client and family prevent dehydration, infection, and pain; maintain adequate nutrition and skin integrity; and restore mobility and psychosocial well-being.

4. Teach the client and family how to assess for evidence of fluid volume deficit. Explain the rationale supporting all fluid therapies and emphasize the need to report immediately all signs and symptoms of fluid imbalance, including weight loss, scanty urine output, and dry mucous membranes.

5. Explain the rationale about asepsis. Instruct caregivers to protect the client from exposure to people with colds or infections and to follow aseptic technique meticulously when caring for the wound. Ensure that the client and family are able to recognize all signs and symptoms of infection, including fever, poor wound healing, purulent drainage, and malaise.

6. Consultation with physical therapy begins early in the treatment plan and continues throughout the long-term rehabilitative process.

7. Explain to the client and family the need for progressive physical activity, and help them establish realistic goals.

8. Explain the rationale supporting the use of splints, pressure support garments, and other assistive devices, and demonstrate how to apply them. Ensure that the client and family understand the importance of reporting any evidence of lack of progress.

9. Identify and answer all questions related to the client's nutritional therapies and maintaining adequate daily calorie intake. Consult with a dietician early in the treatment plan and throughout rehabilitation.

10. Encourage the client and family to express concerns related to pain management. Explain the causes of pain and discomfort and the

POWERPOINT SLIDES

Tables and/or Figures
- **Figure 46-8** Burn Contracture (Source: Courtesy of JPD/Custom Medical Stock Photo, Inc.)

SUGGESTIONS FOR CLASSROOM ACTIVITIES
- Discuss the long-term care of a client with major burns, including discussion of community agencies and web searches for support groups and burn recovery sites.
- If possible invite representatives of a burn recovery or burn support groups to speak to the students.

SUGGESTIONS FOR CLINICAL ACTIVITIES
- Ask students to develop a teaching plan for a client with a major burn.

REFERENCE
- UC Davis Medical Center: Burn recovery. Available at http://www.ucdmc.ucdavis.edu/healthconsumers/pss/burnrecovery/

rationale supporting the use of analgesia. Instruct the client and family to report inadequate pain control. Teach the client and family alternative pain control therapies.

11. Instruct the client and family in the care of the graft and donor sites. Provide the rationale for use of all pressure support garments.
12. Emphasize the need to report any evidence of inadequate wound healing, including altered skin integrity, drainage, swelling, and redness.
13. Encourage the client and family to express their fears and concerns, and provide referrals to appropriate community resources. Powerlessness, anger, guilt, anxiety, and feeling of loss are common reactions to burn injury.
14. Direct the client and family to occupational therapy, social services, clergy, or psychiatric services as appropriate. Suggest helpful resources such as the American Burn Association, American Academy of Facial Plastic and Reconstructive Surgery, and the Phoenix Society for Burn Survivors, Inc.

GENERAL CHAPTER CONSIDERATIONS

1. Have students study and learn key terms listed at the beginning of the chapter.
2. Have students complete end of chapter exercises either in their book or on the MyNursingKit website.
3. Use the Classroom Response Question PowerPoints to assess students prior to lecture.

• Clinical Reasoning Care Map

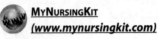

MYNURSINGKIT
(www.mynursingkit.com)

• Websites
• NCLEX® Questions
• Case Studies
• Key Terms

STUDENT WORKBOOK AND RESOURCE GUIDE

• Chapter 46 activities
• *Separate purchase*

PRENTICE HALL NURSE'S DRUG GUIDE

• *Separate purchase*

CLASSROOM RESPONSE QUESTION
POWERPOINTS

TESTBANK

CHAPTER 47
MENTAL HEALTH AND ASSESSMENT

LEARNING OUTCOME 1

Compare and contrast mental health and mental illness.

Concepts for Lecture

1. There are seven important aspects of a mentally healthy person: accurate assessment of reality; healthy self-concept; ability to relate to others; sense of meaning in life; creativity/productivity; control over one's own behavior; and adaptability to change and conflict. The mentally ill person will be lacking to some degree in one or more of these seven important aspects.

2. The person with mental illness might have difficulty differentiating between what really is and what might be and difficulty reasonably predicting the consequences of his or her own behavior (e.g., knowing that if you hit another person, they might hit you back).

3. A person with mental illness might not have a healthy concept of self, which includes realistic appraisal of abilities, function, and appearance, and might not have a positive acceptance of the self as it is.

4. If a person does not have the ability to relate to others in a satisfying way, a person cannot be fully mentally healthy.

5. A fully mentally healthy person will have a sense of what is important in life and what gives life meaning. Many people find a sense of meaning through religion, nature, philosophy, ethics, or service to others. A mentally ill person may have difficulty finding meaning in life.

6. The mentally healthy person does not have to be an artist to be creative. Healthy people can solve problems creatively. The mentally healthy person can interpret experiences abstractly. Persons who are mentally ill may think more concretely (e.g., interpret proverbs concretely). Mentally healthy people want to feel like they are doing something to make a difference to others or to the world, and this is a part of healthy creativity. People who are mentally ill may not be concerned with a sense of productivity or contribution.

7. Mentally healthy people can control their behavior, meaning they can balance conflicts with their instincts, conscience, and reality before they act. Mentally ill people may have difficulty doing this (e.g., mentally ill people may act out violently because they are frustrated at the moment). Mentally healthy people can delay gratification, whereas mentally ill people may have difficulty delaying gratification. Mentally healthy people are more apt to act in a way that helps someone else even if it is difficult for them.

8. Mentally healthy people are adaptable. They can compromise, plan, and be flexible. They can manage conflict successfully and can manage change. The mentally ill person may have difficulty with adaptability.

9. Mental health is a range of behaviors, a relative state, not an absolute thing. Nobody is at the ultimate level of health in every area all the time. A person can have minimal to maximal mentally healthy behavior, whether he or she has a mental disorder or not.

POWERPOINT SLIDES

Tables and/or Figures
- **Figure 47-1** Young Woman With Healthy Self-Concept

SUGGESTIONS FOR CLASSROOM ACTIVITIES

- Based on the premise that mental illness would be an alteration in or absence of the attributes of mental health, elicit from students the characteristics of a client with a mental illness.
- Discuss the idea of mental health and mental illness on a continuum.
- Discuss the prevalence and impact of mental illness on society. Include a discussion of the underdiagnosing of mental illness.

SUGGESTIONS FOR CLINICAL ACTIVITIES

- Ask students to write you a note about their experience, if any, working with or living with people who are mentally ill and any feelings or fears they have in working with the mentally ill. Have one-on-one conferences with the students prior to assigning them to a client who is mentally ill.
- Invite a nurse who works in the mental health clinical area to speak with students about the challenges faced and techniques to use when caring for a client with a mental illness.
- In postconference, have students identify what aspects of mental health seemed to be impaired in the client assigned to them and what aspects of mental health were intact.

LEARNING OUTCOME 2

Describe the relationship between neurotransmission in the brain and mental illness.

Concepts for Lecture

1. Human consciousness, behavior, learning, memory, emotion, and creativity are all the result of physiologic brain functions. Neurotransmission is the communication between neurons conducted by neurotransmitter chemicals. Neurotransmission must occur for the brain to perform normally. An understanding of neurotransmission is the foundation for understanding mental illness.
2. Neurotransmitters are chemical messengers that conduct impulses from one neuron to the next. Neurotransmitters are manufactured in the neuron (nerve cell) and are released from the axon (the part of the nerve cell conveying an impulse away from the cell body) into the synapse (space between the axon and its target cell's dendrite). The neurotransmitter chemical stimulates the dendrite (the part of the neuron that conveys impulses toward the cell body) of the cell after the synapse.
3. The neurotransmitter must fit into a specific receptor site on the surface of the dendrite. The receptor site that is stimulated by the appropriate transmitter opens the ion channel into the dendrite. The ion channel allows for interchange of ions (sodium, potassium, and calcium), which changes the electrical charge of the cell (depolarization). In this way, an electrical impulse passes from one neuron to the next.
4. After the neurotransmitter is released into the synapse, it either excites or inhibits the next neuron (depending on the neurotransmitter). It is either taken back into the axon to be stored for later use (reuptake), or it is inactivated and metabolized by enzymes.
5. When certain neurotransmitters have abnormally high or decreased function, mental disorders result.
6. Acetylcholine is decreased in Alzheimer's and Parkinson's diseases.
7. Dopamine is increased in schizophrenia and mania and decreased in depression and Parkinson's disease.
8. Norepinephrine is decreased in depression and increased in schizophrenia, mania, and anxiety.
9. Serotonin probably plays a role in disorders of schizophrenia and is decreased in depression. Serotonin is possibly decreased in anxiety and obsessive-compulsive disorder.
10. Gamma-aminobutyric acid (GABA) is decreased in anxiety and schizophrenia.
11. Glutamate is implicated in schizophrenia and increased in Alzheimer's disease. See Table 47-1, Neurotransmitters and Their Relationship to Mental Disorders.

LEARNING OUTCOME 3

Explain why psychosocial assessment is important.

Concepts for Lecture

1. Psychosocial assessments are important because nurses treat the whole client—body, mind, and spirit. Each aspect of the person affects the others.
2. In completing the psychosocial assessment, the nurse identifies factors that may affect both psychologic and social functioning.

 **POWERPOINT SLIDES**

Tables and/or Figures

- **Table 47-1** Neurotransmitters and Their Relationship to Mental Disorders

 SUGGESTIONS FOR CLASSROOM ACTIVITIES

- Invite students to begin thinking about the relationship between neurotransmitter abnormalities and pharmacotherapy for mental disorders.
- Invite a Pharm-D or pharmacology professor to come to the class and talk about the relationship between neurotransmitter abnormalities and pharmacotherapy for mental disorders.

 SUGGESTIONS FOR CLINICAL ACTIVITIES

- Assign students to care for clients who have a mental illness. Ask students to review their client's medications targeted for specific symptoms of mental illness and make note of what specific abnormalities of specific neurotransmitters the medication is directed at correcting.
- Ask one of the psychiatrists in the clinical area to talk with the students in postconference about the relationship between the medications they are prescribing and neurotransmitter abnormalities.

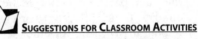 **REFERENCE**

- National Institute of Mental Health: Information about mental illness and the brain. Available at http://science.education.nih.gov/supplements/nih5/mental/guide/info-mental-a.htm

 **POWERPOINT SLIDES**

Tables and/or Figures

- **Table 47-3** Assessing Self-Concept
- **Table 47-4** Assessing Coping skills

3. Information about a client's family and culture is an important part of the psychosocial assessment because family and culture affect each person's health attitudes and behaviors related to health and illness.

4. Culture encompasses the attitudes, beliefs, customs, and behaviors that are passed from one generation to the next. Assessing a person's culture is important because it influences how a person dresses; what they eat; what work they do; their religion, language, customs, family roles, and parenting behavior; the way they relate to others; how they educate their children; their values and attitudes about right and wrong; and the priorities they set for their lives.

5. The psychosocial assessment includes the client's marital status and the members of the client's household because this information helps the healthcare team understand what family roles and responsibilities the client has and what kind of support the client might receive at home.

6. The languages spoken in the client's home are an aspect of psychosocial assessment because language affects the client's ability to relate and communicate with others. The nurse's ability to communicate with the client will affect the quality of nursing assessments, some interventions, and teaching.

7. It is important for nurses to understand that it requires different skills to understand technical or medical language than it does to conduct social conversation. Some clients will be independent for everyday communication but will require an interpreter for informed consent or discharge teaching situations.

8. Religious affiliation is an important psychosocial issue. Clients may have special religious-oriented dietary needs (such as Jewish clients who adhere to kosher dietary laws, Hindus or Seventh-Day Adventists who are vegetarians, Mormons who cannot consume caffeine), and many religious traditions require special foods or restrict foods for certain religious holy days.

9. Religion can be especially important to people when they are ill. Catholics and other Christians may want to be visited by their religious priests or ministers when they are sick. The nurse may be able to help clients by asking if they have any religious needs while they are hospitalized. Some people will want to wear items of religious significance, and others may have traditions that require prayer at specified times or certain hygiene practices. Nurses cannot be expected to know about all potential religious or cultural needs but can discover these issues during the psychosocial assessment.

10. During the psychosocial assessment, it is valuable to ask the client why he or she was admitted because the answer to this question can give the nurse information about the client's perception of his or her situation.

11. Medical history is helpful in psychosocial assessment because the client's health status certainly affects psychosocial functioning. Chronic illnesses provide significant stressors that will affect the client's ability to cope when they are discharged. The client's behavior and relationships with self and others can be affected by health problems.

12. Nurses should consider the client's whole health status, not only the specific issue for which she or he was admitted, when planning for discharge.

13. The use of alcohol or drugs as a way to cope with stress is an unhealthy coping mechanism, even if the client does not have alcohol dependency. The crisis of hospitalization can be an opportunity for a client to change behavior and to begin new ways of coping. The nurse needs to ask every client about alcohol and drug use because occasionally a client will be ready to talk and this will provide a great opportunity to help the client.

SUGGESTIONS FOR CLASSROOM ACTIVITIES

- Break students into small groups to discuss why various aspects of the psychosocial assessment are important.
- Provide forms for psychosocial assessment from a variety of mental healthcare facilities and have students compare the information requested on the various forms to see what information they have in common and what information is on some forms but not on others.
- Invite a nurse who does psychosocial assessments to come and speak to the class about techniques he or she uses to get the data requested on the psychosocial assessment form the nurse's facility uses. Ask the nurse to discuss why the information gathered is important.

SUGGESTIONS FOR CLINICAL ACTIVITIES

- Arrange for students to rotate through an admissions unit of a mental health facility so they can observe a psychosocial assessment being done by a nurse on a newly admitted client. If possible, arrange for the students to do psychosocial assessments under supervision.

REFERENCE

- US Surgeon General: Mental health: Culture, race, and ethnicity. Available at http://www.surgeongeneral.gov/library/mentalhealth/cre/execsummary-6.html

14. Another reason to ask about recent alcohol and drug use on admission is to find out if the client is currently under the influence of intoxicants. Many prescribed medications interact in potentially dangerous ways with alcohol and other drugs. The physician must be notified immediately if the client is currently under the influence of alcohol or other intoxicants.

15. It is important to determine alcohol use history in order to predict the likelihood of alcohol withdrawal syndrome. People who consume large amounts of alcohol regularly are likely to experience elevated vital signs and other symptoms of CNS stimulation if they stop drinking abruptly. The nurse needs to ask how often the client drinks, not if they drink.

16. Assessing the smoking history is important in order to determine risk of respiratory illness and nicotine withdrawal symptoms, such as anxiety, insomnia, and irritability. A smoking history gives the nurse another opportunity for health teaching.

17. Assessing the amount of caffeinated beverages the client drinks regularly is important because if the client drinks large amounts of caffeinated beverages, the client is at risk for caffeine withdrawal when hospitalized. Symptoms of caffeine withdrawal include headache, decreased energy, and constipation.

18. Assessing support systems is important because when clients do not have an adequate social support system of their own, the nurse should contact a social worker who may need to arrange for help through a public agency.

19. Assessment of a client's self-concept is important because a client with very negative self-concept may need additional assessment for depression (see Table 47-3, Assessing Self-Concept). Self-concept includes body image, role performance, identity, and self-esteem.

20. It is important to gather information about the client's coping skills (the behaviors people use to relieve or cope with their stress) because knowledge of the client's usual coping behaviors will help the nurse promote healthy coping behavior or plan for teaching to promote the client's health. Learning to talk with others to express feelings and start problem solving might help the client begin to develop a new healthy way of coping. See Table 47-4, Assessing Coping Skills.

21. The mental status assessment can be considered part of the psychosocial assessment. The mental status assessment is important because the results provide a clearer picture of the client's thinking processes.

22. The mental status assessment includes appearance, orientation, mood and affect, speech characteristics, thought disorders (delusions, obsessions, or phobias), hallucinations, behavior, memory, and judgment/insight.

LEARNING OUTCOME 4

Identify risk factors for mental illness.

Concepts for Lecture

1. Risk factors for mental illness include inability to reach developmental tasks, imbalance of brain neurotransmitters, hopelessness, lack of information about treatment options, inadequate role models for values and behaviors, inadequate coping skills, inadequate resources, substance dependency, exhaustion, extreme stress, and genetic predisposition to mental illness.

POWERPOINT SLIDES

Tables and/or Figures
- **Figure 47-2** Risk Factors for Mental Illness and Factors That Promote Mental Health

SUGGESTIONS FOR CLASSROOM ACTIVITIES
- Relate the risk factors from Figure 47-2 to the aspects of mental health. Ask students to identify any relationship between the two.
- Review the concept of mental health as being on a continuum. Discuss the risk factors in terms of how many need to be present for mental illness to occur.
- Ask students if they can identify other risk factors for mental illness not listed in the text.

SUGGESTIONS FOR CLINICAL ACTIVITIES
- Have students review patient histories in the mental health clinical setting so they can identify risk factors the client had for mental illness. Ask the students to compare the risk factors the client had for mental illness with those provided in the text.

REFERENCE
- Helpguide.org: Risk factors for mental and emotional problems. Available at http://www.helpguide.org/mental/mental_emotional_health.htm#risk

LEARNING OUTCOME 5

Identify factors that promote mental health.

Concepts for Lecture

1. Factors that promote mental health include ability to determine reality accurately, a healthy self-concept, a means of being creative and productive, a positive attitude, ability to manage change/flexibility, adequate rest, sense of meaning in life, control over one's own behavior, satisfying interpersonal relationships, and adequate support.

LEARNING OUTCOME 6

Identify subjective and objective psychosocial assessment data.

Concepts for Lecture

1. Subjective psychosocial assessment data include information about the client's family and culture.
2. The client's perception of the reason for admission is subjective data.
3. Current medical problems described by the client are part of the subjective data.
4. Clients may minimize the amount of alcohol they drink. Information about the use of alcohol or drugs is considered subjective.
5. Social support systems described by the client are subjective.
6. Self-concept is subjective.
7. Coping skills described by the client are subjective data.
8. Objective data includes appearance, motor activity, quality of speech, affect, characteristics of speech, interpersonal behavior, mood, thought processes, cognition, judgment, and abstract or concrete behavior.

GENERAL CHAPTER CONSIDERATIONS

1. Have students study and learn key terms listed at the beginning of the chapter.
2. Have students complete end of chapter exercises either in their book or on the MyNursingKit Website.
3. Use the Classroom Response Question PowerPoints to assess students prior to lecture.

 **POWERPOINT SLIDES**

 **SUGGESTIONS FOR CLASSROOM ACTIVITIES**

- Ask students to interview family members, friends, and professionals about what factors they think promote mental health.
- Have students break into small groups in class to discuss factors they think promote mental health.
- Have students research the topic of factors promoting mental health and have them bring the information they find to class and present briefly on their findings.

 SUGGESTIONS FOR CLINICAL ACTIVITIES

- Ask a social worker and a mental health nurse to talk with students in postconference about factors that promote mental health.

 **POWERPOINT SLIDES**

Tables and/or Figures

- **Table 47-3** Assessing Self-Concept
- **Table 47-4** Assessing Coping Skills

 **SUGGESTIONS FOR CLASSROOM ACTIVITIES**

- Have students work in pairs and sort out subjective from objective data in the psychosocial assessment. Have students discuss why each piece of data is either subjective or objective.

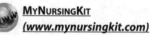 **SUGGESTIONS FOR CLINICAL ACTIVITIES**

- Have students do psychosocial assessments under supervision on the clinical unit. In postconference, discuss the subjective and objective data collected during clinical.

MYNURSINGKIT
(www.mynursingkit.com)

- Websites
- NCLEX® Questions
- Case Studies
- Key Terms

STUDENT WORKBOOK AND RESOURCE GUIDE

- Chapter 47 activities
- *Separate purchase*

PRENTICE HALL NURSE'S DRUG GUIDE

- *Separate purchase*

CLASSROOM RESPONSE QUESTION POWERPOINTS

TESTBANK

CHAPTER 48
CARING FOR CLIENTS WITH COGNITIVE DISORDERS

LEARNING OUTCOME 1

Describe cognitive changes that occur with normal aging.

Concepts for Lecture

1. Aging affects cognition in varying degrees depending on an individual's genetics, past experiences, living environment, life-long nutrition, and physical health.
2. As the brain ages, a small percentage of neurons is lost, so the brain becomes slightly smaller and loses weight.
3. Slight forgetfulness, especially for recent events, is normal.
4. Problem-solving abilities are slowed.
5. Older adults tend to solve problems based on their past life experiences, making them less likely than younger people to try new ways to solve problems.
6. Voluntary movements, reflexes, and reaction time are also slowed due to a decrease in the production of the neurotransmitters that normally assist with impulse conduction.
   See Table 48-1 for normal memory lapses versus serious warning signs of a cognitive disorder.

LEARNING OUTCOME 2

Differentiate between delirium and dementia.

Concepts for Lecture

1. Delirium is a temporary condition that alters the level of consciousness. It may affect the client's ability to focus thoughts, recall past events, understand and use language, or have an accurate perception of the environmental stimuli (APA, 2000).
2. Delirium has multiple causes. It is associated with a variety of general medical conditions, surgery, polypharmacy, infections, and drugs. It is an indicator of serious, life-threatening physiologic processes that can occur at any age, although older adults are at the highest risk.
3. The onset of delirium often indicates a major underlying biochemical imbalance that might be fatal if untreated (e.g., physical brain disorders including dementia or stroke; heart disease; metabolic disorders; infections; postoperative states resulting from anesthesia, blood loss, pain, and other physiologic stressors; substance-related disorders; and extreme psychosocial stressors).
4. Early recognition of delirium is critical. If some causes of delirium are not recognized or treated, the client may have permanent neurologic damage or may die. If delirium is treated early, it is likely to resolve, whereas dementia is not likely to resolve.
5. Dementia is a group of symptoms that occur together and not a disease itself.
6. There are over 100 causes of dementia but 60–80% of those affected have dementia of the Alzheimer's type, also known as Alzheimer's disease. None of the three most common types of dementia–Alzheimer's

POWERPOINT SLIDES

Tables and/or Figures

- **Figure 48-1** Normal Changes of Aging in the Neurologic System

SUGGESTIONS FOR CLASSROOM ACTIVITIES

- Ask students to interview an older person (over 65) and find out what cognitive changes that person thinks has come with aging.

SUGGESTIONS FOR CLINICAL ACTIVITIES

- Assign students to provide care for older adults. Ask students to find out what their assigned clients think about cognitive changes that have come with aging. Ask students to compare a number of older clients to see if some have had more cognitive changes than others and to think about what may have caused the differences.

REFERENCE

- Anstey KJ, Low LF: Normal cognitive changes in aging. Available at http://www.ncbi.nlm.nih.gov/pubmed/15532151

POWERPOINT SLIDES

Tables and/or Figures

- **Table 48-2** Common Causes of Dementia
- **Table 48-3** Comparison of Delirium, Dementia, and Depression

SUGGESTIONS FOR CLASSROOM ACTIVITIES

- Have students break into two groups to differentiate between delirium and dementia. Provide some art materials and poster boards and have students make creative posters demonstrating the differences between delirium and dementia.

SUGGESTIONS FOR CLINICAL ACTIVITIES

- Assign students to care for clients who have delirium and clients who have dementia. Discuss in postconference the differences between delirium and dementia.

type, dementia with Lewy bodies, and vascular dementia—is reversible. (See Table 48-2 for causes of these and other types of dementia.)

7. Causes of dementia include neurodegenerative disorders, vascular abnormalities, toxic or metabolic disorders, immune abnormalities, infections, systemic diseases, seizure disorders, low-pressure hydrocephalus, and drugs.

8. Delirium develops over a short period of time (usually hours or days) and tends to fluctuate during the day. Dementia develops gradually, over years. It is progressive, and there is no cure for dementia.

9. Dementia runs in families, whereas delirium does not.

10. In delirium, the orientation fluctuates, and the client is disoriented, lethargic, or hypervigilant; whereas in dementia, the client has progressive impairment in orientation and all cognitive functions.

11. In delirium, cognition is fluctuating, disorganized, and fragmented, and speech may be slow or fast. In dementia, there is difficulty with abstract thinking, memory impairment, and language and perceptual disturbances.

12. In delirium, behavior may include psychomotor agitation or psychomotor retardation or mixed. In dementia, the client has apraxia and may have refusal to bathe, catastrophic reactions, and wandering.

13. In delirium, the sleep–wake cycle is disturbed, and the cycle may be reversed. In dementia, there are frequent awakenings and sundowning (increased confusion at night).

14. In delirium, the condition is temporary (hours to weeks) if the underlying condition is treated; if not, it may be fatal. In dementia, there is a progressive decline in cognition and abilities. Life expectancy after diagnosis is 8 years.

LEARNING OUTCOME 3

Identify clients at risk for cognitive disorders.

Concepts for Lecture

1. Older adults are at the highest risk for treatable delirium, and most affected individuals are over age 65. It can occur at any age.

2. All surgical clients are at risk for developing delirium.

3. People with diabetes; kidney, liver, or heart disease; or alcohol or other substance dependency are at risk of delirium.

4. Being in the intensive care unit increases the risk of delirium.

5. Chemical, fluid, or electrolyte imbalances also place a client at risk for delirium.

6. Risk factors for vascular dementia include advanced age, history of smoking, hypertension, hyperlipidemia, cardiac dysrhythmias (atrial fibrillation), coronary artery disease, and diabetes mellitus (Box 48-2).

7. The incidence of Alzheimer's disease is increased in families with affected members. Genes have been identified that cause dementia of the Alzheimer's type (DAT). Genes on chromosomes 1, 12, 19, and 21 are related to the code for the development of DAT.

POWERPOINT SLIDES

Tables and/or Figures
- **Box 48-2** Risk Factors for Vascular Dementia

SUGGESTIONS FOR CLASSROOM ACTIVITIES
- Have students visit the library or go online to find an article discussing risk factors for delirium and dementia. Have students bring the articles to class and present briefly on their articles. Make copies of the articles and put them in a binder for students to reference.
- Invite a gerontologist or a nurse practitioner who works with geriatric clients to talk to the class about delirium and dementia and to include a discussion on risk factors for delirium and dementia.

SUGGESTIONS FOR CLINICAL ACTIVITIES
- Assign students to clients in long-term care who have dementia and have students discuss risk factors these clients had for dementia.
- Ask one of the nurses on staff at the long-term care facility to talk in postconference about clients he or she has cared for who had delirium and what risk factors those clients had for delirium.

REFERENCE
- Alzheimer's Association: Vascular dementia. Available at http://www.alz.org/alzheimers_disease_vascular_dementia.asp

Learning Outcome 4

Explain the stages of Alzheimer's disease and their implications for nursing care.

Concepts for Lecture

1. During the early stage of Alzheimer's disease (dementia of the Alzheimer's type [DAT]), the initial sign of the disease is deterioration in memory.
2. Deterioration in memory may go unnoticed by family and friends until it becomes too severe for the client, or sometimes his or her spouse, to cover it up.
3. The early stage usually lasts 2 to 4 years. Antidementia medications are intended to prolong this stage.
4. During the early stage, there is gradual short-term memory impairment, especially for new learning. Forgetfulness is beyond what is normal or usual for people the same age.
5. In the early stage of Alzheimer's disease, people tend to lose initiative and their usual interests.
6. Judgment and orientation to geography are diminished in the early stages of Alzheimer's.
7. The second or middle stage of Alzheimer's disease is usually the longest, lasting 2 to 10 years after the diagnosis.
8. Memory loss and mental confusion worsen in the middle stage of Alzheimer's disease. As remote memory is lost, the client has difficulty recognizing close family and friends.
9. In the middle stage, clients may wander, becoming particularly restless in the late afternoon or early evening.
10. Clients in the middle stage may have difficulty organizing thoughts or thinking logically and may experience hallucinations, delusional thinking, or illusions. Clients in this stage may have expressive or receptive aphasia and apraxia.
11. Behavioral problems in the middle stage may include agitation and aggressiveness.
12. Clients in the middle stage may confabulate, or make up stories, to explain something that they do not remember or know how to answer.
13. During the middle stage, family members often come to the conclusion that they are unable to manage the care of the loved one at home. People who are admitted to long-term care facilities have often experienced severe life stressors.
14. The late stage of Alzheimer's disease may last 1 to 3 years.
15. In the late stage, clients have little memory and are thus unable to process new information.
16. Clients in the late stage may not be able to understand words and forget the meaning of, and how to do, self-care activities.
17. Clients in the late stage are likely immobile and incontinent. At this point, many families are unable to continue to provide care for their loved one at home.
18. In the late stage of Alzheimer's disease, clients may make repetitious sounds instead of speech and may have difficulty eating and swallowing.
19. Some clients in the late stage experience hyperorality, putting anything within reach into their mouths. At this stage, clients are susceptible to choking, pneumonia, and other infections.
20. Some clients in the late stage assume the fetal position. The culmination of this stage is death.

PowerPoint Slides

Tables and/or Figures
- **Figure 48-4** MRI of Person With Alzheimer's (Source: Photo Researchers, Inc.)
- **Figure 48-6** Catastrophic Reaction in Person With Dementia (Source: Getty Images, Inc./ Stone Allstock.)

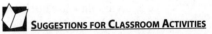

Suggestions for Classroom Activities

- Invite a caregiver for a person who is in stage three of Alzheimer's disease to come to class and talk about what the three stages were like in terms of behaviors, manifestations, and safety issues, and to answer prescreened questions from students. Have students write their questions out, screen them for suitability, and give them to the guest speaker ahead of time. If possible, get two or three caregivers to come to class and see if their experiences have been similar to what is described in the text and similar to each other's experiences.

Suggestions for Clinical Activities

- Assign students to care for clients who are in various stages of Alzheimer's disease and have the students compare the behaviors of the clients in various stages with what they have learned in class about the stages.

LEARNING OUTCOME 5

Safely administer medications to clients with Alzheimer's disease.

Concepts for Lecture

1. The goal of medication therapy is to prolong the early to middle stages of the disease.
2. Because a decreased amount of the neurotransmitter acetylcholine is present in Alzheimer's disease, the medications that inhibit the breakdown of acetylcholine are effective in its treatment. These antidementia drugs are in the family called cholinesterase inhibitors.
3. Cholinesterase inhibitors don't actually increase the amount of acetylcholine; they increase the availability by inhibiting acetylcholinesterase, the enzyme that breaks it down.
4. The brain produces less and less acetylcholine as Alzheimer's disease progresses, so the drugs become less effective as decreasing amounts of the neurotransmitter are available.
5. Current medications for Alzheimer's disease include donepezil (Aricept), a cholinesterase inhibitor that may slow progress of the disease but does not reverse the degenerative process. This medication comes in PO tablets and orally dissolving tablets (ODTs), which are helpful for clients who choke easily or do not like pills. Nursing implications for antidementia agents are provided in Table 48-4.
6. Rivastigmine (Exelon) is a cholinesterase inhibitor that comes in capsules, oral solution, and transdermal patches.
7. Galantamine (Razadyne) is a cholinesterase inhibitor that comes in tablets, extended-release capsules that are given in a single daily dose, and oral solutions.
8. Memantine (Namenda) is an N-methyl-D-aspartate (NMDA) receptor antagonist that may reduce brain cell destruction by reducing glutamate-caused extra calcium entering cells. Memantine (Namenda) comes in tablets and oral solutions given in twice-daily doses.
9. Tacrine (Cognex) is a cholinesterase inhibitor that comes in capsule form and is given four times a day. See nursing implications for antidementia drugs, Table 48-4.
10. Other medications for clients with dementia do not promote cognitive functioning but control the problem behaviors of combativeness, agitation, depression, paranoia, and delusions. These antipsychotic drugs, risperidone (Risperdal), olanzapine (Zyprexa), and haloperidol (Haldol), have been shown to reduce symptoms of hostility, aggression, mistrust, and uncooperativeness in people with dementia.
11. Antipsychotic medications should be used with great caution because one important side effect is blocking acetylcholine receptors, reducing the activity of the neurotransmitter already diminished in Alzheimer's disease. The antipsychotics may also cause postural hypotension, abnormal body movements, neuroleptic malignant syndrome, abnormal glucose metabolism, dry mucous membranes, constipation, and increased risk of cardiac disease in the elderly.

POWERPOINT SLIDES

Tables and/or Figures
- **Table 48-4** Giving Medications Safely: Antidementia Agents

SUGGESTIONS FOR CLASSROOM ACTIVITIES

- Invite a pharmacist or someone from a university pharmacy school to speak to the class about medications for dementia.
- Invite someone from a company that does drug research on antidementia drugs to speak about the research that goes into developing a new drug for dementia and to talk about any new drugs currently in trial testing.

SUGGESTIONS FOR CLINICAL ACTIVITIES

- If possible, rotate students through an experience where they will observe a nurse giving medication to a client with Alzheimer's disease or helping the client in the early stages of Alzheimer's to take their own medication safely. This could be a rotation with a visiting nurse or in an assisted-living facility. Have the students observe the safety measures the nurse takes or puts in place as well as the strategies used to educate the client about the medication and motivate the client to take the medication.
- Assign students to work with clients in various stages of Alzheimer's disease. Supervise them preparing and giving medications to their assigned clients. Talk about nursing implications for the medications and strategies to help clients safely take their medications before administering the medications.

LEARNING OUTCOME 6

Apply the nursing process to the care of clients with cognitive disorders.

Concepts for Lecture

1. Assessing the client with delirium involves assessing the mental state. A classic tool for assessing the mental state of clients is the Folstein Mini-Mental State Examination (MMSE; Figure 48-2). Read the test carefully before administering it, and treat the client with respect and encouragement.

2. The nurse may use the MMSE to establish a baseline of data about the client's cognition. It can then be used as a series of assessments to show whether cognition is improving or declining.

3. The client's family can be an excellent source of information about the course of the client's disease. They will know if the onset was slow or quick, whether the client is oriented at home or not, and whether there are special challenging areas for the client. Consider the family as important allies in the care of the client.

4. A possible nursing diagnosis for a client with delirium is Risk for Injury related to impaired judgment and disorientation, with a possible expected outcome that the client will receive no injuries throughout the hospital stay.

5. Nursing interventions for a nursing diagnosis of Risk for Injury include: (1) placing the client in a room with bright natural light; (2) approaching the client in a calm, reassuring manner; (3) observing the delirious client frequently both day and night; (4) reorienting the client at every opportunity; and (5) maintaining a safe environment, keeping items that would be dangerous for the client to ingest out of the client's reach and keeping the space in the room clear of furniture and clutter.

6. Another possible nursing diagnosis for a client with delirium is Disturbed Thought Processes related to chemical, fluid, or electrolyte imbalances, with a possible expected outcome that the client will become oriented to person, place, and time and have no more episodes of hallucinations or agitation.

7. Nursing interventions for a nursing diagnosis of Disturbed Thought Processes may include: (1) orienting the client at every opportunity by keeping a clock and a calendar in the client's room; (2) calling the person by name and introducing yourself each time you enter the room; (3) using all your resources to determine which medications the client has been taking at home, noting the doses and times and who prescribed each medication, and providing this information to the physician.

8. When a client has hallucinations, the nurse reassures the client that they are not real, tries to keep the client in reality, and talks about simple things in the here-and-now, such as the weather or what the client had for breakfast.

9. Another nursing intervention for a nursing diagnosis of Disturbed Thought Processes is to approach the client calmly, confidently, and caringly when the client's cooperation is needed for procedures. The nurse also needs to explain what is to be done in simplest terms and as gently as possible.

10. The nurse needs to ensure that the client has full physiologic support (e.g., if they are dehydrated, they need to be given fluids).

11. The nurse can evaluate care given a client with delirium by evaluating for safety issues or injuries. The mental status should be evaluated with the MMSE or other consistent tool to see if there is improved orientation and recovery from abnormal thoughts and that medical conditions are being treated.

POWERPOINT SLIDES

Tables and/or Figures

- **Figure 48-2** Folstein Mini-Mental State Examination

Nursing Care Plan: Client With Middle-Stage Alzheimer's Disease

SUGGESTIONS FOR CLASSROOM ACTIVITIES

- Have students break into small groups to review the nursing care plan "Client With Middle-Stage Alzheimer's Disease." Ask the students to list any additional assessment data they would like to have that is not available in the care plan. Have the students match expected outcomes from the list of expected outcomes to the nursing diagnoses on the list of nursing diagnoses. Have each group write nursing interventions for one or two of the nursing diagnoses on the list.

SUGGESTIONS FOR CLINICAL ACTIVITIES

- Assign students to care for clients with a diagnosis of Alzheimer's disease and to prepare an individualized care plan for their assigned clients based on the assessment findings gathered on their clients. Have the students do an evaluation of the outcomes in postconference to see if expected outcomes were met.

12. Normal assessments for health must be performed in clients with dementia but should be organized to fit the best time of day, when the client is most cooperative.

13. Expected outcomes for clients with cognitive impairment include freedom from injury to self or others; maintenance of as much functional (self-care) ability as possible; obtaining safe, effective, and comfortable personal care; and being able to live life and approach death with dignity.

14. A problem the client with dementia may have is wandering. The expected outcome is that the client's activity will be redirected in a positive way. Interventions include trying to understand the client's agenda and, after exploring the client's thought, changing the subject to whatever event is about to occur. Another possible intervention is to put a stop sign on places the client should not go. If the client is at home, a deadbolt can be put on the outside door, pathways can be kept free of clutter, and the client can be allowed to walk as much as he or she desires.

15. Sundowning is another problem the client with dementia may have. Interventions include keeping the house or unit well lit during the day; providing opportunities for the client to exercise every day so the client will be tired enough to go to bed; providing a light evening snack without caffeine; keeping the environmental stimuli low; and turning the television off if the client is not watching it.

16. Refusal to bathe is a problem the client with dementia may experience. Interventions include determining the reason the client is reluctant to bathe, reassuring the client if fear is the reason, remaining calm and matter-of-fact, offering assistance, providing whatever devices the client needs, moving slowly, following the client's old bath routine as closely as possible, having everything ready in advance, and if all else fails, doing a sponge bath.

17. Another problem the client with dementia may have is paranoia/suspicion. Interventions include remembering that being suspicious is not the client's choice but part of the deterioration of the disease, not arguing with the client's suspicions, being reassuring instead of argumentative, and considering buying duplicates of frequently lost items.

18. Clients with dementia may have language difficulties. Interventions include always introducing yourself to the client by name and role each time you enter the room; calling the client by name; approaching the client from the front; making simple statements with few words and simple sentences; allowing lots of time for processing what you have said, and if the client does not understand, repeating yourself exactly at least twice before using new words; working on listening skills; asking the client to point or describe the idea with different words; trying to use procedural memory; keeping a sense of humor; treating the client with respect; and remaining calm.

19. Clients with dementia may have catastrophic reactions that are caused by the disease and are not the client's choice. The best approach is to prevent them from happening. The Mayo Clinic recommends using an "ABC" approach, which includes looking at the antecedent of the problem, reviewing the behavior itself, and looking at the consequences of the behavior. Interventions include not touching a client during an outburst. After the outburst, a gentle touch can be reassuring. The nurse should not hurry clients and needs to provide opportunities and activities where the client can be successful.

20. In evaluating care for clients with Alzheimer's disease, it is important to determine whether unmet goals are too high for the client to reach. It is better to plan realistic help to maintain function or dignity as function declines than to plan for cognitive improvement or other unrealistic goals.

LEARNING OUTCOME 7

Discuss the impact on the caregivers and families of clients with cognitive disorders.

Concepts for Lecture

1. Because dementia of the Alzheimer's type is progressive, has no cure, and runs in families, some people watch their parents die slowly from dementia and then spend years dreading or fearing its onset in themselves. When they hear the diagnosis of Alzheimer's, people are often devastated.
2. It takes a team to care for a client with Alzheimer's disease. One single caregiver cannot do it all.
3. Families of those with Alzheimer's disease experience a great deal of stress.
4. Nurses can be advocates for both client and caregiver by reminding caregivers that they need to take care of themselves. See Box 48-5 for 10 ways for caregivers to stay healthy and reduce stress.

GENERAL CHAPTER CONSIDERATIONS

1. Have students study and learn key terms listed at the beginning of the chapter.
2. Have students complete end of chapter exercises either in their book or on the MyNursingKit Website.
3. Use the Classroom Response Question PowerPoints to assess students prior to lecture.

POWERPOINT SLIDES

Tables and/or Figures
- **Box 48-5** Client Teaching: Ten Ways for Caregivers to Stay Healthy and Reduce Stress

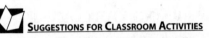

SUGGESTIONS FOR CLASSROOM ACTIVITIES
- Invite family members of individuals with Alzheimer's disease to talk to the class about how their family member having Alzheimer's disease impacts them. Invite some family members who are caregivers and some who are not but who have frequent contact with the individual who has Alzheimer's disease.
- Ask students to work in pairs and talk about how they think it would impact them if they had a family member diagnosed with Alzheimer's disease. Have the groups share with the class as a whole.

SUGGESTIONS FOR CLINICAL ACTIVITIES
- Assign students to care for clients who have Alzheimer's disease. Ask the students to explore with family members and other caregivers how dealing with a person with Alzheimer's disease impacts them. Have students discuss their findings in postconference.

- Clinical Reasoning Care Map

MYNURSINGKIT
(www.mynursingkit.com)
- Websites
- NCLEX® Questions
- Case Studies
- Key Terms

STUDENT WORKBOOK AND RESOURCE GUIDE
- Chapter 48 activities
- *Separate purchase*

PRENTICE HALL NURSE'S DRUG GUIDE
- *Separate purchase*

CLASSROOM RESPONSE QUESTION
POWERPOINTS

TESTBANK

CHAPTER 49
CARING FOR CLIENTS WITH PSYCHOTIC DISORDERS

LEARNING OUTCOME 1

Explain the role of brain neurotransmitters in causing schizophrenia.

Concepts for Lecture

1. Schizophrenia is a thought disorder that affects a person's ability to perceive reality accurately, thereby disrupting normal social functioning.
2. In schizophrenia, there is an imbalance in brain neurotransmitters that normally mediate thought, mood, and behavior.
3. Neurotransmitters and their receptors, especially dopamine, norepinephrine, serotonin, GABA (gamma-aminobutyric acid), and glutamate, are altered in schizophrenia.
4. In schizophrenia, there is an excess of the neurotransmitters dopamine and norepinephrine in the brain.

LEARNING OUTCOME 2

Explain the manifestations and treatment options for clients with schizophrenia.

Concepts for Lecture

1. Characteristic symptoms of schizophrenia as listed in the *Diagnostic and Statistical Manual of Mental Disorders*, 4th edition, Text Revision are delusions, hallucinations, disorganized speech, grossly disorganized or catatonic behavior, and negative symptoms. The client must have two or more of these symptoms to have a diagnosis of schizophrenia.
2. In addition to two or more of the symptoms listed above, the client must have seriously impaired social or occupational function, and the symptoms must have been present for at least 6 months.
3. The symptoms associated with schizophrenia may be placed into three major categories: positive, disorganized, and negative symptoms.
4. Positive (or psychotic) symptoms seem to be an excess or distortion of normal functions. They include hallucinations and delusions.
5. Hallucinations are sensory perceptions that seem real but occur without external stimuli. The client may or may not have the insight that these are not real sensory experiences. Auditory hallucinations are the most common in schizophrenia, and visual hallucinations are the next most common. Hallucinations can also be tactile, gustatory (taste), olfactory (smell), or somatic (involving body sensations).
6. Delusions are fixed false beliefs that persist despite evidence that they are not true.
7. Disorganized thinking is a major feature of schizophrenia. There is an inability to sort and interpret incoming sensory information. There is a resulting inability to respond appropriately. Disorganized thinking is demonstrated in disorganized speech. At its worst, speech becomes "word salad" in which words are thrown together without relationship to each other. Sometimes clients make up new words called neologisms that have no meaning to other people.

POWERPOINT SLIDES

Tables and/or Figures
- **Figure 47-3** Neurotransmission

SUGGESTIONS FOR CLASSROOM ACTIVITIES

- Have students work in small groups. Assign to each group one of the neurotransmitters involved in the development of schizophrenia. Have students research the functions of each neurotransmitter and have a spokesperson from each group present the group's findings to the class.

SUGGESTIONS FOR CLINICAL ACTIVITIES

- Assign students to work with clients who have a diagnosis of schizophrenia. Ask students to review the chart and collect data from observations of and interactions with the client. Have students compare the manifestations they find with what they have learned about neurotransmitters and their role in manifestations of schizophrenia.
- Ask a psychiatrist on the clinical unit to discuss the role of neurotransmitters in the manifestations of schizophrenia in clinical postconference.

REFERENCE

- American Medical Network: Schizophrenia and neurotransmitters. Available at http://www.health.am/psy/more/schizophrenia-and-neurotransmitters

POWERPOINT SLIDES

Tables and/or Figures
- **Table 49-1** Terms Related to Schizophrenia
- **Table 49-2** Types of Delusions
- **Box 49-3** Antipsychotic Medications
- **Table 49-3** Abnormal Involuntary Movement Scale (AIMS)

8. Negative symptoms of schizophrenia, in contrast to the positive ones, involve a deficit or decrease of normal functions. Negative symptoms include flat affect, alogia, and anhedonia.

9. For psychiatric inpatients, the environment or milieu can be used as part of therapy. The environment should be pleasant, simple, and safe. There should be minimal stimulation, no background music, and no loud television, loud talking, or flashing lights because clients already have the stimulation caused by anxiety, fear, or hallucinations.

10. In milieu therapy, consistent nursing staff helps promote development of trust. The nurses also serve as role models for normal behavior. Clients have the opportunity to practice their behavior in the milieu. They have the opportunity to give and receive feedback on behavior. Peer pressure is a powerful incentive for change.

11. Milieu therapy provides structure for client's daily living. Meals and group activities are scheduled. Unit policies are followed consistently. Structure offers a predictable environment that is less stressful for a client with impaired thinking.

12. Medication is not the only treatment, but it is a cornerstone in the treatment of schizophrenia. Antipsychotic medications help relieve the hallucinations, delusion, and disordered thinking associated with the disorder.

13. It is important to assess clients on antipsychotic therapy for abnormal involuntary movement with a scale such as the AIMS (Abnormal Involuntary Movement Scale) to identify symptoms of tardive dyskinesia (TD) early. Anticholinergic drugs can be used to treat extrapyramidal side effects of antipsychotic drugs.

14. Narcoleptic malignant syndrome is a potentially fatal side effect of antipsychotic drugs.

LEARNING OUTCOME 3

Describe the actions and side effects of antipsychotic drugs.

Concepts for Lecture

1. The antipsychotic medications (formerly called neuroleptics) are grouped as either typical (first-generation), atypical (second-generation), or new-generation antipsychotic drugs. See Box 49-3, Antipsychotic Medications.

2. Antipsychotic medications help relieve the hallucinations, delusions, and disordered thinking associated with schizophrenia.

3. The typical antipsychotics tend to be effective in treating psychosis or the positive symptoms of schizophrenia. The typical antipsychotics are especially effective in the treatment of acute psychosis with agitation. The negative symptoms are not very responsive to the typical antipsychotic medications.

4. Side effects of the antipsychotic drugs include extrapyramidal effects (dystonia, dyskinesia, akathisia, and tardive dyskinesia). See Box 49-4 and Table 49-3.

5. Tardive dyskinesia (TD; late onset of abnormal movement) is an extrapyramidal effect that develops after extended antipsychotic drug therapy.

6. TD may be due to development of hypersensitivity to dopamine. It is not caused by the same dopamine–acetylcholine imbalance as the other extrapyramidal symptoms (EPS). It does not respond to anticholinergic medications.

7. Neuroleptic malignant syndrome (NMS) is a potentially fatal side effect of antipsychotic drugs. The major symptoms are high fever,

SUGGESTIONS FOR CLASSROOM ACTIVITIES

• Have students find additional resources discussing milieu therapy. These resources include books, articles, and information on the Internet. Ask students to bring their information to class. Have students break into small groups to discuss milieu therapy and how they see themselves changing their behavior to be therapeutic and part of milieu therapy. Ask students to talk about how their dress and behavior are important when they are part of the milieu.

SUGGESTIONS FOR CLINICAL ACTIVITIES

• Assign the students to observe the clients and staff on a psychiatric inpatient unit and make note of the activities and behaviors indicating the unit milieu. Are these activities and behaviors therapeutic? Why or why not?

REFERENCE

• Focus Alternative Learning Center: Milieu therapy. Available at http://www.focus-alternative.org/milieu.htm

POWERPOINT SLIDES

Tables and/or Figures

• **Box 49-4** Extrapyramidal Side Effects From Antipsychotic Drugs
• **Box 49-5** Assessment: Metabolic Side Effects of Antipsychotic Drugs
• **Table 49-3** Abnormal Involuntary Movement Scale (AIMS)
• **Table 49-4** Anticholinergic Drugs Used to Treat Extrapyramidal Side Effects
• **Box 49-6** Anticholinergic Side Effects

SUGGESTIONS FOR CLASSROOM ACTIVITIES

• Discuss in detail issues connected with pharmacotherapy for the client with schizophrenia. Include length of time needed to see therapeutic effects; client's perception of own health status; and correlation between side effects and adherence issues.
• Ask the students what relationship they see between teaching the client/family about medication and medication adherence. Stress the importance of client/family teaching.
• Divide students into small work groups. Assign each group a particular antipsychotic medication. Have students research major potential side effects of their assigned drugs. Have students discuss why the side effects would increase nonadherence with medication regimen.

muscle rigidity, autonomic instability (unstable blood pressure, diaphoresis, and pale skin), delirium, inability to speak, tremors, and elevated levels of enzymes that indicate muscle damage (CPK). Temperatures may rise as high as 108°F (42.2°C).

8. The antipsychotics also have endocrine side effects. Dopamine inhibits the hormone prolactin, which promotes breast enlargement and milk production. Typical antipsychotics elevate levels of prolactin because they inhibit dopamine. Chronic prolactin elevation can cause decreased libido (sexual drive), breast enlargement (gynecomastia), and galactorrhea (leakage of milk) in women or men. It can also cause menstrual dysfunction in women.

9. The incidence of type 2 diabetes is increased in people with schizophrenia, even in those who are not obese. This increase may be in part due to adverse effects on the endocrine system caused by antipsychotic medications.

10. Monitoring of adverse metabolic effects of atypical (second-generation) antipsychotics should be improved. See Box 49-5, Assessment: Metabolic Side Effects of Antipsychotic Drugs.

11. Anticholinergic side effects often result from the use of antipsychotics See Box 49-6.

12. Clients taking anticholinergic medications for EPS have an increased risk for anticholinergic side effects.

13. Most of the antipsychotics can cause weight gain. Olanzapine (Zyprexa) causes the highest incidence of weight gain. Weight gain with antipsychotics is associated with increased appetite, binge eating, carbohydrate craving, decreased satiety, and changes in food preferences in some clients. Increased insulin may also contribute to weight gain in people taking antipsychotic drugs.

14. The hypotension caused by antipsychotics is an antiadrenergic effect. Normally the blood vessels respond to changes in body position by constricting, ensuring adequate blood flow to the brain. When sympathetic alpha-1 receptors are blocked, the vessels are prevented from responding automatically to body position changes.

15. Orthostatic hypotension occurs when the individual stands up or changes position quickly. It is also called postural hypotension.

16. Antipsychotics may cause increased heart rate as an anticholinergic side effect. They may also cause prolonged conduction time through the heart's electrical system. On EKG, a prolonged QT interval indicates prolonged conduction.

17. The antipsychotics tend to decrease the seizure threshold, so a smaller stimulus is required to cause a seizure in a client taking these medications. Epilepsy or a history of seizures is not a contraindication for the use of antipsychotic drugs, but the physician should be notified of any such history.

18. Some clients taking antipsychotics experience photosensitivity, which is an increased sensitivity to the effects of the sun. Photosensitive clients experience severe sunburn with minimal sun exposure. Dark-skinned as well as light-skinned clients can experience photosensitivity.

19. EPS are the side effects most commonly cited by clients as their reason for noncompliance with antipsychotic medications at home. As a group, the atypical agents cause fewer EPS, less prolactin increase, and less tardive dyskinesia.

20. The atypical antipsychotics treat psychosis effectively in some people who are resistant to the typical antipsychotics.

21. Individually, the atypical antipsychotics have some of the same side effects as the typical agents. Examples are the increased risk of weight gain with olanzapine, increased prolactin with resperidone, and the risk of increased heart conduction time with ziprasidone.

SUGGESTIONS FOR CLINICAL ACTIVITIES

•   Assign students to care for clients with a diagnosis of schizophrenia. Following HIPAA regulations, have students share in postconference the medication regimen for their assigned clients and any difficulties the client has had adhering to the medication regimen (if any are known).
•   Assist students to assess clients with schizophrenia (through observation) and review the chart for side effects of antipsychotic medication therapy. Have students share their findings in postconference.
•   Invite a pharmacist to speak with students about the actions and side effects of the various antipsychotic medications.
•   Invite a nurse to speak with the students about the challenges faced by the medical team in terms of patient adherence with drug therapy for schizophrenia.

REFERENCE

•   National Institute of Mental Health: Mental health medications. Available at http://www.nimh.nih.gov/health/publications/mental-health-medications/complete-index.shtml

22. Clients taking atypical antipsychotics are 9% more likely to have diabetes than people taking typical agents.

23. Clozapine can cause agranulocytosis, a life-threatening decrease in white blood cell production. This effect happens to 1% of the clients who take clozapine.

24. Clozapine is used only for clients who are resistant to treatment with other antipsychotics.

25. All clients receiving clozapine have their WBC measured once per week during the first 6 months of therapy and every other week after that to assess whether their white blood cell count is stable. If a client's WBC drops, clozapine would be permanently discontinued.

26. The new-generation antipsychotic aripiprazole (Abilify, Abilitat) has a stabilizing and modulating effect on brain dopamine. This drug is intended to reduce dopamine transmission when it is too high and to preserve it when it is too low, thus maintaining the dopaminergic–cholinergic balance. Therefore, it causes a lower rate of abnormal involuntary movements (EPS).

27. Several antipsychotic agents are currently available in long-acting decanoate form, which can last up to several weeks and thus increase compliance.

28. Several antipsychotic agents are available in liquid oral concentrate form.

LEARNING OUTCOME 4

Apply the nursing process to the care of clients with schizophrenia or other psychoses.

Concepts for Lecture

1. When prioritizing nursing care in the acute phase of psychosis, treatment should focus on the client's basic needs. Safety, nutrition, and rest are the priorities. Acute symptom management is also important.

2. In psychiatric nursing, the client's potential for violence is assessed first because it is a safety issue. Mentally ill people in general are no more violent than the general public, but there are groups of mentally ill people with increased risk for violence toward others.

3. Certain behaviors may suggest that a client is becoming increasingly agitated and more likely to act out violently. These behaviors are clenched fists, loud talking or yelling, threatening, increasing motor activity, hitting walls or furniture, wincing, or looking afraid.

4. Nurses regularly assess and document the client's behavior, mood, and thought content (reflected in what the client says). All clients with psychosis should be asked directly if they feel like hurting themselves or others.

5. Interpreting the meaning of the client's behaviors can be difficult if the client is from a different culture from the nurse. See Box 49-7 for description of cultural sensitivity issues in psychiatric care. The nurse should always try to interpret client behavior relative to the client's cultural background.

6. When clients are hallucinating, they may not be sure what is real and what is not. Physical touching may be perceived as part of a threatening hallucination. Delusional thinking may make even the well-intentioned nurse seem menacing. Physical assessment may be very stressful for the client. Some clients mistake physical touch for sexual advances.

7. Only priority physical assessments should be done in the acute psychiatric setting.

 **POWERPOINT SLIDES**

Tables and/or Figures
- **Box 49-7** Focus on Diversity: Cultural Care In Psychiatric Nursing
- **Box 49-8** Nursing Care Checklist: Interacting With a Person Who Is Actively Hallucinating

Nursing Care Plan: Client With Schizophrenia

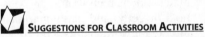 **SUGGESTIONS FOR CLASSROOM ACTIVITIES**
- Discuss in detail the assessment data that would indicate a client is experiencing paranoia or command hallucinations.
- Divide the students into small groups and assign each group a nursing diagnosis given in the chapter. Ask the students to expand on the interventions and the rationales for interventions.

 **SUGGESTIONS FOR CLINICAL ACTIVITIES**
- Have students observe the psychiatric clinical environment. Instruct students to note how the environment is constructed/arranged to promote client and staff safety.
- Ask a nurse on the clinical area to talk with the students in postconference about strategies used on the unit to keep clients and staff safe.

 REFERENCE
- National Institute of Mental Health: Are people with schizophrenia violent? Available at http://www.nimh.nih.gov/health/publications/schizophrenia/are-people-with-schizophrenia-violent.shtml

8. A trusting nurse–client relationship will make it easier for the nurse to gain client cooperation for necessary assessments.

9. The nurse must understand the desired effects and potential side effects of all medications and treatments received by their clients and assess for these.

10. Psychiatric clients may not be able to clearly articulate what is wrong with them. Careful listening is another important nursing skill.

11. It is important to obtain written permission from clients to communicate with anyone about them, including their family members.

12. Data about the client's mental status, observation of the client's behavior and interactions with others, physical assessment findings, and information from family all contribute data for establishing nursing diagnoses.

13. Priority nursing diagnoses that often apply to clients with schizophrenia include Risk for Violence, Self-Directed or Other-Directed; Disturbed Thought Processes; Ineffective Coping; and Impaired Social Interaction.

14. One nursing diagnosis for a client with schizophrenia is Risk for Violence, Self-Directed or Other-Directed, with a possible expected outcome that the client will cause no harm to self or others.

15. Nursing interventions for Risk for Violence, Self-Directed or Other-Directed, include avoiding touching an actively hallucinating client; intervening early as soon as you have identified increased agitation, reassuring clients that they are safe in the hospital; avoiding confronting clients aggressively about their behavior; and when inappropriate behavior arises, telling the client simply and calmly that the behavior is not acceptable and redirecting the client to another activity.

16. Additional interventions for Risk for Violence, Self-Directed or Other-Directed, include starting with less restrictive interventions when clients have inappropriate behavior; trying to talk first then redirect, offering meds, isolating/medicating, and restraining last; maintaining a low-stimulation environment; talking with clients about signs and symptoms of anxiety and agitation and the triggers that start these feelings; discussing options for appropriate behavior and anxiety management techniques; and observing people experiencing paranoia or command hallucinations closely. See Box 49-8 for help on interacting with clients who are actively hallucinating.

17. Another nursing diagnosis for a client with schizophrenia is Disturbed Thought Processes, with a possible expected outcome that the client will have reality-based thinking.

18. Nursing interventions for a nursing diagnosis of Disturbed Thought Processes include looking for the client's strengths and abilities when providing nursing care; reinforcing reality and talking about what is really happening; avoiding arguing with the client about delusional thoughts; encouraging or assisting the client to express feelings of fear or anxiety; and providing validation for the client's feelings.

19. Ineffective Coping is a nursing diagnosis often used for clients with schizophrenia. A possible expected outcome is that the client will take medications as prescribed, will have behavior choices when frustrated other than acting out frustration physically, and will have stress management strategies.

20. Nursing interventions for a nursing diagnosis of Ineffective Coping include establishing a trusting relationship in which the client is safe to express true feelings, especially negative ones; offering medications in a confident way, expecting the client to take them; and teaching clients stress management techniques such as going to their rooms and doing relaxation exercises.

21. Impaired Social Interaction is a nursing diagnosis often used for a client with schizophrenia. A possible expected outcome is that the

client will behave in appropriate ways in social situations and client will maintain contact with family and important friends.

22. Nursing interventions for a nursing diagnosis of Impaired Social Interaction include approaching client with an accepting attitude, being honest and sincere; interacting with the client individually and modeling appropriate social behavior; giving positive reinforcement for client's voluntary interactions with others; and encouraging client to attend group activities in the hospital and accompanying client at first if necessary.

23. When evaluating the effectiveness of nursing care for clients with schizophrenia, the nurse looks to the desired outcomes determining whether the client demonstrates reality-based thinking, performs ADL independently, demonstrates an understanding of medication management, states a plan for self-management of stress or frustration, and interacts effectively with others.

GENERAL CHAPTER CONSIDERATIONS

1. Have students study and learn key terms listed at the beginning of the chapter.
2. Have students complete end of chapter exercises either in their book or on the MyNursingKit website.
3. Use the Classroom Response Question PowerPoints to assess students prior to lecture.

- Clinical Reasoning Care Map

MyNursingKit
(www.mynursingkit.com)

- Websites
- NCLEX® Questions
- Case Studies
- Key Terms

STUDENT WORKBOOK AND RESOURCE GUIDE

- Chapter 49 activities
- *Separate purchase*

PRENTICE HALL NURSE'S DRUG GUIDE

- *Separate purchase*

CLASSROOM RESPONSE QUESTION POWERPOINTS

TESTBANK

CHAPTER 50
CARING FOR CLIENTS WITH MOOD DISORDERS

LEARNING OUTCOME 1

Explain the pathophysiology of mood disorders in relation to brain neurotransmitters.

Concepts for Lecture

1. Depression can have a variety of causes. Major depressive disorder has a genetic component, a brain physiology component, and a psychosocial component. Each contributes to the cause but does not explain the disorder alone.
2. Major depressive disorder is 1.5 to 3 times more common among first-degree biologic relatives of affected people than among the general population.
3. Researchers have found that people who have a variant of the gene that codes for a transporter of serotonin are more likely to develop depression after experiencing stress.
4. People inherit the tendency to respond to life stressors with the development of depression.
5. Brain neurotransmitters such as serotonin, norepinephrine, dopamine, acetylcholine, and gamma-aminobutyric acid (GABA) are likely involved in depression. In depression, the neurotransmitters have reduced function. The fact that antidepressant medications (which increase neurotransmitter function) are so effective is evidence that neurotransmitter function affects mood.
6. Like major depressive disorder, bipolar I disorder tends to recur in families. There is evidence of a genetic etiology but not of a single gene inheritance. First-degree biologic relatives of a person with bipolar disorder have a 4% to 24% chance of having the disease, the same recurrence rate as depression. Any given manic episode is likely to follow a stressor.
7. The brain neurotransmitters norepinephrine and dopamine are implicated in the cause of manic episodes. The same monoamine neurotransmitters whose decreased activity is implemented in depression are increased in mania. Hormones also interact with neurotransmitters in mood disorders. Hypothyroidism is correlated with depression and with rapid cycling of mood between depression and mania.

LEARNING OUTCOME 2

Assess clients for suicidal thinking.

Concepts for Lecture

1. The U.S. Surgeon General published a call to action in 1999 that included the risks for suicide (Box 50-3) and the protective factors for suicide (Box 50-4).
2. Risk factors for suicide include previous suicide attempt; mental disorders; co-existing mental and alcohol or substance abuse disorders; family history of suicide; hopelessness; impulsive and/or aggressive tendencies; barriers to accessing mental health treatment; relationship, social, work,

 **POWERPOINT SLIDES**

Tables and/or Figures

- **Figure 50-1** Positron Emission Tomography (PET) Scan of a Brain Before and After Treatment for Depression (Source: Photo Researchers, Inc.)

 SUGGESTIONS FOR CLASSROOM ACTIVITIES

- Invite a professor from a pharmacy school or a physiologist to talk with the class about the relationship of mood disorders and neurotransmitters.
- Assign students to find articles in the library or online about the relationship of neurotransmitters and mood disorders.

SUGGESTIONS FOR CLINICAL ACTIVITIES

- Assign students to work with clients who have mood disorders. Ask the students to make a list of the client's medications for their mood disorders. Have the students research each medication and state what neurotransmitters are being theoretically affected by each medication. Students can use a variety of resources to find this information (e.g., the hospital pharmacist, the psychiatrist, the Internet, medication inserts, their drug textbook, and other textbooks).

REFERENCE

- National Institutes of Health: Information about mental illness and the brain. Available at http://science.education.nih.gov/ supplements/nih5/mental/guide/ info-mental-a.htm

 **POWERPOINT SLIDES**

Tables and/or Figures

- **Box 50-3** Risk Factors for Suicide
- **Box 50-4** Protective Factors for Suicide
- **Box 50-5** Talking About Suicide

SUGGESTIONS FOR CLASSROOM ACTIVITIES

- Use a transparency of Box 50-3 to discuss risk factors for suicide.

or financial losses; general medical illness; easy access to lethal suicide methods, especially guns; unwillingness to seek help because of the stigma attached to mental and substance abuse disorders and/or suicidal thoughts; influence of significant people; cultural or religious beliefs; local epidemics of suicide that have a contagious influence; and isolation.

3. Protective factors for suicide include effective and appropriate clinical care for mental, physical, and substance abuse disorders; easy access to a variety of clinical interventions and support; restricted access to highly lethal methods of suicide; family and community support; support from ongoing medical and mental healthcare relationships; learned skills in problem solving, conflict resolution, and nonviolent handling of disputes; and cultural and religious beliefs that discourage suicide and support self-preservation instincts.

4. Suicide rates are highest among older adults.

5. Most elderly suicide victims are seen by their primary care provider within a few weeks of the suicide and are experiencing a first episode of mild to moderate depression. This demonstrates a lost opportunity for identifying suicide risk and preventing suicide.

6. Most people with depression, whether they are contemplating suicide or not, benefit from talking about their feelings, especially the frightening ones. Depression makes it hard for people to identify and explain their own feelings. Talking about and clarifying these feelings can help a depressed person gain perspective, interrupt negative thinking, or work on problem solving.

7. Active listening is a powerful tool for nurses to use. Clients often express gratitude for the opportunity to express their feelings about suicide (see Box 50-5: Talking About Suicide).

8. Only when a nurse is aware of a client's suicidal thinking, or suicidal ideation, can the nurse intervene to help the client.

9. The nurse can assess the dangerousness of the client's suicidal thoughts. Thinking "I feel so bad, I wish I were dead" is not as dangerous as "I have a gun at home, and as soon as I am discharged, I plan to shoot myself."

10. The nurse–client relationship is not social. The relationship is a professional relationship where it is important to assess the client's safety and to intervene to protect the client or others, as necessary, so it is important to ask clients if they feel like hurting themselves or others.

11. In the general medical setting, every elderly client with a chronic illness and every client who has the risk factors for suicide listed in Box 50-3 should be asked: "Do you feel like hurting yourself or other people?"

12. After the nurse assesses suicidal ideation, the nurse determines if the client has organized their thoughts about suicide enough to have a plan by asking the client, "Do you have a plan?" The nurse assesses the lethality of the plan by asking, "What is your plan?" The nurse assesses if the client has access to the planned means of suicide by asking if the client has access to the planned method (e.g., "Do you have access to a gun?").

13. The nurse must inform the treatment team of the client's suicide ideation, plan, lethality of the plan, and access to the planned method. Failure to report suicidal ideation constitutes breach of the nurse's legal and ethical duty to protect the client.

- Discuss the factors that relate to the elderly client with a chronic illness. Ask students to give examples of chronic illnesses that lead to depression and thus potential for thoughts of suicide.
- Discuss the nurse's responsibility in reporting a client who has clear thoughts, intention, a plan, and means to commit suicide, to the treatment team.

Suggestions for Clinical Activities

- Have the students write about their fears and insecurities about assessing a client for suicide. Have the students also write about any experiences they have had with suicidal persons and about any family members or friends who committed suicide. Ask the students to give this "confidential" information to you. Hold private mini-conferences with students to discuss with them what they have written.
- Invite members of the treatment team to speak with students about how their individual roles as team members ensure the safety of the client with a plan for committing suicide.

References

- Agency for Healthcare Research and Quality: Screening for suicide risk. Available at: http://www.ahrq.gov/clinic/3rduspstf/suicide/suiciderr.htm
- American Academy of Family Physicians: Evaluation and treatments of patients with suicidal ideation. Available at http://www.aafp.org/afp/990315ap/1500.html

Learning Outcome 3

Safely and effectively administer antidepressant medications and mood stabilizing medications.

Concepts for Lecture

1. Medications have been shown to be effective for all types of depression. However, there is no single medication that works for everyone.

2. Antidepressants require 2–6 weeks to achieve full effect; often, several drugs are tried in an attempt to find effective treatment.

3. Some people experience no improvement with antidepressant medications, and others experience intolerable side effects. In some cases, side effects may be useful (e.g., a client who has trouble sleeping may be given an antidepressant with sedating effects at bedtime).

4. Depression appears to involve reduced neurotransmitter function in brain synapses and changes in receptors on brain neurons.

5. Antidepressants may be organized into four groups: tricyclic antidepressants (TCAs) and related cyclic agents; selective serotonin reuptake inhibitors (SSRIs); other novel antidepressants; and monoamine oxidase inhibitors (MAOIs).

6. The tricyclics were the first choice of treatment for depression from the 1950s until the 1990s. Although antidepressant medications have proven to be very effective, they do have limitations. They have numerous side effects, including dry mouth, orthostatic hypotension, increased heart rate, constipation, urinary hesitancy or retention, dilatation of pupils (mydriasis), blurred vision, dry eyes, and photophobias.

7. Clients with narrow-angle glaucoma may develop increased eye pressure due to pupil dilation when they take medications with anticholinergic side effects. The nurse should notify the physician if the client has a history of glaucoma.

8. The tricyclic antidepressants can be fatal in overdose. Because suicide is a risk of depression, the healthcare team must consider the possibility of the use of antidepressants by a client as a method of suicide.

9. Since the 1990s, SSRIs are usually prescribed if a client has significant suicidal thinking, a history of suicide attempts, or impulse control problems. The SSRIs are usually the first-choice drugs for the treatment of depression because they have fewer side effects than the other types of antidepressants, and they are just as effective. See Table 50-1 for the nursing implications of antidepressant drugs.

10. Tricyclic and related drugs include amitriptyline (Elavil), amoxapine (Asendin), clomipramine (Anafranil), desipramine (Norpramin), doxepin (Sinequan), imipramine (Tofranil), maprotiline (Ludiomil), nortriptyline (Pamelor), protriptyline (Vivactil), and trimipramine (Surmontil).

11. TCAs block the reuptake of serotonin and norepinephrine. The nursing implications include assessing for side effects, such as sedation, orthostatic hypotension, weight gain, anticholinergic effects, tachycardia, or cardiac dysrhythmias. The nurse needs to assess vital signs and mental status, notify the physician if the client has glaucoma, assess for suicidal thinking, and know that older adults require lower doses and to use with caution in the elderly who are more likely to have side effects.

12. Selective serotonin reuptake inhibitors (SSRIs) include citalopram (Celexa), escitalopram (Lexapro), fluoxetine (Prozac), fluvoxamine (Luvox), paroxetine (Paxil), and sertraline (Zoloft).

13. SSRIs inhibit reuptake of serotonin and are used to treat depression, panic disorder (paroxetine), obsessive compulsive disorder (fluvoxamine, fluoxetine), premenstrual dysphoric disorder, bulimia nervosa (fluoxetine), anxiety (paroxetine), and PTSD (sertraline).

 **PowerPoint Slides**

Tables and/or Figures

- **Table 50-1** Giving Medications Safely: Antidepressants
- **Table 50-2** Giving Medications Safely: Mood Stabilizers
- **Box 50-6** Focus on Older Adults: Antidepressants and the Older Adult
- **Box 50-9** Lithium Side Effects and Toxicity

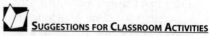 **Suggestions for Classroom Activities**

- Divide the students into small workgroups. Assign each group a specific medication used to treat mood disorders. Have students identify the one side effect that would most likely lead to noncompliance with therapy. Have students discuss how they would work with the client to help the client communicate with the prescribing psychiatrist and be adherent to the prescribed medication regimen.
- Have a pharmacist or psychiatrist speak to the students about common medication combinations/regimens used to treat mood disorders.

Suggestions for Clinical Activities

- Assign students to care for clients with mood disorders. Have the students choose one medication from their client's medication regimen and develop a teaching brochure for that medication.

14. Nursing implications for SSRIs include assessing for side effects, such as nausea, loose stools, sexual side effects (decreased libido), headache, anxiety or sedation, insomnia, slight anticholinergic symptoms, and orthstatic hypotension. The nurse needs to assess vital signs and mental status. There is a low potential for harm in overdose. The dosage in the elderly needs to be decreased.

15. Novel antidepressants inhibit reuptake of norepinephrine, dopamine, and/or serotonin. They are used to treat insomnia (trazodone), anxiety disorder (reboxetine), and depression and as an aid to stop smoking (bupropion). Nursing implications include assessing for side effects, such as anxiety, nausea, agitation, sedation, weight loss, increased blood pressure (venlafaxine), seizures (bupropion), and insomnia.

16. The monoamine oxidase inhibitors (MAOIs) block the enzyme monoamine oxidase that breaks down neurotransmitters. MAOIs are used to treat depression that is not responsive to other agents.

17. Nursing implications for MAOIs include awareness that MAOIs can cause hypertensive crisis when the client eats foods high in tyramine and can have a drug interaction with other antidepressants, meperidine, general anesthetics, sympathomimetics, bronchodilators, and methylphenidate. The nurse needs to assess vital signs and mental status. MAOIs can be fatal in overdose.

18. The first MAOI available in a transdermal patch is selegiline. At the lowest dose (6 mg), the client does not require the diet restrictions of the other MAOIs. Moclobemide (Manerix) is an MOA-A inhibitor. It is a reversible selective inhibitor of MAO-A used to treat depression. This medication does not have the hypertensive side effects of MAOIs. This medication is not to be given with MAOIs or narcotics.

19. Older clients with depression tend to respond well to antidepressant drugs. Special nursing implications include knowing that the elderly require lower doses due to decreased metabolic efficiency; elders are at increased risk for orthostatic hypotension, which increases their risks for falls and injury; and if older adults are dehydrated, they are at increased risk for medication side effects.

20. When SSRIs are combined with antipsychotics, extrapyramidal symptoms are increased. Serotonin syndrome, a potentially fatal result of excess serotonin activity, can result from combining SSRIs with MAOIs, St. John's wort, or tryptophan.

21. A 2-week "wash-out" period should occur between the use of SSRIs or TCAs and MAOIs. If the nurse suspects serotonin syndrome, the nurse needs to hold the SSRI and notify the physician immediately.

22. The nurse stresses to clients taking MAOIs that they must avoid foods high in tyramine, which include aged cheese, foods containing aged cheese, preserved meats, liver and other organ meats, broad fava beans, sauerkraut, banana peel, draft beer, red wine, soy sauce, and yeast or protein extract products. Coffee, cola, and tea should be consumed in moderation.

23. The symptoms of bipolar depression are the same as those in clients who have depression alone (unipolar depression). The depression associated with bipolar disorder does not respond well to antidepressant medications alone. Antidepressants given with either lithium or divalproex (an anticonvulsant) have been found to be effective in stabilizing mood.

24. Lithium, a naturally occurring element, was the first mood-stabilizing drug. Target symptoms of mania include irritability, euphoria, pressured speech, flight of ideas, motor hyperactivity, aggressive behavior, grandiosity, delusions, impulsiveness, and hallucinations.

25. It is thought that lithium corrects an ion exchange abnormality in the neuron and normalizes neurotransmitter function.

26. Lithium has a narrow therapeutic range, and toxicity is close to therapeutic blood levels. The therapeutic range is 0.5–1.5 mEq/L. Lithium

levels are drawn weekly initially, then every 2 months. The client needs to maintain stable sodium intake, fluid and electrolyte balance, and mental status. Lithium is categorized as pregnancy category D.

27. The classes of drugs used to treat manic episodes are mood stabilizers (antimanic agents), anticonvulsants (that act as mood stabilizers), benzodiazepines (to decrease anxiety and agitation while the other drugs are starting to work), and antipsychotics (if the client has psychotic symptoms).

28. In addition to a mood stabilizer, an antidepressant is often prescribed, often in lower doses than for people who have depression alone. The dose is kept low because antidepressant medications can trigger a manic episode in a person with bipolar disorder.

29. Lithium includes lithium carbonate, eskalith, eskalith CR, lithonate, and lithotabs. Nursing implications include using these drugs with caution in the elderly and in people with thyroid diseases and diabetes. The nurse needs to assess the client for toxicity.

30. Mood stabilizers include valproic acid (Depakene), sodium valproate (Depacon), divalproex sodium (Depakote), carbamazepine (Tegretol), and lamotragine (Lamictal).

31. With the anticonvulsant mood stabilizers, the nursing interventions include assessing for side effects and monitoring liver function and mental status. When giving valproate, the medication in the liquid form is to be mixed with juice to reduce mouth irritation. With carbamazepine, the client is monitored for bone marrow suppression. With lamotrigine, the client is monitored for Stevens-Johnson syndrome. Valproate is a pregnancy category D drug, and the others are pregnancy category C.

LEARNING OUTCOME 4

Apply the nursing process to clients with mood disorders.

Concepts for Lecture

1. Mood is reflected in the client's behavior and speech. A mental health assessment on admission provides baseline information on the client with a mood disorder. Over time, briefer assessments of pertinent parts of mental status can be compared to the original assessment to document client progress.

2. The client's cultural background is an important aspect of assessment. See Box 50-12 for the relationship between culture and symptoms of depression.

3. One possible nursing diagnosis is Risk for Self-Directed Violence, with an expected outcome that the client will not harm self.

4. Nursing interventions for Risk for Self-Directed Violence include assessing mental status, including suicidal ideation; if the client has suicidal ideation, assessing for a suicide plan and whether the client has the means to complete the plan; sharing information about suicidal thinking with the treatment team; removing potentially dangerous items from the client's area; assessing client's safety frequently during the night; remaining with a client who is having feelings about harming self; and creating a "no harm" contract with the client.

5. Another possible nursing diagnosis for a client with a mood disorder is Risk for Other-Directed Violence. A possible expected outcome is that the client will not harm others.

6. Nursing interventions for Risk for Other-Directed Violence include remaining calm; providing a low-stimulation environment for a client who is manic; and making expectations for client behavior clear to

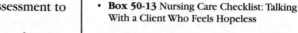
POWERPOINT SLIDES

Tables and/or Figures
- **Box 50-10** Geriatric Depression Scale (Short Form)
- **Box 50-11** Beck Depression Inventory (Short Form)
- **Box 50-12** Focus on Diversity: Is Depression the Same Everywhere?
- **Box 50-13** Nursing Care Checklist: Talking With a Client Who Feels Hopeless

Nursing Care Plan: Client With Depression

SUGGESTIONS FOR CLASSROOM ACTIVITIES
- Using the nursing diagnoses given in the chapter, elicit from students the nursing interventions they believe will address them.
- Discuss how a nurse develops a trusting relationship with a client who has a mood disorder, in order to do an accurate assessment and develop a nursing care plan with the client.

SUGGESTIONS FOR CLINICAL ACTIVITIES
- Assign students to care for clients with major depressive disorder and bipolar disorders in the manic phase. Have students compare and contrast the plans of care for these clients.
- Assist students to understand the critical elements of the plan of care for a client exhibiting violent behavior.

the client as soon as possible. Staff members need to be consistent in their expectations of the client.

7. Additional interventions for a nursing diagnosis of Risk for Other-Directed Violence include observing client closely and responding quickly to increasing agitation, starting with least restrictive approach (redirection, PRN medication, isolation, and finally restraint as a last resort); and minimizing group activities for client in mania; providing appropriate opportunities for physical activity, with walking as the ideal activity, although the client may prefer another activity such as ping-pong or basketball.

8. A possible nursing diagnosis for a client with mood disorder is Impaired Social Interaction. A possible expected outcome might be that the client will interact individually with staff and peers and participate in group activities.

9. Nursing interventions for a nursing diagnosis of Impaired Social Interaction include establishing a trusting relationship with the client, spending some time each shift interacting with the client individually, providing structured activities to allow the client with depression to interact with others, and encouraging the client to participate.

10. Another nursing diagnosis for clients with depression is Imbalanced Nutrition, with a possible expected outcome that the client will maintain admission body weight (or gain a specified amount of weight, as indicated).

11. Interventions for a nursing diagnosis of Imbalanced Nutrition may include offering lighter foods, snacks, and liquids if the client is lethargic and overweight; discussing the value of regular exercise in improving one's spirits; encouraging the client to set a plan of regular, light exercise; offering fluids frequently and small amounts of nutritious foods; and providing nutritious "finger foods" if the client is highly active, pacing, or too busy to eat.

12. Another nursing diagnosis for a client with depression is Hopelessness, with a possible expected outcome that the client will express feelings and make statements indicating hope that the future will be better.

13. Nursing interventions for a nursing diagnosis of Hopelessness include allowing the client to talk about feelings and life events, using therapeutic communication techniques to help client see that she or he has survived difficulties in the past and that she or he has strengths, and teaching client about the disorder and medications and that the treatment team will not give up hope until the client feels better. See Box 50-13 for ideas about using therapeutic communication as an intervention for a client who feels hopeless.

GENERAL CHAPTER CONSIDERATIONS

1. Have students study and learn key terms listed at the beginning of the chapter.
2. Have students complete end of chapter exercises either in their book or on the MyNursingKit Website.
3. Use the Classroom Response Question PowerPoints to assess students prior to lecture.

- Clinical Reasoning Care Map

 **MYNURSINGKIT (www.mynursingkit.com)**

- Websites
- NCLEX® Questions
- Case Studies
- Key Terms

 STUDENT WORKBOOK AND RESOURCE GUIDE

- Chapter 50 activities
- *Separate purchase*

PRENTICE HALL NURSE'S DRUG GUIDE

- *Separate purchase*

 CLASSROOM RESPONSE QUESTION POWERPOINTS

 TESTBANK

CHAPTER 51
CARING FOR CLIENTS WITH ANXIETY DISORDERS

LEARNING OUTCOME 1

Collect subjective and objective data about client's anxiety.

Concepts for Lecture

1. Anxiety and fear cause the same physiologic responses, which are the result of sympathetic nervous system manifestation.
2. Manifestations of sympathetic stimulation (Box 51-1) include objective symptoms of increase blood glucose, increased heart rate, increased blood pressure, dilated pupils, cool skin, piloerection, and decreased GI motility.
3. There are four degrees of anxiety (mild, moderate, severe, and panic), and each has different subjective effects and observable behavior. See Table 51-2.
4. Generalized anxiety disorder is characterized by excessive anxiety and worry occurring on most days for at least 6 months. The client with generalized anxiety disorder has to have at least three of the following symptoms: restlessness, fatigue, difficulty concentrating, irritability, muscle tension, and disturbed sleep.
5. A diagnosis of generalized anxiety disorder in children requires only one of the above symptoms in addition to the persistent anxiety.
6. Clients with generalized anxiety disorder report they feel significant stress, have difficulty controlling the worry, or have related impairment in social or occupational functioning (subjective data).
7. Clients with panic disorder have recurrent, unexpected panic attacks followed by at least 1 month of persistent concern about having another one.
8. A panic attack is characterized by an episode of intense fear or discomfort. During this episode, four or more of the following are present: palpitations, pounding heart, or increased heart rate; sweating; trembling or shaking; sensations of shortness of breath or smothering; feeling of choking; chest pain or discomfort; nausea or abdominal distress; feeling dizzy, unsteady, light-headed, or faint; derealization (feeling of unreality) or depersonalization (being detached from oneself); fear of losing control or going crazy; fear of dying; paresthesias (numbness or tingling); and chills or hot flashes.
9. Agoraphobia is characterized by anxiety about being in places or situations where escape may be difficult (or embarrassing) or when help might not be available in the case of a panic attack.
10. Agoraphobia is commonly associated with panic disorder. It can result in severe impairment in social and occupational functioning when the individual avoids multiple anxiety-producing situations.
11. Clients with obsessive-compulsive disorder have obsessive thoughts that commonly involve dirt and germs, numbers or counting, symmetry and order, ideas that are against the individual's religious beliefs, or sexual thoughts that are disgusting to the affected individual. Examples of compulsive rituals are cleaning, hand washing, touching or doing things in a certain order, or praying.
12. There is no pleasure for the affected individual in performing the compulsive rituals, only temporary relief from the anxiety caused by not doing these things.

POWERPOINT SLIDES

Tables and/or Figures
- **Box 51-1** Manifestations of Sympathetic Stimulation
- **Table 51-2** Four Degrees of Anxiety
- **Table 51-3** Specific Phobia Names
- **Figure 51-2** Potential Anxiety-Producing Events
- **Figure 51-3** The Sympathetic Nervous System Responds in the Same Way to Fear of an Alligator as to General Anxiety
- **Figure 51-5** OCD Shown in Typical Situations
- **Figure 51-6** Veterans Experiencing Military Sexual Trauma at Risk for PTSD
- **Box 51-3** Military Sexual Trauma

SUGGESTIONS FOR CLASSROOM ACTIVITIES

- Have students break into small groups to compare and contrast normal anxiety and anxiety disorders.
- Ask students to share examples of instances when they experienced "normal" anxiety.
- Discuss the changes in vital signs that would be seen in a client with an anxiety disorder. Describe the degree of elevation in vital signs that occurs as anxiety progresses from mild anxiety to panic.

SUGGESTIONS FOR CLINICAL ACTIVITIES

- Assign students to care for clients with anxiety disorders. Have students observe their assigned clients for manifestations of anxiety. Have students ask their clients to describe the anxiety they have experienced at its worst.

REFERENCES

- Anxiety Disorders Association of America: Homepage. Available at http://www.adaa.org/
- National Institutes of Health: Anxiety disorders. Available at http://www.nimh.nih.gov/health/topics/anxiety-disorders/index.shtml

13. Posttraumatic stress disorder (PTSD) is a debilitating condition that follows an extreme traumatic stressor. The person's response to the event must involve intense fear, helplessness, or horror.

14. The characteristic symptoms of PTSD include the following, which are present for more than 1 month: persistent reexperiencing of the traumatic event; avoidance of stimuli associated with the trauma; numbing of general responsiveness; and increased arousal (difficulty sleeping, nightmares, exaggerated startle response, and hypervigilance or alertness for danger).

15. People with PTSD commonly have repeated intrusive memories or dreams of the event. Some people experience flashbacks in which they relive the event, believing that it is actually happening. A flashback may include sights, sounds, smells, or feelings from the traumatic event.

16. People affected with PTSD feel distressed by situations that remind them of the event and avoid these situations.

17. People with PTSD may have difficulty with interpersonal relationships. They may have difficulty trusting or being affectionate.

18. Military sexual trauma refers to both sexual harassment and sexual assault in a military setting. Victims of military sexual trauma are at increased risk for PTSD.

19. Social phobia, also called social anxiety disorder, is characterized by a marked and persistent fear of social or performance situations in which embarrassment may occur. A phobia is a persistent and irrational fear.

20. With social phobia, exposure to the social or performance situation almost always results in an immediate anxiety reaction.

21. Social phobia only exists if the fear, avoidance, or anxiety about encountering the social situation interferes significantly with the affected individual's daily routine or social, academic, or occupational life or if the person is markedly distressed by the disorder.

22. Physical symptoms often accompany the anxiety in social phobia. These include blushing, excessive sweating, nausea, GI distress, tremors, and difficulty talking.

23. Specific phobias include the phobia of blood or needles. The extreme fear in the phobia of blood or needles may result in the vasovagal response. The client's heart and respiratory rates initially increase due to sympathetic stimulation. When the vagus nerve is stimulated, the heart rate and blood pressure fall, potentially resulting in a loss of consciousness.

LEARNING OUTCOME 2

Apply the nursing process to the care of clients with anxiety disorders.

Concepts for Lecture

1. During the nursing history, the nurse may identify that the client has a general medical condition that commonly has anxiety as a symptom. In these clients, treating the general medical disorders treats anxiety symptoms.

2. The nurse assesses for the physical symptoms of anxiety, which usually begin with increased heart rate, blood pressure, and respiratory rate, and assesses the level of anxiety.

3. The nursing assessment always includes how clients respond to their illnesses, how clients respond to the treatments, and what factors cause or worsen anxiety, if these are observed.

 **POWERPOINT SLIDES**

Tables and/or Figures
- **Box 51-4** General Medical Conditions Associated With Anxiety
- **Box 51-7** Assessment: Questions to Assess Coping Methods
- **Box 51-8** Client Teaching: Progressive Relaxation Exercise

Nursing Care Plan: Client With Generalized Anxiety Disorder

4. In the intervention phase of the nursing process, the nurse will help the client recognize factors that increase and decrease anxiety as a way of improving the client's insight.

5. The nurse responsible for the care of clients who receive medication must know the desired effects and potential side effects of those medications. The nurse assesses the client's response to medication.

6. If a client is experiencing an episode of anxiety, the nurse assesses the client's perception of the threat represented by the situation.

7. The client's use of alcohol or drugs as self-medication for anxiety at home should be assessed.

8. A client with a history of insomnia or the regular use of medications for sleep needs to be assessed because it may indicate chronic anxiety.

9. Information about the client's usual coping methods can be helpful in planning care for the anxious client.

10. The nurse's own anxiety level is another important assessment because when the nurse is anxious, it is much easier for the client to feel anxious.

11. Anxiety is a nursing diagnosis and a possible expected outcome is that the client will discuss feelings of anxiety and potential desire to harm self.

12. Nursing interventions for a nursing diagnosis of Anxiety could include assessing for risk of self-harm; observing closely and providing safe environment; having a calm, nonthreatening attitude while caring for the client; assuring the client that he or she is safe; maintaining a low-stimulation environment; and keeping communication simple and direct.

13. Ineffective Coping is another nursing diagnosis often used for a client with anxiety. A possible expected outcome is that the client will verbalize strategies to interrupt anxiety.

14. Nursing interventions for a nursing diagnosis of Ineffective Coping include encouraging the client to express feelings; providing time for one-on-one interaction and establishing a trusting relationship; using therapeutic communication techniques; helping client to explore factors that lead to anxiety; exploring options for responding adaptively to stressors and practicing them if possible; teaching the client to recognize anxiety as it develops and taking control of stopping the anxiety from escalating (relaxation or breathing techniques, exercises, meditation); and teaching the client to use progressive relaxation as a coping strategy.

15. Another nursing diagnosis for a client with anxiety is Post-Trauma Syndrome, with a possible expected outcome that the client will discuss feelings and verbalize situations that increase the sense of threat, fear, or anxiety.

16. Nursing interventions for Post-Trauma Syndrome include assessing the degree of anxiety or fear and the degree of threat perceived by the client; staying calm and staying with the client; keeping communication simple; assisting client to correct any distortions of thinking; helping the client identify coping behaviors that have been useful in the past; and identifying supportive people in the client's life.

17. Evaluation involves gathering data to ascertain if the expected outcomes were met. It is not the goal of the nurse to relieve all anxiety. Some anxiety is a necessary protective mechanism that allows people to be alert. Nurses try to help clients understand themselves, so they can learn new coping skills and keep anxiety at a manageable level.

SUGGESTIONS FOR CLASSROOM ACTIVITIES

- Discuss the medical conditions found in Box 51-4 that may produce the symptoms of anxiety. Review how this type of anxiety is different from that which is found in anxiety disorders. Ask students if they have worked with clients who had anxiety associated with a medical disorder or if they have seen this in family members or had experience with anxiety associated with a medical disorder themselves.

- Encourage a class discussion on how the anxiety level of the nurse may exacerbate feelings of anxiety in the client. Ask the students to come up with situations in the clinical setting when it is especially important for the nurse to be perceived as calm by the client.

- Break the students into small groups of three or four and have each group discuss in detail the nursing interventions for one or more of the nursing diagnoses in the text and ascertain why these interventions are important.

SUGGESTIONS FOR CLINICAL ACTIVITIES

- In a preclinical conference, generate a discussion with students about their own anxiety in the clinical setting. Have the students identify strategies that they will use to cope with or reduce their anxiety. In postconference, ask students to describe how their strategies worked and what other strategies they may have come up with to deal with their own anxiety.

- Assign students to care for clients who have been identified as having anxiety. Have students create a plan of care for their assigned clients.

- Role model for the students the concept of therapeutic use of self as a means of developing a therapeutic relationship with clients.

LEARNING OUTCOME 3

Explain the role of coping mechanisms in the management of anxiety.

Concepts for Lecture

1. People use coping behaviors to adapt to or manage stress or change.
2. To control anxiety, people develop patterns of coping behavior. Coping behaviors can be adaptive (healthy or likely to lead to positive resolution) or maladaptive (unhealthy). A person who uses active problem solving, while considering the rights of others, is using coping behavior adaptively. A client who expresses negative or aggressive behavior toward others is using maladaptive coping behaviors.
3. Some methods of coping are part of our conscious thoughts, while others are unconscious. People use both conscious coping behaviors and unconscious defense mechanisms that may also be adaptive or maladaptive. See Table 51-4 for specific examples of defense mechanisms.
4. Defense mechanisms include acting out, altruism, anticipation, compensation, denial, displacement, dissociation, humor, intellectualization, projection, rationalization, reactive formation, regression, repression, sublimation, and suppression.

LEARNING OUTCOME 4

Plan nonpharmacologic nursing interventions to treat or prevent client anxiety.

Concepts for Lecture

1. Each anxiety disorder is treated specifically, but generally, the most effective nonpharmacologic nursing intervention is cognitive-behavioral therapy (CBT).
2. In CBT, clients are helped to change thinking patterns that contribute to their anxieties.
3. Cognitive therapy includes education about the physiology behind anxiety reactions.
4. The goal of the behavioral part of CBT is to change the client's reaction to anxiety-provoking situations. One behavioral approach is to teach the client deep-breathing or relaxation techniques to use in situations expected to provoke anxiety as a means of interrupting the automatic anxiety response.
5. In exposure therapy, clients confront the thing they fear. One approach called exposure and response prevention is often used in OCD. For example, if clients fear dirt and germs, the therapist may have the client dirty their hands and wait a given amount of time before washing while the therapist helps the client cope with resulting anxiety so the client experiences a coping success.
6. Other types of exposure exercises involve techniques such as encouraging a person with social phobia to spend a set amount of time in a feared social situation while fighting the desire to run away.
7. The therapist may assign the client to make a small social error to see how others will respond, followed by the therapist discussing the reaction of others and helping the client see that the fear of judgment by others is not as brutal as the client feared.

 POWERPOINT SLIDES

Tables and/or Figures
- **Table 51-4** Defense Mechanisms

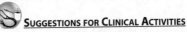 **SUGGESTIONS FOR CLASSROOM ACTIVITIES**

- Write the names of each defense mechanism, along with a description of the defense mechanism, on separate pieces of paper. Have students break into small groups. Each group will get a piece of folded paper with the name and description of a defense mechanism. Each group will design and present a skit depicting the defense mechanism they received. The remaining students will guess which defense mechanism is being presented.

 SUGGESTIONS FOR CLINICAL ACTIVITIES

- Assign students to care for clients who have been identified as having anxiety. Ask the students to identify any coping behaviors their client is using to deal with anxiety.

 REFERENCE

- About.com: Defense mechanisms. Available at http://psychology.about.com/od/theoriesofpersonality/ss/defensemech.htm

 **POWERPOINT SLIDES**

Tables and/or Figures
- **Box 51-8** Client Teaching: Progressive Relaxation Exercises

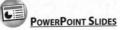 **SUGGESTIONS FOR CLASSROOM ACTIVITIES**

- Discuss cognitive-behavioral therapy (CBT), including overall goal and dual aspects.
- Invite a clinical nurse practitioner who conducts CBT with clients to talk to the class about CBT.
- Ask students to share examples of negative thinking expressed either by a client during a clinical experience or by other anonymous persons associated with the student.
- Ask students to think about how erroneous negative thinking can lead to avoidance. Include the concept of this becoming a self-perpetuating problem/issue.
- Break students into small groups to discuss the concept of resilience, how they might improve their own resilience, and how this might affect their work with clients who have anxiety.

8. Repeated practice of exposure exercises and discussion of feelings and coping techniques with the therapist can help reduce social phobia.
9. Behavioral therapy alone has been used effectively to treat social phobia. The client might be gradually exposed to the feared object or situation. For example, initially the exposure may be only to a picture of the object or situation, and gradually, the client comes to face the feared object or situation. The therapist usually goes with the client to provide support and guidance.
10. The therapist may also work with the client to promote resilience. The resilience factors are self-efficacy, high functional ability, independence with activities of daily living, good self-rated health, and a positive outlook on life.

LEARNING OUTCOME 5

Safely administer antianxiety (anxiolytic) and sedative hypnotic agents.

Concepts for Lecture

1. Medications from several classifications treat anxiety effectively.
2. Medications should not be used when more adaptive approaches could realistically solve the problem.
3. Despite the potential hazards of antianxiety drugs for a few clients, there are many situations in which they are indicated. Most anxiety disorders require a combination of medication and psychotherapy for effective treatment.
4. Benzodiazepines (BZs) are used for anxiety, insomnia, alcohol withdrawal, skeletal muscle relaxation, acute management of seizures, severe agitation, social phobia, generalized anxiety disorder, and panic disorder.
5. The target symptoms for the antianxiety drugs are nervousness, sweating, increased heart rate, sense of dread, fearfulness, phobias, compulsiveness, nausea, vomiting, diarrhea, dizziness, irritability, headache, and dry mouth.
6. The target symptoms for sedative-hypnotics are insomnia and sleep disorders.
7. Long-acting BZ antianxiety agents include alprazolam (Xanex), chlordiazepoxide (Librium), clonazepam (Klonopin), clorazepate (Tranxene), diazepam (Valium), and prazepam (Centrax). Intermediate-acting BZs include halazepam (Pamipam), lorazepam (Ativan), and oxazepam (Serax).
8. Occasionally, clients will have a paradoxical response (contradictory, opposite from expected response) to the BZs. Instead of relaxation, they experience agitation or unstable emotions.
9. The elderly, children, and people with brain damage are at increased risk of a paradoxical response to a BZ. When a client has a paradoxical reaction, the BZ should be discontinued.
10. Dependence and tolerance are important concerns with the BZs. Prolonged use of BZs causes a decrease in GABA receptors. When the BZ is discontinued abruptly, the CNS is stimulated and unable to inhibit or regulate itself. It is important for a client to slowly withdraw from BZs rather than abruptly stop the medication.
11. Overdoses of BZs alone are not commonly fatal. Fatalities more often involve the combination of BZs and alcohol and/or other CNS depressants.
12. The long-acting sedative-hypnotic agents include prazepam (Centrax), flurazepam (Dalmane), and quazepam (Doral). The intermediate-acting

SUGGESTIONS FOR CLINICAL ACTIVITIES

- In the psychiatric clinical setting, arrange for students to each have an opportunity to observe the use of CBT by a trained practitioner. Have students discuss their observations during postconference.

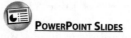
REFERENCES

- National Association of Cognitive-Behavioral Therapists: What is cognitive behavioral therapy? Available at http://nacbt.org/whatiscbt.htm
- National Alliance on Mental Illness: Cognitive behavioral therapy. Available at http://www.nami.org/Template.cfm?Section=About_Treatments_and_Supports&template=/ContentManagement/ContentDisplay.cfm&ContentID=7952

POWERPOINT SLIDES

Tables and/or Figures
- **Table 51-5** Benzodiazepine Antianxiety and Sedative-Hypnotic Agents
- **Box 51-5** Non-Benzodiazepine Antianxiety and Sedative-Hypnotic Agents

SUGGESTIONS FOR CLASSROOM ACTIVITIES

- Have students prepare a notebook, in a three-ring binder, of information about the benzodiazepine and non-benzodiazepine antianxiety and sedative-hypnotic agents. Students can collect information from a variety of sources such as drug information inserts, pharmacy information sheets, the Internet, and their drug textbook. Instruct students to list nursing implications for each drug or highlight this information in yellow in the information they collected.

SUGGESTIONS FOR CLINICAL ACTIVITIES

- Assign students to give medications to clients who are taking benzodiazepine and non-benzodiazepine antianxiety and/or sedative-hypnotic agents. Ask students to verbalize or produce their written nursing implications for these medications.

REFERENCES

- Health Central: Anxiety drug information. Available at http://www.healthcentral.com/anxiety/find-drug.html
- National Institutes of Health: Mental health medications. Available at http://www.nimh.nih.gov/health/publications/mental-health-medications/complete-index.shtml

sedative-hypnotics include oxazepam (Serax), estazolam (ProSom), and temazepam (Restoril). The short-acting sedative-hypnotic agents include triazolam (Halcion). See Table 51-5.

13. Non-benzodiazepine antianxiety agents include the classification aza-spirone, whose generic name is buspirone and trade name is BuSpar, and propranolol (Inderol). The non-benzodiazepine sedative-hypnotic agents include imidazopyridine or zolpidem (Ambien), pyrazolopy-rimidine, or zaleplon (Sonata), and the antihistamine diphenhy-dramine (Benadryl). See Box 51-5.

14. Antihistamines, such as diphenhydramine (Benadryl), can be used for their sedating effects. Their advantage is that they do not cause dependence, although they are not as effective as the BZs. With pro-longed use, clients become tolerant to the sedating side effect of anti-histamines.

15. The barbiturates, such as secobarbital and pentobarbital, are rarely used. The sedative hypnotic agents described above are more effec-tive and safer.

16. The barbiturates cause dependence and tolerance and have a danger-ous withdrawal syndrome. They are dangerous in overdose and can cause fatalities due to interactions with alcohol and other CNS depressants.

GENERAL CHAPTER CONSIDERATIONS

1. Have students study and learn key terms listed at the beginning of the chapter.

2. Have students complete end of chapter exercises either in their book or on the MyNursingKit Website.

3. Use the Classroom Response Question PowerPoints to assess students prior to lecture.

- Clinical Reasoning Care Map

MYNURSINGKIT
(www.mynursingkit.com)

- Websites
- NCLEX® Questions
- Case Studies
- Key Terms

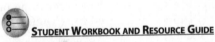

STUDENT WORKBOOK AND RESOURCE GUIDE

- Chapter 51 activities
- *Separate purchase*

PRENTICE HALL NURSE'S DRUG GUIDE

- *Separate purchase*

CLASSROOM RESPONSE QUESTION
POWERPOINTS

TESTBANK

CHAPTER 52
CARING FOR CLIENTS WITH PERSONALITY DISORDERS

LEARNING OUTCOME 1

Identify the major features of personality disorders.

Concepts for Lecture

1. There are five basic personality traits in every person. An individual's personality expresses each trait somewhere along the continuum between the two extremes of each trait. The five basic personality traits are extroversion, agreeableness, conscientiousness, emotional stability, and openness.
2. While the normal range of human behavior, feelings, and thought is broad, it is possible for personality to be outside the normal range.
3. A personality disorder is an enduring pattern of inner experience and behavior that has the following characteristics: it deviates markedly from the expectations of the individual's culture; it is pervasive and inflexible; it begins in adolescence or young adulthood; it is stable over time; and it leads to distress for the individual or impairment of functioning.
4. A person's personality significantly affects how a person responds to life events, including illness. A client's culture also affects the client's behavior and personality.
5. It is important to consider a client's cultural background when interpreting behavior. See Box 52-1.
6. For a personality disorder to be present, the individual's symptoms cannot be caused by a general medical disorder or by substance abuse.
7. The American Psychiatric Association describes 10 specific types of personality disorders that are grouped into three clusters by their similarities. The clusters are as follows: Cluster A, odd and eccentric; Cluster B, dramatic and emotional; and Cluster C, anxiety and fear-based personality disorders.
8. There are four main categories of features common to all personality disorders: impaired self-identity, distorted thinking patterns, blunted/distorted emotions, and impulsive/inflexible behavior.

LEARNING OUTCOME 2

Adapt the nurse–client relationship to the special concerns of the client who has a personality disorder.

Concepts for Lecture

1. It can be very challenging to care for people with personality disorders. Personality disorders are difficult to treat because personality is resistant to change and there are no medications that affect personality directly.
2. Nurses often find it frustrating to work with clients who have disorders of personality. Over time, these clients have developed maladaptive methods of coping with life. Clients with personality disorders can be manipulative, socially inappropriate, and difficult.

POWERPOINT SLIDES

Tables and/or Figures
- **Box 52-1** Focus on Diversity: Personality and Culture
- **Table 52-1** Personality Disorders by Cluster

SUGGESTIONS FOR CLASSROOM ACTIVITIES

- Divide students into three groups; one group will discuss the personality disorders in Cluster A, a second group will discuss personality disorders in Cluster B, and the third group will discuss Cluster C personality disorders. Provide the groups with some reference materials on personality disorders. Each group will designate a secretary to write down everything the group knows about the personality disorders within their cluster. After a set amount of time, each group will present what they know about the personality disorders in their cluster.

SUGGESTIONS FOR CLINICAL ACTIVITIES

- Assign the students to an inpatient psychiatric unit or a community mental health center. Ask the staff to identify clients with diagnosed personality disorders. Ask students to observe the behavior of these clients and to compare their behaviors with those described in the textbook.
- Ask the nurse on the psychiatric inpatient unit or community mental health center to describe the features of personality disorders.

REFERENCE

- Family Practice Notebook: Cluster B personality disorder. Available at http://www.fpnotebook.com/Psych/Behavior/ClstrBPrsnltyDsrdr.htm

POWERPOINT SLIDES

Tables and/or Figures
- **Table 52-1** Personality Disorders by Cluster
- **Figure 52-2** People With Antisocial Personality Disorder Think Rules and Laws Do Not Apply to Them
- **Figure 52-3** Self-Injury as a Coping Mechanism by a Man With Borderline Personality Disorder
- **Figure 52-4** Dramatic Dress and Exaggerated Emotions of Clients With Histrionic Personality Disorder

3. Direct communication with clear expectations for client behavior and clear and consistent limits is important for clients who have personality disorders.

4. Nurses who work with clients who have personality disorders must understand themselves first and understand their professional responsibilities to be most effective.

5. Nurses must have the insight to know what type of behavior causes them stress, so they can act rather than react to the client's behaviors.

6. The nurse must remember that the goal of the nurse is to provide professional care, not to be the friend of the client.

7. Objective understanding of personality disorders will help nurses take an objective approach to client care.

8. When working with a client with paranoid personality disorder, the nurse must keep in mind that despite the client's aggressive appearance, the inner feelings are often fear and insecurity.

9. The client with feelings of fear and insecurity often responds to reassurances about their safety. The client with paranoid personality disorder is often very aware of power relationships, so the client may respond better to information directly from the physician or charge nurse rather than from the staff nurse.

10. Clients with paranoid personality disorder, schizoid personality disorder, and schizotypal personality disorder do not enjoy being with other people. However they require enough interpersonal contact to keep them oriented to reality, but not so much that they cannot cope.

11. The risk of alcoholism is 21 times greater for the client with antisocial personality disorder than for the general population. The role of the LVN/LPN with these clients is notifying the physician if the client makes the nurse aware of either the antisocial personality disorder or alcoholism. The best personal approach to the client with antisocial personality disorder is a direct one. The nurse should share perceptions about the emotional consequences of the client's behavior for others. The staff must cooperate to consistently apply the treatment plan and facility policies.

12. Clients with borderline personality disorder tend to respond best to a predictable, structured environment. The nurse can offer suggestions for "things to try" instead of hurting self (e.g., talk to someone, delay your decision for 5 minutes, etc.).

13. The nurse can help clients with histrionic personality disorder to focus on themselves for problem solving, rather than expecting others to fulfill all their needs.

14. The client with narcissistic personality disorder can be helped to develop coping skills that involve independent problem solving without exploitation of others.

15. Work with clients who have avoidant personality disorder focuses on improving self-esteem, developing a trusting relationship, developing adaptive coping skills, and improving social skills.

16. The challenge in working with clients who have dependent personality disorder is to support these clients to make their own decisions without giving advice on how to act.

17. When working with clients with obsessive-compulsive personality disorder, the focus of treatment is on how the client is affected by the disorder in such areas as coping, sleeping, nutrition, and interpersonal relationships.

SUGGESTIONS FOR CLASSROOM ACTIVITIES

- Invite a psychiatric clinical nurse specialist to talk to the class about how to adapt the nurse–client relationship to the special concerns of the client with a personality disorder. Ask students to write questions they have about the nurse–client relationship in working with clients who have personality disorders. Give the questions to the speaker in advance.

- Ask students to choose a book about a person who has a personality disorder or a book about living with or working with people who have a personality disorder. Have the students turn in a written report and give a brief presentation to the class.

SUGGESTIONS FOR CLINICAL ACTIVITIES

- Pair students with a nurse working on a psychiatric inpatient unit or in an outpatient psychiatric setting so the students can observe the approaches the nurse uses with clients who have personality disorders. Have students present in postconference or in writing the approaches they think are effective in building and maintaining a nurse–client relationship with a client who has a personality disorder.

REFERENCE

- National Institutes of Health: Borderline personality disorder. Available at http://www.nimh.nih.gov/health/publications/borderline-personality-disorder-fact-sheet/index.shtml

LEARNING OUTCOME 3

Collect and document information about client behaviors related to personality disorders.

Concepts for Lecture

1. Each personality disorder in the three clusters of personality disorders has its own particular behavioral features.
2. When working with clients who have Cluster A odd/eccentric personality disorders, the nurse will collect information about the client's mental status, anxiety level, and ability to cooperate with others and document this information objectively.
3. The nurse will collect data that indicate the client's thought processes and document it. This may be in the form of a quote such as, "Client states 'Leave the light on. I want to see if someone is coming to get me.'" Behavior may also be documented objectively (e.g., "Client is in the bathroom with the door closed yelling, 'Stay away, don't hurt me.'")
4. When working with clients who have Cluster B personality disorders who are often at risk for violence to themselves (borderline personality disorder) or at risk for violence toward others (antisocial personality), the nurse will gather information about behaviors indicating these risks.
5. The nurse working with clients with Cluster B personality disorders will collect data about clients' mental status and behavior and document it specifically and objectively. This might be in the form of a quote, for example, "Client states 'I can't possibly take this medication unless the chief of surgery brings it to me.'"
6. The nurse working with clients with Cluster C personality disorders will collect data about the client's functional ability, mental status, and interpersonal relationships and document this information objectively. The nurse will describe client behavior and statements that reflect mental status or client's responses to interventions.

LEARNING OUTCOME 4

Apply the nursing process to clients with personality disorders.

Concepts for Lecture

1. The priorities of care with clients who have personality disorders in Cluster A (odd/eccentric: paranoid personality disorder, schizoid personality disorder, and schizotypal personality disorder) are to maintain professional boundaries and facility policies and to provide reassurance about the plan of care.
2. Assessment of clients with personality disorders in Cluster A includes collecting subjective and objective data about the client's mental status, observing and describing the client's verbal and nonverbal behavior objectively in the chart, paying particular attention to the client's anxiety level and ability to cooperate with others, and asking about medications the client takes at home.
3. One nursing diagnosis for a client with a personality disorder in Cluster A (odd/eccentric) is Disturbed Thought Processes. A possible expected outcome for Disturbed Thought Processes is that the client will engage in reality-based verbalizations, expressing concerns that are based in reality.

POWERPOINT SLIDES

Tables and/or Figures

- **Figure 52-1** Vicious Cycle of Personality Disorders
- **Figure 52-2** People With Antisocial Personality Disorder Think Rules and Laws Do Not Apply to Them
- **Figure 52-3** Self-Injury as a Coping Mechanism by a Man With Borderline Personality Disorder
- **Figure 52-4** Dramatic Dress and Exaggerated Emotions of Clients With Histrionic Personality Disorder

SUGGESTIONS FOR CLASSROOM ACTIVITIES

- Assign students to one of three groups and give each group one of the clusters of personality disorders. Have students review the behaviors of persons with each of the personality disorders within their assigned cluster. Have students document objectively some behaviors that might be observed in clients in each personality disorder. Each group can take turns reading their documentation and having the rest of the class guess which personality disorder the group is documenting on.

SUGGESTIONS FOR CLINICAL ACTIVITIES

- Assign students to care for clients with diagnosed personality disorders or significant traits of the disorders. If this is not possible, then have students observe clients with these disorders or traits. Ask the students to chart the clients' behaviors objectively.

POWERPOINT SLIDES

Tables and/or Figures

- **Box 52-2** Corrective Statements for Distorted Thoughts
- **Box 52-3** Nursing Care Checklist: Preventing Personality Disordered Clients from Upsetting the Unit

Nursing Care Plan: Client With Borderline Personality Disorder

SUGGESTIONS FOR CLASSROOM ACTIVITIES

- Divide the students into three groups and give each group one of the clusters of personality disorders. Ask each group to review the nursing process for one or more of the personality disorders, as presented in the chapter. Ask students to add to the list of data to be collected the possible nursing diagnoses and specific interventions the group thinks would be helpful in working with a person with this particular personality disorder or disorders. Ask each group to choose a discussion leader, a recorder, and someone to present their discussion to the class.

4. Nursing interventions for a nursing diagnosis of Disturbed Thought Processes include not ignoring the client's suspicions, but not overemphasizing the fears of the client either; approaching clients with a matter-of-fact, professional attitude; reassuring clients that they are safe and the staff is making every effort to provide accurate, quality care for them; adhering strictly to the rules of the organization; and trying some corrective statements to help the client toward more realistic thinking. See Box 52-2.

5. Impaired Social Interaction is another nursing diagnosis used with clients who have Cluster A personality disorders. A possible expected outcome for Impaired Social Interaction is that the client will participate in brief interactions with the nurse and other healthcare staff.

6. Nursing interventions for a nursing diagnosis of Impaired Social Interaction include making interpersonal interactions with the client brief and nonthreatening; assigning consistent staff to work with this client; providing low-stress opportunities for clients to be with other people, such as eating at a table with others at mealtime; and providing some social skills training, such as redirecting behavior that is socially inappropriate.

7. Evaluation of whether the client is achieving nursing care outcomes involves collecting the following data: how the client interacts with others, verbal and nonverbal behavior, and anxiety level.

8. The priorities of nursing care for clients with Cluster B dramatic/emotional personality disorders (antisocial personality disorder, borderline personality disorder, histrionic personality disorder, and narcissistic personality disorder) include encouraging independent problem-solving and maintaining professional boundaries.

9. Some clients with Cluster B personality disorders are at risk for violence toward themselves (borderline personality) and violence toward others (antisocial personality). In assessing these clients, the nurse needs to collect data about the clients' mental status and behavior and document client behavior specifically and objectively.

10. Sometimes, clients with personality disorders in Cluster B can disrupt an entire nursing unit with their behavior. To prevent personality-disordered clients from upsetting the unit, use the following strategies: make the rules clear; stick to the rules consistently; when a client is causing staff to be upset, have a conference; include the client in problem solving; and remember who is the client and who is the professional. See Box 52-3.

11. A nursing diagnosis for a client with a Cluster B personality disorder is Risk for Self-Directed Violence. A possible expected outcome is that the client will not harm self.

12. Nursing interventions for a nursing diagnosis of Risk for Self-Directed Violence include helping the client identify early internal symptoms of distress (such as pounding heart, sense of uneasiness, nervousness, etc.); writing the cues of distress listed by the client on a card and giving it to the client; teaching the client skills for tolerating a stressful event; using the five senses exercise to help people who have used self-harm for coping to find more enduring and adaptive ways to comfort themselves; and telling all clients who have thoughts about self-harm or suicide to notify the staff if they feel like hurting themselves.

13. Another nursing diagnosis often used for clients with Cluster B personality disorders is Risk for Other-Directed Violence, with a possible expected outcome that the client will not harm others and will comply with unit policies.

14. Nursing interventions for a nursing diagnosis of Risk for Other-Directed Violence include observing the client for increasing agitation or frustration; directing clients away from others into their rooms if clients become agitated; not tolerating verbal abuse but, instead,

SUGGESTIONS FOR CLINICAL ACTIVITIES

- Assign students to care for a client with a personality disorder in a clinical area or to observe clients with a personality disorder. Have students review the care plan in their assigned client's chart and to also write their own care plan for their client.

calmly redirecting the client or stating that the behavior is not acceptable; applying the rules consistently; and getting help when a client is violent.

15. The focus of care when working with clients with Cluster C personality disorders is providing a safe, professional atmosphere in which the client can express anxieties and identify needs.

16. When assessing the client with Cluster C personality disorders, the role of the nurse is to help clients deal with the effects of the disorder. The nurse collects information about the client's functional ability, mental status, and interpersonal relationships. Family members may be a source of information about the client's functional ability at home.

17. A nursing diagnosis for clients with Cluster C personality disorders is Anxiety, with a possible expected outcome that the client will discuss feelings of anxiety and identify situations that precipitate anxiety.

18. Nursing interventions for a nursing diagnosis of Anxiety include helping clients identify the situations associated with their anxiety; helping anxious or dependent clients practice asking for what they need; giving positive reinforcement when clients identify their needs; giving clients choices about their care whenever possible; encouraging clients to express their true feelings; reducing environmental stimuli; and promoting a trusting relationship with the client.

19. Evaluating nursing care relates to resolving the effects the disorders have on clients. Nurses intervene based on the individual client's needs and evaluate whether the client achieved the following desired outcomes: effective, adaptive coping behavior; no harm to self or others; adequate sleep to feel rested during the day; appropriate interactions with other people; making positive statements about self; taking initiative to solve problems; following unit rules; asking for help directly and appropriately; and engaging in reality-based thinking.

GENERAL CHAPTER CONSIDERATIONS

1. Have students study and learn key terms listed at the beginning of the chapter.
2. Have students complete end of chapter exercises either in their book or on the MyNursingKit Website.
3. Use the Classroom Response Question PowerPoints to assess students prior to lecture.

* Clinical Reasoning Care Map

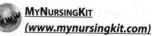

MYNURSINGKIT
(www.mynursingkit.com)
* Websites
* NCLEX® Questions
* Case Studies
* Key Terms

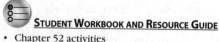

STUDENT WORKBOOK AND RESOURCE GUIDE
* Chapter 52 activities
* *Separate purchase*

PRENTICE HALL NURSE'S DRUG GUIDE
* *Separate purchase*

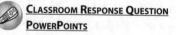

CLASSROOM RESPONSE QUESTION
POWERPOINTS

TESTBANK

CHAPTER 53
CARING FOR CLIENTS WITH SUBSTANCE ABUSE OR DEPENDENCY

LEARNING OUTCOME 1

Explain substance abuse, substance dependency, tolerance, and withdrawal.

Concepts for Lecture

1. The DSM-IV-TR describes substance abuse as a maladaptive pattern of substance use despite adverse outcomes. It results in significant impairment or distress manifested by one or more of the following: (1) inability to fulfill major role obligations at work, school, or home; (2) recurrent substance use in physically hazardous situations; (3) recurrent legal or interpersonal problems; and (4) continued use despite persistent social and interpersonal problems caused by use of the substance, such as fights or arguments with partner about intoxication.

2. Substance dependency is more severe than substance abuse. It is a maladaptive pattern of substance use leading to significant impairment or distress, manifested by three or more of the following: tolerance to the substance; withdrawal syndrome; substance taken in higher amounts or for longer periods than intended; unsuccessful or persistent desire to decrease or control use; a great deal of time spent in obtaining, using, and recovering from effects of the substance; reduction of important social, occupational, or recreational activities due to substance use; and continued substance use despite knowledge of a persistent physical or psychological problem that is likely caused by the substance.

3. With continued use, the user develops tolerance to alcohol. This means that increasing amounts of alcohol are needed to achieve the same effect or the same amount of alcohol causes less effect.

4. If an individual drinks large amounts of alcohol regularly, the CNS experiences depression. Through its mechanism for maintaining homeostasis, the depressed CNS increases its own stimulation. The individual then requires more alcohol to achieve intoxication of the stimulated CNS.

5. The process of increasing tolerance develops over years of alcohol dependency, until the individual must drink almost constantly to avoid the distressing symptoms of CNS stimulation.

6. When the alcohol-dependent individual stops drinking, the CNS is still stimulated. The homeostatic mechanism that balanced the depressant effects of the alcohol takes time to return to normal. Meanwhile, the individual suffers withdrawal symptoms.

7. The alcohol withdrawal syndrome includes elevated vital signs, anxiety, tremors, diaphoresis, slurred speech, GI disturbances (vomiting, cramping, diarrhea), ataxia, nystagmus, disorientation, and, at its most severe hallucinations, seizures, and death.

8. Alcohol withdrawal syndrome usually lasts about 4 days. See Table 53-1 for withdrawal symptoms.

POWERPOINT SLIDES

Tables and/or Figures
- **Box 53-1** Manifestations of Alcohol Intoxication by Blood Alcohol Concentration

SUGGESTIONS FOR CLASSROOM ACTIVITIES
- Break students into small groups and have them compare and contrast substance abuse and dependency.
- Invite a recovering alcoholic and an addictionologist (if you have one in your area) to come and talk with the class about substance abuse, substance dependency, tolerance, and withdrawal.

SUGGESTIONS FOR CLINICAL ACTIVITIES
- Have students arrange to visit an open Alcoholics Anonymous (AA) meeting on their own as one of their clinical experiences. Ask students to pay attention to what participants are saying and compare their past drinking behaviors and other behaviors with the textbook definitions of substance abuse, substance dependency, tolerance, and/or withdrawal.
- Arrange for students to sit in during assessments of people with substance problems prior to admission to a treatment facility. Ask the students to be alert for clues that the prospective client/clients are having problems with substance abuse or dependency, tolerance, or withdrawal.

REFERENCE
- National Institute on Drug Abuse. The science of drug abuse. Available at http://www.drugabuse.gov/

LEARNING OUTCOME 2

Collect information from clients who are using commonly abused drugs.

Concepts for Lecture

1. Assess the substance abuse history of every client. Notify the physician of recent use or regular use so appropriate measures can be taken to adjust does of prescribed medication.
2. The nurse must present a nonjudgmental attitude and be accepting of clients as people, whether they use drugs or not.
3. A general screening tool for whether a client has problems with alcohol is the CAGE questionnaire. Further inquiry is indicated if the client answers "yes" to any one of the questions on the CAGE.
4. See Box 53-4 for an assessment for substance abuse. Questions on the assessment include: How many cigarettes a day do you smoke? How often do you drink alcohol? About how much do you drink? What kind of drugs do you use that are not prescribed? What is your method of use? What purpose do these substances serve for you (relaxation, fun, to help you get through the day)?
5. The question that asks the client what purpose the substance serves promotes the nurse's ability to help the client find other choices for coping or entertainment.
6. Additional questions to ask the client include: Have you had any problems because of drinking or drug use (social, job, or legal)? When was the last time you used alcohol or any drug, what was it, and how much?
7. The DSM-IV-TR lists 11 substances of abuse. These commonly abused substances include alcohol; opioids; sedatives, hypnotics, and anxiolytics; cocaine; amphetamine and similar drugs; hallucinogens; phencyclidine (PCP) and similar drugs; inhalants; and cannabis. See Table 53-1: Comparison of Commonly Abused CNS Depressants and Stimulants.

LEARNING OUTCOME 3

Identify adverse effects caused by interactions between commonly abused substances and medications used in medical care.

Concepts for Lecture

1. Medical management includes prescription of medications and therefore must include consideration of drug interactions and cross-tolerance.
2. Clients who have used drugs or alcohol recently are at risk for additive effects with prescribed drugs.
3. Commonly prescribed medications that cause additive CNS depression are the narcotic analgesics, sedatives, benzodiazepines, sleep agents, and anesthetic agents.
4. A person who is dependent on heroin or alcohol will be tolerant not only to these, but to other CNS depressants as well. This phenomenon is called cross-tolerance.
5. Cross-tolerance is important to the anesthesiologist, who may find that the client needs more than the usual anesthetic to put him to sleep.
6. Cross-tolerance is important to physicians and nurses because clients who are tolerant to CNS depressants may need a higher than usual analgesic dose to relieve pain.

POWERPOINT SLIDES

Tables and/or Figures
- **Box 53-4** Assessment: Substance Use
- **Table 53-1** Comparison of Commonly Abused CNS Depressants and Stimulants

SUGGESTIONS FOR CLASSROOM ACTIVITIES

- Describe the techniques used by the nurse to obtain subjective assessment data from a client who is suspected of substance abuse. Give examples of open-ended questions.
- Assign each student a commonly abused CNS depressant or stimulant. Ask students to research their substance, write a report on the substance and abuse and dependence associated with the drug, and give a short verbal presentation in class at a scheduled date.

SUGGESTIONS FOR CLINICAL ACTIVITIES

- Assign students to care for clients with substance abuse problems. Role model the techniques to be used when gathering subjective data. Have students practice open-ended questions with peers.
- In the traditional medical/surgical clinical rotation, have students care for clients who have long-term health issues related to alcohol abuse, for example, cirrhosis or cardiomyopathy.

REFERENCE

- National Institutes of Health: Alcohol alert. Available at http://pubs.niaaa.nih.gov/publications/aa56.htm

POWERPOINT SLIDES

SUGGESTIONS FOR CLASSROOM ACTIVITIES

- Invite an emergency room physician and/or nurse to talk with the class about the situations they see involving people taking prescription medication and substances of abuse together.

SUGGESTIONS FOR CLINICAL ACTIVITIES

- Arrange for students to tour a substance abuse treatment facility and, while there, to have a presentation by staff on the importance of understanding cross-tolerance as well as some experiences staff have had dealing with clients who use substances of abuse and prescription medication.
- Assign students to care for clients in the medical/surgical hospital who are diagnosed with substance abuse problems as well as medical problems. Have the students review the chart and interview the client to learn what prescription medications they take and what substances have been abused in what amount and the resulting effects on the client's health.

LEARNING OUTCOME 4

Provide appropriate nursing interventions for a client in drug or alcohol withdrawal.

Concepts for Lecture

1. Substance dependency treatment has two major phases: acute and rehabilitation. In the acute phase, the person may be in a hospital or another inpatient or outpatient setting. The client often enters treatment while intoxicated.
2. Detoxification, or removal of the substance from the body, begins the acute phase. The withdrawal syndrome also occurs acutely. Medical and nursing support are often needed during withdrawal.
3. Medications are used in the acute phase of treatment to provide safe withdrawal.
4. For clients whose primary substance of abuse is alcohol, vitamin B_1 is given to prevent Wernicke-Korsakoff's syndrome.
5. Alcohol withdrawal is usually managed with a benzodiazepine anxiolytic agent, which is given in a decreasing dose over several days to treat and prevent withdrawal.
6. Alcohol and barbiturate withdrawals can be life threatening.
7. The second phase of substance dependency continues indefinitely.
8. Medications used in the rehabilitation phase of treatment are for the purpose of preventing relapse.
9. Disulfiram (Antabuse) may be prescribed to deter clients from drinking alcohol. It causes a severe, uncomfortable reaction when the client drinks (flushing, throbbing, headache, nausea, and vomiting).
10. Methadone, a synthetic opiate, is used as a replacement for heroin. The goal is to prevent the risks of intravenous drug use as methadone is given orally.
11. Naltrexone (ReVia) is an opioid antagonist used to treat opiate overdose. It has been found to reduce the cravings for alcohol in abstinent clients.
12. Clonidine (Catapres) is an antihypertensive drug given to clients with opiate dependence to prevent some of the symptoms of withdrawal.
13. Nurses should take the client's blood pressure before each dose and hold the drug if the client is hypotensive.

LEARNING OUTCOME 5

Apply the nursing process to clients experiencing substance abuse or dependency.

Concepts for Lecture

1. A nursing diagnosis for clients who are abusing or are dependent on substances is Risk for Injury related to alcohol withdrawal. A possible expected outcome is that the client will have stable vital signs within the normal range and will not suffer injury due to alcohol withdrawal.
2. A nursing intervention for a nursing diagnosis of Risk for Injury related to alcohol withdrawal is taking vital signs frequently. If the vital signs are elevated, medicate the client with benzodiazepines according to physician's orders. Additional interventions include assessing for other withdrawal symptoms (anxiety, agitation, sweating, nausea, vomiting, tremors, and ataxia); offering small amounts of fluids frequently but not pushing fluids if the client is nauseated and offering high-calorie foods; maintaining a low-stimulation environment for the client; and

POWERPOINT SLIDES

SUGGESTIONS FOR CLASSROOM ACTIVITIES

- Review the concept that delirium tremens is considered to be a medical emergency.
- Ask students to share their ideas on how the nurse keeps the client in withdrawal safe.
- Invite a nurse who works with clients detoxifying from alcohol or other drugs to come to speak with the class about pharmacologic and nonpharmacologic management of the client in withdrawal.

SUGGESTIONS FOR CLINICAL ACTIVITIES

- Arrange for students to rotate through a treatment facility that detoxifies clients withdrawing from alcohol or other drugs. Ask students to observe and keep a log of their experiences and thoughts about the withdrawal process and the nursing care of clients who are withdrawing.

REFERENCES

- National Institute of Neurological Disorders and Stroke: NINDS Wernicke-Korsakoff syndrome information page. Available at http://www.ninds.nih.gov/disorders/wernicke_korsakoff/wernicke-korsakoff.htm
- National Institutes of Health: Detoxification from alcohol and other drugs. Available at http://www.ncbi.nlm.nih.gov/bookshelf/br.fcgi?book=hssamhsatip&part=A39784

POWERPOINT SLIDES

Tables and/or Figures
- **Box 53-4** Assessment: Substance Use

Nursing Care Plan: Client With Ineffective Coping

SUGGESTIONS FOR CLASSROOM ACTIVITIES

- Divide students into small groups and ask them to review the nursing diagnoses suggested in the text. Have the students identify nursing interventions for these nursing diagnoses.
- Ask students to discuss how the nurse would decrease environmental stimuli in these settings and in the home setting.

encouraging expression of feelings about drinking or about what the client is experiencing.

3. Another nursing diagnosis for an individual with substance abuse or dependency is Deficient Knowledge (Substance Abuse and Its Consequences), with a possible expected outcome that the client will list or acknowledge the consequences of substance abuse.

4. Nursing interventions for a nursing diagnosis of Deficient Knowledge include assessing what clients know and what they need to learn; teaching clients about the process of drug abuse and dependency and how people use drugs for coping, recreation, and company; and reviewing the consequences to the client of substance use.

5. A third nursing diagnosis for individuals with substance abuse or dependency is Ineffective Coping, with a possible expected outcome that the client will have a plan for healthy alternatives to substance use for coping.

6. Nursing interventions for Ineffective Coping include helping plan for new healthy coping strategies to replace substance use; helping make a list of fun, recreational activities; and helping clients identify their resources for various needs and stressful situations.

7. Other nursing diagnoses that commonly apply to people with substance use disorders are Compromised or Disabled Family Coping; Chronic Low Self-Esteem; Powerlessness; Fear; Ineffective Denial; Imbalanced Nutrition: Less than Body Requirements; Disturbed Sleep Pattern; Social Isolation; Spiritual Distress; Disturbed Sensory Perception; and Risk for Violence.

8. To evaluate whether nursing interventions for clients with substance-use disorders are effective, look at the outcomes. Desired outcomes include the following: client will have a plan for healthy alternatives to substance use for coping; client will identify resources for obtaining help when need; client will identify risk factors for relapse and plan for relapse prevention; client will identify and verbalize feelings; client will assume responsibility for own behavior; and client will use peer support to maintain sobriety.

GENERAL CHAPTER CONSIDERATIONS

1. Have students study and learn key terms listed at the beginning of the chapter.

2. Have students complete end of chapter exercises either in their book or on the MyNursingKit Website.

3. Use the Classroom Response Question PowerPoints to assess students prior to lecture.

SUGGESTIONS FOR CLINICAL ACTIVITIES

- Seek permission for students to attend a meeting of a peer support group for persons with substance abuse problems.
- Arrange for students to tour one or more substance abuse treatment programs.

- Clinical Reasoning Care Map

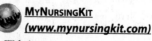
MYNURSINGKIT
(www.mynursingkit.com)

- Websites
- NCLEX® Questions
- Case Studies
- Key Terms

STUDENT WORKBOOK AND RESOURCE GUIDE

- Chapter 53 activities
- *Separate purchase*

PRENTICE HALL NURSE'S DRUG GUIDE

- *Separate purchase*

CLASSROOM RESPONSE QUESTION POWERPOINTS

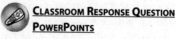
TESTBANK